MY GRAMMAR COACH

내신기출 N제 중2

KB211709

| 교재
내용
문의 | 교재 내용 문의는 EBS 중학사이트
(mid.ebs.co.kr)의 교재 Q&A
서비스를 활용하시기 바랍니다. | 교 재
정오표
공 지 | 발행 이후 발견된 정오 사항을 EBS
중학사이트 정오표 코너에서 알려 드립니다.
교재학습자료 → 교재 → 교재 정오표 | 교재
정정
신청 | 공지된 정오 내용 외에 발견된 정오 사항이 있다면
EBS 중학사이트를 통해 알려 주세요.
교재학습자료 → 교재 → 교재 선택 → 교재 Q&A |

중학 내신 영어 해결사
MY COACH 시리즈

MY GRAMMAR COACH

내신기출 N제 중2

이 책의 **구성과 특징**

＼ 첫째,

13종 교과서의 문법 요목 및 전국 중학교 시험 문제를 분석하여 구성 (p. 5~8 교과서 문법 연계표 참고)

＼ 둘째,

단원별 세분화된 요목으로 최대한 간단하게 문법 설명 제시

❶ 챕터별 세분화된 문법 요목

종합적인 이해에 앞서 세분화된 각각의 문법 요목에 대한 충분한 학습이 이루어지도록 유닛이 구성되었습니다.

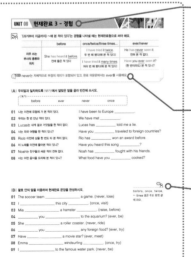

❷ 학습 지시 및 문법 핵심 정리

문법에 관한 긴 설명을 배제하고 어떻게 학습해야 하는지가 간단하게 제시되고, 해당하는 문법의 핵심만 한눈에 볼 수 있도록 정리되어 있습니다.

❸ 주의 및 참고

핵심 문법 정리만으로 부족할 수 있는 참고 사항 및 주의 사항이 세심하게 제시되어 있습니다.

❹ 문제 풀이 팁

막상 문제를 풀 때는 배운 내용이 기억나지 않거나, 배운 내용을 적용하기 힘든 경우들이 있습니다. 이를 위해 Coaching Tip을 통해 다시 한번 문법 설명이 제공됩니다.

STRUCTURE & FEATURES

\ **셋째,**
주관식 위주의 풍부한 드릴 문제 제시 및 세심한 코칭

\ **넷째,**
서술형 비율을 높인 중간고사 · 기말고사 실전문제

\ **다섯째,**
추가 연습할 수 있는 워크북 제공

\ **여섯째,**
문제 해결의 단서와 주의 포인트를 짚을 수 있는 정답과 해설

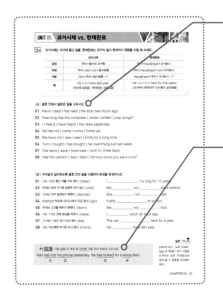

⑤ 주관식 위주의 드릴 문제

해당 문법에 대한 집중적인 연습 및 완벽한 이해를 위해 해당 문법 요목에 가장 효과적인 주관식 위주의 연습 문제가 제시됩니다.

⑥ 내신 기출 맛보기

챕터 끝에서 종합적인 실전 문제를 풀기 전에, 배운 내용을 바로바로 실전형으로 풀어 볼 수 있게 구성되었습니다. 해당 문법이 내신 문제화 되었을 때 어떻게 나올 수 있는지를 미리 만나 보며, 학습에 대한 동기 부여가 될 수 있습니다.

⑦ 챕터별 중간고사 · 기말고사 실전문제

세분화된 유닛들로 충분한 학습을 한 후에 종합적으로 챕터별 실전문제를 풀 수 있습니다. 교과서별 중간고사 · 기말고사 시험 범위를 확인하여 시험 대비에도 도움이 될 것입니다. (객관식 25문항 + 주관식 25문항)

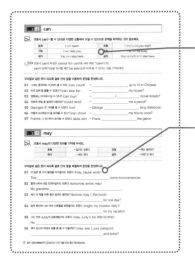

워크북

⑧ 유닛별 문법 요약

본문에서 배웠던 각 유닛의 문법을 요약하여 배운 내용을 상기해 볼 수 있습니다.

⑨ 유닛별 추가 연습 문제

유닛별 추가 연습 문제를 통해 부족했던 부분들을 확실하게 보충할 수 있습니다.

⑩ 챕터별 중간고사 · 기말고사 실전문제

종합적인 문제 풀이를 할 수 있도록 워크북에도 추가적인 챕터별 실전문제가 수록되어 있습니다. 교과서별 중간고사 · 기말고사 시험 범위를 확인하여 시험 대비에도 도움이 될 것입니다. (객관식 15문항 + 주관식 15문항)

⑪ 정답과 해설

정답과 함께, 문제 해결에 필요한 필수 문법 및 주의할 포인트를 확인 학습할 수 있습니다.

중2 영어 교과서 문법 연계표

YBM(박)		GRAMMAR COACH	
단원	문법	Chapter	Unit
1	to부정사의 형용사적 용법	4	6
1	명사절을 이끄는 접속사 that	10	9
2	의문사 + to부정사	4	4
2	원급 비교 as ~ as	7	1
3	사역동사	9	9
3	조건을 나타내는 if	10	4
4	관계대명사 주격	12	1, 2
4	명사 -thing + 형용사	6	7
S1	간접의문문	14	7
S1	최상급	7	7
5	수동태	3	1
5	so ~ that	10	7
6	가주어 it	4	2
6	not only ~ but also	10	2
7	to부정사 목적격보어	9	7
7	관계대명사 목적격	12	3
8	현재완료	1	6~9
8	조동사 may	2	2
S2	지각동사	9	8
S2	too ~ to	4	10

YBM(송)		GRAMMAR COACH	
단원	문법	Chapter	Unit
1	최상급	7	7
1	to부정사의 부사적 용법	4	7, 8
2	to부정사의 형용사적 용법	4	6
2	사역동사 make	9	9
3	의문사 + to부정사	4	4
3	관계대명사 who	12	1
4	현재완료	1	6~9
4	조건을 나타내는 if	10	4
5	부가의문문	14	8, 9
5	수동태	3	1
6	so ~ that	10	7
6	관계대명사 목적격	12	3
7	지각동사	9	8
7	가주어 it	4	2
8	to부정사 목적격보어	9	7
8	명사를 수식하는 분사	5	8
9	관계부사	12	10, 11
9	간접의문문	14	7

천재(정)		GRAMMAR COACH	
단원	문법	Chapter	Unit
1	to부정사의 형용사적 용법	4	6
1	명사절을 이끄는 접속사 that	10	9
2	조건을 나타내는 if	10	4
2	지각동사	9	8
3	현재완료	1	6~9
3	접속사 though	10	8
4	관계대명사의 주격, 목적격	12	1~3
4	관계대명사의 생략	12	8
5	의문사 + to부정사	4	4
5	5형식	9	6~10
6	a few / a little	6	8
6	수동태	3	1
7	명사를 수식하는 분사	5	8
7	가주어 it	4	2
8	so ~ that	10	7
8	사역동사	9	9

천재(이)		GRAMMAR COACH	
단원	문법	Chapter	Unit
1	관계대명사 주격	12	1, 2
1	조건을 나타내는 if	10	4
2	관계대명사 목적격	12	3
2	의문사 + to부정사	4	4
3	가주어 it	4	2
3	to부정사의 형용사적 용법	4	6
4	수동태	3	1
4	원급 비교 as ~ as	7	1
5	to부정사 목적격보어	9	7
5	before / after	10	3
6	사역동사	9	9
6	too ~ to	4	10
7	현재완료	1	6~9
7	명사를 수식하는 분사	5	8
8	최상급	7	7
8	간접의문문	14	7

금성(최)		GRAMMAR COACH	
단원	문법	Chapter	Unit
1	조건을 나타내는 if	10	4
	부가의문문	14	8, 9
2	의문사 + to부정사	4	4
	so that	10	7
3	to부정사의 형용사적 용법	4	6
	동사를 강조하는 do	14	3
4	간접의문문	14	7
	수동태	3	1
5	enough to	4	11
	현재완료	1	6~9
6	관계대명사 주격	12	1, 2
	가주어 it	4	2
7	관계대명사 목적격	12	3
	관계대명사 what	12	9
8	too ~ to	4	10
	가정법 과거	13	1~3

미래엔(최)		GRAMMAR COACH	
단원	문법	Chapter	Unit
1	관계대명사 주격	12	1, 2
	시간을 나타내는 접속사	10	3
2	현재완료	1	6~9
	each	6	4
3	to부정사의 형용사적 용법	4	6
	가주어 it	4	2
4	관계대명사 목적격	12	3
	so ~ that	10	7
5	조건을 나타내는 if	10	4
	원급 비교 as ~ as	7	1
6	수동태의 시제	3	2~4
	명사 -thing + 형용사	6	7
7	5형식	9	6~10
	사역동사	9	9
8	지각동사	9	8
	to부정사 목적격보어	9	7

비상(김)		GRAMMAR COACH	
단원	문법	Chapter	Unit
1	동명사	5	1
	5형식	9	6~10
2	조건을 나타내는 if	10	4
	to부정사 목적격보어	9	7
3	수동태	3	1
	to부정사의 형용사적 용법	4	6
4	관계대명사 주격	12	1, 2
	지각동사	9	8
5	현재완료	1	6~9
	관계대명사 목적격	12	3
6	가주어 it	4	2
	원급 비교 as ~ as	7	1
7	사역동사	9	9
	간접의문문	14	7
8	so ~ that	10	7
	명사를 수식하는 분사	5	8

지학사(민)		GRAMMAR COACH	
단원	문법	Chapter	Unit
1	부정대명사	6	1~4
	조건을 나타내는 if	10	4
2	의문사 + to부정사	4	4
	관계대명사 주격	12	1, 2
3	관계대명사 목적격	12	3
	to부정사 목적격보어	9	7
4	명사 -thing + 형용사	6	7
	현재완료	1	6~9
5	수동태	3	1
	조동사가 있는 수동태	3	6
6	so ~ that	10	7
	원급 비교 as ~ as	7	1
7	가주어 it	4	2
	how come	8	4
8	사역동사	9	9
	양보를 나타내는 접속사	10	8

다락원(강)		GRAMMAR COACH	
단원	문법	Chapter	Unit
1	수량형용사 a few, a little	6	8
	목적의 so that	10	7
	비교급	7	4
2	반복 어구 생략(등위접속사)	10	1
	지각동사	9	8
	to부정사 – 감정의 원인	4	8
3	each	6	4
	가주어 it, 진주어 to부정사	4	2
	분사구문	11	3~6
4	현재완료 시제	1	6~9
	양보 부사절을 이끄는 though	10	8
	5형식 문장(keep, make)	9	6
5	관계대명사 who, which	12	1, 2
	전치사의 목적어(동명사)	5	6
	too ~ to	4	10
6	의문사가 있는 간접의문문	14	7
	비교급 강조 much	7	4
	사역동사	9	9
7	의문사 + to부정사	4	4
	don't need to	2	4
	원급 비교 as ~ as	7	1
8	상관접속사	10	2
	one ~, the other ~	6	2
	대동사 do(비교급)	7	1
9	used to	2	7
	so ... that ~	10	7
	접속사 as	10	3, 6

이 책의 **차례**

연계표를 확인하여 나의 영어 교과서에 나오는 문법을 체크(✔)하고, 그 부분을 집중적으로 공부하세요.

CONTENTS

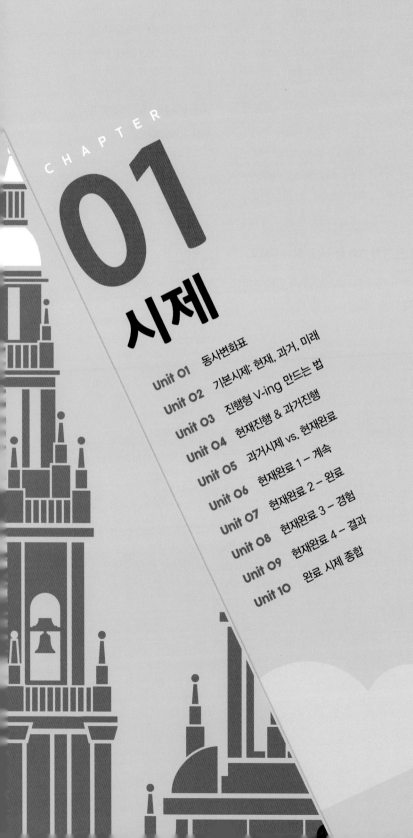

CHAPTER

01

시제

UNIT 01 동사변화표

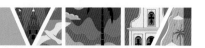

주어가 3인칭 단수일 때, 동사의 현재형을 만드는 방법을 알아 두세요.

대부분의 동사	-s	rise – rises (올라가다, 뜨다) leave – leaves (떠나다, 남기다)	save – saves (구하다, 아끼다) plan – plans (계획하다)
-o, -s, -x, -sh, -ch로 끝나는 동사	-es	finish – finishes (마치다) teach – teaches (가르치다)	miss – misses (놓치다, 그리워하다) relax – relaxes (긴장을 풀다)
자음+y로 끝나는 동사	y를 i로 바꾸고 -es	cry – cries (울다) study – studies (공부하다)	try – tries (해 보다, 애쓰다) worry – worries (걱정하다)
모음+y로 끝나는 동사	-s	play – plays (놀다) enjoy – enjoys (즐기다)	buy – buys (사다)
불규칙 동사	be have	be – am/are/is (~이다, ~하다) have – has (가지다, 먹다)	

동사의 과거형과 과거분사형이 같은 규칙 변화 동사들을 알아 두세요.

대부분	-ed	accept – accepted – accepted (받아들이다) add – added – added (더하다)
-e로 끝나는 동사	-d	disagree – disagreed – disagreed (동의하지 않다) believe – believed – believed (믿다) die – died – died (죽다) decide – decided – decided (결정하다) lie – lied – lied (거짓말하다)
단모음+단자음으로 끝나는 동사	마지막 자음 하나 더 쓰고 -ed	drop – dropped – dropped (떨어뜨리다) plan – planned – planned (계획하다)
자음+y로 끝나는 동사	y를 i로 바꾸고 -ed	carry – carried – carried (들고 있다, 나르다) marry – married – married (결혼하다) hurry – hurried – hurried (서두르다) study – studied – studied (공부하다) try – tried – tried (해 보다, 애쓰다) worry – worried – worried (걱정하다)
모음+y로 끝나는 동사	-ed	delay – delayed – delayed (미루다, 연기하다) play – played – played (놀다) stay – stayed – stayed (머물다)

|A| 다음 동사의 규칙 과거형과 과거분사를 쓰면서 외우시오.

01 accept	– _____ – _____			**32** move	– _____ – _____	
02 accomplish	– _____ – _____			**33** need	– _____ – _____	
03 agree	– _____ – _____			**34** pass	– _____ – _____	
04 allow	– _____ – _____			**35** plan	– _____ – _____	
05 believe	– _____ – _____			**36** play	– _____ – _____	
06 borrow	– _____ – _____			**37** prefer	– _____ – _____	
07 carry	– _____ – _____			**38** pull	– _____ – _____	
08 close	– _____ – _____			**39** push	– _____ – _____	
09 collect	– _____ – _____			**40** raise	– _____ – _____	
10 copy	– _____ – _____			**41** remember	– _____ – _____	
11 cover	– _____ – _____			**42** save	– _____ – _____	
12 cry	– _____ – _____			**43** show	– _____ – _____	
13 decide	– _____ – _____			**44** smell	– _____ – _____	
14 depend	– _____ – _____			**45** smile	– _____ – _____	
15 delay	– _____ – _____			**46** sound	– _____ – _____	
16 disagree	– _____ – _____			**47** start	– _____ – _____	
17 drop	– _____ – _____			**48** stay	– _____ – _____	
18 enjoy	– _____ – _____			**49** stop	– _____ – _____	
19 enter	– _____ – _____			**50** study	– _____ – _____	
20 fail	– _____ – _____			**51** thank	– _____ – _____	
21 finish	– _____ – _____			**52** touch	– _____ – _____	
22 found	– _____ – _____			**53** try	– _____ – _____	
23 happen	– _____ – _____			**54** use	– _____ – _____	
24 hope	– _____ – _____			**55** visit	– _____ – _____	
25 hurry	– _____ – _____			**56** wait	– _____ – _____	
26 join	– _____ – _____			**57** walk	– _____ – _____	
27 laugh	– _____ – _____			**58** want	– _____ – _____	
28 learn	– _____ – _____			**59** wash	– _____ – _____	
29 lie (거짓말하다)	– _____ – _____			**60** watch	– _____ – _____	
30 look	– _____ – _____			**61** work	– _____ – _____	
31 marry	– _____ – _____			**62** worry	– _____ – _____	

동사의 불규칙 과거형과 과거분사형은 암기해야 해요.

정해진 규칙 없이 변하는 동사의 과거형과 과거분사형	
am, is – was – been (~이다, ~하다)	lead – led – led (이끌다)
are – were – been (~이다, ~하다)	leave – left – left (떠나다)
become – became – become (~이 되다)	lend – lent – lent (빌려주다)
begin – began – begun (시작하다)	lie – lay – lain (눕다, 누워 있다)
bind – bound – bound (묶다)	lose – lost – lost (지다, 잃다)
bite – bit – bitten (물다)	make – made – made (만들다)
bleed – bled – bled (피를 흘리다)	mean – meant – meant (의미하다)
blow – blew – blown (바람이 불다)	meet – met – met (만나다)
break – broke – broken (깨뜨리다)	pay – paid – paid (지불하다)
bring – brought – brought (가져오다)	ride – rode – ridden (타다)
build – built – built (짓다, 건설하다)	ring – rang – rung (울리다)
buy – bought – bought (사다)	rise – rose – risen (떠오르다)
catch – caught – caught (잡다)	run – ran – run (달리다)
choose – chose – chosen (선택하다)	say – said – said (말하다)
come – came – come (오다)	see – saw – seen (보다)
do – did – done (하다)	sell – sold – sold (팔다)
draw – drew – drawn (그리다)	send – sent – sent (보내다)
drink – drank – drunk (마시다)	shoot – shot – shot (쏘다)
drive – drove – driven (운전하다)	sing – sang – sung (노래하다)
eat – ate – eaten (먹다)	sit – sat – sat (앉다)
fall – fell – fallen (떨어지다)	sleep – slept – slept (자다)
feed – fed – fed (먹이를 주다)	speak – spoke – spoken (말하다)
feel – felt – felt (느끼다)	spend – spent – spent (시간/돈을 쓰다)
fight – fought – fought (싸우다)	stand – stood – stood (일어서다)
find – found – found (발견하다)	steal – stole – stolen (훔치다)
fly – flew – flown (날다)	swim – swam – swum (수영하다)
forget – forgot – forgotten (잊다)	take – took – taken (타다, 받다)
forgive – forgave – forgiven (용서하다)	teach – taught – taught (가르치다)
get – got – got/gotten (얻다, 사다)	tell – told – told (말하다)
give – gave – given (주다)	think – thought – thought (생각하다)
go – went – gone (가다)	throw – threw – thrown (던지다)
grow – grew – grown (자라다)	understand – understood – understood (이해하다)
have – had – had (가지다, 먹다)	
hear – heard – heard (듣다)	wake – woke – waken (일어나다)
hold – held – held (잡다)	wear – wore – worn (입다)
keep – kept – kept (간직하다, 유지하다)	win – won – won (이기다)
know – knew – known (알다)	write – wrote – written (쓰다)
lay – laid – laid (놓다)	

현재형과 과거형과 과거분사형이 같은 동사도 외워 두세요.

현재형, 과거형, 과거분사형이 같은 동사	bet – bet – bet (내기를 걸다) cost – cost – cost (비용이 들다) cut – cut – cut (자르다) hit – hit – hit (치다) hurt – hurt – hurt (다치게 하다)	let – let – let (~하게 하다) put – put – put (두다, 놓다) read [riːd] – read [red] – read [red] (읽다) shut – shut – shut (닫다) spread – spread – spread (퍼지다)

|B| 다음 동사의 불규칙 과거형과 과거분사형을 쓰면서 외우시오.

01 am, is – _____ – _____
02 are – _____ – _____
03 become – _____ – _____
04 begin – _____ – _____
05 bet – _____ – _____
06 bind – _____ – _____
07 bite – _____ – _____
08 bleed – _____ – _____
09 blow – _____ – _____
10 break – _____ – _____
11 bring – _____ – _____
12 build – _____ – _____
13 buy – _____ – _____
14 catch – _____ – _____
15 choose – _____ – _____
16 come – _____ – _____
17 cost – _____ – _____
18 cut – _____ – _____
19 do – _____ – _____
20 draw – _____ – _____
21 drink – _____ – _____
22 drive – _____ – _____
23 eat – _____ – _____
24 fall – _____ – _____
25 feed – _____ – _____
26 feel – _____ – _____
27 fight – _____ – _____

28 find – _____ – _____
29 fly – _____ – _____
30 forget – _____ – _____
31 forgive – _____ – _____
32 get – _____ – _____
33 give – _____ – _____
34 go – _____ – _____
35 grow – _____ – _____
36 have – _____ – _____
37 hear – _____ – _____
38 hit – _____ – _____
39 hold – _____ – _____
40 hurt – _____ – _____
41 keep – _____ – _____
42 know – _____ – _____
43 lay – _____ – _____
44 lead – _____ – _____
45 leave – _____ – _____
46 lend – _____ – _____
47 let – _____ – _____
48 lie (눕다) – _____ – _____
49 lose – _____ – _____
50 make – _____ – _____
51 mean – _____ – _____
52 meet – _____ – _____
53 pay – _____ – _____
54 put – _____ – _____

55 read	– _____ – _____	70 spend	– _____ – _____
56 ride	– _____ – _____	71 spread	– _____ – _____
57 ring	– _____ – _____	72 stand	– _____ – _____
58 rise	– _____ – _____	73 steal	– _____ – _____
59 run	– _____ – _____	74 swim	– _____ – _____
60 say	– _____ – _____	75 take	– _____ – _____
61 see	– _____ – _____	76 teach	– _____ – _____
62 sell	– _____ – _____	77 tell	– _____ – _____
63 send	– _____ – _____	78 think	– _____ – _____
64 shoot	– _____ – _____	79 throw	– _____ – _____
65 shut	– _____ – _____	80 understand	– _____ – _____
66 sing	– _____ – _____	81 wake	– _____ – _____
67 sit	– _____ – _____	82 wear	– _____ – _____
68 sleep	– _____ – _____	83 win	– _____ – _____
69 speak	– _____ – _____	84 write	– _____ – _____

실전 TIP

found는 '설립하다'라는 동사이기도 하고 find의 과거형이기도 하다는 걸 외워 두세요.

내신 기출 다음 동사 변화형이 틀린 것은?

① find (찾다) – finded – finded

② found (설립하다) – founded – founded

③ lay (놓다) – laid – laid

④ lie (거짓말하다) – lied – lied

⑤ lie (누워 있다) – lay – lain

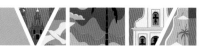

기본시제를 표현하는 동사의 형태 및 부정문, 의문문의 어순을 정확히 파악하세요.

시제	상황	긍정문의 동사 형태		부정문	의문문
현재	현재 상태, 습관, 반복, 진리	be동사	am, are, is	be(현재)+not	Be(현재)+주어 ~?
		일반동사	동사원형(+s)	do(es)+not+원형	Do(es)+주어+원형 ~?
과거	과거의 동작, 상태	be동사	was, were	be(과거)+not	Be(과거)+주어 ~?
		일반동사	원형+ed / 불규칙	did+not+원형	Did+주어+원형 ~?
미래	미래의 일	will+동사원형		will+not+원형	Will+주어+원형 ~?
		be going to+동사원형		be 뒤에 not을 씀	Be만 주어 앞에 씀

주의 시제를 판단할 때는 문맥이나 문장의 시간 부사를 파악해야 해요.

참고 시간, 조건의 부사절에서 미래는 현재시제로 표현하는 것에 주의하세요.
When he ~~will come~~ comes back, we will start.

|A| 다음 동사의 3인칭 현재 단수형과 과거형을 차례대로 쓰시오.

01 be   – _____ – _____   **11** do   – _____ – _____

02 find   – _____ – _____   **12** let   – _____ – _____

03 keep   – _____ – _____   **13** hide   – _____ – _____

04 read   – _____ – _____   **14** feed   – _____ – _____

05 watch   – _____ – _____   **15** go   – _____ – _____

06 forgive – _____ – _____   **16** have – _____ – _____

07 believe – _____ – _____   **17** stop   – _____ – _____

08 fly   – _____ – _____   **18** know – _____ – _____

09 hit   – _____ – _____   **19** study – _____ – _____

10 leave   – _____ – _____   **20** make – _____ – _____

|B| 밑줄 친 단어를 알맞은 형태로 바꾸시오.

주어와 시제에 따라 동사의 형태가 달라지니, 주어와 동사에 늘 유의해야 해요!

01 I will <u>woke</u> up late tomorrow.   _____

02 She is going to <u>plays</u> soccer this weekend.   _____

03 Tom <u>sended</u> me a letter yesterday.   _____

04 The boy <u>go</u> to school at 8:00.   _____

05 Will the airplane <u>arrives</u> at the airport tonight?   _____

06 New York have a lot of famous restaurants. _____

07 World War II starts in 1939. _____

08 My little sister is not speak English very well. _____

09 They doesn't study late at night yesterday. _____

10 My dad be going to leave the city today. _____

11 Until he will finish his work, they will wait for him. _____

|C| 괄호 안의 단어를 이용하여 대화를 완성하시오.

01 A: _____ you hungry now? (be)

02 B: Yes. I _____ very hungry. (be)

03 I _____ lunch. (have)

04 A: I _____ two sandwiches 30 minutes ago. (buy)

05 B: I _____ sandwiches. (love)

06 A: I _____ you one if you want. (give)

07 _____ you _____ it? (want)

08 B: Yes, please. _____ you _____ it now? (have, be going to)

09 A: I _____ one 5 minutes ago. (eat)

10 I _____ hungry, too. (be)

실전 TIP

현재, 과거, 미래 시제를 바르게 썼는지 확인하세요.

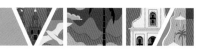

동사에 -ing를 붙일 때의 규칙을 알아 두세요.

대부분의 동사	-ing	call (부르다, 전화하다) – calling	
-e로 끝나는 동사	e를 빼고 -ing	make (만들다) – making	
-ie로 끝나는 동사	ie를 y로 바꾸고 -ing	die (죽다) – dying tie (묶다) – tying	lie (거짓말하다; 눕다) – lying
1음절이며, 단모음+단자음으로 끝나는 동사	마지막 자음을 하나 더 쓰고 -ing	get (얻다) – getting run (달리다) – running win (이기다) – winning stop (멈추다) – stopping swim (수영하다) – swimming	put (놓다) – putting sit (앉다) – sitting cut (자르다) – cutting shop (쇼핑하다) – shopping
2음절이지만 강세가 뒤에 있는 동사	마지막 자음을 하나 더 쓰고 -ing	begin (시작하다) – beginning regret (후회하다) – regretting	forget (잊다) – forgetting

|A| 다음 동사의 -ing형을 쓰면서 외우시오.

01 arrive – _____
02 bake – _____
03 begin – _____
04 believe – _____
05 bring – _____
06 call – _____
07 camp – _____
08 climb – _____
09 close – _____
10 come – _____
11 control – _____
12 dance – _____
13 die – _____
14 drive – _____
15 fly – _____
16 get – _____
17 give – _____
18 have – _____
19 lie – _____
20 listen – _____

21 love – _____
22 make – _____
23 play – _____
24 put – _____
25 read – _____
26 ride – _____
27 run – _____
28 save – _____
29 say – _____
30 shop – _____
31 sing – _____
32 sit – _____
33 smile – _____
34 stop – _____
35 study – _____
36 swim – _____
37 take – _____
38 teach – _____
39 win – _____
40 write – _____

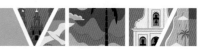

'~하고 있다'와 같이 진행 중인 동작을 나타낼 때는 진행형 〈be+V-ing〉로 써야 해요.

현재진행	am/are/is+V-ing	She is having breakfast now. They are not going to school now. I am leaving for Jeju tomorrow. (현재진행이 가까운 미래에 예정된 일을 표현하기도 함)
과거진행	was/were+V-ing	She was having breakfast at that time. Were they going to school that day?

🙁 **주의** 소유나 상태를 나타내는 동사(have, want, know, like, believe 등)는 진행형으로 쓸 수 없어요.
하지만 have가 '먹다'라는 의미일 때는 진행형이 가능해요.

|A| 밑줄 친 부분이 현재시제라면 현재진행으로, 과거시제라면 과거진행으로 바꾸시오.

01 It rains. → ＿＿＿＿＿＿＿＿　　**09** I take a shower. → ＿＿＿＿＿＿＿＿

02 We go to school. → ＿＿＿＿＿＿＿＿　　**10** He drank juice. → ＿＿＿＿＿＿＿＿

03 She opens it. → ＿＿＿＿＿＿＿＿　　**11** They played it. → ＿＿＿＿＿＿＿＿

04 It snowed. → ＿＿＿＿＿＿＿＿　　**12** They laugh. → ＿＿＿＿＿＿＿＿

05 Tom and I run. → ＿＿＿＿＿＿＿＿　　**13** He eats an apple. → ＿＿＿＿＿＿＿＿

06 Mom and I swam. → ＿＿＿＿＿＿＿＿　　**14** We stood there. → ＿＿＿＿＿＿＿＿

07 I bought a book. → ＿＿＿＿＿＿＿＿　　**15** She closed the door. → ＿＿＿＿＿＿＿＿

08 You sing a song. → ＿＿＿＿＿＿＿＿　　**16** You listened to him. → ＿＿＿＿＿＿＿＿

|B| 우리말과 일치하도록 괄호 안의 말을 이용하여 문장을 완성하시오.

🗨 Tip – 진행형의 부정문은 〈be동사+not+V-ing〉의 형태로, 의문문은 〈(의문사+)be동사+주어+V-ing ~?〉의 형태로 써야 해요.

01 나는 지금 바닥을 쓸고 있다. (sweep)　　I ＿＿＿＿＿＿＿＿＿＿ the floor now.

02 엄마는 나무에 물을 주고 계셨다. (water)　　My mom ＿＿＿＿＿＿＿＿＿＿ trees.

03 그들은 자기소개하고 있었다. (introduce)　　They ＿＿＿＿＿＿＿＿＿＿ themselves.

04 너는 점심을 먹고 있니? (have)　　＿＿＿＿＿＿ you ＿＿＿＿＿＿ lunch?

05 선생님이 나를 기다리고 계시니? (wait)　　＿＿＿＿＿＿ the teacher ＿＿＿＿＿＿ for me?

06 그녀는 오븐에 무엇을 굽고 있었나요? (bake)　　What ＿＿＿＿＿＿ she ＿＿＿＿＿＿ in the oven?

07 나는 전화 통화를 하고 있지 않아. (talk)　　I ＿＿＿＿＿＿＿＿＿＿ on the phone.

08 그 요리사는 요리하고 있었니? (cook)　　＿＿＿＿＿＿ the chef ＿＿＿＿＿＿?

09 그들은 방을 청소하고 있지 않았다. (clean)　　They ＿＿＿＿＿＿＿＿＿＿ the room.

UNIT 05 과거시제 vs. 현재완료

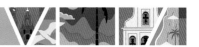

과거시제는 과거에 끝난 일을, 현재완료는 과거의 일이 현재까지 영향을 미칠 때 쓰세요.

	과거시제	현재완료
긍정	주어+동사의 과거형	주어+have[has]+과거분사
부정	주어+did+not+동사원형	주어+have[has]+not+과거분사
의문	Did+주어+동사원형 ~?	Have[Has]+주어+과거분사 ~?
예	He lived here last year. (작년에 살았음 / 현재와는 상관없음)	He has lived here for five years. (과거부터 현재까지 5년 동안 살아왔음)

|A| 괄호 안에서 알맞은 말을 고르시오.

01 Kevin (read / has read) the story two hours ago.

02 How long has the composer (wrote / written) pop songs?

03 I (heard / have heard) the news yesterday.

04 He has not (came / come) home yet.

05 We have not (saw / seen) Emily for a long time.

06 Yumi (bought / has bought) her swimming suit last week.

07 The twins (were / have been) sick for three days.

08 Has the cartoon (was / been) famous since you were a kid?

|B| 우리말과 일치하도록 괄호 안의 말을 이용하여 문장을 완성하시오.

01 나는 10년 동안 개를 키워 왔다. (raise)　I ＿＿＿＿＿＿＿＿ my dog for 10 years.

02 우리는 전에 거기에 방문한 적이 없다. (visit)　We ＿＿＿＿＿ not ＿＿＿＿＿ there before.

03 그녀는 아직 결정하지 못했다. (decide)　She ＿＿＿＿＿ not ＿＿＿＿＿ yet.

04 Kathy는 학교에 갔다(그래서 지금 없다). (go)　Kathy ＿＿＿＿＿＿＿＿ to school.

05 우리는 그것을 배우지 못했다. (learn)　We ＿＿＿＿＿ not ＿＿＿＿＿ that.

06 나는 1시간 전에 점심을 먹었다. (have)　I ＿＿＿＿＿ lunch an hour ago.

07 그 차는 1년간 여기 있어 왔다. (be)　The car ＿＿＿＿＿＿＿ here for a year.

08 그는 지난해에 여기로 이사 왔다. (move)　He ＿＿＿＿＿ here last year.

실전 TIP

yesterday, last week, ago 등 특정한 과거 시점을 표현하는 말은 현재완료와 함께 쓸 수 없음을 유의해야 해요.

내신 기출 다음 밑줄 친 부분 중 어색한 것을 찾아 바르게 고치시오.

Ken has lost his phone yesterday. He has looked for it since then.
　　①　　②　　　　③　　　　④

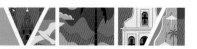

UNIT 06 현재완료 1 – 계속

 for 또는 since가 있다면 '(과거부터 현재까지 계속) ~해 왔다'는 의미로 현재완료형을 써야 해요.

	for (~ 동안)	since (~ 이후로)
뒤에 오는 말	for+기간	since+과거 시점/과거 문장
예문	He has lived here for five years.	He has lived here since last year. He has lived here since he was born.

|A| 문장의 빈칸에 for나 since 중 알맞은 것을 쓰시오.

01 He has learned it _____ one year.

02 It has been popular _____ the1900s.

03 He has had this car _____ last year.

04 I have worn glasses _____ six years.

05 He has enjoyed it _____ 2009.

06 Alice has studied art _____ four years.

07 They have dated _____ a week.

08 We have worked together _____ 2020.

09 I have studied here _____ two years.

10 She has been sick _____ Friday.

11 I have known her _____ I was a kid.

12 We haven't seen Steve _____ a year.

13 Mr. Kim has taught me _____ 2020.

14 How have you been _____ then?

|B| 밑줄 친 부분에서 틀린 곳을 찾아 바르게 고치시오.

01 Kelly liked animals since she was a kid. → _____

02 I have been friends with Emily last year. → _____

03 They have play baseball for two years. → _____

04 Ms. Park have worked as a volunteer since November. → _____

05 Jisu and I have known each other since ten years. → _____

06 My brother and I have lived here since children. → _____

07 My dad drove this car for more than ten years. → _____

08 She have known the secret since last week. → _____

09 It has four months since I left Paris. → _____

'(과거에 시작한 일을 현재에) 이미/막/아직 ~했다'라는 표현은 현재완료형으로 써야 해요.

	already (이미, 벌써)	just (막, 방금)	yet (아직 – 부정문에서)
자주 쓰는 부사와 위치	have+already+과거분사	have+just+과거분사	haven't+과거분사 ~ yet.
예문	She has already heard it. 이미 들었다	I have just finished it. 막 끝냈다	He hasn't read it yet. 아직 읽지 않았다

|A| 우리말과 일치하도록 빈칸에 알맞은 동사를 쓰시오.

01 비행기는 이미 인도로 떠났다. (leave)   The plane _____ to India.

02 그는 이제 막 새 전화기를 샀다. (buy)   He _____ a new phone.

03 너는 숙제를 끝마쳤니? (finish)   _____ your homework?

04 나는 아직 그것을 받지 못했다. (receive)   I _____ it _____.

05 그녀는 방금 이메일 한 통을 받았다. (get)   She _____ an email.

06 그녀는 벌써 머리를 감았니? (wash)   _____ her hair?

07 그들은 아직 도착하지 않았다. (arrive)   They _____.

08 봄이 이미 왔어. (come)   Spring _____.

|B| 괄호 안의 말을 이용하여 문장을 완성하시오.

현재완료와 어울려 쓰는 부사의 위치에 주의하세요.

01 The show _____. (begin, already)

02 We _____. (yet, decide)

03 I _____ this book. (read, just)

04 She has _____ home. (come back, just)

05 _____ you _____ a soccer game? (finish, just)

06 The movie _____. (start, just)

07 He _____ my secret to people. (already, tell)

08 My aunt _____ a mother. (just, become)

09 The store _____. (yet, open)

현재완료 3 - 경험

📖 '(과거부터 지금까지) ~해 본 적이 있다'는 경험을 나타낼 때는 현재완료형으로 써야 해요.

자주 쓰는 부사의 종류와 위치	before	once/twice/three times...	ever/never
	She has heard it before. 전에 들은 적이 있다	I have tried it twice. 두 번 해 봤다[해 본 적 있다]	He has never seen it. 전혀 본 적 없다
	She hasn't heard it before. 전에 들은 적이 없다	I have tried it many times. 여러 번 해 봤다[해 본 적 있다]	Have you ever seen it? (한 번이라도) 본 적 있니?

😊참고 never는 자체적으로 부정의 의미가 포함되어 있고, 완료 의문문에서는 ever를 사용해요.

|A| 우리말과 일치하도록 |보기|에서 알맞은 말을 골라 빈칸에 쓰시오.

┌ 보기 ┐
| before | ever | never | once |

01 나는 이전에 유럽에 가 본 적이 있다.　　　　I have been to Europe _____.

02 우리는 한 번 만난 적이 있다.　　　　　　　We have met _____.

03 Lucas는 내게 결코 거짓말을 한 적이 없다.　Lucas has _____ told me a lie.

04 너는 외국 여행을 한 적이 있니?　　　　　　Have you _____ traveled to foreign countries?

05 Rio는 이전에 상을 한 번도 타 본 적이 없다.　Rio has _____ won an award before.

06 이 노래를 이전에 들어본 적이 있니?　　　　　Have you heard this song _____?

07 Noah는 친구들과 싸운 적이 전혀 없다.　　　Noah has _____ fought with his friends.

08 너는 어떤 음식을 요리해 본 적이 있니?　　　What food have you _____ cooked?

|B| 괄호 안의 말을 이용하여 현재완료 문장을 완성하시오.

before, once, twice, ~ times 등은 주로 문장 끝에 와요.

01 The soccer team _____ a game. (never, lose)

02 I _____ this city _____. (once, visit)

03 Mia _____ a hamster _____. (raise, before)

04 _____ you _____ to the aquarium? (ever, be)

05 She _____ a roller coaster. (never, ride)

06 _____ you _____ any foreign food? (ever, try)

07 Have _____ a movie star? (ever, meet)

08 Emma _____ windsurfing _____. (once, try)

09 I _____ to the famous water park. (never, be)

UNIT 09   현재완료 4 – 결과

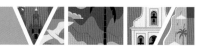

'(과거에 ~한 결과 현재) ~하다'라는 의미를 만들 때 현재완료형을 써야 해요.

	과거	현재완료
비교	She lost her bag. 잃어버렸다	She has lost her bag. 잃어버렸다 (그래서 지금 없다)
	(과거 발생, 현재 상황 모름)	(과거 발생, 그 결과가 현재까지 이어짐)

'~에 가고 없다'와 '~에 가 본 적 있다'를 구분해서 사용할 수 있어야 해요.

	have gone to (결과)	have been to (경험)
예문	She has gone to Canada. ~에 가 버렸다	She has been to Canada. ~에 가 본 적이 있다
주의	'가서 (그 결과) 현재 여기에 없다'라는 의미로 I(나), We(우리)를 주어로는 쓰지 않아요.	'가 본 적이 있다'라는 의미지만, go가 아닌 be를 쓴다는 것에 주의하세요.

|A| 빈칸에 have[has] been 또는 have[has] gone을 쓰시오.

01 They are not here. They _____ to Thailand.

02 I _____ to Canada before.

03 _____ you _____ to the United States?

04 _____ she _____ to her hometown? I don't see her anymore.

05 I'm alone here. Everyone _____ to the party.

|B| 두 문장이 같은 뜻이 되도록 빈칸에 알맞은 말을 쓰시오.

01 I lost my bag. So I don't have it now.   → I _____ my bag.

02 He went to Africa. So he is not here now.   → He _____ to Africa.

03 Someone stole my wallet. And I can't find it.   → Someone _____ my wallet.

04 James is not here now. He left for Japan.   → James _____ for Japan.

05 She lost her glasses. And she doesn't have them.   → She _____ her glasses.

06 The power went out. So it is still dark.   → The power _____ out.

07 Someone took my shoes. So I don't have them now. → Someone _____ my shoes.

08 I went to Hawaii last year. It was my first time.   → I _____ to Hawaii once.

09 She forgot my name. And she still doesn't remember it. → She _____ my name.

계속	I have learned Chinese since last month.
	• for는 '~동안'의 의미로 지속된 기간 / since는 '~이후로, ~부터'의 의미로 특정 시점이 기준
완료	I have just finished the homework.
	• 주로 just, already, yet, finally 등과 함께 사용
경험	She has tried Thai food before.
	• ever, never, before, often, once, ~ times 등과 함께 사용
결과	She has lost her expensive bag.
	• 〈have gone to〉 (~에) 가 버려서 (여기에) 없다 / 〈have been to〉 ~에 가 본 적이 있다

|A| 괄호 안의 단어를 이용하여 현재완료 문장을 완성하고, 각 문장이 어떤 용법으로 쓰였는지 쓰시오.

01 Olivia has _____ her homework _____. (finish, yet)　　　[　　　]

02 _____ have you _____ English? (how long, study)　　　[　　　]

03 I _____ my ticket, so I can't get on the train. (lose)　　　[　　　]

04 My family and I _____ Jeju several _____. (be, times)　　　[　　　]

|B| 우리말과 일치하도록 괄호 안의 말을 바르게 배열하시오.

현재완료와 자주 쓰는 already, yet, just, ever, for, since 등의 의미와 쓰임에 유의하고, 특정 시점을 가리키는 when, last week, yesterday, ~ ago 등은 과거시제와 어울려 씀을 기억하세요.

01 너는 전에 그 박물관에 가 본 적이 있니? (ever, you, have, visited)

_____ the museum before?

02 서점은 아직 문을 열지 않았다. (has, yet, not, opened)

The bookstore _____.

03 우리는 이미 수학 숙제를 다 끝마쳤다. (we, already, finished, have)

_____ our math homework.

04 우리 농구 팀은 시합에서 한 번도 져 본 적이 없다. (lost, never, has, a game)

My basketball team _____.

05 Sue와 나는 작년부터 이곳에서 의학을 공부했다. (since, studied, have)

Sue and I _____ medicine here _____ last year.

06 그는 벌써 우리에게 파티 초대장을 보내 왔다. (sent, us, already, has)

He _____ an invitation to the party.

실전 TIP

과거의 어느 한 시점을 나타낼 때는 현재완료로 쓸 수 없다는 것에 유의하세요.

내신 기출 다음 밑줄 친 부분 중 어색한 것을 찾아 바르게 고치시오.

She <u>has never been</u> to foreign countries. She <u>has lived</u> in Korea since
　　　　①　　　　　　　　　　　　　　　　　　②

she <u>has been</u> born.
　　③

중간고사·기말고사 실전문제

학년과 반		이름		객관식	/ 25문항	주관식	/ 25문항

01 다음 중 동사의 변화형이 옳지 <u>않은</u> 것은?

① stay – stayed – stayed
② hurry – hurried – hurried
③ wait – wait – wait
④ enjoy – enjoyed – enjoyed
⑤ drop – dropped – dropped

02 다음 빈칸에 들어갈 말로 알맞은 것은?

The class _____ start at 10 a.m.

① will be
② is being
③ is going to
④ is going
⑤ was

03 우리말을 영어로 옮길 때 빈칸에 알맞은 것은?

우리 오빠는 전에 유럽에 가 본 적이 있다.
My brother _____ Europe before.

① is in
② was in
③ went to
④ has been to
⑤ has gone to

04 다음 중 어법상 <u>어색한</u> 것을 <u>모두</u> 고르시오.

① I was taking a shower when you called me.
② My father was having a wonderful hat.
③ The bread was smelling very good.
④ I was thinking about her.
⑤ She was listening to music at that time.

05 다음 밑줄 친 부분 중 어법상 <u>어색한</u> 것을 <u>모두</u> 고르시오.

① He <u>took</u> his son to school this morning.
② Linda <u>lied</u> on the sofa when I visited her.
③ Mom <u>read</u> my favorite book last night.
④ We <u>win</u> first prize last week.
⑤ He <u>woke</u> up early this morning.

06~07 다음 밑줄 친 부분의 용법이 나머지 넷과 <u>다른</u> 것을 고르시오.

06 ① He <u>has</u> just <u>arrived</u> at the party.
② I <u>haven't finished</u> my homework yet.
③ The bus <u>has</u> just <u>left</u> the bus stop.
④ They <u>haven't seen</u> each other for a long time.
⑤ He <u>has</u> already <u>opened</u> the store.

07 ① I <u>have lost</u> my wallet on the bus.
② I <u>have been</u> to India twice.
③ He <u>hasn't read</u> the *Harry Potter* series before.
④ I <u>have eaten</u> durian before.
⑤ <u>Have</u> you <u>heard</u> about the accident at the corner?

08~12 다음 중 어법상 어색한 것을 고르시오.

08 ① I was listening to K-pop now.
② Water boils at 100℃.
③ Jane will come to my birthday party next Thursday.
④ My father went fishing last summer.
⑤ She goes to church every Sunday.

09 ① How long have you been in this class?
② He has been jobless since he lost his job.
③ She doesn't talk to me since yesterday.
④ I have never studied hard in my life.
⑤ Have you ever seen a pelican before?

10 ① The chef has cooked the beef for four hours.
② Have you done the laundry yet?
③ James has raised a cat for three years.
④ We go to the mountain twice a year.
⑤ When have you baked this cake?

11 ① I have broken the box yesterday.
② She has sold lemonade on the street for two hours.
③ I have known him for ten years.
④ He rode on a train two days ago.
⑤ Mike stayed up late last night to study for the exam.

12 ① I have been to the Louvre Museum once.
② I went to Disneyland last Sunday.
③ I have swim in the pool for one hour.
④ It has rained a lot since this Monday.
⑤ A thief broke into her house last night.

13 다음 빈칸에 들어갈 말이 바르게 짝지어진 것은?

> 1. Taylor Swift _____ a famous singer now.
> 2. She _____ born in 1989.
> 3. She _____ over 100 songs since she became a singer.

① is – is – write
② is – was – wrote
③ is – was – has written
④ was – is – is writing
⑤ was – was – has written

14~17 다음 중 어법상 올바른 것을 고르시오.

14 ① I haven't already eaten the cake.
② Alice has worn her glasses for five years.
③ She hasn't eaten meat since three years.
④ My mom has had her garden for last year.
⑤ I have seen her two weeks ago.

15 ① She has just began to exercise.
② When have you met him?
③ How long did you played the game so far?
④ She has never been to Hong Kong.
⑤ Chris have never eaten Thai food.

16 ① He has left for Busan next week.
② She is going to a movie with her mom now.
③ What time were you coming to the party tomorrow?
④ I'm going to go shopping with my friend last weekend.
⑤ Jimin has just arrived at the station five minutes ago.

17 ① Andy worked in his workplace for five years.
② I saved my pocket money since I was 10.
③ She has traveled to Japan last year.
④ Jay has loved Mary for his entire life.
⑤ Tom has invented the machine in 2001.

18 다음 중 밑줄 친 부분이 어법상 어색한 것은?

① Jia has studied English for two years.
② John has been a member of the team since 2017.
③ He has painted the room for two hours.
④ I have lived in my hometown since I was born.
⑤ She has learned to dance for last year.

19 다음 중 어법상 어색한 문장의 개수는?

1. Nate hasn't finished dinner yet.
2. Rachel has eaten not any meat because she is a vegetarian.
3. How long does it rained?
4. My father has already cooked the breakfast.

① 없음   ② 1개   ③ 2개   ④ 3개   ⑤ 4개

20~21 다음 중 어법상 올바른 문장의 개수를 고르시오.

20
1. Tom hasn't cleaned the house for three weeks.
2. When I saw him on the street, he was talking to someone.
3. I'm going to have lunch with Jenny next Monday.
4. She has studied science hard last night.

① 없음   ② 1개   ③ 2개   ④ 3개   ⑤ 4개

21
1. I have never seen such a beautiful woman in my life.
2. She has sent a message to her boyfriend two hours ago.
3. When did you brush your teeth?
4. I have bought a nice T-shirt yesterday.

① 없음   ② 1개   ③ 2개   ④ 3개   ⑤ 4개

22 다음 중 어법상 어색한 문장으로 짝지어진 것은?

ⓐ Have you ever traveled to another country?
ⓑ We have visited our hometown last week.
ⓒ Amy has won the gold medal in 2019.
ⓓ I watched the TV program yesterday.
ⓔ I have met the movie star twice.

① ⓐ, ⓒ   ② ⓑ, ⓒ   ③ ⓑ, ⓓ
④ ⓒ, ⓓ   ⑤ ⓓ, ⓔ

23 다음 글의 밑줄 친 ⓐ~ⓔ 중 어법상 어색한 것은?

BTS ⓐ is one of the famous artists in the world now. They ⓑ have won many awards around the world. They ⓒ have written many songs so far. They also ⓓ have given a speech at the UN in 2018. Their fans love them very much, so they ⓔ bought a forest for BTS as a birthday present in 2019.

① ⓐ   ② ⓑ   ③ ⓒ   ④ ⓓ   ⑤ ⓔ

24 다음 대화의 밑줄 친 ⓐ~ⓔ 중 어법상 어색한 것은?

> A: ⓐ Have you ever been to Taiwan before?
> B: Yes, I have. ⓑ I stayed in Taipei for three days one year ago.
> A: ⓒ What have you done on the last day of your trip?
> B: ⓓ I had dinner with my family at a nice restaurant. The food was delicious.
> A: Oh, it sounds great! I want to go to Taiwan, too!
> B: ⓔ You will like the city if you go there.

① ⓐ   ② ⓑ   ③ ⓒ   ④ ⓓ   ⑤ ⓔ

25 다음 중 빈칸에 들어갈 말이 바르게 짝지어진 것은?

> When I saw something on my way home, I ___(A)___ on the street. It was a cute puppy! I ___(B)___ for its home for days, but I ___(C)___ it yet.

    (A)   (B)   (C)
① was walking–have looked–haven't found
② was walking–   looked   – didn't find
③   walked   –   looked   –haven't found
④ am walking –have looked– didn't find
⑤ am walking –   looked   –haven't found

26~27 다음 빈칸에 괄호 안의 말을 알맞은 형태로 쓰시오.

26 Brian hasn't _____ (travel) abroad.

27 Has Kim _____ (buy) anything at the shopping mall?

28~30 다음 문장에서 어법상 어색한 부분을 찾아 바르게 고치시오.

28 I haven't played the guitar when I was in high school.

_____ → _____

29 Mr. Anderson has lived in Texas since his entire life.

_____ → _____

30 I am talking on the phone when Mom knocked on the door.

_____ → _____

31 다음 대화의 밑줄 친 우리말과 일치하도록 괄호 안의 말을 이용하여 문장을 완성하시오.

> A: 너는 이전에 이 게임을 해 본 적 있니?
>   (play, ever, game)
> B: Yes, I have. It is very exciting.

_____ before?

32 다음 우리말과 일치하도록 괄호 안의 말을 바르게 배열하시오.

> 지난달부터 눈이 많이 내렸다.
> (snowed, last month, it, has, since, a lot)

_____

33~34 다음 빈칸에 괄호 안의 말을 알맞은 형태로 넣어 대화를 완성하시오.

33 A: Can Susan play with us, Mrs. Smith?
B: No, she can't. She _____ _____ her homework yet. (not, finish)

34 A: What were your friends doing when you arrived at the party?
B: They _____ _____. (dance)

35~37 다음 우리말과 일치하도록 문장을 완성하시오.

35 그는 이미 가게 문을 닫았다.
He _____ _____ _____ the store.

36 나는 이 책상을 5년째 갖고 있다.
I _____ _____ this desk _____ five years.

37 그녀는 멕시코로 가 버렸다.
She _____ _____ to Mexico.

38~39 다음 문장에서 어법상 어색한 부분을 고쳐 완전한 문장을 쓰시오.

38 Thomas Edison has invented the phonograph in 1877.
→ _____

39 We will be late if we will be stuck in a traffic jam!
→ _____

40~41 다음 문장이 어법상 어색하지 않으면 〇를, 어색한 부분이 있으면 밑줄을 치고 바르게 고치시오.

40 (1) She has already read the book.
→ _____

(2) Jane Austen has written *Pride and Prejudice* in 1813.
→ _____

(3) He has studied Japanese for last month.
→ _____

41 (1) She has lost her job last month.
→ _____

(2) We have studied English for five years.
→ _____

(3) He has lost his wallet. He has to buy a new one.
→ _____

42~43 다음 우리말과 일치하도록 괄호 안의 말을 이용하여 문장을 완성하시오.

42 그 기차는 이미 역을 떠나버렸다.
The train (leave, already) the station.
→ _____

43 그는 그녀를 10년째 알아오고 있다.
He (know) her for ten years.
→ _____

44~45 다음 두 문장을 현재완료를 이용해서 한 문장으로 만드시오.

44
> My father went to Russia for his work.
> He isn't here now.

_____

45
> Cathy loved to sing when she was young.
> She still loves to sing now.

_____

46 주어진 |조건|을 이용하여 우리말을 영어로 옮기시오.

> |조건|
> 1) 현재완료를 사용할 것
> 2) 단어 story, hear, such a, funny, never 를 사용할 것
> 3) 8단어를 사용할 것

나는 이렇게 웃긴 이야기를 들어본 적이 없어.

_____

47~48 다음 문장을 지시대로 바꿔 쓰시오.

47 She has worked as a pilot.
   (1) 부정문으로

   _____

   (2) 의문문으로

   _____

48 They have already arrived home.
   (1) 부정문으로

   _____

   (2) 의문문으로

   _____

49 다음 글의 밑줄 친 ⓐ~ⓔ 중 어법상 어색한 것을 골라 기호를 쓰고 바르게 고치시오.

> Seoul ⓐ is a beautiful city. I was born in Seoul in 2007. I ⓑ have visited many places such as Kyungbokgung palace and Insa-dong. Last weekend, I ⓒ went to the night market near the Han River and I had a great time. I think foreigners ⓓ will love Seoul like I do if they ⓔ will visit.

_____ → _____

50 다음은 Jamie와 Amy가 경험해 본 것을 나타낸 표이다. 표를 보고 현재완료시제로 문장을 완성하시오.

	Jamie	Amy
grow flowers	×	○
eat a waffle	○	○
see a dolphin	○	×

Jamie has never grown flowers, but Amy
_____.

Jamie and Amy _____
_____.

Jamie has seen a dolphin, but Amy
_____.

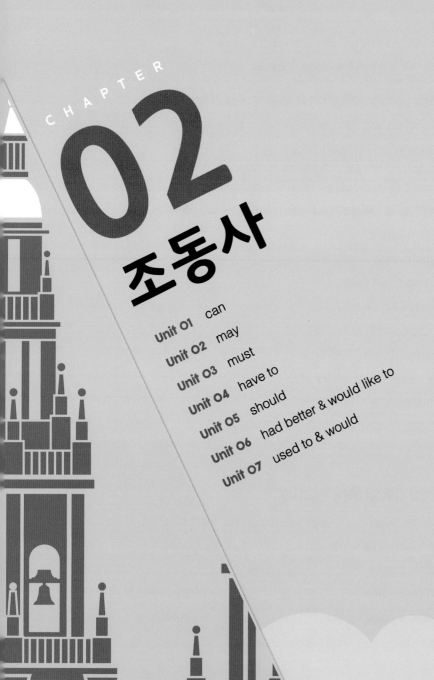

CHAPTER

02

조동사

UNIT 01　can

조동사 can(~할 수 있다)은 다양한 상황에서 쓰일 수 있으므로 문맥을 파악하는 것이 중요해요.

능력	I can swim.	요청	Can[Could] you wait?
가능	I can help you.	추측	He can be busy.
허가	You can stay here.	금지	You cannot[can't] stay here.

🙁 **주의** 조동사 can의 부정은 cannot 또는 can't로 써야 해요. *cann't (×)

🙂 **참고** could는 can의 과거시제로도 쓰고, 정중한 요청을 나타낼 때도 써요.

can이 능력/가능을 의미할 때만 be able to와 바꾸어 쓸 수 있다는 것을 기억하세요.

능력/가능	I can swim. = I am able to swim.
허가	You can stay. ≠ You are able to stay.(×)

|A| 문장에서 can 또는 could가 어떤 의미를 나타내는지 고르시오.

01 Can you do me a favor? (능력 / 요청)

02 This machine can wash the dishes. (허가 / 능력)

03 You can come to me anytime. (능력 / 허가)

04 Could you pass me the salt? (요청 / 허가)

05 What can we do to save the Earth? (능력 / 허가)

06 She can speak four languages. (능력 / 허가)

07 You can use my computer if you want. (허가 / 능력)

08 Can you please turn up the volume? (허가 / 요청)

|B| 우리말과 일치하도록 괄호 안의 말을 이용하여 문장을 완성하시오.

01 너는 바이올린을 연주할 수 있니? (can, play) _____ the violin?

02 여기에서 우회전하면 안 된다. (can, turn right) You _____ here.

03 그들이 5시까지 올 수 있나요? (able, come) _____ they _____ by 5:00?

04 제가 여기서 사진을 찍어도 되나요? (can, take) _____ a picture here?

05 여기서 떠들면 안 된다. (can, make a noise) You _____ here.

06 그 아기는 걷지 못한다. (able, walk) The baby _____.

07 나는 그것을 풀 수 있었다. (solve) I _____ it.

08 나는 그것을 기억해 낼 수 없었다. (remember) I _____ it.

09 라디오 좀 꺼 주실래요? (could, turn off) _____ you _____ the radio?

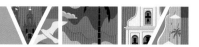

조동사 may의 다양한 의미를 기억해 두세요.

추측	～일지도 모른다	The story may be true.　The story may not be true.
허가	～해도 된다	You may come in.
요청	～해도 될까요?	May I borrow your umbrella?
금지	～하면 안 된다	You may not come in.

주의 may의 부정은 may not으로 쓰고, 축약하지 않아요.

|A| 문장에서 may 또는 may not이 추측, 허가, 요청, 금지 중 어떤 의미를 나타내는지 쓰시오.

01 You may take pictures here.　[　] **05** It may snow tonight.　[　]

02 This may not be a good idea.　[　] **06** May I sit here?　[　]

03 You may not enter this room.　[　] **07** May I have your order?　[　]

04 She may be on her way here.　[　] **08** Tony may like Japanese food.　[　]

|B| 우리말과 일치하도록 괄호 안의 말을 바르게 배열하시오.

may의 부정문은 〈may not+동사원형〉, 의문문은 〈May+주어+동사원형 ～?〉으로 써요.

01 그녀는 힘든 시간을 보낼지도 모른다. (have, may, she)

_____ a hard time.

02 그는 비 오는 날을 좋아하지 않을지도 모른다. (may, not, days, like, rainy)

He _____.

03 제가 당신의 이메일 주소를 받을 수 있을까요? (I, have, may, address)

_____ your email _____?

04 네가 요청하면 그가 너에게 사과할지도 모른다. (may, you, apologize to)

He _____ if you ask.

05 뭔가 잘못될지도 모른다. (might, go, something)

_____ wrong.

might는 may보다 약한 추측을 나타내요.

06 수업 중에는 화장실에 가면 안 된다. (may, go to, not, you)

_____ the bathroom during class.

실전 TIP

may not이 추측의 의미인지, 금지의 의미인지를 파악하세요.

내신 기출 다음 밑줄 친 부분 중 의미가 다른 하나는?

① You may not be here.

② It may not be fresh.

③ He may not be busy.

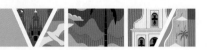

UNIT 03 must

'~해야만 한다'라는 의무나, '~임에 틀림없다'라는 강한 추측을 표현할 때 조동사 must를 쓰세요.

의무	~해야만 한다	We must follow the rules.
강한 추측	~임이 틀림없다	She must be rich.
강한 금지	~하면 안 된다	You must not tell a lie.

주의 부정의 강한 추측은 can't[cannot](~일 리가 없다)로 써요. The story can't be true.

|A| |보기|에서 알맞은 말을 하나씩 골라 괄호 안의 조동사와 함께 문장을 완성하시오.

형용사(happy, hungry, tired)나 명사를 보어로 쓸 때는 앞에 be동사를 써요.

보기			
happy	tell anyone	swim here	drive fast
hungry	Mina	tired	buy a ticket

01 You _____. But try to eat slowly. (must)

02 The event is not free. You _____. (must)

03 Mina is in New York now. That _____! (can't) '~일 리 없다'는 can't be로 써요.

04 The sign says "No swimming". We _____. (must)

05 It is a top secret. You _____. (must)

06 Jane won first prize. She _____. (must)

07 You worked too hard. You _____. (must)

08 You _____. It is a school zone. (must)

|B| 우리말과 일치하도록 괄호 안의 말을 이용하여 문장을 완성하시오.

01 너는 9시 전에는 문을 열면 안 된다. (must, open)

You _____ the door before 9:00.

02 저 가수는 십 대들 사이에서 인기가 많은 것이 분명하다. (must, be)

The singer _____ popular among teenagers.

03 너는 초콜릿을 좋아하는 게 분명하다. (must, like)

You _____ chocolate.

04 우리가 10시까지 돌아가야 하나요? (must, go back)

_____ we _____ by 10:00?

05 이 시간에 사람들이 이렇게 많을 리가 없다. (can't, be)

There _____ this many people at this time.

06 여기에 쓰레기를 버리면 안 된다. (must, throw away)

You _____ trash here.

UNIT 04 have to

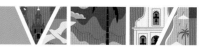

have[has] to는 의미상 must와 바꾸어 쓰지만, 부정문은 서로 다른 의미인 것에 주의해야 해요.

	must		have to	
긍정문	We must pay.	의무	We have to pay.	~해야 한다(의무)
부정문	We must not pay.	금지	We don't have to pay.	~할 필요가 없다(불필요)
의문문	Must we pay?	의무	Do we have to pay?	~해야 합니까?(의무)

주의 주어가 3인칭 단수면 has to로 써야 하며, 과거(~했어야 했다)는 had to로 써요.

have[has] to의 의문문은 〈Do[Does]+주어+have to+동사원형 ~?〉의 어순으로 써요.

참고 have to는 need to로 바꾸어 쓸 수 있어요. We don't have[need] to pay.

|A| 문장을 지시대로 바꾸시오.

01 I have to clean up the mess. (과거형으로) → _____.

02 We need to cancel it. (부정문으로) → _____.

03 He has to prepare dinner. (의문문으로) → _____?

04 You have to be polite. (부정문으로) → _____.

05 They have to listen carefully. (과거형으로) → _____.

06 Billy has to go to bed. (부정문으로) → _____.

07 I need to change clothes. (의문문으로) → _____?

08 She has to take a rest. (미래형으로) → _____.

'~해야 할 것이다'는 will have to로 써요.

|B| 우리말과 일치하도록 have to를 알맞은 형태로 바꾸고 괄호 안의 말을 이용하여 문장을 완성하시오.

01 우리 가족은 서울로 이사 가야 했다. (move)

My family _____ to Seoul.

02 우리는 여기 도서관 안에서 조용히 해야 한다. (be quiet)

We _____ here in the library.

03 Audrey는 시험을 쳐야 할 것이다. (take)

Audrey _____ a test.

04 우리는 미래에 대해 너무 많이 걱정할 필요는 없다. (worry)

We _____ too much about the future.

05 내가 매일 개를 씻겨야 하나요? (wash)

_____ I _____ my dog every day?

06 우리는 음료수 값을 내지 않아도 됐다. (pay)

We _____ for the drinks.

UNIT 05   should

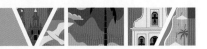

조동사 should는 '~하는 게 좋겠다, ~해야 한다'라는 뜻으로 충고나 제안을 할 때 써야 해요.

~해야 한다, ~하는 편이 좋겠다	You should wash your hands.
~하지 않는 게 좋겠다, ~해서는 안 된다	You shouldn't[should not] play games too much.
~하는 게 좋을까?, ~해야 하나?	Should I take the bus? – Yes, you should. / No, you shouldn't.

|A| should와 shouldn't 중에 알맞은 말을 골라 빈칸에 쓰시오.

01 You _____ run in the classroom.

02 We _____ turn off the lights when we go out.

03 You _____ ask your parents for good advice.

04 You _____ eat too much fast food.

05 He _____ stay in bed and rest.

06 You _____ travel alone during the night.

07 You _____ talk on the phone in the library.

08 Jessica _____ brush her teeth before she goes to bed.

|B| 괄호 안의 말과 should를 이용하여 대화를 완성하시오.

01 A: We _____ water and electricity. (save)

B: Right. I want to save the Earth, too.

02 A: You _____ too late. (stay up)

B: OK. I will go to bed right now.

03 A: _____ I _____ all these symbols? (memorize)

B: Not all of them.

04 A: Joanne is very angry at me.

B: You _____ to her. (apologize)

05 A: This math problem is too difficult.

B: You _____ your teacher how to solve it. (ask)

06 A: Is it okay if I eat now?

B: You _____ before you wash your hands. (eat)

조동사 should의 부정형은
〈shouldn't[should not]+
동사원형〉으로 금지를 나타
내며, 의문형은 〈Should+
주어+동사원형 ~?〉으로 표
현해야 해요.

다음 조동사 표현들을 익히세요.

	had better	would like to
의미	～하는 게 낫다 (should보다 강한 충고)	～하고 싶다, ～하기 원한다 (≒ want to)
긍정/축약	You had better <u>go</u> now. You'd better	I would like to <u>stay</u>. I'd like to
부정	You'd better <u>not</u> go now.	I would <u>not</u> like to stay.
의문	*<u>Should</u> I go now?	Would you like to stay?

주의 had better는 의문문으로 잘 쓰지 않아요. 거의 should를 사용하여 의문문을 만들어요.

참고 would like 다음에는 명사가, would like to 다음에는 동사원형이 와요.

|A| 빈칸에 들어갈 말을 |보기|에서 골라 쓰시오.

|보기|
would like to   wouldn't like to   had better   had better not

01 I have seen it. I didn't like it. So I _____ watch it again.

02 You smell bad. You _____ take a shower.

03 The weather is fantastic! I _____ go on a picnic.

04 What _____ you _____ do on your birthday?

05 I _____ have pizza. I love pizza.

06 You _____ eat desserts. You're on a diet.

07 I _____ go to Jeju if it's okay with you.

08 It's raining cats and dogs. You _____ go out.

|B| 우리말과 일치하도록 had better 또는 would like to와 괄호 안의 말을 이용하여 문장을 완성하시오.

01 너는 그의 말을 듣는 게 나을 거야. (listen)   You _____ to him.

02 너는 어떤 나라를 여행하고 싶니? (travel)   What country _____?

03 너는 같은 실수를 하지 않는 게 나을 거다. (make)   You _____ the same mistake.

04 너는 아파 보여. 지금 잠자리에 드는 게 낫겠어. (go)   You look sick. You _____ to bed now.

05 나는 스파게티와 스테이크를 먹고 싶어요. (have)   I _____ spaghetti and steak.

06 여기에 앉으실래요? (sit)   _____ here?

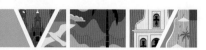

'(과거에) ～하곤 했다'와 같이 과거의 반복하던 일은 used to와 would로 쓰세요.

	used to (～하곤 했다)	would (～하곤 했다)
예문	I used to go there on Sunday. 일요일에 거기에 가곤 했다.	I would go there when it rained. 비가 오면 거기에 가곤 했다.
주의	used to 앞에 be동사를 쓰면 다른 의미가 돼요. be used to+명사: ～에 익숙하다 be used to+동사: ～하는 데 사용되다	과거의 상태를 나타낼 때는 would를 못 써요. There would be a tree. (×) → used to be He would live here. (×) → used to live

주의 과거의 습관적 행동을 나타내는 would는 상태 동사인 be, feel, taste, hear, have, live, love, like, want, understand, know, agree, believe 등과 같이 쓸 수 없고 used to를 써야 해요.

|A| 괄호 안의 말 중에서 알맞은 것을 모두 고르시오.

be, have, like, love, know, live 등의 상태 동사는 used to와 써야 해요.

01 There (used to / would) be a tall building here.

02 They (used to / would) live in this town.

03 We (used to / would) go to a movie every Sunday.

04 There (used to / would) be a store at the corner.

05 My grandpa (used to / would) be a police officer.

06 Luna (used to / would) be very shy.

07 I (used to / would) have many friends.

08 I (used to / would) play the guitar when I was free.

|B| 우리말과 일치하도록 used to나 would를 써서 문장을 완성하시오.

01 거실에 오래된 소파가 있었다.

There ＿＿＿＿＿＿＿＿＿＿ be an old sofa in the living room.

02 우리 할아버지는 주말에 야구 경기를 보러 가시곤 했다.

My grandpa ＿＿＿＿＿＿＿＿＿＿ go to a baseball game on weekends.

03 그녀는 축구팬이었다.

She ＿＿＿＿＿＿＿＿＿＿ be a fan of soccer.

04 이 나라는 매우 가난했지만, 지금은 매우 부유하다.

This country ＿＿＿＿＿＿＿＿＿＿ be very poor, but it is very rich now.

05 나는 시간이 있을 때마다 엄마에게 전화하곤 했다.

Whenever I had time, I ＿＿＿＿＿＿＿＿＿＿ call my mom.

06 우리가 더 어렸을 때는 벽에 우리 사진이 붙어 있곤 했다.

There ＿＿＿＿＿＿＿＿＿＿ be our photos on the wall when we were younger.

중간고사·기말고사 실전문제

객관식 (01~25) / 주관식 (26~50)

정답과 해설 · 9쪽

학년과 반	이름	객관식	/ 25문항	주관식	/ 25문항

01~02 다음 빈칸에 들어갈 말로 알맞은 것을 고르시오.

01

> It's cold outside. You _____ wear your jacket, or you will catch a cold.

① should not   ② may not
③ had better   ④ don't have to
⑤ can't

02

> She _____ play the guitar two years ago, but now she can.

① could   ② couldn't   ③ can
④ can't   ⑤ was able to

03~04 다음 빈칸에 공통으로 들어갈 말을 고르시오.

03

> 1. You _____ not run in the library.
> 2. He worked very hard yesterday. He _____ be very tired now.

① used to   ② must   ③ had better
④ would   ⑤ may

04

> 1. _____ I have this hamburger?
> 2. It _____ not be true!
> 3. _____ you help me?

① Can[can]   ② May[may]
③ Would[would]   ④ Must[must]
⑤ Should[should]

05 다음 중 주어진 문장의 밑줄 친 부분과 의미가 같은 것은?

> I want to have this bag.

① She would wear a beautiful ring.
② I would go fishing with my friends.
③ Would you do me a favor?
④ We would like to book a flight.
⑤ I went to see a movie last night.

06 다음 중 주어진 문장의 밑줄 친 부분과 의미가 같은 것은?

> You may not touch this jar. It's expensive.

① You must touch this jar.
② You don't have to touch this jar.
③ You can't touch this jar.
④ You would not touch this jar.
⑤ You had better touch this jar.

07~08 다음 대화의 밑줄 친 부분에 알맞은 문장을 고르시오.

07

> A: I'm worried about the game tomorrow.
> B: 너는 걱정할 필요가 없어. We are the best team in our school.

① You don't have to worry about that.
② You must not worry about that.
③ You should not worry about that.
④ You should worry about that.
⑤ You may not worry about that.

08

> A: Who is that man next to the window?
> B: I'm not sure. <u>그는 새로 오신 영어 선생님일지도 몰라.</u>

① He had better not be the new English teacher.
② He must be the new English teacher.
③ He has to be the new English teacher.
④ He may be the new English teacher.
⑤ He must not be the new English teacher.

09 다음 중 대화의 연결이 자연스럽지 <u>않은</u> 것은?

① A: Should I take this medicine?
  B: No, you don't have to.
② A: Look! The window is broken. Who did this?
  B: We had better call the police.
③ A: Can I clean this table now?
  B: No, I can't.
④ A: Do I have to do it now?
  B: Yes, you should do.
⑤ A: Where are you going this summer?
  B: I'm not sure. I may go to Busan.

10 다음 대화의 빈칸에 들어갈 말로 가장 적절한 것은?

> A: You look so tired. You haven't slept enough because of the test. You had better _____.
> B: You're right. I need to rest.

① studying hard so late
② study hard so late
③ not study hard so late
④ not studying hard so late
⑤ not studied hard so late

11 다음 중 앞뒤의 연결이 자연스럽지 <u>않은</u> 것은?

① She is absent today. She must be sick.
② It's hot inside. We had better open the window.
③ She speaks Chinese well. She may come from China.
④ You don't have to pay. It's a gift.
⑤ I used to play soccer when I was young. I still play it.

12 다음 밑줄 친 부분의 의미가 나머지와 넷과 <u>다른</u> 것은?

① You <u>must</u> stretch your body before swimming.
② We <u>must</u> keep quiet in the museum.
③ You practiced hard, so you <u>must</u> win the game.
④ You <u>must</u> clean your room every day.
⑤ We <u>must</u> study hard for a test.

13~14 다음 중 어법상 올바른 것을 고르시오.

13 ① She can't get up yesterday, so she was late for school.
② She must leaves home early tomorrow.
③ You had better read a lot of books if you want to be a writer.
④ When Tina was young, she can make a lot of friends.
⑤ He had to hurry now if he doesn't want to be late.

14 ① She must takes some medicine.
② Birds can flies very high in the sky.
③ The boy could ran so fast.
④ He will can hold a concert next month.
⑤ You should be careful when you use this knife.

15~17 다음 중 어법상 어색한 것을 고르시오.

15 ① You must be able to solve this problem.
② I would like to eat pizza, but now I don't.
③ I must not miss this chance.
④ We should wash hands before dinner.
⑤ You may go to the playground.

16 ① May I check your ticket?
② I'm hungry. I would like to eat something.
③ She's smart. She must be able to solve the problem.
④ She will be able to show the new design.
⑤ You can study hard if you want to pass the test.

17 ① The car used to be clean, but now it is dirty.
② I would go hiking with my father when I was a child.
③ My father used to watch TV every night.
④ My aunt would be a singer.
⑤ Rachel used to walk to school.

18 다음 대화의 빈칸에 들어갈 말이 바르게 짝지어진 것은?

> A: Hi, _____(A)_____ you help me?
> B: Sure. What do you need?
> A: I _____(B)_____ buy a ticket to Sokcho.
> B: The last bus to Sokcho departs soon! You _____(C)_____ hurry if you want to catch it.

	(A)	(B)	(C)
①	can	– would like to	– had better not
②	may	– would	– have to
③	can	– would like to	– have to
④	may	– would	– should
⑤	can	– would like to	– had to

19 다음 빈칸 ⓐ~ⓔ에 들어갈 말로 적절한 것은?

> • You _____ⓐ_____ do your homework if you want to play games.
> • You _____ⓑ_____ come to my party if you don't want to.
> • She _____ⓒ_____ like him, or she wouldn't give him an expensive present.
> • Tom _____ⓓ_____ arrive at the airport on time.
> • I _____ⓔ_____ go to the dentist yesterday because I had a toothache.

① ⓐ – must not   ② ⓑ – must not
③ ⓒ – should not   ④ ⓓ – has to
⑤ ⓔ – have to

20~21 다음 중 어법상 올바른 문장의 개수를 고르시오.

20
> 1. Mary would be very shy when she was a child.
> 2. He didn't eat his onions. He may not like onions.
> 3. You must stop watching TV.
> 4. This movie must be very boring.

① 없음   ② 1개   ③ 2개
④ 3개   ⑤ 4개

21
> 1. Mark was able to make a coding language.
> 2. You can't take photos here.
> 3. You had better arriving at the station early.
> 4. He can able to write his name in English.

① 없음   ② 1개   ③ 2개
④ 3개   ⑤ 4개

22~23 다음 중 어법상 어색한 문장의 개수를 고르시오.

22
> 1. I would like to volunteer at the animal shelter.
> 2. I saw many people visiting Mr. Harrison's house. He must be very busy now.
> 3. You look very sick. You had better see a doctor.
> 4. You shouldn't throw food at the animals in the zoo.

① 없음　　　② 1개　　　③ 2개
④ 3개　　　⑤ 4개

23
> 1. I used to living in Mexico when I was young.
> 2. People can't live without air.
> 3. We must follow the law.
> 4. You had better careful when you cross the street.

① 없음　　　② 1개　　　③ 2개
④ 3개　　　⑤ 4개

24 다음은 Sarah의 과거와 현재의 습관이다. 표의 내용을 바르게 설명한 것은?

	과거(매일)	현재(매일)
ride a bike	○	×
feed her dog	×	○
take a bath	○	○
play the guitar	×	×

① Sarah rides a bike every day.
② Sarah takes a bath every day.
③ Sarah used to play the guitar.
④ Sarah doesn't feed her dog anymore.
⑤ Sarah would feed her dog.

25 다음은 Hannah와 Jake가 해야 할 일과 하지 말아야 할 일의 목록이다. 표의 내용을 바르게 설명한 것은?

	Hannah	Jake
해야 할 일	study English	wash the dishes
하지 말아야 할 일	eat too much candy	play computer games too much

① Hannah has to wash the dishes.
② Jake must study English.
③ Jake must not wash the dishes.
④ Hannah should not eat too much candy.
⑤ Jake has to play computer games.

26~28 다음 우리말과 일치하도록 괄호 안의 말을 이용하여 문장을 완성하시오.

26
> 나는 어릴 때 피아노를 잘 쳤다. (can)

I _____ play the piano well when I was young.

27
> 우리는 택시를 타는 것이 낫겠다. (take)

We _____ _____ _____ a taxi.

28
> 그녀는 그렇게 일찍 일어날 필요가 없다.
> (have to)

She _____ _____ _____ get up so early.

29~30 다음 우리말과 일치하도록 괄호 안의 말을 바르게 배열하시오.

29
> 소금 좀 건네주시겠어요?
> (pass, the salt, could, please, you, me)

_____

30
> 제가 얼마를 지불해야 하나요?
> (I, do, pay, have to, how much)

_____

31~33 다음 |보기|에서 밑줄 친 부분의 의미를 골라 그 기호를 쓰시오.

┌─|보기|────────────────────────────┐
│ ⓐ 능력 · 가능　　ⓑ 금지　　ⓒ 요청 │
└──────────────────────────────────┘

31 You <u>can't</u> dive deep into the sea alone.

_____

32 Whales <u>can</u> dive deep into the sea.

_____

33 <u>Can</u> you dive with me into the sea?

_____

34~35 다음 |보기|와 같이 두 문장의 의미가 같도록 바꾸어 쓰시오.

┌─|보기|────────────────────────────┐
│ I want a cup of tea.   │
│ = I would like a cup of tea.   │
│ I want to have dinner with you.   │
│ = I would like to have dinner with you.   │
└──────────────────────────────────┘

34 Do you want some more water?

= _____

35 I want to order a cheeseburger.

= _____

36~39 다음 문장의 어법상 <u>어색한</u> 부분을 찾아 바르게 고치시오.

36 She mays went to the airport now.

_____ → _____

37 We would be good friends, but we don't talk to each other anymore.

_____ → _____

38 You will can see dolphins when you go to Jeju.

_____ → _____

39 You should being nice to your friends.

_____ → _____

40~41 다음 문장이 어법상 어색하지 않으면 ○를, <u>어색한</u> 부분이 있으면 밑줄을 치고 바르게 고치시오.

40 (1) I would like some coffee, please.

→ _____

(2) We had better not using plastic.

→ _____

(3) You should brush your teeth before going to bed.

→ _____

41 (1) She musts not drink too much soda.

→ _____

(2) He used to being a soccer player.

→ _____

(3) The driver have to drive more carefully.

→ _____

42~43 다음 문장에서 어법상 어색한 부분을 고쳐 완전한 문장을 쓰시오.

42 He could watched the movie yesterday.

→ _____

43 I will must move to another place next year.

→ _____

44~46 다음 문장을 지시대로 바꿔 쓰시오.

44 Eric must fill in the form for immigration.
(의문문으로)

→ _____

45 He had better bring an umbrella. (부정문으로)

→ _____

46 You are going to visit Vietnam this summer.
(의문문으로)

→ _____

47~48 주어진 |조건|을 이용하여 우리말을 영어로 옮기시오.

47 ┤조건├
  • want to를 쓰지 않고, 같은 의미의 다른 단어를 쓸 것
  • 단어 travel, around the world, all을 사용할 것
  • 9단어를 사용할 것

나는 세계 여행을 하고 싶다.

_____

48 ┤조건├
  • should를 사용할 것
  • 단어 an ambulance, call을 사용할 것
  • 5단어를 사용할 것

우리가 구급차를 불러야 할까?

_____

49 다음은 지민이와 소영이가 작년에 할 수 있었던 것과 할 수 없었던 것을 나타낸 표이다. 표를 보고 빈칸에 알맞은 말을 쓰시오.

	Jimin	Soyoung
solve the riddle	×	○
play the ocarina	×	×

Jimin _____ solve the riddle last year, but Soyoung _____. Jimin and Soyoung _____ play the ocarina last year.

50 다음 글의 밑줄 친 ⓐ~ⓔ 중 어법상 어색한 것을 골라 기호를 쓰고 바르게 고치시오.

Cinderella ⓐ has to work very hard every day. She heard there would be the prince's birthday party. She wants to go there, too. But her stepmother says, "You ⓑ must not go to the party if you ⓒ can finish your work." She thinks she ⓓ may not go to the party because of lots of works. Suddenly, a fairy appears and helps her. She thinks she ⓔ will be able to go to the party.

→ _____

CHAPTER

03
수동태

Unit 01   수동태의 의미와 형태

Unit 02   수동태의 과거시제

Unit 03   수동태의 미래시제

Unit 04   수동태 시제 종합

Unit 05   by 이외의 전치사를 쓰는 수동태

Unit 06   조동사가 있는 수동태

Unit 07   수동태의 부정문과 의문문

Unit 08   4형식 문장의 수동태

Unit 09   5형식 문장의 수동태

Unit 10   지각동사와 사역동사의 수동태

Unit 11   동사구 수동태

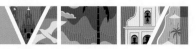
| 능동태 ↓ 수동태 | Many people love Pengsoo.

 Pengsoo is loved by many people. | 많은 사람이 펭수를 사랑한다. 〈Many people에 초점〉

 펭수는 많은 사람에 의해 사랑받는다. 〈Pengsoo에 초점〉 |

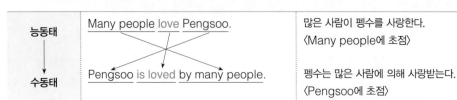

아래 순서에 따라 수동태 문장을 만드세요.

Step ①	목적어를 주어 자리로 옮겨요.	인칭대명사라면 주격으로 써야 해요.
Step ②	동사를 〈be+과거분사〉로 써요.	be동사는 주어의 인칭, 수에 맞추고 시제도 표현해요.
Step ③	동사 뒤에 〈by+행위자〉를 써요.	인칭대명사라면 by 뒤에 목적격으로 써야 해요. 행위자가 중요하지 않으면, 생략도 가능해요.

수동태로 쓸 수 없는 동사들을 기억하세요.

목적어(행위의 대상)가 없는 자동사: happen, occur, arrive, die, appear, smell 등

소유나 상태를 나타내는 타동사: have, fit, lack, resemble, cost 등

|A| 괄호 안의 단어를 알맞은 형태로 바꾸어 빈칸에 쓰시오.

01 He is _____ by me. (invite)

02 The letter was _____ by Minsu. (type)

03 The play was _____ last winter in Seoul. (perform)

04 English is _____ in many countries. (speak)

05 This newspaper is _____ every morning. (deliver)

06 Plastics, paper, and glass are _____. (recycle)

07 All of the rooms are _____ every day. (clean)

08 The song is _____ by many people around the world. (sing)

09 Pandas are _____ by laws. (protect)

10 A lot of rice is _____ and _____ in Asia. (grow, eat)

|B| 우리말과 일치하도록 괄호 안의 말을 이용하여 문장을 완성하시오.

01 싱싱한 채소가 날마다 우리 집으로 배달된다. (deliver)

Fresh vegetables _____ to my house every day.

수동태는 〈be동사+p.p(+by+행위자)〉로 표현하는데, 행위자가 we, you, they, people처럼 일반적인 사람일 때는 종종 생략해요.

02 맛있는 쿠키와 파이가 우리 엄마에 의해 구워진다. (bake)

Delicious cookies and pies _____ my mom.

03 다양한 영화들이 영화관에서 상영된다. (screen)

Various movies _____ at the theater.

04 그들은 가수가 되기 위해 전문가들에 의해 훈련받는다. (train)

They _____ to become singers _____ professionals.

05 다양한 약이 질병을 치료하기 위해 개발되고 사용된다. (invent, use)

Various medicines _____ to cure disease.

06 이번 달이 끝나기 전에 단 이틀이 남았다. (leave)

Only two days _____ before the end of this month.

|C| 문장을 수동태로 바꾸시오.

01 Ted cleans the floor.

→ The floor _____.

02 My little brother messes up my house.

→ My house _____.

03 People respect Ms. Park.

→ Ms. Park _____.

04 Many women copy the princess' dresses.

→ The princess' dresses _____.

05 Dr. White leads the study.

→ The study _____.

06 In the factory, robots do all the work.

→ In the factory, all the work _____.

07 Worker bees make honey.

→ Honey _____ worker bees.

08 The company supports some developing countries.

→ Some developing countries _____ the company.

실전 TIP

동사의 변화형과 수동태로
표현하지 않는 동사를 확인
하세요.

내신기출 다음 중 틀린 문장을 <u>모두</u> 고르시오.

① I am always surprised by my little sister's jokes.

② These days, a lot of songs are made by teenagers.

③ The best player of the year is chosen by many fans.

④ The beautiful house with a garden is had by my family.

⑤ The sports magazine is read by more than one million people.

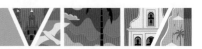
수동태로 과거시제를 표현할 때는 be동사만 과거형(was, were)으로 쓰세요.

능동태	Many people loved the book.	많은 사람이 그 책을 사랑했다.
수동태	The book was loved by many people.	그 책은 많은 사람에 의해 사랑받았다.

|A| 괄호 안에서 알맞은 말을 고르시오.

01 It (was invented / invented) in 1879.

02 Sam (wrote / was written) the book.

03 The tower (was built / built) in 1910.

04 I (were planted / planted) these trees.

05 The bread (was baked / baked) today.

06 My bike (stole / was stolen) yesterday.

07 This soup (cooked / was cooked) by him.

08 She (designed / was designed) this dress.

09 Edison (was invented / invented) it in 1879.

10 The book (was written / wrote) by Sam.

11 People (was built / built) the tower in 1910.

12 These trees (were planted / planted) by me.

13 I (was baked / baked) the bread today.

14 The man (stole / was stolen) my bike.

15 He (cooked / was cooked) the soup.

16 This dress (designed / was designed) by her.

|B| 문장을 수동태로 바꾸시오.

01 Mozart composed over 500 works throughout his life.

→ _____ throughout his life.

02 Gustave Eiffel built the Eiffel Tower in 1889.

→ _____ Gustave Eiffel in 1889.

03 They performed the opera last Christmas in New York.

→ _____ last Christmas in New York.

04 We canceled our trip due to the heavy rain.

→ _____ due to the heavy rain.

05 Leonardo da Vinci painted *the Mona Lisa* in 1503.

→ _____ by Leonardo da Vinci in 1503.

06 They broadcasted his speech all over the country.

→ _____ all over the country.

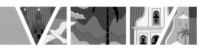

🔍 수동태로 미래시제를 표현할 때는 be동사만 will be로 쓰세요.

능동태	Many people will love the book.	많은 사람이 그 책을 사랑할 것이다.
↓		
수동태	The book will be loved by many people.	그 책은 많은 사람에 의해 사랑받을 것이다.

|A| 괄호 안의 단어를 사용하여 미래시제 문장을 완성하시오.

01 The door ＿＿＿＿＿＿＿＿＿＿＿＿＿＿ by Mr. Kim tomorrow. (repair)

02 Lunch ＿＿＿＿＿＿＿＿＿＿＿＿ at one o'clock. (serve)

03 The museum ＿＿＿＿＿＿＿＿＿＿＿＿ in Seoul next year. (build)

04 The project ＿＿＿＿＿＿＿＿＿＿＿ by my team soon. (finish)

05 The tickets for the concert ＿＿＿＿＿＿＿＿＿＿＿＿ on the Internet. (sell)

06 New uniforms ＿＿＿＿＿＿＿＿＿＿＿ next semester. (introduce)

07 Trees and flowers ＿＿＿＿＿＿＿＿＿＿＿＿ by students. (plant)

|B| 우리말과 일치하도록 괄호 안의 말을 이용하여 문장을 완성하시오.

🗨 수동태의 미래시제는 〈will+ be+p.p.(+by+행위자)〉 로 써요.

01 노벨 평화상이 오늘 수여될 것이다. (award)

The Nobel Peace Prize ＿＿＿＿＿＿＿＿＿＿＿＿＿ today.

02 신문과 잡지가 당신의 객실로 배달될 것입니다. (deliver)

The newspaper and magazine ＿＿＿＿＿＿＿＿＿＿＿ to your room.

03 책상과 의자가 2층으로 옮겨질 것이다. (move)

The desks and chairs ＿＿＿＿＿＿＿＿＿＿＿＿ to the second floor.

04 그 문제는 우리 부모님이 해결해 주실 것이다. (solve)

The problem ＿＿＿＿＿＿＿＿＿＿＿ my parents.

05 건조한 날씨 덕분에 빨래가 금방 마를 것이다. (dry)

The laundry ＿＿＿＿＿＿＿＿＿＿＿＿ quickly, thanks to the dry weather.

06 조만간 초대장이 너에게 발송될 것이다. (send)

The invitation ＿＿＿＿＿＿＿＿＿＿＿＿ to you sooner or later.

🎓 **실전 TIP**

시제가 무엇인지, 능동인지 수동인지 확인하세요.

내신 기출 ▶ 다음 빈칸에 알맞은 것은?

The school festival ＿＿＿＿＿＿＿ next Sunday.

① hold ② held ③ was held
④ will be held ⑤ will be holding

현재	am/are/is+과거분사	Pengsoo is loved by many people.
과거	was/were+과거분사	The light bulb was invented in the 1880s.
미래	will be+과거분사	A lot of food will be prepared for the party.

|A| 문장을 수동태로 바꾸시오.

01 We will save the Earth.　　　　→ The Earth ＿＿＿＿＿＿＿＿＿＿＿＿.

02 My grandparents raised me.　　→ I ＿＿＿＿＿＿＿＿＿＿＿ my grandparents.

03 Mr. Kim will repair the elevator.　→ ＿＿＿＿＿＿＿＿＿＿＿ Mr. Kim.

04 Picasso painted this artwork.　　→ ＿＿＿＿＿＿＿＿＿＿＿ Picasso.

05 People speak Chinese in Taiwan.　→ Chinese ＿＿＿＿＿＿＿＿＿ in Taiwan.

06 They will provide drinks for free.　→ Drinks ＿＿＿＿＿＿＿＿＿＿ for free.

07 He installed the new computer.　→ The new computer ＿＿＿＿＿＿＿＿＿.

08 I will keep all my promises.　　→ All my promises ＿＿＿＿＿＿＿＿.

|B| 우리말과 일치하도록 괄호 안의 말을 이용하여 문장을 완성하시오.

01 그녀의 웨딩드레스는 유명한 디자이너에 의해 만들어졌다. (make)

Her wedding dress ＿＿＿＿＿＿＿＿＿＿＿ a famous designer.

02 사진과 동영상이 네 스마트폰에 자동으로 저장된다. (save)

Photos and videos ＿＿＿＿＿＿＿＿＿＿＿ automatically to your smartphone.

03 한국 중학교는 1960년에 설립되었다. (establish)

Hankuk Middle School ＿＿＿＿＿＿＿＿＿＿＿ in 1960.

04 당신이 동의하지 않으면 당신의 정보는 수집되지 않을 것이다. (collect)

Your information ＿＿＿＿＿＿＿＿＿＿＿ unless you agree.

05 아름다운 시 한 편이 우리 엄마에 의해 쓰였다. (write)

A beautiful poem ＿＿＿＿＿＿＿＿＿＿＿ my mom.

06 선발 대회의 결과는 내일 아침에 발표될 것이다. (announce)

The results of the contest ＿＿＿＿＿＿＿＿＿＿＿ tomorrow morning.

UNIT 05 by 이외의 전치사를 쓰는 수동태

 전치사 by가 아닌 다른 전치사와 자주 사용되는 수동태 관용 구문을 외우세요.

be made from ~으로 만들어지다 (재료 성질이 변함)	be worried about ~에 대해 걱정하다
be made of ~으로 만들어지다 (재료 성질이 안 변함)	be covered with ~으로 덮여 있다
be known for ~으로[때문에] 알려져 있다	be pleased with ~에 기뻐하다
be known to ~에게 알려져 있다	be satisfied with ~에 만족하다
be known as ~으로서 알려져 있다	be tired of ~에 싫증이 나다
be filled with ~으로 가득 차 있다 (=be full of)	be surprised at ~에 놀라다
be excited about ~에 흥분하다	be interested in ~에 흥미가 있다

|A| 괄호 안에서 알맞은 말을 고르시오.

01 Her hands are covered (with / on) mud.

02 I am tired (with / of) living in this city.

03 Your name will be known (to / of) the world.

04 Everyone was surprised (at / with) the news.

05 She will be pleased (with / on) my gift.

06 Ice cream is made (from / to) milk.

07 I am interested (in / on) making robots.

08 The doors are made (of / on) wood.

09 Dan was satisfied (with / by) his new school.

10 Their house is filled (of / with) happiness.

|B| 우리말과 일치하도록 괄호 안의 말을 이용하여 문장을 완성하시오.

01 나는 전통 문화에 관심이 많다. (interest)

I _____ traditional culture so much.

02 좋은 와인은 신선한 포도로 만들어진다. (make)

Good wine _____ fresh grapes.

03 여러분은 그 영화의 결말에 흥분하게 될 것이다. (excite)

You _____ the movie's ending.

04 이 공은 고무로 만든 것이다. (make)

This ball _____ rubber.

05 우리 부모님은 우리 팀의 승리에 기뻐하셨다. (please)

My parents _____ my team's victory.

06 모든 사람이 그의 요리 솜씨에 놀랄 것이다. (surprise)

Everyone _____ his cooking skills.

> be made of는 물리적 변화가 있을 때, be made from은 화학적 변화가 있을 때 '~으로 만들어지다'라는 뜻을 표현해요.

내신 기출 빈칸에 들어갈 말이 <u>다른</u> 하나는?

① The room was filled _____ flowers.

② His clothes were covered _____ dust.

③ You will be surprised _____ the truth.

> **실전 TIP**
> 수동태 관용 표현을 다시 한 번 확인하세요.

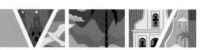

수동태의 미래시제와 마찬가지로 다양한 조동사를 이용해서 수동태 문장을 만들 수 있어야 해요.

능동태	Many people <u>might love</u> the book.	많은 사람이 그 책을 사랑할지 모른다.
↓ 수동태	The book <u>might be loved</u> by many people.	그 책은 많은 사람에 의해 사랑받을지 모른다.

|A| 우리말과 일치하도록 |보기|에서 알맞은 말을 골라 빈칸에 쓰시오.

┌ 보기 ┐
may be finished	could be delayed	should be carried	can be solved
can be prepared	must be returned	should be protected	must be kept

01 동물은 보호받아야 한다.   Animals _____.

02 교칙은 반드시 지켜져야 한다.   School rules _____.

03 배달이 지연될 수도 있다.   Deliveries _____.

04 그 프로젝트는 내일 끝날지도 모른다. The project _____ tomorrow.

05 그 문제는 곧 해결될 수 있다.   The problem _____ soon.

06 책은 일주일 안에 반드시 반납되어야 한다. The books _____ in a week.

07 아침 식사는 곧 준비될 수 있다.   Breakfast _____ soon.

08 이 상자는 안전하게 옮겨져야 한다.   This box _____ safely.

|B| 밑줄 친 부분에 유의하여 문장을 수동태로 바꾸시오.

조동사가 있는 수동태는 〈조동사+be+p.p.(+by+행위자)〉의 어순으로 쓰며, 조동사 뒤에는 반드시 be동사의 원형인 be가 와야 해요.

01 We <u>should</u> make right decisions for everyone.

→ _____ for everyone.

02 We <u>can</u> eat this fish without cooking.

→ _____ without cooking.

03 We <u>might</u> find wild animals in this area.

→ _____ in this area.

04 Drivers <u>must</u> observe the speed limit.

→ _____.

05 You <u>should</u> wipe this mirror softly.

→ _____.

06 We <u>can</u> see the island from far away.

→ _____.

UNIT 07 수동태의 부정문과 의문문

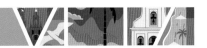

수동태의 부정과 의문도 be동사로 나타내지만, 조동사가 있다면 조동사를 이용해야 해요.

	be+과거분사	조동사+be+과거분사
긍정	The book is loved by all.	The book can be loved by all.
부정	The book is **not** loved by all.	The book can**not** be loved by all.
의문	Is the book loved by all?	Can the book be loved by all?

참고 조동사가 있는 모든 문장은 조동사를 이용하여 부정문과 의문문, 그리고 그 대답을 만들어요.

|A| 괄호 안의 지시대로 주어진 문장을 바꾸시오.

01 The train was delayed. (부정) → _____

02 The book will be printed in Korea. (의문) → _____

03 Rooms are cleaned every day. (부정) → _____

04 It is delivered in the morning. (의문) → _____

05 The letter was written by me. (부정) → _____

06 The ring was found on the bed. (의문) → _____

07 You will be surprised at the news. (부정) → _____

08 They are invited to the party. (의문) → _____

|B| 괄호 안의 말을 이용하여 대화를 완성하시오.

01 **A:** Could you move this sofa?

    B: Sorry, but this sofa _____. It's too heavy. (cannot, move)

02 **A:** I like this painting. It's Monet's work.

    B: No. This _____ Monet. It's Pissarro's. (not, paint)

수동태 의문문은 〈(의문사+)be동사+주어+p.p.(+by+행위자) ~?〉 또는 〈(의문사+)조동사+주어+be+p.p.(+by+행위자) ~?〉로 표현해야 해요.

03 **A:** When _____ breakfast _____? (will, serve)

    B: Breakfast will be delivered to your room at 9 a.m.

04 **A:** The work should be done by tomorrow.

    B: Sorry, but it _____ by tomorrow. (cannot, do)

05 **A:** How was the movie? Did you like it?

    B: No. I _____ the movie. (not, satisfy)

06 **A:** _____ English _____ in France? (speak)

    B: No. English is not spoken in France. They speak French.

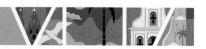

UNIT 08 　4형식 문장의 수동태

4형식 문장의 목적어 2개(간접목적어, 직접목적어)를 주어로 수동태 문장을 쓸 수 있어야 해요.

	간접목적어(~에게)를 주어로 쓸 때	직접목적어(~을)를 주어로 쓸 때
능동태 → 수동태	She gave them a card. They were given a card by her.	She gave them a card. A card was given to them by her.
주의	직접목적어는 동사 뒤에 그대로 쓰고, 능동태의 주어는 〈by+행위자〉로 넣을 수 있어요.	능동태의 간접목적어(~에게)를 〈전치사+사람〉으로 써야 해요.

> 주의 직접목적어를 주어로 할 때, 간접목적어 앞의 전치사는 동사에 따라 다르므로 주의하세요.

give, tell, send, show, teach, sell, write	to	A card was given to them.
get, make, buy, cook	for	Curry was cooked for us.
ask의 직접목적어가 question이나 favor일 때	of	A question was asked of me.

> 주의 make, buy, get, send, bring, write, cook 등의 동사는 직접목적어만 주어로 써요.

|A| 빈칸에 알맞은 전치사를 쓰시오.

01 The letter was written ＿＿＿＿＿＿ you by her.

02 A question was asked ＿＿＿＿＿＿ her by James.

03 The sports car was sold ＿＿＿＿＿＿ him by the dealer.

04 A cup of coffee was given ＿＿＿＿＿＿ the lady.

05 The sneakers were bought ＿＿＿＿＿＿ him by his grandpa.

06 Chicken soup was cooked ＿＿＿＿＿＿ the children.

07 History is taught ＿＿＿＿＿＿ the students by Mr. Willis.

08 Your passport should be shown ＿＿＿＿＿＿ the staff.

09 An umbrella was given ＿＿＿＿＿＿ the girl by her mom.

10 A favor was asked ＿＿＿＿＿＿ the speaker by one of the people.

11 Invitation cards will be sent ＿＿＿＿＿＿ the attendees by the boss.

|B| 문장을 수동태로 바꾸시오.

01 Jenny showed me her drawing.　→ Jenny's drawing ＿＿＿＿＿＿＿＿＿＿＿＿.

02 Someone sent me a long letter.　→ A long letter ＿＿＿＿＿＿＿＿＿＿＿＿.

03 Mr. Jeon bought Rosy new shoes. → New shoes ＿＿＿＿＿＿＿＿＿＿＿＿.

04 The chef cooked us spaghetti. → Spaghetti _____.

05 His girlfriend made him a cake. → A cake _____.

06 They gave the winner flowers. → The winner _____.

07 A stranger asked me my name. → I _____.

|C| 우리말과 일치하도록 괄호 안의 말을 바르게 배열하시오.

01 운이 좋게도, Jessica는 많은 기회를 받았다. (given, opportunities, a lot of, was)

Luckily, Jessica _____.

02 나는 우리 할머니에게서 따뜻한 이야기를 들었다. (told, a warm story, was, by)

I _____ my grandma.

03 이 초대 카드들은 Greg이 너희들에게 썼다. (to, written, you, were, by)

These invitation cards _____ Greg.

04 그녀의 이모가 그녀에게 예쁜 새 드레스를 사 주셨다. (by, her, was, bought, for)

A pretty new dress _____ her aunt.

05 그들은 피카소의 훌륭한 그림들을 보게 되었다. (were, Picasso's, shown, great paintings)

They _____.

06 많은 질문이 팬들로부터 그 가수에게 쏟아졌다. (asked, of, were, the singer)

Many questions _____ by her fans.

실전 TIP

간접목적어가 주어인지, 직접목적어가 주어인지를 먼저 파악하고 수동태로 만들어 보세요.

내신 기출 다음 문장을 수동태로 바꿀 때 빈칸에 알맞은 말을 쓰시오.

Stella told me the news about the accident.

→ I _____ about the accident by Stella.

→ The news about the accident _____ by Stella.

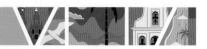

UNIT 09   5형식 문장의 수동태

5형식 문장의 목적어를 주어로 수동태 문장을 쓰는 방법을 알아 두세요.

목적격보어가 명사/형용사/to부정사일 때	
능동태	He made her happy / a doctor.	He told them to save money.
수동태	She was made happy / a doctor by him.	They were told to save money by him.

😊 참고 능동태의 목적어를 주어로 쓰고, 수동태 동사를 쓴 후, 목적격보어를 그대로 써요.

|A| 문장을 수동태로 바꾸시오.

01 People call him Little Bunny. → He _____.

02 Noah keeps the place clean. → The place _____ Noah.

03 Her song made us happy. → We _____ her song.

04 They elected Lucas the president. → Lucas _____ them.

05 My parents taught me to be kind. → I _____ my parents.

06 They found only one man alive. → Only one man _____.

07 The trainer told them to exercise. → They _____ the trainer.

08 The staff asked the boy not to run. → The boy _____ the staff.

💬 목적격보어로 to부정사의 부정인 not to run이 쓰였어요.

|B| 우리말과 일치하도록 괄호 안의 말을 이용하여 문장을 완성하시오.

💬 5형식 문장을 수동태로 바꿀 때, 목적격보어는 〈be동사 +p.p.〉 뒤에 이어서 그대로 써요.

01 모든 승객들은 안전벨트를 매라는 요청을 받는다. (ask, fasten)

All passengers _____ their seat belts.

02 Roy는 Teddy의 무례한 행동으로 인해 화가 났다. (make, angry)

Roy _____ Teddy's rude behavior.

03 학생들은 아무것도 만지지 말라는 경고를 받았다. (warn, not, touch)

Students _____ anything.

04 그녀는 떠나지 말라고 들었다. (tell, leave, not)

She _____.

05 그들은 불에서 떨어져 있으라는 경고를 받았다. (warn, stay away)

They _____ from fire.

06 사람들은 혼자 여행하지 말라는 조언을 듣는다. (advise, not, travel)

People _____ alone.

UNIT 10 지각동사와 사역동사의 수동태

지각동사나 사역동사가 있는 5형식 문장을 수동태로 쓸 때 목적격보어의 형태에 주의하세요.

	목적격보어가 원형부정사인 지각동사	목적격보어가 원형부정사인 사역동사
능동태	We saw the boys take their bags.	He made the driver stop.
수동태	The boys were seen to take their bags.	The driver was made to stop by him.
주의	목적격보어로 쓴 원형부정사는 수동태에서 to부정사로 써요. 단, 목적격보어가 분사일 때는 그대로 분사를 써요. The boys were seen playing soccer.	

|A| 괄호 안에서 알맞은 말을 고르시오.

01 He was seen (to enter / enter) the house.

02 They were made (to stay / staying) indoors.

03 You were seen (shop / shopping) at the supermarket.

04 Tiffany was made (to feel / feel) anxious before the test.

05 The window was heard (break / breaking).

|B| 문장을 수동태로 바꾸시오.

01 Her song makes me sing along.

→ _____ .

02 We saw the thief stealing the shoes.

→ _____ .

03 We heard some dogs barking outside.

→ _____ .

04 They made the workers move the stone.

→ _____ .

05 The police saw a man driving too fast.

→ _____ .

06 The instructor made me wear a life jacket.

→ _____ .

> 지각동사와 사역동사의 목적격보어로 쓰인 동사원형은 수동태에서 to부정사로 바뀌지만, 지각동사의 현재분사 목적격보어는 그대로 써요.

실전 TIP 목적격보어가 to부정사든 원형부정사든 수동태에서는 모두 to부정사로 써야 해요.

내신 기출 다음 빈칸에 공통으로 알맞은 말을 쓰시오.

- Everyone must be made _____ keep the traffic rules.
- Children are not allowed _____ play with toy guns in the country.

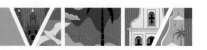

UNIT 11 동사구 수동태

동사구를 수동태로 전환할 때는 동사구를 하나의 단어처럼 취급해서 항상 붙여서 써야 해요.

능동태	Some girls laughed at the boy.	몇몇 소녀들이 그 소년을 비웃었다.
수동태	The boy was laughed at by some girls.	그 소년은 몇몇 소녀들에 의해 비웃음을 당했다.

참고 다음의 동사구를 외워 두세요.

laugh at ~을 비웃다	check out ~을 대출하다	run over ~을 차로 치다
look after ~을 돌보다	turn on ~을 켜다	bring up ~을 양육하다, 키우다
take care of ~을 돌보다, 처리하다	turn off ~을 끄다	pay for ~에 대해 지불하다
turn down ~을 거절하다	turn down ~의 소리를 줄이다	look down on ~을 무시하다
hand in ~을 제출하다	put off ~을 미루다[연기하다]	

|A| |보기|에서 알맞은 전치사나 부사를 골라 빈칸을 채우시오.

보기
out   off   for   over   down

01 Tickets must be paid _____ in advance.

02 The match was put _____ because of the weather.

03 The man was run _____ by a big truck.

04 The volume should be turned _____ now.

05 Only one book can be checked _____ at a time.

|B| 우리말과 일치하도록 괄호 안의 말을 이용하여 문장을 완성하시오.

01 과거에 여자들은 남자들에게 무시당했다. (look down on)

In the past, women _____ men.

02 그 공포 영화는 관람객들에게 비웃음을 받았다. (laugh at)

The horror movie _____ the audience.

03 이곳에 있는 아이들은 자원봉사자들의 보살핌을 받는다. (take care of)

The children here _____ volunteers.

04 우리는 서로 존중하도록 양육되었다. (bring up)

We _____ to respect each other.

05 그들의 결혼식은 9월까지 연기되었다. (put off)

Their wedding _____ until September.

06 네 수업료는 부모님이 지불해 주셨다. (pay for)

Your tuition fee _____ your parents.

중간고사·기말고사 실전문제

학년과 반	이름	객관식	/ 25문항	주관식	/ 25문항

01~02 다음 빈칸에 들어갈 말로 알맞은 것을 고르시오.

01
> The table _____ by him.

① moved
② was moved
③ be moved
④ are moved
⑤ is moving

02
> A: Who made this paper doll?
> B: It _____ by me.

① made   ② has made   ③ was made
④ is making   ⑤ be made

03~04 다음 빈칸에 들어갈 말이 바르게 짝지어진 것을 고르시오.

03
> A: Who _____(A)_____ my wallet?
> B: It _____(B)_____ by the man beside you.

	(A)	(B)
①	were stealing	– was stolen
②	were stolen	– stole
③	stole	– has stolen
④	stole	– was stolen
⑤	was stolen	– was stealing

04
> 1. I was surprised _____(A)_____ the scary mask.
> 2. I was interested _____(B)_____ playing the guitar.

(A) (B)
① at – by
② by – by
③ in – in
④ by – at
⑤ at – in

05 다음 글의 빈칸에 들어갈 말이 바르게 짝지어진 것은?

> D.O. is a member of the famous K-pop group EXO. The group has won many awards for their songs. D.O. is also known _____(A)_____ an actor. He is known _____(B)_____ the movie *Along with the Gods* and now he is known _____(C)_____ many K-pop fans as well as K-drama fans.

(A) (B) (C)
① as – to – for
② as – for – to
③ for – as – to
④ for – to – as
⑤ to – for – as

06 다음 빈칸에 들어갈 말로 알맞지 <u>않은</u> 것은?

> This art work was _____ by him.

① drown   ② painted   ③ drawn
④ bought   ⑤ colored

07 다음 빈칸에 공통으로 들어갈 말로 알맞은 것은?

> 1. He was worried _____ me when I was sick.
> 2. They are excited _____ the news.

① to   ② by   ③ for
④ with   ⑤ about

08~09 다음 빈칸에 들어갈 말이 나머지 넷과 다른 것을 고르시오.

08 ① About 70% of the surface of the Earth is covered _____ water.
② He was made to feed the dog _____ his mother.
③ She was seen to break into the store _____ the police officer.
④ The door was closed with a big noise _____ the wind.
⑤ The musician was loved _____ the audience.

09 ① This table is made _____ plastic.
② The box is full _____ candies and cookies.
③ She is tired _____ working all day.
④ He is satisfied _____ his new computer.
⑤ Some questions were asked _____ her by me.

10 다음 문장을 능동태로 바르게 바꾼 것은?

The blue jeans were worn by Jane.

① Jane was wore the blue jeans.
② Jane worn the blue jeans.
③ Jane wore the blue jeans.
④ Jane is wore the blue jeans.
⑤ Jane could wear the blue jeans.

11~12 다음 우리말을 영어로 바르게 옮긴 것을 고르시오.

11

그 빵집은 Sarah에 의해 깨끗이 유지되었다.

① The bakery kept cleaned by Sarah.
② The bakery was keeping clean by Sarah.
③ The bakery was kept clean by Sarah.
④ The bakery was cleaned by Sarah.
⑤ The bakery was been kept clean by Sarah.

12

이 지붕은 언제 수리되었니?

① When were this roof repaired?
② When will this roof be repaired?
③ When this roof was repaired?
④ When was this roof repaired?
⑤ When are this roof repaired?

13~14 다음 중 어법상 올바른 것을 고르시오.

13 ① She is resembled by her father.
② The accident is happened on the street.
③ He is arrived at the bus station too late.
④ The apple pie is smelled good.
⑤ The suitcase is delivered on time.

14 ① Was the guy hated by all his friends?
② The concert hall was built not in Spain.
③ When were the kids find in the forest?
④ What time will the money be able to give to me?
⑤ The small shoes could be not worn by me.

15~18 다음 중 어법상 <u>어색한</u> 것을 고르시오.

15 ① The secret was told to me by her.
② The cat was brought of me by mom.
③ The fantastic world was shown to me.
④ The red dress was bought for her by me.
⑤ Many questions were asked of her by him.

16 ① The child could be treated more gently.
② The plates should be washed after you have dinner.
③ The reason may be told by him.
④ She could not be ride a horse when she was young.
⑤ She must be given first prize because she did the best.

17 ① I was made borrow the book by her.
② I was seen singing loudly by my mom.
③ He was heard crying in his room by her.
④ I was asked to answer the questions.
⑤ They were taught to be polite in the class.

18 ① My sister was taken care of by my aunt.
② She was laughed at by her classmates.
③ The music was turned off by the teacher.
④ The homework was handed in the student.
⑤ The request was turned down by my boss.

19 다음 중 수동태로 바르게 옮기지 <u>못한</u> 것은?

① Nari showed her boss the new product.
   → The new product was shown to her boss by Nari.
② We must follow the rules.
   → The rules must be followed by us.
③ My parents call me sweet pea.
   → I am called sweet pea by my parents.
④ She cleaned the road.
   → The road was cleaned.
⑤ She cut her beautiful long hair.
   → Her beautiful long hair is cut.

20~21 다음 중 어법상 올바른 문장의 개수를 고르시오.

20
> 1. The wedding ring was made to her by him.
> 2. The new design will be shown at the conference.
> 3. The letter sent to my mother by me.
> 4. Latin America discovered by Christopher Columbus in 1492.

① 없음   ② 1개   ③ 2개
④ 3개   ⑤ 4개

21
> 1. The kitchen was cleaned by her.
> 2. The dog was bathed by Jenny.
> 3. The road was covered by snow.
> 4. This swimsuit is fit me well.

① 없음   ② 1개   ③ 2개
④ 3개   ⑤ 4개

22 다음 중 어법상 어색한 문장으로 짝지어진 것은?

> ⓐ An invitation card is sent me.
> ⓑ The laundry were doing by Lisa.
> ⓒ Jane was invited to the party.
> ⓓ I was cleaning the room.
> ⓔ The building was destroyed by the dynamite.

① ⓐ, ⓑ
② ⓑ, ⓒ
③ ⓐ, ⓑ, ⓒ
④ ⓑ, ⓓ, ⓔ
⑤ ⓑ, ⓒ, ⓔ

23~24 다음 중 어법상 어색한 문장의 개수를 고르시오.

23

> 1. The tall tree cut last weekend.
> 2. *Gulliver's Travels* were written by Jonathan Swift in 1726.
> 3. People are spoken Chinese in Malaysia.
> 4. The laptop was broke by my brother.

① 없음
② 1개
③ 2개
④ 3개
⑤ 4개

24

> 1. The old house needs to be painting.
> 2. The room is filled with pink roses.
> 3. I was made be happy by the present.
> 4. I was made to move the boxes by him.

① 없음
② 1개
③ 2개
④ 3개
⑤ 4개

25 다음 글의 밑줄 친 ⓐ~ⓔ 중 어법상 어색한 것은?

> Leonardo Da Vinci ⓐ was born in Italy. He was a genius. He ⓑ was interesting in painting, engineering, sculpture, and science. *The Mona Lisa* ⓒ was painted by him in 1452 and *The Last Supper* ⓓ was drawn from 1495 to 1498. These two paintings ⓔ are known to many people around the world.

① ⓐ
② ⓑ
③ ⓒ
④ ⓓ
⑤ ⓔ

26~27 다음 우리말과 일치하도록 괄호 안의 말을 이용하여 문장을 완성하시오.

26

> 그 선풍기는 Mina에 의해 켜졌다. (turn on)

The fan ＿＿＿＿＿＿＿ ＿＿＿＿＿＿＿ ＿＿＿＿＿＿＿ by Mina.

27

> 그 회의는 스미스 씨에 의해 연기되었다. (put off)

The meeting ＿＿＿＿＿＿＿ ＿＿＿＿＿＿＿ ＿＿＿＿＿＿＿ by Mr. Smith.

28 다음 빈칸 (A), (B)에 괄호 안의 말을 각각 알맞은 형태로 쓰시오.

> • The work must be ＿＿(A)＿＿ (do) by tomorrow.
> • Thousands of stamps were ＿＿(B)＿＿ (collect) by Mr. Smith.

(A) ＿＿＿＿＿＿＿ (B) ＿＿＿＿＿＿＿

29~33 다음 |보기|에서 빈칸에 알맞은 전치사를 골라 쓰시오.

┌보기├─────────────
   with   of   from   about
└──────────────────────

29 She is pleased _____ the good news.

30 The sculpture is made _____ stone.

31 I'm worried _____ my math test tomorrow.

32 This shoes are made _____ rubber.

33 I'm tired _____ studying Spanish every day.

34~35 다음 우리말과 일치하도록 괄호 안의 말을 바르게 배열하시오.

34
┌────────────────────────
많은 물고기들이 그 어부에게 잡힌다.
(fish, many, by, are, caught, the fisherman)
└────────────────────────

─────────────────────

─────────────────────

35
┌────────────────────────
나의 아버지는 일주일 동안 그 간호사에 의해 보살핌을 받았다.
(my father, by, was, for, taken care of, the nurse, one week)
└────────────────────────

─────────────────────

─────────────────────

36~37 다음 문장을 수동태로 바꿔 쓰시오.

36 My aunt took me to the library.

→ _____

_____

37 The soldiers attacked the enemy.

→ _____

_____

38~40 다음 문장에서 어법상 어색한 부분을 찾아 바르게 고치시오.

38 This grocery store built two years ago.

_____ → _____

39 When are you born?

_____ → _____

40 Was the movie star appear on the stage?

_____ → _____

41~42 다음 문장에서 어법상 어색한 부분을 고쳐 완전한 문장을 쓰시오.

41 Whom was this song written?

→ _____

42 The blue bird was had by Junho.

→ _____

43~44 다음 밑줄 친 부분이 어법상 맞으면 ○를, 어색하면 바르게 고치시오.

43 (1) Can I <u>worn</u> my glasses in the water?

→ _____

(2) Jeju is known <u>by</u> its beautiful scenery.

→ _____

(3) The car was stolen <u>by</u> the man next door.

→ _____

44 (1) The huge amount of gold <u>were finding</u> under the sea.

→ _____

(2) A lot of energy should <u>save</u> for the planet.

→ _____

(3) This TV is made <u>by</u> Korea.

→ _____

45~46 다음 |보기|와 같이 질문에 맞는 답을 쓰시오.

|보기|
A: Who invented the telephone?
B: (1) Alexander Graham Bell <u>invented the telephone</u>.
　 (2) The telephone <u>was invented by Alexander Graham Bell</u>.

45 A: Who made this cupcake?
　 B: (1) Jina _____.
　　 (2) This cupcake _____.

46 A: Who read this newspaper?
　 B: (1) My brother _____.
　　 (2) The newspaper _____.

47~48 다음 문장을 지시대로 바꿔 쓰시오.

47 The plan must be changed for the best result. (부정문으로)

→ The plan _____
changed for the best result.

48 My husband gave me the ring. (수동태로)

→ The ring _____
by my husband.

49 주어진 |조건|을 이용하여 다음 문장을 수동태로 바꿔 쓰시오.

|조건|
• 수동태를 사용할 것
• 주어가 the pizza가 될 것
• 9단어를 사용할 것

The chef cooked me the pizza.

→ _____

50 다음 글의 밑줄 친 ⓐ~ⓔ 중 어법상 어색한 것을 골라 기호를 쓰고 바르게 고치시오.

The movie *Wonder* has changed my life. I used to be very shy when I was in elementary school. I ⓐ<u>was laughed at</u> by my friends because I was too small. I ⓑ<u>was worried about</u> going to school before going to bed every night. When I saw this movie, I thought that the boy in the movie could understand how I felt. After seeing the movie, I ⓒ<u>was asked</u> my brother to exercise together. I ⓓ<u>was helped</u> by my mother's food to become tall. Now I ⓔ<u>am pleased with</u> my life.

_____ → _____

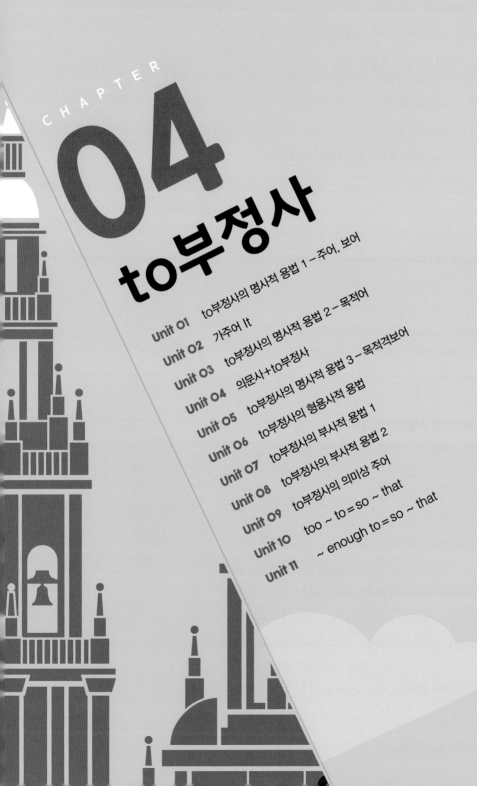

CHAPTER

04

to부정사

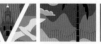

동사를 명사(~하기, ~하는 것)처럼 사용하려면 〈to＋동사원형〉의 형태로 만들어야 해요.

명사 역할 – 주어	명사 역할 – 보어
To become a scientist takes years.	My dream is to become a scientist.
과학자가 되는 것은 수년이 걸린다.	나의 꿈은 과학자가 되는 것이다.

😊 참고 부정사란 '정해진 품사가 없다'는 뜻으로 명사, 형용사, 부사로 쓰여요.

😟 주의 • to부정사는 뒤에 목적어나 부사구를 취할 수 있다.
      • to부정사 주어는 3인칭 단수 취급한다.
      • to부정사의 부정은 to 앞에 not을 쓴다.

|A| |보기|에서 알맞은 말을 골라 to부정사로 만들어 문장을 완성하시오.

보기
travel   eat   protect   invent   say   learn   keep

01 _____ vegetables is necessary for health.

02 _____ a foreign language is not easy.

03 _____ "Thank you" is important.

04 His dream is _____ a flying car.

05 My dream is _____ around the world.

06 _____ the traffic rules is dangerous.

07 His duty as a police officer is _____ people.

|B| 우리말과 일치하도록 괄호 안의 말을 바르게 배열하시오.

> to부정사는 3인칭 단수로 취급한다는 점에 유의하세요.

01 그의 취미는 가족들과 함께 캠핑을 가는 것이다. (go, is, to, camping)
His hobby _____ with his family.

02 최고의 방법은 서로 이해하는 것이다. (to, each other, understand)
The best way is _____.

03 개를 산책시키는 일은 그녀의 일과 중 하나다. (her dog, to, is, walk)
_____ one part of her daily routine.

04 Joy의 소망은 친구들과 함께 콘서트에 가는 것이다. (a concert, is, to, go to)
Joy's hope _____ with her friends.

05 컴퓨터 게임을 하는 것은 너의 눈에 안 좋다. (play, to, computer games, is)
_____ not good for your eyes.

06 내 방학 계획은 제주도를 여행하는 것이다. (Jeju, to, travel in, is)
My plan for the vacation _____.

UNIT 02 가주어 It

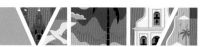

to부정사 주어는 문장 뒤로 옮길 수 있는데, 이때 가(짜)주어 It을 주어 자리에 넣어야 해요.

to부정사를 주어 자리에 쓸 때	가주어 It을 쓸 때
To become a scientist takes years.	It takes years to become a scientist.
과학자가 되는 것은 수년이 걸린다.	과학자가 되는 것은 수년이 걸린다.

참고 주어 자리에 쓴 It을 가주어라고 하고, 뒤에 쓴 to부정사를 진주어라고 해요.

|A| 가주어 It으로 시작하는 문장으로 바꾸시오.

01 To go skiing is exciting.　　　　→ It _____.

02 To study English is important.　　→ It _____.

03 To go to a movie is my hobby.　　→ It _____.

04 To exercise every day is good for you.　→ It _____.

05 To get a perfect score is my goal.　→ It _____.

06 To travel around the country is fun.　→ It _____.

|B| 우리말과 일치하도록 가주어 It과 괄호 안의 말을 이용하여 문장을 완성하시오.

가주어 It은 항상 문장의 맨 앞에 위치하며 3인칭 단수라는 점에 유의하세요.

01 헬멧을 쓰지 않는 것은 위험하다. (wear)

_____ dangerous _____ a helmet.

02 다른 문화를 이해하는 것은 중요하다. (understand)

_____ important _____ other cultures.

03 너 없이 박물관에 가는 것은 재미가 없었다. (visit)

_____ fun _____ a museum without you.

04 매일 일기를 쓰는 것은 어려운 일이 아니다. (write)

_____ difficult _____ a diary every day.

05 사전을 이용하는 것은 유용할 수 있다. (can, use)

_____ be helpful _____ a dictionary.

06 이 드레스를 사는 데에는 돈이 많이 들지 않는다. (buy)

_____ not cost much money _____ this dress.

실전 TIP
주어로 쓴 to부정사는 3인칭 단수 취급한다는 데 유의하세요.

내신 기출 다음 빈칸에 공통으로 알맞은 것은?

To fasten a seat belt _____ necessary.
= It _____ necessary to fasten a seat belt.

① be　　② is　　③ are　　④ do　　⑤ does

UNIT 03 to부정사의 명사적 용법 2 – 목적어

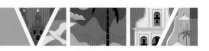

to부정사를 목적어(명사)로 쓸 수 있는 기본 동사들을 파악하세요.

want/would like 원하다	hope 바라다	plan 계획하다	refuse 거절하다
wish 소망하다	promise 약속하다	choose 선택하다	learn 배우다
expect 예상하다	agree 동의하다	decide 결정하다	need ~할 필요가 있다

참고 명사를 주어, 목적어, 보어 자리에 쓰듯이, 명사적 용법의 to부정사도 목적어 자리에 쓸 수 있어요.

|A| |보기|에서 알맞은 말을 골라 빈칸에 to부정사 형태로 쓰시오.

> |보기|
> make　　be　　leave　　have　　cook　　move　　meet　　put off

01 I wanted _____ a good time with you.

02 I hope _____ all of you soon.

03 Sometimes, Jane wishes _____ alone.

04 We are planning _____ to another city.

05 Would you like _____ a message?

06 I promise _____ the same mistake again.

07 Did you learn _____ spaghetti?

08 I cannot agree _____ the project.

'~하지 않는 것'을 의미하는 to부정사의 부정형은 to 앞에 not을 써요.

|B| 우리말과 일치하도록 괄호 안의 말을 이용하여 문장을 완성하시오.

01 우리는 미래를 위해 계획을 세울 필요가 있다. (need, make)

We _____ plans for the future.

02 나는 공항에 1시에 도착할 것으로 예상한다. (expect, arrive)

I _____ at the airport at one o'clock.

03 나는 지금 당장 찬물로 샤워하고 싶다. (want, take)

I _____ a cold shower right now.

04 이번 주말에 너는 조부모님을 뵈러 갈 계획이니? (plan, visit)

Are you _____ your grandparents this week?

05 수미는 2년 전에 바이올린 연주를 배웠다. (learn, play)

Sumi _____ the violin two years ago.

06 그들은 내일 소풍을 가지 않기로 결정했다. (decide, not, go)

They _____ on a picnic tomorrow.

UNIT 04 의문사 + to부정사

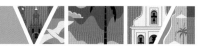

의문사 뒤에 to부정사를 써서 하나의 명사처럼 쓸 때, 문맥에 맞게 알맞은 의문사를 써야 해요.

what+to부정사	무엇을 ~할지	when+to부정사	언제 ~할지
which+to부정사	어느 것을 ~할지	where+to부정사	어디에서 ~할지
who(m)+to부정사	누가[누구를] ~할지	how+to부정사	어떻게 ~할지, ~하는 법

참고 〈의문사+to부정사〉는 〈의문사+주어+should+동사원형〉으로 바꿔 쓸 수도 있어요.

I don't know how to get there. 그곳에 가는 방법

= how I should get there 내가 그곳에 어떻게 가야 하는지

|A| 두 문장의 뜻이 같도록 빈칸에 알맞은 말을 쓰시오.

01 Tom learned _____. = Tom learned how he should swim.

02 I will tell you when to start. = I will tell you _____.

03 Teddy asked me _____. = Teddy asked me how he should spell it.

04 We are not sure where to go. = We are not sure _____.

05 Let me know _____. = Let me know which I should press.

06 I know how to use this machine. = I know _____.

07 I am not sure _____. = I am not sure who I should invite.

08 Tell me what to buy for my mom. = Tell me _____.

|B| 우리말과 일치하도록 괄호 안의 말과 to부정사를 이용하여 문장을 완성하시오.

〈의문사+to부정사〉는 명사적 용법으로 쓰이므로, 문장에서 주어, 보어, 목적어가 될 수 있어요.

01 이 지도는 우리에게 공항까지 가는 방법을 보여 준다. (get)

This map shows us _____ to the airport.

02 나는 방학 때 어디로 갈지 확실하지 않다. (go)

I am not sure _____ for my vacation.

03 다음으로 뭘 해야 하는지 네게 말해 줄게. (do)

I will tell you _____ next.

04 문제는 어디서 그를 만나야 하는가이다. (him, meet)

The problem is _____.

05 김 선생님은 영어로 쓰는 방법을 내게 가르쳐 주셨다. (write)

Mr. Kim taught me _____ in English.

06 언제 영어 공부를 시작해야 하는지가 나의 첫 번째 질문이다. (start)

_____ learning English is my first question.

UNIT 05　to부정사의 명사적 용법 3 – 목적격보어

목적격보어로 to부정사를 쓰는 동사들을 외워 두세요.

어순	주어	to부정사를 목적격보어로 쓰는 5형식 동사	목적어	목적격보어(to부정사)
예문	I	want, ask, tell, expect, allow, advise, order, get, help	him	to come
의미	나는	~한다	~이/~에게	~하라고 / ~하기를 / ~하는 것을

🗨️ **주의** help는 목적격보어로 to부정사와 to가 없는 원형부정사 둘 다 쓰지만, 원형부정사를 더 자주 써요.
She helped the children (to) make paper boats.

|A| 괄호 안의 단어를 알맞은 형태로 바꾸어 빈칸에 쓰시오.

01 A strange man asked _____ him the way. (I, show)

02 The doctor told _____ about his health. (he, not, worry)

03 They didn't expect _____ Lucy. (he, marry)

04 Becky will help _____ my little sister. (I, take care of)

05 He warned _____ bothering the boy. (the kids, stop)

|B| 우리말과 일치하도록 괄호 안의 말을 이용하여 문장을 완성하시오.

01 내 친구는 나에게 같이 쇼핑하러 가자고 요청했다. (ask, go shopping)
My friend _____ with her.

02 그 코치는 선수들에게 너무 많이 먹지 말라고 충고했다. (advise, the players, eat)
The coach _____ too much.

03 그는 아무도 그 호수를 헤엄쳐서 건너지 못하게 했다. (allow, no one, swim)
He _____ across the lake.

04 이 책은 학생들이 한국 역사에 대해 배우도록 돕는다. (help, learn)
This book _____ about Korean history.

05 우리 부모님은 항상 나에게 최선을 다하라고 말씀하신다. (tell, do my best)
My parents always _____.

06 그녀는 그들이 오늘 올 것이라고 기대했다. (expect, come)
She _____ today.

실전 TIP 👨‍🎓

help는 목적격보어로 to부정사와 원형부정사를 쓸 수 있어요.

내신기출 다음 빈칸에 들어갈 수 없는 것은?

This material will help you _____ the rule.

① remember　　　② to remember　　　③ remembering

UNIT 06　to부정사의 형용사적 용법

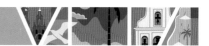

to부정사는 형용사처럼 명사를 꾸밀 수 있는데, 이때 어순에 주의하세요.

어순	형용사	명사	형용사	형용사 역할 to부정사
일반적인 명사의 경우	many	books		to read
-thing/-one/-body의 경우		something	interesting	(~해야 할, ~할)

to부정사가 수식하는 명사가 to부정사구에 포함된 전치사의 목적어라면 전치사도 함께 써야 해요.

수식하는 명사와 to부정사의 관계	명사	형용사 역할 to부정사	참고
단순 수식		to like me (나를 좋아해 줄)	
to부정사 동사의 목적어	friends	to trust (믿을 수 있는)	trust friends (동사의 목적어)
to부정사 전치사의 목적어		to talk with (같이 이야기할)	talk with friends (전치사의 목적어)

|A| 밑줄 친 부분을 바르게 고치시오.

01 There is no time <u>wasting</u>.　　　→ _____

02 We have a lot of work <u>do</u>.　　　→ _____

03 I need some friends to <u>understand</u>.　　　→ _____

04 Do you have time <u>talked</u> with me?　　　→ _____

05 There is medicine <u>stopping</u> the pain.　　　→ _____

06 He bought a new printer <u>use to</u> in his office.　　　→ _____

07 You need time <u>to thinking</u> about the problem.　　　→ _____

의미상 '(내가) 이해할 친구가 필요하다'보다는 '나를 이해해 줄 친구가 필요하다'가 더 적절해요.

|B| 우리말과 일치하도록 괄호 안의 말을 바르게 배열하시오.

01 나 너에게 말할 중요한 게 있어. (to, important, tell, something, you)

I have _____.

02 Cathy는 파티에 입고 갈 만한 예쁜 새 드레스가 필요하다. (pretty, wear, to, dress)

Cathy needs a new _____ for the party.

03 겨울은 스키를 즐기기에 최고의 계절이다. (skiing, to, enjoy, season)

Winter is the best _____.

04 차가운 마실 거라도 줄까? (something, drink, to, cold)

Do you want _____?

05 그에게는 버려야 할 나쁜 습관이 하나 있다. (get rid of, habit, bad, to)

He has one _____.

06 모든 사람에게는 대화를 함께 나눌 좋은 누군가가 필요하다. (someone, talk with, to, nice)

Everyone needs _____.

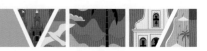

to부정사가 주어, 목적어, 보어가 아니라면, 부사의 역할을 하는 것으로 판단하세요.

부사적 to부정사의 의미	부사 역할 to부정사	같은 표현
~하기 위해서 (목적)	I exercise to lose weight.	= in order to lose weight
		= so as to lose weight
~하지 않기 위해서 (목적)	I try hard not to fail.	= in order not to fail
		= so as not to fail

|A| |보기|에서 알맞은 말을 골라 to부정사의 형태로 바꾸어 빈칸에 쓰시오.

┌─|보기|────────────────────────────────┐
ask   pass   stay   buy   arrive   win   learn   send
└──────────────────────────────────────┘

01 You should study hard _____ the exam.

02 We went to the department store _____ shoes.

03 I need a phone _____ text messages.

04 They came to Korea _____ Taekwondo.

05 All people need exercise _____ healthy.

06 She took a taxi _____ there in time.

07 Minho practiced soccer _____ the match.

08 I called my teacher _____ about the test result.

|B| 우리말과 일치하도록 괄호 안의 말을 바르게 배열하시오.

01 우리는 일출을 보기 위해 아침 일찍 일어났다. (see, to, the sunrise)

We woke up early in the morning _____.

02 그 아기는 넘어지지 않기 위해서 천천히 걸었다. (so, not, to, as, fall)

The baby walked slowly _____.

03 그들은 집으로 돌아가기 위해 첫 기차에 탑승했다. (home, get back, to)

They got on the first train _____.

04 Lucas는 늦지 않기 위해 학교까지 뛰어갔다. (in, not, order, late, be, to)

Lucas ran to school _____.

05 표를 사려면 줄을 서서 기다려야 한다. (the ticket, buy, to)

You must wait in a line _____.

06 그들은 매주 토요일마다 산책하기 위해 공원에 간다. (to, in, take a walk, order)

They go to the park _____ every Saturday.

> '~하지 않기 위해서'는 〈(in order/so as) not to+동사원형)으로 표현한다는 것을 알아 두세요.

부사적 용법의 to부정사는 '~하기 위해서(목적)'라는 뜻 외에 다음과 같은 의미로도 쓰이므로 문맥에 맞게 해석해야 해요.

부사적 to부정사의 의미	부사 역할 to부정사	의미
'~하게 되어 …한' (감정의 원인)	I'm happy to see you again.	다시 만나서 행복한
'~하기에 …한' (형용사 수식)	This sentence is hard to understand.	이해하기에 어려운
'~하다니 …한' (판단의 근거)	She must be clever to think of such an idea.	그런 생각을 하다니 영리한
'~해서 (결국) …하다' (결과)	The poor girl grew up to be a famous star. The sea turtle lived to be 188 years old.	자라서 (결국) 스타가 되었다 188살까지 살았다

|A| 밑줄 친 to부정사의 용법을 |보기|에서 고르고 우리말로 해석하시오.

|보기|
a. ~하게 되어   b. ~하기에(는)   c. ~하다니   d. (결국) ~하다

01 Japanese is not difficult to learn. → ( ) _____

02 I was stupid to say such a word. → ( ) _____

03 I want to grow up to be like my mother. → ( ) _____

04 This city is not too dangerous to travel alone. → ( ) _____

05 We tried our best, only to fail. → ( ) _____

06 Those books are very interesting to read. → ( ) _____

07 I am sorry to say this. → ( ) _____

08 My brother grew up to become a firefighter. → ( ) _____

09 This dress is beautiful to wear for the party. → ( ) _____

10 I am blessed to make friends with you. → ( ) _____

11 Mushroom soup is good to eat in the morning. → ( ) _____

12 She must be happy to get the present. → ( ) _____

13 James is hard to satisfy. → ( ) _____

14 Dogs are not easy to take care of. → ( ) _____

15 This juice is a little too cold to drink. → ( ) _____

|B| |보기|와 같이 to부정사를 이용하여 두 문장을 한 문장으로 연결하시오.

┌─|보기|────────────────────────────────
│ I hear the news. + I am sorry.
│ → I am sorry to hear the news.
└──────────────────────────────────────

01 We won the contest. + We were happy.

→ _____.

02 He met his teacher again. + He was glad.

→ _____.

03 I don't have the opportunity. + I am disappointed

→ _____.

04 I was invited to the party. + I was pleased.

→ _____.

05 They went to the amusement park. + They were really excited.

→ _____.

06 Everyone heard the sudden noise. + Everyone was surprised.

→ _____.

|C| 우리말과 일치하도록 괄호 안의 말을 바르게 배열하시오.

01 하나는 자라서 훌륭한 과학자가 되었다. (a great scientist, to, become)

Hana grew up _____.

02 그는 잠에서 깨어나 좋은 소식을 들었다. (hear, to, woke up)

He _____ the good news.

03 그렇게 커다란 물고기를 잡다니 그 어부는 운이 좋았다. (fish, such a large, catch, to)

The fisher was lucky _____.

04 나는 학교까지 달려갔지만, 결국은 학교에 지각했다. (for school, be, late, to)

I ran to school only _____.

> only to부정사는 '~하지만 결국 …하다'라는 의미임을 알아 두세요.

05 그녀는 열심히 공부했지만, 시험에는 떨어졌다. (to, fail, the exam)

She studied hard only _____.

06 혼자 여행하다니 유나는 틀림없이 용감하다. (travel, by herself, to)

Yuna must be brave _____.

> **실전 TIP**
> to부정사의 의미가 '~하다니 …한'이라는 '판단'인지 '~해서 결국 …하다'라는 '결과'인지 파악해야 해요.

┌───
│ (내신 기출) 다음 밑줄 친 부분의 의미가 <u>다른</u> 하나는?
│ ① You are so smart <u>to solve this math problem</u>.
│ ② My grandfather lived <u>to be one hundred years old</u>.
│ ③ She must be crazy <u>to turn down an offer like that</u>!
└───

UNIT 09 to부정사의 의미상 주어

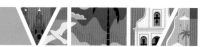

to부정사의 행위를 하는 주체가 따로 있을 때, 그 행위의 주체자를 표시하는 방법을 알아 두세요.

주어가 행위자	She was happy to see Paul. 그녀는 폴을 보게 되어 행복했다.	She = to see의 행위자
일반적인 행위자	The book is hard to read. 그 책은 (사람들이) 읽기 어렵다.	to read의 행위자 → 사람들
특정 행위자	The book is hard for children to read. 그 책은 아이들이 읽기 어렵다.	to read의 행위자 → children

참고 for children과 같이 to부정사의 행위자를 의미상 주어라고 해요.

의미상 주어는 대부분 〈for+행위자〉의 형태로 to부정사 바로 앞에 쓰지만, of를 쓸 때를 주의하세요.

사람의 성격이나 성품을 나타내는 형용사	의미상 주어	to부정사
kind, wise, polite, honest, nice, clever, generous, foolish, silly, rude, careless	of you	to say that
~하다	네가	그런 말을 하다니

|A| of와 for 중에 알맞은 말을 골라 빈칸에 쓰시오.

01 It is kind _____ you to say so.

02 It's important _____ me to achieve it.

03 It was stupid _____ her to trust him.

04 It was difficult _____ James to get a job.

05 It's generous _____ him to help the poor.

06 It's nice _____ you to teach me.

07 It was foolish _____ me to go there.

08 It was hard _____ me to focus.

|B| 우리말과 일치하도록 괄호 안의 말을 이용하여 문장을 완성하시오.

〈of+목적격〉의 형태로 의미상의 주어를 나타내는 형용사에 유의하세요.

01 네가 그 이유를 설명한 것은 친절했다. (kind, explain)

It was _____ the reason.

02 한국인들이 일본어를 공부하는 것은 쉽다. (Koreans, easy, study)

It is _____ Japanese.

03 나에게 사실을 말해 주다니 너는 정직하구나. (honest, tell)

It is _____ me the truth.

04 이 호수에서 아이들이 수영하는 것은 위험할 수 있다. (dangerous, swim, children)

It can be _____ in this lake.

05 나의 무례함을 용서해 주다니 그는 관대했다. (forgive, generous)

It was _____ my rudeness.

06 부모님으로부터 조언을 구하다니 너는 현명했다. (advice, seek, wise)

It was _____ from your parents.

〈too ~ to부정사〉를 〈so ~ that〉 구문으로 바꾸어 쓸 수 있어야 해요.

too ~ to ... …하기에는 너무 ~하다	I was too tired to study.	나는 공부하기에는 너무 피곤했다.
so ~ that ... 매우 ~해서 …하다	= I was so tired that I couldn't study.	나는 매우 피곤해서 공부할 수 없었다.

주의 〈so ~ that ...〉 구문에서 that 이하는 시제와 문맥에 맞게 쓰세요.

|A| 두 문장이 같은 뜻이 되도록 빈칸에 알맞은 말을 쓰시오.

01 It was _____ for him _____. = It was so late that he couldn't call.

02 You are _____ it. = You are so young that you can't watch it.

03 It was too dark for me to read. = It was _____.

04 The soup is _____. = The soup is so hot that she can't eat it.

05 He is _____ a player. = He is so short that he can't be a player.

06 This is too big for you to wear. = This is _____ it.

07 It's too cold for us to swim. = It's _____.

|B| 우리말과 일치하도록 괄호 안의 말을 이용하여 문장을 완성하시오.

01 우리 학교는 내가 걸어가기에는 너무 멀다. (walk, far, me)

My school is _____ to.

02 나는 매우 슬퍼서 울음을 그칠 수가 없었다. (sad, that, stop)

I was _____ crying.

03 그 음식은 어린 아이들이 먹기에는 너무 매웠다. (spicy, little children, eat)

The food was _____.

04 그 선수는 경주에서 우승하기에는 너무 느렸다. (slow, win)

The athlete was _____ the race.

05 이 시는 매우 길어서 우리가 외울 수 없다. (long, memorize, we, that)

This poem is _____ it.

06 그녀는 더 이상 집중하기에는 너무 졸렸다. (sleepy, concentrate)

She was _____ more.

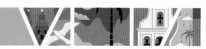

UNIT 11 ~ enough to = so ~ that

〈~ enough+to부정사〉역시 〈so ~ that〉 구문으로 바꾸어 쓸 수 있어야 해요.

~ enough to ... …하기에 충분히 ~하다	He is smart enough to solve it.	그것을 풀기에 충분히 똑똑하다.
so ~ that ... 매우 ~해서 …하다	= He is so smart that he can solve it.	매우 똑똑해서 그것을 풀 수 있다.

주의 〈so ~ that ...〉 구문에서 that 이하는 시제와 문맥에 맞게 쓰세요.

|A| 두 문장이 같은 뜻이 되도록 빈칸에 알맞은 말을 쓰시오.

01 I'm strong enough to lift the box. = I'm _____ the box.

02 He _____. = He's so brave that he will fight back.

03 He is rich enough to buy a house. = He is _____ a house.

04 He became _____. = He became so healthy that he can go out.

05 She ran _____ him. = She ran so fast that she could catch him.

06 They studied hard enough to pass. = They studied _____.

|B| 우리말과 일치하도록 괄호 안의 말과 enough to를 이용하여 문장을 완성하시오.

01 그녀는 버스를 잡을 수 있을 만큼 충분히 일찍 왔다. (catch, early)

She came _____ the bus.

02 그는 모든 사람이 믿을 수 있을 만큼 정직하다. (honest, believe, for, everyone)

He is _____.

03 이 바나나들은 우리가 먹을 수 있을 만큼 충분히 익지 않았다. (ripe, for, eat, us)

These bananas are not _____.

04 너는 너 자신을 챙길 수 있을 만큼 충분히 나이가 들었다. (old, take)

You are _____ care of yourself.

05 우리가 소풍 갈 수 있을 만큼 날씨가 충분히 따뜻하다. (warm, go, us, for)

The weather is _____ on a picnic.

06 우리 엄마는 좋은 요리사가 될 만큼 요리를 잘 하신다. (be, well)

My mom cooks _____ a good cook.

> to부정사의 의미상 주어는 enough와 to부정사 사이에 와요.

실전 TIP
'너무 ~해서 …하지 못하다'와 '~할 만큼 충분히 …하다'의 표현을 생각해 보세요.

내신 기출 다음 빈칸에 공통으로 들어갈 알맞은 말을 쓰시오.

- My dad was too tired _____ get up early.
- She is smart enough _____ put the puzzle together.

중간고사·기말고사 실전문제

객관식 (01~25) / 주관식 (26~50)

학년과 반		이름		객관식	/ 25문항	주관식	/ 25문항

01~03 다음 빈칸에 들어갈 말로 알맞은 것을 고르시오.

01

> A: Could you please let me know
> _____ to turn on this machine?
> B: Oh, you can just push that button.

① what　　② why　　③ when
④ how　　⑤ that

02

> He promised _____ my birthday again.

① not forgetting　　② not forget
③ not to forget　　④ forget not to
⑤ forget not

03

> She is strong _____ to become a triathlete.
> *triathlete: 철인 3종 경기 선수

① too　　② enough　　③ so
④ very　　⑤ much

04 다음 문장의 밑줄 친 It과 쓰임이 같은 것은?

> It is impossible to walk on water.

① It's sunny today.
② It's 3 o'clock.
③ It's dangerous to drive in the rain.
④ What is it?
⑤ I made it last night.

05 다음 빈칸에 들어갈 말이 나머지 넷과 다른 것은?

① It is careless _____ her to tell your secret to others.
② It is generous _____ you to help the homeless.
③ It is rude _____ him to say so.
④ It is honest _____ you not to lie to me.
⑤ It is fun _____ her to watch the comedy show.

06~07 다음 중 밑줄 친 부분의 용법이 나머지 넷과 다른 것을 고르시오..

06 ① Jack has so many things to do.
② There are many places to visit in the world.
③ I study Spanish to travel to Spain in the future.
④ Elizabeth really needs someone to talk with.
⑤ She has a plan to buy a beautiful vase.

07 ① Sam wanted to play the guitar.
② It was exciting to sing aloud together.
③ To feel the breeze is good.
④ My hobby is to read books.
⑤ To see gorillas, we went to the zoo.

08 다음 문장의 밑줄 친 부분과 용법이 같은 것은?

> I was pleased to meet them again.

① She is happy to have a family like hers.
② He lived to be ninety years old.
③ This frying pan is convenient to cook with.
④ She danced on the floor to please her mother.
⑤ The game was difficult to play.

09~10 다음 문장의 밑줄 친 부분과 용법이 다른 것을 고르시오.

09

> I'm going to the library to borrow books.

① I need some sugar to make apple jam.
② It is impossible to believe the news.
③ She turned on the lamp to find her ring.
④ I set an alarm to wake up early.
⑤ He quit his job to achieve his dream.

10

> Tom asked me to buy some bread.

① The athlete practiced hard to win the race.
② Her wish is to see Santa Clause.
③ I wish to have a turtle as my pet.
④ To invite a friend to my house is my dream.
⑤ It is hard to meet Robert these days.

11 다음 두 문장이 같은 뜻이 되도록 할 때, 빈칸에 알맞은 것은?

> Can you tell me how I should donate my money?
> = Can you tell me _____ donate my money?

① how   ② used to   ③ what to
④ what   ⑤ how to

12~13 다음 우리말을 영어로 바르게 옮긴 것을 고르시오.

12

> 그녀는 누울 충분한 공간이 없었다.

① She didn't have enough space to lie.
② She hasn't enough space to lie on.
③ She didn't have enough space to lie on.
④ She didn't have space enough to lie.
⑤ She didn't have space enough to lie on.

13

> 나는 너무 무서워서 밤길을 혼자 걸을 수 없다.

① I'm too scared to walking alone on the street at night.
② I'm too scared how to walk alone on the street at night.
③ I'm too scared not to walk alone on the street at night.
④ I'm too scared to walk alone on the street at night.
⑤ I'm enough scared to walk alone on the street at night.

14 우리말과 일치하도록 빈칸에 알맞은 말을 넣을 때, ⓒ 에 들어갈 말은?

> • 네가 일찍 일어나지 않는 것은 좋지 않다.
> = It is not good ___ⓐ___ ___ⓑ___
> ___ⓒ___ ___ⓓ___ ___ⓔ___ up early.

① to ② for ③ not
④ get ⑤ you

---

15 ① Jim decided not to move to New York.
② He refused not going to the hospital because he has no money.
③ He was so sad that he can see not his mother in the hospital.
④ Jane went to bed early not so as to be late for school.
⑤ She exercises regularly in order not to fat.

16 ① I hope to see Jina tomorrow and playing together.
② She wants to heat the room because it's cold inside.
③ To watching the football game is exciting.
④ The teacher told the students clean the classroom.
⑤ Mike refused going to the theater because he was sick.

---

17 ① You are too young to ride this bicycle.
② This road is bad to drive on.
③ He is strong enough to beat his rival.
④ It is wise of you not to fight with her.
⑤ There are lots of places play in Seoul.

18 ① She is too weak to carry this box.
② She gave me the paper to write on.
③ It's boring to watch online classes all day.
④ I'd like to learn how to make wooden toys.
⑤ We need something to wear warm.

19 ① It's easy for me to run very fast.
② It's impossible of me to find the answer.
③ It's careless of you to fall on the ground.
④ It's fun for us to play computer games.
⑤ It's friendly of you to be nice to everyone.

20~21 다음 중 어법상 <u>어색한</u> 문장의 개수를 고르시오.

20

ⓐ I want you talking with me all night.
ⓑ Is he known to be the people?
ⓒ He promised get up early every morning.
ⓓ Jamie told me to wait at the door.

① 없음   ② 1개   ③ 2개
④ 3개   ⑤ 4개

21

ⓐ I want to buy some fruit at the store.
ⓑ He ordered me going to bed early.
ⓒ We are ready eat dinner!
ⓓ You are too lazy to get up early.

① 없음   ② 1개   ③ 2개
④ 3개   ⑤ 4개

22 다음 중 밑줄 친 부분의 용법이 같은 것끼리 짝지어진 것은?

ⓐ Mom brought a dog <u>to make</u> it my friend.
ⓑ I like <u>to run</u> every morning with my dog.
ⓒ Is it important <u>to eat</u> well when I'm sick?
ⓓ We went to the beach <u>to swim</u> yesterday.
ⓔ Tom has enough money <u>to buy</u> a new watch.

① ⓐ, ⓑ   ② ⓐ, ⓔ   ③ ⓑ, ⓒ
④ ⓑ, ⓔ   ⑤ ⓒ, ⓓ

23 다음 중 문장 전환이 올바르지 <u>못한</u> 것은?

① He was so tired that he couldn't stay up late at night.
　→ He was too tired of staying up late at night.
② Jinny walked to the beach to see the sunset.
　→ Jinny walked to the beach in order to see the sunset.
③ The girl is so tall that she can reach the cabinet.
　→ The girl is tall enough to reach the cabinet.
④ Can you tell me where to go next?
　→ Can you tell me where I should go next?
⑤ It's tough to work in a foreign country.
　→ To work in a foreign country is tough.

24 다음 대화의 빈칸에 들어갈 말이 바르게 짝지어진 것은?

A: I'm worried about the vocal test next week. Can you advise me ___(A)___ improve my singing skills?
B: Of course. I'll give you some tips. Firstly, I ask you ___(B)___ voice training every day.
A: Great idea. I don't know ___(C)___ eat to improve my voice.
B: You should drink a lot of water. I think onion soup is also good for your voice.
A: Thanks a lot! It is really helpful.
B: I hope you get a good score.

	(A)	(B)	(C)
①	how to	practice	what to
②	how to	to practice	what to
③	what to	practice	how to
④	what to	to practice	how to
⑤	what to	to practice	what to

25 다음 글의 밑줄 친 ⓐ~ⓔ 중 쓰임이 같은 것끼리 짝 지어진 것은?

〈CHEF WANTED〉
We are looking for a new chef of our restaurant! Those skilled in cooking Korean dishes can apply for the position.

We promise ⓐ to provide plenty of rewards and many opportunities ⓑ to introduce your new menu to our visitors.

ⓒ To apply for the position, you will have to tell us or present some documents ⓓ to prove your work experience. We hope ⓔ to work together soon!

① ⓑ, ⓔ   ② ⓑ, ⓒ   ③ ⓐ, ⓓ
④ ⓐ, ⓔ   ⑤ ⓒ, ⓔ

26 다음 우리말과 일치하도록 괄호 안의 말을 이용하여 문장을 완성하시오.

Katherine은 요리하는 것을 배우고 있는 중이다. (learn, cook)

Katherine is _____ _____ _____.

27~28 다음 우리말과 일치하도록 괄호 안의 말을 바르게 배열하시오.

27
언제 공원에서 만날지 계획을 하자.
(to, at the park, let's, plan, when, meet)

_____

28
그녀는 이번 여름에는 산에 가지 않기로 결정했다.
(this summer, she, go to, not, decided, the mountain, to)

_____

29~31 다음 문장에서 밑줄 친 부분의 의미를 |보기|에서 골라 쓰시오.

|보기|
ⓐ 감정의 원인   ⓑ 결과   ⓒ 목적   ⓓ 판단

29 He grew up to be a musician.
→ _____

30 She must be foolish not to solve this problem.
→ _____

31 Minji was disappointed to miss the chance.
→ _____

32~34 다음 문장에서 어법상 어색한 부분을 고쳐 완전한 문장을 쓰시오.

32 I told my sister to passes me the ball.
→ _____

33 I ask him to lend me a pen to write.
→ _____

34 He goes on a diet in order lose weight.

→ _____

35~39 다음 문장의 빈칸에 |보기|에서 알맞은 말을 골라 쓰시오.

|보기|
| for | of | to | too |

35 It is necessary _____ us to check your temperature.

36 You should exercise regularly _____ be healthy.

37 This bottle is closed _____ tightly to open.

38 It is mean _____ him to tease the little boy.

39 YouTube is one of the easiest ways for teenagers _____ watch their favorite singers.

40~41 다음 두 문장의 의미가 같도록 괄호 안의 말을 이용하여 바꾸어 쓰시오.

40 I'm so strong that I can lift heavy stones. (enough)

= I'm _____

_____

41 To study psychology costs a lot of money. (It)

= _____

_____

42~45 다음 문장의 빈칸에 |보기|에서 알맞은 의문사를 골라 쓰시오.

|보기|
| what | where | when | how |

42 I don't know _____ to go. Should we go to the east, or to the west?

43 A: Do you know _____ to meet Becky for a meeting?
B: Yes, at one o'clock.

44 A: Can you tell me _____ to get to the convenient store near here?

B: You can go straight just one block and then you'll find it.

45 Don't tell me _____ to do! I'm old enough to know what I'm doing.

46~47 다음 문장이 어법상 어색하지 않으면 ○를, 어색한 부분이 있으면 밑줄을 치고 바르게 고치시오.

46 (1) I turned off the radio so as to not listen to the music.

→ _____

(2) She was enough shy to talk with strangers.

→ _____

(3) Mom explained what to cook a fried chicken.

→ _____

47 (1) I have something fresh to eat.

→ _____

(2) She had better wear socks to protect her feet.

→ _____

(3) It was meaningful of me to have dinner with you.

→ _____

48~49 주어진 |조건|을 이용하여 다음 문장을 바꿔 쓰시오.

48 ┤조건├

1) to부정사를 사용할 것
2) too를 사용할 것
3) 9단어를 사용할 것

The house was so big that I couldn't clean it by myself.

= _____

_____

49 ┤조건├

1) to부정사를 사용할 것
2) 의문사 what을 사용할 것
3) 8단어를 사용할 것

Tim's dog has died. I don't know what I should say to him.

= Tim's dog has died. _____

_____

50 다음 글의 밑줄 친 ⓐ~ⓕ 중 어법상 어색한 것을 골라 기호를 쓰고 바르게 고치시오.

When I was young, my dream was ⓐ to go to space. I asked my father ⓑ how to become an astronaut. He told me ⓒ to study math and science and ⓓ exercising regularly. It was hard for me ⓔ to pass the test to become an astronaut of NASA. But I could make my dream come true after all. Now I'm planning ⓕ to travel to Mars. I'm proud of myself.

_____ → _____

05

동명사와 분사

동사를 명사처럼 쓸 때는 동사를 to부정사로 만들거나 동명사(V-ing)로 만드세요.

구분	명사 역할 – 주어	명사 역할 – 보어
to부정사	**To become a scientist** takes years. 과학자가 <u>되는 것은</u> 수년이 걸린다.	My dream is **to become a scientist**. 나의 꿈은 <u>과학자가 되는 것</u>이다.
동명사	Becoming a scientist takes years. 과학자가 <u>되는 것은</u> 수년이 걸린다.	My dream is becoming a scientist. 나의 꿈은 <u>과학자가 되는 것</u>이다.

참고 V-ing 만드는 법은 현재진행을 만드는 것과 같으므로, Chapter 01 Unit 03을 참고하세요.
주어와 보어 역할을 하는 to부정사와 동명사는 의미가 같아요.

|A| |보기|에서 알맞은 말을 골라 빈칸에 동명사 형태로 쓰시오.

| 보기 |
| listen   eat   drink   take   become   teach   go |

01 My plan for this vacation is _____ skiing.

02 _____ to classical music is my favorite hobby.

03 My dream is _____ the best actress in the world.

04 _____ a shower every day is necessary in summer.

05 My mom's job is _____ English to students.

06 _____ warm tea can make you feel relaxed.

07 _____ vegetables is good for your health.

|B| 두 문장이 같은 뜻이 되도록 동명사를 이용하여 빈칸에 알맞은 말을 쓰시오.

동명사로 된 주어는 단수 취급한다는 점에 유의하세요.

01 It is not easy to learn foreign languages.

= _____ is not easy.

02 My plan for this weekend is to go to a movie.

= My plan for this weekend is _____.

03 One of Jimin's hobbies is to draw pictures of her dog.

= One of Jimin's hobbies is _____.

04 It takes a lot of effort to keep a friendship.

= _____ takes a lot of effort.

05 Mr. Smith's job is to design cars and motorbikes.

= Mr. Smith's job is _____.

06 It is Ken's aim to win first place at the contest.

= _____ at the contest is Ken's aim.

UNIT 02 명사로 쓰이는 동명사 2-동사의 목적어

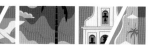

to부정사만 목적어로 쓸 수 있는 동사들이 있듯이, 동명사만 목적어로 쓰는 동사를 파악하세요.

enjoy 즐기다	keep 계속 ~하다	imagine 상상하다	practice 연습하다
avoid 피하다	quit 그만 두다	deny 부정하다	give up ~을 포기하다
finish 마치다	mind 신경 쓰다	suggest 제안하다	stop ~하기를 멈추다

|A| 밑줄 친 동명사가 문장에서 하는 역할을 |보기|에서 골라 빈칸에 번호를 쓰시오.

┌보기┐
ⓐ 주어   ⓑ 보어   ⓒ 동사의 목적어

01 Joy enjoys <u>watching</u> animation.   [   ]

02 <u>Drinking</u> enough water is necessary.   [   ]

03 Did you finish <u>doing</u> your homework?   [   ]

04 <u>Putting</u> on gloves will keep you warm.   [   ]

05 My favorite activity is <u>playing</u> basketball.   [   ]

|B| 우리말과 일치하도록 괄호 안의 말을 이용하여 문장을 완성하시오.

동명사를 목적어로 취하는 동사들을 다시 확인하세요.

01 너는 같은 음식을 먹는 게 꺼려지니? (eat, mind)

Do you _____ the same food?

02 너는 여가 시간에 무엇을 하는 것을 즐기니? (enjoy, do)

What do you _____ in your free time?

03 나는 다시 그와 함께 일하는 것을 상상할 수 없다. (work, imagine, can)

I _____ with him again.

04 나는 이 보고서 작성을 한 시간 안에 마칠 수 있다. (finish, write, can)

I _____ this report within an hour.

05 그는 옳은 일을 하는 것을 포기하지 않을 것이다. (do, give up, will)

He _____ the right thing.

06 밤에 자전거를 탈 때는 어두운 색을 입는 것을 피해야 한다. (wear, avoid, should)

You _____ dark colors when you ride a bike at night.

실전 TIP

동명사가 주어로 쓰였는지, 보어로 쓰였는지, 목적어로 쓰였는지 확인해 보세요.

내신 기출 다음 밑줄 친 부분의 쓰임이 <u>다른</u> 하나는?

① Do you mind <u>opening</u> the windows?

② Joy's wish is <u>traveling</u> around the world.

③ He didn't give up <u>becoming</u> a soccer player.

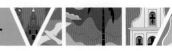

UNIT 03 동명사와 to부정사 목적어 – 의미가 같은 경우

동사에 따라 목적어를 to부정사를 쓸지, 동명사를 쓸지, 아니면 둘 다 쓸 수 있는지를 파악하세요.

to부정사만 목적어로 취하는 동사	want, wish, expect, hope, promise, need, plan, choose, decide, refuse, learn, agree
동명사만 목적어로 취하는 동사	enjoy, keep, imagine, practice, avoid, quit, deny, give up, finish, mind, suggest, stop
둘 다를 목적어로 취하는 동사	like, love, hate, prefer, begin, start, continue

|A| 괄호 안에서 동사의 목적어로 알맞은 말을 모두 고르시오.

01 He enjoys (to play / playing) chess.

02 She decided (to leave / leaving).

03 He promised (to come / coming).

04 I suggested (to go / going) there.

05 She denied (to say / saying) that.

06 We like (to go / going) shopping.

07 She gave up (to see / seeing) him.

08 It began (to rain / raining).

09 I expect (to meet / meeting) them soon.

10 He stopped (to eat / eating) junk food.

|B| 우리말과 일치하도록 괄호 안의 말을 이용하여 문장을 완성하시오.

01 Tom은 이틀 더 머무르기를 선택했다. (choose, stay)

Tom _____ two more days.

02 날이 어두워지기 시작했다. (get dark, start)

It _____.

03 우리는 공원에서 계속 산책했다. (keep, take a walk)

We _____ at the park.

04 그들은 그 프로젝트를 연기하기로 동의했다. (agree, delay)

They _____ the project.

05 음악 좀 꺼 주시겠어요? (turn off, mind)

Would you _____ the music?

06 우리 할머니는 주말 저녁에 TV 드라마 시청을 즐기신다. (watch, enjoy)

My grandma _____ TV dramas on weekend evenings.

> 문장의 본동사를 기준으로 본동사보다 이전에 발생한 일은 동명사 형태로, 나중에 발생하는 일은 to부정사 형태로 쓴다는 대략적인 개념을 이해해야 해요.

실전 TIP

동명사와 to부정사를 모두 목적어로 취하는 동사를 확인하세요.

(내신 기출) 다음 빈칸에 공통으로 들어갈 수 있는 것은?

• Suddenly, she _____ crying loudly.

• They _____ to argue with each other.

① began   ② decided   ③ finished

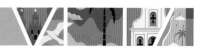

UNIT 04 동명사와 to부정사 목적어 – 의미가 다른 경우

목적어가 to부정사일 때와 동명사일 때 의미가 달라지는 동사에 주의하세요.

	to부정사	동명사
remember	I remembered to call him. 전화해야 한다는 걸 기억했다	I remembered calling him. 전화했던 걸 기억했다
forget	I forgot to call him. 전화해야 하는 걸 잊었다	I forgot calling him. 전화했다는 걸 잊었다
try	I tried to call him. 전화하려고 노력했다	I tried calling him. 전화를 (한번) 시도해 봤다
regret	I regretted to call him. 전화하게 되어 유감이었다/안타까웠다	I regretted calling him. 전화했던 걸 후회했다

> 주의 stop은 동명사를 목적어로 취하며, 〈stop+to부정사〉는 '~하기 위해 멈추다'라는 의미로, 이때 to부정사는 목적어가 아니라 부사(~하기 위해)로 쓰인 것임을 알아 두세요.
> I stopped calling him. 전화하는 걸 그만뒀다
> I stopped to call him. 전화하기 위해 멈췄다

|A| 밑줄 친 부분의 의미를 우리말로 쓰시오.

01 We stopped to have some food. _____

02 You should remember to buy some milk and bread. _____

03 We regret to inform you of the death of your dog. _____

04 You'd better not forget to take the medicine on time. _____

05 Teresa really regrets not listening to her teacher. _____

06 Do you remember visiting Paris in 2017? _____

|B| 괄호 안의 단어를 알맞은 형태로 바꾸어 빈칸에 쓰시오.

to부정사와 동명사를 모두 목적어로 취하는 동사들은 대체로 목적어가 과거의 일이라면 동명사를, 미래의 일이라면 to부정사를 써요.

01 Do you remember _____ to the concert last year? (go)

02 I can't forget _____ a talk with you at the party two years ago. (have)

03 Please stop _____ a noise. It's too noisy here. (make)

04 Remember _____ your umbrella. It is going to rain soon. (bring)

05 She regrets _____ badly when she was younger. (behave)

06 Don't forget _____ me when you arrive at the airport. (call)

07 I'm too tired. Let's stop _____ a rest. (take)

08 The customer tried _____ the machine before buying it. (use)

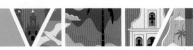

UNIT 05 동명사와 to부정사 목적어 종합

to부정사 목적어와 동명사 목적어에 대해 종합적으로 학습하세요.

to부정사만 목적어로 취하는 동사	want, wish, expect, hope, promise, need, plan, choose, decide, refuse, learn, agree
동명사만 목적어로 취하는 동사	enjoy, keep, imagine, practice, avoid, quit, deny, give up, finish, mind, suggest, stop
둘 다 취하고 의미가 같은 동사	like, love, hate, prefer, begin, start, continue
둘 다 취하지만 의미가 다른 동사	remember, forget, try, regret

|A| 밑줄 친 부분이 어법상 맞으면 ○를 쓰고, 틀리면 바르게 고치시오.

01 Do you <u>mind opening</u> the doors? → (   )

02 Will you <u>promise doing</u> your best? → (   )

03 Do you <u>enjoy to traveling</u> all around the country? → (   )

04 How could you <u>refuse to help</u> the poor? → (   )

05 Can you <u>imagine to have</u> no friends? → (   )

|B| 우리말과 일치하도록 괄호 안의 말을 이용하여 문장을 완성하시오.

01 아기는 배가 고파서 울기 시작했다. (start, cry)

The baby _____ because she felt hungry.

02 너희는 미래에 대해 생각해 볼 수 있도록 멈추는 게 좋겠다. (stop, think)

You'd better _____ about your future.

03 나는 더 좋은 점수를 얻기 위해서 열심히 공부하고 싶다. (study hard, want)

I _____ to get better grades.

04 너는 바이올린 연주 배웠던 거 기억하니? (remember, learn)

Do you _____ how to play the violin?

05 우리는 서로 돕고 이해해야 한다. (need, help)

We _____ and understand each other.

06 어떻게 해야 우리가 이기적으로 되는 것을 피할 수 있지? (become, avoid)

How can we _____ selfish?

> 동사에 '~하는 것을, ~하기를, ~한 것을'이라는 목적어가 필요할 때, 어떤 형태의 목적어를 취하는지 알아야 해요.

실전 TIP

to부정사를 목적어로 취할 수 없는 동사를 찾으세요.

내신 기출 다음 빈칸에 들어갈 수 <u>없는</u> 것은?

We _____ to go to the art museum this weekend.

① want ② plan ③ enjoy ④ agree ⑤ decide

UNIT 06 전치사의 목적어 & 동명사 관용표현

동명사와 자주 쓰이는 관용표현을 외워 두세요.

go -ing	~하러 가다	be worth -ing	~할 가치가 있다
How[What] about -ing?	~하는 게 어때?	have trouble -ing	~하는 데 어려움이 있다
be busy -ing	~하느라 바쁘다	feel like -ing	~하고 싶다
spend+시간/돈+-ing	시간/돈을 ~하는 데 쓰다	It is no use -ing	~해 봐야 소용없다
look forward to -ing	~하기를 기대하다	on[upon] -ing	~하자마자 (= as soon as)
be used to -ing	~에 익숙하다	cannot help -ing	~할 수밖에 없다
Thank you for -ing	~한 것에 대해 감사하다	by -ing	~함으로써

참고 동명사는 to부정사와 달리, 전치사의 목적어로도 쓸 수 있어요.

참고 〈can't help -ing〉는 〈can't help but+동사원형〉으로도 쓸 수 있어요.

I can't help laughing. (웃지 않을 수 없다) = I can't help but laugh.

|A| 우리말과 일치하도록 |보기|에서 알맞은 표현을 골라 문장을 완성하시오.

┌─보기┐
on -ing   go -ing   can't help -ing
be worth -ing   what about -ing be no use -ing
└──────┘

01 그는 그녀와 사랑에 빠지지 않을 수 없었다. (fall)

He _____ in love with her.

02 그의 가족은 신선한 공기와 야생 생물을 즐기기 위해 캠핑하러 갔다. (camp)

His family _____ to enjoy the fresh air and wildlife.

03 정보를 위해 인터넷을 검색하는 게 어떨까? (search)

_____ the Internet for information?

04 겸손하게 지내는 것은 칭찬을 받을 만하다. (be praised)

Staying modest _____.

05 쏟아진 우유를 두고 울어 봐야 소용없다. (cry)

It _____ over spilt milk.

06 역에 도착하자마자, 그는 표를 샀다. (arrive at)

_____ the station, he bought a ticket.

|B| 괄호 안에 주어진 말을 이용하여 문장을 현재시제로 완성하시오.

01 Becky _____ early in the morning. (get up, be used to)

02 She _____ always _____ the housework. (do, be busy)

03 Don't _____ computer games. (play, much time, spend)

04 Jessica _____ new friends at school. (make, have trouble)

05 I _____ you in person. (look forward to, meet)

06 Ted _____ at home today because he is tired. (stay, feel like)

전치사의 목적어로 동사가 올 때는 동명사로 써요.

|C| 우리말과 일치하도록 괄호 안의 말을 이용하여 문장을 완성하시오.

01 너는 네 개를 돌보는 일에 책임이 있다. (be responsible for, take care of)

You _____ your dog.

02 제게 이런 기회를 주셔서 감사합니다. (thank you for, give)

_____ me this opportunity.

03 Joy는 노래를 작곡하는 일을 잘한다. (be good at, compose)

Joy _____ songs.

04 심각한 교통 체증은 우리가 제시간에 도착하는 것을 막았다. (prevent ~ from, arrive)

Heavy traffic _____ on time.

05 나는 나 혼자 외국 여행을 하는 것을 꿈꾼다. (dream of, travel)

I _____ abroad by myself.

06 그들은 과학 실험을 하는 것에 흥미가 있다. (be interested in, do)

They _____ a science experiment.

07 학생들은 처음으로 견학을 가는 일에 마음이 들떠 있었다. (be excited about, go)

The students _____ on a field trip for the first time.

실전 TIP

전치사의 목적어로 to부정사는 올 수 없어요.

내신기출 다음 중 틀린 문장을 찾아 바르게 고치시오.

① The sky went dark and it started to rain.

② She apologized for not to keep her promise.

③ You should remember to call us when you arrive!

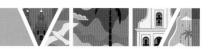

UNIT 07 현재분사 vs. 과거분사

동사를 형용사(명사 수식, 보어 역할)처럼 쓰기 위해서는 현재분사나 과거분사로 만들어야 해요.

		현재분사	과거분사
형태		동사+-ing	과거분사형 (-ed 또는 불규칙 형태)
의미		~하는 (능동)	~된, ~당한 (수동)
역할	명사 수식	falling leaves 떨어지는	fallen leaves 떨어진
	보어	The news is shocking. 충격적인	People are shocked. 충격 받은

참고 V-ing와 과거분사형(p.p.)은 여러 용도로 쓰인다는 걸 기억하세요.

V-ing		p.p.	
진행형	He is singing now. 노래하는 중이다	수동태	The car is fixed. 고쳐졌다
동명사	Singing is fun. 노래하기는 재미있다	완료형	He has already fixed it. 이미 고쳤다
현재분사	a singing bird 노래하는 새	과거분사	the fixed car 고쳐진 차

|A| 괄호 안의 단어를 알맞은 분사 형태로 바꾸어 빈칸에 쓰시오.

현재분사는 능동의 의미, 과거분사는 수동의 의미를 가진다는 사실을 유념하세요.

01 The man _____ on the sofa is my father. (sit)

02 I like the boy _____ behind the teacher. (stand)

03 The shoes were _____ in Italy. (make)

04 They sell _____ cars to customers. (use)

05 The door is _____, so I can't come into the house. (lock)

06 Could you please fix this _____ window? (break)

07 Do you know the tall girl _____ Jimin? (name)

08 The train _____ for Busan was delayed. (leave)

|B| 우리말과 일치하도록 괄호 안의 말을 이용하여 문장을 완성하시오.

01 선수들이 운동장에서 뛰고 있었다. (run) The players were _____ on the track.

02 편지 한 통이 그 책상에 남겨져 있었다. (leave) A letter was _____ on the desk.

03 네 자전거는 곧 수리될 것이다. (repair) Your bike will be _____ soon.

04 이 소설은 한 학생에 의해 집필되었다. (write) This novel was _____ by a student.

05 나는 그 파티에 초대받지 못했다. (invite) I wasn't _____ to the party.

06 그들은 악수를 하고 있니? (shake) Are they _____ hands?

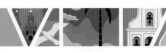

분사는 목적어나 부사(구)를 취할 수 있고, 이때는 명사를 뒤에서 수식한다는 것을 알아 두세요.

현재분사	명사 앞	Do you know the running dog? 달리고 있는 개
	명사 뒤	Do you know the dog running in the park? 공원에서 달리고 있는 개
과거분사	명사 앞	My uncle will fix the broken window. 깨진 창
	명사 뒤	My uncle will fix the window broken by a boy. 소년에 의해 깨진 창

|A| 우리말과 일치하도록 괄호 안의 말을 이용하여 빈칸을 채우시오.

01 걸어 다니는 사전 (walk, dictionary)　　　a _____

02 울고 있는 저 아기 (cry, baby)　　　that _____

03 그가 만든 모든 노래 (make, song)　　　all the _____ by him

04 영어로 쓰인 책 한 권 (write, book)　　　a _____ in English

05 쓰러진 나무 (fall, tree)　　　a _____

06 노래를 부르고 있는 그 소녀 (sing, girl)　　　the _____ a song

07 이 썩은 계란 (rot, egg)　　　this _____

08 떨리는 목소리로 (tremble, voice)　　　in a _____

분사가 명사를 단독으로 수식하는 경우에는 명사 앞에 위치하고, 다른 수식어구와 함께 쓰이는 경우에는 명사 뒤에 위치함을 알아 두세요.

|B| 주어진 문장과 같은 뜻이 되도록 빈칸을 채워 문장을 완성하시오.

01 We know the boy. He is leaning against a tree.

= We know _____.

02 There are a lot of toys. They are displayed on the shelf.

= There are a lot of _____.

03 Apples were picked this morning. They taste very good.

= The _____ taste very good.

04 The president was Tony Smith. He was elected yesterday.

= _____ was Tony Smith.

05 A woman is introducing him. She is his teacher.

= _____ is his teacher.

06 A woman is waiting at the gate. She is my mother.

= _____ is my mother.

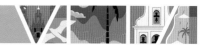

UNIT 09 보어로 쓰이는 분사

분사를 형용사처럼 보어로 쓸 때, 주어나 목적어와의 관계가 능동인지 수동인지 파악하세요.

주격 보어	현재분사	The news is surprising. 놀라게 하는, 놀라운	news = surprising 관계
	과거분사	We are surprised by the news. 놀람을 당한, 놀란	We = surprised 관계
목적격 보어	현재분사	I heard someone calling my name. 부르는	someone = calling 관계
	과거분사	I heard my name called. 불려지는	my name = called 관계

|A| 괄호 안에서 알맞은 말을 고르시오.

01 I want to get my hair (cutting / cut) today.

02 He looked (exhausting / exhausted) after the soccer match.

03 They could enter the house because the door was (breaking / broken).

04 This movie was so (boring / bored) that I couldn't help falling asleep.

05 The boy got his left leg (breaking / broken) in the accident.

06 Didn't you hear your name (calling / called)?

07 She found her new school (interesting / interested).

08 A lot of fans saw their favorite singer (dancing / danced) on the stage.

|B| 우리말과 일치하도록 괄호 안의 말을 이용하여 문장을 완성하시오.

01 그의 엄마는 그의 새로운 보라색 머리를 보고 충격을 받게 되었다. (become, shock)

His mom _____ to see his new purple hair.

02 우리는 돌고래 몇 마리가 바다에서 수영하고 있는 것을 보았다. (see, swim)

We _____ some dolphins _____ in the ocean.

03 그녀는 모든 창문이 누군가에 의해 열린 것을 발견했다. (find, open)

She _____ all the windows _____ by someone.

04 우리 엄마는 나의 옷을 세탁해 주셨다. (have, wash)

My mom _____ my clothes _____.

05 나는 눈사람처럼 보이기 위해 온몸을 하얀색으로 칠했다. (get, paint)

I _____ my whole body _____ white to look like a snowman.

06 Emily는 그녀의 휴대전화가 공원 벤치에 남겨져 있는 것을 발견했다. (find, leave)

Emily _____ her cell phone _____ on the bench at the park.

과거분사는 지각동사와 사역동사의 목적격보어로도 써요. 이때, 목적어와 목적격보어는 수동 관계라는 점을 유의하세요.

감정 동사를 분사로 만들 때, 감정을 유발하는지, 느끼는지를 판단하여 분사의 형태를 결정하세요.

감정을 표현하는 동사	감정을 유발 → 현재분사	감정을 느낌 → 과거분사
interest 흥미를 끌다	interesting 흥미를 갖게 하는	interested 흥미를 느끼는
excite 신나게 하다	exciting 신나게 하는	excited 신이 난
tire 피곤하게 하다	tiring 피곤하게 하는	tired 피곤한
shock 충격을 주다	shocking 충격적인	shocked 충격을 받은
move 감동시키다	moving 감동적인	moved 감동한
disappoint 실망시키다	disappointing 실망스러운	disappointed 실망한
confuse 혼란시키다	confusing 혼란스럽게 하는	confused 혼란스러운
frighten 겁먹게 하다	frightening 겁먹게 하는	frightened 겁먹은
puzzle 당황하게 하다	puzzling 당황하게 하는	puzzled 당황한
satisfy 만족시키다	satisfying 만족시키는	satisfied 만족한
surprise 놀라게 하다	surprising 놀라게 하는[놀라운]	surprised 놀란
bore 지루하게 하다	boring 지루하게 하는[지루한]	bored 지루함을 느끼는
please 기쁘게 하다	pleasing 기쁨을 주는	pleased 기쁜
embarrass 당황하게 하다	embarrassing 당황하게 하는	embarrassed 당황한, 난처한
amaze 놀라게 하다	amazing 놀라게 하는[놀라운]	amazed 놀란
fascinate 매료시키다	fascinating 매력적인	fascinated 매료된
depress 우울하게 하다	depressing 우울하게 하는	depressed 우울해진
relax 느긋하게 쉬다	relaxing 느긋하게 하는	relaxed 느긋한, 편안한

|A| 우리말과 일치하도록 위의 표에서 알맞은 말을 골라 빈칸에 쓰시오.

01 지루하게 하는 사람 a _____ person

02 실망한 고객들 _____ customers

03 당황스러운 실수 an _____ mistake

04 만족한 손님 a _____ guest

05 혼란스러운 정보 _____ information

06 감동적인 소설 a _____ novel

07 매력적인 도시 a _____ city

08 피곤한 얼굴 a _____ face

09 흥미로운 이야기 an _____ story

10 당황스러운 질문들 _____ questions

11 만족스러운 결과 a _____ result

12 놀란 표정 an _____ look

13 실망스러운 공연 a _____ performance

14 흥분된 얼굴 an _____ face

15 놀라운 소식 _____ news

16 신나는 게임 an _____ game

17 우울해진 십대들 _____ teenagers

18 놀라운 선물 a _____ present

19 당황한 표정 a _____ expression

20 평온해진 분위기 a _____ mood

|B| 우리말과 일치하도록 괄호 안의 말을 올바른 형태로 바꾸어 빈칸을 채우시오.

01 그 소식은 놀라웠다. (surprise)

The news was _____.

02 그 호텔의 서비스는 매우 만족스러웠다. (satisfy)

The hotel's service was very _____.

03 우리 모두는 그 연극에 감동 받았다. (move)

We all were _____ by the play.

04 그들은 그 교통사고에 충격을 받았다. (shock)

They were _____ by the car accident.

05 그는 난처한 질문에는 대답하지 않았다. (embarrass)

He did not answer the _____ questions.

06 비는 언제나 사람들을 우울하게 한다. (depress)

The rain always makes people feel _____.

|C| |보기|와 같이 감정 분사를 이용하여 빈칸을 채우시오.

> ┤보기├
> Her letter surprised her friends. (be surprised at)
> → Her friends <u>were surprised at</u> her letter. Her letter was <u>surprising</u>.

01 The city fascinated many tourists. (be fascinated by)

The city was _____. Many tourists _____ the city.

02 The food satisfied customers. (be satisfied with)

Customers _____ the food. The food was _____.

03 Emily's test result pleased her. (be pleased with)

Emily _____ her test result. Emily's test result was _____.

04 The nuclear war frightened all the people. (be frightened by)

All the people _____ the nuclear war. The nuclear war was _____.

실전 TIP 🎓

감정 분사를 쓸 때는 수식을 받는 대상과의 관계가 능동인지 수동인지 반드시 확인해야 해요.

내신 기출 다음 빈칸에 들어갈 말로 바르게 짝지어진 것은?

- Don't be _____ by today's failure.
- These _____ instructions are not helpful at all.
- You shocked us with your _____ talent.

① frustrating – confused – amazed
② frustrated – confused – amazing
③ frustrated – confusing – amazing

현재분사와 동명사는 형태가 같아서, 문맥상 그 쓰임과 의미를 구분할 수 있어야 해요.

	현재분사	동명사
명사 앞	running man 뛰고 있는 남자	running shoes 달리기 신발 *뛰고 있는 신발(X)
	washing woman 세탁하고 있는 여자	washing machine 세탁기 *세탁하고 있는 기계(X)
be의 보어	The news is surprising. 소식은 놀랍다	My hobby is dancing. 취미는 춤추기이다
	The movie was boring. 영화는 지루했다	The plan is going to Jeju. 계획은 가는 것이다

|A| 밑줄 친 부분의 쓰임이 동명사인지 현재분사인지 고르시오.

01 Playing the piano is my favorite hobby.　　　　(현재분사 / 동명사)

02 How many sleeping rooms are there?　　　　(현재분사 / 동명사)

03 The problem was not having enough time.　　　　(현재분사 / 동명사)

04 The story we heard was touching.　　　　(현재분사 / 동명사)

05 Her work was disappointing at first.　　　　(현재분사 / 동명사)

06 I bought a pair of walking boots.　　　　(현재분사 / 동명사)

07 You need an exercising space.　　　　(현재분사 / 동명사)

08 Look at this smiling baby.　　　　(현재분사 / 동명사)

|B| 문장의 밑줄 친 부분이 형용사인지 동명사인지 고르고, 문장을 우리말로 해석하시오.

현재분사는 형용사 역할을 하며, 동명사는 명사 역할을 한다는 점 잊지 마세요.

01 My hobby is jumping rope.

(현재분사 / 동명사) → _____

02 A lot of people in Africa need clean drinking water.

(현재분사 / 동명사) → _____

03 I'm interested in designing dresses.

(현재분사 / 동명사) → _____

04 The little girl was frightened by the barking dog.

(현재분사 / 동명사) → _____

05 Her goal is winning an Olympic gold medal.

(현재분사 / 동명사) → _____

06 You should wait for your turn in the waiting room.

(현재분사 / 동명사) → _____

중간고사·기말고사 실전문제

객관식 (01~25) / 주관식 (26~50)

정답과 해설 · 22쪽

| 학년과 반 | 이름 | 객관식 | / 25문항 | 주관식 | / 25문항 |

01~03 다음 빈칸에 들어갈 말로 알맞은 것을 고르시오.

01

She must remember _____ a present for her mother's birthday next week.

① buying ② to buy ③ buy
④ buys ⑤ bought

02

He called the police because he found his bicycle _____ by someone.

① stealing ② stole ③ stealed
④ stolen ⑤ steal

03

Everybody was pleased with the _____ experience at the stadium.

① excited ② to excite ③ exciting
④ excite ⑤ excitement

04 다음 빈칸에 들어갈 말로 알맞지 않은 것은?

Mike _____ reading a book.

① keeps ② likes ③ stopped
④ finished ⑤ plans

05 다음 글의 빈칸에 들어갈 말이 바르게 짝지어진 것은?

1. I can keep _____ over five hours.
2. Don't open the door without _____.

① shopping – knocking
② shopping – to knock
③ to shop – knocking
④ to shop – to knock
⑤ to shop – not knocking

06~07 다음 우리말을 영어로 바르게 옮긴 것을 고르시오.

06

그는 축구선수가 되기 위해 노력했다.

① He tried to becoming a football player.
② He tried becoming a football player.
③ He tried to become a football player.
④ He tried not to become a football player.
⑤ He tried becomes a football player.

07

나는 따뜻한 물 없이 샤워하는 데 어려움을 겪는다.

① I have trouble to take a shower without warm water.
② I have trouble not taking a shower without warm water.
③ I have trouble take a shower without warm water.
④ I have trouble taking a shower with warm water.
⑤ I have trouble taking a shower without warm water.

08 다음 두 문장이 같은 뜻이 되도록 할 때, 빈칸에 알맞은 것은?

> I couldn't help laughing at his joke.
> = I couldn't help but _____ at his joke.

① to laugh   ② laughing
③ laugh   ④ laughed
⑤ being laughed

09 다음 중 우리말 해석이 잘못된 것은?

① The firefighter tried to put out a fire.
그 소방관은 불을 끄기 위해 노력했다.
② My mother stopped to buy some flowers.
우리 엄마는 꽃을 사기 위해 멈춰 섰다.
③ I remember swimming in the sea last summer.
나는 지난여름 바다에서 수영한 것을 기억한다.
④ She regrets not telling her father the truth.
그녀는 아버지에게 진실을 말하지 않은 것을 후회한다.
⑤ Do you forget traveling in Spain with me?
너는 나와 스페인 여행할 것을 잊었니?

10 다음 문장의 밑줄 친 부분과 쓰임이 같은 것은?

> She was cooking pasta for her children.

① I'm going skiing with my friends altogether.
② When I took a shower, I was listening to my favorite song.
③ I already spent too much money buying new items.
④ On hearing the news, he bursted into tears.
⑤ Saving money for the trip to Jeju is our goal of this year.

11~12 다음 중 밑줄 친 부분의 쓰임이 나머지 넷과 다른 것을 고르시오.

11 ① You can use my shopping cart.
② I have to take Mr. Ha's writing class tomorrow.
③ My father bought me dancing shoes.
④ I see my sister sleeping in her bedroom.
⑤ I'd like to try on this shirt in the fitting room.

12 ① Taking a nap is good for your health.
② Your battery is running out.
③ Traveling abroad costs a lot of money.
④ I like taking pictures of nature.
⑤ Tom's dream is becoming an artist.

13 다음 짝지어진 문장의 의미가 서로 다른 것은?

① a) Jane started to clean the room.
   b) Jane started cleaning the room.
② a) Mike prefers to eat noodles for lunch.
   b) Mike prefers eating noodles for lunch.
③ a) I love to watch romantic movies when I'm sad.
   b) I love watching romantic movies when I'm sad.
④ a) Jim stopped to look for his wallet in the classroom.
   b) Jim stopped looking for his wallet in the classroom.
⑤ a) Tina continued to work at her office at night.
   b) Tina continued working at her office at night.

14 다음 빈칸에 들어갈 말로 알맞은 것은?

> He looks forward _____ his new workplace.

① visit   ② to visit   ③ visited
④ to visiting   ⑤ being visited

15 다음 중 밑줄 친 부분의 용법이 같은 것끼리 짝지어진 것은?

> ⓐ I like the boy standing next to Mina.
> ⓑ I can't go to the beach without wearing sunglasses.
> ⓒ The news was very surprising.
> ⓓ Sam hates talking to strangers.
> ⓔ How about having dinner at John's house?

① ⓐ, ⓑ   ② ⓐ, ⓓ   ③ ⓑ, ⓒ
④ ⓐ, ⓔ   ⑤ ⓑ, ⓔ

16~17 다음 중 어법상 올바른 것을 고르시오.

16 ① Being not on time is rude to anyone.
② Eating too many cookies are bad for your health.
③ Sleeping alone at night is very scary.
④ I consider eating not candies anymore.
⑤ Does this book interesting or boring?

17 ① He remembered to live in LA ten years ago.
② My aunt tried wearing a necklace at a jewelry shop.
③ Did you forget closing the window?
④ I don't regret to buy a jacket yesterday.
⑤ We stopped shopping when we found a shopping mall.

18~20 다음 중 어법상 어색한 것을 고르시오.

18 ① My favorite food is frying chicken.
② The boy lying down on the grass is John.
③ Tom thinks classical music is very boring.
④ I had an embarrassing moment yesterday.
⑤ Joe was depressed because he failed the exam.

19 ① I look forward to working with you.
② I feel like going swimming this Sunday.
③ I'd like to drinking a cup of water, please.
④ We postponed visiting the museum until next week.
⑤ He is used to using apps on his smartphone.

20 ① Being able to ride a bike is very exciting.
② Bill tries to avoid to sleep too late.
③ I can enter the room by showing my ID card.
④ She began to run when she saw a dog.
⑤ We practiced playing badminton in the park.

21 다음 대화에서 밑줄 친 부분이 어법상 어색한 것은?

① A: The movie was so boring.
   B: I agree. I almost slept.
② A: Are you interested in math?
   B: No, I hate math!
③ A: My father allowed me to go camping.
   B: Oh, you must be excited.
④ A: What did you do yesterday?
   B: I ran so hard and it was tiring.
⑤ A: The flower festival was amazed.
   B: Yes, I think the parade was the best.

22~23 다음 중 어법상 어색한 문장의 개수를 고르시오.

22

> ⓐ Can you see the girl raising her hands?
> ⓑ Hannah keeps to play the violin.
> ⓒ That may be the stolen table.
> ⓓ I'm satisfying with the nice room of this hotel.

① 없음　　　② 1개　　　③ 2개
④ 3개　　　⑤ 4개

23

> ⓐ The police officer prevented the crowd from gathering in front of the police office.
> ⓑ His job is catching fish in the sea.
> ⓒ Tony suggested not moving to another place.
> ⓓ Would you mind to change the schedule?

① 없음　　　② 1개　　　③ 2개
④ 3개　　　⑤ 4개

24 다음 대화의 빈칸에 들어갈 말이 바르게 짝지어진 것은?

> A: It was a great concert. The music was ___(A)___.
> B: Yes, I think so, too. The second keyboard player's playing was also ___(B)___.
> A: Was there a second keyboard player? I didn't know that.
> B: Did you see the woman ___(C)___ next to the singer?
> A: Now I remember. She was great!

	(A)		(B)		(C)
①	touching	–	fascinating	–	stood
②	touching	–	fascinated	–	stands
③	touching	–	fascinating	–	standing
④	touched	–	fascinated	–	stood
⑤	touched	–	fascinating	–	standing

25 다음 글의 밑줄 친 ⓐ~ⓔ 중 용법이 나머지 넷과 다른 것은?

> A: It's very hot today! I want ⓐ to go to the swimming pool. How about you?
> B: I feel like ⓑ going swimming, too. Let's go together.
> A: OK, what do we need ⓒ to pack?
> B: We should bring a swimsuit and swimming glasses.
> A: Alright. I'm ready. I'm ⓓ calling a taxi.
> B: Great... oh, wait! I forgot ⓔ to bring my swimming cap. Here it is. We can go now.

① ⓐ　　　② ⓑ　　　③ ⓒ
④ ⓓ　　　⑤ ⓔ

26~27 다음 우리말과 일치하도록 괄호 안의 말을 이용하여 문장을 완성하시오.

26

> 너는 일본어로 쓰인 그 소설을 읽었니?
> (write)

Did you read the novel _____ in Japanese?

27

> 나는 그 영화를 보면서 울 수밖에 없었다.
> (could, help)

I _____ _____ crying while watching the movie.

28~30 다음 우리말과 일치하도록 괄호 안의 말을 바르게 배열하시오.

28

> 나는 이번 주말에 머리를 자를 것이다.
> (cut, will, I, have, my hair, this weekend)

_____

29 나의 할머니는 정원에서 꽃을 키우는 것을 좋아하셨다.
(growing, in the garden, liked, flowers, my grandmother)

_____

30 너의 실수를 사과하는 것은 소용없다.
(apologizing for, use, it, your mistake, no, is)

_____

31~35 다음 문장에서 어법상 어색한 부분을 찾아 바르게 고치시오.

31 It is interested to read this book.

_____ → _____

32 Do you mind to turn on the light?

_____ → _____

33 He forgot turning off the light when he left home.

_____ → _____

34 I finished washing the dishes and do the laundry.

_____ → _____

35 Thank you for give us this opportunity.

_____ → _____

36~39 다음 두 문장을 한 문장으로 연결할 때, 빈칸에 알맞은 말을 분사를 쓰시오.

36 The man is an artist. He is painting a flower.

→ The man _____ a flower is an artist.

37 This cake tastes good. It was baked by Susie.

→ This cake _____ by Susie tastes good.

38 I sometimes visit this store. It was built five years ago.

→ I sometimes visit this store _____ five years ago.

39 I made a chair. It was given to my sister.

→ The chair _____ by me was given to my sister.

40 다음 문장을 지시대로 바꿔 쓰시오.

I'm used to using a knife and fork together. (부정문으로)

→ _____

41~42 다음 문장에서 어법상 어색한 부분을 고쳐 완전한 문장을 쓰시오.

41 It is a sword using in the battle with France.

→ _____

42 The horror movie made me frightening.

→ _____

43~44 다음 문장이 어법상 어색하지 않으면 ○를, 어색한 부분이 있으면 밑줄을 치고 바르게 고치시오.

43 (1) I saw the boy shouting at me.

　　→ _____

(2) I don't mind to skip the meal if you want.

　　→ _____

(3) I'll bring the laptop computer repaired by my dad.

　　→ _____

44 (1) It is worth paying for this dress.

　　→ _____

(2) I'll try doing my best in the game tomorrow.

　　→ _____

(3) Practicing help you become the best player.

　　→ _____

45~47 다음 문장의 밑줄 친 부분과 쓰임이 같은 것을 |보기|에서 골라 쓰시오.

┤보기├
ⓐ To eat well is very important.
ⓑ This book is boring.
ⓒ I want to be a teacher.

45 My father's job is helping the poor children.

　　→ _____

46 I denied helping him because he was mean.

　　→ _____

47 Helping each other makes the better world.

　　→ _____

48~49 주어진 |조건|을 이용하여 우리말을 영어로 옮기시오.

48 ┤조건├
1) 분사를 목적격보어로 쓸 것
2) 단어 see, dance, the Tango, yesterday 를 필요하면 이용하여 쓸 것
3) 7단어를 사용할 것

나는 어제 그녀가 탱고를 추는 것을 보았다.

_____

_____

49 ┤조건├
1) 동명사를 사용할 것
2) 단어 give up, climb, the mountain, because of, the weather를 쓸 것
3) 10단어를 사용할 것

그들은 날씨 때문에 등산하는 것을 포기했다.

_____

_____

50 다음 글의 밑줄 친 ⓐ~ⓔ 중 어법상 어색한 것을 골라 기호를 쓰고 바르게 고치시오.

A: I'm considering ⓐ to buy a new car.
B: I think you should call Jake. His job is ⓑ repairing ⓒ broken cars. He knows all about cars.
A: Really? I thought he is a salesman.
B: He quit ⓓ selling computers last year and started ⓔ studying to become an engineer.
A: Thank you for your advice. I'll call him.

_____ → _____

06

대명사, 형용사, 부사

UNIT 01 부정대명사 1

정해지지 않은 불특정한 사람이나 물건을 가리킬 때는 부정대명사 one을 사용해야 해요.

부정대명사	정해지지 않은 것을 가리킴	one	I need a shirt. I'll buy one. (정해지지 않은 셔츠)	단수
		ones	I need shoes. I'll buy ones. (정해지지 않은 신발)	복수
인칭대명사	정해진 것을 가리킴	it	I bought a shirt. I like it. (내가 산 그 셔츠)	단수
		they	I bought shoes. I like them. (내가 산 그 신발)	복수

'모든, 모두'를 쓸 때는 all, '둘 다, 양 쪽 모두'를 쓸 때는 both로 써야 해요.

구분	의미	부정대명사	부정형용사	수
all	전부 모든	all of 복수명사/셀 수 없는 명사 ~(들)의 전부/모두	all 복수명사/셀 수 없는 명사 모든 ~	셀 수 없는 명사는 단수 취급
both	둘 다 둘 다의	both of 복수명사 ~들 둘 다	both 복수명사 둘 다의 ~들	복수 취급

|A| 빈칸에 one(s)과 it 중 알맞은 말을 골라 쓰시오.

01 I lost my bike. Help me find _____.

02 These are big. I want smaller _____.

03 I like carrot cake. _____ tastes good.

04 I prefer this _____ to that _____.

05 It's too heavy for the little _____.

06 We watched a game. We enjoyed _____.

|B| 우리말과 일치하도록 |보기|에서 알맞은 말을 골라 빈칸에 쓰시오.

| 보기 |
| one   ones   it   all   both |

01 두 선수 모두 경기에서 이기기 위해 최선을 다했다.

_____ players did their best to win the game.

02 나는 복숭아를 하나 먹고 싶어. 너도 하나 먹을래?

I would like to have a peach. Are you having _____, too?

03 너희 두 사람 다 오늘 피곤해 보인다.

_____ of you look tired today.

04 그 관객들 모두 그 영화가 지루하다고 생각했다.

_____ of the audience found the movie boring.

05 나의 흰색 원피스가 더러워져서, 오늘 그것을 빨아야 한다.

My white dress got dirty, so I have to wash _____ today.

06 그 수리공은 더러워진 옷을 새것으로 갈아입었다.

The repairman changed dirty clothes for clean _____.

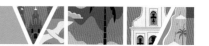

UNIT 02 부정대명사 2

정해진 범위(2개, 3개) 내에서 하나씩 가리킬 때 one, another, the other를 써요.

구분	부정대명사	의미	수	예문
2개 중	one	하나	단수	One is red.
	the other	나머지 하나		The other is blue.
3개 중	one	하나		One is red.
	another	또 다른 하나		Another is blue.
	the other	나머지 하나		The other is yellow.

참고 other(그 밖의 다른, 그 밖의 다른 것) 앞에 the가 붙으면 특정한 것이 되므로 '나머지'라는 의미가 돼요.

|A| |보기|에서 알맞은 말을 골라 빈칸에 쓰시오.

┌ 보기 ┐
one   the other   another   it

01 I don't like this _____. Please show me _____.

02 There were two pieces of pizza. She ate one. You can have _____.

03 She has two pets. One is a cat, and _____ is very small.

04 She has three sons. _____ is a vet, _____ is a nurse, and _____ is a scientist.

|B| 우리말과 일치하도록 빈칸에 알맞은 말을 넣으시오.

문장에서 가리키는 대상의 개수를 먼저 파악해야 부정대명사 표현이 쉬워져요.

01 그녀는 우산이 필요했다. 그래서 내가 그녀에게 하나 줬다.

She needed an umbrella. So I gave _____ to her.

02 나는 우산을 가지고 있었다. 그리고 내가 그것을 그녀에게 줬다.

I had an umbrella. And I gave _____ to her.

03 이곳에는 파란색 바지밖에 없지만, 나는 분홍색 바지를 원한다.

There are only blue pants here, but I want pink _____.

04 이 주스는 정말 맛이 좋네요. 한 잔 더 마실 수 있을까요?

This juice tastes really good. Can I have _____?

05 너는 두 가지 선택권이 있다. 하나는 여기 머무는 것이고, 나머지 하나는 떠나는 것이다.

You have two choices. _____ is staying here, and _____ is leaving here.

06 나는 세 명의 펜팔이 있다. 한 명은 영국인, 다른 하나는 캐나다인, 나머지는 미국인이다.

I have three pen pals. _____ is English, _____ is Canadian, and _____ is American.

여러 개가 있는 상황에서 쓸 수 있는 표현을 알아 두세요.

구분	부정대명사	의미	수	예문
여러 개 중	some	몇몇	복수	Some are red.
	others	다른 몇몇		Others are blue.
	the others	나머지 모두		The others are yellow.

each other와 one another의 차이점을 알아 두세요.

each other	둘이 서로	Amy and Sally looked at each other. 둘이 서로
one another	셋 이상일 때 서로	We had to help one another. 서로서로

|A| 문장에서 틀린 부분을 찾아 밑줄 긋고 바르게 고치시오.

01 There are two rings. One is silver, and another is gold. → _____

02 She has four dolls. One is a teddy bear, and the others is Barbie dolls. → _____

03 There are ten towels. Some are white, and the other are brown. → _____

04 Some is left-handed and the others are right-handed. → _____

|B| 우리말과 일치하도록 괄호 안의 말과 부정대명사를 이용하여 문장을 완성하시오.

some ~, others …는 '어떤 것들은, 또 어떤 것들은'이라고 자주 표현돼요.

01 그 두 사람은 서로에 대해 거의 모른다. (know, hardly)

The two men _____ _____ _____ _____.

02 차 한 잔 더 드시겠어요? (tea, cup of)

Would you like _____ _____ _____ _____?

03 어떤 노트북은 비싸지만, 또 어떤 것들은 저렴하다. (laptop computers)

_____ _____ _____ are expensive, but _____ are cheap.

04 나는 편지 두 통을 받았다. 하나는 언니에게서, 나머지 한 통은 엄마에게서 온 것이었다.

I have got two letters. _____ was from my sister and _____ _____ was from my mom.

05 가끔은 동물들도 서로서로 도우려고 한다. (help)

Sometimes, animals try to _____ _____ _____.

실전 TIP

그냥 '다른 사람들'인지, '나머지 사람들'인지 구분해 보세요.

내신기출 다음 빈칸에 들어갈 말이 다른 하나는?

① We should always consider _____.

② Some people love to live with pets while _____ don't.

③ Among seven students, some wear glasses while _____ don't.

다양한 부정대명사의 쓰임을 알아두세요.

구분	의미	부정대명사	부정형용사
each	(하나하나) 각각(의)	each of 복수명사 ~들의 각각 (하나하나)	each 단수명사 (하나하나) 각각의 ~
every	매, 다, 모든	X	every 단수명사 모든 ~
some	몇몇(의), 약간(의) (긍정, 권유)	some of 복수명사/셀 수 없는 명사 ~(들)의 몇몇(일부)	some 복수명사/셀 수 없는 명사 몇몇(일부)의 ~(들)
any	어떤 ~도, 조금이라도 (부정, 의문)	any of 복수명사/셀 수 없는 명사 ~(들)의 어떤 것이라도, 조금이라도	any 복수명사/셀 수 없는 명사 어떤 ~(들)도, 조금의 ~이라도

|A| 문장에서 틀린 부분을 찾아 밑줄 긋고 바르게 고치시오.

01 Are there some problems? → _____

02 Each teams has its own symbol. → _____

03 Any students want to wear school uniforms. → _____

04 Every classroom in the school were clean and neat. → _____

05 Some of the pages in this book is missing. → _____

06 I don't want some more. → _____

|B| 우리말과 일치하도록 |보기|에서 알맞은 말을 골라 문장을 완성하시오.

┌ 보기 ├─────────────────────────────────┐
| each   every   some   any |
└──┘

01 차와 빵을 좀 드실래요? Would you like _____ tea and bread?

02 모든 여자 아이들이 분홍색을 좋아하는 것은 아니다. Not _____ girl likes pink.

03 나는 돈을 좀 모아서 가난한 나라의 아이들을 도와줄 것이다.

I will save _____ money to help children in poor countries.

04 그는 너무나 슬퍼서 하루 종일 어떤 음식도 전혀 먹지 않았다.

He felt so sad that he did not eat _____ food all day.

05 너희는 각각 달라서, 서로를 존중해야 한다.

_____ of you is different, so you should respect each other.

실전 TIP

every 뒤에는 항상 단수명사가 온다는 것을 다시 한번 상기하세요.

(내신 기출) 다음 문장에서 틀린 부분을 찾아 고치시오. (2군데)
Every children are able to achieve his or her full potential.
　　　①　　　　②　　　　③　　　　④　　　　⑤

UNIT 05　재귀대명사

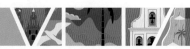

'나 자신', '그녀 자신'과 같은 재귀대명사의 형태를 알아 두세요.

주어		재귀대명사 (~ 자신)	주어		재귀대명사 (~들 자신)
단수	I	myself	복수	we	ourselves
	you	yourself		you	yourselves
	he	himself			
	she	herself		they	themselves
	it	itself			

재귀대명사를 어떤 경우에 사용하는지 파악하세요.

재귀	주어와 목적어가 같을 때	I love myself. (○) I love ~~me~~. (×)	목적어이므로 생략 ×
강조	'직접'이라는 의미로 강조할 때	We made the cake (ourselves). We (ourselves) made the cake.	강조 역할로 생략 ○

|A| 빈칸에 알맞은 재귀대명사를 쓰고, 생략할 수 있으면 ○, 없으면 ×를 쓰시오.

01 Look at _____ in the mirror before you go out.　[　　]

02 Does he love you _____, not your background?　[　　]

03 The children cleaned the house _____.　[　　]

04 I call _____ Little Genius.　[　　]

05 She wrote this letter to you _____.　[　　]

06 Jessi, please introduce _____ to us.　[　　]

> 재귀대명사가 주어를 강조할 때에는 주어 바로 뒤나 문장 끝에 와요.

|B| 우리말과 일치하도록 재귀대명사와 괄호 안의 말을 이용하여 문장을 완성하시오.

01 너희는 너희 스스로를 알고 사랑해야 한다. (love)

　　You must know and _____.

02 그는 같은 실수를 저질러서 스스로에게 화가 났다. (angry at)

　　He was _____ for making the same mistake.

03 내가 직접 그 문제를 처리할 것이다. (take care of)

　　I _____ will _____ the problem.

04 그녀는 여름 그 자체는 좋아하지만, 땀에 젖는 건 싫어한다. (summer, like)

　　She _____, but hates being wet with sweat.

05 우리는 우리 스스로 해내서 행복했다. (make it)

　　We felt happy to _____.

UNIT 06 재귀대명사 관용표현

재귀대명사를 포함한 다음 관용표현을 알아 두세요.

for oneself	혼자 힘으로, 스스로	talk to oneself	혼잣말하다
by oneself	홀로, 혼자서(= alone)	enjoy oneself	즐거운 시간을 보내다
of itself	저절로	make oneself at home	편하게 지내다
in itself	본래, 그 자체가	help oneself to	~을 마음껏 먹다
beside oneself	제정신이 아닌	kill oneself	자살하다

|A| 괄호 안에서 알맞은 말을 고르시오.

01 She always talks to (herself / yourself), "Do your best."

02 (Help / Drink) yourselves to fresh juice and salad.

03 Learning is always good (in / on) itself.

04 I made this robot for (myself / itself) for the first time.

05 It can be dangerous for you to travel to Europe by (yourself / you).

06 All the children enjoyed (themselves / them) at the water park.

|B| 우리말과 일치하도록 재귀대명사 관용표현을 이용하여 문장을 완성하시오.

재귀대명사와 함께 쓰여 관용표현을 완성하는 전치사를 외워 두어야 해요.

01 그는 걱정으로 제정신이 아니었다.

He was _____ with worry.

02 어떻게 문이 저절로 열릴 수 있지?

How could the door open _____?

03 그녀는 혼자서 그 일을 끝마칠 수 없었다.

She couldn't finish the work _____.

04 오늘은 먹고 싶은 것이라면 무엇이든지 마음껏 먹어도 돼.

Today, you can _____ anything you want to eat.

05 그 꼬마 아이가 이 노래를 혼자 힘으로 작곡했나요?

Did the little boy write this song _____?

06 Brown 씨는 Emily에게 자기 집처럼 편하게 지내라고 말했다.

Ms. Brown told Emily to _____.

실전 TIP

누구에게 하는 말인지, 단수인지 복수인지를 파악해야 해요.

내신 기출 다음 빈칸에 공통으로 알맞은 말을 쓰시오.

• Help _____ to the coffee and salad.

• You are a strong boy. You can do if for _____.

UNIT 07 -thing + 형용사

명사를 수식하는 형용사의 위치를 잘 파악하세요.

형용사의 위치	예문
형용사+명사	a useful book 유용한 책
명사+형용사구	a book useful for kids 아이들에게 유용한 책
-thing/-one/-body+형용사	nothing wrong 잘못된 것이 없음
-thing/-one/-body+형용사+to부정사(형용사적)	something important to know 알아야 할 중요한 것

주의 -thing, -one, -body로 끝나는 명사는 뒤에서 형용사가 수식해요.

|A| 밑줄 친 부분을 바르게 고치시오.

01 I want to do <u>good something</u> for the Earth. → _____

02 There is <u>worse nothing</u> than being lonely. → _____

03 He doesn't have <u>cold anything</u> to drink. → _____

04 The <u>thing main</u> is to believe in yourself. → _____

05 Do you have <u>special someone</u> in your mind? → _____

06 Would you recommend <u>funny something</u> to see? → _____

07 There must be <u>things heavy</u> in your bag. → _____

08 There was not <u>interesting anything</u> to watch on TV. → _____

|B| 우리말과 일치하도록 괄호 안의 말을 이용하여 문장을 완성하시오.

01 나는 유명한 누군가를 친구로 사귀고 싶다. (famous)

　 I want to make friends with _____.

02 걱정하지 마. 심각한 건 그 어떤 것도 없어. (serious)

　 Don't worry. There isn't _____.

03 오늘은 중요한 일이 아무것도 없다. (important)

　 There is _____ today.

04 사과는 하기 쉬운 일이 아니다. (easy)

　 Apologizing is not the _____ to do.

05 우리는 흥미로운 무언가를 경험할 수 있다. (interesting)

　 We can experience _____.

06 나는 어제 그가 아름다운 누군가와 데이트하는 모습을 봤다. (beautiful)

　 I saw him go out with _____ yesterday.

07 그는 아들을 돌볼 믿을 만한 어떤 사람도 찾지 못했다. (to look after, reliable)

　 He didn't find _____ his son.

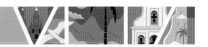

명사의 수와 양을 나타내는 수량형용사를 기억해 두세요.

의미	수량 형용사	+ 명사	예시	주의
많은	many	+ 셀 수 있음	I have many books.	• 명사의 종류에 상관없이 a lot of 나 lots of를 쓸 수 있음 • much는 주로 부정문에서 씀
	much	+ 셀 수 없음	I don't have much time.	
조금/ 약간 있는	a few	+ 셀 수 있음	I have a few books.	• 명사의 종류에 상관없이 some (긍정, 권유)이나 any(부정, 의문)를 쓸 수 있음
	a little	+ 셀 수 없음	I have a little time.	
거의 없는	few	+ 셀 수 있음	I have few books.	• 부정의 의미를 포함하고 있음
	little	+ 셀 수 없음	I have little time.	

|A| 문장에서 틀린 부분을 찾아 밑줄 긋고 바르게 고치시오.

01 She has a lot of friend in her school. → _____

02 I want any soup and fried eggs for breakfast. → _____

03 There were so much traffic that he was late. → _____

04 The street is quiet today. There are little people on the street. → _____

05 Saving the Earth is really important for much reasons. → _____

06 It will take a lot of times to solve the puzzles. → _____

07 Do you have any question about today's lesson? → _____

08 There was few salt left. We need to buy more. → _____

|B| 우리말과 일치하도록 수량형용사와 괄호 안의 말을 이용하여 문장을 완성하시오.

뒤에 나오는 명사가 셀 수 있는지 셀 수 없는지, 긍정인지 부정인지 파악해야 해요.

01 우물에는 물이 거의 없었다. (water)

There was _____ in the well.

02 너희 학교에는 학생이 얼마나 많이 있니? (students)

How _____ does your school have?

03 나는 이 문제에 대해 생각해 볼 시간이 좀 필요하다. (time)

I need _____ to think about this issue.

04 핫초코가 너무 달면 우유를 조금 넣으세요. (milk)

Add _____ if the hot chocolate is too sweet.

05 그 일을 완성하는 데에는 겨우 몇 분밖에 안 걸릴 것이다. (minute)

It will take only _____ to finish the work.

06 그는 동료들로부터 어떠한 정보도 얻지 못했다. (information)

He couldn't get _____ from his coworkers.

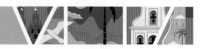

부사가 수식하는 말들과 부사의 위치를 알아 두세요.

형용사 수식	형용사 바로 앞	He is my very good friend.
다른 부사 수식	수식하는 부사 바로 앞	He speaks too slowly.
동사 수식	문장 뒤	Snails move slowly.
문장 전체 수식	문장 앞	Fortunately, there is a solution.

부사는 very처럼 자체가 부사인 것도 있지만, 대부분 형용사에 -ly를 붙여 만들어요.

대부분의 경우	+ -ly	real → really safe → safely	sudden → suddenly careful → carefully
자음+y로 끝나는 경우	y를 i로 바꾸고+-ly	easy → easily heavy → heavily	happy → happily angry → angrily
-le로 끝나는 경우	e를 없애고+-ly	simple → simply	gentle → gently

🗨️ 주의 〈명사+-ly〉는 형용사예요. lovely 사랑스러운 / friendly 상냥한 / timely 시기적절한 / daily 매일의

형용사와 부사의 형태가 같은 단어들에 유의하세요.

early	이른 / 일찍	high	높은 / 높이
late	늦은 / 늦게	hard	어려운, 딱딱한 / 열심히
fast	빠른 / 빠르게	near	가까운 / 가까이
long	긴 / 길게, 오래	pretty	예쁜 / 꽤

🗨️ 주의 -ly가 붙어 다른 뜻이 되는 단어들에 유의하세요.
lately 최근에 / hardly 거의 ~않다 / highly 매우, 대단히 / nearly 거의 / closely 면밀히

|A| 괄호 안에서 알맞은 말을 고르시오.

01 Her dress was so (beautiful / beautifully).

02 Joanne had a (simple / simply) breakfast today.

03 I heard a (strange / strangely) sound in my room.

04 Could you take a (quick / quickly) look at this?

05 Snow White and the prince lived (happy / happily) ever after.

06 (Fortunate / Fortunately), the heavy rain stopped.

07 Think (careful / carefully) before you make a decision.

08 The little boy is sleeping (peaceful / peacefully).

|B| 우리말과 일치하도록 |보기|에서 알맞은 말을 골라 쓰고, 형용사인지 부사인지 표시하시오.

많은 부사가 -ly로 끝나지만, 의미가 달라지는 경우도 있다는 점에 유의하세요.

|보기|

high	highly	late	lately

01 최근에 달을 본 적이 있나요?

Have you seen the moon _____? (형용사 / 부사)

02 캥거루는 매우 높게 점프할 수 있다.

Kangaroos can jump very _____. (형용사 / 부사)

03 그녀는 회의에 늦어서 사과했다.

She was _____ for the meeting, so she apologized.

(형용사 / 부사)

04 그는 미술관의 예술품에 매우 감명 받았다.

He was _____ impressed by the artworks in the gallery.

(형용사 / 부사)

05 비행기는 폭설로 인해 늦게 도착했다.

The airplane arrived _____ due to the heavy snow. (형용사 / 부사)

06 그 오래된 성당은 천장이 매우 높다.

The old cathedral has very _____ ceilings. (형용사 / 부사)

|C| 우리말과 일치하도록 빈칸에 알맞은 말을 쓰시오.

01 갑자기 아기가 울음을 터뜨렸다.

_____, the baby burst out crying.

02 거의 백 명 정도의 사람들이 줄을 서서 기다리고 있다.

_____ one hundred people are waiting in a line.

03 나는 이번 시험을 위해 열심히 공부하기로 결심했다.

I decided to study _____ for this test.

04 그들은 서로를 거의 모른다.

They _____ know each other.

05 머리가 길고 검은 그 소녀가 나의 가장 친한 친구이다.

The girl with _____ dark hair is my best friend.

06 나는 우리 조부모님이 오래 사시면 좋겠다.

I want my grandparents to live _____.

실전 TIP

〈형용사+-ly〉 형태의 부사인지, 〈명사+-ly〉 형태의 형용사인지 확인해 보세요.

내신 기출 다음 중 품사가 <u>다른</u> 하나는?

① really ② lately ③ finally ④ friendly ⑤ brightly

UNIT 10 빈도부사

얼마나 자주(빈도)인지에 따라서 부사를 알맞게 선택해야 해요.

빈도	100%	80–90%	60%	30–40%	10%	0%
부사	always	usually	often	sometimes	hardly/seldom	never
	항상	보통, 대개	종종, 자주	가끔, 때때로	거의 ~않다	절대 ~않다

빈도부사를 쓰는 위치에 주의하세요.

be동사 뒤	She is never late.
일반동사 앞	She never comes late.
조동사가 있다면 조동사 뒤	She will never be late.

주의 hardly, seldom, rarely, never는 이미 부정의 의미가 있으므로, 따로 not을 쓰지 않는다는 것에 유의하세요.

|A| 괄호 안의 빈도부사가 들어갈 알맞은 위치를 고르시오.

01 (always) You ① should ② be careful ③ when you ride a bike.

02 (never) Minsu ① is ② late for ③ an appointment.

03 (usually) She ① comes back ② home ③ very late.

04 (seldom) He ① scolds ② his children ③ these days.

05 (often) Tom ① called ② his parents ③ to say hello.

06 (hardly) They ① go ② out ③ these days.

|B| 우리말과 일치하도록 괄호 안의 말을 바르게 배열하여 문장을 완성하시오.

01 무지개는 보통 비가 그친 뒤 볼 수 있다. (be, usually, can, seen)

Rainbows _____ after rain.

02 나는 항상 네게 달려갈 준비가 돼 있다. (always, am, ready to, run)

I _____ to you.

03 우리 아빠는 주말에 주로 낚시하러 가신다. (goes, often, fishing)

My dad _____ on weekends.

04 나는 내 목표를 이룰 때까지 절대 포기하지 않을 것이다. (will, give up, never)

I _____ until I achieve my goal.

05 대구에는 작년 겨울에 눈이 거의 안 왔다. (snowed, hardly, last winter)

It _____ in Daegu.

06 Frederick은 때때로 이상한 행동을 한다. (strange, sometimes, does, something)

Frederick _____ .

중간고사·기말고사 실전문제

객관식 (01~25) / 주관식 (26~50)

정답과 해설 · 26쪽

학년과 반	이름	객관식	/ 25문항	주관식	/ 25문항

01~02 다음 빈칸에 들어갈 말로 알맞은 것을 고르시오.

01

> I don't need _____ advice from him.

① some　　② any　　③ few
④ a few　　⑤ many

02

> Can you give me _____ chance?

① the other　　② it　　③ each
④ another　　⑤ every

03 다음 문장의 밑줄 친 부분과 바꿔 쓸 수 있는 것은?

> We couldn't get a lot of information from him.

① much　　② few　　③ a little
④ a few　　⑤ little

04 다음 빈칸에 들어갈 말로 알맞지 <u>않은</u> 것은?

> She is smiling very _____.

① lovely　　② brightly　　③ happily
④ softly　　⑤ beautifully

05~06 다음 빈칸에 들어갈 말이 바르게 짝지어진 것은?

05

> There were two apples in the basket. My brother ate ___(A)___ and gave ___(B)___ to me.

	(A)		(B)
①	one	–	ones
②	some	–	others
③	one	–	some
④	some	–	another
⑤	one	–	the other

06

> 1. To become a good player, you must not make ___(A)___ mistakes.
> 2. I went out with ___(B)___ friends last night.

	(A)		(B)
①	any	–	any
②	any	–	some
③	some	–	some
④	some	–	any
⑤	some	–	a little

07 다음 중 밑줄 친 단어가 수식하는 대상이 <u>다른</u> 것은?

① He runs <u>fast</u>.
② You must get up <u>early</u>.
③ She made a <u>pretty</u> paper doll.
④ The bird flew <u>high</u> in the sky.
⑤ A boat came <u>close</u> to us.

08~09 다음 우리말을 영어로 바르게 옮긴 것을 고르시오.

08

> Danny는 가끔 우리 집에 방문한다.

① Danny usually visits our home.
② Danny never visits our home.
③ Danny sometimes visits our home.
④ Danny seldom visits our home.
⑤ Danny always visits our home.

09

> Mike는 돈이 거의 없어서 그 재킷을 사지 못했다.

① Mike couldn't buy the jacket because he had a few money.
② Mike shouldn't buy the jacket because he had a little money.
③ Mike couldn't buy the jacket because he had few money.
④ Mike shouldn't buy the jacket because he had no money.
⑤ Mike couldn't buy the jacket because he had little money.

10 다음 중 밑줄 친 부분을 생략할 수 없는 것을 모두 고르시오.

① I painted the wall of my room myself.
② I love myself just as I am.
③ Can you fix this machine yourself?
④ She introduced herself to me.
⑤ He himself built this house.

11 다음 질문에 대한 대답으로 가장 어색한 것은?

> How often do you watch a movie?

① I seldom watch a movie every day.
② I usually watch a movie every weekend.
③ I sometimes watch a movie at night.
④ I often watch a movie on the weekend.
⑤ I always watch a movie before I sleep.

12~13 다음 중 어법상 올바른 것을 고르시오.

12 ① My brother never eat carrots.
② You can't never see her again.
③ Claire often gets up late in the morning.
④ I meet sometimes Sohee in the library.
⑤ We couldn't hardly eat any food yesterday.

13 ① She didn't have some food last night.
② I can lend you any money if you need it.
③ Do you have some question about me?
④ Would you like to have some juice?
⑤ We need any fruit for breakfast.

14~17 다음 중 어법상 어색한 것을 고르시오.

14 ① They were talking with others.
② Both of them are able to swim.
③ There wasn't anyone in the park.
④ Every books written by her is great.
⑤ Please don't do anything right now.

15 ① The baby seldom drank the milk.
② Skydiving is sometimes dangerous.
③ He always is gentle to his students.
④ She usually rides a bike to her school.
⑤ My father often goes fishing by himself.

16 ① I bought something warm to wear.
② He has many things interesting to show.
③ I looked for someone strong to move this heavy box.
④ He feels lonely because he has nobody close to him.
⑤ Would you like to have something cold?

17 ① Both my feet was frozen in the cold weather.
② Each girl needs to gather in front of the building.
③ All of the students in the school are not allowed to enter this place.
④ All the money in my pocket was stolen this morning.
⑤ Every athlete usually practices running in the gym.

18 다음 대화에서 밑줄 친 부분이 어법상 어색한 것은?

① A: Are these books on the table yours?
   B: No, the ones on the bookshelf are mine.
② A: Where did you find this ring?
   B: I found it under the sofa.
③ A: Can I have some coffee, please?
   B: Sure. Do you want any more cookies?
④ A: I don't remember where I put my hat.
   B: Where did you see it last?
⑤ A: This shirt is too small. Do you have a bigger one?
   B: Sorry, we don't.

19~20 다음 중 어법상 어색한 문장의 개수를 고르시오.

19
ⓐ I understand only a few Korean words.
ⓑ Do you have some plans for the weekend?
ⓒ The seeds in the capsule will never disappear.
ⓓ How many apples do you need?

① 없음　② 1개　③ 2개　④ 3개　⑤ 4개

20
ⓐ Those are not her pants. The ones in the box are hers.
ⓑ I bought a few flowers at the flower shop.
ⓒ I couldn't hardly move my head.
ⓓ Each of the tubes were made of rubber.

① 없음　② 1개　③ 2개　④ 3개　⑤ 4개

21 다음 중 밑줄 친 단어의 역할이 같은 것끼리 짝지어진 것은?

ⓐ Why are you so late? The class is over.
ⓑ The train passed the station fast.
ⓒ This town is big enough for many people to live in.
ⓓ As the rive r is very long, lots of cities can be found along it.

① ⓐ, ⓑ　　② ⓐ, ⓒ　　③ ⓐ, ⓓ
④ ⓑ, ⓓ　　⑤ ⓒ, ⓓ

22~23 다음 대화의 빈칸에 들어갈 말이 바르게 짝지어진 것은?

22
1. I'm planning to buy a computer. It's okay to buy a used ___(A)___ if it's still working well.
2. The model didn't have ___(B)___ time to change her clothes.
3. Thanks to his help, ___(C)___ lives were saved from the fire yesterday.

	(A)		(B)		(C)
①	one	–	much	–	many
②	it	–	many	–	little
③	them	–	much	–	a little
④	one	–	many	–	much
⑤	it	–	much	–	few

23

Mary: Stop fighting ___(A)___ ! What's wrong with you?
Jack: Kevin threw the ball first!
Kevin: I threw ___(B)___ because I tried to say hi to him. I'm sorry if I made you angry.
Jack: I didn't know that. I'm sorry, too.
Mary: It's good to hear that. We have to be nice to ___(C)___ .
Jack: You're right.

	(A)	(B)	(C)
①	one another	one	each other
②	one another	it	each other
③	each other	one	each other
④	each other	it	one another
⑤	each other	one	one another

24 다음 표를 보고, 빈도부사를 바르게 쓴 문장으로 알맞은 것은?

How often do you go to the park?				
	Spring	Summer	Fall	Winter
Sarah	○	○	○	○
Jack	○	×	×	×
Tom	×	×	×	×
Amy	○	×	○	×

① Sarah hardly goes to the park all year.
② Tom always goes to the park every season.
③ Amy never goes to the park.
④ Jack seldom goes to the park all year.
⑤ Sarah never goes to the park in winter.

25 다음 대화의 밑줄 친 ⓐ~ⓔ 중 어법상 올바른 것은?

A: Hey, Amy! I don't have ⓐ some time to wash the dishes.
B: I'll do ⓑ one instead of you.
A: Thank you for saying so.
B: It's not a big deal. Do you need ⓒ anything else?
A: I'd like to ask you to find my jeans.
B: Where did you see ⓓ ones last?
A: I don't know. Maybe ⓔ anywhere in my bedroom.

① ⓐ　② ⓑ　③ ⓒ　④ ⓓ　⑤ ⓔ

26~29 괄호 안의 단어를 알맞은 위치에 넣어 문장을 다시 쓰시오.

26 She couldn't find anything in his art. (special)

→ _____

27 There are many things to experience in Korea. (exciting)

→ _____

28 I will forget this moment in my life. (never)

→ _____

29 She loses confidence when she is criticized. (often)

→ _____

30~31 다음 우리말과 일치하도록 괄호 안의 말을 바르게 배열하시오.

30
> 나는 그에게 편하게 지내라고 말했다.
> (him, himself, make, told, at home, to, I)

_____

31
> 우리는 컴퓨터 게임을 하는 데 너무 많은 시간을 쓰지 말아야 한다.
> (time, playing, we, spend, too much, computer games, not, should)

_____

32 다음 문장을 지시대로 바꿔 쓰시오.

You often watched cartoons on TV when you were young. (의문문으로)

→ _____

33~36 다음 빈칸에 |보기|에서 알맞은 말을 골라 쓰시오.

┌ 보기 ├─────────────────────────┐
a few   few   little   some   any
└──────────────────────────────────┘

33 Do you have _____ ideas to solve this problem?

34 Only _____ people agreed with him.

35 He is thirsty, but he has _____ water to drink in his bottle.

36 We have _____ onions, so we need to buy _____.

37~41 다음 빈칸에 |보기|에서 알맞은 말을 골라 쓰시오.

┌ 보기 ├─────────────────────────────┐
one   another   the other
some   the others
└──────────────────────────────────────┘

37 My friend is _____ of the twins.

38 I lost three balls and I found only one. I don't know where to look for _____.

39 There were a dozen eggs. _____ were used to make fried eggs, and others were used to bake a pie.

40 Ms. Scott is explaining the French Revolution to two students. _____ is reading the textbook. _____ is watching her.

41 My mom baked some chocolate cookies. I tried one, but I'm still hungry. I need to have _____.

42~43 다음 문장에서 어법상 어색한 부분을 찾아 바르게 고치시오.

42 She bought myself a beautiful doll.

_____ → _____

43 I don't care about what the others think about me.

_____ → _____

44~45 다음 문장에서 어법상 어색한 부분을 고쳐 완전한 문장을 쓰시오.

44 We don't have many light to find the gold earrings.

→ _____

_____

45 Those cats are very cute! I like the white cat and the two orange them.

→ _____

_____

46~47 다음 문장이 어법상 어색하지 않으면 ○를, 어색한 부분이 있으면 밑줄을 치고 바르게 고치시오.

46 (1) Are there some questions about today's lesson?

→ _____

(2) When you boil eggs, put some salt in the water.

→ _____

(3) I made strawberry juice. Would you like some?

→ _____

47 (1) I thought we had only a few hours.

→ _____

(2) These sunglasses are too big. I need small one.

→ _____

(3) I sent her a message and I want to know if she read one.

→ _____

48~49 주어진 |조건|을 이용하여 우리말을 영어로 옮기시오.

48
|조건|
1) 수량형용사 lots of를 사용할 것
2) 단어 have, things, do, now를 필요하면 활용하여 쓸 것
3) 8단어를 사용할 것

나는 지금 할 일이 많다.

_____

49
|조건|
1) 수량형용사 a few를 사용할 것
2) 단어 years, later, come back, from the journey를 필요하면 활용하여 쓸 것
3) 10단어를 사용할 것

몇 년이 지난 후, 그는 그 여행에서 돌아왔다.

_____

50 다음 글의 밑줄 친 ⓐ~ⓔ 중 어법상 어색한 것을 골라 기호를 쓰고 바르게 고치시오.

Ms. Franklin is a businesswoman. She was poor when she was young. After she turned 20, she worked ⓐ hard. She did ⓑ many things to make money. She earned ⓒ a lot of money by ⓓ herself and became the CEO of her company. She must be very proud of ⓔ her.

_____ → _____

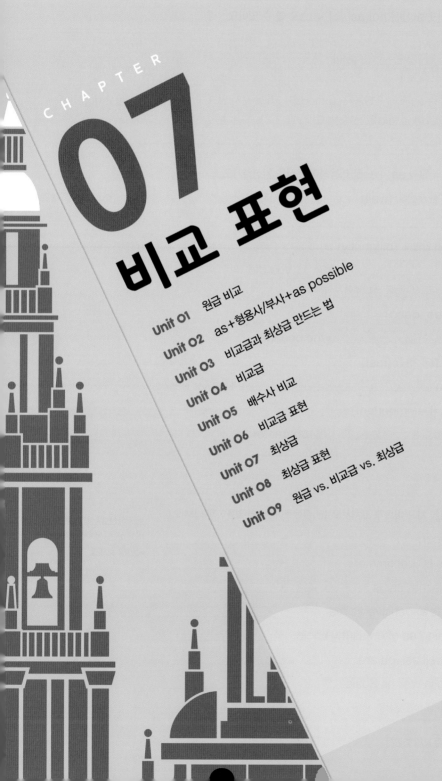

UNIT 01 원급 비교

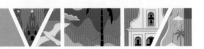

'~만큼 …한[하게]'는 〈as+형용사/부사+as〉로 표현하세요.

형용사	She is	as	kind	as	him[he is].
부사	She can swim		well		him[he can].

부정문(~만큼 …하지 않다[못하다])은 not as[so] ~ as로 쓸 수 있어요.

형용사	She isn't	as[so]	kind	as	him[he is].
부사	She didn't study		hard		him[he did].

> 주의 문장에 일반동사가 쓰인 경우, as 뒤에 일반동사(studied)를 그대로 쓰지 않고, 이를 대신하는 대동사 do를 써요. 이때 주어와 시제에 맞게 do, does, did를 선택하세요.

|A| 우리말과 일치하도록 괄호 안의 말과 as ~ as를 이용하여 문장을 완성하시오.

01 나는 Joy만큼 영어를 잘 말하지는 못한다. (well)

I can't speak English _____ Joy.

02 그녀는 너만큼 부지런하게 일하지 않았다. (diligently)

She didn't work _____ you did.

as you worked라고 하지 않고, 대동사 did를 쓰는 것에 주의하세요.

03 그들의 사랑은 바다만큼 깊다. (be, deep)

Their love _____ the ocean.

04 전기 자동차가 일반 자동차만큼 빨리 가니? (fast)

Does an electric car go _____ a regular car?

05 외모는 인성만큼 중요하지 않다. (be, important)

Appearance _____ character.

|B| 문장에서 틀린 부분을 찾아 밑줄 치고 바르게 고치시오. (단, 틀린 곳이 없으면 '없음'이라고 쓰시오.)

비교하는 대상은 무엇인지, 비교하는 동사는 무엇인지 확인해 보세요.

01 My bike is as new as your. → _____

02 I can jump as highly as 60 centimeters. → _____

03 This car goes as fast as that car is. → _____

04 Your mobile phone is as expensive as me. → _____

05 My dad doesn't go fishing as often as my uncle. → _____

06 She does not sing as well as you are. → _____

07 Mike didn't play the violin well as Susie. → _____

08 You drew as well as Picasso was. → _____

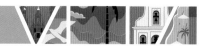

〈as+형용사/부사+as〉를 이용한 다음 표현을 익혀 두세요.

as ~ as possible 가능한 한 ~하게	Please call me as quickly as possible. 가능한 한 빨리
	I tried to go there as often as possible. 가능한 한 자주
as ~ as 주어+can[could] 주어가 할 수 있는 만큼 ~하게	Please call me as quickly as you can. 당신이 할 수 있는 만큼 빨리
	I tried to go there as often as I could. 내가 할 수 있었던 한 자주

주의 〈as ~ as〉 뒤에 〈주어+can[could]〉를 쓸 때 알맞은 주어와 시제로 쓰세요.

|A| 괄호 안의 단어를 바르게 배열하여 문장을 완성하시오.

01 They visit their grandparents _____. (as, possible, as, often)

02 We should always study _____. (can, as, we, hard, as)

03 Laugh _____. (as, possible, much, as)

04 Try to speak _____. (possible, as, loud, as)

05 It's time to run _____. (can, as, as, fast, you)

06 My parents want to look _____. (possible, as, as, young)

|B| 두 문장의 뜻이 같도록 문장을 완성하시오.

01 Jenny spoke as slowly as possible.

= Jenny spoke _____.

02 We'll repair this machine as quickly as we can.

= We'll repair this machine _____.

03 You'd better send an email as soon as possible.

= You'd better send an email _____.

04 Please keep the fruits as cool as they can.

= Please keep the fruits _____.

05 You have to leave for Seoul as early as you can.

= You have to leave for Seoul _____.

06 We answered the questions as politely as possible.

= We answered the questions _____.

〈as+형용사/부사+as+주어〉 다음에 오는 can/could는 주절의 시제에 일치시켜야 해요.

실전 TIP

주절의 시제가 현재인지 과거인지 확인해야 해요.

내신 기출 다음 중 틀린 것을 골라 바르게 고치시오.

The <u>old woman</u> <u>tried to</u> write her <u>name</u> as <u>clearly</u> as she <u>can</u>.

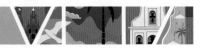

형용사나 부사의 비교급과 최상급을 만드는 방법을 알아 두세요.

형용사/부사의 형태		원급	비교급	최상급
대부분	-er / -est	tall	taller	tallest
-e로 끝남	-r / -st	nice	nicer	nicest
-y로 끝남	y를 삭제 -ier / -iest	early	earlier	earliest
「단모음+단자음」으로 끝남	자음 추가 -er / -est	hot	hotter	hottest
-ous, -ful, -ive, -ing 등 형용사	more / most+원급	famous exciting	more famous more exciting	most famous most exciting
형용사+ly 부사		slowly	more slowly	most slowly

주의 〈명사+ly = 형용사〉는 y를 삭제하고 -ier / -iest를 붙여요.
friendly(친절한) – friendlier – friendliest   lovely(사랑스러운) – lovelier - loveliest

불규칙 변화하는 형용사/부사의 비교급과 최상급은 암기해야 해요.

원급	비교급	최상급
good (좋은) / well (잘)	better (더 좋은, 더 잘)	best (가장 좋은)
bad/ill (나쁜) / badly (나쁘게)	worse (더 나쁜)	worst (가장 나쁜)
many (수가 많은) / much (양이 많은)	more (더 많은)	most (가장 많은)
little (적은)	less (더 적은)	least (가장 적은)

|A| 다음 단어들의 비교급과 최상급을 쓰면서 외우시오.

01 유능한　　able　　　　　　– ＿＿＿＿＿＿ – ＿＿＿＿＿＿

02 화난　　　angry　　　　　　– ＿＿＿＿＿＿ – ＿＿＿＿＿＿

03 나쁜　　　bad　　　　　　　– ＿＿＿＿＿＿ – ＿＿＿＿＿＿

04 나쁘게　　badly　　　　　　– ＿＿＿＿＿＿ – ＿＿＿＿＿＿

05 아름다운　beautiful　　　　– ＿＿＿＿＿＿ – ＿＿＿＿＿＿

06 큰　　　　big　　　　　　　– ＿＿＿＿＿＿ – ＿＿＿＿＿＿

07 따분한　　boring　　　　　– ＿＿＿＿＿＿ – ＿＿＿＿＿＿

08 용감한　　brave　　　　　　– ＿＿＿＿＿＿ – ＿＿＿＿＿＿

09 밝은　　　bright　　　　　　– ＿＿＿＿＿＿ – ＿＿＿＿＿＿

10 바쁜　　　busy　　　　　　– ＿＿＿＿＿＿ – ＿＿＿＿＿＿

11 조심하는　careful　　　　　– ＿＿＿＿＿＿ – ＿＿＿＿＿＿

12	조심하여	carefully	– _____	– _____
13	싼	cheap	– _____	– _____
14	깨끗한	clean	– _____	– _____
15	차가운	cold	– _____	– _____
16	편안한	comfortable	– _____	– _____
17	위험한	dangerous	– _____	– _____
18	맛있는	delicious	– _____	– _____
19	어려운	difficult	– _____	– _____
20	근면한, 성실한	diligent	– _____	– _____
21	더러운	dirty	– _____	– _____
22	쉬운	easy	– _____	– _____
23	쉽게	easily	– _____	– _____
24	흥미로운	exciting	– _____	– _____
25	비싼	expensive	– _____	– _____
26	유명한	famous	– _____	– _____
27	뚱뚱한	fat	– _____	– _____
28	어리석은	foolish	– _____	– _____
29	신선한	fresh	– _____	– _____
30	친절한	friendly	– _____	– _____
31	좋은	good	– _____	– _____
32	잘생긴	handsome	– _____	– _____
33	행복한	happy	– _____	– _____
34	어려운	hard	– _____	– _____
35	건강한	healthy	– _____	– _____
36	무거운	heavy	– _____	– _____
37	도움이 되는	helpful	– _____	– _____
38	뜨거운	hot	– _____	– _____
39	아픈	ill	– _____	– _____
40	중요한	important	– _____	– _____
41	재미있는	interesting	– _____	– _____
42	게으른	lazy	– _____	– _____
43	가벼운	light	– _____	– _____
44	양이 적은	little	– _____	– _____
45	긴	long	– _____	– _____
46	사랑스러운	lovely	– _____	– _____

47	낮은	low	– _____	– _____
48	운이 좋은	lucky	– _____	– _____
49	수가 많은	many	– _____	– _____
50	양이 많은	much	– _____	– _____
51	좋은	nice	– _____	– _____
52	시끄러운	noisy	– _____	– _____
53	나이 많은, 오래된	old	– _____	– _____
54	예의 바른	polite	– _____	– _____
55	가난한	poor	– _____	– _____
56	인기 있는	popular	– _____	– _____
57	예쁜	pretty	– _____	– _____
58	조용한	quiet	– _____	– _____
59	부유한	rich	– _____	– _____
60	무례한	rude	– _____	– _____
61	슬픈	sad	– _____	– _____
62	안전한	safe	– _____	– _____
63	심각한, 진지한	serious	– _____	– _____
64	얕은	shallow	– _____	– _____
65	마른	skinny	– _____	– _____
66	느린	slow	– _____	– _____
67	천천히	slowly	– _____	– _____
68	화창한	sunny	– _____	– _____
69	맛있는	tasty	– _____	– _____
70	끔찍한	terrible	– _____	– _____
71	두꺼운	thick	– _____	– _____
72	얇은	thin	– _____	– _____
73	못생긴	ugly	– _____	– _____
74	유용한	useful	– _____	– _____
75	귀중한	valuable	– _____	– _____
76	약한	weak	– _____	– _____
77	잘	well	– _____	– _____
78	넓은	wide	– _____	– _____
79	현명한	wise	– _____	– _____
80	어린, 젊은	young	– _____	– _____

UNIT 04 비교급

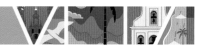

비교 표현 '~보다 더 …한[하게]'는 〈비교급+than ~〉으로 써야 해요.

비교 포인트	예문	의미
형용사 비교급+than	She is taller than her mom.	그녀는 그녀의 엄마보다 더 키가 크다.
부사 비교급+than	She can run faster than her dad.	그녀는 그녀의 아빠보다 더 빠르게 달릴 수 있다.

😊 **참고** than은 '~보다'라는 의미의 전치사예요.

😟 **주의** 비교급을 강조하여 '훨씬 더'라고 할 때, 비교급 앞에 much, even, far, still, a lot을 써요.
* very는 쓸 수 없음에 주의하세요.

|A| 괄호 안에서 알맞은 말을 고르시오.

01 My little brother is as (smart / smarter) as Edison.

02 Summer vacation was (shorter / more short) than winter vacation.

03 Your room has become a lot (clean / cleaner) than before.

04 This computer is (very / much) better than mine.

05 I went to school later than I (was / did) yesterday.

06 This jacket is less (expensive / more expensive) than that coat.

07 Ann can run less fast than (Jack can / Jack do).

'~보다 덜 …한'은 〈less+형용사/부사+than〉으로 표현해요.

|B| 우리말과 일치하도록 괄호 안의 말을 이용하여 문장을 완성하시오.

01 행복은 돈보다 훨씬 더 중요하다. (important, even)

Happiness is _____ money.

02 쥐가 개보다 냄새를 더 잘 맡을 수 있다. (smell, well)

Mice can _____ dogs can.

03 한국에서는 야구가 축구보다 더 인기가 있니? (popular)

Is baseball _____ soccer in Korea?

04 그곳까지 버스로 가는 편이 지하철로 가는 것보다 더 쉽다. (easy)

Going there by bus _____ going there by subway.

05 내가 제일 좋아하는 가수는 네가 제일 좋아하는 가수보다 더 노래를 잘한다. (sing, well)

My favorite singer _____ your favorite one.

실전 TIP 🎓
very는 비교급을 강조할 때는 사용할 수 없어요.

【내신 기출】 다음 빈칸에 very를 쓸 수 없는 것은?

① The boy is _____ smart and polite.

② James earns _____ more money than Mike.

③ The woman was _____ pleased to hear the news.

'~보다 …배 더 ~한[하게]'는 〈as+원급+as〉 또는 〈비교급+than〉 앞에 배수사를 붙이세요.

주어+동사	배수(사)	원급/비교급	비교 대상	의미
Regular pizza is	three times	as thick as	thin pizza.	얇은 피자보다 3배 더 두꺼운
		thicker than		
Math is	a hundred times	as difficult as	history.	역사보다 100배 더 어려운
		more difficult than		

참고 '배수사'란 〈숫자+times(~배)〉라고 배수를 나타내는 말이에요. three times(3배), ten times(10배) 등으로 표현해요. 단, 2배는 twice라고 표현한다는 데 유의하세요.

|A| 우리말과 일치하도록 |보기|의 말과 배수사 비교 표현을 이용하여 문장을 완성하시오.

| 보기 |
| large   long   well   old   expensive   bright |

01 아기들은 어른들보다 잠을 두 배 더 오래 잔다. Babies sleep _____ as adults.

02 그 나라는 한국보다 여섯 배 더 크다. That country is _____ as Korea.

03 이 자전거는 내 것보다 다섯 배 더 비싸다. This bike is _____ than mine.

04 우리 이모는 나보다 세 배 더 연세가 많으시다. My aunt is _____ than me.

05 이 동물은 인간보다 일곱 배 더 잘 본다. This animal sees _____ than people.

06 이 방은 다른 방보다 두 배 더 밝다. This room is _____ as other rooms.

|B| 두 문장이 같은 뜻이 되도록 원급 또는 비교급을 이용하여 문장을 완성하시오.

01 The Arctic has warmed three times faster than the whole world.

= The Arctic has warmed _____ as the whole world.

02 This library has eight times as many books as my school does.

= This library has _____ than my school does.

03 You are a hundred times as pretty as this rose.

= You are _____ than this rose.

04 Learning English was ten times easier than learning Chinese.

= Learning English was _____ as learning Chinese.

05 The Earth is four times bigger than the moon.

= The Earth is _____ as the moon.

06 An African elephant is twelve times as heavy as a polar bear.

= An African elephant is _____ than a polar bear.

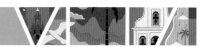

UNIT 06 비교급 표현

다음 비교급을 이용한 유용한 표현을 알아 두세요.

표현	〈the+비교급 ~, the+비교급 ...〉	〈비교급+and+비교급〉
의미	~하면 할수록 더 …하다	점점 더 ~한[하게]
예문	The darker it is, the brighter stars shine. 더 어두울수록, 별은 더 빛난다	It's getting colder and colder. 점점 더 추워지고 있다
	The sooner, the better. 더 빠를수록, 더 좋다 (뒤의 주어와 동사 생략 가능)	She will become more and more popular. 점점 더 인기를 얻을 것이다

|A| 우리말과 일치하도록 괄호 안의 말을 이용하여 문장을 완성하시오.

01 날씨가 점점 더 더워지고 있다. (hot)　　It's getting _____.

02 그는 점점 더 빨리 걷기 시작했다. (fast)　　He began to walk _____.

03 한국은 점점 더 강해지고 있다. (strong)　　Korea is getting _____.

04 점점 더 많은 사람들이 모여들었다. (many)　　_____ people gathered together.

05 그 표는 점점 더 비싸졌다. (expensive)　　The ticket became _____.

3음절 이상이라서 단어 앞에 more를 붙이는 형용사는 '점점 더 ~한/하게'를 표현할 때 〈more and more+형용사/부사〉의 어순으로 나타낸다는 점을 알아두세요.

06 나는 점점 더 신이 났다. (excited)　　I got _____.

|B| 두 문장이 같은 뜻이 되도록 〈the+비교급, the+비교급〉을 이용하여 바꾸시오.

01 As you get more, you want more.

= _____ you get, _____ you want.

02 If we laugh more, we become happier.

= _____ we laugh, _____ we become.

03 As I listened to his song more, I felt more relaxed.

= _____ I listened to his song, _____ I felt.

04 If you try to save the world more, the world will be cleaner.

= _____ you try to save the world, _____ the world will be.

05 As it got darker outside, it became colder.

= _____ it got outside, _____ it became.

06 If you go to bed later, waking up will be more difficult.

= _____ you go to bed, _____ waking up will be.

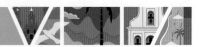

다음 최상급 표현을 알아 두세요.

표현	〈the+최상급〉	〈one of the+최상급+복수명사〉
의미	가장 ~한[하게]	가장 ~한 것들 중 하나
예문	Mina is the tallest student in the class. 반에서 키가 가장 큰 학생	Seoul is one of the busiest cities in Asia. 서울은 가장 분주한 도시들 중 하나
	It's the most difficult of all the questions. 그 모든 문제들 중 가장 어려운	Math is one of the most difficult subjects. 수학은 가장 어려운 과목들 중 하나

참고 최상급 뒤에는 〈in+단수명사(장소나 집단): ~에서〉 또는 〈of+복수명사: ~들 중에서〉가 올 수 있어요.

|A| 우리말과 일치하도록 괄호 안의 말을 이용해 문장을 완성하시오.

01 너의 인생에서 최고의 순간은 언제였니? (good, moment)

When was _____ in your life?

02 Amy가 세 자매 중에 가장 어리다. (young, sister)

Amy is _____.

03 말은 인류의 가장 사랑받는 파트너들 중 하나였다. (beloved, partner)

A horse was _____ of mankind.

04 휴대전화는 최고의 발명품들 중 하나다. (good, invention)

The mobile phone is _____.

05 Lucas는 우리 반에서 가장 부지런한 학생이다. (diligent, student)

Lucas is _____ in my class.

06 New York은 세계에서 가장 분주한 도시 중 하나다. (busy, city, world)

New York is _____.

〈one of the+최상급〉 뒤에 오는 명사는 반드시 복수형으로 써야 해요.

|B| 문장에서 틀린 부분을 찾아 밑줄 긋고 바르게 고치시오.

01 The more, the best. → _____

02 To win the game, you should jump the high. → _____

03 Santorini Island is one of the beautiful island. → _____

04 He is one of the best singer in the world. → _____

05 Stella is the kindest student of my class. → _____

06 You are one of the happiest man in the world. → _____

07 What is the biggest in all animals? → _____

08 This is the most popular of his song. → _____

최상급 뒤에 in이나 of를 써서 비교하는 대상의 범위를 나타낼 수 있어요.

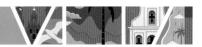

원급과 비교급을 이용하여 최상급의 의미를 표현하는 방법을 알아 두세요.

최상급	Tom is the fastest (boy) in his class.	Tom이 가장 빠르다.
원급	= No (other) boy is as fast as Tom.	= Tom만큼 빠른 소년은 없다.
비교급	= No (other) boy is faster than Tom.	= Tom보다 더 빠른 소년은 없다.
	= Tom is faster than any other boy.	= Tom은 다른 어떤 소년보다 빠르다.
	= Tom is faster than all the other boys.	= Tom은 다른 모든 소년들보다 빠르다.

|A| 두 문장이 같은 뜻이 되도록 빈칸을 채우시오.

〈비교급+than any other〉 뒤에는 단수명사, 〈비교급+than all the other〉 뒤에는 복수명사가 온다는 점에 유의하세요.

01 No other friend understands me better than you.

= You _____.

02 This is the shortest and easiest way.

= No other _____ than this.

03 Love is the most important thing in life.

= Love is _____ other thing.

04 For me, writing a letter is the most difficult thing.

= For me, no other _____ as writing a letter.

05 No other season is as beautiful as fall.

= No other _____ than fall.

06 A computer is the best invention in the world.

= A computer is better _____ in the world.

|B| 괄호 안의 단어를 바르게 배열하여 최상급의 의미가 되도록 문장을 완성하시오.

01 No other _____ as my dress. (as, dress, beautiful, is)

02 I like English _____. (subjects, the, other, than, all, more)

03 _____ as he does. (fast, no, other, swims, student, as)

04 I love ice cream _____. (dessert, other, more, than, any)

05 _____ than this song. (popular, more, is, other, no, song)

06 Prague is _____ city. (any, more, attractive, other, than)

07 No other _____ now. (happier, do, I, person, feels, than)

08 _____ Jupiter in the solar system. (is, than, other, no, planet, larger)

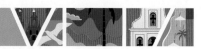

형용사/부사의 원급, 비교급, 최상급에 관한 기본 사항을 표에서 확인한 후 종합적으로 연습하세요.

구분	형태	의미	참고
원급	as ~ as ...	…만큼 ~한[하게]	as ~ as 사이에는 원급을 써요.
비교급	-er[more ~] than ...	…보다 더 ~한[하게]	전치사 than과 함께 써요.
최상급	the -est[most ~] of/in ...	…에서/중에서 가장 ~한[하게]	최상급 앞에 the를 붙여요.

|A| 문장에서 틀린 부분을 찾아 밑줄 긋고 바르게 고치시오.

01 You look very more healthier these days. → _____

02 Paris is one of the most popular city in the world. → _____

03 He ran as fastest as possible to catch the bus. → _____

04 The machine was not more useful as I expected. → _____

05 The more difficult the test is, harder I will study. → _____

06 A full moon is nine times bright as a half moon. → _____

07 No other teachers is as kind as my English teacher. → _____

|B| 우리말과 일치하도록 괄호 안의 말을 이용하여 문장을 완성하시오.

01 아이스크림은 케이크만큼 맛있다. (delicious)

Ice cream is _____ cake.

02 오늘 그녀는 어제보다 기분이 훨씬 더 좋다. (much, well)

Today, she feels _____ yesterday.

03 내 손은 저 아기의 손보다 두 배 더 크다. (big)

My hands are _____ that baby's ones.

04 로미오와 줄리엣은 역사상 최고 인기 영화 중 하나다. (popular)

Romeo and Juliet is _____ in history.

05 피아노를 더 많이 연습할수록, 나는 더 자신감을 갖게 됐다. (confident)

The more I practiced the piano, _____ I became.

06 그 어떤 나라도 러시아만큼 크지 않다. (large)

_____ as Russia.

실전 TIP

원급 비교인지 비교급 비교인지 최상급 비교인지 확인해 보세요.

내신기출 다음 중 빈칸에 interesting이 들어갈 수 있는 것은?

① No other book is as _____ as *Harry Porter* in the world.

② No other book is _____ than *Harry Porter* in the world.

③ *Harry Porter* is _____ than all the other books in the world.

중간고사·기말고사 실전문제

객관식 (01~25) / 주관식 (26~50)

정답과 해설 · 31쪽

학년과 반		이름		객관식	/ 25문항	주관식	/ 25문항

01 다음 중 원급 – 비교급 – 최상급 형태가 <u>잘못된</u> 것은?

① exciting – more exciting – most exciting
② good – better – best
③ light – more light – most light
④ much – more – most
⑤ weak – weaker – weakest

02~03 다음 빈칸에 들어갈 말로 알맞은 것을 고르시오.

02

This book is _____ than that book.

① more bored
② more boring
③ the most boring
④ the most bored
⑤ any more boring

03

A basketball is _____ than a baseball.

① more bigger
② big
③ biggest
④ bigger
⑤ the most biggest

04~05 다음 빈칸에 들어갈 말이 바르게 짝지어진 것을 고르시오.

04

1. She can run _____ than I can.
2. This stick is as _____ as a knife.

① more fast – sharp
② faster – sharp
③ fast – sharp
④ fast – sharper
⑤ faster – sharpest

05

1. How bigger is this table _____ that table?
2. This apple isn't _____ sweet as that one.

① than – more
② as – so
③ so – as
④ than – so
⑤ so – than

06~07 다음 우리말을 영어로 바르게 옮긴 것을 고르시오.

06

그는 내가 본 중에 가장 잘생긴 배우이다.

① He is the most handsome actor I have ever seen.
② He is the most handsomest actor I have ever seen.
③ He is the more handsome actor I have ever seen.
④ He is most handsome actor I have ever seen.
⑤ He is handsome actor I have ever seen.

07

나의 할아버지는 나보다 다섯 배 더 연세가 많다.

① My grandfather is five times as older than me.
② My grandfather is five times as older than mine.
③ My grandfather is five times more old than me.
④ My grandfather is five times as old as me.
⑤ My grandfather is five times old as me.

08 다음 빈칸에 공통으로 들어갈 말로 알맞은 것은?

> 1. The sugar in this juice is _____ than that in this tea.
> 2. I eat kimbab _____ often than sushi.

① little   ② least   ③ fewer
④ few   ⑤ more

09 다음 |보기|의 밑줄 친 much와 의미가 같은 것은?

> |보기|
> He was much younger than I thought.

① You must not eat too much sugar.
② I don't have much money to buy a new bag.
③ Don't drink too much Coke.
④ She has much more time than me.
⑤ Thank you so much for your help!

10 다음 문장과 의미가 같은 것은?

> This game is less boring than that book.

① This game isn't so boring than that book.
② This game isn't boring at all.
③ This game is as boring as that book.
④ That book isn't more boring than this game.
⑤ That book is more boring than this game.

11 다음 중 문장의 의미가 나머지 넷과 다른 것은?

① Mango is the sweetest fruit for me.
② Mango is as sweet as other fruit for me.
③ No other fruit is sweeter than mango for me.
④ No other fruit is so sweet as mango for me.
⑤ Mango is sweeter than any other fruit for me.

12~13 다음 중 어법상 올바른 것을 고르시오.

12 ① His house is larger than my house.
② He climbed the mountain as high as possibly.
③ My dress is more beautiful than her.
④ She is as not charming as her sister.
⑤ Tim speaks as slow as Ken does.

13 ① Your computer is convenient than mine.
② I told her my phone number as clearly than possible.
③ This ring is very more expensive than any other ring.
④ He is one of the smartest scientists in the world.
⑤ The room became coldest and coldest.

14~16 다음 중 어법상 어색한 것을 고르시오.

14 ① He is far more famous than his rival is.
② The most he spent his money, the poorest he became.
③ John is one of the nicest people on our team.
④ Please call me back as soon as possible.
⑤ Mom is worried about my health the most.

15 ① He studied even harder than I did last night.
② She seemed very tired when I saw her.
③ I hate Tom because he is a lot rude person.
④ I think this hat is much better than that one.
⑤ This house is very old and dirty.

16 ① This book is as thick as that book.
② This road is the worse to drive on.
③ This food tastes as good as that food.
④ I have to sleep earlier today.
⑤ This pizza is less delicious than that pasta.

17 다음 중 어법상 올바른 문장의 개수는?

ⓐ Please call me back as soon as possible.
ⓑ The weather is getting colder and colder.
ⓒ Mom is the funniest person in my family.
ⓓ He is one of most popular singers in the world.

① 없음   ② 1개   ③ 2개
④ 3개   ⑤ 4개

[18~19] 다음 중 어법상 어색한 문장의 개수를 고르시오.

18

ⓐ He painted much well than I did.
ⓑ The red dress isn't so beautiful as the yellow one.
ⓒ My pants are less beautiful than hers.
ⓓ No other man is funnier as the comedian.

① 없음   ② 1개   ③ 2개
④ 3개   ⑤ 4개

19

ⓐ *Three Idiots* is one of famous Indian movies in the world.
ⓑ This is the more interesting show of all the shows I've ever seen.
ⓒ I finished reading as early as she does.
ⓓ The hotter the weather becomes, the faster the iceberg melts.

① 없음   ② 1개   ③ 2개
④ 3개   ⑤ 4개

[20~21] 다음 빈칸에 들어갈 말이 바르게 짝지어진 것을 고르시오.

20

1. I like candy ___(A)___ more than gum.
2. You grew flowers ___(B)___ beautifully.
3. She is as friendly ___(C)___ you.

	(A)	(B)	(C)
①	very	– even	– than
②	so	– far	– that
③	as	– as	– a lot
④	a lot	– very	– as
⑤	any	– a lot	– very

21

A: You look very ___(A)___ .
B: I had a car accident last week, so I was in the hospital.
A: That's too bad. Do you feel ___(B)___ now?
B: Yeah, I'm good. We should cross the street ___(C)___ at night.

	(A)	(B)	(C)
①	worst	– worse	– most carefully
②	ill	– better	– more carefully
③	worse	– bad	– most carefully
④	great	– good	– very carefully
⑤	good	– greatest	– more carefully

22 다음 두 문장의 의미가 서로 <u>다른</u> 것은?

① a) If you exercise more often regularly, you will become healthier.
  b) The more often you exercise regularly, the healthier you will become.
② a) He could speak Spanish less fluently than me.
  b) He couldn't speak Spanish as fluently as me.
③ a) The tuna salad is the most delicious food in this restaurant.
  b) No other food is as delicious as the tuna salad in this restaurant.
④ a) Her daughter is taller than her son.
  b) Her son is as short as her daughter.
⑤ a) This shirt is three times as large as that shirt.
  b) This shirt is three times larger than that shirt.

<u>23~24</u> 다음 표를 보고, 내용과 <u>다른</u> 것을 고르시오.

	Height	Weight
Judy	160 cm	46 kg
Jimmy	170 cm	60 kg
Sheryl	155 cm	55 kg
Steve	180 cm	80 kg

23 ① Jimmy is shorter than Steve.
② Of the four, no one is taller than Steve.
③ Sheryl isn't as tall as Jimmy.
④ Steve isn't taller than Jimmy.
⑤ Judy isn't shorter than Sheryl.

24 ① Of the four, no one is heavier than Steve.
② Judy is the lightest one of the four.
③ Jimmy is lighter than Steve.
④ Judy isn't heavier than Steve.
⑤ Sheryl isn't heavier than Judy.

25 다음 중 뜻이 같은 문장끼리 짝지어진 것은?

ⓐ Jiho's score was higher than Sora's.
ⓑ Sora's score was as low as Jiho's.
ⓒ Jiho's score was the highest of all.
ⓓ Sora's score wasn't so high as Jiho's.
ⓔ Sora's score was lowest in the class.

① ⓐ, ⓑ   ② ⓐ, ⓓ   ③ ⓑ, ⓒ
④ ⓒ, ⓓ   ⑤ ⓐ, ⓔ

<u>26~27</u> 다음 우리말과 일치하도록 괄호 안의 말을 바르게 배열하시오.

26
그녀는 그보다 열 배나 돈을 많이 번다.
(more, times, than, money, earns, she, he, ten, does)

_____

27
과학은 가장 어려운 과목들 중 하나이다.
(science, subjects, of, the, most, is, one, difficult)

_____

<u>28~29</u> 다음 우리말과 일치하도록 괄호 안의 말을 이용하여 문장을 완성하시오.

28 세상에서 가장 빠른 동물은 무엇이니?
What is _____ animal in the world?
(fast)

29 그는 그녀보다 행복해 보인다.

He looks _____ than her. (happy)

30~31 다음 빈칸에 괄호 안의 말을 알맞은 형태로 쓰시오.

30 The painter paints water paintings _____ than oil paintings. (well)

31 Love is _____ than any other thing. (important)

32~33 다음 두 문장의 뜻이 같도록 빈칸에 알맞은 말을 쓰시오.

32 My father is the busiest man in the world.

= _____ other man is _____ than my father in the world.

33 If you read more books, you will be smarter.

= _____ books you read, _____ you will be.

34~38 다음 |보기|에서 알맞은 단어를 골라 빈칸에 쓰시오.

┌보기┐
very   as   than   even   less
└───────────────────────────┘

34 Jane's hairband is _____ prettier than mine.

35 Mr. Ericson's class is _____ interesting than Mr. Thomson's.

36 No other girl is skinnier _____ Gahee in our class.

37 He always likes pizza _____ much.

38 I don't meet him so often _____ you do.

39 다음 |보기|에 주어진 단어를 활용하여 빈칸에 각각 알맞은 말을 쓰시오.

┌보기┐
comfortable: 편안한
• He said that it is ___(A)___ chair in his room.
• I had a headache, so I sat on the chair. I felt ___(B)___ than before.
• This chair is very ___(C)___ .
└───────────────────────────┘

(1) (A) _____

(2) (B) _____

(3) (C) _____

40 다음 문장을 지시대로 바꿔 쓰시오.

Sarah can ride a bike as well as I can. (부정문으로)

→ _____

41~43 다음 문장에서 어법상 어색한 부분을 찾아 바르게 고치시오.

41 They walked on ice as carefully as possibly.

_____ → _____

42 He threw the ball high than me.

_____ → _____

43 She is a very kindest person.

_____ → _____

44~45 다음 문장에서 어법상 어색한 부분을 고쳐 완전한 문장을 쓰시오.

44 The computer was very more expensive than I expected.

→ _____

45 He hopes to become handsome than before.

→ _____

46~47 다음 문장이 어법상 어색하지 않으면 ○를, 어색한 부분이 있으면 밑줄을 치고 바르게 고치시오.

46 (1) This question is more difficult than all the other question.

→ _____

(2) He is the greatest football players in Korea.

→ _____

(3) The problems were solved more and more easily with his help.

→ _____

47 (1) He looks healthier than before.

→ _____

(2) Seoul is one of the largest city in the world.

→ _____

(3) This orange looks fresher as that apple.

→ _____

48~49 주어진 |조건|을 이용하여 우리말을 영어로 옮기시오.

48 ┤조건├

1) 〈비교급+and+비교급〉 표현을 사용할 것
2) 단어 the bag, slowly, get, heavy를 필요하면 활용하여 쓸 것
3) 7단어를 사용할 것

그 가방은 천천히 점점 더 무거워졌다.

_____

49 ┤조건├

1) 최상급을 사용할 것
2) 단어 good, person, for the job을 필요하면 활용하여 쓸 것
3) 8단어를 사용할 것

그녀는 그 일에 가장 적합한 사람이다.

_____

50 다음 글의 밑줄 친 ⓐ~ⓔ 중 어법상 어색한 것을 골라 기호를 쓰고 바르게 고치시오.

I have four dogs. They are Bambi, Coco, Toto, and Mongja. Bambi is ⓐ the oldest dog, but he's very energetic. Coco is bigger than ⓑ all the other dogs, but she still behaves like a small puppy. Toto is ⓒ very smart and I believe she is one of ⓓ the smartest dog in the world. Mongja is ⓔ the funniest dog among my dogs. She makes me feel happy all the time.

_____ → _____

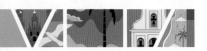

UNIT 01   who/what 의문문

사람 또는 사물에 대한 구체적인 정보를 요구할 때 쓰는 의문사를 알아 두세요.

의문사 who의 의미와 쓰임			의문사 what의 의미와 쓰임		
누구	보어	Who is she?	무엇	보어	What is this?
누가	주어	Who knows you?	무엇이	주어	What makes you mad?
누구를	목적어	Who(m) do you know?	무엇을	목적어	What do you like?

참고 어떤 것, 어느 쪽을 물을 때는 which를 사용하고 선택 가능한 것들을 or로 연결해요.
Which do you want, tea or juice?

의문사가 있는 의문문의 어순에 주의하세요.

be동사 의문사 의문문	의문사+be동사+주어 ~?
일반동사 의문사 의문문	의문사+조동사[do 조동사]+주어+동사원형 ~?

주의 의문사가 주어일 경우에는 동사 뒤에 따로 주어를 쓰지 않아요. Who washed the dishes?

|A| |보기|와 같이 주어진 대답의 밑줄 친 부분을 묻는 질문을 완성하시오.

┌─ 보기 ├──────────────────────────────────────
│   Who is your favorite singer? – My favorite singer is IU.
└──

01 _____ the window?   – James broke it.
02 _____ you buy?   – I bought a new backpack.
03 _____ your homeroom teacher?   – My homeroom teacher is Mr. Jeon.
04 _____ caused the problem?   – TV caused the problem.
05 _____ you want to play with?   – I want to play with Mike.

|B| 우리말과 일치하도록 괄호 안의 단어를 바르게 배열하여 문장을 완성하시오.

01 너는 여가 시간에 무엇을 하니? (do, what, do, you)
_____ in your free time?

02 누가 너에게 그 이야기를 했니? (told, who)
_____ you the story?

03 빨간색과 보라색 중에 어떤 게 네 칫솔이니? (one, is, which)
_____ your toothbrush, the red one or the purple one?

04 누가 이 컴퓨터를 고칠 수 있을까? (can, fix, who)
_____ this computer?

05 너는 누구를 가장 좋아하니? (like, you, do, who)
_____ the most?

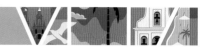

다양한 정보를 물을 수 있는 의문사들을 알아 두세요.

when	언제	When is the exam? When do you go to bed?	why	왜	Why are you sad? Why do you like it?
where	어디 어디서[에, 로]	Where is the bathroom? Where do you study?	how	어떤 어떻게	How was your weekend? How do you go there?

|A| |보기|와 같이 주어진 대답의 밑줄 친 부분을 묻는 질문을 완성하시오.

┌─보기┤
When is your birthday? - My birthday is November 5.
└─

01 _____ you live?   – I live in Seoul.

02 _____ call me?   – I called to say hello to you.

03 _____ the train leave? – It left two minutes ago.

04 _____ the movie?   – It was as great as I expected.

05 _____ Judy from?   – She is from Russia.

|B| 우리말과 일치하도록 괄호 안의 말을 이용하여 문장을 완성하시오.

01 너의 제주도 여행은 어땠니? (trip)

_____ to Jeju?

02 너는 언제 시간이 나니? (available, be)

_____?

03 너는 그동안 어떻게 지냈니? (have been)

_____ doing?

04 너희 둘은 언제 처음 만났니? (meet)

_____ you two first _____ each other?

05 내가 어디에서 표를 살 수 있을까? (buy)

_____ tickets?

06 그녀는 왜 그렇게 하기로 결정했을까? (decide)

_____ to do so?

의문사와 조동사가 함께 있는 의문문은 〈의문사+조동사+주어+동사원형 ~?〉으로 표현해요.

실전 TIP

알맞은 의문사를 찾기 위해서는 어떻게 대답하고 있는지를 확인해야 해요.

┌ **내신 기출** 빈칸에 각각 알맞은 의문사를 쓰시오.

• _____ did you get here? - I came here by subway.

• _____ do you like better, pink or blue? - I like blue better.

'얼마나 ~한[하게]'라고 물을 때는 〈how+형용사/부사〉로 쓰세요.

의미	How	형용사/부사	의문문
얼마나 자주	How	often	do you go to the library?
몇 살[얼마나 늙은/오래된]	How	old	is your brother?
얼마나 긴[길게]/오래	How	long	does it take to go there?
(수) 얼마나 많이	How	many	do you have?
(가격/양이) 얼마(나 많이)	How	much	is the ticket?
얼마나 먼	How	far	is the market?

주의 How many/much는 뒤에 명사를 쓸 수 있고, 〈How many/much+명사〉까지가 하나의 의문사예요.

How many books do you have? *many+셀 수 있는 명사

How much time do you have? *much+셀 수 없는 명사

|A| 〈How+형용사/부사〉를 이용해서 대화의 질문을 완성하시오.

01 A: _____ is the Great Wall of China? B: It is about 2.700 kilometers long.

02 A: _____ people did you invite to the party? B: I invited ten people.

03 A: _____ is the N Seoul Tower? B: It is 236 meters tall.

04 A: _____ sugar do you need? B: I need a spoonful of sugar.

05 A: _____ do you exercise? B: I exercise once a week.

06 A: _____ is the nearest bus stop? B: It is about one minute away.

|B| 우리말과 일치하도록 괄호 안의 말을 이용하여 문장을 완성하시오.

01 지하철역까지 가는 데 시간이 얼마나 걸리니? (take)

_____ to get to the subway station?

02 이 가방 값으로 내가 얼마를 내야 할까? (should, pay for)

_____ this bag?

03 얼마나 많은 나라가 이번 올림픽에 참가하지? (take part in, country)

_____ these Olympic Games?

04 너희 가족은 얼마나 자주 영화를 보러 가니? (go)

_____ to a movie?

05 우리가 얼마나 오래 일몰을 기다려야 하지? (should, wait for)

_____ the sunset?

06 사진 속의 이 아기는 몇 살이니? (baby)

_____ in the picture?

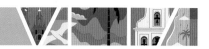

UNIT 04 how come 의문문

how come은 why와 비슷한 의미지만, 뒤에 나오는 어순이 다른 점에 주의하세요.

의미	How come	+ 평서문 어순	Why	+ 의문문 어순
도대체 왜, 어째서, 어쩌다	How come	you are angry?	= Why	are you angry?
	How come	you called her?	= Why	did you call her?

참고 How come은 How did it come (that) ~ (어쩌다 ~하게 되었나?)라는 표현에서 did it을 생략해서 쓰는 말로 (that)절에 평서문을 써야 해요.

|A| 두 문장이 같은 뜻이 되도록 빈칸에 알맞은 말을 쓰시오.

01 How come she is always late?　=＿＿＿＿＿＿＿＿＿＿ always late?

02 How come there are so many people?　=＿＿＿＿＿＿＿＿＿＿ so many people?

03 ＿＿＿＿＿＿＿＿＿＿ the window?　= Why did you break the window?

04 ＿＿＿＿＿＿＿＿＿＿ still sleeping?　= Why is he still sleeping?

05 How come you skipped lunch today?　=＿＿＿＿＿＿＿＿＿＿ lunch today?

06 ＿＿＿＿＿＿＿＿＿＿ absent?　= Why were you absent?

|B| 우리말과 일치하도록 괄호 안의 말을 이용하여 문장을 완성하시오.

〈How come+주어+동사 ~?〉는 의문문이지만, 주어와 동사의 어순이 바뀌지 않고 평서문처럼 써요.

01 어쩌다 내 전화기가 고장이 났을까? (be, how come, my phone)

＿＿＿＿＿＿＿＿＿＿＿＿ out of order?

02 그녀는 도대체 왜 항상 검정색 옷만 입지? (how come, wear black)

＿＿＿＿＿＿＿＿＿＿＿＿ all the time?

03 어째서 너희가 서로를 알고 있니? (how come, you two, know)

＿＿＿＿＿＿＿＿＿＿＿＿ each other?

04 도대체 왜 너는 여기 매일 들르니? (drop by, how come)

＿＿＿＿＿＿＿＿＿＿＿＿ here every day?

05 너는 왜 매일 밤늦게까지 안 자는 거야? (why, stay up late)

＿＿＿＿＿＿＿＿＿＿＿＿ every night?

06 도대체 왜 우리 아빠는 항상 피곤해 하실까? (how come, always, feel)

＿＿＿＿＿＿＿＿＿＿＿＿ tired?

실전 TIP

How come과 Why 의문문의 어순을 다시 한 번 확인하세요.

내신 기출 동사 know를 이용하여 문장을 완성하시오.

How come he ＿＿＿＿＿ everything about me?

= Why ＿＿＿＿＿ he ＿＿＿＿＿ everything about me?

UNIT 05 what과 how를 이용한 감탄문

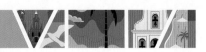

감탄문은 의문사 what 또는 how로 만든다는 걸 기억하세요.

구분	감탄의 대상		어순	참고
What 감탄문	명사	셀 수 없을 때	What(+형용사)+명사(+주어+동사)!	〈주어+동사〉는 생략하는 경우가 많음
		셀 수 있는 단수	What+a/an(+형용사)+단수명사(+주어+동사)!	
		셀 수 있는 복수	What(+형용사)+복수명사(+주어+동사)!	
How 감탄문	형용사/부사		How+형용사/부사(+주어+동사)!	

|A| 빈칸에 What과 How 중 알맞은 것을 쓰시오.

01 _____ a nice dress (it is)!

02 _____ large (this room is)!

03 _____ fast (the man runs)!

04 _____ old computers (they have)!

05 _____ easy (the exam was)!

06 _____ a kind girl (she is)!

07 _____ cold water (this is)!

08 _____ delicious (these dishes are)!

09 _____ expensive (the ring is)!

10 _____ an interesting movie (it is)!

11 _____ early (she gets up)!

12 _____ great players (they are)!

|B| 우리말과 일치하도록 괄호 안의 단어를 바르게 배열하여 문장을 완성하시오.

감탄문에서 what 뒤에는 명사가 오지만 how 뒤에는 명사가 오지 않아요.

01 이것들은 정말 맛있는 사과들이구나! (what, these, delicious, apples, are)

_____!

02 이 사과들은 정말 맛있구나! (how, these, delicious, apples, are)

_____!

03 그것은 정말 높은 건물이구나! (it, building, is, what, tall, a)

_____!

04 이 배낭은 정말 무겁구나! (this backpack, how, is, heavy)

_____!

05 정말 좋은 날씨구나! (weather, it, nice, what, is)

_____!

06 별이 정말 밝게 빛나는구나! (the stars, brightly, how, shine)

_____!

07 시간이 정말 빠르게 지나가는구나! (fast, how, goes by, time)

_____!

08 그는 정말 비싼 휴대전화를 가지고 있구나! (he, an, what, cellphone, has, expensive)

_____!

중간고사·기말고사 실전문제

객관식 (01~25) / 주관식 (26~50)

정답과 해설 · 35쪽

학년과 반		이름		객관식	/ 25문항	주관식	/ 25문항

01~02 다음 빈칸에 들어갈 말로 알맞은 것을 고르시오.

01

_____ ate my chocolate cookies?

① What ② Where ③ Whom
④ When ⑤ Who

02

_____ didn't you tell me the truth?

① How ② Why ③ Whom
④ How come ⑤ What

03~04 다음 빈칸에 들어갈 말이 바르게 짝지어진 것을 고르시오.

03

1. _____ can they meet Mr. Han tomorrow? 2. _____ do you love her?

① Where – When ② Who – Why
③ When – Where ④ Whom – How
⑤ Where – Why

04

1. _____ time do you eat dinner? 2. _____ do I get to the post office?

① When – Where ② When – How
③ What – How ④ Which – Where
⑤ What – Where

05 다음 빈칸에 공통으로 들어갈 말로 알맞은 것은?

1. _____ did you go to Jeju? 2. _____ is Mike's birthday?

① How ② Why ③ When
④ Where ⑤ What

06 다음 중 빈칸에 들어갈 동사가 나머지 넷과 <u>다른</u> 것은?

① _____ he arrive at the airport on time yesterday?

② _____ you sick when Tom visited your home?

③ _____ Mike eat dinner with you last night?

④ _____ your mom swim in the pool this morning?

⑤ _____ you closely look in the mirror? There's still something on your face.

07 다음 중 밑줄 친 <u>What</u>의 쓰임이 나머지 넷과 <u>다른</u> 것은?

① <u>What</u> kind of sports do you like the most?

② <u>What</u> a good boy you are!

③ <u>What</u> is your grandmother's first name?

④ <u>What</u> can I do for you?

⑤ <u>What</u> are you talking about?

08~09 다음 우리말을 영어로 바르게 옮긴 것을 고르시오.

08

너는 Tommy를 얼마나 많이 사랑하니?

① How do you love Tommy?
② How big do you love Tommy?
③ How many do you love Tommy?
④ How much do you love Tommy?
⑤ How come you love Tommy?

09

어째서 그 파티에 가지 않았니?

① How come didn't you go to the party?
② Why you didn't go to the party?
③ How come you didn't go to the party?
④ How did you not go to the party?
⑤ Why did you not go to the party?

10 다음 질문에 대한 대답으로 가장 적절한 것은?

How often do you exercise in the gym?

① Yes, I exercise a lot.
② I go to the gym by bus.
③ I will go to the gym tomorrow.
④ No, I don't exercise at all.
⑤ I hardly exercise in the gym.

11 다음 질문에 대한 대답으로 적절하지 <u>않은</u> 것은?

What does he do for a living?

① He's a furniture designer.
② His job is a job manager.
③ He lives in Busan with his parents.
④ He works as a live show host.
⑤ He's teaching English in a middle school.

12 다음 대화의 질문으로 가장 알맞은 것은?

A: _____
B: I usually walk to school.

① Are you going to school?
② Do you go to school in the morning?
③ Will you go to school with me?
④ How do you go to school?
⑤ Why do you go to school by bus?

13~14 다음 중 어법상 올바른 것을 고르시오.

13 ① Which number is this apartment?
② I heard a scream five minutes ago. How happened?
③ What do you eat more often, bread or rice?
④ What room is the bathroom in this house?
⑤ Which color do you use for your painting more often, blue or red?

14 ① How high and great is Seorak mountain!
② Why you didn't come to my birthday party last weekend?
③ What beautiful garden with many flowers it is!
④ How big was the bear you saw at the zoo?
⑤ Which flavor do you prefer, lemon and grape?

15 다음 중 대화가 자연스럽지 <u>않은</u> 것은?

① A: What do you <u>think</u> about this movie?

B: I think it's great.

② A: Why do you like this movie?

B: I like this movie very much.

③ A: How small this kitten is!

B: Yes, it is so cute!

④ A: Do you have a brother?

B: Yes, I do.

⑤ A: Have you ever been to Rome?

B: Yes, I have.

16~17 다음 중 어법상 <u>어색한</u> 것을 고르시오.

16 ① When are you going to Bangkok?

② What bring you here? Do you live around here?

③ Where have you been? I was worried!

④ Why is he shouting at us from across the street?

⑤ Who is that boy singing merrily on the stage?

17 ① What interesting movies it is!

② How did you find this gold ring?

③ I feel like going hiking. How's the weather today?

④ How come you decided to move to Jeju?

⑤ How could the stranger enter this building?

18 다음 중 어법상 올바른 문장의 개수는?

ⓐ What is bigger, beans or corn?

ⓑ What huge a waterfall it is!

ⓒ What made you the best player?

ⓓ Which way will you turn, left or right?

① 없음 ② 1개 ③ 2개

④ 3개 ⑤ 4개

19 다음 두 문장의 의미가 서로 <u>다른</u> 것은?

① a) Why do you think so?

b) What makes you think so?

② a) What do you do?

b) What are you doing?

③ a) What did you do that for?

b) Why did you do that?

④ a) How come she doesn't like cheese?

b) Why doesn't she like cheese?

⑤ a) How's it going?

b) How are you?

20~21 다음 중 어법상 <u>어색한</u> 문장의 개수를 고르시오.

20

ⓐ How longer is a kilogram than a gram?

ⓑ When did you come to the party?

ⓒ What's the weather like today?

ⓓ What is the point of his speech?

① 없음 ② 1개 ③ 2개

④ 3개 ⑤ 4개

21

ⓐ It's raining every day in London these days! How come does it rain in Seoul?

ⓑ Which is more exciting, bungee jumping or sky diving?

ⓒ How long is the boy?

ⓓ Do you usually stay home or go out on the weekend?

① 없음 ② 1개 ③ 2개

④ 3개 ⑤ 4개

22 다음 표의 내용을 바탕으로 질문과 답변이 올바르지 않은 것은?

Time	Subject	Teacher	Place
8:00 a.m.	Society	Mr. Han	Room A
9:00 a.m.	English	Mr. Choi	Room B
1:00 p.m.	Math	Ms. Ahn	Room C
2:00 p.m.	Science	Ms. Park	Room D

① A: Who's going to teach in Room C?
　 B: It's Ms. Ahn.
② A: Where will Mr. Han teach society?
　 B: He will teach it in Room A.
③ A: When does Ms. Park teach science?
　 B: She teaches it at two o'clock.
④ A: What subject does Mr. Choi teach?
　 B: It's math.
⑤ A: Is Mr. Han going to teach society?
　 B: Yes, he is.

[23~24] 다음 대화의 빈칸에 들어갈 말이 바르게 짝지어진 것을 고르시오.

23
A: Can you see those people?
B: What a big crowd! ____(A)____ did they gather here?
A: They came to see celebrities.
B: ____(B)____ is coming?
A: It's TWICE!
B: Really? They are one of my favorite singers. ____(C)____ lucky I am!

	(A)	(B)	(C)
①	Why	– Who	– How
②	How come	– What	– How
③	Why	– What	– How
④	How come	– Who	– What
⑤	Why	– Who	– What

24
A: ____(A)____ time is the last show?
B: It starts at 9:00 o'clock.
A: ____(B)____ long is the show?
B: It's one-hour show.
A: ____(C)____ much is the ticket?
B: It's ten dollars.

	(A)	(B)	(C)
①	What	– How	– What
②	How	– What	– How
③	When	– Where	– Would
④	How	– What	– What
⑤	What	– How	– How

25 다음 대화의 밑줄 친 ⓐ~ⓔ 중 어법상 어색한 것은?

A: ⓐ How was your trip to Turkey?
B: It was great! I visited many sites of ancient Turkish culture. ⓑ What beautiful places they were!
A: Did you try a lot of new food?
B: Sure. I liked Turkish Delight the most.
A: ⓒ What kind of food it is?
B: It's a traditional Turkish dessert. ⓓ How sweet it was! I brought some for you.
A: Thanks! ⓔ How interesting your trip seems!

① ⓐ　　② ⓑ　　③ ⓒ　　④ ⓓ　　⑤ ⓔ

[26~27] 다음 우리말과 일치하도록 괄호 안의 말을 이용하여 문장을 완성하시오.

26 어젯밤 여기서 무슨 일이 일어났니? (happen)
What _____ here last night?

27 그녀는 애플 망고를 좋아하니? (like)
_____ she _____ apple mangoes?

28~32 다음 |보기|에서 알맞은 단어를 골라 빈칸에 쓰시오.

┌ 보기 ├─────────────────────┐

How　　　What　　　Who

Why　　　When　　　Where

└──────────────────────────┘

28 _____ well does she play the piano?

29 _____ size are your pants?

30 _____ can I buy a ticket to enter the museum? Is it beside the front door?

31 _____ was the first time he walked?

32 _____ kicked the ball at my window and broke it?

33~34 다음 우리말과 일치하도록 괄호 안의 말을 바르게 배열하시오.

33
┌────────────────────────────┐

다음 승리자는 누가 될 수 있을까?

(the next winner, be able to, will, who, be)

└────────────────────────────┘

_____

34
┌────────────────────────────┐

어째서 어젯밤에 늦게까지 깨어 있었니?

(stayed up late, you, how, last night, come)

└────────────────────────────┘

_____

35~38 다음 |보기|에서 알맞은 단어를 골라 빈칸에 쓰시오.

┌ 보기 ├─────────────────────┐

What　　　Which　　　How

└──────────────────────────┘

35 _____ is your favorite TV program?

36 _____ book do you like the best among those on the bookshelf?

37 _____ far is Kenya from Seoul?

38 _____ is the weather like in Australia?

39~41 다음 지시대로 밑줄 친 부분을 묻는 질문을 쓰시오.

39 Her dog's name is Bambi.
(의문사 what을 사용한 의문문으로)

→ _____

40 They visited Disneyland yesterday.
(의문사 when을 사용한 의문문으로)

→ _____

41 Heejin has lived in Italy for 10 years.
(의문사 how를 사용한 의문문으로)

→ _____

42~44 다음 문장에서 어법상 어색한 부분을 찾아 바르게 고치시오.

42 Why you didn't come to the exhibition last night?

_____ → _____

43 Where do you from, Japan or Korea?

_____ → _____

44 Whom came last in the race yesterday?

_____ → _____

45~46 다음 문장에서 어법상 어색한 부분을 고쳐 완전한 문장을 쓰시오.

45 What did you saw when you were out?

→ _____

46 What do you want to eat, pizza and fried chicken?

→ _____

47 다음 문장이 어법상 어색하지 않으면 ○를, 어색한 부분이 있으면 밑줄을 치고 바르게 고치시오.

(1) What a mysterious universe we live in!

→ _____

(2) How you don't read this novel? It's funny!

→ _____

(3) What was the first time you and Minji met?

→ _____

48~49 주어진 |조건|을 이용하여 우리말을 영어로 옮기시오.

48 ┌ 조건 ┐
1) 의문사 how를 사용할 것
2) 단어 tall, new, building, Hanoi를 필요하면 활용하여 쓸 것
3) 8단어를 사용할 것

하노이에 있는 그 새로운 빌딩은 얼마나 높니?

_____

_____

49 ┌ 조건 ┐
1) 의문사 which로 시작하는 문장을 쓸 것
2) 단어 you, direction, mean, North, or, South를 필요하면 활용하여 쓸 것
3) 8단어를 사용할 것

북쪽과 남쪽 중 어느 방향을 의미하는 거니?

_____

_____

50 다음 대화의 밑줄 친 ⓐ~ⓔ 중 어법상 어색한 것을 골라 기호를 쓰고 바르게 고치시오.

A: Mom, I'm home. I'm hungry. ⓐ What food is in the kitchen?
B: I baked some pizza and bread. ⓑ Which do you want?
A: I want both of them. They are really good! ⓒ How delicious this pizza is!
B: Thank you. ⓓ What was school?
A: I got an A+ on math exam.
B: ⓔ What great news! I'm proud of you.

_____ → _____

09

문장의 형식

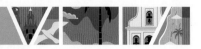

문장을 구성하는 5대 요소, 즉 주어, 동사(서술어), 목적어, 보어, 수식어를 외워 두세요.

문장 구성 요소	역할	예문
주어	문장의 주체 (~은/는, ~이/가)	The teacher teaches science.
동사(서술어)	주어의 상태, 동작 서술 (~이다, ~하다)	The teacher teaches science.
목적어	동작의 대상 (~을/를, ~에게)	The teacher teaches us science.
보어	주어나 목적어 보충 설명	He is a teacher. The teacher makes us happy.
수식어	명사, 동사, 문장 수식	The new teacher teaches science in school.

|A| 문장에서 밑줄 친 부분이 주어, 동사, 목적어, 보어 중에 어떤 역할인지 |보기|에서 골라 쓰시오.

┌ 보기 ┐
주어: S   동사: V   목적어: O   보어: C
└────┘

01 I don't like fast food.   [   ]   **09** My uncle is a vet.   [   ]
02 Kelly cooks well.   [   ]   **10** I bought a new pen.   [   ]
03 I am Korean.   [   ]   **11** You look very sad.   [   ]
04 This sofa feels soft.   [   ]   **12** The boy became happy.   [   ]
05 I trust him.   [   ]   **13** His song is great.   [   ]
06 The show was fantastic.   [   ]   **14** He heard a dog barking.   [   ]
07 We can't see anything.   [   ]   **15** Her dress is black.   [   ]
08 Sora and I are best friends.   [   ]   **16** They enjoy playing ball.   [   ]

|B| 우리말과 일치하도록 괄호 안의 단어를 바르게 배열하여 문장을 완성하시오.

문장의 각 요소가 있어야 할 자리에 유의하세요.

01 5분 후에 수업이 시작한다. (in, the class, five minutes, starts)

_____.

02 나의 부모님은 두 분 다 선생님이시다. (teachers, both my parents, are)

_____.

03 이 음식은 안 좋은 냄새가 난다. (good, this food, smell, doesn't)

_____.

04 새들이 나뭇가지 위에서 노래하고 있다. (singing, are, birds, on a branch)

_____.

05 그는 그녀에게 장미 백 송이를 사 주었다. (her, bought, one hundred roses, he)

_____.

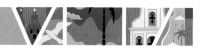

〈주어+동사〉 뒤에 어떤 말이 오는가에 따라 1, 2, 3형식으로 구분하세요.

	문장의 구성 요소	예문	참고
1형식	〈주어+동사〉	〈The train arrived〉 (on time). 〈She is sleeping〉 (on the sofa).	주어, 동사만으로 완전한 문장
2형식	〈주어+동사〉+보어	〈The train is〉 long. 〈She became〉 a nurse.	보어가 없으면 불완전한 문장
3형식	〈주어+동사〉+목적어	〈The train takes〉 us (to Busan). 〈She wants〉 some juice.	목적어(~을, ~에게)가 필요한 문장

참고 부사, 전치사구는 문장 구성 요소에서 제외해요.

|A| |보기|와 같이 문장을 문장 성분별로 나누고, 각각의 문장 성분을 쓰시오.

┌ 보기 ┐
I / drank / orange juice / in the kitchen. → 주어+동사+목적어+수식어구

01 He became a great scientist. → _____

02 The show ends in one hour. → _____

03 Water freezes at 0 ℃. → _____

04 Her face turned red. → _____

05 Joy looks happy today. → _____

|B| 우리말과 일치하도록 괄호 안의 단어를 바르게 배열하여 문장을 완성하고, 몇 형식인지 쓰시오.

01 하늘에 보름달이 떴다. (rose, the full moon)

_____ in the sky.   [   ] 형식

02 그들은 한국에서 가장 유명한 가수들이다. (the most famous, are, they, singers)

_____ in Korea.   [   ] 형식

03 Teddy는 오늘 늦게 일어났다. (woke up, Teddy, late)

_____ today.   [   ] 형식

04 그 공포 영화는 정말 무서웠다. (was, very scary, the horror movie)

_____.   [   ] 형식

05 나의 언니는 고등학생이다. (a high school student, older sister, my, is)

_____.   [   ] 형식

06 그녀의 작은 아기가 울고 있었다. (was, little baby, her, crying)

_____.   [   ] 형식

UNIT 03 감각동사 + 형용사

be동사와 감각동사가 취하는 보어의 종류와 그 의미를 파악하세요.

보어를 취하는 동사		보어	의미
be동사	be, am, are, is, was, were	명사, 형용사	~이다, ~다
감각동사	feel, look, sound, smell, taste	형용사	~하게 느끼다, ~하게 보이다, ~한 소리가 나다, ~한 냄새가 나다, ~한 맛이 나다

😊 참고 감각동사 뒤에 명사를 쓰려면 〈감각동사+like+명사〉로 쓰면 돼요.

He looks smart. → He looks like a smart person.

그 외에 보어를 취하는 일반동사와 그 의미를 알아 두세요.

become	~이 되다, ~해지다	keep	~하게 유지하다	turn	~으로 변하다, ~해지다
get	~해지다	remain	~한 채로 있다	appear	~인 것 같다

|A| 문장에서 틀린 부분에 밑줄 긋고 바르게 고치시오.

01 Why do you look so sadly today? → _____

02 This milk smells sourly. → _____

03 I don't feel comfortably on this chair. → _____

04 The mushroom soup tasted salt. → _____

05 Your car doesn't sound like very good. → _____

06 The cloud looks a sheep. → _____

|B| 우리말과 일치하도록 괄호 안의 말을 이용하여 문장을 완성하시오.

01 그 장난감은 진짜 자동차처럼 보였다. (real) The toy _____ car.

02 나는 그들을 보면 기분 좋게 느껴진다. (good) I _____ when I see them.

03 라면은 늘 냄새가 좋다. (awesome) Ramen always _____.

04 너는 공주처럼 보인다. (princess) You _____.

05 그것은 이상하게 들릴지도 모른다. (strange) It may _____.

06 그 아이스크림은 우유 맛이 난다. (milk) The ice cream _____.

실전 TIP 🎓

보어로는 부사가 절대 올 수 없어요.

내신 기출 우리말을 영작한 문장에서 틀린 부분을 찾아 고쳐 쓰시오.

너 지금 몹시 불안해 보여.

= You look very nervously now.
①   ②   ③   ④   ⑤

UNIT 04　3형식 & 4형식

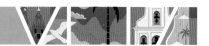

3형식 타동사 다음의 목적어로 올 수 있는 다양한 말들을 알아 두세요.

목적어로 쓸 수 있는 말	예문	해석
명사/대명사	I want a book. / I call him.	~을, ~에게
to부정사	I want to read a book.	~하기를 / ~하는 것을
동명사	I like reading a book.	~하기를 / ~하는 것을
명사절	I know that you like books.	~이라는 것을

목적어 두 개('~에게'와 '~을')를 취하는 4형식 동사들과 그 어순을 알아 두세요.

4형식 어순	4형식 동사 (수여동사: ~에게 …을 ~해 주다)		간접목적어	직접목적어
	give, make, show, send, ask, tell, lend, get, bring, teach, buy, cook 등		~에게	…을

주의 목적어가 1개 있으면 3형식, 목적어(간접목적어, 직접목적어)가 2개 있으면 4형식이에요.

|A| 문장의 목적어에 밑줄 긋고 문장이 몇 형식인지 쓰시오.

01 He sent me mail.　　[　]

02 She lent her friend money.　　[　]

03 She showed Tony the way.　　[　]

04 He likes going there.　　[　]

05 He opened the shop in 2002.　　[　]

06 I finished my math homework.　　[　]

07 Dad washed the dishes.　　[　]

08 We gave him a present.　　[　]

|B| 우리말과 일치하도록 괄호 안의 말을 바르게 배열하여 문장을 완성하시오.

01 그녀는 똑같은 실수를 저질렀다. (the same mistake, made)

　　She _____.

02 우리 할머니는 내게 당근 케이크를 만들어 주셨다. (a carrot cake, me, made)

　　My grandma _____.

03 저희에게 물을 좀 주실 수 있나요? (some water, us, give)

　　Could you _____?

04 Beth는 내게 그녀의 비밀을 말해 주었다. (told, me, her secret)

　　Beth _____.

05 Becky는 내게 항상 질문을 많이 한다. (questions, a lot of, asks, me)

　　Becky always _____.

06 내게 음료수를 한 잔 더 갖다 줄래? (me, bring, another drink)

　　Could you _____?

4형식 문장은 〈수여동사+간접목적어+직접목적어〉의 어순으로 써요.

UNIT 05 3~4형식 전환

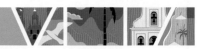

4형식 문장을 3형식 문장으로 바꿔 쓸 수 있는데, 이때 어순과 전치사에 주의하세요.

	일반 수여동사	직접목적어	to	
3형식 어순	get, make, buy, cook, build, find	(~을)	for	간접목적어
	ask, inquire	question, favor	of	

|A| 문장에 쓰인 동사에 유의하여 빈칸에 to, for, of 중 알맞은 전치사를 쓰시오.

01 He bought some flowers _____ me.

02 Please pass the salt _____ me.

03 May I ask a favor _____ you?

04 He wrote a long letter _____ his teacher.

05 Sara made a hat _____ her baby.

06 Jessica lent her skirt _____ her sister.

07 My dad often cooks steaks _____ us.

08 She gave detailed instructions _____ them.

|B| 3형식 문장은 4형식으로, 4형식 문장은 3형식으로 바꿔 쓰시오.

01 Lucas, pass the ball to another player right now.

= _____.

02 Did you make me this birthday card?

= _____?

03 He taught how to play the violin to me.

= _____.

04 The driver showed the police his driver's license.

= _____.

05 Tom asked a lot of questions of me.

= _____.

06 She reads her baby bedtime stories.

= _____.

4형식 문장을 3형식으로 바꿀 때는 동사에 따라 간접목적어 앞에 나오는 전치사가 달라짐에 유의하세요.

UNIT 06 5형식 1 - 명사, 형용사

목적격보어로 명사나 형용사를 쓰는 5형식 동사를 알아 두세요.

	명사/형용사를 목적격보어로 쓰는 5형식 동사	목적어	목적격보어
5형식 어순	make, call, name, find, keep, elect, think, believe, consider 등	~을, ~이/가	명사, 형용사

|A| 우리말과 일치하도록 괄호 안에서 알맞은 말을 고르시오.

01 그녀를 혼자 내버려 두지 마.　　Don't leave (her alone / alone her).

02 그는 그 고양이를 Mia라고 이름 지었다.　　He named (the cat Mia / Mia the cat).

03 나는 그 책이 재미있다는 것을 알았다.　　I found the book (interesting / interestingly).

04 그들은 나를 천재라고 부른다.　　They call (a genius me / me a genius).

05 맛있는 음식은 나를 행복하게 한다.　　Delicious food makes me (happy / happily).

06 그들은 그를 영웅으로 생각한다.　　They think (a hero him / him a hero).

07 네 손을 항상 깨끗하게 유지해라.　　Always keep your hands (clean / cleanly).

08 그들은 그를 대표로 만들었다.　　They made (a leader him / him a leader).

|B| 우리말과 일치하도록 괄호 안의 말을 바르게 배열하여 문장을 완성하시오.

5형식 문장에서 목적어와 목적격보어의 순서가 바뀌지 않도록 유의하세요.

01 그녀의 칭찬은 나를 자신감 있게 만들었다. (confident, me, made)

Her compliment _____.

02 규칙적인 운동은 너를 건강하게 지켜줄 것이다. (keep, will, healthy, you)

Regular exercise _____.

03 너희들은 왜 James를 척척박사라고 부르니? (Mr. Know-It-All, James, call)

Why do you _____?

04 내 친구들과 나는 그 게임이 정말 어렵다는 걸 알았다. (found, really difficult, the game)

My friends and I _____.

05 사람들은 종종 미국을 "용광로"라고 부른다. (call, America, a melting pot)

People often _____.

06 두꺼운 외투와 목도리가 나를 따뜻하게 지켜 주었다. (warm, me, kept)

The thick coat and muffler _____.

UNIT 07 5형식 2 – to부정사

목적격보어로 to부정사를 쓰는 동사들을 알아 두세요.

5형식 어순	to부정사를 목적격보어로 쓰는 5형식 동사	목적어	목적격보어
	want, ask, tell, expect, enable, encourage allow, advise, order, get, permit, force	~에게, ~이/가	to부정사 (~하기를/~하라고)

참고 to부정사의 부정은 to 앞에 not을 쓰면 돼요.

|A| 문장에서 <u>틀린</u> 부분에 밑줄 긋고 바르게 고치시오.

01 The teacher allowed us use computers. → _____

02 The flight attendant asked me taking a seat. → _____

03 Why do you keep secret it? → _____

04 He didn't tell you to being careful. → _____

05 My family and friends make me happily. → _____

06 No one expected her win the contest. → _____

07 My parents want me becoming a violinist. → _____

08 She ordered them stayed quiet. → _____

|B| 우리말과 일치하도록 괄호 안의 말을 이용하여 문장을 완성하시오.

01 나는 너희가 나와 함께 테니스 동아리에 가입하기를 원한다. (want, join)

I _____ the tennis club with me.

02 우리 엄마는 나에게 창문을 다 열라고 부탁하셨다. (ask, open)

My mom _____ all the windows.

03 경찰은 강도들에게 손을 위로 들라고 명령했다. (order, put, the robbers)

The police officer _____ their hands up.

04 우리 부모님은 내가 휴대전화 게임을 하는 것을 허락하지 않으신다. (allow, play)

My parents _____ mobile games.

05 우리는 항상 우리 자신을 깨끗하게 유지해야 한다. (ourselves, keep, clean)

We should _____.

06 의사 선생님은 나에게 충분한 휴식을 취하라고 조언하셨다. (advise, get)

The doctor _____ enough rest.

본동사의 시제가 과거여도 목적격보어는 to부정사 형태를 유지해요.

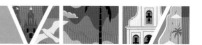
 지각동사가 취할 수 있는 목적격보어의 종류와 그 의미를 잘 파악하세요.

	지각동사	목적어	목적격보어	의미
5형식 어순	feel, see, watch, hear, listen to, smell, notice 등	~이/가	원형부정사	목적어가 ~하는 것을 (능동)
			현재분사	목적어가 ~하고 있는 것을 (진행 강조)

|A| 괄호 안에서 알맞은 말을 <u>모두</u> 고르시오.

01 What made Ellie (sad / sadness)?

02 Katie saw her pet cat (scratch / to scratch) his head.

03 I listened to the singer (sing / to sing) my favorite song.

04 Sophia smelled the wood (burn / burning) in the fireplace.

05 He heard someone (knock / knocking) on the door.

06 My parents allowed me (buy / to buy) a new bag.

07 I saw the babies (cry / crying) on the street.

08 Mia felt somebody (touch / to touch) her hair.

|B| |보기|와 같이 두 문장을 한 문장으로 연결하시오.

> **|보기|**
> I saw a rabbit. It was eating some carrots.
> → I saw a rabbit eating some carrots.

01 I smelled the food. It was burning in the kitchen.

→ _____.

02 Aiden felt someone. Someone was looking at him.

→ _____.

03 Emma heard her dog. It was barking in a loud voice.

→ _____.

04 We listened to a parrot. It was speaking some words.

→ _____.

05 Bella watched several elephants. They were crossing the road.

→ _____.

06 I saw Charles. He was running at the park.

→ _____.

UNIT 09 5형식 4 - 사역동사

사역동사(~에게 …하도록 시키다)는 목적격보어로 원형부정사나 과거분사를 쓰세요.

	사역동사	목적어	목적격보어	의미
5형식 어순	make, have (~이 …하게 시키다)	~이/가	원형부정사	목적어가 ~하게 만들다/시키다
			과거분사	목적어가 ~되도록 만들다/시키다
	let (~이 …하게 두다)		원형부정사	목적어가 ~하게 두다
			to be 과거분사	목적어가 ~되도록 두다

참고 let의 문장은 allow의 문장으로 바꿔 쓸 수 있는데, 이때 목적격보어의 형태에 주의하세요.
She let her children play near the lake. 아이들이 호수 가까이에서 놀게 놔뒀다
= She allowed her children to play near the lake.

|A| |보기|에서 알맞은 단어를 하나씩 골라 빈칸에 알맞은 형태로 쓰시오.

|보기|
| plant | have | clean | talk | play | come |

01 The staff told them _____ quietly.

02 We saw monkeys _____ chess.

03 Mr. Kim had us _____ the tree.

04 My parents make me _____ my room.

05 Please let me _____ one more chance.

06 Don't let them _____ into your room.

|B| 우리말과 일치하도록 괄호 안의 말을 이용하여 문장을 완성하시오.

본동사를 먼저 파악해야 알맞은 목적격보어의 형태를 결정할 수 있어요.

01 폭설은 우리가 하루 종일 집에 머물게 했다. (make, stay)

The heavy snow _____ home all day.

02 그 과학자는 로봇이 음식을 서빙하게 했다. (have, serve)

The scientist _____ a robot _____ food.

03 우리 엄마는 내가 혼자서 여행하게 두지 않으실 것이다. (let, travel)

My mom will _____ by myself.

04 그 하얀 드레스는 Joy가 더 아름다워 보이게 했다. (make, look)

The white dress _____ more beautiful.

05 내가 잠시 그것에 대해 생각 좀 하게 해 주세요. (let, think)

_____ about it for a while.

실전 TIP
목적격보어를 확인하고 원형부정사를 목적격보어로 취할 수 없는 동사를 찾아보세요.

내신 기출 빈칸에 들어갈 수 없는 동사 2개를 고르시오.

The English teacher _____ us repeat the English words.

① had ② let ③ told ④ made ⑤ wanted

UNIT 10 5형식 5 – help/get

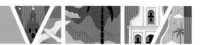

 help의 목적격보어로는 원형부정사나 to부정사를 쓰세요.

	사역동사	목적어	목적격보어	의미
5형식 어순	help (~이 …하도록 돕다)	~이/가	원형부정사	목적어가 ~하도록 돕다
			to부정사	
			(to) be 과거분사	목적어가 ~되도록 돕다 (수동)
	get (~이 …하도록 시키다)		to부정사	목적어가 ~하게 만들다
			과거분사	목적어가 ~되도록 만들다

> 주의 5형식의 get은 '시키다'라는 사역의 의미지만, 목적격보어로 to부정사를 쓰고 수동의 의미일 때는 과거분사를 써요.
> She got her husband to take out the trash. 그녀의 남편에게 쓰레기를 내다 버리게
> She got the trash taken out (by her husband). 쓰레기가 (그녀의 남편에 의해) 내다 버려지게

|A| 괄호 안에서 알맞은 말을 <u>모두</u> 고르시오.

01 My teacher got us (arrive / to arrive) on time.

02 Chloe helped an old lady (move / to move) a chair.

03 His boss got him (making / to make) reservations.

04 Kate helped her friends (clean / cleaned) the classroom.

05 What made Toby (feel / feeling) so sleepy today?

06 I helped my mom (to wash / washing) the dishes.

07 The pharmacist got Elena (take / to take) the medicine three times a day.

|B| 우리말과 일치하도록 괄호 안의 말을 이용하여 문장을 완성하시오.

01 그의 노래들은 우리가 긴장을 풀고 밤에 잘 잘 수 있도록 도와준다. (help, relax, sleep)

His songs _____ tight at night.

02 낯선 사람이 네 집에 들어오게 두지 말라. (let, come, strangers)

Don't _____ into your house.

03 간호사는 환자들이 마스크를 쓰도록 했다. (get, wear)

The nurse _____ the patients _____ their masks.

04 충분한 물을 마시는 일은 사람들이 건강을 유지하는 데 도움이 된다. (help, keep)

Drinking enough water _____ people _____ healthy.

05 정원의 꽃들은 나를 상쾌하게 했다. (make, feel)

The flowers in the garden _____ refreshed.

06 우리 부모님은 내가 조부모님께 안부 전화를 드리게 했다. (get, say hello).

My parents _____ to my grandparents on the phone.

UNIT 11 목적격보어의 다양한 형태 확인

대표적인 5형식 동사들의 주요 목적격보어의 형태를 전체적으로 확인하세요.

동사	목적격보어
make, call, name, find, keep, elect, think, believe, consider	명사, 형용사
want, ask, tell, expect, enable, encourage, allow, advise, order, get, permit, force	to부정사
지각동사 feel, see, watch, hear, listen to, smell, notice	원형부정사, 현재분사
사역동사 make, have, let	원형부정사, 과거분사
help	to부정사, 원형부정사
get	to부정사, 과거분사

|A| |보기|에서 알맞은 단어를 하나씩 골라 빈칸에 알맞은 형태로 쓰시오.

┌─보기┐
| pick   win   shake   give   clean   take |

01 Maria wanted me _____ her up at her house.

02 Let me _____ you my opinion about it.

03 I felt the building _____ back and forth.

04 I'll help you _____ care of your baby.

05 I didn't expect myself _____ the contest.

06 The teacher got Nova _____ the restroom.

|B| 우리말과 일치하도록 괄호 안의 말을 이용하여 문장을 완성하시오.

01 수의사는 내가 매일 개를 산책시키도록 했다. (have, walk)

The vet _____ my dog every day.

02 선생님은 항상 우리에게 열심히 연습하고 최선을 다하라고 말씀하신다. (tell, practice)

The teacher always _____ hard and do our best.

03 사람들은 그 수영 선수를 "마린 보이"라고 부른다. (call, Marine Boy)

People _____ the swimmer _____.

04 Kai는 호텔 직원에게 수건을 좀 더 달라고 요청했다. (ask, give)

Kai _____ the hotel staff _____ her more towels.

05 Tom은 그의 친구들이 한 시간 넘게 자기를 기다리게 했다. (make, wait)

Tom _____ for him for more than one hour.

06 땀을 흘리는 것은 네가 몸을 시원하게 유지하는 데 도움이 된다. (help, keep, cool)

Sweating _____ your body _____.

|C| 두 문장을 한 문장으로 연결하시오.

01 I saw a lot of dolphins. They were swimming in the sea.

→ I _____ in the sea.

02 Susie finished her work. Henry helped her to do that.

→ Henry _____ her work.

03 The entire audience watched Levi. He won first place in the race.

→ The entire audience _____ in the race.

04 My mom arranged books on the bookshelf. I helped her to do that.

→ I _____ on the bookshelf.

05 Jack ordered some fried chicken. Aria made him do so.

→ Aria _____ some fried chicken.

06 Ava's dad heard Ava. She played the violin so well.

→ Ava's dad _____ so well.

07 A blind man crossed the street. Leo helped him to do that.

→ Leo _____.

|D| 우리말과 일치하도록 괄호 안의 말을 이용하여 문장을 완성하시오.

01 Mila의 친구들은 Mila를 "꼬마 백설공주"라고 부른다. (call, Little Snow White)

Mila's friends _____.

02 Oliver의 편지는 내가 호주에 있는 그에게 전화하게 했다. (got, call, him)

Oliver's letter _____ in Australia.

03 나는 그녀가 약속을 지킬 것이라고 기대하지 않는다. (expect, keep her promise)

I don't _____.

04 아이들은 그 만화 영화가 정말 재미있다고 생각했다. (found, so interesting)

The children _____ the animation movie _____.

05 Camila는 누군가 그녀의 머리카락을 잡아당기고 있는 것을 느꼈다. (felt, someone, pull)

Camila _____ her hair.

실전 TIP

동사를 잘 보고, 그에 맞는 목적격보어의 형태를 기억해 보세요.

내신 기출 빈칸에 알맞은 말로 짝지어진 것을 고르시오.

• Elena heard her little brother _____ her name.

• My parents don't allow me _____ out late at night.

• The police officers make drivers _____ to the speed limit.

① call – go – to keep
② calling – to go – keep
③ calling – to go – to keep

중간고사·기말고사 실전문제

학년과 반	이름	객관식	/ 25문항	주관식	/ 25문항

01~02 다음 빈칸에 들어갈 말로 알맞은 것을 고르시오.

01
> We thought the problem _____.

① ease ② easy ③ easily
④ high ⑤ highly

02
> Hyoju asked me _____ the tennis club.

① joining ② join ③ joined
④ to join ⑤ joins

03~04 다음 빈칸에 들어갈 말로 알맞지 <u>않은</u> 것을 고르시오.

03
> Samantha looked very _____ when I saw her yesterday.

① healthy ② lively ③ calmly
④ lovely ⑤ funny

04
> The man _____ visitors follow the rules.

① had ② got ③ made
④ let ⑤ helped

05 다음 빈칸에 공통으로 들어갈 말로 알맞은 것은?

> 1. She _____ him some clothes to wear.
> 2. The flight attendant _____ him to show his passport.

① made ② let ③ told
④ gave ⑤ got

06~07 다음 빈칸에 들어갈 말이 바르게 짝지어진 것을 고르시오.

06
> 1. The photographer asked the girl _____ more actively.
> 2. Let me _____ you how to contact Mr. Kim.

① pose – tell ② to pose – to tell
③ to pose – tell ④ pose – to tell
⑤ to pose – telling

07
> 1. They will let you _____ home now.
> 2. He saw the bat _____ from the cave.

① go – flying ② to go – fly
③ to go – flying ④ go – to fly
⑤ going – fly

08~09 다음 우리말을 영어로 바르게 옮긴 것을 고르시오.

08 나는 네가 내 책을 지금 돌려주길 원한다.

① I want you return my book now.
② I want you to return my book now.
③ I want to return my book by you now.
④ I want return my book by you now.
⑤ I want you to return your book now.

09 그 히트곡은 그녀를 유명한 가수로 만들어 주었다.

① The hit song made her famous.
② The hit song made she a famous singer.
③ The hit song made her a famous singer.
④ The hit song made her famous a singer.
⑤ The hit song made her sing a famous.

10~11 다음 중 문장의 형식이 나머지 넷과 다른 것을 고르시오.

10 ① The water was getting hotter and hotter.
② The princess was sleeping beautifully in the castle.
③ This tastes like chocolate cake.
④ These eggs at the store look very fresh.
⑤ I got wet because of the rain yesterday.

11 ① I asked the clerk the price of the luggage bag.
② Amy cooked the nice breakfast for us.
③ Mom bought an alarm clock for me not to be late for school.
④ May I ask some questions of you?
⑤ He will give a scholarship to the smartest student.

12~13 다음 문장과 형식이 같은 문장을 고르시오.

12 He lives in Australia with his family.

① I invited Mary to my birthday party.
② My dogs got sick at the same time.
③ They didn't say a word that night.
④ The crocodile moves very fast.
⑤ The sky turned dark blue after sunset.

13 She saw her face in the mirror.

① You should keep the secret of the new boss.
② We didn't go out because of the cold weather.
③ She gave her daughter a bunch of flowers for a birthday present.
④ I smelled something burning in the kitchen.
⑤ My coach ordered me not to miss the chance.

14 다음 빈칸에 들어갈 전치사가 나머지 넷과 다른 것은?

① The salesman sold a car _____ the customer.
② I'll buy these cheese cookies _____ you.
③ Will you write a letter _____ me in Spain?
④ He teaches French _____ us.
⑤ The author showed his work _____ them.

15~16 다음 중 어법상 올바른 것을 고르시오.

15 ① His story sounds like very interesting.
② Can I buy this bag to you?
③ He called me Bunny when I was young.
④ I didn't listen to Peter to speak in German.
⑤ Jaemin looks very friend to everyone.

16 ① The nutritionist got them eat well in the hospital.
② The actress smiles bright in the film.
③ The potato chips of this restaurant tastes very crispy.
④ My sister has loved Jessica's brother for a long time.
⑤ The hairpin makes her more attractively.

17 다음 중 문장 전환이 올바른 것은?

① Will you give me your old backpack?
→ Will you give your old backpack for me?
② He has to write a letter to his parents.
→ He has to write his parents a letter.
③ I'll make you a decorated postcard.
→ I'll make a decorated postcard you.
④ James lent me his uniform because mine was dirty.
→ James lent his uniform for me because mine was dirty.
⑤ The reporter asked our opinions of us.
→ The reporter asked us to our opinions.

18~19 다음 중 어법상 어색한 것을 고르시오.

18 ① Harry built a museum his grandchildren.
② I expected him to come to my exhibition.
③ Can you get a warm blanket for me?
④ He told me to enjoy swimming in the sea.
⑤ The teacher helped me to get a good score.

19 ① He helped me understand the sentence in Thai.
② My mom doesn't let me play too long.
③ He made me to find the right way to go out.
④ Why didn't he tell you to apply for this job?
⑤ He advised me to walk more for my health.

20 다음 중 어법상 올바른 문장의 개수는?

ⓐ Emma looks lovely and lively.
ⓑ Your promise sounds like a lie.
ⓒ She advised me to take medicine.
ⓓ You always make him smiles.

① 없음　　　② 1개　　　③ 2개
④ 3개　　　⑤ 4개

21 다음 중 어법상 어색한 문장의 개수는?

ⓐ I couldn't have her listened to my advice.
ⓑ She ordered us finish cleaning the room.
ⓒ Practicing every day will help you becoming healthy.
ⓓ The sound of rain made us feeling good.

① 없음　　② 1개　　③ 2개
④ 3개　　⑤ 4개

22 다음 중 문장의 형식이 같은 것끼리 짝지어진 것은?

ⓐ I usually go to school by bus.
ⓑ I felt a strange man watching me all day.
ⓒ Mary was swimming in the water.
ⓓ She touched the soft silk yellow dress.
ⓔ You should follow the rules.

① ⓐ, ⓑ　　② ⓐ, ⓒ　　③ ⓑ, ⓓ
④ ⓒ, ⓓ　　⑤ ⓑ, ⓔ

23 다음 중 |보기|의 밑줄 친 made와 쓰임이 같은 것은?

┤보기├
My grandmother made us blueberry pie.

① The host of the party made the hall clean.
② Their songs made me happy and calm.
③ She made a beautiful flower bouquet.
④ The carpenter made me a wooden chair.
⑤ We made a house for the stray cats.

24 다음 대화의 빈칸에 들어갈 말이 바르게 짝지어진 것은?

A: I think I gained weight.
B: No, you still look 　(A)　 .
A: I don't think so. How do I lose weight?
B: Well, I usually advise dieters 　(B)　 every day. How about going swimming?
A: Sounds 　(C)　 !

	(A)	(B)	(C)
①	slim	– to exercise	– great
②	fat	– exercise	– a plan
③	wonderfully	– to exercise	– like
④	beautiful	– exercise	– good
⑤	funny	– to exercise	– nicely

25 다음 글의 밑줄 친 ⓐ~ⓔ 중 어법상 어색한 것은?

My father always ⓐ told me to listen to my own voice. I didn't understand his words when I was young. ⓑ Sometimes I feel confused when others ⓒ make me follow their rules or ⓓ behave as they want. Now I understand my father's words and I'm trying to listen to my own voice. ⓔ It helps me to feel freely at any time.

① ⓐ　② ⓑ　③ ⓒ　④ ⓓ　⑤ ⓔ

26~27 다음 빈칸에 괄호 안의 말을 알맞은 형태로 쓰시오.

26 I've never heard her _____. (sing)

27 The movie made all of us _____. (cry)

32 <u>To tell you the truth</u>, we don't like the new captain.

→ _____

28~32 다음 밑줄 친 부분의 문장 성분을 |보기|에서 골라 쓰시오.

┌ 보기 ┐
ⓐ 주어 ⓑ 동사 ⓒ 목적어 ⓓ 보어 ⓔ 수식어
└────────────────────────┘

33~34 다음 우리말과 일치하도록 괄호 안의 말을 바르게 배열하시오.

28 He suddenly appeared <u>this morning</u>.

→ _____

33
당신의 아이들을 조용히 시켜 주세요.
(keep, please, quiet, your kids)

_____
_____

29 He lived <u>in a boat</u> on the river for a while.

→ _____

34
나의 할아버지는 언제나 나를 영웅이라고 불렀다.
(always, me, a hero, my grandfather, called)

_____
_____

30 Don't make me <u>feel annoyed</u> with that noise.

→ _____

35~38 다음 빈칸에 알맞은 전치사를 |보기|에서 골라 쓰시오.

┌ 보기 ┐
to   for   of
└────────────────────────┘

31 My mom always told me <u>many bedtime stories</u>.

→ _____

35 May I ask a favor _____ you?

36 He sent two emails _____ us.

37 He bought some flowers _____ her.

38 Could you pass the salt _____ me?

39~40 다음 |보기|와 같이 두 문장을 한 문장으로 쓰시오.

┌─ 보기 ├─
I watched Jim. He was playing the guitar.
→ I watched Jim playing the guitar.
└────────────────────────────

39 He heard the song. Mary was singing it.

→ He _____

_____

40 I didn't allow dogs to come in. Sam told me to do that.

→ Sam _____

_____

41~42 다음 문장을 3형식은 4형식으로, 4형식은 3형식으로 바꿔 쓰시오.

41 Did he show his photo album to you?

→ _____

_____

42 Have you bought your parents a present before?

→ _____

_____

43~45 다음 문장에서 어법상 어색한 부분을 찾아 바르게 고치시오.

43 Would you bring that white towel me?

_____ → _____

44 The clown in the amusement park looked a ghost.

_____ → _____

45 The woman had the driver to arrive at the airport as early as possible.

_____ → _____

46~47 다음 문장에서 어법상 어색한 부분을 고쳐 완전한 문장을 쓰시오.

46 We sang cheerful at the concert altogether last weekend.

→ _____

_____

47 The new president made people living better than before.

→ _____

_____

48 다음 문장이 어법상 어색하지 않으면 ○를, 어색한 부분이 있으면 밑줄을 치고 바르게 고치시오.

(1) I want myself being confident.

→ _____

(2) It sounds a very moving story.

→ _____

(3) I could feel my mom touching my cheek when I was sleeping.

→ _____

49 주어진 |조건|을 이용하여 우리말을 영어로 옮기시오.

┌─|조건|─────────────────────
│ 1) 동사 make를 쓸 것
│ 2) 단어 only, can, happy, when, sad를 필요하면 활용하여 쓸 것
│ 3) 10단어를 사용할 것
│ 4) 축약형을 사용하지 말 것
└────────────────────────────

내가 슬플 때 오직 너만 날 행복하게 만들 수 있어.

_____

_____

50 다음 중 문장의 형식이 같은 두 문장을 찾아 기호를 쓰시오.

┌────────────────────────────
│ ⓐ Please keep quiet in the library while others are reading books.
│ ⓑ He made a beautiful necklace for his girlfriend.
│ ⓒ He couldn't make the students get out of the building.
│ ⓓ This stick will help you to stand firmly.
│ ⓔ He got me the best ham I've ever had.
└────────────────────────────

_____ , _____

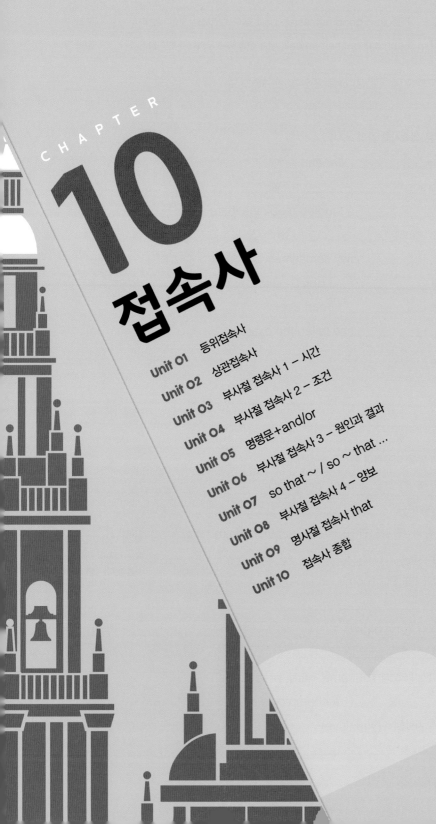

CHAPTER

10
접속사

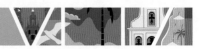

앞뒤에 오는 말의 의미를 파악하여 접속사 and(그리고), but(그러나), or(또는)로 연결하세요.

and	~와, 그리고	Jane and Tom are friends. Jane과 Tom은	단어와 단어
but	~이지만, 그러나	It looked good but tasted bad. 좋아 보였지만, 맛이 나빴다	구와 구
or	또는, ~이거나	I can call or she can call. 내가 전화하거나, 그녀가 전화하거나	절과 절

참고 등위접속사란 단어와 단어, 구와 구, 절과 절을 대등하게 연결하는 말이에요.

|A| 빈칸에 and, but, or 중 알맞은 접속사를 골라 쓰시오.

01 I have been to France _____ Japan.

02 Did you see Asher in person _____ on TV?

03 Emily went to America _____ studied medicine there.

04 Which one do you prefer, black _____ white?

05 Jessie is attractive _____ noisy sometimes.

06 My sister likes spaghetti _____ I don't.

07 Logan entered the room _____ read books.

08 Sophia studied hard _____ she failed the exam.

|B| 우리말과 일치하도록 괄호 안의 말을 이용하여 문장을 완성하시오.

01 어느 경기에서든지, 언제나 승자와 패자가 있다. (a loser, a winner)

In every game, there is always _____.

02 너는 어디로 가고 싶니? 부산, 제주, 아니면 강원도? (Busan, Gangwon, Jeju)

Where do you want to go to _____?

03 너는 여기 머물러도 되고, 나와 같이 가도 된다. (come with me)

You can stay here _____.

04 Liam은 매우 슬펐지만, 울지 않았다. (cry, didn't)

Liam felt very sad _____.

05 Amelia는 열심히 연습해서 챔피언이 되었다. (became, hard, practiced)

Amelia _____ a champion.

06 네가 완벽하지는 않지만, 나는 너를 사랑한다. (you, love)

You are not perfect _____.

세 개 이상의 단어를 나열할 때는 마지막 단어 앞에 접속사를 쓴다는 점 기억하세요.

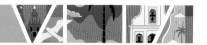

서로 상관이 있는 것들을 묶어 주는 상관접속사의 종류와 의미를 알아 두세요.

상관접속사	의미	상관접속사	의미
both A and B	A와 B 둘 다	not A but B	A가 아니라 B
either A or B	A 또는 B	not only A but (also) B	A뿐만 아니라 B도
neither A nor B	A도 B도 아닌	= B as well as A	A와 마찬가지로 B도

참고 not only A but (also) B는 B as well as A로 쓸 수 있어요.

상관접속사로 이루어진 말이 주어일 때 주어와 동사의 수일치에 주의하세요.

상관접속사	수일치	예문
both A and B	복수 취급	Both Tom and Sara are busy.
either A or B		Either I or she has to go.
neither A nor B		Neither his brothers nor his sister knows you. *모른다(부정)
not A but B	B에 수일치	Not Tom but his parents have a car.
not only A but (also) B		Not only Tom but also his sisters are coming.
= B as well as A		= His sisters, as well as Tom, are coming

|A| 괄호 안에서 알맞은 말을 고르시오.

01 Either Eugene (or / nor) Lucas is American.

02 It is not sunny (nor / but) rainy today.

03 You can enjoy both skiing (and / also) swimming.

04 Sue is famous (not / but) only as a movie star but also as a singer.

05 You can either go to a movie (or / and) go shopping.

06 This shirt is neither beautiful (nor / or) cheap.

07 I will wear (either / neither) a black dress or a pink one.

08 Helen Keller could (either / neither) hear nor see.

|B| 우리말과 일치하도록 괄호 안의 말과 상관접속사를 이용하여 문장을 완성하시오.

01 Elena는 부모님을 만날 수도 없었고, 전화를 드릴 수도 없었다. (meet, call)

Elena could _____ her parents.

02 Emily는 스페인어뿐만 아니라 독일어도 공부하고 있다. (German, Spanish)

Emily is learning _____.

03 나는 가능하다면 휴대전화나 카메라를 살 것이다. (a camera, a mobile phone)

I will buy _____ if possible.

04 그 식당의 피자는 맛있을 뿐만 아니라 저렴하기도 하다. (delicious, cheap)

The restaurant's pizza is _____.

05 이 제품은 아이들과 어른들 모두에게 사랑받는다. (by, kids, adults)

This product is loved _____.

06 Luke는 의사가 아니라 수의사가 되고 싶다. (a doctor, a vet)

Luke wants to be _____.

|C| 어법상 어색한 부분을 찾아 밑줄 긋고 바르게 고치시오.

01 Not only I but also my sister are sick today.   → _____

02 Both Maya and Camila is great soccer players.   → _____

03 Kim won the gold medal not for himself but in Korea.   → _____

04 Either iced coffee or hot coffee are good for me.   → _____

05 Ryan wants to learn not only how to ski also how to swim. → _____

06 I will either sleep or watching TV this afternoon.   → _____

07 I can speak neither Japanese or Chinese.   → _____

08 The teacher, as well as the students, were satisfied with the result.

→ _____

as well as를 제외하면 상관접속사로 연결된 문장에서 동사는 동사와 더 가까이 있는 주어의 수에 일치시켜야 한다는 사실 꼭 기억하세요. 단, both A and B는 항상 복수동사를 써요.

|D| 두 문장이 같은 뜻이 되도록 빈칸에 알맞은 상관접속사를 쓰시오.

01 Ella is not to blame. Lucas is not to blame, either.

= _____ Ella _____ Lucas is to blame.

02 I will go to the zoo. Or I will go to the park.

= I will go to _____ the zoo _____ the park.

03 Ethan likes going to a movie. I like going to a movie, too.

= _____ Ethan _____ I like going to a movie.

04 My sister is Gianna. Luna is not my sister.

= My sister is _____ Luna _____ Gianna.

05 He was a great scientist as well as an excellent painter.

= He was _____ an excellent painter _____ a great scientist.

06 Scarlett is good at singing. She is good at dancing, too.

= Scarlett is good at _____ singing _____ dancing.

실전 TIP

both A and B는 둘 모두를 가리키므로, 항상 복수동사와 함께 써요.

내신기출 다음 중 어법상 어색한 것은?

① Not I but she has to apologize to him.

② Both vegetables and meat is good for your health.

③ Neither James nor Layla likes playing with balls.

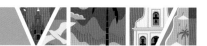

시간을 나타내는 부사절 접속사를 익혀 두세요.

시간 접속사	의미	예문	주의
when	~할 때, ~하면	We will leave when he comes.	will come (X)
before	~하기 전에	Take off your shoes before you enter.	
after	~한 후에	After I got home, I took a nap.	
while	~하는 동안	While I was waiting for a bus, I met some friends.	
as	~할 때, ~하면서	She listened to music as she was preparing food.	
until	~할 때까지	The female will sit on the eggs until they hatch.	will hatch (X)

🙁 **주의** 시간을 나타내는 부사절에서는 현재시제가 미래시제를 대신해요.

|A| 괄호 안에서 알맞은 접속사를 고르시오.

01 We can see a rainbow (before / after) it stops raining.

02 Please turn off the lights (until / before) you go out.

03 My mom washed the dishes (until / while) I was sleeping.

04 Call me (when / after) you have free time.

05 You should wash your hands (after / while) you come back home.

06 Ted ate some popcorn (as / until) he watched a movie.

07 I will wait for you (before / until) you come back to me.

08 (While / When) Olivia made the mistake, she broke into tears.

|B| 우리말과 일치하도록 괄호 안의 말과 알맞은 접속사를 이용하여 문장을 완성하시오.

01 수영장에 뛰어들기 전에 너는 준비운동을 해야 한다. (you, the pool, dive into)

You have to warm up your body _____.

02 Mia는 음식을 다 먹고 나서 양치를 했다. (eating, finished, she)

Mia brushed her teeth _____.

03 내가 어렸을 때, 우리 가족과 나는 부산에 살았다. (was, little, I)

_____, my family and I lived in Busan.

04 나는 학교까지 걸어가다가 Noah를 만났다. (walked to, I, school)

_____, I met Noah.

05 운전하는 동안에는 전화를 사용하지 마시오. (driving, you, are)

Don't use your phone _____.

06 Lucas는 졸릴 때까지 책을 많이 읽을 것이다. (feels, he, sleepy)

Lucas will read a lot of books _____.

💬 시간을 나타내는 접속사가 사용된 부사절에서는 현재시제로 미래를 나타내요.

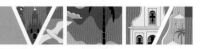
앞뒤 문맥을 확인하여 if를 써야 하는지, 반대의 의미인 unless를 써야 하는지를 판단하세요.

if	~한다면	If it rains tomorrow, we will not go on a picnic.	비 오면, 안 간다
unless	~하지 않는다면	Unless it rains tomorrow, we will go on a picnic.	비 안 오면, 간다
	= if ~ not	= If it doesn't rain tomorrow, we will go on a picnic.	

주의 조건을 나타내는 부사절에서도 현재시제가 미래시제를 대신해요.

|A| 두 문장이 같은 뜻이 되도록 if 또는 unless를 쓰시오.

01 Let's play outside _____ it doesn't rain.

= Let's play outside _____ it rains.

02 You will fail the exam _____ you don't study hard.

= You will fail the exam _____ you study hard.

03 The food will be spoiled _____ it is kept cool.

= The food will be spoiled _____ it isn't kept cool.

04 We can borrow books _____ the library is not closed.

= We can borrow books _____ the library is closed.

05 You will be tired _____ you get enough sleep.

= You will be tired _____ you don't get enough sleep.

06 You can't enter the hall _____ you have a ticket.

= You can't enter the hall _____ you don't have a ticket.

07 You may catch a cold _____ you don't wash your hands often.

= You may catch a cold _____ you wash your hands often.

|B| 우리말과 일치하도록 괄호 안의 말을 이용하여 문장을 완성하시오.

01 서두르지 않으면, 우리는 학교에 지각할 것이다. (unless, hurry)

We will be late for school _____.

02 네게 자유 시간이 있다면, 우리 같이 놀자. (free time, have)

Let's play together _____.

03 만약 거기에 가고 싶다면, 너는 미리 표를 예매해야 한다. (want to, there, go)

You should book the ticket in advance _____.

04 만약 밖이 너무 추우면, 우리는 집 안에 머무를 것이다. (cold, too, outside, is)

We will stay inside the house _____.

05 네가 제시간에 도착하지 않는다면, 우리는 너 없이 갈 것이다. (if, arrive, on time)

We will go without you _____.

UNIT 05 　명령문 + and/or

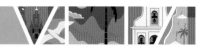

명령문 뒤에 and를 쓸 때와 or를 쓸 때 반대의 의미가 되는 것에 주의해야 해요.

명령문+and	~해라, 그러면 ~할 것이다	Hurry, and you will not be late. 서두르면 늦지 않을 것이다
명령문+or	~해라, 그렇지 않으면 ~할 것이다	Hurry, or you will be late. 서두르지 않으면 늦을 것이다

〈명령문+and/or〉는 의미에 맞게 조건문 if/unless 문장으로 바꿔 쓸 수 있어야 해요.

Hurry, and you will not be late.	= If you hurry, you will not be late.
Hurry, or you will be late.	= Unless you hurry, you will be late.

|A| 빈칸에 and와 or 중 알맞은 말을 쓰시오.

01 Exercise regularly, _____ you will be healthy.

02 Help to save the animals, _____ they will be in danger.

03 Push the button, _____ the movie will start.

04 Please be on time, _____ you cannot participate in the event.

05 Please be quiet, _____ she will begin her speech.

|B| 두 문장이 같은 뜻이 되도록 문장을 완성하시오.

if와 unless가 있는 문장을 명령문으로 바꿀 때는 어떤 접속사가 어울리는지 생각해 보세요.

01 If you follow the rules, you will be safe.

= Follow the rules, _____.

02 Unless you watch out on the ice, you may fall on the street.

= Watch out on the ice, _____.

03 If you take a warm shower, you will feel better.

= Take a warm shower, _____.

04 If you don't apologize to Gianna, she will get angry at you.

= Apologize to Gianna, _____.

05 Unless you wear a thick coat, you will catch a cold.

= Wear a thick coat, _____.

06 Unless you give up, you will be the champion someday.

= Don't give up, _____.

실전 TIP

명령문과 명령문 뒤의 의미가 '그러면'인지 '그렇지 않으면'인지 파악해 보세요.

내신기출 다음 빈칸에 들어갈 말이 <u>다른</u> 하나는?

① Grab the chance, _____ you will regret it.

② Study hard, _____ you will pass the exam.

③ Get up right now, _____ you will miss the bus.

앞뒤 문맥에 맞게 접속사 so(그래서 ~)를 쓸지, because(~ 때문에)를 쓸지 판단하세요.

so+결과	그래서 ~	It was very dark, so we couldn't see anything.	
because+원인	~ 때문에	She had to take a taxi because she was so tired.	= as[since]

주의 because[as, since]는 접속사로 뒤에 문장을 쓰고, because of는 전치사이므로 뒤에 (동)명사(구)를 써야 해요.
The roads were slippery because[as, since] it snowed. 눈이 내렸기 때문에
= The roads were slippery because of the snow. 눈 때문에

|A| 우리말과 일치하도록 괄호 안의 말을 이용하여 문장을 완성하시오.

01 나는 책 읽는 것을 좋아해서 도서관에 자주 간다. (the library)

I like reading books, _____ often.

02 공기 오염 때문에 지구는 점점 더 따뜻해지고 있다. (air pollution)

The Earth is getting warmer and warmer _____.

03 Lucas는 모두에게 친절하기 때문에, 그의 반 친구들 모두 그를 좋아한다. (kind to everyone, as)

_____, all of his classmates like him.

04 Mark는 너무 부끄러워서 얼굴이 빨개졌다. (turn red, his face)

Mark was too shy, _____.

05 Linda는 나의 가장 친한 친구이기 때문에, 나는 그녀에게 내 비밀을 다 말한다. (since, best friend)

_____, I tell her all my secrets.

|B| |보기|에서 알맞은 말을 골라, because나 because of를 이용하여 문장을 완성하시오.

보기		
the huge fire	the noise	she loves skiing
he was sick	I love animals	

01 A lot of people lost their homes _____.

02 I will be a vet _____.

03 The baby couldn't sleep _____.

04 She likes winter the most _____.

05 We visited our grandpa _____.

실전 TIP
빈칸 뒤에 오는 말이 명사(구)인지 〈주어+동사〉의 절인지 확인해 보세요.

내신 기출 빈칸에 들어갈 말이 <u>다른</u> 하나는?

① The field trip was postponed _____ bad weather.
② It will take a long time to get there _____ heavy traffic.
③ Amanda was very happy _____ she won the final game.

UNIT 07 so that ~ / so ~ that ...

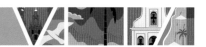

〈so that ~〉과 〈so ~ that ...〉의 쓰임과 의미를 혼동하지 마세요.

so that ~	~하도록, 하기 위해서	He saved money so that he can buy a house. 그는 집을 살 수 있도록 돈을 저축했다.
so 형용사/부사 that ...	너무[매우] ~해서 …하다	He became so rich that he can buy the house. 그는 매우 부유해져서 그 집을 살 수 있다.

😊 **참고** so ~ that ...(너무[매우] ~해서 …하다)은 의미상 too ~ to ... 또는 ~ enough to ...로 바꿔 쓸 수 있어요.
He became <u>rich</u> enough to buy the house.

|A| 두 문장이 같은 뜻이 되도록 〈so that ~〉이나 〈so ~ that ...〉 구문을 이용하여 빈칸에 알맞은 말을 쓰시오.

01 I took the subway to arrive early.　　→ I took the subway _____.

02 I was tired. I couldn't get up early.　　→ I was _____.

03 The food is too spicy for me to eat.　　→ The food is _____.

04 Emily studied hard to get a good mark. → Emily studied hard _____.

|B| 우리말과 일치하도록 괄호 안의 말과 〈so that ~〉이나 〈so ~ that ...〉 구문을 이용하여 문장을 완성하시오.

01 음악이 너무 시끄러워서 나는 네 목소리를 들을 수 없었다. (loud, hear your voice)

The music was _____.

02 그 집에 들어가기 위해 그녀는 신발을 벗었다. (enter, the house)

She took off her shoes _____.

> 💬 so that 전후의 시제 일치에 신경 써야 해요.

03 커피는 너무 써서 아이들은 그것을 마실 수 없다. (bitter, drink)

Coffee is _____.

04 어떤 사람들은 더 잘 보기 위해 안경을 쓴다. (see better)

Some people wear glasses _____.

05 바다가 너무 깊어서 우리는 그 안에서 수영할 수 없다. (deep, swim in)

The sea is _____.

06 우리는 해돋이를 보기 위해 5시에 일어났다. (watch, the sunrise)

We got up at five o'clock _____.

> **실전 TIP** 🎓
> 문제가 어떻게 어려워서 풀지 못하는지, 왜 스페인어를 배우고 있는지, 왜 식당에 갔는지 알아보세요.

내신 기출 빈칸에 공통으로 들어갈 말을 쓰시오.

• The question is _____ difficult that she can't solve it.

• I am learning Spanish _____ that I can travel to Spain.

• James went to the restaurant _____ that he could eat spaghetti.

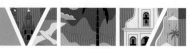

UNIT 08   부사절 접속사 4 - 양보

🔍 '비록 ~이지만, 비록 ~일지라도'라는 양보의 표현은 접속사 though를 쓰세요.

though	비록 ~이지만, 비록 ~일지라도	Though she failed several times, she never gave up.
		= Although[Even though] ~
but	하지만	= She failed several times, but she never gave up.

😦 주의 because ~하기 때문에 …한다 (순접)   vs.   though ~할지라도 …한다 (역접)

|A| 문맥에 맞게 빈칸에 because와 though 중에서 알맞은 말을 쓰시오.

01 _____ it was a holiday, my dad went to work.

02 _____ I am not that rich, I am so happy every day.

03 _____ Emma felt so sad, she cried alone.

04 _____ Elijah was sick, he didn't see a doctor.

05 _____ the work was difficult, Aria gave it up.

06 _____ Ethan is so young, he helps his parents to do the housework.

07 _____ the weather was bad, the airplane couldn't take off.

08 _____ Mia and Luna often fight, they are best friends.

|B| 우리말과 일치하도록 괄호 안의 말을 이용하여 문장을 완성하시오.

💬 though, although, even though 뒤에는 완전한 문장이 와야 함을 잊지 마세요.

01 비록 눈이 많이 올지라도, 우리는 소풍을 갈 것이다. (snow, a lot)

_____, we will go on a picnic.

02 Ella는 아름답지만, 불행해 보인다. (beautiful)

_____, she looks unhappy.

03 그 노래는 아주 오래되었는데도 불구하고, 여전히 많은 사람들에게서 사랑받는다. (very old, the song)

_____, it is still loved by many people.

04 그는 세계적으로 유명한 스타지만, 여전히 겸손하다. (a world-famous star)

_____, he is still humble.

05 민수는 한국인이지만, 한국말을 전혀 하지 못한다. (Korean)

_____, he cannot speak any Korean.

06 우리는 자매인데도 불구하고, 매우 다르게 생겼다. (sisters)

_____, we look very different.

UNIT 09 명사절 접속사 that

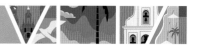

접속사 that(~하다는 것) 뒤에 하나의 절(문장)을 써서 하나의 명사처럼 사용하세요.

that절	의미: 그가 늦게 일어난다는 것	주의
주어	That he gets up late is unbelievable.	that절은 단수 취급
목적어	No one knows (that) he gets up late.	목적어 that절의 that은 생략 가능
보어	The truth is that he gets up late.	

😊 참고 주어 자리의 that절은 가주어 It을 그 자리에 쓰고, 진짜 주어는 문장 뒤로 옮길 수 있어요.

→ It is unbelievable that he gets up late.

|A| 두 문장을 한 문장으로 연결하시오.

01 No one is perfect. + I know that.

→ I know _____.

02 Our team won the gold medal. + That is the good news.

→ The good news is _____.

03 He didn't join us. + It was disappointing.

→ It was _____.

04 You should not break the rules. + That is the point.

→ The point is _____.

05 He won an Oscar. + It was amazing.

→ _____ was amazing.

06 You need some time to take a rest. + I think so.

→ I think _____.

07 Kimchi is good for your health. + It is true.

→ _____ is true.

08 He made a mistake. + He had to admit that.

→ He had to admit _____.

09 We don't have enough time. + That is the fact.

→ The fact is _____.

10 Ted gave me a present. + It was unexpected.

→ It was _____.

|B| 우리말과 일치하도록 that과 괄호 안의 말을 바르게 배열하여 문장을 완성하시오.

01 어떤 사람들은 고기가 여러분의 건강에 좋지 않다고 생각한다. (for your health, meat, is, good, not)

Some people think _____.

02 돌고래가 아픈 구성원들을 돕는다는 것은 흥미롭다. (dolphins, the sick members, help)

_____ is interesting.

03 문제는 우리에게 지도자가 없다는 것이다. (we, no leader, have)

The problem is _____.

04 집이 없는 사람들이 많다는 것이 안타깝다. (there, many homeless people, are)

It is a pity _____.

05 진실은 그가 또 약속을 어겼다는 것이었다. (broke, he, his promise)

The truth was _____ again.

06 우리나라가 올해 올림픽을 개최할 것이라는 점이 흥미진진하다. (hold, our country, will)

It is exciting _____ the Olympic Games this year.

07 많은 사람들은 인터넷이 최고의 발명품 중 하나라고 믿는다. (the Internet, one, is)

Many people believe _____ of the best inventions.

|C| 우리말과 일치하도록 괄호 안의 말을 이용하여 문장을 완성하시오.

01 이게 옳은 결정이라고 생각하나요? (think)

_____ the right decision?

02 내게 너와 같은 좋은 친구가 있다는 건 축복이야. (is, a good friend, have, like you)

_____ a blessing.

03 많은 아이들이 전쟁에서 부모를 잃었다는 것이 슬펐다. (a lot of, children, lost, sad)

It _____ their parents in wars.

04 엄마의 의견은 내가 의사가 되어야 한다는 것이다. (a doctor, should be)

My mom's opinion _____.

05 어떤 고양이들은 서로 다른 두 가지 색의 눈을 가지고 있다는 것이 흥미롭다. (interesting, some cats, have)

It _____ two different colored eyes.

내신 기출 다음 밑줄 친 부분 중 생략할 수 있는 것은?

① It is certain <u>that</u> my parents love me a lot.
② The fact is <u>that</u> the Earth is being destroyed.
③ They couldn't believe <u>that</u> he told them a lie.
④ It was surprising <u>that</u> Lucas became the winner.
⑤ <u>That</u> you two don't know each other is strange.

실전 TIP

명사절이 목적어 역할을 할 때, 접속사 that을 생략할 수 있다는 것을 기억하세요.

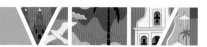

UNIT 10 접속사 종합

접속사 각각의 의미를 다시 한번 확인하세요.

and	~와, 그리고	but	~이지만, 그러나	or	또는, ~이거나
not only A but also B (= B as well as A)	A뿐만 아니라 B도	both A and B	A와 B 둘 다	either A or B	A 또는 B
neither A nor B	A도 B도 아닌	not A but B	A가 아니라 B	when	~할 때, ~하면
before	~하기 전에	after	~한 후에	while	~하는 동안
as	~할 때, ~하면서	until	~할 때까지	if	~한다면
unless	~하지 않는다면	because/as/since	~ 때문에	so	그래서 ~
so that ~	~하도록, ~하기 위해서	so ~ that ...	너무[매우] ~해서 ...하다	(even) though	비록 ~일지라도 (= although)
명령문, and	~해라, 그러면	명령문, or	~해라, 안 그러면	명사절 that	~하다는 것

|A| 어법상 어색한 부분을 찾아 밑줄 긋고 바르게 고치시오.

01 My opinion is this we should start the work right now. → _____

02 Not only I but also my sister like the song. → _____

03 Did you turn off the lights after you went out? → _____

04 Unless you don't wake up now, you will be late. → _____

05 Read a lot of books, or you can get valuable knowledge. → _____

06 I visited Liam so that I can celebrate his birthday. → _____

07 The movie became popular because its attractive characters. → _____

|B| 우리말과 일치하도록 괄호 안의 말을 이용하여 문장을 완성하시오.

접속사를 사용할 때에는 동사의 시제에 유의해야 해요.

01 날씨가 너무 덥지도 않고 너무 춥지도 않다. (too, hot, cold)

The weather is _____.

02 표가 없으면 박물관에 입장할 수 없다. (have, a ticket, unless)

You can't enter the museum _____.

03 목도리를 하고 장갑을 껴, 그렇지 않으면 너는 감기에 걸릴지도 몰라. (may, a cold, catch)

Wear a muffler and gloves, _____.

04 나는 우리가 지구를 지키기 위해 무언가 해야 한다고 생각한다. (need to, do)

_____ something to save the Earth.

05 비록 그 일이 쉽지 않더라도, 나는 포기하지 않을 것이다. (the work, easy)

_____, I will not give it up.

중간고사·기말고사 실전문제

객관식 (01~25) / 주관식 (26~50)

학년과 반		이름		객관식	/ 25문항	주관식	/ 25문항

01~02 다음 빈칸에 들어갈 말로 알맞은 것을 고르시오.

01

This novel is interesting, _____ it is too long.

① and   ② so   ③ but
④ or   ⑤ both

02

_____ you are not tall, you are fast enough to become a basketball player.

① Although   ② If   ③ As
④ Because   ⑤ That

03 다음 빈칸에 들어갈 말로 알맞은 것을 <u>모두</u> 고르시오.

Sarah was late for school _____ she got up late this morning.

① although   ② so   ③ because
④ as   ⑤ even though

04~05 다음 빈칸에 공통으로 들어갈 말로 알맞은 것을 고르시오.

04

Eat _____ sleep well, _____ you'll become healthy.

① or   ② and   ③ but
④ so   ⑤ nor

05

1. I drank a lot of coffee yesterday, _____ I couldn't sleep at all.
2. He was _____ tired that he couldn't stay up late.

① but   ② and   ③ as
④ so   ⑤ or

06~07 다음 빈칸에 들어갈 말이 바르게 짝지어진 것을 고르시오.

06

1. I like both orange juice _____ apple juice.
2. We can go there by either bus _____ taxi.

① and – but   ② and – or
③ but – and   ④ or – and
⑤ so – but

07

1. Dave was absent today _____ he was sick.
2. She didn't know the word, _____ she looked it up in the dictionary.

① since – so   ② so – because
③ and – as   ④ so – but
⑤ before – after

[08~09] 다음 우리말을 영어로 바르게 옮긴 것을 고르시오.

08
> 나는 꽃뿐만 아니라 새도 좋아한다.

① I like either birds or flowers.
② I like not birds but flowers.
③ I like but birds not flowers.
④ I like birds as well as flowers.
⑤ I like neither flowers nor birds.

09
> 그 게임이 끝났을 때, 우리는 흥분했다.

① Before the game was over, we were excited.
② As the game was over, we were exciting.
③ When the game was over, we were excited.
④ Until the game was over, we were excited.
⑤ After the game was over, we were exciting.

10 다음 중 밑줄 친 that을 생략할 수 있는 것은?

① My dream is that I travel to Mars in 10 years.
② You have to wear that purple sweater.
③ It is surprising that Mike and Brian are twins.
④ I didn't know that Sarah's mom is a teacher.
⑤ What was that suitcase in front of the room?

11 다음 문장의 밑줄 친 부분과 의미가 같은 것은?

> If Harry doesn't hurry, he can't buy the bread.

① Unless Harry doesn't hurry
② When Harry doesn't hurry
③ Unless Harry will hurry
④ When Harry will not hurry
⑤ Unless Harry hurries

12 다음 중 밑줄 친 since의 의미가 나머지 넷과 다른 것은?

① Since you are so young, you can't live by yourself.
② Since I don't have money, I have to work hard.
③ Since I was eight, I have lived in this house.
④ I can bake cookies since it's very easy.
⑤ I don't like to eat dinner since I'm still full.

13 다음 문장의 밑줄 친 As와 쓰임이 같은 것은?

> As you came early, you can leave now.

① She used to be ill as a child.
② This play isn't as interesting as that play.
③ Eric's painting is as good as Hansol's.
④ I order you to leave this place as a boss.
⑤ They ran fast as they heard the sound of an explosion.

14 다음 문장의 빈칸에 들어갈 접속사와 같은 접속사를 쓸 수 있는 것은?

> Clean your room, _____ you can't have dinner.

① Don't worry about Suho _____ he is smart and strong.
② Either Jake _____ Susan can go there with you.
③ I can't believe _____ Minho failed to be an athlete.
④ Keep your room warm, _____ you will get better.
⑤ Both Donald _____ Joe are funny friends.

15 다음 중 어법상 올바른 것은?

① I'm good at not only math also science.
② I enjoyed the concert as it was delayed.
③ If it's summer, it's not very hot this year.
④ Neither I nor he don't want to sleep.
⑤ I used to walk alone before it became dark.

16~18 다음 중 어법상 <u>어색한</u> 것을 고르시오.

16 ① Finish your homework, or you can watch YouTube.
② The fruits won't be ripe until it's warm.
③ Both dogs and cats are cute and lovely.
④ He'll call you when he arrives at his house.
⑤ You can have tea while you are waiting.

17 ① Either I or he visits Mr. Han's apartment.
② The restaurant is closed because it's a holiday.
③ We will have lunch after the class will be over.
④ You can't come in unless you knock on the door.
⑤ I can't see outside as there's no window.

18 ① Both Mary and I learn singing and dancing.
② I went out before I turned off all the lights.
③ Ben didn't study hard, so he got bad scores.
④ I saw a dog while I was sitting on the chair.
⑤ When I crossed the street, I saw Mike and his dog.

19 다음 중 어법상 올바른 문장의 개수는?

> ⓐ It's so funny so I can't help laughing.
> ⓑ Neither earrings nor a necklace were stolen.
> ⓒ Both my mom and I cried while we were watching a sad movie.
> ⓓ Unless we ate dinner, we took a walk for a while.

① 없음 ② 1개 ③ 2개 ④ 3개 ⑤ 4개

20~21 다음 중 어법상 <u>어색한</u> 문장의 개수를 고르시오.

20

ⓐ She likes neither candy nor chocolate.
ⓑ We couldn't go out because the rain.
ⓒ I'll choose either a blue or red T-shirt.
ⓓ We talked about the movie when we came home.

① 없음   ② 1개   ③ 2개   ④ 3개   ⑤ 4개

21

ⓐ The room was hot although I turned off the heater.
ⓑ The problem is what we lost our baggage.
ⓒ You will have dinner after I will finish my work.
ⓓ This problem is too difficult that I can't solve it.

① 없음   ② 1개   ③ 2개   ④ 3개   ⑤ 4개

22 다음 중 같은 뜻의 문장끼리 짝지어진 것은?

ⓐ You can see not only tigers but also bears.
ⓑ You can see neither tigers nor bears.
ⓒ You can see bears as well as tigers.
ⓓ You can see either tigers or bears.

① ⓐ, ⓑ   ② ⓐ, ⓓ   ③ ⓐ, ⓒ
④ ⓑ, ⓓ   ⑤ ⓒ, ⓓ

23 다음 두 문장의 의미가 서로 같은 것을 <u>모두</u> 고르시오.

① a) Because you ate a lot, you must be full now.
   b) As you ate a lot, you must be full now.
② a) He ran fast so that he could catch the bus.
   b) He ran too fast to catch the bus.
③ a) I want to meet not Somi, but Jiyoung.
   b) I want to meet Jiyoung as well as Somi.
④ a) Hurry up, and you'll catch the train.
   b) You'll catch the train unless you hurry up.
⑤ a) I was sleeping when the doorbell rang.
   b) I was sleeping as the doorbell rang.

24 다음 대화의 빈칸에 들어갈 말이 바르게 짝지어진 것은?

A: Mom, do you know where Cathy is?
B: She may be in her room ____(A)____ at the gym.
A: I've already checked her room, ____(B)____ she's not there.
B: Why are you looking for her?
A: ____(C)____ she borrowed my pants, I want to ask her to return them.
B: I saw the pants in her room. I'll get them for you.
A: Thanks.

	(A)		(B)		(C)
①	and	–	and	–	Although
②	or	–	or	–	Because
③	and	–	but	–	Since
④	or	–	but	–	As
⑤	and	–	or	–	When

25 다음 글의 밑줄 친 ⓐ~ⓔ 중 어법상 어색한 것을 **모두** 고르시오.

> It's the last day of this year ⓐ but I have good memories of this year. I usually like ⓑ either summer and autumn, ⓒ but I liked winter the most this year. It's ⓓ because I went skiing with my family and it was a very good time. This summer was much hotter than before, ⓔ so I couldn't enjoy the summer activities enough. I hope it won't be as hot next summer.

① ⓐ   ② ⓑ   ③ ⓒ   ④ ⓓ   ⑤ ⓔ

26~27 다음 우리말과 일치하도록 괄호 안의 말을 이용하여 문장을 완성하시오.

26 비록 내가 바쁘더라도, 너를 극장에 데려다 주겠다. (busy)

_____ _____ _____, I'll take you to the theater.

27 나도 Irene도 시험을 통과하지 못했다. (pass)

_____ I _____ Irene _____ the test.

28~31 다음 |보기|에서 빈칸에 알맞은 접속사를 골라 쓰시오.

> |보기|
> if   when   that   unless   since

28 _____ you exercise regularly, your body will become weak.

29 _____ you were reading the book, I came in this room.

30 _____ it was your birthday, I bought a bunch of flowers for you.

31 You will see the stars _____ the weather is good.

---

32 다음 우리말과 일치하도록 괄호 안의 말을 바르게 배열하시오.

> 나는 Jim이 아니라 Jack과 파티에서 춤을 췄다. (but, with Jim, I, not, with Jack, at the party, danced)

_____

_____

---

33 다음 |보기|와 같이 두 문장을 접속사를 이용하여 한 문장으로 쓰시오.

> |보기|
> The sofa was so big. I couldn't move it by myself.
> → The sofa was so big that I couldn't move it by myself.

I was so thrilled with the music. I couldn't say anything.

→ _____

_____

34~36 다음 밑줄 친 that절의 문장 성분과 같은 것을 |보기|에서 골라 쓰시오.

┌─| 보기 |─────────────────────
ⓐ We heard that you won first prize.
ⓑ That we help each other is important.
ⓒ The problem is that we didn't save the
   file.
└──────────────────────────────

34 That you held my hands was a touching
moment.

→ _____

35 The fact is that you don't have any
disease.

→ _____

36 They learned that Peru is in South
America.

→ _____

37~38 다음 문장의 밑줄 친 부분을 지시대로 바꿔 같은
뜻의 완전한 문장으로 쓰시오.

37 Try to help others, and you can make the
world better. (접속사 if 사용)

→ _____

_____

38 We have to save water to protect the
planet. (접속사 so that 사용)

→ _____

_____

39~40 다음 문장의 밑줄 친 as와 의미가 같은 접속사를
|보기|에서 골라 쓰시오.

┌─| 보기 |─────────────────────

   because   when   until

└──────────────────────────────

39 We called the police as we saw the
accident.

→ _____

40 We couldn't hear each other as the
people shouted loudly.

→ _____

41~43 다음 문장에서 어법상 어색한 부분을 찾아 바르게
고치시오.

41 He is not only kind but also friend to anyone.

_____ → _____

42 Tom's friends, as well as Tom, goes to the
movies on weekends.

_____ → _____

43 Did you hear it Stacy had a car accident?

_____ → _____

44 다음 문장에서 어법상 어색한 부분을 고쳐 완전한 문
장을 쓰시오.

You should knock on the door after you
enter.

→ _____

_____

45~46 다음은 Eunhee의 어제 일과표이다. 표를 보고 주어진 접속사를 이용하여 질문에 알맞은 답을 완전한 문장으로 쓰시오.

10:00 ~ 10:30	feed her dog
10:30 ~ 11:40	take an online class
11:40 ~ 12:00	take a rest
12:00 ~ 13:00	have lunch

45 Q: What did Eunhee do at 10:30? (after)

A: _____

_____

46 Q: What did Eunhee do before noon? (before)

A: _____

_____

47 다음 문장이 어법상 어색하지 않으면 ○를, 어색한 부분이 있으면 밑줄을 치고 바르게 고치시오.

(1) Fasten your seat belt, and you will be safe.

→ _____

(2) Though I don't have time, I can't pick you up.

→ _____

(3) When you arrive at the airport, give us a call.

→ _____

48~49 주어진 |조건|을 이용하여 다음 문장을 바꿔 쓰시오.

48 ┤조건├
1) 접속사 as well as를 사용할 것
2) 단어 rope, thick, long를 쓸 것
3) 8단어를 사용할 것

이 줄은 길 뿐만 아니라 굵다.

_____

_____

49 ┤조건├
1) 접속사 unless를 사용할 것
2) 단어 sick, go, the concert를 쓸 것
3) 10단어를 사용할 것
4) 축약형을 사용하지 말 것

네가 아프지 않다면, 너는 콘서트에 갈 수 있다.

_____

_____

50 밑줄 친 접속사가 같은 뜻으로 쓰인 문장 두 개를 골라 기호를 쓰시오.

ⓐ They have to rewrite the report <u>as</u> it had too many errors.
ⓑ I was surprised <u>when</u> a stranger came and talked to me.
ⓒ You can learn Spanish <u>if</u> you want.
ⓓ He got well <u>since</u> you took care of him.
ⓔ She didn't stop working <u>although</u> she had a toothache.

_____ , _____

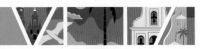

UNIT 01 현재분사

동사를 형용사(명사 수식, 보어 역할)처럼 쓰기 위해서는 동사에 -ing를 붙여 현재분사로 만드세요.

형태	V+-ing	의미	~하는 (능동)

참고 분사란 동사에 -ing(현재분사)나 -ed(과거분사)를 붙여서, 형용사처럼 사용할 수 있는 말이에요.

목적어나 부사(구)를 취할 수 있는 현재분사의 위치와 역할을 알아 두세요.

명사 수식	명사 앞	falling leaves 떨어지는 나뭇잎들
	명사 뒤	leaves falling on the table 탁자에 떨어지는 나뭇잎들
보어	주격	The news is shocking. 충격적인
	목적격	I saw them playing soccer. 그들이 축구하는 걸 봤다.

참고 목적격보어로 현재분사를 쓸 수 있는 동사는 지각동사예요. (see, watch, hear, feel...)

|A| 우리말과 일치하도록 |보기|에 있는 단어를 현재분사로 이용하여 문장을 완성하시오.

┌ 보기 ┐
stand   interest   dance   talk   write   surprise

01 춤추는 인형을 보아라.　　　　　　　　Look at the _____ doll.

02 나무 앞에 서 있는 소년이 있다.　　　　There is a boy _____ in front of a tree.

03 오늘은 놀라운 소식이 있다.　　　　　　We have _____ news today.

04 그 쇼는 흥미로워 보인다.　　　　　　　The show looks _____.

05 나는 그녀가 편지를 쓰고 있는 것을 보았다.　　I saw her _____ a letter.

06 소미는 엄마가 통화하는 소리를 들었다.　　Somi heard her mom _____ on the phone.

|B| 우리말과 일치하도록 괄호 안의 말을 바르게 배열하여 문장을 완성하시오.

01 그것은 실망스러운 공연이었다. (performance, disappointing)

That was a _____.

02 사진에서 Noah 옆에 앉아 있는 이 소녀는 누구니? (next to, who, is, sitting, this girl)

_____ Noah in the picture?

03 그 연설은 너무 지루하게 들린다. (too, sounds, boring)

The speech _____.

04 누가 저 울고 있는 아기를 돌볼 수 있지? (baby, take care of, that, crying)

Who can _____?

05 나는 Jennie가 문에 노크하고 있는 것을 보았다. (knocking on, the door)

I saw Jennie _____.

수식어구와 함께 쓰일 때에 현재분사는 명사 뒤에 위치한다는 사실을 기억하세요.

UNIT 02 과거분사

🔤 동사를 수동의 의미를 나타내는 형용사로 쓸 때는 동사의 과거분사형을 활용하세요.

형태	과거분사형 (-ed 또는 불규칙 형태)	의미	～된, ～당한 (수동)

🔤 부사(구)를 취할 수 있는 과거분사의 위치와 역할을 알아 두세요.

명사 수식	명사 앞	fallen leaves 떨어진 나뭇잎들
	명사 뒤	leaves fallen on the table 탁자에 떨어진 나뭇잎들
보어	주격	People are shocked. 충격 받은
	목적격	I had my hair cut. 머리카락이 잘려지게 했다.

😊참고 목적격보어로 과거분사를 쓸 수 있는 동사는 사역동사(make, have), 지각동사 등이 있어요.

|A| 괄호 안에서 알맞은 말을 고르시오.

01 His face looked (puzzled / puzzling).

02 The price was (raised / raising) again.

03 He hated the (tired / tiring) work.

04 You look (worried / worrying) today.

05 We watched the (thrilled / thrilling) movie.

06 I was (shocked / shocking) by her behavior.

|B| 우리말과 일치하도록 괄호 안의 말을 바르게 배열하여 문장을 완성하시오.

01 최근에 Oliver는 오래된 팝송에 관심을 갖게 되었다. (has, become, interested in)

Recently, Oliver _____ some old pop songs.

02 그 편지는 반으로 접혀져 있었다. (was, in half, folded)

The letter _____.

03 오늘 아침 내게 보내진 그 선물은 나를 매우 행복하게 했다. (to me, the present, sent)

_____ this morning made me very happy.

04 Elijah는 그 영화에 깊이 감동받아 눈물을 흘렸다. (the movie, was, deeply moved, by)

Elijah _____, so he shed tears.

05 나는 집에 오는 길에 누군가 울고 있는 소리를 들었다. (crying, heard, I, someone)

_____ on my way home.

06 눈으로 뒤덮인 저 지붕을 보아라. (the roof, snow, covered with)

Look at _____.

실전 TIP

실망시키는 건지 실망한 건지, 황당하게 하는 건지 황당해진 건지 확인해 보세요.

내신기출 다음 빈칸에 괄호 안의 말을 알맞은 형태의 분사로 쓰시오.

• He felt _____ by his poor grades. (disappoint)

• She was put in an _____ situation. (embarrass)

부사절 〈접속사＋주어＋동사〉를 분사를 이용하여 간결하게 줄여 쓰는 방법을 익히세요.

	분사구문 만드는 법	
1	부사절의 접속사 생략	~~As~~ Jane got off the bus, she said goodbye.
2	부사절과 주절의 주어가 같다면, 부사절 주어 생략	~~Jane~~ got off the bus, she said goodbye.
3	동사를 현재분사(-ing)로 바꿈 * 주어를 명확히 밝히기 위해 she 대신 Jane으로 씀	**Getting** off the bus, Jane said goodbye.

참고 접속사의 의미를 분명하게 하고 싶을 때는 접속사를 생략하지 않고 쓰기도 해요.

참고 부사절의 be동사는 분사구문에서 being으로 쓰고 생략할 수도 있어요.

|A| 두 문장이 같은 뜻이 되도록 분사구문을 이용하여 문장을 완성하시오.

01 While she looked at me, she smiled.　= _____, she smiled.

02 Since I have a lot to do, I got up early.　= _____, I got up early.

03 When I met you again, I felt so pleased.　= _____, I felt so pleased.

04 Because she was surprised, she cried out.　= _____, she cried out.

05 If you reach the top, you will find them.　= _____, you will find them.

06 After he said hello to me, he got on the bus. = _____, he got on the bus.

07 While she relaxed, she listened to music.　= _____, she listened to music.

08 As she is short, she can't reach it.　= _____, she can't reach it.

|B| 우리말과 일치하도록 괄호 안의 말을 이용하여 분사구문을 완성하시오.

01 외출하면서, 우리 엄마는 모든 전등을 다 끄셨다. (leave, the house)

_____, my mom turned off all the lights.

02 노래를 하면서, 그 가수는 무대 위로 올라왔다. (sing, a song)

_____, the singer came on the stage.

03 표를 구할 수 있기를 바라면서, 나는 매표소로 달려갔다. (hope to, get, a ticket)

_____, I ran to the ticket office.

04 공항에 도착했을 때, Maya는 그녀가 가장 좋아하는 영화배우를 봤다. (the airport, arrive at)

_____, Maya saw her favorite movie star.

05 한 블록 직진해서 가면, 당신은 은행을 발견할 것이다. (go straight, one block)

_____, you will find a bank.

06 충분한 시간이 있었기 때문에, 우리는 우리 차례를 기다렸다. (have, enough, time)

_____, we waited for our turn.

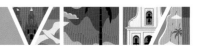

UNIT 04 분사구문 1 – 때, 이유

접속사가 없는 분사구문은 주절과의 관계를 파악하여 문맥에 맞게 해석해야 해요.

분사구문	주절과의 관계	의미
Arriving there, she saw Tom.	때	= When she arrived there, 도착했을 때
Being tired, he went to bed.	이유	= Because[Since / As] he was tired, 피곤했기 때문에

참고 부사절이 부정문이면 분사 앞에 not이나 never를 써야 해요.

As I didn't know what to say, I kept silent. = Not knowing what to say, I kept silent.

|A| 우리말과 일치하도록 |보기|의 말을 이용하여 분사구문을 완성하시오.

┌─ 보기 ┐
After she found me   While he took a bath
When she took a walk   Because he missed the train
└─────────────┘

01 기차를 놓쳐서 우리 아빠는 화가 났다.　＿＿＿＿＿＿＿＿＿＿＿＿＿, my dad got angry.

02 나를 발견하고 나서, 그녀는 내 품에 달려와 안겼다.　＿＿＿＿＿＿＿＿＿＿＿, she ran into my arms.

03 목욕을 하면서, Andy는 노래를 불렀다.　＿＿＿＿＿＿＿＿＿＿＿＿＿, Andy sang a song.

04 산책할 때, Joy는 유기견을 발견했다.　＿＿＿＿＿＿＿＿＿＿＿＿＿, Joy found a homeless dog.

|B| 우리말과 일치하도록 괄호 안의 말을 이용하여 문장을 완성하시오.

01 뜨거운 물을 쏟는 바람에, 그의 바지가 다 젖어버렸다. (the hot water, spill)

＿＿＿＿＿＿＿＿＿＿＿＿＿＿＿＿＿＿＿＿, he got his pants wet.

02 약속을 지키지 않았기 때문에, 나는 Luna에게 사과를 해야 했다. (not, keep, my promise)

＿＿＿＿＿＿＿＿＿＿＿＿＿＿＿＿＿＿＿＿, I had to apologize to Luna.

03 차 안에 앉아서, 우리 가족은 다함께 영화를 봤다. (sit in, our car)

＿＿＿＿＿＿＿＿＿＿＿＿＿＿＿＿＿＿＿＿, my family watched a movie together.

04 밖에서 농구를 한 뒤, 우리 모두는 목이 매우 말랐다. (play, basketball, outside)

＿＿＿＿＿＿＿＿＿＿＿＿＿＿＿＿＿＿＿＿, we all were so thirsty.

05 벤치에 앉아서, Kate는 개미들을 관찰했다. (the bench, sit on)

＿＿＿＿＿＿＿＿＿＿＿＿＿＿＿＿＿＿＿＿, Kate observed ants.

실전 TIP

'때'를 설명하는 말인지, '이유'를 설명하는 말인지 확인하세요.

내신기출 다음 밑줄 친 부분과 주절과의 관계가 다른 하나는?

① Having to study for the test, I am so busy.
② Being best friends, we understand each other well.
③ Going to the bookstore, I read the best-selling book.

분사구문이 의미상 '~하면'의 조건이나 '비록 ~일지라도'라는 양보를 나타낼 때를 주의하세요.

분사구문	주절과의 관계	의미
Turning right, you will see it.	조건	= If you turn right, 우회전하면
Though being young, she is thoughtful.	양보	= Though she is young, 비록 어리지만

참고 양보를 나타내는 분사구문은 의미를 명확히 하기 위해 접속사를 생략하지 않고 쓰는 경우가 많아요.

|A| 두 문장이 같은 뜻이 되도록 〈If/(Al)Though+주어+동사〉의 형태로 문장을 바꾸시오.

01 Though living near the sea, I can't swim.

= _____, I can't swim.

02 Exercising regularly, you'll get healthier.

= _____, you'll get healthier.

03 Listening to this music, you'll feel relaxed.

= _____, you'll feel relaxed.

04 Although feeling hungry, she skipped lunch.

= _____, she skipped lunch.

|B| 우리말과 일치하도록 괄호 안의 말과 분사구문을 이용하여 문장을 완성하시오.

01 정말 춥다고 느꼈지만, 그에게는 두꺼운 외투가 없었다. (though, feel, so cold)

_____, he didn't have a thick coat.

02 이 책을 읽으면, 우리는 인생의 의미를 발견하게 될 것이다. (this book, read)

_____, we will find the meaning of life.

03 날마다 열심히 연습하면, 언젠가 너는 최고가 될 수 있다. (practice, hard, every day)

_____, you can reach the top someday.

04 밝게 웃고 있었지만, 그녀는 울고 싶었다. (smile, brightly, though)

_____, she wanted to cry.

05 모든 등불을 끄면, 너희는 반짝이는 별을 더 잘 볼 수 있다. (all, turn off, the lights)

_____, you can see the twinkling stars better.

양보를 나타내는 분사구문은 분사 앞에 (al)though를 남겨둘 수 있음을 알아 두세요.

실전 TIP

'~하면'인지, '~이지만, 비록 ~하더라도'인지 확인하세요.

내신 기출 밑줄 친 부분과 주절과의 관계가 다른 하나는?

① Although being very tired, she cooked for her family.

② Though living in America, he can't speak English well.

③ Buying this T-shirt, you can get another one for free.

 분사구문으로 '~하는 동안, ~하면서'의 동시동작이나 '~하고 나서'라는 연속상황을 나타낼 수 있어야 해요.

분사구문	주절과의 관계	의미
Driving a car, you shouldn't eat.	동시동작	= While[As] you drive a car, 운전하면서
He studied hard, passing the exam.	연속상황	= and passed the exam 그리고 합격했다

|A| 우리말과 일치하도록 |보기|의 말을 분사구문으로 바꾸어 문장을 완성하시오.

> **보기**
> say "cheese"   go out   look at the sky
> call my name   clean the house   board the plane

01 하늘을 바라보면서 나는 노래를 불렀다.   _____, I sang a song.

02 그녀는 불을 끄고 나서 밖으로 나갔다.   She turned off the light, _____.

03 내 이름을 부르면서 그는 내게 공을 던졌다.   _____, he threw the ball toward me.

04 그녀는 작별인사를 하고 나서 비행기에 올랐다.   She said good-bye, _____.

05 "치즈"라고 말하면서 그녀는 사진을 찍었다.   _____, she took a picture.

06 아빠는 창문을 열고서 집 청소를 하셨다.   Dad opened the window, _____.

|B| 두 문장이 같은 뜻이 되도록 분사구문을 이용하여 문장을 완성하시오.

01 He got dressed, and looked at himself in the mirror.

   = He got dressed, _____.

02 While Lina had lunch, she watched an animation movie.

   = _____, Lina watched an animation movie.

03 They warmed up their bodies, and jumped into the sea.

   = They warmed up their bodies, _____.

04 Joy winked, and gave a big smile.

   = Joy winked, _____.

05 As she surfed the Internet, she called her mom.

   = _____, she called her mom.

06 This bus leaves here at two o'clock, and arrives in Seoul at four.

   = This bus leaves here at two o'clock, _____.

중간고사·기말고사 실전문제

학년과 반	이름	객관식	/ 25문항	주관식	/ 25문항

01~02 다음 빈칸에 들어갈 말로 알맞은 것을 고르시오.

01

> Who is the woman _____ on the bench?

① sat   ② sit   ③ sitting
④ seating   ⑤ to sit

02

> I like to read novels _____ in Chinese.

① wrote   ② to write   ③ writing
④ write   ⑤ written

03~05 다음 두 문장의 의미가 같도록 빈칸에 들어갈 말로 알맞은 것을 고르시오.

03

> Though being rich, he feels very lonely.
> = _____ he is rich, he feels very lonely.

① As   ② So
③ Even though   ④ Since
⑤ When

04

> After she put on my coat, she went outside.
> = _____ my coat, she went outside.

① Puts on   ② Put on   ③ Putting on
④ Putting   ⑤ Being put on

05

> Climbing the mountain, we saw a blue bird.
> = _____ we were climbing the mountain, we saw a blue bird.

① Though   ② Since   ③ Until
④ While   ⑤ If

06~07 다음 빈칸에 들어갈 말이 바르게 짝지어진 것을 고르시오.

06

> 1. She looked _____ because of her low scores.
> 2. The room was _____ with boxes.

① depressed – filled   ② depressing – full
③ excited – filling   ④ exciting – filled
⑤ impressed – filling

07

> He stopped _____ computer games because it's _____.

① playing – bored   ② playing – boring
③ to play – excited   ④ to play – boring
⑤ playing – exciting

08~09 다음 우리말을 영어로 바르게 옮긴 것을 고르시오.

08

> 그 개는 밤비라고 불린다.

① The dog was called Bambi.
② The dog calls Bambi.
③ The dog has called Bambi.
④ The dog is called Bambi.
⑤ The dog called Bambi.

09

> 그 버스는 한 시에 떠났고, 네 시에 도착했다.

① The bus left at one, arriving at four.
② The bus left at one while it arrived at four.
③ The bus left at one since it arrived at four.
④ The but leaving at one, arriving at four.
⑤ The bus was leaving at one, arriving at four.

10 다음 밑줄 친 단어의 쓰임이 나머지 넷과 다른 것은?

① He sang songs playing the guitar on the street.
② I enjoyed watching football on weekends.
③ Feeling sad, she prayed for the poor.
④ I was thinking about the math problem.
⑤ Yelling at me, he looked angry.

11~12 다음 문장의 밑줄 친 부분과 의미가 같은 것은?

11

> Turning left, you should see the department store.

① If you will turn left
② When you will turn left
③ When you turned left
④ If you turn left
⑤ Unless you turn left

12

> Because Sarah fell from the ladder, she went to the hospital.

① Fell from the ladder
② Has fallen from the ladder
③ Fallen from the ladder
④ Being fallen from the ladder
⑤ Falling from the ladder

13 다음 중 어법상 올바른 것은?

① This delicious pie was made by Mrs. Kim.
② He was gone to school by bus.
③ Tom has showed his new artwork to me.
④ They were giving a timetable from their teacher.
⑤ It's excited for me to meet your brother.

14~15 다음 중 어법상 어색한 것을 고르시오.

14 ① Living in the city, he is very busy.
② Not to study hard, he failed the test.
③ Being smart, she passed the exam.
④ Though having many things to do, we didn't cancel the picnic.
⑤ Covered with snow, the lake was frozen.

15 ① My grandmother was watching TV, having some snacks.
② Being shocked, I couldn't say a word.
③ I saw the girl talking with Sharon yesterday.
④ Spent a long time with him, she knows well about him.
⑤ Looking at his face in the mirror, Junho smiled.

16 다음 중 문장의 해석이 옳지 <u>않은</u> 것은?

① When crossing the street, she saw a dog barking.
길을 건너면서, 그녀는 개 한 마리가 짖고 있는 것을 보았다.

② Not having confidence, she couldn't say anything.
확신이 없어서, 그녀는 아무 말도 하지 못했다.

③ Though learning to swim, I'm afraid of water.
수영하는 법을 배웠지만, 나는 물이 무섭다.

④ Turning left, you can see the store.
좌회전했기 때문에 너는 그 가게를 볼 수 있다.

⑤ As being tired of studying English, I learn to study Spanish.
영어를 공부하는 것이 지겨워져서, 나는 스페인어를 배운다.

17 다음 중 어법상 바르게 고치지 <u>못한</u> 것은?

① She helped me <u>washed</u> the dishes.
(→ washing)

② I felt my mom <u>touched</u> my hands.
(→ touching)

③ Did you see the bird <u>to fly</u> in the sky?
(→ flying)

④ I got my hair <u>cutting</u> as it was too long.
(→ cut)

⑤ He has visited the exhibition <u>holding</u> by the National Gallery.   (→ held)

18 다음 중 밑줄 친 부분이 어법상 <u>어색한</u> 것은?

① <u>Though</u> being winter, it's warm this year.

② <u>Though</u> having money, I can buy that suitcase.

③ <u>Though</u> not exercising at all, he is slim and healthy.

④ <u>Though</u> falling on the ground, he kept running to the finish line.

⑤ <u>Though</u> being slow, it is still working.

19 다음 중 밑줄 친 부분을 어법상 바르게 고친 것은?

① <u>Enter</u> the classroom, I saw my friends.
(→ Entered)

② <u>Interesting</u> in the book, I ordered it.
(→ Interested)

③ <u>Raise</u> in the country, she can grow plants.
(→ Raising)

④ <u>Shock</u> by the news, everyone kept silent.
(→ Shocking)

⑤ <u>Walk</u> in the forest, I saw a squirrel.
(→ Walked)

20 다음 중 어법상 올바른 문장의 개수는?

ⓐ Not having so shy, she hid herself behind the curtain.
ⓑ Being chew gum, he played the baseball.
ⓒ Having not money, he couldn't buy the shoes.
ⓓ Born in a rich family, he became a millionaire.

① 없음   ② 1개   ③ 2개   ④ 3개   ⑤ 4개

21 다음 중 어법상 어색한 문장의 개수는?

ⓐ Asked my opinion, I was embarrassed.
ⓑ Getting on the bus, I dropped my wallet.
ⓒ Not wanting to sleep, I drank coffee.
ⓓ Hoping to buy a new jacket, I'm saving money.

① 없음　② 1개　③ 2개　④ 3개　⑤ 4개

22 다음 중 어법상 올바른 문장끼리 짝지어진 것은?

ⓐ Badly hurt, the crocodile died after all.
ⓑ The chocolate cookies baked by my mom tasting good.
ⓒ Talking on the phone, she explained the shortest way to her house.
ⓓ Hearing the audience applause, I was really touched.

① ⓐ, ⓑ　　② ⓑ, ⓒ　　③ ⓐ, ⓑ, ⓒ
④ ⓐ, ⓒ, ⓓ　⑤ ⓑ, ⓒ, ⓓ

23~24 다음 빈칸에 들어갈 말이 바르게 짝지어진 것은?

23

1. ＿＿＿＿＿＿＿ he finished his homework, he played the computer game.
2. ＿＿＿＿＿＿＿ Susan, I was very happy.
3. ＿＿＿＿＿＿＿ thirsty, you can have some water.

① Although – Met – Being
② While – Meeting – Been
③ After – Met – Being
④ Though – Meeting – Been
⑤ After – Meeting – Being

24

A: How do I look?
B: You look ＿＿(A)＿＿ ! Do you have special plans?
A: I'm going to a classical music concert.
B: That sounds great! Will you go alone?
A: I'm going with Brian. The tickets were ＿＿(B)＿＿ by his uncle. I'm considering ＿＿(C)＿＿ dinner. Do you know any good restaurants?
B: I recommend Billy's Steak in the downtown area. I hope you have a great time.

	(A)	(B)	(C)
①	fascinating	given	bought
②	fascinated	giving	bought
③	fascinated	given	buying
④	fascinating	giving	bought
⑤	fascinating	given	buying

25 다음 글의 밑줄 친 ⓐ~ⓔ 중 어법상 어색한 것을 모두 고르시오.

I went camping with my family last Saturday. ⓐ Left the house, we realized that it was raining. ⓑ Thinking that the road would be slippery, my father drove very carefully. The rain fell harder ⓒ when we arrived at the mountain. ⓓ Though being worried about the safety, we kept going. We safely climbed the mountain, ⓔ stayed at the mountain cabin at night.

① ⓐ　　　② ⓑ　　　③ ⓒ
④ ⓓ　　　⑤ ⓔ

26~28 다음 빈칸에 괄호 안의 말을 알맞은 형태로 쓰시오.

26 We're looking at the painting _____ by her. (draw)

27 _____ on the street, I met Jimmy. (walk)

28 _____ by his propose, she started crying. (touch)

29~31 다음 문장의 밑줄 친 부분의 의미를 |보기|에서 골라 쓰시오.

| 보기 |
| ⓐ 이유   ⓑ 양보   ⓒ 시간   ⓓ 조건 |

29 <u>Not hungry</u>, he ate only an apple for dinner.

→ _____

30 <u>Downloading the audio file</u>, you can listen to it.

→ _____

31 <u>Although working hard</u>, he couldn't be promoted.

→ _____

32~33 다음 우리말과 일치하도록 괄호 안의 말을 바르게 배열하시오.

32
> 정원에서 자라고 있는 꽃들은 피는 중이다.
> (blooming, the flowers, are, growing, in the garden)

_____

33
> 간식을 전혀 먹지 않아서, 그녀는 날씬해졌다.
> (having, became, she, any snacks, thin, not)

_____

34~36 다음 우리말과 일치하도록 밑줄 친 분사구문을 부사절로 바꿔 쓰시오.

34
> 지금 바쁘지 않으면, 나랑 함께 해변에 가고 싶니?
> <u>Not busy now</u>, do you want to go to the beach with me?

_____, do you want to go to the beach with me?

35
> 뉴스를 보시면서, 나의 아버지는 커피를 드신다.
> <u>Watching the news program</u>, my father drinks coffee.

_____, he drinks coffee.

36

> 1925년에 세워진 후, 동대문 운동장은 서울의 명소가 되었다.
> Built in 1925, Dongdaemun Stadium became a landmark of Seoul.

_____,
Dongdaemun Stadium became a landmark of Seoul.

37~40 다음 문장에서 어법상 <u>어색한</u> 부분을 찾아 바르게 고치시오.

37 Crossed her arms, Cindy sang a song softly.

_____ → _____

38 Got tired of waiting, I canceled the reservation.

_____ → _____

39 He made me feel annoying yesterday.

_____ → _____

40 Turned on the radio, she listened to classical music.

_____ → _____

41~43 다음 두 문장을 분사구문을 이용하여 한 문장으로 쓰시오. (단, 앞 문장을 분사구문으로 만드시오.)

41 She walked to her office. She was talking on the phone.

→ _____

_____

42 He found an old coin in his pocket. He was curious.

→ _____

_____

43 The shop is decorated with flowers. The shop looked fascinating.

→ _____

_____

44~45 다음 문장이 어법상 어색하지 않으면 ○를, <u>어색한</u> 부분이 있으면 밑줄을 치고 바르게 고치시오.

44 (1) The wall was painting by the children.

→ _____

(2) Being scared, I couldn't say anything.

→ _____

(3) Don't knowing what to do, he called his teacher.

→ _____

45 (1) He waved smiles at me.

→ _____

(2) The man sat on the chair was reading newspaper.

→ _____

(3) Arriving at the port, I knew the ship had already gone.

→ _____

46~47 다음 문장에서 어법상 어색한 부분을 고쳐 완전한 문장을 쓰시오.

46 We made some products by using recycling plastic.

→ _____

_____

47 Injuring in the war, the soldier had scars.

→ _____

_____

48~49 주어진 |조건|을 이용하여 우리말을 영어로 옮기시오.

48 ┌조건┐
1) 분사구문을 사용할 것
2) 접속사를 넣을 것
3) 단어 hungry, not, eat, anything을 활용할 것
4) 7단어를 사용할 것
5) 축약형을 사용하지 말 것
└─────────────────┘

나는 배가 고팠지만 아무것도 먹지 않았다.

_____

_____

49 ┌조건┐
1) 분사구문을 사용할 것
2) 접속사를 넣을 것
3) 단어 dog, lie on, her lap, loved, feel, safe를 활용할 것
4) 11단어를 사용할 것
└─────────────────┘

그녀의 개는 그녀의 무릎 위에 누워 있는 동안, 안전하고 사랑받는다고 느꼈다.

_____

_____

50 다음 각 문장에서 생략되었을 접속사를 |보기|에서 골라 쓰시오.

┌보기┐
When   Before   Because
└─────────────────────────┘

ⓐ Entering the museum, she bought a ticket.
ⓑ Calling me, he asked her my phone number.
ⓒ Not living here a long time, I'm not used to the currency of this country yet.
ⓓ Called by me, she was cooking in the kitchen.
ⓔ Being poor, he couldn't afford to pay for it.

ⓐ _____
ⓑ _____
ⓒ _____
ⓓ _____
ⓔ _____

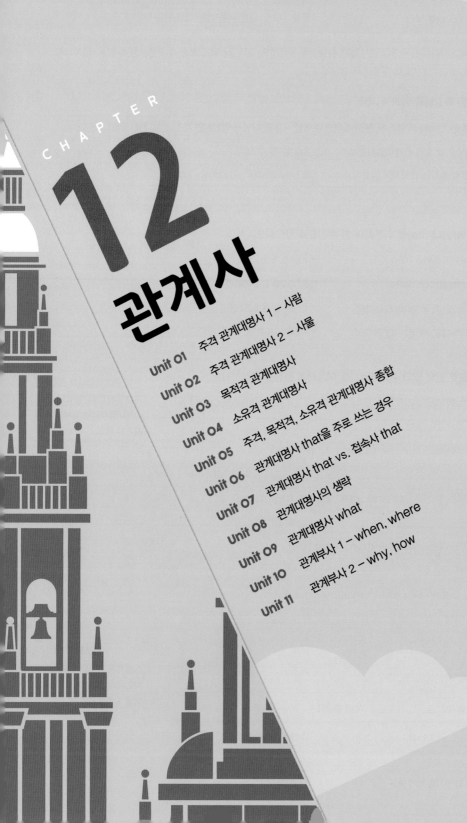

CHAPTER

12

관계사

두 개의 문장에 같은 사람이 있을 때, 관계대명사 who[that]를 써서 두 문장을 연결하세요.

I met the boy. 나는 그 소년을 만났다.	관계대명사로 연결	I met the boy who[that] knows you. 나는 너를 아는 그 소년을 만났다.
He knows you. 그는 너를 안다.		

😊 참고 the boy를 선행사라고 부르며, 관계대명사절이 선행사를 수식하는 형태가 되므로 관계대명사절을 형용사절이라고도 불러요.

다음 관계대명사 관련 특징들을 알아 두세요.

1	문장을 연결하는 접속사 역할과 뒤 문장의 대명사 역할 – 주격 대명사 역할이면 주격 관계대명사라고 부른다.
2	선행사가 사람일 때 주격 관계대명사는 who 또는 that을 쓸 수 있다.
3	관계대명사절의 동사는 선행사에 맞춘다. I met the boy who[that] knows you.

|A| 두 문장을 관계대명사 who나 that을 이용하여 한 문장으로 만드시오.

01 I like the girl. + She is kind to me.　→ I like the girl _____.

02 I have a friend. + He sings well.　→ I have a friend _____.

03 I have a sister. + She is 2 years older.　→ I have a sister _____.

04 I saw a man. + He was wearing a hat.　→ I saw a man _____.

|B| 우리말과 일치하도록 괄호 안의 말과 관계대명사를 이용하여 문장을 완성하시오.

> 주격 관계대명사가 쓰인 관계대명사절의 동사의 수는 관계대명사의 선행사에 일치시켜야 해요.

01 나는 전에 나의 영어 선생님이셨던 그 선생님을 만났다. (used to, English teacher)

I met the teacher _____.

02 이 대학교에 다니는 모든 학생들은 다 여자다. (attend, university)

All the students _____ women.

03 나무 옆에 서 있는 저 소녀는 지민이다. (stand, next to, the tree, be)

The girl _____ is Jimin.

04 안경을 쓰고 있는 저 사람을 너는 아니? (the man, wear, be)

Do you know _____?

05 우리 엄마는 추리 소설을 쓰는 작가다. (write, mystery novels)

My mom is an author _____.

> **실전 TIP** 🎓
> 선행사가 단수인지 복수인지 확인해서 알맞지 않은 동사형을 찾아보세요.

내신 기출 다음 빈칸에 들어갈 수 없는 것은?

> Jennie is the friend who _____ me a lot.

① likes　　　② helps　　　③ understand

UNIT 02 주격 관계대명사 2 – 사물

🔍 두 개의 문장에 같은 사물이 있을 때, 관계대명사 which[that]를 써서 두 문장을 연결하세요.

I like the shirt. 나는 그 셔츠를 좋아한다.	관계대명사로	I like the shirt which[that] has no buttons.
It has no buttons. 그것은 단추가 없다.	연결	나는 단추가 없는 그 셔츠를 좋아한다.

😊참고 the shirt가 선행사이며, 관계대명사 which[that]는 접속사와 대명사(it, 주어)의 역할을 하고 있어요.
관계대명사 that은 선행사가 사람이냐 사물이냐에 관계없이 둘 다 쓸 수 있어요.

|A| 괄호 안에서 알맞은 말을 고르시오.

01 Jessie has a cat that (have / has) odd eyes.

02 This is the song (which / who) is popular among teenagers.

03 I know one man who (raise / raises) more than ten dogs.

04 Anyone who (want / wants) to stay healthy should exercise regularly.

05 I found some doors (who / that) were in need to repair.

06 The man (which / who) saved my family from the fire was Mr. Garcia.

|B| 우리말과 일치하도록 괄호 안의 말과 관계대명사를 이용하여 문장을 완성하시오.

> 관계대명사절의 동사와 선행사의 일치에 유의해야 해요. 선행사가 -thing, -body로 끝나는 대명사일 경우에는 which, who를 사용할 수도 있지만, 주로 that을 사용하는 것도 참고해 두세요.

01 그녀는 자기가 만든 드레스를 입고 있었다. (made by, herself)

She was wearing a dress _____.

02 Tony에게는 그를 특별하게 만드는 무언가가 있다. (something, make, special)

Tony has _____.

03 너는 너와 많이 닮은 누군가를 만나 본 적이 있니? (someone, resemble)

Have you ever met _____ a lot?

04 이것은 가족의 소중함에 관한 책이다. (about, the importance)

This is a book _____ of family.

05 우리 엄마는 옷을 사랑하는 패션 디자이너다. (a fashion designer, clothes)

My mom is _____.

06 대기 오염은 반드시 해결되어야 하는 한 가지 문제이다. (one problem, must, solve)

Air pollution is _____.

🎓 **실전 TIP**
선행사가 사람인지 사물인지 확인해 보세요.

내신 기출 다음 빈칸에 which나 who 중 알맞은 말을 쓰시오.

- The singer _____ is singing on the stage is my favorite.
- Look at the beautiful castle _____ was built two hundred years ago.

UNIT 03 목적격 관계대명사

관계대명사가 목적격 대명사의 역할을 할 때는 목적격 관계대명사를 쓰세요.

The boy knows you. 그 소년은 너를 안다.	관계대명사로 연결	The boy who(m)[that] I met knows you.
I met him. 나는 그를 만났다.		내가 만난 그 소년은 너를 안다.

참고 The boy가 선행사이며, 관계대명사 who(m)[that]는 접속사와 대명사(him, 목적어)의 역할을 하고 있어요.

다음 관계대명사 관련 특징들을 알아 두세요.

	사람 선행사	사물 선행사	사물 또는 사람
주격 관계대명사	who	which	that
목적격 관계대명사	who(m)	which	

|A| 두 문장을 관계대명사 who(m)나 which, that을 이용하여 한 문장으로 만드시오.

01 This is the girl. + I saw her yesterday.　→ This is the girl _____.

02 This is the mountain. + We climb it often. → This is the mountain _____.

03 It is the city. + Many tourists visit it.　　→ It is the city _____.

04 The boy came to the party. + I like him.

→ The boy _____ came to the party.

05 The flowers smelled good. + He bought them for me.

→ The flowers _____ smelled good.

06 Do you remember the song? + We used to sing it together.

→ Do you remember the song _____?

|B| 우리말과 일치하도록 괄호 안의 말과 관계대명사를 이용하여 문장을 완성하시오.

선행사가 사물인지, 사람인지 잘 구별해서 알맞은 관계대명사를 고르세요.

01 태민은 내가 매우 많이 좋아하는 가수다. (like)

Taemin is the singer _____ very much.

02 이것은 내가 감기 때문에 먹는 약이다. (for, take, a cold)

This is the medicine _____.

03 김연아는 내가 가장 존경하는 스케이터다. (respect, the most)

Yuna Kim is the skater _____.

04 그녀는 많은 베스트셀러 책을 집필한 작가다. (write, best-selling books, many)

She is the writer _____.

05 나는 Annie가 어제 내게 보낸 이메일을 읽고 있는 중이다. (send)

I am reading the email _____ yesterday.

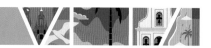

UNIT 04 　소유격 관계대명사

두 문장의 공통된 부분이 소유의 관계일 때, 소유격 관계대명사 whose를 쓰세요.

The boy knows you. 그 소년은 너를 안다.	관계대명사로 연결	The boy whose eyes are big knows you.
His eyes are big. 그의 눈은 크다.		눈이 큰 그 소년이 너를 안다.

참고 The boy가 선행사이며, 소유격 관계대명사 whose는 접속사와 소유격 대명사(his)의 역할을 하고 있어요.

|A| 문장에서 어법상 어색한 부분을 찾아 밑줄 긋고 바르게 고치시오.

01 Mom is the person whom loves me the most. → _____

02 This is *the Mona Lisa* who Leonardo da Vinci drew. → _____

03 I know a boy whom dream is to be a baseball player. → _____

04 Dennis is the best actor which everyone loves. → _____ 　최상급은 주로 관계대명사

05 France is the country who I want to visit. → _____ 　that과 함께 써요.

06 I like the woman who hair is long and blond. → _____

|B| 두 문장을 관계대명사 whose를 이용하여 한 문장으로 만드시오. 　소유격 관계대명사 뒤에는 반드시 명사가 온다는 사실 을 유념하세요.

01 I have a friend. + Her eyes are blue.

→ I have a friend _____.

02 He lives in the house. + Its roof is painted red.

→ He lives in the house _____.

03 A boy is looking for you. + His name is Ken.

→ A boy _____ is looking for you.

04 They raise a dog. + Its hair is white and long.

→ They raise a dog _____.

05 Please pass me that book. + Its cover is green.

→ Please pass me that book _____.

06 My teacher is a wise man. + His advice is always helpful.

→ My teacher is a wise man _____.

UNIT 05 주격, 목적격, 소유격 관계대명사 종합

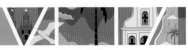

 선행사의 종류에 따른 주격, 목적격, 소유격 관계대명사를 종합적으로 연습하세요.

선행사의 종류에 따른 주격, 목적격, 소유격 관계대명사를 알아 두세요.

	사람 선행사	사물 선행사	사물 또는 사람
주격 관계대명사	who	which	that
목적격 관계대명사	who(m)	which	
소유격 관계대명사	whose		

|A| 빈칸에 알맞은 관계대명사를 쓰시오.

01 Winter is the season _____ Susan likes the most.

02 The little boy _____ I saw on the street was crying.

03 The baby _____ eyes are twinkling like stars is Lucas.

04 Do you remember the lady _____ saved you yesterday?

05 Switzerland is the country _____ nature is very beautiful.

|B| 두 문장을 관계대명사를 이용하여 한 문장으로 만드시오.

01 Ted is the player. + He was selected as the MVP.

→ Ted is the player _____.

02 This is the car. + My dad wants to buy this.

→ This is the car _____.

03 He is a man. + His heart is full of thanks.

→ He is a man _____.

04 Josh is the man. + I can always trust him.

→ Josh is the man _____.

05 They are the glasses. + Emily used to wear them.

→ They are the glasses _____.

06 I raise a dog. + It wags its tail when he sees me.

→ I raise a dog _____ when he sees me.

> 관계대명사를 이용해 두 문장을 한 문장으로 연결할 때는 주어와 동사의 수일치에 유의해야 해요.

실전 TIP

둘 다 목적격 관계대명사가 쓰인 문장이므로, 관계사절에 목적어가 있으면 안 된다는 데 유의하세요.

내신기출 문장에서 어법상 어색한 부분을 고치시오.

• She wants to eat the cookie that you made it. _____

• I am wearing the T-shirt that I bought it yesterday. _____

관계대명사를 who(m)나 which가 아닌, that을 주로 쓰는 경우에 주의하세요.

선행사	사람+사물	Look at the man and his dog that are running.
	최상급이나 서수	This is my best friend that I've known for 15 years.
	the only, the very, the same 등	He is the only child that can make them proud.
	all, much, little, any, no 등	The money was all that she had.
	-thing인 대명사	She gave him everything that she could give.

|A| 괄호 안에서 가장 알맞은 말을 고르시오.

01 This is all (whose / whom / that) I know about Sophia.

02 This is the first book (whom / that / which) I have written.

03 There was some food (whose / who / which) the dog could eat.

04 The only reason (which / that / whom) I chose this dress is its color.

05 We don't have any information (who / whom / that) you want to know.

06 Do you have many friends (which / who / whom) will help you in need?

07 Do you see the girl and the pet (whom / that / which) are sitting on the sofa?

08 France is the most beautiful country (who / whom / that) I have ever visited.

|B| 우리말과 일치하도록 괄호 안의 말과 관계대명사를 이용하여 문장을 완성하시오.

주로 관계대명사 that을 동반하는 선행사를 외워 둬야 해요.

01 그들은 자신들에게 필요한 건 다 가지고 있다. (everything, need)

They have _____.

02 그것은 그녀가 아는 유일한 단어였다. (the only word, know)

It was _____.

03 이것은 내가 받은 첫 번째 러브레터다. (the first love letter, receive)

This is _____.

04 이것이 바로 우리가 토론해야 하는 두 번째 요점이다. (the second point, need to, discuss)

This is _____.

05 길을 건너고 있던 그 여성과 그녀의 개에게 무슨 일이 생겼나요? (dog, woman, cross, be)

What happened to _____ the street?

06 그녀는 그녀의 아기를 행복하게 하는 모든 것을 알고 있다. (everything, make, happy)

She knows _____.

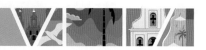
that의 역할이 관계대명사인지 명사절을 이끄는 접속사인지를 구분하세요.

that의 역할		예문	비교
관계대명사	형용사적 역할 – 선행사 수식	The movie that I saw was fun. 내가 본 그 영화는 재미있었다.	that이 접속사와 대명사의 역할을 함 → 따라서 that 뒤에 문장 요소가 빠져 있음 (I saw X) → 목적격 대명사 빠짐
접속사	명사적 역할 – 주어, 목적어, 보어	I heard that the movie was fun. 나는 그 영화가 재미있었다는 것을 들었다.	that이 절을 이끄는 접속사의 역할을 함 → 따라서 that 뒤에 문장 요소가 다 있음 (the movie was fun)

참고 that은 지시대명사나 지시형용사로도 쓰여요.

That is my bag. 〈지시대명사〉 / That bag is mine. 〈지시형용사〉

|A| 밑줄 친 that과 쓰임이 같은 것을 |보기|에서 골라 알맞은 기호를 쓰시오.

┌ 보기 ┐
ⓐ I read the book that you lent me.   ⓑ I know that you don't lie to me.
└─────┘

01 I believe that we can do it together.   [   ]

02 I found the key that you lost yesterday.   [   ]

03 I think that you have to take a rest.   [   ]

04 This is something that must be kept secret. [   ]

|B| 우리말과 일치하도록 괄호 안의 말과 that을 이용하여 문장을 완성하시오.

01 나는 그녀에게 빌려준 돈을 받지 못했다. (the money, lend)

I didn't get back _____.

02 문제는 바로 그것을 하기에는 네가 너무 어리다는 것이다. (too, young, to do it)

The problem is _____.

03 나는 내가 가진 모든 것을 네게 줄 수 있다. (everything, have)

I can give _____ to you.

04 우리 선생님은 우리가 규칙을 따라야 한다고 늘 말씀하신다. (should, follow the rules)

Our teacher always tells us _____.

실전 TIP

that절이 명사처럼 쓰였는지, 형용사처럼 쓰였는지 확인하세요. 또는 that절이 완전한 문장인지 아닌지로도 알 수 있어요.

내신 기출 다음 밑줄 친 부분의 쓰임이 다른 하나는?

① It is true that she is good at dancing.

② I heard that you are a big fan of soccer.

③ There were some cookies that he baked for himself.

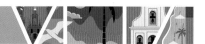

UNIT 08 관계대명사의 생략

 관계대명사를 생략할 수 있는 경우들을 알아 두세요.

목적격 관계대명사 생략 가능		The boy ~~who(m)~~ I met knows you.	
관계대명사의 동사가 진행형일 때	〈관계대명사＋be동사〉 생략 가능	The boy ~~who is~~ singing is Ben.	분사가 명사를 뒤에서 수식하는 문장이 됨
관계대명사의 동사가 수동태일 때		The boy ~~who is~~ invited is Ben.	

|A| 문장에서 생략할 수 있는 부분에 밑줄을 그으시오.

01 Look at the baby who is sitting on the bench.

02 She is the girl who we met at the park.

03 That person who is running toward us is my cousin.

04 Why don't we visit the zoo that Susie recommended?

05 Look at the sentences that are underlined in red.

06 I am eating the cake which you bought for me.

07 It was a special house which was made of ice.

08 Where can I find the T-shirt that I saw in the magazine?

whom이 아닌 who가 목적격 관계대명사로 사용되어도 생략할 수 있어요.

|B| 우리말과 일치하도록 괄호 안의 말을 바르게 배열하여 문장을 완성하시오.

01 교실을 청소하고 있는 저 소녀는 누구니? (the girl, the classroom, cleaning)

Who is ＿＿＿＿＿＿＿＿＿＿＿＿＿＿＿＿＿＿＿?

02 나는 그녀가 작곡한 모든 노래를 좋아한다. (all, the songs, by her, composed)

I like ＿＿＿＿＿＿＿＿＿＿＿＿＿＿＿＿＿＿＿.

03 그것은 닭고기와 토마토, 그리고 양파로 만든 수프이다. (chicken, soup, made of)

It is ＿＿＿＿＿＿＿＿＿＿＿＿＿＿＿＿＿＿＿, tomatoes, and onions.

04 초록색 스웨터를 입은 귀여운 강아지를 좀 봐. (a green sweater, wearing, the cute dog)

Look at ＿＿＿＿＿＿＿＿＿＿＿＿＿＿＿＿＿＿＿.

05 나는 100년 전에 지어진 탑 앞에서 사진을 찍었다. (one hundred years ago, a tower, built)

I took a picture in front of ＿＿＿＿＿＿＿＿＿＿＿＿＿＿＿＿＿＿＿.

06 그녀는 부모님이 그녀에게 사 주신 목걸이를 잃어버렸다. (her parents, had bought, the necklace, for her)

She lost ＿＿＿＿＿＿＿＿＿＿＿＿＿＿＿＿＿＿＿.

UNIT 09   관계대명사 what

선행사가 없을 때는 관계대명사 what을 쓰세요.

관계대명사		예문	비교
that	선행사가 있음	The movie (that) I saw was fun. 내가 본 그 영화는 재미있었다.	
what	선행사가 없음	What I saw was fun. 내가 본 것은 재미있었다.	= The one[thing] that I saw was fun.

😊 참고 관계대명사 what은 '~한 것'의 의미로, the one[thing] that[which]로 바꿔 쓸 수 있어요.

|A| 두 문장이 같은 뜻이 되도록 빈칸에 알맞은 말을 쓰시오.

01 What I want is the truth.   = _____ is the truth.

02 The thing that I ordered is juice.   = _____ is juice.

03 This is what we can do.   = This is _____.

04 The thing that she wanted was a rose.   = _____ was a rose.

05 The thing that made me mad was this.   = _____ was this.

06 His concert ticket is the thing that I need. = His concert ticket is _____.

|B| 우리말과 일치하도록 괄호 안의 말과 which 또는 what을 이용하여 문장을 완성하시오.

01 내가 말하고 있는 것에 좀 귀 기울여 들어줘. (be, say)

Please listen carefully to _____.

02 그를 특별하게 만드는 것은 그의 밝은 미소다. (make, special)

_____ is his bright smile.

03 그것은 내가 십 년 넘게 길러온 나의 개다. (have raised)

It is _____ for more than ten years.

> 관계대명사 what은 앞에 선행사가 있다면 절대 쓸 수 없음을 기억하고, 그때는 관계대명사 which나 that을 사용할 수 있음을 알아 두세요.

04 그녀는 자신이 어제 한 일을 후회하고 있다. (do)

She regrets _____.

05 그림 그리는 것은 내가 여가 시간에 주로 하는 일이다. (usually, do, in my free time)

Drawing a picture is _____.

🎓 **실전 TIP**

빈칸의 접속사가 선행사를 포함하는지 아닌지를 확인해 보세요.

내신 기출 다음 빈칸에 들어갈 말이 생략될 수 없는 것은?

① Taking a warm shower is _____ makes me relaxed.

② This is my best friend _____ I've known for 15 years.

③ The movie _____ we saw last night wasn't very good.

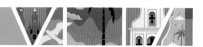

선행사가 시간, 장소인 경우에는 〈접속사+부사(구)〉의 역할을 하는 관계부사를 쓰세요.

관계부사	두 문장	관계부사가 있는 한 문장	참고
when	The 25th is the day.	The 25th is the day when we first met.	〈접속사+부사구(on that day)〉 역할
	We first met on that day.		
where	This is the park.	This is the park where we had fun.	〈접속사+부사구(in the park)〉 역할
	We had fun in the park.		

😊 **참고** the time, the place, the day와 같이 일반적인 선행사는 선행사나 관계부사 둘 중 하나만 써도 돼요.
  → It is the day when / [the day / when] we met.

😊 **참고** 관계부사 when과 where는 〈전치사+관계대명사〉로 바꿔 쓸 수 있어요.
  The 25th is the day on which we first met.   This is the park in which we had fun.
  하지만 관계대명사 자리에 that은 쓸 수 없어요.

|A| 빈칸에 알맞은 관계부사를 쓰시오.

01 This is the hospital _____ my mom works.

02 November was the month _____ Joy was born.

03 I don't know the place _____ she is now.

04 I want to know the date _____ it was made.

05 This is the playground _____ we enjoyed jumping rope.

06 Do you remember the day _____ we first went to school?

|B| 두 문장을 관계부사를 이용하여 한 문장으로 연결하시오.

01 My grandma was born in 1950. The Korean War broke out in that year.

  → My grandma was born in 1950 _____.

02 This is the village. A lot of rich people live in this village.

  → This is the village _____.

03 Last Tuesday was the day. We moved to a new house on that day.

  → Last Tuesday was _____.

💬 the day, the place처럼 관계부사의 선행사가 일반적인 명사인 경우에는 자주 생략해요.

04 This is the ticket office. You can buy the ticket at this place.

  → This is the ticket office _____.

05 Now is the time. You should give your opinion now.

  → Now is the time _____.

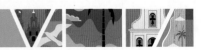

선행사가 이유나 방법인 경우에도 〈접속사+부사(구)〉의 역할을 하는 관계부사를 쓰세요.

관계부사	두 문장	관계부사가 있는 한 문장	주의
why	That is the reason. He is mad for that reason.	That is the reason why he is mad.	〈접속사+부사구(for that reason)〉 역할
how	I found the way. He solved it in that way.	I found the way ~~how~~ he solved it. I found ~~the way~~ how he solved it.	the way, how 둘 중 하나만 써요.

😊 참고 the reason과 같이 일반적인 선행사는 선행사나 관계부사 둘 중 하나만 써도 돼요.
→ This is the reason why [the reason / why] he is mad.

😊 참고 관계부사 why와 how도 〈전치사+관계대명사〉로 바꿔 쓸 수 있어요.
That is the reason for which he is mad. I found the way in which he solved it.
역시 관계대명사 자리에 that은 쓸 수 없어요.

|A| 빈칸에 알맞은 관계부사를 쓰시오.

01 Please tell me the reason _____ you were absent yesterday.

02 The teacher explained _____ rainbows are made.

03 It showed _____ they solved the problems.

04 He told us the reason _____ he had to leave early.

05 I want to know _____ this machine works.

06 The reason _____ we are here is to help the homeless dogs.

|B| 우리말과 일치하도록 괄호 안의 말을 이용하여 문장을 완성하시오.

01 네가 귀가하는 방법을 말해 줄 수 있겠니? (get back home)

Could you describe _____ ?

02 나는 그녀가 사진을 잘 찍는 방법을 알고 싶다. (take, good pictures)

I want to know _____.

03 가을에 나뭇잎 색깔이 붉게 되는 이유가 뭘까? (leaves, turn red, fall)

What is the reason _____?

04 네가 수학을 잘하게 된 방법을 우리에게도 알려줘. (become, good at, math)

Let us know _____.

05 너는 네가 시험에 떨어진 이유를 알고 싶니? (fail the test)

Do you want to know _____?

💬 구어체에서는 관계부사 why와 선행사 the reason 중 한 가지만 쓰는 경우가 많아요.

중간고사·기말고사 실전문제

객관식 (01~25) / 주관식 (26~50)

정답과 해설·51쪽

학년과 반		이름		객관식	/ 25문항	주관식	/ 25문항

01~03 다음 빈칸에 들어갈 말로 알맞은 것을 고르시오.

01
Is it Sam _____ is playing the guitar?

① which ② whom ③ whose
④ what ⑤ who

02
I wrote a book _____ is about my travels in Asia.

① whom ② whose ③ what
④ which ⑤ thing

03
Do you know the way _____ I can get to the post office?

① where ② how ③ that
④ which ⑤ in which

04 다음 빈칸에 들어갈 말로 알맞지 <u>않은</u> 것은?

This is the _____ which I saw.

① bear ② man ③ box
④ rock ⑤ name

05 다음 빈칸에 공통으로 들어갈 말로 알맞은 것은?

1. I heard _____ John moved to Chicago.
2. He is the only one _____ knows my secret.

① what ② when ③ that
④ who ⑤ where

06~07 다음 빈칸에 들어갈 말이 바르게 짝지어진 것은?

06
The elderly lady _____ I _____ with before is my grandmother.

① who – talks ② which – talking
③ whom – talk ④ that – talked
⑤ which – talked

07
1. I don't know _____ I want.
2. The girl _____ name is Cindy is friendly.

① what – whose ② which – the
③ that – which ④ that – whose
⑤ what – that

08 다음 우리말을 영어로 바르게 옮긴 것은?

햄버거를 먹고 있는 저 소녀가 내 여동생이다.

① That girl that eating a hamburger is my sister.
② That girl who eating a hamburger is my sister.
③ That girl whom eats a hamburger is my sister.
④ That girl who is eating a hamburger is my sister.
⑤ That girl which is eating a hamburger is my sister.

09 다음 우리말을 영어로 옮겼을 때 어법상 어색한 것은?

> 그녀는 내가 빌려준 물건을 돌려주지 않았다.

① She didn't return what I lent.
② She didn't return the thing which I lent.
③ She didn't return which I lent.
④ She didn't return the thing that I lent.
⑤ She didn't return the thing I lent.

10 다음 중 밑줄 친 that을 생략할 수 있는 것은?

① I know that he is going hiking today.
② We have to move that table together.
③ It is surprising that we can go to the moon.
④ I bought a pan that looks strong and heavy.
⑤ Minsu is the one that won first prize.

[11~12] 다음 두 문장을 한 문장으로 바르게 연결한 것을 고르시오.

11
> • These are grapes.
> • I picked them in the yard.

① These are grapes who I picked in the yard.
② These are grapes that I picked in the yard.
③ These are grapes whom I picked in the yard.
④ These are grapes what I picked in the yard.
⑤ These are grapes in which I picked the yard.

12
> • I brought an umbrella.
> • It helps Jane not to get wet.

① I brought an umbrella who helps Jane not to get wet.
② I brought an umbrella to which helps Jane not to get wet.
③ I brought an umbrella that it helps Jane not to get wet.
④ I brought an umbrella what helps Jane not to get wet.
⑤ I brought an umbrella which helps Jane not to get wet.

[13~14] 다음 중 밑줄 친 단어의 쓰임이 나머지 넷과 다른 것을 고르시오.

13 ① Jihun told me where I could buy the bag.
② Tom found the bus where I lost my card.
③ Matt didn't know where I was that night.
④ Where Jiho saw Michael was the question.
⑤ I will ask her where she was studying then.

14 ① I took care of my grandmother who is in the hospital.
② Do you know who your teacher is?
③ They saw the boy who sings on the street.
④ Do you know the woman who teaches English?
⑤ I miss my cousins who I met last year.

15~16 다음 문장의 밑줄 친 that의 쓰임과 같은 것을 고르시오.

15

> The boy rolled the ball that is Minho's.

① He drew some paintings that Susie wanted.

② I heard the song that my friend recommended.

③ That's the girl that I talked about.

④ Did you see the boy that Max fought with?

⑤ She is the author that owns this bookstore.

16

> She ate the dinner that he made in the kitchen.

① It is exciting that you made a film.

② The shoes that I'm wearing are too small.

③ I understand that you can't come.

④ You should know that this is the last chance.

⑤ She weaved that beautiful sweater for herself.

17 다음 중 어법상 바르게 고친 것은?

① Jack wrote the day that he meets Jane.
(→ on that)

② I have a friend whom name means sky.
(→ who)

③ Open to the first page which is in the text book. (→ that)

④ The girl which jumps in the gym is Jenny.
(→ whom)

⑤ Remember the way how you found the way. (→ where)

18~19 다음 중 어법상 어색한 것을 고르시오.

18 ① I read the story who he wrote last year.

② He remembers the clerk who was very nice.

③ They're looking for the man whom they fired.

④ That man is the one who is responsible for safety.

⑤ The information that I found online was wrong.

19 ① This is my sister whose fingers are thin.

② I had a bag my father bought for me.

③ She likes the city in that she lives.

④ He is the only child that Jinny has.

⑤ I found the memo she gave to me.

20 다음 중 어법상 바르게 고치지 못한 것은?

① He gave me something which was very heavy. (→ that)

② I watched a film what was about global warming. (→ which)

③ Do you know that is the biggest country?
(→ what)

④ The girl whom danced with you is Marie.
(→ who)

⑤ Tell me the reason in that I can't use this.
(→ for that)

21 다음 중 어법상 올바른 것은?

① It is the third floor how the shop is located.

② It is Tom whom is the best player of us.

③ She is my role model which is a K-pop star.

④ The book is his who is on the bookshelf.

⑤ He is the one whom I trust the most in my life.

22 다음 중 어법상 올바른 문장의 개수는?

> ⓐ The only thing that never change is my love for you.
> ⓑ This is the first trip who I've ever had.
> ⓒ Joe, who exercising regularly, is healthy.
> ⓓ I can give you everything what you want.

① 없음　② 1개　③ 2개　④ 3개　⑤ 4개

23 다음 중 어법상 어색한 문장의 개수는?

> ⓐ We saw the super model who was very tall and fashionable.
> ⓑ He likes the dress what she is wearing today.
> ⓒ I'm looking for a place where I can read a book.
> ⓓ I love you just the way you are.

① 없음　② 1개　③ 2개　④ 3개　⑤ 4개

24 다음 대화의 빈칸에 들어갈 말이 바르게 짝지어진 것은?

> A: Did you see the film ___(A)___ Michelle recommended?
> B: No, I didn't. Can you tell me the story?
> A: It is about a boy's lost dog ___(B)___ tried to return home. It was a very touching movie.
> B: I'd like to watch it.
> A: I heard that it is on TV next Thursday ___(C)___ you will visit me.

	(A)	(B)	(C)
①	what	that	on that
②	that	which	when
③	which	who	on which
④	that	which	which
⑤	which	who	when

25 다음 글의 밑줄 친 ⓐ~ⓔ 중 어법상 어색한 것은?

> He is a famous inventor ⓐ who invented many useful things. The most popular thing ⓑ that he invented is a cordless cleaner. This new cleaner ⓒ which changed people's lifestyle helps us to clean very easily. The inventions ⓓ which is made by this inventor are thought as innovation. He keeps trying to invent ⓔ many new things that can help us.

① ⓐ　② ⓑ　③ ⓒ　④ ⓓ　⑤ ⓔ

[26~27] 다음 우리말과 일치하도록 괄호 안의 말과 관계사를 이용하여 문장을 완성하시오.

26 우리는 우리 집 앞에 서 있는 그 눈사람을 만들었다.

We built the snowman _____ _____ in front of our house. (stand)

27 그는 운전하면서 가장 아름다운 그 길을 택할 것이다.

While driving, he'll take the road _____ _____ the most beautiful. (be)

[28~31] 다음 문장의 밑줄 친 단어의 쓰임을 |보기|에서 골라 쓰시오.

> |보기|
> ⓐ 의문사　　ⓑ 관계대명사　　ⓒ 관계부사

28 <u>What</u> you did to her was wrong.

→ _____

29 March is the month <u>when</u> my father comes.

→ _____

30 <u>How</u> do you feel when you see a rainbow?

→ _____

31 The staff didn't hear <u>where</u> to meet for the business meeting.

→ _____

32~33 다음 우리말과 일치하도록 괄호 안의 말을 바르게 배열하시오.

32
> 무엇이 당신이 산 가장 좋은 것입니까?
> (thing, you, is, that, what, bought, the best, ?)

_____

33
> 판다는 대나무 먹는 것을 즐기는 동물이다.
> (an animal, which, enjoys, a panda, is, eating bamboo)

_____

34~35 다음 |보기|와 같이 두 문장을 관계부사를 이용하여 한 문장으로 쓰시오.

> ┌ 보기 ┐
> • Italy is the country.
> • I bought the souvenirs there.
> → Italy is the country where I bought the souvenirs.

34 • My mom didn't tell me the reason.
　　• My sister was angry for that reason.

→ _____

_____

35 • He taught his kids the way.
　　• His grandfather sailed the boat in the way.

→ _____

_____

36~37 다음 문장에서 생략되었을 관계대명사를 넣어 문장을 다시 쓰시오.

36 It is Kate singing in the yard.

→ _____

37 She is the only one Matt has been waiting for.

→ _____

38~39 다음 문장에서 생략되었을 관계부사를 넣어 문장을 다시 쓰시오.

38 He misses his hometown he was born.

→ _____

39 I don't remember the day we first met.

→ _____

40~42 다음 문장에서 어법상 <u>어색한</u> 부분을 찾아 바르게 고치시오.

40 My brother's friend who name is Billy is like a hero.

_____ → _____

41 Can you lend me the novel *Jane Eyre* who you recommended?

_____ → _____

42 This city is the place for which she was born and raised.

_____ → _____

43~45 다음 문장의 밑줄 친 that의 쓰임과 같은 것을 |보기|에서 골라 쓰시오.

┌─|보기|─────────────────────┐
ⓐ I like bananas that are a little sweet.
ⓑ Do you understand the words that he said?
ⓒ I didn't know that you left for Vietnam.
└───────────────────────────┘

43 Can you believe that he became a model?

→ _____

44 I love this cake that Susan made for me.

→ _____

45 We should know the rules that everyone has to follow.

→ _____

46~47 다음 문장에서 어법상 어색한 부분을 고쳐 완전한 문장을 쓰시오.

46 A library is the place in where people read books.

→ _____

_____

47 Can you tell me the reason in which you lied?

→ _____

_____

48 다음 문장이 어법상 어색하지 않으면 ○를, 어색한 부분이 있으면 밑줄을 치고 바르게 고치시오.

(1) She didn't believe which he said at the restaurant.

→ _____

(2) Did you receive the letter which I sent to you?

→ _____

49 주어진 |조건|을 이용하여 우리말을 영어로 옮기시오.

┌─|조건|─────────────────────┐
1) 관계부사를 쓸 것
2) 단어 a lot of, love, play the guitar를 쓸 것
3) 10단어를 사용할 것
└───────────────────────────┘

많은 사람들이 그가 기타 치는 방법을 사랑한다.

_____

_____

50 다음 중 밑줄 친 부분을 생략할 수 있는 문장의 기호를 쓰시오.

┌───────────────────────────┐
ⓐ The student added the scores which he got on the tests.
ⓑ The diamond necklace which was bright and shiny was stolen.
ⓒ They visited the place where Syrian refugees were living.
ⓓ She knows the writer who has won many awards.
ⓔ Could you let me know the day when Sarah will come?
└───────────────────────────┘

_____ , _____ , _____

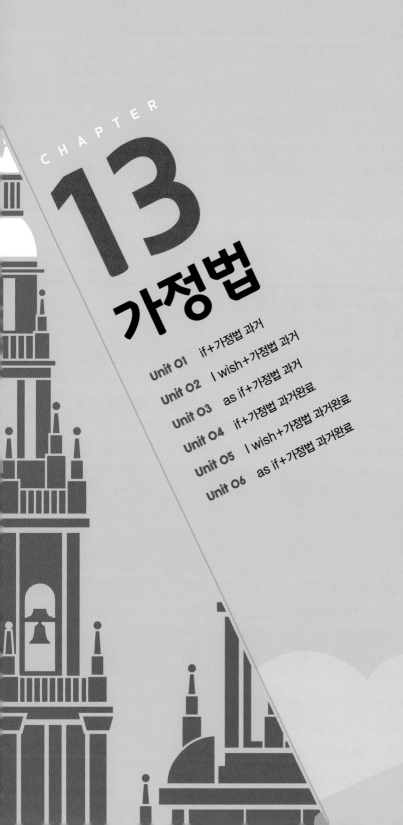

현재 사실의 반대를 가정할 때는 가정법 동사(일반동사 과거형, be동사 were)를 쓰세요.

일반 동사	현재 사실	I don't have time so I can't go.	시간이 없어서 갈 수 없다.
	반대 가정	┌ don't have의 반대/과거 If I had time, I could go. └ can't go의 반대/과거	내가 시간이 있다면, 갈 수 있을 텐데.
be 동사	현재 사실	He is not healthy, so he won't join.	건강하지 않아서 합류하지 않을 거다.
	반대 가정	┌ is not의 반대/과거(were만 사용) If he were healthy, he would join. └ won't join의 반대/과거	그가 건강하다면, 합류할 텐데.

참고 가정법은 단순히 반대를 가정하는 것이 아니라, 안타까움, 후회, 유감을 표현하기 위해 사용해요.

주의 가정이 아니라, 실현 가능한 단순 조건을 나타낼 때는 동사를 과거형으로 쓰지 않아요.

구분	if절	주절
단순 조건문	현재	미래
가정법 과거	과거형 / were	would/could/might+동사원형

|A| 괄호 안의 단어를 알맞은 형태로 바꿔 가정법 과거 문장을 완성하시오.

01 If it _____ (be) sunny, we _____ (will go) on a picnic.

02 If I _____ (know) your phone number, I _____ (will talk) to you on the phone.

03 If we _____ (go) to the same school, we _____ (will play) together every day.

04 If she _____ (be) stronger, she _____ (will help) her mom move the sofa.

05 If you _____ (be, not) busy, you _____ (can spend) time with us.

06 If we _____ (learn) Spanish, we _____ (can talk) with the Spanish student.

|B| 문장을 가정법 문장으로 바꾸시오.

가정법 과거는 현재 사실의 반대를 가정하지만, 동사는 반드시 과거시제로 써요.

01 As you don't want juice, I will not get it for you.

= _____, I would get it for you.

02 Because I don't know the way to the station, I can't show you the way.

= _____, I could show you the way.

03 As I am not an eagle, I can't fly high.

= _____, I could fly high.

04 Because there is air, we can live.

= _____, we could not live.

05 As we are healthy, we can enjoy sports every day.

= _____, we couldn't enjoy sports every day.

06 Because he is kind to everyone, he is always loved.

= _____, he would not always be loved.

|C| 우리말과 일치하도록 괄호 안의 말을 이용하여 문장을 완성하시오.

01 내가 미국에 있다면, 나는 나이아가라 폭포를 보러 갈 텐데. (in America)

_____, I would go to see Niagara Falls.

02 수영장이 있다면, 우리는 종일 수영할 수 있을 텐데. (swim)

If there were a pool, _____ all day.

03 날씨가 좋으면, 우리는 밖에서 캐치볼을 할 것이다. (play catch)

If the weather is good, _____ outside.

04 만약 네가 눈이 좋다면, 너는 그를 발견할 수 있을 텐데. (have good eyesight)

_____, you could find him.

05 내가 만약 현명한 결정을 내린다면, 나는 그것을 후회하지 않을 텐데. (regret)

If I made a wise decision, _____ it.

06 너 같은 좋은 친구가 없다면, 나는 매우 심심할 텐데. (a good friend, have)

_____ like you, I would feel very bored.

07 부모님이 한가하시면, 나는 함께 행복한 휴일을 보낼 것이다. (my parents, free)

_____, I will have a happy holiday with them.

|D| 문장의 밑줄 친 부분을 바르게 고치시오.

01 If it is winter, we could build a snowman together. → _____

02 What would you do if you have one million dollars? → _____

03 If I had a robot, I will let it cook for me. → _____

04 If I win the lottery, I could help the poor. → _____

05 If I was a teacher, I would give you good advice. → _____

06 If you were ten years older, what will you become? → _____

실전 TIP

조건문인지 가정법 문장인지 동사의 형태를 보고 확인하세요. 조건문의 미래는 현재 시제로 표현한다는 데 유의하세요.

내신 기출 다음 중 어법상 어색한 것은?

① If you practice hard, you will pass the test.

② If she will not be busy, she will come to the festival.

③ If I had more money, I could buy the car for my dad.

UNIT 02   I wish+가정법 과거

'만약 ~이라면 좋을 텐데'라고 할 때는 〈I wish＋가정법 동사〉로 표현하세요.

일반 동사	현재 사실	I don't <u>have</u> a brother.	형제가 없다.
	유감/아쉬움	I wish I <u>had</u> a brother. └ 가정법 과거(현재 사실의 반대)	형제가 있다면 좋을 텐데.
be 동사	현재 사실	Sujeong <u>is not</u> here.	수정이가 여기 없다.
	유감/아쉬움	I wish Sujeong ~~was~~ were here. └ 가정법 과거 be동사 were	수정이가 여기 있으면 좋을 텐데.

😊 참고 사실과 반대되는 일에 대한 유감, 아쉬움의 표현이므로 가정법 동사를 써요.

|A| 우리말과 일치하도록 괄호 안의 단어를 알맞은 형태로 바꾸시오.

01 내가 너만큼 키가 크면 좋을 텐데.   I wish I _____ as tall as you. (be)

02 내게 휴대전화가 있다면 좋을 텐데.   I wish I _____ a mobile phone. (have)

03 내가 우주로 여행할 수 있다면 좋을 텐데.   I wish I _____ to space. (can travel)

04 내가 새 자전거를 사면 좋을 텐데.   I wish I _____ a new bicycle. (buy)

05 서울에 눈이 많이 오면 좋을 텐데.   I wish it _____ a lot in Seoul. (snow)

06 오늘이 휴일이라면 좋을 텐데.   I wish it _____ a holiday today. (be)

07 그가 가족들과 함께 더 많은 시간을 보낼 수 있다면 좋을 텐데.

   I wish he _____ more time with his family. (can spend)

|B| 두 문장이 같은 뜻이 되도록 문장을 완성하시오.

> 직설법을 가정법으로, 가정법을 직설법으로 전환할 때는 시제에 유의해야 해요.

01 I'm sorry (that) I can't speak a lot of foreign languages.

   = I wish _____.

02 I wish there were many students in this class.

   = I'm sorry (that) _____.

03 I'm sorry (that) I am not good at eating spicy food.

   = I wish _____.

04 I wish I could go skiing with you.

   = I'm sorry (that) _____.

05 I'm sorry (that) I can't enter Harvard University.

   = I wish _____.

06 I wish I could help you clean the classroom.

   = I'm sorry (that) _____.

UNIT 03 　 as if+가정법 과거

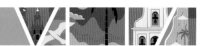

'마치 ~인 것처럼'이라고 쓸 때는 〈as if+가정법 동사〉로 표현하세요.

일반 동사	현재 사실	He can't do it now.	지금 할 수 없다.
	마치 ~처럼	He acts as if he ~~did~~ could do it now. └ 조동사를 과거로 써요.	지금 할 수 있는 것처럼 행동한다.
be 동사	현재 사실	She is not a doctor.	의사가 아니다.
	마치 ~처럼	She talks as if she were a doctor. └ 가정법 과거(현재 사실의 반대)	마치 의사인 것처럼 말한다.

참고 사실과 반대되는 일에 대한 표현이므로 가정법 동사를 써요.

|A| 우리말과 일치하도록 |보기|에서 알맞은 말을 골라 빈칸에 올바른 형태로 바꿔 쓰시오.

| 보기 |
| I am flying in the sky. 　　He knows everything. 　　I am a baby. |
| He is a chef. 　　　　　　We are in heaven. 　　　She is an American. |

01 마치 내가 아기인 것처럼 나를 대하지 마. 　　Don't treat me _____.

02 난 마치 내가 하늘을 날고 있는 것처럼 느껴. 　　I feel _____.

03 Sam은 마치 자기가 요리사인 것처럼 요리한다. 　　Sam cooks _____.

04 그녀는 마치 자기가 미국인인 것처럼 말한다. 　　She speaks _____.

05 그는 마치 자기가 모든 것을 다 아는 것처럼 행동한다. 　　He behaves _____.

06 우리는 마치 우리가 천국에 있는 것처럼 느낀다. 　　We feel _____.

|B| 두 문장이 같은 뜻이 되도록 문장을 완성하시오.

〈as if+가정법 과거〉로 문장을 전환할 때는 현재 사실의 반대를 과거시제로 써요.

01 In fact, he doesn't understand me well.

= He talks _____.

02 In fact, they enjoy playing computer games.

= They behave _____.

03 In fact, I am not younger than you.

= You treat me _____.

04 In fact, there is a serious problem.

= Billy speaks _____.

05 In fact, you don't know everything about life.

= Don't talk _____.

06 In fact, he is not a famous movie star.

= He acts _____.

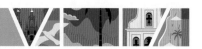

과거 사실의 반대를 가정할 때는 가정법 동사를 과거완료형으로 쓰세요.

일반 동사	과거 사실	I didn't have time, so I couldn't go.	시간이 없어서 갈 수 없었다.
	반대 가정	┌ didn't have의 반대 had+have의 완료형 had If I had had time, I could have gone. └ couldn't go의 반대/완료형	시간이 있었다면, 갈 수 있었을 텐데.
be 동사	과거 사실	He was not healthy, so he didn't join.	건강하지 않았어서 합류 안 했다.
	반대 가정	┌ was not의 반대/완료형 If he had been healthy, he would have joined. └ 조동사가 없을 때 would	그가 건강했다면, 합류했을 텐데.

참고 가정법은 단순히 반대를 가정하는 것이 아니라, 안타까움, 후회, 유감을 표현하기 위해 사용해요.

주의 가정법 과거와 과거완료의 동사 형태에 주의하세요.

구분		if절	주절
가정법 과거	현재 사실 반대 가정	과거형/were	would/could/might+동사원형
가정법 과거완료	과거 사실 반대 가정	had+과거분사형	would/could/might+have+과거분사형

|A| 괄호 안의 단어를 알맞은 형태로 바꿔 가정법 과거완료 문장을 완성하시오.

01 If I _____ (have) a mobile phone, I _____ (will, call) you.

02 If you _____ (practice) harder, you _____ (can, win) the contest.

03 If they _____ (be) Korean, they _____ (can, use) chopsticks.

04 If she _____ (walk) more carefully, she _____ (may not, fall) on the floor.

05 If I _____ (wake up) earlier, I _____ (can, catch) the school bus.

06 If it _____ (snow) a lot, we _____ (will, enjoy) skiing last winter.

|B| 우리말과 일치하도록 |보기|에서 알맞은 말을 골라 빈칸에 알맞은 형태로 쓰시오.

보기					
speak	play	live	be	fall	bake

01 만약 우리가 같은 나라에 살았더라면, 서로 더 자주 만났을 텐데.

_____ in the same country, we would have met each other more often.

02 오븐이 고장 나지 않았더라면, 우리 엄마가 우리에게 빵을 구워 주셨을 텐데.

If the oven had not broken down, _____ bread for us.

03 내가 영어를 잘했더라면, 그 외국인에게 길 안내를 해 줬을 텐데.

_____ English well, I would have shown the foreigner the way.

04 어제 비가 안 왔더라면, 우리는 밖에서 축구를 할 수 있었을 텐데.

If it had not rained yesterday, _____ soccer outside.

05 내가 힘이 더 셌었더라면, 이 상자를 들어올릴 수 있었을 텐데.

_____ stronger, I could have lifted this box.

06 그 영화가 재미있었더라면, 우리가 영화를 보다가 잠들지는 않았을 텐데.

If the movie had been interesting, _____ asleep during it.

|C| 두 문장이 같은 뜻이 되도록 문장을 완성하시오.

01 Because I didn't live in the countryside, I couldn't see a lot of stars.

= _____ in the countryside, _____ a lot of stars.

02 If you had told the news to me, I would have congratulated you.

= _____ the news to me, _____ you.

03 As the weather was not warm, we didn't go on a picnic.

= _____ warm, _____ on a picnic.

04 If he had run faster, he could have won the gold medal.

= _____ faster, _____ the gold medal.

05 Because the math exam was difficult, I couldn't get full marks.

= _____ difficult, _____ full marks.

|D| 문장의 밑줄 친 부분을 바르게 고치시오.

01 If I had prepared well for the test, I would <u>feel</u> more confident. → _____

02 If I <u>had</u> a car, I could have taken you home. → _____

03 If I had <u>able</u> to cook, I would have cooked delicious food for you. → _____

04 If you had gone to see a doctor, you <u>will</u> have got over your cold. → _____

05 If she had looked out the window, she <u>can</u> have found me. → _____

실전 TIP

가정법 과거인지, 가정법 과거완료인지 확인해야 해요.

내신 기출 다음 빈칸에 들어갈 말이 바르게 짝지어진 것은?

- If we _____ the same age, we could take the same class.
- If I had brought my swimsuit, I _____ in the sea.
- If you _____ me advice, I could have got a better result.

① were – could have swum – gave
② had been – could swim – had given
③ were – could have swum – had given

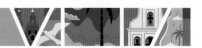

'만약 ~였다면 좋았을 텐데'라고 할 때는 〈I wish + 가정법 과거완료〉로 표현하세요.

일반 동사	과거 사실	I didn't see him.	그를 못 봤다.
	유감/아쉬움	I wish I had seen him └ 가정법 과거완료(과거 사실의 반대)	그를 봤다면 좋았을 텐데.
be 동사	과거 사실	Sujeong was not here.	수정이가 여기 없었다.
	유감/아쉬움	I wish Sujeong had been here. └ 가정법 과거완료(과거 사실의 반대)	수정이가 여기 있었다면 좋았을 텐데.

|A| 괄호 안의 말을 이용하여 가정법 과거완료 문장을 완성하시오.

01 I wish I _____ with you in Canada. (be)

02 I wish I _____ nicely to my friends. (behave)

03 I wish you and I _____ more often. (exercise)

04 I wish I _____ a lot of English books. (read)

05 I wish more people _____ this party. (join)

06 I wish I _____ his birthday. (not, forget)

07 I wish I _____ the same school as Jennie. (attend)

08 I wish the bookstore _____ earlier this morning. (open)

|B| 두 문장이 같은 뜻이 되도록 문장을 완성하시오.

가정법 과거완료 문장을 직설법 문장으로 바꿀 때는 시제에 유의하세요.

01 I wish I had woken up early this morning.

= I'm sorry that _____ this morning.

02 I'm sorry that I spilled the water on the keyboard.

= I wish _____ on the keyboard.

03 I wish I had listened to my parents.

= I'm sorry that _____.

04 I'm sorry that you were not satisfied with our food.

= I wish _____.

05 I wish there had been enough time to take pictures.

= I'm sorry that _____ to take pictures.

06 I'm sorry that I didn't bring my umbrella with me.

= I wish _____ with me.

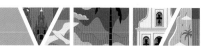
'마치 ~이었던 것처럼'이라고 쓸 때는 〈as if+가정법 과거완료〉로 표현하세요.

일반 동사	과거 사실	He didn't see me.	나를 못 봤다.
	마치 ~처럼	He talks as if he had seen me. └ 과거 사실의 반대 가정	마치 나를 봤던 것처럼 말한다.
be 동사	과거 사실	Sujeong was not here.	여기 없었다.
	마치 ~처럼	Sujeong acts as if she had been here. └ 과거 사실의 반대 가정	마치 여기 있었던 것처럼 행동한다.

|A| 두 문장이 같은 뜻이 되도록 빈칸에 알맞은 말을 쓰시오.

01 You talk as if you had lived in Europe. = In fact, _____ Europe.

02 In fact, you didn't help me. = Don't speak _____.

03 He always talks as if he had become a president. = In fact, _____.

04 In fact, she didn't do her best. = She behaves _____.

05 Michael speaks as if he had arrived on time. = In fact, _____.

06 In fact, she didn't see a UFO. = She acts _____.

07 You are eating dinner as if you had not had lunch. = In fact, _____.

08 In fact, he didn't participate in the meeting. = He talks _____ the meeting.

|B| 우리말과 일치하도록 괄호 안의 말을 이용하여 문장을 완성하시오.

as if를 기준으로, 앞에는 동사의 현재형이 오고, 뒤에는 과거완료형이 온다는 사실 기억하세요.

01 Sam은 마치 자기가 경기에서 이겼던 것처럼 말한다. (speak, win the game)

Sam _____.

02 그는 자기가 모든 문제를 해결했던 것처럼 말한다. (talk, solve all the problems)

He _____.

03 Joy는 마치 자기가 그 책을 다 읽었던 것처럼 말한다. (talk, finish reading the book)

Joy _____.

04 그녀는 마치 자기가 직접 그 음식을 요리했던 것처럼 행동한다. (act, cook the food, herself)

She _____.

05 그 아이들은 마치 자기들이 창문을 깨지 않았던 것처럼 말한다. (talk, break the window)

The children _____.

06 너는 마치 네가 그 미술 수업을 들었던 것처럼 말한다. (talk, take the art class)

You _____.

중간고사·기말고사 실전문제

학년과 반	이름	객관식	/ 25문항	주관식	/ 25문항

01~03 다음 빈칸에 들어갈 말로 알맞은 것을 고르시오.

01

If he _____ the game, he would buy us dinner.

① won   ② win   ③ wins
④ has won   ⑤ have won

02

This doll looks as if it _____ alive.

① was   ② has been   ③ being
④ were   ⑤ been

03

If you _____ to Paris, you must visit the Eiffel Tower.

① went   ② have been ③ will go
④ have gone ⑤ go

04~05 다음 빈칸에 공통으로 들어갈 말로 알맞은 것을 고르시오.

04

1. _____ you are a student, you should study hard.
2. You look _____ if you liked Mary.

① If[if]   ② So[so]
③ When[when]   ④ As[as]
⑤ Because[because]

05

1. If I _____ a chance, I wouldn't have missed it.
2. I wish I _____ a bicycle when I was young.

① had given   ② had had
③ have had   ④ have
⑤ have given

06~08 다음 빈칸에 들어갈 말이 바르게 짝지어진 것을 고르시오.

06

1. If I _____ your ring, I would call you.
2. I wish I _____ a dog.

① find – had   ② found – have
③ found – had   ④ find – had
⑤ will find – have

07

1. If you _____ her, you would change your mind.
2. If she _____ tired, she would sleep.

① knew – were   ② knew – was
③ know – is   ④ know – were
⑤ knows – was

08

If I _____ the fire, I _____ 119.

① saw – called
② have seen – called
③ have seen – called
④ had seen – have called
⑤ had seen – would have called

11

만약 그 가방이 비싸지 않다면, 내가 살 수 있을
텐데.

① If the bag wasn't expensive, I could buy
it.
② If the bag wasn't expensive, I could
have bought it.
③ If the bag weren't expensive, I could
have bought it.
④ If the bag weren't expensive, I could
buy it.
⑤ If the bag hasn't been expensive, I
could have bought it.

09~11 다음 우리말을 영어로 바르게 옮긴 것을 고르시오.

09

내가 그를 도와줄 수 있다면 좋을 텐데.

① I wish I will help him.
② I wish I could have helped him.
③ I wish I would help him.
④ I wish I could help him.
⑤ I wish I had helped him.

12 다음 중 밑줄 친 단어의 쓰임이 나머지 넷과 <u>다른</u> 것은?

① I wish I <u>were</u> beautiful.
② I could wear this dress if I <u>were</u> taller.
③ If you <u>were</u> brave, you could save the
dog.
④ They behave as if they <u>were</u> animals.
⑤ We <u>were</u> frightened as we heard the
story.

13~14 다음 문장을 가정법으로 바르게 옮긴 것을 고르시오.

13

As I'm not good at running, I want to
run as fast as Minho does.

① I wish I run as fast as Minho.
② I wish I can run as fast as Minho.
③ I wish I could run as fast as Minho.
④ I wish I could have run as fast as Minho.
⑤ I wish I ran as fast as Minho.

10

그녀는 마치 나를 잘 아는 것처럼 말한다.

① She talks as if she had known me well.
② She talked as if she knew me well.
③ She talks as if she knew me well.
④ She talked as if she had known me well.
⑤ She talks as if she knows me well.

14

Because she doesn't understand the question, she can't answer.

① If she understands the question, she can answer.

② If she understood the question, she can answer.

③ If she understood the question, she could answer.

④ If she had understood the question, she could have answered.

⑤ If she had understood the question, she could answer.

15 다음 중 문장의 앞뒤 연결이 의미상 어색한 것은?

① I don't like Jack because he is very rude. I wish he weren't so rude.

② I miss my grandmother who passed away last month. I wish I could see her again.

③ There is a new movie. But I don't have time. I wish I had time to watch it.

④ I can't eat peanuts because I'm allergic to them. I wish I could eat them.

⑤ I'm so busy now. I wish I had not been so busy.

16 다음 중 어법상 올바른 것은?

① If you are here, I could take you to the river.

② He's looking at me as if he doesn't know me.

③ If she didn't have her son, she would be sad.

④ I wish I had been in Europe now.

⑤ He describes the river as if he is there.

17~18 다음 중 어법상 어색한 것을 고르시오.

17 ① If I had won, they would have been happy.

② I wish I could drink some cold juice.

③ If I could visit Disneyland, I would be excited.

④ He talks as if he became the king.

⑤ She looks as if she is alone here.

18 ① If it didn't snow, we could go outside.

② If I had the accident, I wouldn't be alive.

③ If you looked here, you would have found it.

④ I wish to quit my job because I'm too tired.

⑤ He always talks as if he were smart.

19 다음 밑줄 친 ⓐ~ⓔ 중 어법상 어색한 것을 모두 고르시오.

If I ⓐ had known him better, I ⓑ wouldn't had let him ⓒ did the job. I promise I ⓓ will never have him ⓔ do it again.

① ⓐ ② ⓑ ③ ⓒ ④ ⓓ ⑤ ⓔ

20 다음 두 문장의 뜻이 서로 같지 <u>않은</u> 것은?

① a) As you can't come inside, you have to wait here.
   b) If you could come inside, you wouldn't have to wait here.

② a) She isn't pretty, but she speaks like she is.
   b) She speaks as if she were pretty.

③ a) You can't get good scores unless you study hard.
   b) If you studied hard, you couldn't get good scores.

④ a) I didn't eat anything, and I am hungry now.
   b) I wish I had eaten something.

⑤ a) Clean your room, or you can't eat dinner.
   b) If you clean your room, you can eat dinner.

21 다음 중 어법상 바르게 고치지 <u>못한</u> 것은?

① I wish I <u>can watch</u> TV right now.
       (→ had watch)

② I would <u>have thanked</u> Sam if I met him.
       (→ thank)

③ If I <u>have</u> a pen, I could write a memo.
      (→ had)

④ If I <u>have</u> a bicycle, I could go to school faster.
      (→ had)

⑤ Kai acts as if <u>doesn't eat</u> my bread.
       (→ hadn't eaten)

22 다음 중 어법상 올바른 문장의 개수는?

ⓐ If I were your mom, I would let you go.
ⓑ I wish I could go to the gym and exercise.
ⓒ I would have given it to you if I had it.
ⓓ I wish he would not lie about the test.

① 없음 ② 1개 ③ 2개 ④ 3개 ⑤ 4개

23 다음 중 어법상 <u>어색한</u> 문장의 개수는?

ⓐ If he jumped as highly as possible, he could touch the ceiling.
ⓑ He looks as if he liked me very much.
ⓒ I wish my novel were finished.
ⓓ If I had a passport, I could have traveled to another country.

① 없음 ② 1개 ③ 2개 ④ 3개 ⑤ 4개

24 다음 대화의 빈칸에 들어갈 말이 바르게 짝지어진 것은?

A: Did you hear that Sora went to Jeju?
B: Wow, I envy her. I wish I ___(A)___ in Jeju, too!
A: What would you do if you ___(B)___ to Jeju?
B: I ___(C)___ go to the beach and swim. How about you?
A: I would climb Halla Mountain and eat delicious food.

	(A)	(B)	(C)
①	were	went	would
②	was	had gone	would
③	were	have gone	would
④	were	had gone	will
⑤	was	went	will

25 다음 글의 밑줄 친 ⓐ~ⓔ 중 어법상 어색한 것은?

My best friend Noah moved to another city. Because ⓐ we were always together, I feel lonely without him. ⓑ I really wish he were here. ⓒ If his place were near, I would visit him on weekends. But his place is too far from here. So we talk a lot on the phone. On the phone, ⓓ he talks as if he doesn't miss me. But actually, ⓔ he calls me more than I call him.

① ⓐ   ② ⓑ   ③ ⓒ   ④ ⓓ   ⑤ ⓔ

26~27 다음 우리말과 일치하도록 괄호 안의 말을 이용하여 문장을 완성하시오.

26 Sarah는 춤을 잘 추는 것처럼 보인다. (be)
Sarah looks as if she _____ good at dancing.

27 만약 엄마가 내가 뭘 했는지 아신다면, 매우 화를 내실 거다. (know, be)
If my mom _____ what I have done, she _____ really mad.

28~31 다음 문장의 빈칸에 |보기|에서 알맞은 말을 골라 쓰시오. (단, |보기|의 말은 한 번씩만 쓸 것)

┌ 보기 ┐
would   if   as   could
└─────┘

28 I wish I _____ go with you now.

29 _____ I had time, I would help you.

30 _____ I didn't have money, I couldn't buy the jacket.

31 I _____ visit my grandmother if I went to Sokcho.

32~34 다음 우리말과 일치하도록 괄호 안의 말을 바르게 배열하시오.

32
내가 더 건강했었다면 좋았을 텐데.
(I, been, healthier, wish, I, had)

_____

_____

33
내가 그의 집이 어딘지 안다면, 지금 거기 갈 텐데.
(I, where, would, I, if, knew, is, now, his house, go there)

_____

_____

34

> 나의 집이 더 컸었다면, 나는 큰 개를 키울 수 있었을 텐데.
> (bigger, could, my house, been, a big dog, have, had, if, raised, I)

_____

_____

35~37 다음 문장을 주어진 표현으로 시작하는 가정법으로 바꿔 쓰시오.

35 Because he spent too much money, he became poor.

→ If _____

_____

36 Today is Monday, but I hope it's Friday.

→ I wish _____

_____

37 As it rained a lot, we canceled the game.

→ If _____

_____

38~39 다음 두 문장의 의미가 같도록 문장을 완성하시오.

38 He's so young that he can't play with his sisters. (older 이용)

= If he _____

_____

---

39 I didn't save enough money to buy the pants.

= I wish I _____

_____

40~44 다음 문장에서 어법상 어색한 부분을 찾아 바르게 고치시오.

40 I would pay for dinner if I had had money now.

_____ → _____

41 If you sleep over tonight, I tell you the story.

_____ → _____

42 I wish I met him there yesterday.

_____ → _____

43 The cat walks as if it is a tiger.

_____ → _____

44 If we had caught the bus, we would have been late.

_____ → _____

45~46 다음 문장에서 어법상 어색한 부분을 고쳐 완전한 문장을 쓰시오.

45 He talks as if he didn't do anything wrong before.

→ _____

_____

46 If I had left early yesterday, I could meet you.

→ _____

_____

47 다음 문장이 어법상 어색하지 않으면 ◯를, 어색한 부분이 있으면 밑줄을 치고 바르게 고치시오.

(1) If she wasn't sick, she could go skiing.

→ _____

(2) If you can have one superpower, what would you choose?

→ _____

(3) If you don't run, you will miss the train.

→ _____

48~49 주어진 |조건|을 이용하여 우리말을 영어로 옮기시오.

48 ┤조건├
1) if를 사용할 것
2) 단어 the weather, be, good, go fishing을 필요하면 활용하여 쓸 것
3) 9단어를 사용할 것

만약 날씨가 좋으면, 나는 낚시하러 갈 수 있을 텐데.

_____

_____

49 ┤조건├
1) as if를 사용할 것
2) 단어 act, be, a detective를 필요하면 활용하여 쓸 것
3) 9단어를 사용할 것

그는 마치 탐정이었던 것처럼 행동한다.

_____

_____

50 다음 글의 밑줄 친 ⓐ~ⓔ 중 어법상 어색한 것을 골라 기호를 쓰고 바르게 고치시오.

My dream was to become a writer, but my parents wanted me to be a soldier. Now I'm a soldier, but sometimes ⓐ I wish I had kept writing when I was young. If I could go back, ⓑ I would have become a writer. The funny thing is that ⓒ my son acts as if he were a writer! I told him to become whatever he wants to be. ⓓ I will just support him if he is happy with his job. ⓔ I expect to see my children enjoying their life.

_____ → _____

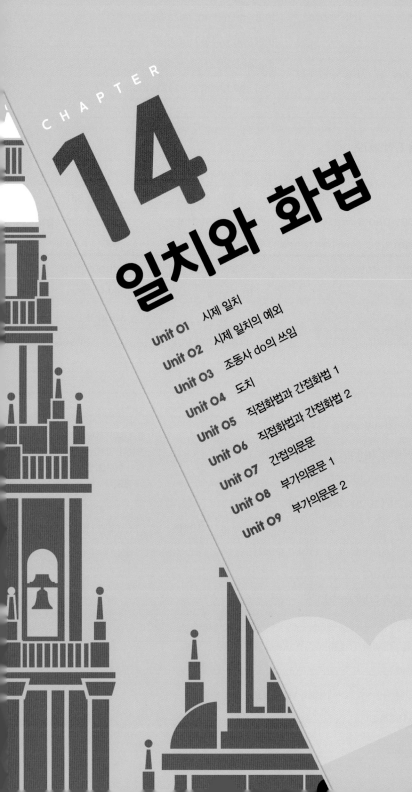

14
일치와 화법

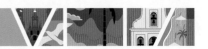

주절의 시제와 종속절의 시제의 기본적인 관계를 알아 두세요.

주절 시제	종속절의 시제		예문
현재	모든 시제 가능	He knows	that you are honest.
			that you did not tell a lie.
			that you will tell the truth.
과거	과거나 과거완료 가능	He thought	that she was in London.
			that she had gone to London.

|A| 주절의 시제를 과거로 바꿔서 문장을 완성하시오.

01 I know why you feel sad.　　　　→ I _____ why you _____ sad.

02 She says that she heard you sing.　→ She _____ that she _____ you sing.

03 He tells us that there are many parks. → He _____ us that there _____ many parks.

04 The teacher finds out that I am sick.　→ The teacher _____ that I _____ sick.

05 We believe that we will win the game. → We _____ that we _____ the game.

06 I hope that you are alive.　　　　　→ I _____ that you _____ alive.

07 Gary thinks you left without a word.　→ Gary _____ you _____ without a word.

08 I am afraid that you may be absent.　→ I _____ afraid that you _____ absent.

|B| 우리말과 일치하도록 괄호 안의 말을 이용하여 문장을 완성하시오.

01 그는 테니스 클럽 활동이 흥미롭다고 생각했다. (think, be, interesting)

He _____ that the tennis club activity _____.

02 나는 버스가 부산으로 떠났다는 것을 알았다. (know, leave for)

I _____ that the bus _____ Busan.

03 나는 모든 선수들이 최선을 다했다고 믿는다. (believe, do their best)

I _____ that all the players _____.

04 우리는 네가 성공할 것이라고 확신한다. (be, succeed)

We _____ sure that you _____.

05 Teddy는 자기가 실수를 했다는 것을 깨달았다. (realize, make a mistake)

Teddy _____ that he _____.

06 우리는 그 축제가 매년 열린다는 것을 안다. (know, be held, yearly)

We _____ that the festival _____.

종속절의 시제가 주절의 시제보다 앞서는지, 혹은 동일한지 여부를 먼저 따져 보아야 해요.

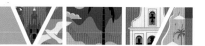

항상 현재시제를 쓰는 경우와 항상 과거시제를 쓰는 경우에 유의하세요.

항상 현재	진리, 사실, 속담, 현재의 습관 등	He knew that the Earth is round.	둥글다는 것을 알았다.
		He told us that he likes to draw pictures.	좋아한다고 말했다.
		She said that blood is thicker than water.	더 진하다고 말했다.
항상 과거	역사적 사실	I will learn how Armstrong landed on the moon.	어떻게 착륙했는지 배울 거다.

|A| 문장에서 어법상 어색한 부분을 찾아 밑줄 긋고 바르게 고치시오.

01 The little children learned that leaves turned red in autumn.   → _____

02 I didn't know why Jane is angry at me.   → _____

03 The teacher said that the Korean War had broken out in 1950.   → _____

04 We learned that water froze at 0 ℃.   → _____

05 My grandma said that good medicine was bitter in the mouth.   → _____

06 The boy didn't know that oil and water did not mix.   → _____

07 I believed that a rolling stone gathered no moss.   → _____

|B| 주절의 시제를 과거로 바꿔서 문장을 완성하시오.

주절의 시제와는 상관없이 항상 현재시제 또는 과거시제로 써야 하는 경우들을 알아야 해요.

01 We know that Shakespeare wrote about 37 plays.

→ We _____.

02 We learn that the biggest planet is Jupiter.

→ We _____.

03 The students learn that Mount Everest is the tallest mountain.

→ The students _____.

04 We find out that a spider has eight legs.

→ We _____.

05 The newspaper says that Dokdo is a Korean island.

→ The newspaper _____.

06 It says that Queen Victoria became queen at the age of 18.

→ It _____.

실전 TIP

우리가 배운 시점보다 훨씬 이전에 일어난 일이지만 역사적 사실은 항상 과거로 표현해야 해요.

내신 기출 문장에서 어법상 어색한 부분을 찾아 고치시오.

We learned that Christopher Columbus had discovered America in 1492.

UNIT 03 조동사 do의 쓰임

do는 조동사로도 쓰일 수 있다는 것을 알아 두세요.

do의 쓰임		예문	주의
본동사	~하다	He does his homework.	그는 숙제를 한다.
조동사	강조 (정말)	He does study hard.	주어/시제에 맞게 do/does/did+동사원형
	부정문	He does not study hard.	주어/시제에 맞게 do/does/did+not+동사원형
	의문문	Does he study hard?	주어/시제에 맞게 Do/Does/Did+주어+동사원형 ~?

참고 조동사가 있는 문장에는 항상 동사원형을 써요.

|A| 문장의 밑줄 친 do/does/did와 역할이 같은 것을 |보기|에서 찾아 알맞은 기호를 쓰시오.

┌─보기─────────────────────────────────────┐
│ I always do my best. [ⓐ]   I do love you. [ⓑ] │
└──┘

01 I will do the cleaning today.   [   ]

02 My dad does his business in Canada.   [   ]

03 Children do love playing in the yard.   [   ]

04 I did try to break the bad habit.   [   ]

05 She learned how to do the work.   [   ]

06 Amy does hate eating vegetables.   [   ]

07 Jessica did like the history book.   [   ]

|B| 우리말과 일치하도록 조동사 do와 괄호 안의 말을 이용하여 문장을 완성하시오.

주어의 인칭과 시제에 유의하여 do의 형태를 결정해야 해요.

01 그는 소란을 피우지 않기 위해 정말 노력했다. (try to, not)

He _____ make any noise.

02 할머니의 음식은 정말로 맛있는 냄새가 났다. (smell)

My grandma's food _____ delicious.

03 나는 정말로 항상 우리 부모님을 신뢰한다. (trust, always)

I _____ my parents.

04 우리 아빠와 삼촌은 정말로 겨울 낚시를 좋아한다. (like)

My dad and uncle _____ fishing in winter.

05 우리 모두는 사랑의 힘을 정말 믿는다. (believe in)

We all _____ the power of love.

06 그 볶음밥은 정말로 너무 매웠다. (taste)

The fried rice _____ spicy.

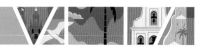

부사(구)나 전치사구를 강조하기 위해 문장 앞에 쓸 때, 그 뒤는 〈동사+주어〉의 어순으로 도치시키세요.

문장 앞에 쓰는 말	도치: 〈부사(구)+동사+주어〉	다양한 강조의 의미
Here / There	Here comes the bus.	(드디어, 이제) 버스가 온다.
	There goes the last bus.	(이런) 마지막 버스가 가는구나.
전치사구	Across the street is the shop.	길 건너편이 그 가게야.
	Down the hill ran the boy.	언덕 아래로 그 소년이 뛰었어.

😊 참고 도치구문은 문맥에 따라 유연하게 해석하도록 하세요.

😟 주의 Here나 There의 경우, 주어가 대명사일 때는 그대로 〈주어+동사〉가 돼요.

Here it comes.   There it goes.

|A| 밑줄 친 부분을 강조하는 도치구문으로 바꿔 쓰시오.

01 The baby played under a tree. → _____ .

02 The bank is behind the tower. → _____ .

03 The bird is on my shoulder. → _____ .

04 The dog hid under the bed. → _____ .

05 The children walked up the hill. → _____ .

06 Our school bus went there. → _____ .

07 She comes there. → _____ .

|B| 괄호 안의 말을 바르게 배열하여 부사구를 강조하는 도치 문장을 쓰시오.

01 원숭이 한 마리가 군중 속으로 뛰어갔다. (ran, a monkey, into, the crowd)

_____

02 하늘에 무지개가 있다. (in, a rainbow, is, the sky)

_____

03 달이 구름 뒤로 사라졌다. (the moon, behind, the clouds, disappeared)

_____

04 인천행 마지막 버스가 저기에 간다. (for Incheon, the last bus, there, goes)

_____

05 우리 텐트는 산 정상에 있었다. (our tent, at the top, was, of the mountain)

_____

06 다리 아래로 한강이 흐른다. (the Han River, under, flows, the bridge)

_____

직접화법의 문장을 간접화법으로 바꿔 쓸 때 다음 단계에 따라 고쳐 쓰세요.

직접화법	Jinsu said to me, "You look so tired now."	
step 1	전달 동사 바꾸기	say to me → told me / say → say
step 2	따옴표(" ")를 없애고 that절로 쓰기	*that은 생략 가능
step 3	that절의 주어를 전달자의 입장으로 바꾸기	"You" → "I"
step 4	시제를 전달자의 입장으로 바꾸기	"look" → looked *said와 같은 시제
step 5	시간, 장소 부사(구)를 전달자의 입장으로 바꾸기	"now" → then
간접화법	Jinsu told me (that) I looked so tired then.	

 직접화법은 있는 그대로 전달하는 것이고, 간접화법은 전달자의 입장으로 고쳐 쓴 말이에요.
→ 전달자의 입장에서는 You가 I이며, look이 looked가 돼요.

 간접화법으로 바꿔 쓸 때 주의해야 할 시제 및 부사(구)를 알아 두세요.

전달 동사의 시제	현재(say)	따옴표 안의 동사 = 간접화법 that절의 동사
	과거(said)	현재 → 과거 / 과거 → 과거완료 / 현재완료 → 과거완료

now → then	today → that day	tonight → that night
this[these] → that[those]	here → there	ago → before
yesterday → the previous day / the day before	tomorrow → the next day / the following day	last night → the previous night / the night before

---

|A| 문장을 간접화법으로 바꿀 때 빈칸에 알맞은 말을 쓰시오.

01 She said, "I will go tomorrow." → She said that she would go ＿＿＿＿＿＿＿＿.

02 He said, "I like this robot." → He said that he liked ＿＿＿＿＿＿＿＿ robot.

03 My dad said, "I will stay here." → My dad said that he would stay ＿＿＿＿＿＿＿＿.

04 The girl said, "I am hungry now." → The girl said that she was hungry ＿＿＿＿＿＿＿＿.

|B| 문장을 간접화법으로 바꾸시오.

01 Joy said to me, "I want you to join me."
→ Joy ＿＿＿＿＿＿＿＿ that ＿＿＿＿＿＿＿＿＿＿＿＿.

02 Ms. Lee said to us, "I am happy with your present."
→ Ms. Lee ＿＿＿＿＿＿＿＿ that ＿＿＿＿＿＿＿＿＿＿＿＿.

03 Lisa said, "I have to change my clothes."
→ Lisa ＿＿＿＿＿＿＿＿ that ＿＿＿＿＿＿＿＿＿＿＿＿.

04 He said, "I got up at seven this morning."

→ He _____ that _____.

05 They said, "We enjoyed the party."

→ They _____ that _____.

06 My aunt said to me, "I like your painting."

→ My aunt _____ that _____.

|C| 문장을 직접화법으로 바꾸시오.

01 She told me that she had had a heavy lunch.

→ She _____, "_____."

02 Emily said that she could pass the test that day.

→ Emily _____, "_____."

03 The guests said that they didn't like that food.

→ The guests _____, "_____."

04 Dan told us that he would go to France the following week.

→ Dan _____, "_____."

💬 직접화법의 next week[month]는 간접화법에서 the following week[month]로 써요.

05 He told me that he was sorry for being rude.

→ He _____, "_____."

06 The lady told me that she had seen me on TV the previous night.

→ The lady _____, "_____."

|D| 문장에서 어법상 어색한 부분을 찾아 밑줄 긋고 바르게 고치시오.

01 The teacher said that *Hangeul* had been invented in 1443.　　　→ _____

02 The player said that he can win the game that night.　　　→ _____

03 My friend said me that she would visit her grandparents.　　　→ _____

04 Joanne told us that she has met her favorite singer.　　　→ _____

실전 TIP 🎓

간접화법으로 바꿀 때 시제
일치에 신경 써야 해요.

내신 기출 다음 중 문장 전환이 올바르지 않은 것은?

① The man said, "It'll take ten minutes from now."

→ The man said that it would take ten minutes from then.

② Somi said, "I'll visit China next week."

→ Somi said that she would visit China the following week.

③ Maria said to me, "I'm going to a movie."

→ Maria told me that she is going to a movie.

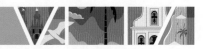
의문문을 간접화법으로 바꿔 쓸 때는 다음 단계에 따라 고쳐 쓰세요.

직접화법	She said to him, "Where do you live now?"	
step 1	전달동사를 ask로 바꾸기	said → asked / said to him → asked him
step 2	that을 쓰지 않고, 의문사를 접속사로 쓰기	asked him where
step 3	의문사 뒤에 〈주어+동사〉의 어순으로 쓰기	asked him where (you live)
step 4	의문사 없는 의문문은 if/whether를 쓰기	asked him if/whether ~ (~인지 아닌지 물었다)
step 5	주어, 동사, 부사(구)를 전달자의 입장으로 바꾸기	"you" → he, "live" → lived, "now" → then
간접화법	She asked him where he lived then.	

주의 의문사가 없는 의문문은 접속사 if나 whether를 쓴다는 것에 주의하세요.

직접화법	He said to me, "Have you been to Busan?" "부산에 가 본 적 있어?"라고 말했다.
간접화법	He asked me if[whether] I had been to Busan. 부산에 가 본 적이 있냐고 물었다.

|A| 문장에서 어법상 어색한 부분을 찾아 밑줄 긋고 바르게 고치시오.

01 The teacher asked me if I have the book. → _____

02 She asked me whether I will go to the meeting. → _____

03 My mom asked me who can come to my party. → _____

04 The girl asked me how tired was I. → _____

05 The man told whether I felt tired. → _____

06 The lady asked me who helped me the previous day. → _____

07 He asked me that I could lend him my pen. → _____

08 The foreigner asked her what time was it. → _____

|B| 문장을 간접화법으로 바꾸시오.

01 The woman said to me, "Why did you choose this school?"

→ The woman _____ me _____.

02 Our teacher said, "Who is making a noise now?"

→ Our teacher _____.

03 He said to Jane, "May I sit next to you?"

→ He _____ Jane _____.

04 She said to me, "What are you interested in?"

→ She _____ me _____.

05 Helena said to me, "Did you get your hair cut?"

→ Helena _____ me _____ .

06 The man said to us, "How long are you staying here?"

→ The man _____ us _____ .

|C| 문장을 직접화법으로 바꾸시오.

01 My mom asked us what we were doing then.

→ My mom said to us, "_____?"

02 Anna asked me whether I liked my school.

→ Anna said to me, "_____?"

03 He asked me if my family was doing well.

→ He said to me, "_____?"

04 Joanne asked us where we were planning to visit.

→ Joanne said to us, "_____?"

05 She asked me who made me feel angry.

→ She said to me, "_____?"

06 I asked him how I could get to the bank.

→ I said to him, "_____?"

07 My dad asked me if I had finished my homework.

→ My dad said to me, "_____?"

|D| 우리말과 일치하도록 괄호 안의 말을 이용하여 문장을 완성하시오.

01 선생님은 내게 중국어를 배운 적이 있는지 물어보셨다. (learn Chinese)

The teacher asked me _____ .

02 그녀는 내게 점심으로 무엇을 먹는지 물었다. (have, for lunch)

She asked me _____ .

03 그는 내게 그 멕시코 음식을 즐겼는지 물었다. (the Mexican food, enjoy)

He asked me _____ .

04 나는 그 남자에게 내가 언제 다음 버스를 탈 수 있는지 물었다. (get the next bus)

I asked the man _____ .

05 그녀는 내게 그 케이크가 맛있는지 물었다. (taste good)

She asked me _____ .

06 의사 선생님은 그녀에게 약을 먹었는지 물어보셨다. (take the medicine)

The doctor asked her _____ .

UNIT 07 간접의문문

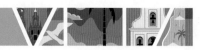

의문사 의문문을 평서문 어순으로 써서 '~인지 말해 줘', '~인지 궁금해'와 같이 쓰세요.

의문사 여부	직접의문문	간접의문문	
의문사 있음	Where <u>did</u> <u>you</u> stay?	Tell me where <u>you</u> <u>stayed</u>.	어디 묵었는지 말해 줘.
		I wonder where <u>you</u> stayed.	어디 묵었는지 궁금해.
의문사 없음	<u>Did</u> <u>you</u> <u>stay</u> here?	Tell me if <u>you</u> <u>stayed</u> here.	여기 묵었는지 아닌지 말해 줘.
		I wonder whether <u>you</u> <u>stayed</u> here.	여기 묵었는지 아닌지 궁금해

주의 의문사가 없는 의문문은 if/whether를 써서 간접의문문을 만들어요.
의문사가 주어인 경우에는 어순이 바뀌지 않아요. She wanted to know <u>who</u> wrote the essay.

생각이나 추측을 나타내는 동사(think, believe, imagine, guess, suppose)의 간접의문문에 주의하세요.

직접의문문	think, believe suppose, guess 등의 동사가 있는 간접의문문	
Where did you stay?	Do you **think** ~~where he stayed~~? (X)	
	Where do you **think** he stayed? (O)	그가 어디에 묵었다고 생각해?
Who is she?	Do you **suppose** ~~who she is~~? (X)	
	Who <u>do you</u> **suppose** she is? (O)	그녀가 누구라고 추측해?

|A| 두 문장을 한 문장으로 연결하여 간접의문문을 만들 때, 빈칸에 알맞은 말을 쓰시오.

종속절에 조동사가 있는 경우에 유의하세요.

01 Please tell me. + Are you ready?

→ Please tell me _____.

02 Let me know. + How old are you?

→ Let me know _____.

03 My teacher knows. + What is this book about?

→ My teacher knows _____.

04 Could you tell me? + How will you fix this problem?

→ Please tell me _____.

|B| 두 문장을 한 문장으로 연결하시오.

01 Do you think? + What is it?　　　　　　→ _____?

02 Do you believe? + Who can help you?　　→ _____?

03 Do you think? + How can I keep warm?　→ _____?

04 Do you suppose? + What time will she arrive? → _____?

05 Do you think? + Where did you lose the bag?　→ _____?

06 Do you guess? + Why is this not working?　→ _____?

|C| 우리말과 일치하도록 괄호 안의 말을 바르게 배열하여 문장을 완성하시오.

01 너는 어제 Thomas에게 무슨 일이 일어났는지 아니? (know, you, do, what, happened)

_____ to Thomas yesterday?

02 내가 어디에서 하차해야 하는지 내게 말해 줘. (tell, where, me, please, should, I, get)

_____ off.

03 의사 선생님은 내가 왜 열이 나는지 알고 계셨다. (why, the doctor, I, knew, had)

_____ a fever.

04 나는 Sam이 내 선물을 좋아할지 잘 모르겠다. (will, not, I'm, whether, Sam, like, sure)

_____ my present.

05 그를 어디에서 마지막으로 봤는지 내게 얘기해 줄 수 있겠니? (tell, you, where, you, can, me, saw)

_____ him last?

06 나는 네가 나를 얼마나 사랑하는지 궁금해. (wonder, how much, love, you, I)

_____ me.

07 그가 약속을 지킬지는 의문이다. (doubtful, is, it, if, keep, will, he)

_____ his promise.

08 내일 날씨가 화창할지는 아무도 모른다. (knows, will, the weather, no one, if, be)

_____ sunny tomorrow.

|D| 문장에서 어법상 어색한 부분을 찾아 밑줄 긋고 바르게 고치시오.

01 Please tell me why did you tell me a lie.　→ _____

02 How do you think old I am?　→ _____

03 When do you know she learned how to swim?　→ _____

04 I told him where he would stay during the summer.　→ _____

05 Do you believe who he is?　→ _____

실전 TIP
생각이나 추측을 나타내는 동사들만 간접의문문의 의문사가 문장 맨 앞으로 갈 수 있어요.

내신 기출 다음 중 문장 전환이 바르지 않은 것은?

① Do you think? + When can we eat lunch?
　→ When do you think we can eat lunch?
② Do you guess? + What is she watching now?
　→ What do you guess she is watching now?
③ Could you tell me? + Why did you change your mind?
　→ Why could you tell me you changed your mind?

UNIT 08 부가의문문 1

평서문 뒤에 '그렇지?' 또는 '그렇지 않니?'라고 확인을 구하는 부가의문문의 사용법을 알아 두세요.

	평서문,	+ 부가의문문	예문
be동사	긍정	+ 부정 의문 be동사	She <u>is</u> wise, isn't she?
	부정	+ 긍정 의문 be동사	She isn't wise, <u>is</u> she?
일반동사	긍정	+ 부정 의문 do동사	She **has** a bike, doesn't she?
	부정	+ 긍정 의문 do동사	She <u>doesn't have</u> a bike, does she?

주의 대답은 긍정이면 무조건 Yes, 부정이면 무조건 No로 해야 해요.

A: She is wise, isn't she?

B: Yes, she is. (현명함) / No, she isn't. (현명하지 않음)

|A| 빈칸에 알맞은 부가의문문을 쓰시오.

01 Emily is a really good student, _____?

02 You skipped breakfast, _____?

03 The children don't like kimchi, _____?

04 You are not afraid of dogs, _____?

05 Dad always works late, _____?

06 This soup tastes good, _____?

07 The performance was fantastic, _____?

08 His mom and dad are American, _____?

|B| 부가의문문과 그에 맞는 대답으로 대화를 완성하시오.

부가의문문이 부정문 형태일 때는 항상 축약형으로만 써야 해요.

01 **A**: Your mom works at a hospital, _____?

   B: _____. She is a teacher.

02 **A**: You were not surprised by the news, _____?

   B: _____. The news was very shocking.

03 **A**: These shoes are not yours, _____?

   B: _____. They are my sister's shoes.

04 **A**: You were sick yesterday, _____?

   B: _____. I had a fever.

05 **A**: Amanda didn't come to the party, _____?

   B: _____. She was busy.

06 **A**: Those books are written in English, _____?

   B: _____. They are written in Korean.

UNIT 09 부가의문문 2

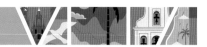

조동사가 있는 문장이나, 명령문, 청유문의 부가의문문을 만드는 방법에 유의하세요.

	평서문,	+ 부가의문문	예문
조동사	긍정	+ 부정 의문 조동사	She **can ride** a bike, can't she?
	부정	+ 긍정 의문 조동사	She **can't ride** a bike, can she?
명령문	긍정	will you?	**Be** quiet, will you?
	부정		Don't touch it, will you?
청유문	긍정	shall we?	Let's start the game, shall we?
	부정		Let's not do it, shall we?

주의 부가의문문에서 am의 부정은 aren't로 한다는 것에 주의하세요. I **am** too late, aren't I?

|A| 빈칸에 알맞은 부가의문문을 쓰시오.

01 You will join the club, _____?

02 She should not go out now, _____?

03 He can swim in the sea, _____?

04 Be careful of cars, _____?

05 You can't speak Spanish, _____?

06 Let's go there, _____?

07 We should wait, _____?

08 Pay attention to him, _____?

|B| 우리말과 일치하도록 괄호 안의 말을 이용하여 문장을 완성하시오.

01 우리는 마지막 버스를 탈 수 있어, 그렇지 않니? (can, catch)

_____ the last bus, _____?

02 나는 정말 똑똑해, 그렇지 않아? (so, smart)

I am _____, _____?

03 너희들은 여기에서 축구를 하면 안 돼, 그렇지 않니? (should, play soccer)

_____ here, _____?

04 우리 그 문제에 대해서는 얘기하지 말자, 어때? (talk about)

_____ the problem, _____?

05 좀 더 인내심을 가져, 알겠니? (more patient)

_____, _____?

명령문은 주어 you가 생략돼 있는 형태이므로, 부가의문문의 주어는 항상 you를 사용해요.

실전 TIP
부가의문문의 동사와 인칭대명사를 하나씩 확인하세요.

내신 기출 다음 중 어법상 옳은 문장은?

① You and your sister love swimming, isn't they?
② They will not go shopping on the weekend, will they?
③ Your brother didn't go on a picnic with you, did you?

중간고사·기말고사 실전문제

학년과 반	이름	객관식	/ 25문항	주관식	/ 25문항

01~03 다음 빈칸에 들어갈 말로 알맞은 것을 고르시오.

01

> She is worried about me, _____ she?

① is
② isn't
③ who
④ will
⑤ does

02

> I told mom that I _____ in my room.

① were
② would
③ will be
④ was
⑤ am

03

> I _____ like to go swimming a lot.

① will
② want
③ do
④ could
⑤ am

04~06 다음 빈칸에 들어갈 말이 바르게 짝지어진 것을 고르시오.

04

> 1. Do you know who _____ on the moon first?
> 2. I heard the news _____ false.

① lands - is
② landed - were
③ landed - was
④ lands - is
⑤ land - was

05

> She _____ me that he _____ come to the party.

① told - will
② will tell - does
③ tell - hadn't
④ has told - does
⑤ told - wouldn't

06

> 1. He said that he _____ going to take a trip to Europe.
> 2. I will tell you _____ is going to visit us.

① was - who
② would - who
③ is - she
④ did - whom
⑤ will - that

07~08 다음 빈칸에 공통으로 들어갈 말로 알맞은 것을 고르시오.

07

> 1. He acts as _____ he liked me.
> 2. Can you tell me _____ you can join our club?

① which
② that
③ if
④ so
⑤ who

08

> A: I'm too short, _____ I?
> B: No, you _____ short. You look perfect!

① were   ② are   ③ am
④ weren't   ⑤ aren't

11 다음 대화의 빈칸에 알맞은 것은?

> A: Do you know _____?
> B: Yes, it is written on her notebook.

① how her name wrote
② what her name is
③ which is her name
④ what is her name
⑤ whether her name is

09~10 다음 우리말을 영어로 바르게 옮긴 것을 고르시오.

09

> 나는 그녀가 몇 시에 떠날 예정인지 궁금해.

① I wonder what time she is going to leave.
② I wonder what time is she going to leave.
③ I wonder her what time is going to leave.
④ I wonder what time is going her to leave.
⑤ I wonder she is going to leave what time.

12 다음 밑줄 친 if의 쓰임이 나머지 넷과 다른 것은?

① I wonder if he eats dinner or not.
② He asked me if I could ride a horse.
③ She can't tell if he finished his homework.
④ He will call you if he comes home.
⑤ I'm not certain if I can go out tonight.

13~14 다음 문장을 간접 화법으로 바꿀 때, 빈칸에 알맞은 것을 고르시오.

13

> He said to me, "I'm going to your house now."
> → He _____.

① told that I was going to your house then
② said to me to go to my house then
③ said that he was going to my house now
④ told me to go to my house now
⑤ told me that he was going to my house then

10

> 그는 내게 그날 그의 의자를 돌려 달라고 말했다.

① He told me, "Return my chair that day."
② He said, "Return my chair today."
③ He said to me, "I returned your chair."
④ He told me to return his chair that day.
⑤ He told me to return my chair that day.

14

> Jane said, "I'll visit his house tomorrow."
> → Jane _____.

① told that she will visit his house tomorrow

② said that she visited his house the next day

③ said that she will visit his house the next day

④ said that she would visit his house the next day

⑤ told that she would visit his house the next day

15 다음 두 문장을 한 문장으로 바르게 연결한 것은?

> Do you think? + When did she arrive?

① Do you think when she did arrive?

② Do you think when she arrived?

③ When do you think she arrived?

④ When do you think she did arrive?

⑤ When you think she arrived?

16 다음 중 어법상 올바른 것은?

① I did practiced hard so that I could win the game.

② That movie which we just saw was really wonderful, isn't it?

③ Helen asked me to bring her bag when I visited her in the hospital.

④ Mr. Kim told that the World War II had started in 1939.

⑤ How come did you break the window?

[17~18] 다음 중 어법상 어색한 것을 고르시오.

17 ① She enjoy the event very much, doesn't she?

② Can you tell me how the fight started?

③ You liked to see stars at night, didn't you?

④ I don't understand why he told the secret.

⑤ I realized that she had gone by herself.

18 ① I'm calling the man whom I met yesterday.

② Do you remember what he was wearing?

③ I learned that a lizard regrows a lost tail.

④ I'm not sure if he is single or married.

⑤ Sally doesn't like apples, is she?

19 다음 대화 중 어법상 어색한 것은?

① A: I'm not sure if he is coming.
   B: He said that he would come.

② A: What did she say to you at the airport?
   B: She told me that she would miss me.

③ A: When do you suppose Sarah will call?
   B: Maybe tonight.

④ A: You didn't steal the ring, did you?
   B: Yes, I didn't.

⑤ A: I want to know if she got better.
   B: Yes, she is fully recovered now.

20 다음 중 어법상 올바른 문장의 개수는?

ⓐ I asked Julie how I could make her feel better.
ⓑ Who do you think is that girl?
ⓒ We weren't allowed to open the window even though the room was hot.
ⓓ It's time to taste what he has cooked.

① 없음　　② 1개　　③ 2개
④ 3개　　⑤ 4개

21 다음 중 어법상 바르게 고치지 <u>못한</u> 것을 <u>모두</u> 고르시오.

① I wonder if <u>does he eat</u> the hamburger.
　　(→ did he eat)
② Let's meet in front of the tower, <u>will</u> we?
　　(→ shall)
③ The UFO <u>did appeared</u> in the sky.
　　(→ was appeared)
④ I wonder if Henna will <u>comes</u> to our party.
　　(→ come)
⑤ You can tell me who <u>did break</u> the window.
　　(→ broke)

<u>22~23</u> 다음 중 어법상 <u>어색한</u> 문장의 개수를 고르시오.

22

ⓐ I'd like to know what you think about it.
ⓑ I didn't know that Columbus discovered America in 1492.
ⓒ He told me that the bus comes every ten minutes.
ⓓ Here are they on the floor.

① 없음　　② 1개　　③ 2개
④ 3개　　⑤ 4개

23

ⓐ I heard he had already left for Paris.
ⓑ I did enjoyed the picnic with my friends.
ⓒ There are lots of sheep in the meadow.
ⓓ Down the hall is the waiting room.

① 없음　　② 1개　　③ 2개
④ 3개　　⑤ 4개

24 다음 대화의 빈칸에 들어갈 말이 바르게 짝지어진 것은?

A: Do you know why Ethan is angry?
B: I heard that he ___(A)___ a fight with his girlfriend.
A: ___(B)___ do you think he can make up with her?
B: I think he has to apologize for his mistake.
A: What did he do?
B: He ___(C)___ to me that he forgot her birthday.
A: That's too bad. He had better call her now.
　　*make up with somebody : ~와 화해하다

	(A)	(B)	(C)
①	had	How	told
②	has	Who	told
③	has	Why	told
④	had	Who	said
⑤	had	How	said

25 다음 대화의 밑줄 친 ⓐ~ⓔ 중 어법상 어색한 것은?

> A: ⓐ Do you know where Miae is?
> B: ⓑ I thought she is in the living room.
> A: No, she's not there.
> B: ⓒ She left a message, didn't she?
> A: No, she didn't leave any message.
> B: ⓓ I'm worried that she has lost her way because she's just moved to this town.
> A: ⓔ We need to call the police, don't we?

① ⓐ   ② ⓑ   ③ ⓒ
④ ⓓ   ⑤ ⓔ

26~27 다음 문장에 이어질 부가의문문을 완성하시오.

26 Let's play tennis, _____?

27 He could move the heavy box, _____ _____?

28~29 다음 우리말과 일치하도록 괄호 안의 말을 이용하여 문장을 완성하시오.

28 그는 내가 다음 달에 이탈리아에 갈 것을 안다. (go)
He knows that I _____ _____ to Italy next month.

29 Jack은 어젯밤 자기가 낯선 사람을 봤다고 말했다. (see)
Jack said that he _____ _____ a stranger last night.

30~31 다음 우리말과 일치하도록 괄호 안의 말을 바르게 배열하시오.

30
> Jimmy는 나에게 내가 충분히 잤는지 물어보았다. (asked, I, had, Jimmy, if, slept enough, me)

_____

31
> 너는 그가 얼마나 오래 달릴 수 있다고 추측하니? (run, he, you, guess, can, do, how long)

_____

32~33 다음 |보기|와 같이 두 문장을 한 문장으로 쓰시오.

> ┤보기├
> Do you know? + When does the class start?
> → Do you know when the class starts?

32 Can you tell me? + Why did you cry last night?

→ _____

33 Do you suppose? + How did he become a super star?

→ _____

34~35 다음 밑줄 친 부분을 조동사 do를 이용하여 강조하는 문장으로 바꿔 쓰시오.

34 I <u>remembered</u> what my teacher had told me.

→ _____

_____

35 We <u>see</u> the thousands of stars in the sky.

→ _____

_____

36~37 다음 두 문장의 의미가 같도록 문장을 완성하시오.

36 The bus is coming here now.

= Here _____.

37 She was singing on the stage.

= On _____.

38~39 다음 |보기|와 같이 직접화법을 이용하여 문장을 바꾸어 쓰시오.

|보기|
He said that he was coming home then.
→ He said, "I'm coming home now."

38 I asked her if she had read that novel.

→ _____

39 He said that he could join us that day.

→ _____

40~43 다음 문장에서 어법상 <u>어색한</u> 부분을 찾아 바르게 고치시오.

40 I wondered why he won't tell me the truth.

_____ → _____

41 Do you know when will Matt come?

_____ → _____

42 She did called you many times while you were out.

_____ → _____

43 A: That tiger is very big.
B: Watch out! Here comes it!

_____ → _____

44~45 다음 문장에서 어법상 <u>어색한</u> 부분을 고쳐 완전한 문장을 쓰시오.

44 Paul said me, "Please call me now."

→ _____

_____

45 Can you tell me when does the show end?

→ _____

_____

46 다음 문장이 어법상 어색하지 않으면 ○를, 어색한 부분이 있으면 밑줄을 치고 바르게 고치시오.

(1) We hoped you will become the champion.

→ _____

(2) I knew my mom always listens to music.

→ _____

(3) I learned that a cheetah could run 120 km per hour.

→ _____

47~48 다음 이력서를 참고하여 간접의문문으로 대화를 완성하시오.

Résumé
- Name: Seojin Cheon
- Major: classical music
- Work experience: Teaching at a school of music for five years
- Hobbies: Reading, watching movies

47 A: Can you tell me _____

_____?

B: I like reading and watching movies.

48 A: Can I ask _____

_____?

B: For five years.

49 주어진 |조건|을 이용하여 우리말을 영어로 옮기시오.

조건
1) 조동사 do를 활용할 것
2) 단어 trust, among, his friends를 쓸 것
3) 7단어를 사용할 것

Max는 그의 친구들 중 Tom을 정말 신뢰한다.

_____

_____

50 다음 중 어법상 어색한 문장을 모두 고르시오.

ⓐ Do you know whom did he invite?
ⓑ How do you think you can fix everything?
ⓒ I heard that he was called a trouble maker.
ⓓ I prayed for his recovery all night after I knew he was wounded.
ⓔ I can tell you that he does likes you very much.
ⓕ Around the corner sang they merrily and happily.

_____, _____, _____

필독

중학 국어로 수능 잡기

✦ **필독** 중학 국어로 수능 잡기 시리즈

문학 ─ 비문학 독해 ─ 문법 ─ 교과서 시 ─ 교과서 소설

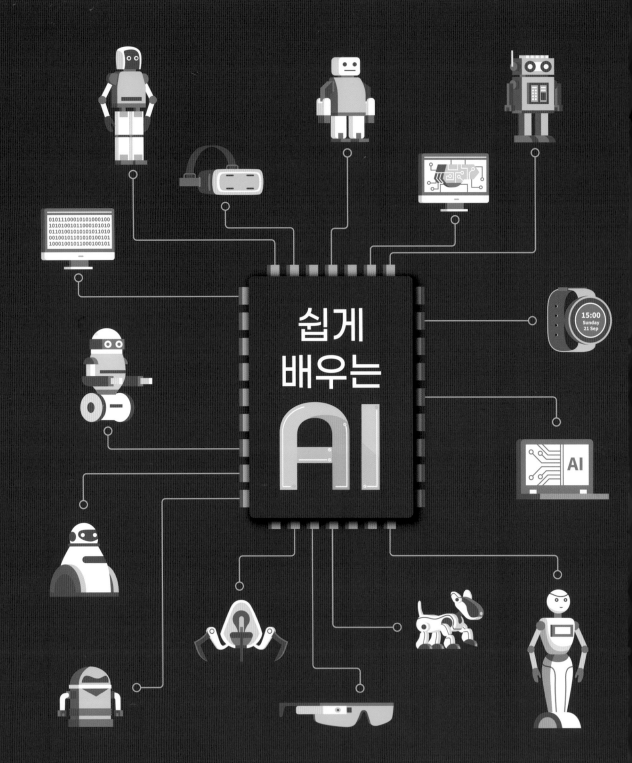

쉽게
배우는
AI

교육과정과 융합한
쉽게 배우는
인공지능(AI) 입문서

초등   중학   고교

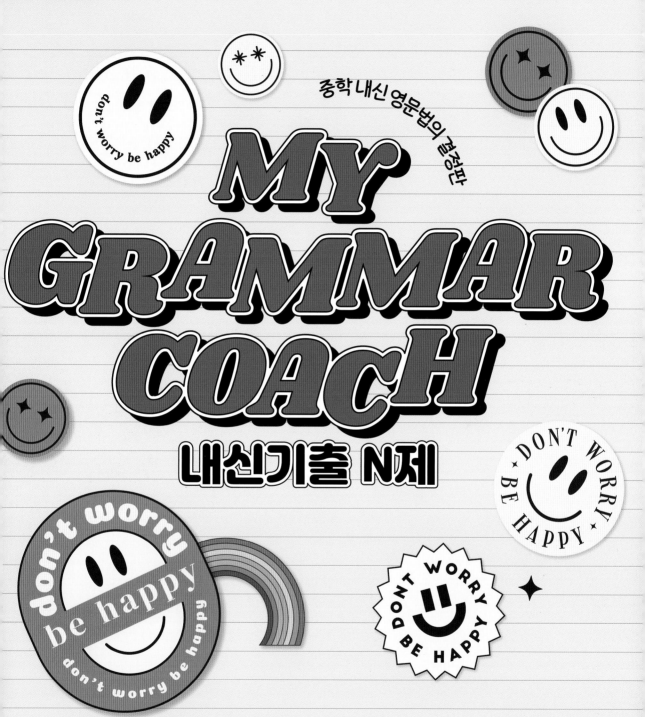

EBS

중|학|도|역|시 **EBS**

중학 내신 영문법의 결정판

MY GRAMMAR COACH

내신기출 N제

don't worry be happy

don't worry be happy

DON'T WORRY BE HAPPY

DON'T WORRY BE HAPPY

Workbook

중2

MY GRAMMAR COACH

내신기출 N제 중2

Workbook

시제

주어가 3인칭 단수일 때, 동사의 현재형

대부분의 동사	-s
-o, -s, -x, -sh, -ch로 끝나는 동사	-es
자음+y로 끝나는 동사	y를 i로 바꾸고 -es
모음+y로 끝나는 동사	-s
불규칙 동사	be – am/are/is have – has

동사의 규칙 과거형과 과거분사형

대부분의 동사	-ed
-e로 끝나는 동사	-d
단모음+단자음으로 끝나는 동사	자음 하나 더 쓰고 -ed
자음+y로 끝나는 동사	y를 i로 바꾸고 -ed
모음+y로 끝나는 동사	-ed

|A| 다음 동사의 규칙 과거형과 과거분사형을 쓰면서 외우시오.

01 accept – _____ – _____
02 accomplish – _____ – _____
03 agree – _____ – _____
04 allow – _____ – _____
05 believe – _____ – _____
06 borrow – _____ – _____
07 carry – _____ – _____
08 close – _____ – _____
09 collect – _____ – _____
10 copy – _____ – _____
11 cover – _____ – _____
12 cry – _____ – _____
13 decide – _____ – _____
14 depend – _____ – _____
15 delay – _____ – _____
16 disagree – _____ – _____
17 drop – _____ – _____
18 enjoy – _____ – _____
19 fail – _____ – _____
20 finish – _____ – _____
21 found – _____ – _____
22 happen – _____ – _____
23 hope – _____ – _____
24 hurry – _____ – _____
25 join – _____ – _____
26 laugh – _____ – _____

27 learn – _____ – _____
28 lie(거짓말하다) – _____ – _____
29 look – _____ – _____
30 marry – _____ – _____
31 plan – _____ – _____
32 play – _____ – _____
33 prefer – _____ – _____
34 raise – _____ – _____
35 remember – _____ – _____
36 save – _____ – _____
37 smile – _____ – _____
38 stay – _____ – _____
39 stop – _____ – _____
40 study – _____ – _____
41 thank – _____ – _____
42 touch – _____ – _____
43 try – _____ – _____
44 use – _____ – _____
45 visit – _____ – _____
46 wait – _____ – _____
47 walk – _____ – _____
48 want – _____ – _____
49 wash – _____ – _____
50 watch – _____ – _____
51 work – _____ – _____
52 worry – _____ – _____

|B| 다음 동사의 불규칙 과거형과 과거분사형을 쓰면서 외우시오.

01	am, is	– _____	– _____	**39**	lend	– _____	– _____
02	are	– _____	– _____	**40**	let	– _____	– _____
03	become	– _____	– _____	**41**	lie(누워 있다)	– _____	– _____
04	begin	– _____	– _____	**42**	lose	– _____	– _____
05	break	– _____	– _____	**43**	make	– _____	– _____
06	bring	– _____	– _____	**44**	mean	– _____	– _____
07	build	– _____	– _____	**45**	meet	– _____	– _____
08	buy	– _____	– _____	**46**	pay	– _____	– _____
09	catch	– _____	– _____	**47**	put	– _____	– _____
10	choose	– _____	– _____	**48**	read	– _____	– _____
11	come	– _____	– _____	**49**	ride	– _____	– _____
12	cost	– _____	– _____	**50**	ring	– _____	– _____
13	cut	– _____	– _____	**51**	rise	– _____	– _____
14	do	– _____	– _____	**52**	run	– _____	– _____
15	draw	– _____	– _____	**53**	pay	– _____	– _____
16	drink	– _____	– _____	**54**	say	– _____	– _____
17	drive	– _____	– _____	**55**	see	– _____	– _____
18	eat	– _____	– _____	**56**	sell	– _____	– _____
19	fall	– _____	– _____	**57**	send	– _____	– _____
20	feel	– _____	– _____	**58**	sing	– _____	– _____
21	fight	– _____	– _____	**59**	sit	– _____	– _____
22	find	– _____	– _____	**60**	sleep	– _____	– _____
23	fly	– _____	– _____	**61**	speak	– _____	– _____
24	forget	– _____	– _____	**62**	spend	– _____	– _____
25	forgive	– _____	– _____	**63**	spread	– _____	– _____
26	get	– _____	– _____	**64**	stand	– _____	– _____
27	give	– _____	– _____	**65**	steal	– _____	– _____
28	go	– _____	– _____	**66**	swim	– _____	– _____
29	grow	– _____	– _____	**67**	take	– _____	– _____
30	have	– _____	– _____	**68**	teach	– _____	– _____
31	hear	– _____	– _____	**69**	tell	– _____	– _____
32	hit	– _____	– _____	**70**	think	– _____	– _____
33	hurt	– _____	– _____	**71**	throw	– _____	– _____
34	keep	– _____	– _____	**72**	understand	– _____	– _____
35	know	– _____	– _____	**73**	wake	– _____	– _____
36	lay	– _____	– _____	**74**	wear	– _____	– _____
37	lead	– _____	– _____	**75**	win	– _____	– _____
38	leave	– _____	– _____	**76**	write	– _____	– _____

기본시제: 현재, 과거, 미래

기본시제를 표현하는 동사의 형태 및 부정문, 의문문의 어순을 정확히 파악하세요.

시제	긍정문의 동사 형태		시제	긍정문의 동사 형태	
현재	be동사	am, are, is	과거	be동사	was, were
	일반동사	동사원형(+s)		일반동사	원형+ed / 불규칙

주의 미래의 일은 조동사 will이나 be going to를 이용해요. 단, 시간, 조건의 부사절에서 미래는 현재시제로 표현한다는 것에 주의하세요. When he ~~will come~~ comes back, we will start.

밑줄 친 단어를 알맞은 형태로 바꿔 쓰시오.

01 I find my dog an hour ago. → _____

02 Is it going to rains soon? → _____

03 Water freeze at 0℃. → _____

04 Are you going to eating it? → _____

05 I visit her last weekend. → _____

06 Rachel sayed hello to me. → _____

07 I am busy yesterday. → _____

08 I was 14 years old now. → _____

09 We rided bikes last week. → _____

10 When he will come, we'll leave. → _____

UNIT 03 진행형 V-ing 만드는 법

동사에 -ing를 붙일 때의 규칙을 알아 두세요.

대부분의 동사	-ing	call – calling
-e로 끝나는 동사	e를 빼고 -ing	make – making
-ie로 끝나는 동사	ie를 y로 바꾸고 -ing	die – dying
1음절이며, 단모음+단자음으로 끝나는 동사	마지막 자음을 하나 더 쓰고 -ing	get – getting
2음절이지만 강세가 뒤에 있는 동사	마지막 자음을 하나 더 쓰고 -ing	begin – beginning

다음 동사의 -ing형을 쓰면서 외우시오.

01 arrive – _____

02 begin – _____

03 believe – _____

04 bring – _____

05 climb – _____

06 close – _____

07 come – _____

08 control – _____

09 die – _____

10 drive – _____

11 fly – _____

12 get – _____

13 give – _____

14 lie – _____

15 play – _____

16 put – _____

17 ride – _____

18 run – _____

19 say – _____

20 shop – _____

21 sit – _____

22 stop – _____

23 study – _____

24 swim – _____

UNIT 04　현재진행 & 과거진행

'~하고 있다'와 같이 진행 중인 동작을 나타낼 때는 진행형 〈be+V-ing〉로 써야 해요.

현재진행	am/are/is+V-ing	She is having breakfast now.
과거진행	was/were+V-ing	She was having breakfast at that time.

우리말과 같은 뜻이 되도록 괄호 안의 말을 이용하여 문장을 완성하시오.

01 Joy는 소설을 읽고 있었다. (read)　　→ Joy _____ a novel.

02 아이들이 농구를 하고 있다. (play)　　→ The children _____ basketball.

03 우리는 그때 휴식을 취하고 있었다. (take)　→ We _____ a rest at that time.

04 아기들은 지금 뭐 하고 있니? (do)　　→ _____ the babies _____ now?

05 John은 TV를 시청하고 있지 않았다. (watch)　→ John _____ TV.

06 우리는 지금 운동을 하고 있지 않다. (exercise)　→ We _____ now.

07 너는 시계를 보고 있었니? (look)　　→ _____ you _____ at the clock?

08 그는 버스를 운전하고 있지 않았다. (drive)　→ He _____ a bus.

09 Emily는 스트레칭을 하고 있지 않았다. (stretch) → Emily _____ her body.

UNIT 05　과거시제 vs. 현재완료

과거시제는 과거에 끝난 일을, 현재완료는 과거의 일이 현재까지 영향을 미칠 때 쓰세요.

	과거시제	현재완료
긍정	주어+동사의 과거형	주어+have[has]+과거분사
부정	주어+did+not+동사원형	주어+have[has]+not+과거분사
의문	Did+주어+동사원형 ~?	Have[Has]+주어+과거분사 ~?

우리말과 같은 뜻이 되도록 괄호 안의 말을 이용하여 문장을 완성하시오.

01 나는 어제 머리를 감지 않았다. (wash)　　→ I _____ my hair yesterday.

02 그는 한 시간 전에 버스에 탔다. (get)　　→ He _____ on the bus one hour ago.

03 나는 아직 그것을 다 끝내지 못했다. (finish) → I _____ not _____ it yet.

04 그는 그 노래를 몇 년 전에 작곡했다. (write) → He _____ the song a few years ago.

05 그들은 2일 동안 아무것도 먹지 못했다. (eat) → They _____ for two days.

06 Jenny는 오늘 아침에 열이 났다. (have)　→ Jenny _____ a fever this morning.

07 너는 아프리카에 가 본 적이 있니? (be)　→ _____ your ever _____ to Africa?

08 나는 지난주에 그 영화를 봤다. (watch)　→ I _____ the movie last week.

09 그는 20년 동안 여기서 일해 왔다. (work)　→ He _____ here for 20 years.

현재완료 1 - 계속

for 또는 since가 있다면 '(과거부터 현재까지 계속) ~해 왔다'라는 의미의 현재완료형으로 써야 해요.

	for(~ 동안)	since(~ 이후로)
뒤에 오는 말	for+기간	since+과거 시점/과거 문장
예문	He has lived here for five years.	He has lived here since last year. He has lived here since he was born.

밑줄 친 부분에서 **틀린** 곳을 찾아 바르게 고치시오.

01 We did not see Helen since last Tuesday. → _____

02 I have this bag for three years. → _____

03 I have loved the song for I was three years old. → _____

04 We were knowing each other since 2020. → _____

05 The building was here since 1984. → _____

06 You've been sick for last week. → _____

07 The author worked on this novel for two years. → _____

08 Have you lived in this city for last year? → _____

09 How long have they stay at this hotel? → _____

현재완료 2 - 완료

'(과거에 시작한 일을 현재에) 이미/막/아직 ~했다'라는 표현은 현재완료형으로 써야 해요.

	already(이미)	just(막, 방금)	yet(아직 – 부정문에서)
자주 쓰는 부사와 위치	have+already+과거분사	have+just+과거분사	haven't+과거분사 ~ yet
예문	She has already heard it.	I have just finished it.	He hasn't read it yet.

괄호 안의 말을 바르게 배열하여 문장을 완성하시오.

01 The singer _____ very famous. (become, already, has)

02 We _____ a present for our teacher. (bought, just, have)

03 The bus _____ the bus stop. (left, already, has)

04 His performance _____ . (started, has, just)

05 They _____ their dinner. (just, finished, have)

06 My bike _____ . (just, down, broken, has)

07 The man _____ the watch. (has, bought, already)

08 _____ your birthday cards? (you, already, have, got)

09 _____ your homework yet? (you, finished, haven't)

현재완료 3 – 경험

'(과거부터 지금까지) ~해 본 적이 있다'는 경험을 나타낼 때는 현재완료형으로 써야 해요.

	before	once/twice/three times ...	ever/never
자주 쓰는 부사의 종류와 위치	She has heard it before. 전에 들은 적 있다	I have tried it twice. 두 번 해 봤다[해 본 적 있다]	He has never seen it. 전혀 본 적 없다
	She hasn't heard it before. 전에 들은 적 없다	I have tried it many times. 여러 번 해 봤다[해 본 적 있다]	Have you ever seen it? (한 번이라도) 본 적 있니?

괄호 안의 말을 이용하여 현재완료 문장을 완성하시오.

01 Liam _____ his own money _____. (before, never, make)

02 I _____ that horror movie _____. (twice, watch)

03 Have you _____ anything on the Internet? (ever, buy)

04 My family _____ to Italy _____. (three times, be)

05 Teddy _____ a horse _____. (before, ride)

06 Have _____ a sunrise like this? (ever, see)

07 They _____ mountain climbing _____. (several times, go)

08 We _____ badminton before. (never, play)

09 Have you _____ to a foreigner? (ever, speak)

현재완료 4 – 결과

'(과거에 ~한 결과가 현재) ~하다'라는 의미를 만들 때 현재완료형으로 써야 해요.

	과거	현재완료
비교	She lost her bag. 잃어버렸다	She has lost her bag. 잃어버렸다 (그래서 지금 없다)
	(과거 발생, 현재 상황 모름)	(과거 발생, 그 결과가 현재까지 이어짐)

'~으로 가 버려서 (이곳에) 없다'와 '~에 가 본 적 있다'를 구분해서 사용할 수 있어야 해요.

비교	have gone to(결과) ~으로 가 버렸다	have been to(경험) ~에 가 본 적이 있다

다음 두 문장이 같은 뜻이 되도록 빈칸에 알맞은 말을 쓰시오.

01 Jake went to Berlin. He is not here. → Jake _____ to Berlin.

02 She moved to Busan. She's not here. → She _____ to Busan.

03 He lost his bike. He doesn't have it. → He _____ his bike.

04 Chris is not here. He left for Hawaii. → Chris _____ for Hawaii.

05 I left my purse on the bus. I don't have it. → I _____ my purse on the bus.

현재완료 시제의 네 가지 의미와 쓰임을 파악하세요.

계속	과거부터 현재까지 계속 되어 온 일(계속 ~해 왔다)
완료	과거부터 시작되어 현재에 완료된 일(이미/막/아직 ~했다)
경험	과거부터 현재까지의 경험(~한 적이 있다)
결과	과거에 발생한 일의 결과가 현재까지 영향을 미침(~해 버렸다)

|A| 다음 밑줄 친 부분의 용법을 |보기|에서 찾아 쓰시오.

┌ 보기 ┐

| 계속 | 완료 | 경험 | 결과 |

01 Have you ever been to Jeju Island? _____

02 They have been busy since last week. _____

03 Jane has already arrived at the dorm. _____

04 His uncle has worked in Japan since 2020. _____

05 My sister has lost her dog at the park. _____

|B| 우리말과 같은 뜻이 되도록 괄호 안의 말을 배열하여 문장을 완성하시오.

01 나는 이전에 집에서 새를 키워 본 적이 있다. (raised, before, have)

I _____ a bird in my house _____.

02 그들은 미국에 있는 학교로 갔다. (to, gone, have)

They _____ a school in America.

03 이 도시에서 얼마나 오랫동안 비가 내리고 있니? (long, how, rained, has, it)

_____ in this city?

04 전등이 나가서 우리는 아무것도 볼 수 없다. (out, gone, has)

The light _____, so we cannot see anything.

05 나는 내가 가장 아끼는 반지를 잃어버렸다. (have, I, lost)

_____ my favorite ring.

06 박 선생님은 대학교에서 10년 동안 과학을 가르쳐 왔다. (science, taught, has, for)

Mr. Park _____ at a university _____ ten years.

01 다음 중 동사의 변화형이 옳지 <u>않은</u> 것은?

① found – founded – founded
② see – saw – seen
③ speak – spoke – spoken
④ make – made – maden
⑤ hide – hid – hidden

02 다음 빈칸에 들어갈 말로 알맞은 것은?

> I _____ the piano since I was a child.

① play   ② plays
③ have played   ④ has played
⑤ will play

03 다음 대화의 빈칸에 들어갈 말로 알맞은 것은?

> A: Have you ever seen a gorilla?
> B: No, _____.

① I didn't   ② I have
③ I haven't   ④ I don't
⑤ I ate too much

04 다음 중 빈칸에 들어갈 말의 쓰임이 나머지 넷과 <u>다른</u> 것은?

① I _____ lived in Seoul for five years.
② I _____ already read this book.
③ I _____ studied Spanish for one year.
④ I _____ a beautiful red dress.
⑤ I _____ seen this animation before.

05 다음 중 밑줄 친 부분의 의미가 나머지 넷과 <u>다른</u> 것은?

① We <u>are going to</u> get on the train.
② Mike <u>is going to</u> church now.
③ It <u>is going to</u> snow this weekend.
④ I'm <u>going to</u> buy a new car tomorrow.
⑤ She <u>is going to</u> meet her friend next Thursday.

06 다음 우리말을 영어로 옮길 때 빈칸에 알맞은 것은?

> 나는 어제 저녁 엄마가 설거지 하는 것을 도와드렸다.
> I _____ my mom wash the dishes last evening.

① help   ② helps
③ helped   ④ will help
⑤ have helped

[07~08] 다음 중 밑줄 친 부분의 용법이 나머지 넷과 다른 것을 고르시오.

07 ① She <u>has</u> never <u>been</u> to Mexico.
② <u>Have</u> you ever <u>seen</u> the Colosseum?
③ I <u>have</u> never <u>studied</u> Japanese.
④ I <u>have</u> once <u>lived</u> in San Francisco.
⑤ They <u>have lost</u> their luggage, so they are looking for it.

08 ① Julia <u>has been</u> in the hospital for three months.

② I <u>have been</u> on the soccer team since 2019.

③ He is not here as he <u>has gone</u> out for shopping.

④ How long <u>have</u> you <u>lived</u> in Seoul?

⑤ They <u>have donated</u> thousands of dollars to charity for ten years.

[09~10] 다음 중 어법상 어색한 문장을 고르시오.

09 ① They held a concert in 2017.

② I have known him since I was young.

③ Bora has studied Spanish for ten years.

④ I was good at basketball when I was young.

⑤ Shakespeare has written many stories in the 17th century.

10 ① When you go to Bali, it will be fun.

② I will not go to her birthday party.

③ I'm going to visit Toronto this Saturday.

④ He will call you tomorrow.

⑤ If it will snow heavily, the airport closes.

[11~12] 다음 중 어법상 올바른 문장을 고르시오.

11 ① When we were in the park, a boy is looking for his dog.

② He has visited Africa four years ago.

③ I haven't heard that sound last month.

④ A bird flew into my house yesterday.

⑤ She has lived in France since two years.

12 ① I'm studying English these days.

② Michael Jackson has died in 2009.

③ She taught Chinese at a high school now.

④ She has read this book two days ago.

⑤ The sun rose in the east every morning.

13 다음 중 어법상 <u>어색한</u> 문장의 개수는?

ⓐ I have been to the theater yesterday.
ⓑ Have you already read this newspaper?
ⓒ I don't finished the task yet.
ⓓ Have you hear about the woman in the forest?

① 없음　② 1개　③ 2개　④ 3개　⑤ 4개

14 다음 중 밑줄 친 부분이 어법상 어색한 것은?

A: ① Have you finished packing your bag?
B: Yes, ② I have. What time ③ are we going to arrive at Hawaii?
A: At 10:30 a.m. We ④ will be able to see the beautiful ocean in ten hours if there ⑤ will be no problem.

15 다음 중 어법상 올바른 문장끼리 바르게 짝지어진 것은?

ⓐ She has come home from her vacation last night.
ⓑ Tom has slept for six hours since he came home.
ⓒ The elephant has lived in the zoo since three years.
ⓓ We have just arrived at the station.
ⓔ He has left the house yesterday.

① ⓐ, ⓑ   ② ⓑ, ⓓ   ③ ⓐ, ⓒ
④ ⓒ, ⓓ   ⑤ ⓐ, ⓔ

[16~18] 다음 괄호 안에 주어진 말을 알맞은 형태로 고쳐 쓰시오.

16 He has _____ on the ground. He is in the hospital now. (fall)

17 Nick has not _____ his homework yet. (finish)

18 She _____ for Germany 3 years ago. (leave)

[19~21] 다음 문장에서 어법상 어색한 부분을 찾아 바르게 고치시오.

19 They knew each other for ten years.

_____ → _____

20 He hasn't come home from work already.

_____ → _____

21 I have spent one hour playing with my friend since 2 p.m.

_____ → _____

22 다음 문장과 뜻이 같도록 빈칸에 알맞은 말을 쓰시오.

She will visit the museum next week.

= She _____ going _____ visit the museum next week.

23 우리말과 뜻이 같도록 괄호 안의 말을 바르게 배열하시오.

> 아빠가 집에 돌아오는 길에, 언덕에서 종소리가 울리고 있었다.
> (when, my father, on his way, home, was, a bell, ringing, on the hill, was)

_____

_____

24 우리말과 뜻이 같도록 빈칸을 채워 문장을 완성하시오.

> 그녀는 이전에 디즈니랜드에 가 본 적이 없다.

She _____ _____ _____
Disneyland before.

25 우리말과 뜻이 같도록 괄호 안의 말을 이용하여 문장을 완성하시오.

> 너희는 얼마 동안 수학을 공부했니?

How long you (study) math?

→ _____

_____

26 다음 대화의 밑줄 친 우리말과 뜻이 같도록 괄호 안의 말을 이용하여 문장을 완성하시오.

> A: 내 여자 친구가 영국으로 가 버렸어. (go)
> B: I'm sorry to hear that.

My girlfriend _____ England.

[27~28] 다음 두 문장을 현재완료를 이용하여 한 문장으로 만드시오.

27
> • My uncle and his wife moved to Chicago two years ago.
> • They still live there now.

My uncle and his wife _____
Chicago for two years.

28
> • My brother began to work at the bank last year.
> • He still works at the bank.

My brother _____ at the bank
for a year.

[29~30] 주어진 |조건|을 이용하여 우리말을 영어로 바꾸시오.

29 ┤조건├
> 1. be going to를 사용할 것
> 2. 단어 close, bakery를 사용할 것
> 3. 7단어를 사용할 것

Tom은 자신의 빵집 문을 닫을 예정이다.

→ _____

_____

30 ┤조건├
> 1. 현재완료시제를 사용할 것
> 2. 단어 their relatives, last year, meet을 사용할 것
> 3. 9단어를 사용할 것

그들은 지난해부터 친척들을 만나지 못하고 있다.

→ _____

_____

조동사

UNIT 01 │ can

조동사 can(~할 수 있다)은 다양한 상황에서 쓰일 수 있으므로 문맥을 파악하는 것이 중요해요.

능력	I can swim.	요청	Can[Could] you wait?
가능	I can help you.	추측	He can be busy.
허가	You can stay here.	금지	You cannot[can't] stay here.

주의 조동사 can의 부정은 cannot 또는 can't로 써야 해요. *cann't (X)

can이 능력/가능을 의미할 때만 be able to와 바꿔 쓸 수 있다는 것을 기억하세요.

우리말과 같은 뜻이 되도록 괄호 안의 말을 이용하여 문장을 완성하시오.

01 그녀는 중국어로 10까지 셀 수 있다. (can, count) → _____ up to 10 in Chinese.

02 우리 집에 좀 들를 수 있겠니? (can, stop by) → _____ my house?

03 영화표는 어디에서 살 수 있니? (can, buy) → _____ I _____ movie tickets?

04 저에게 연필 좀 빌려주시겠어요? (could, lend) → _____ me a pencil?

05 George는 먼 거리를 뛸 수 있었다. (run) → George _____ long distances.

06 어떻게 요리하는지 좀 보여 줄 수 있니? (can, show) → _____ me how to cook?

07 Frank는 그 경기에서 승리할 수 없었다. (able, win) → Frank _____ the game.

UNIT 02 │ may

조동사 may의 다양한 의미를 기억해 두세요.

추측	~일지도 모른다	요청	~해도 될까요?
허가	~해도 된다	금지	~하면 안 된다

우리말과 같은 뜻이 되도록 괄호 안의 말을 배열하여 문장을 완성하시오.

01 이 일은 몇 가지 불편을 야기할지도 모른다. (may, cause, work)

This _____ some inconveniences.

02 할머니께서 내일 도착하실지도 모른다. (tomorrow, arrive, may)

My grandma _____.

03 제가 이 책을 하루 동안 빌려도 될까요? (borrow, may, I, this book)

_____ for one day?

04 방학 동안에 나는 아마 사촌들을 방문할지도 모른다. (might, my cousins, visit, I)

_____ for my vacation.

05 그는 아마 Judy의 남동생일지도 모른다. (may, Judy's, be, little brother)

He _____.

06 제가 당신의 여권과 표를 좀 볼 수 있을까요? (may, see, I, your passport)

_____ and ticket?

UNIT 03 | must

'~해야만 한다'라는 의무나, '~임에 틀림없다'라는 강한 추측을 표현할 때 조동사 must를 쓰세요.

의무	강한 추측	강한 금지
~해야만 한다	~임이 틀림없다	~하면 안 된다
We must follow the rules.	She must be rich.	You must not tell a lie.

주의 부정의 강한 추측은 can't[cannot](~일 리가 없다)로 써요. The story can't be true.

우리말과 같은 뜻이 되도록 괄호 안의 말을 이용하여 문장을 완성하시오.

01 우리는 나가는 길을 찾아야 한다. (find) → We _____ a way out.

02 그 소문이 사실일 리가 없다. (be) → The rumor _____ true.

03 당신은 이곳에 절대 주차하면 안 된다. (park) → You _____ here.

04 너는 창문을 닫아야 한다. (close) → You _____ the window.

05 제가 당신의 개를 산책시켜야 하나요? (walk) → _____ I _____ your dog?

06 뭔가 잘못된 일이 있는 게 분명하다. (be) → There _____ something wrong.

UNIT 04 | have to

have[has] to는 의미상 must와 바꿔 쓰지만, 부정문은 서로 다른 의미인 것에 주의해야 해요.

긍정	~해야 한다	We must[have to] pay.
부정	~해서는 안 된다	We must not pay. ≠ We don't have to pay. (~할 필요가 없다)
의문	~해야 합니까?	Do we have to[Must we] pay?

주의 주어가 3인칭 단수면 has to로 써야 하며, 과거(~했어야 했다)는 had to로 써요.

참고 have to는 need to로 바꿔 쓸 수 있어요. We don't have[need] to pay.

우리말과 같은 뜻이 되도록 have to를 알맞은 형태로 바꿔 빈칸을 채우시오.

01 그녀는 택시를 잡기 위해서 빨리 뛰어가야 했다.

She _____ run fast to catch the taxi.

02 그들은 아침 일찍 일을 시작해야 하니?

_____ they _____ start their work early in the morning?

03 Aaron은 운전하는 법을 배워야 했다.

Aaron _____ learn how to drive.

04 너는 얼마나 오랫동안 기다려야 했니?

How long _____ you _____ wait?

05 너는 들어오기 전에 문에 노크할 필요 없다.

You _____ knock on the door before you enter.

UNIT 05　should

조동사 should는 '~하는 게 좋겠다, ~해야 한다'라는 뜻으로 충고나 제안을 할 때 써야 해요.

긍정	~하는 편이 좋겠다, ~해야 한다	You should wash your hands.
부정	~하지 않는 게 좋겠다, ~해서는 안 된다	You shouldn't[should not] play games too much.
의문	~하는 게 좋을까?, ~해야 하나?	Should I take the bus? – Yes, you should. / No, you shouldn't.

괄호 안의 말과 should를 이용하여 대화를 완성하시오.

01 A: I have a fever.

　　B: You ＿＿＿＿＿＿＿＿＿＿ a doctor right now. (see)

02 A: The show starts at 5 o'clock.

　　B: Oops! We ＿＿＿＿＿＿＿＿＿＿! (hurry up)

03 A: You ＿＿＿＿＿＿＿＿＿＿ friends. (make fun of)

　　B: Sorry. I will not do that again.

04 A: Tomorrow is Oliver's birthday!

　　B: ＿＿＿＿＿＿＿＿＿＿ we ＿＿＿＿＿＿＿＿＿＿ for him? (what, buy)

05 A: It's already nine o'clock. It's too dark.

　　B: Right. We ＿＿＿＿＿＿＿＿＿＿ home. (go back)

UNIT 06　had better & would like to

다음 조동사 표현들을 익히세요.

	had better(~하는 게 낫다)	would like to(~하고 싶다, ~하기 원한다)
긍정/축약	You had better go now. You'd better	I would like to stay. I'd like to
부정	You'd better not go now.	I would not like to stay.
의문	*Should I go now?	Would you like to stay?

주의 had better는 의문문으로 잘 쓰지 않아요. 거의 should를 사용하여 의문문을 만들어요.

우리말과 같은 뜻이 되도록 괄호 안의 말과 had better 또는 would like to를 이용하여 문장을 완성하시오.

01 너는 한 번 시도해 보는 게 좋겠다. (give)　　→ You ＿＿＿＿＿＿＿＿ it a try.

02 나는 집에 돌아가고 싶지 않다. (return)　　→ I ＿＿＿＿＿＿＿＿ home.

03 그녀는 쉬는 게 좋겠다. (take a rest)　　→ She ＿＿＿＿＿＿＿＿.

04 그는 너의 목소리를 듣고 싶어 한다. (hear)　　→ He ＿＿＿＿＿＿＿＿ your voice.

05 너는 이번에는 가지 않는 게 좋겠다. (go)　　→ You ＿＿＿＿＿＿＿＿ this time.

06 나는 더 넓은 집으로 이사가고 싶다. (move)　　→ I ＿＿＿＿＿＿＿＿ to a bigger house.

UNIT 07 | used to & would

'(과거에) ~하곤 했다'와 같이 과거의 반복하던 일은 used to와 would로 쓰세요.

	used to(~하곤 했다)	would(~하곤 했다)
예문	I used to go there on Sunday. 나는 일요일에 거기에 가곤 했다.	I would go there when it rained. 나는 비가 오면 거기에 가곤 했다.
주의	used to 앞에 be동사를 쓰면 다른 의미가 돼요. be used to+명사: ~에 익숙하다 be used to+동사: ~하는 데 사용되다	과거의 상태를 나타낼 때는 would를 못 써요. There would <u>be</u> a tree. (×) → used to be He would <u>live</u> here. (×) → used to live

🗨️ **주의** 과거의 습관적 행동을 나타내는 would는 상태 동사인 be, feel, taste, hear, have, live, love, like, want, understand, know, agree, believe 등과 같이 쓸 수 없고 used to를 써야 해요.

우리말과 같은 뜻이 되도록 used to 또는 would를 이용하여 문장을 완성하시오.

01 나는 어렸을 때 매년 여름마다 바닷가에 가곤 했다.

When I was little, I _____ every summer.

02 이전에는 모퉁이에 커다란 슈퍼마켓이 있었다.

There _____ a big supermarket on the corner.

03 Noah는 한가할 때마다, 만화책을 읽곤 했다.

Whenever Noah was free, she _____ comic books.

04 이전에 나는 여동생을 이해하곤 했는데, 지금은 그녀를 이해할 수 없다.

I _____ my sister, but I can't understand her now.

05 Lucy는 금발 머리를 하고 있었는데 지금 그녀는 검정 머리이다.

Lucy _____ blond hair, but she has black hair now.

06 내가 더 어렸을 때는 김치를 싫어했었지만 지금은 매우 좋아한다.

I _____ kimchi when I was younger, but now I love it.

[01~02] 다음 밑줄 친 부분과 바꿔 쓸 수 있는 말을 고르시오.

01

> She wants to get your phone number.

① would likes to
② like to
③ woulds like to
④ would like to
⑤ would like

02

> She couldn't sleep well last night.

① was able not to
② couldn't able to
③ wasn't able to
④ couldn't be able to
⑤ wasn't able

03 다음 빈칸에 공통으로 들어갈 말로 알맞은 것은?

> • _____ you give me some cookies?
> • I _____ read comic books when I was little, but now I don't read them.

① May[may]
② Must[must]
③ Can[can]
④ Would[would]
⑤ Should[should]

04 다음 문장의 밑줄 친 may와 뜻이 같은 것은?

> You may borrow my computer.

① You may use these pictures.
② The solution may not work.
③ She may not drink coffee.
④ She may live in the apartment.
⑤ This notebook may be Tom's.

05 다음 밑줄 친 부분과 바꿔 쓸 수 있는 말은?

> • Can I help you?
> • Can I try this on?

① Do
② May
③ Will
④ Should
⑤ Would

[06~07] 다음 우리말을 영어로 바르게 옮긴 것을 고르시오.

06

> 너는 이 교실에서 간식을 먹으면 안 된다.

① You must eat snacks in this classroom.
② You don't have to eat snacks in this classroom.
③ You can't not eat snacks in this classroom.
④ You can't eat snacks in this classroom.
⑤ You not must eat snacks in this classroom.

07 이 건물에서 벗어날 다른 문이 있는 게 틀림없다.

① There used to be another gate to get out of this building.
② There can't be another gate to get out of this building.
③ There may be another gate to get out of this building.
④ There would be another gate to get out of this building.
⑤ There must be another gate to get out of this building.

08 다음 중 밑줄 친 부분의 의미가 나머지 넷과 다른 것은?

① She has lived in many countries. She can speak five languages.
② You can't drink anything in the museum.
③ Jack practiced a lot, but he couldn't pass the test.
④ Amy could sing very well last year, and she still can.
⑤ I could make robots when I was young.

[09~10] 다음 중 어법상 어색한 문장을 고르시오.

09 ① He hasn't to go to see a doctor if he is fine.
② You may not talk in the library.
③ You must not eat this cake before you finish your homework.
④ You had better not go outside at night.
⑤ He may not live in New York now.

10 ① I would like to get your advice.
② Would you like more information?
③ Would you like go to the shopping mall?
④ I would like to reserve a room.
⑤ I would like to thank you for coming to my party.

[11~12] 다음 중 어법상 올바른 문장을 고르시오.

11 ① He can swims very well.
② Will Tony comes here?
③ May I using the restroom first?
④ She mays know about him.
⑤ I will stay at the hotel until next week.

12 ① It is raining, so I can't not go to the beach.
② There is an exam tomorrow. She must not be late.
③ He doesn't may find the door.
④ You haven't to eat dinner if you are not hungry.
⑤ She hadn't better go out at night alone.

13 다음 짝지어진 두 문장의 의미가 서로 다른 것은?

① We don't have to apologize to him.
→ We must not apologize to him.
② You must clean the room first.
→ You have to clean the room first.
③ We have to take a rest for a while.
→ We had better take a rest for a while.
④ You had better run fast, or you will be late.
→ If you don't run fast, you will be late.
⑤ I had better not eat too much for my health.
→ I should not eat too much for my health.

14 다음 밑줄 친 ⓐ~ⓓ 중 어법상 어색한 것은?

Last weekend, I ⓐwas able to get two concert tickets of Black Pink, so I went to the concert with my friend. I said we ⓑhad to hurry because of the traffic jam. Fortunately, we ⓒshould arrive on time. When they started singing loudly, my friend told me something. I ⓓcouldn't hear her because it was too noisy. But we enjoyed the concert.

① 없음   ② ⓐ   ③ ⓑ
④ ⓒ   ⑤ ⓓ

15 다음은 수진이의 2년 전과 현재에 할 수 있는 것과 할 수 없는 것을 보여 주는 표이다. 표의 내용을 바르게 설명한 것은?

	2년 전	현재
run fast	×	○
sing well	○	○
play the violin	×	×

① Sujin couldn't sing well two years ago.
② Sujin can run fast now.
③ Sujin could play the violin two years ago.
④ Sujin could run fast two years ago.
⑤ Sujin can play the violin now.

[16~17] 우리말과 뜻이 같도록 빈칸에 알맞은 조동사를 쓰시오.

16
너는 날씨가 더울 때는 물을 마시는 게 낫다.

You _____ _____ drink water when the weather is hot.

17
저는 사과 주스를 마시고 싶습니다.

I _____ _____ to drink some apple juice.

[18~19] 우리말과 뜻이 같도록 괄호 안의 말을 이용하여 문장을 완성하시오.

18
저는 오래 기다려야만 하나요? (have to)

_____ I _____ _____ wait for a long time?

19
나는 너무 늦게 도착해서 병원에 계신 할머니를 볼 수 없었다. (can)

I _____ see my grandmother in the hospital because I arrived too late.

20 우리말과 뜻이 같도록 괄호 안의 말을 바르게 배열하시오.

만약 건강해지고 싶다면, 너는 매일 운동을 해야 한다. (should, exercise, every day, healthy, if, you, want to, you, be)

_____

_____

[21~22] |보기|와 같이 두 문장의 뜻이 같도록 문장을 완성하시오.

┌─ 보기 ─────────────────────────────┐
She can build a house by herself.
= She is able to build a house by herself.
└───────────────────────────────────┘

21 I couldn't find any food in the kitchen.

= _____

_____

22 Could he get to the top of the mountain?

= _____

_____

[23~24] 다음 문장에서 어법상 <u>어색한</u> 부분을 찾아 바르게 고치시오.

23 You don't have to cross the street when the traffic light is red.

_____ → _____

24 He has better not eat sweets too much.

_____ → _____

[25~28] 우리말과 뜻이 같도록 |보기|의 말과 괄호 안의 동사를 이용하여 문장을 완성하시오.

┌|보기|─────────────────────┐
must   may   have to
└────────────────────────────┘

25 그 학생들은 디즈니랜드에 가게 되어 신이 난 게 틀림없다. (be)

The students _____ _____
excited to go to Disneyland.

26 너는 그 책을 읽을 필요가 없다. (read)

You _____ _____ _____

_____ that book.

27 내가 집에 없을 수도 있어. (be)

I _____ _____ _____

at home.

28 재민이는 팔이 부러져 병원에 가야 했다. (go)

Jaemin broke his arm, so he _____

_____ _____ to the hospital.

[29~30] 주어진 |조건|을 이용하여, 우리말을 영어로 바꾸시오.

29 ┌|조건|─────────────────────┐
1. 조동사 can을 쓰지 않고, 같은 의미의 단어로 바꿀 것
2. 단어 go, Jongro, to, myself, by를 사용할 것
3. 8단어를 사용할 것
└────────────────────────────┘

나는 혼자서 종로에 갈 수 있다.

→ _____

_____

30 ┌|조건|─────────────────────┐
1. used to를 사용할 것
2. 단어 there, a, post office, here를 사용할 것
3. 8단어를 사용할 것
└────────────────────────────┘

여기에는 예전에 우체국이 있었다.

→ _____

_____

수동태

UNIT 01   수동태의 의미와 형태

能동태와 수동태 문장의 어순과 동사의 형태를 확인하세요.

능동태 → 수동태	Many people [love] Pengsoo. Pengsoo [is loved] by many people.	많은 사람들이 펭수를 사랑한다. 〈Many people에 초점〉 펭수는 많은 사람들에 의해 사랑받는다. 〈Pengsoo에 초점〉

참고 〈by+행위자〉는 행위자가 중요하지 않으면, 생략도 가능해요.

우리말과 같은 뜻이 되도록 괄호 안의 말을 이용하여 문장을 완성하시오.

01 수백 개의 기사들이 기자들에 의해 작성된다. (write)

Hundreds of articles _____ journalists.

02 매우 많은 물고기들이 이 강에서 잡힌다. (catch)

A lot of fish _____ in this river.

03 모든 고객들에게 최상의 서비스가 제공된다. (provide)

The best services _____ to all customers.

04 어젯밤에 Toby는 엄마에게 심하게 혼났다. (scold)

Toby _____ severely _____ his mom last night.

05 이 프로젝트를 위해 많은 시간과 노력이 소요된다. (consume)

A lot of time and effort _____ for this project.

06 애니메이션 영화는 많은 어린이들에게 사랑을 받는다. (love)

Animation movies _____ many children.

UNIT 02   수동태의 과거시제

수동태로 과거시제를 나타낼 때 〈was/were+과거분사〉의 형태로 써야 해요.

능동태 → 수동태	Many people [loved] the book. The book [was loved] by many people.	많은 사람들이 그 책을 사랑했다. 그 책은 많은 사람들에 의해 사랑받았다.

다음 문장을 수동태로 바꿔 쓰시오.

01 People found dinosaur fossils in my town. → Dinosaur fossils _____ in my town.

02 A lot of girls loved the song. → The song _____ .

03 Joy's friends planned several events. → Several events _____ .

04 He signed the contract. → The contract _____ .

05 People spread the bad news. → The bad news _____ .

06 The school posted a list of students. → A list of students _____ .

UNIT 03 수동태의 미래시제

수동태로 미래시제를 나타낼 때 〈will be+과거분사〉의 형태로 써야 해요.

능동태	Many people will love the book.	많은 사람들이 그 책을 사랑할 것이다.
↓ 수동태	The book will be loved by many people.	그 책은 많은 사람들에 의해 사랑받을 것이다.

우리말과 같은 뜻이 되도록 괄호 안의 말을 이용하여 문장을 완성하시오.

01 연극은 중앙 극장에서 공연될 것이다. (perform)

The play _____ at the Central Theater.

02 쿠키와 빵이 우리 엄마에 의해 곧 구워질 것이다. (my mom, bake)

Cookies and bread _____ soon.

03 당신이 가장 좋아하는 노래가 식당에서 틀어질 것이다. (play)

Your favorite song _____ in the restaurant.

04 그 대회의 우승자는 백 명의 시청자들에 의해 선발될 것이다. (select)

The winner of the contest _____ one hundred viewers.

05 새로운 달력이 내일부터 인쇄될 것이다. (print)

The new calendar _____ from tomorrow.

06 월드컵 경기는 많은 축구 팬들이 시청할 것이다. (watch)

The World Cup games _____ many soccer fans.

UNIT 04 수동태 시제 종합

현재	am/are/is+과거분사	Pengsoo is loved by many people.
과거	was/were+과거분사	The light bulb was invented in the 1880s.
미래	will be+과거분사	A lot of food will be prepared for the party.

우리말과 같은 뜻이 되도록 괄호 안의 말을 이용하여 문장을 완성하시오.

01 비행기에서 비빔밥이 제공될 것이다. (serve) → *Bibimbap* _____ on the plane.

02 그 TV는 트럭에 의해 배달되었다. (deliver) → The TV _____ a truck.

03 새 신발들은 1층에 진열돼 있다. (display) → New shoes _____ on the 1st floor.

04 그 보물은 그에 의해 발견되었다. (discover) → The treasure _____ him.

05 꽃이 정원에 심어질 것이다. (plant) → Flowers _____ in the garden.

06 선물이 너에게 보내질 것이다. (send) → A gift _____ to you.

UNIT 05   by 이외의 전치사를 쓰는 수동태

 전치사 by가 아닌 다른 전치사와 자주 사용되는 수동태 관용 구문을 외우세요.

be made from ~으로 만들어지다(재료 성질이 변함)	be worried about ~에 대해 걱정하다
be made of ~으로 만들어지다(재료 성질이 안 변함)	be covered with ~으로 덮여 있다
be known for ~으로[때문에] 알려져 있다	be pleased with ~에 기뻐하다
be known to ~에게 알려져 있다	be satisfied with ~에 만족하다
be known as ~으로서 알려져 있다	be tired of ~에 싫증이 나다
be filled with ~으로 가득 차 있다(=be full of)	be surprised at ~에 놀라다
be excited about ~에 흥분하다	be interested in ~에 흥미가 있다

우리말과 같은 뜻이 되도록 괄호 안의 말을 이용하여 문장을 완성하시오.

01 그 비밀이 모두에게 알려졌다. (know) → The secret _____ everybody.

02 모두가 그 속도에 놀랐다. (surprise) → Everyone _____ the speed.

03 그녀의 눈은 눈물로 가득 찼다. (fill) → Her eyes _____ tears.

04 그 산은 눈으로 덮여 있다. (cover) → The mountain _____ snow.

05 나는 똑같은 점심에 싫증이 난다. (tire) → I _____ the same lunch.

06 당신은 우리 서비스에 만족할 겁니다. (satisfy) → You _____ our service.

UNIT 06   조동사가 있는 수동태

 수동태의 미래시제와 마찬가지로, 다양한 조동사를 이용해서 수동태 문장을 만들 수 있어야 해요.

능동태	Many people might love the book.	많은 사람들이 그 책을 사랑할지 모른다.
↓ 수동태	The book might be loved by many people.	그 책은 많은 사람들에 의해 사랑받을지 모른다.

밑줄 친 부분에 유의하여 다음 문장을 수동태로 바꿔 쓰시오.

01 I can finish my homework. → _____

02 Teresa can do it. → _____

03 They should fix the computer. → _____

04 They might change the plans. → _____

05 He might release his new song. → _____

06 You should keep this in a refrigerator. → _____

UNIT 07 수동태의 부정문과 의문문

수동태의 부정과 의문도 be동사로 나타내지만 조동사가 있다면 조동사를 이용해야 해요.

	be+과거분사	조동사+be+과거분사
긍정	The book is loved by all.	The book can be loved by all.
부정	The book is **not** loved by all.	The book can**not** be loved by all.
의문	Is the book loved by all?	Can the book be loved by all?

괄호 안의 말을 이용하여 수동태 문장을 완성하시오.

01 _____ the first phone _____? (when, invented)

02 _____ you _____ the result? (please)

03 _____ she _____ foreign cultures? (interest)

04 The homework _____ yet. (not, finish)

05 Good memories _____. (not, erase, will)

06 _____ the cake _____ by 7? (bake, can)

UNIT 08 4형식 문장의 수동태

4형식 문장의 목적어 2개(간접목적어, 직접목적어)를 주어로 수동태 문장을 쓸 수 있어야 해요.

	간접목적어(~에게)를 주어로 쓸 때	직접목적어(~을)를 주어로 쓸 때
능동태	She gave them a card.	She gave them a card.
↓ 수동태	They were given a card by her.	A card was given to them by her.

(주의) 직접목적어를 주어로 할 때, 간접목적어 앞의 전치사는 동사에 따라 달라요. give, send 등의 동사는 전치사 to가, make, buy 등의 동사는 for가 어울린다는 데 유의하세요.

우리말과 같은 뜻이 되도록 괄호 안의 말을 배열하여 문장을 완성하시오.

01 그 책은 우리 할아버지가 아빠에게 사 주셨다. (was, for, by, bought, my dad)

The book _____ my grandpa.

02 그 환자는 의사에게 많은 약을 받았다. (lots of, was, medicine, given, by)

The patient _____ a doctor.

03 문자 메시지가 미나에게서 내게 발송되었다. (by, was, sent, me, to)

A text message _____ Mina.

04 수프와 빵이 당신에게 주어질 것이다. (given, you, to, will, be)

Soup and bread _____.

05 우리는 박 선생님으로부터 수학을 배운다. (are, math, by, taught)

We _____ Ms. Park.

5형식 문장의 수동태

5형식 문장의 목적어를 주어로 수동태 문장을 쓰는 방법을 알아 두세요.

목적격보어가 명사/형용사/to부정사일 때	
능동태 He made her happy / a doctor .	He told them to save money .
↓	
수동태 She was made happy / a doctor by him.	They were told to save money by him.

참고 능동태의 목적어를 주어로 쓰고, 수동태 동사를 쓴 후, 목적격보어를 그대로 써요.

괄호 안의 말을 이용하여 수동태 문장을 완성하시오.

01 Bathrooms _____. (should, keep clean)

02 Daniel _____ his friends. (call, was, an angel)

03 She _____ less sugar. (advise, eat, was)

04 The plane _____ here at noon. (expect, arrive)

05 My cat _____ Chris _____ me. (was, name)

06 I _____ and wait here. (tell, sit down, was)

지각동사와 사역동사의 수동태

지각동사나 사역동사가 있는 5형식 문장을 수동태로 쓸 때 목적격보어의 형태에 주의하세요.

	목적격보어가 원형부정사인 지각동사	목적격보어가 원형부정사인 사역동사
능동태	We saw the boys play soccer .	He made the driver stop .
↓		
수동태	The boys were seen to play soccer .	The driver was made to stop by him.
주의	목적격보어로 쓰인 원형부사는 수동태에서 to부정사로 써요. 단, 목적격보어가 분사일 때는 분사를 그대로 써요. The boys were seen playing soccer.	

다음 문장을 수동태로 바꿔 쓰시오.

01 Their teacher makes the students practice jumping rope.

→ _____

02 She heard the phone ringing in her pocket.

→ _____

03 Mom makes me wipe the floor every Saturday.

→ _____

04 I saw you arrive at the airport.

→ _____

05 People saw the building shaking heavily.

→ _____

동사구를 수동태로 전환할 때는 동사구를 하나의 단어처럼 취급하여 항상 함께 붙여서 써야 해요.

능동태	Some girls laughed at the boy.	몇몇 소녀들이 그 소년을 비웃었다.
수동태	The boy was laughed at by some girls.	그 소년은 몇몇 소녀들에 의해 비웃음을 당했다.

참고 다음의 동사구를 외워 두세요.

laugh at ~을 비웃다	check out ~을 대출하다	run over ~을 차로 치다
look after ~을 돌보다	turn on ~을 켜다	bring up ~을 양육하다, 키우다
take care of ~을 돌보다, 처리하다	turn off ~을 끄다	pay for ~에 대해 지불하다
turn down ~을 거절하다	turn down ~의 소리를 줄이다	rely on ~에 의지하다
hand in ~을 제출하다	put off ~을 미루다[연기하다]	look for ~을 찾다

우리말과 같은 뜻이 되도록 괄호 안의 말을 이용하여 문장을 완성하시오.

01 갑자기 음악의 소리가 줄여졌다. (turn down)

Suddenly, the music _____.

02 지난주에 그 애완용 물고기들은 Stacy에게 보살핌을 받았다. (take care of)

The pet fish _____ Stacy last week.

03 그 올림픽 경기는 전쟁 때문에 연기되었다. (put off)

The Olympic Games _____ the war.

04 그의 제안은 그의 상사에게 항상 거절당했다. (turn down, always)

His proposals _____ his boss.

05 내가 좀 더 키가 작아서 나는 Eugene에게 무시당했다. (look down on)

I _____ Eugene because I was shorter.

06 그 강아지는 도로에서 차에 치였다. (run over)

The dog _____ a car on the road.

07 여러분의 과제는 내일 제출되어야만 해요. (hand in)

Your homework _____ tomorrow.

[01~02] 다음 빈칸에 공통으로 들어갈 말을 고르시오.

01
- She was satisfied _____ the delicious food.
- The shoes are covered _____ dirt.

① by   ② at   ③ of
④ with   ⑤ in

02
- I _____ English at the middle school last year.
- I was _____ not to steal other people's belongings by my parents.

① caught   ② taught   ③ bought
④ thought   ⑤ fought

03 다음 우리말을 영어로 바르게 옮긴 것은?

이 사진은 Mary에게 찍혔다.

① This photo took by Mary.
② This photo was taken by Mary.
③ This photo was taking by Mary.
④ This photo been taken by Mary.
⑤ This photo has been taking by Mary.

04 다음 주어진 문장을 능동태로 바르게 바꾼 것은?

Harry Potter was written by Joan Rowling.

① Joan Rowling writes *Harry Potter*.
② Joan Rowling written *Harry Potter*.
③ Joan Rowling wrote *Harry Potter*.
④ Joan Rowling is wrote *Harry Potter*.
⑤ Joan Rowling could write *Harry Potter*.

05 다음 중 수동태로 바꿀 수 없는 것은?

① You must take care of your dog.
② Heejin always keeps the room clean.
③ I have a yellow umbrella.
④ He asked his father some questions.
⑤ She cooked us a steak for dinner.

06 다음 밑줄 친 부분 중 생략할 수 있는 것은?

① The shoes are sold <u>by people</u> in many countries.
② The door was shut <u>by the man</u> in the black suit.
③ *The Water Lily Pond* was painted <u>by Claude Monet</u>.
④ The cookies were baked <u>by that woman</u>.
⑤ The blue box was made <u>by our teacher</u> during the class.

07 다음 빈칸에 들어갈 말이 바르게 짝지어진 것은?

> · The rabbit ____(A)____ by the hunter.
> · The store will ____(B)____ next week.
> · The girl ____(C)____ a necklace around her neck.

	(A)	(B)	(C)
①	was caught –	closed –	wore
②	was caught –	be closed –	worn
③	was caught –	be closed –	wore
④	caught –	closed	– was wearing
⑤	caught –	closed –	wearing

[08~09] 다음 중 어법상 올바른 문장을 고르시오.

08 ① The news are announced by the reporter yesterday.
② The entrance fee will be payed by me.
③ She was took to school by her mother.
④ The CD released last month.
⑤ The wooden chair was made by us.

09 ① The patient was looked after by his son.
② The movie will release next Monday.
③ When did the concert held?
④ The apple was been eaten by a bird.
⑤ The song will be singing by her.

[10~11] 다음 중 어법상 어색한 문장을 고르시오.

10 ① The knife should be used very carefully.
② The meat should not be overcooked.
③ The announcement must not be released today.
④ The law must is followed by people.
⑤ The computer will be used in the next class.

11 ① The love letter was written to me by Minsu.
② I was given a present by my friend.
③ Jina was made the wine with grapes by Tom.
④ A message was sent to her by me.
⑤ The breakfast was cooked for me by my grandmother.

12 다음 대화 중 어법상 어색한 것은?

① A: Did you find your cat?
   B: Yes, it was found on the roof.
② A: Have you finished the homework?
   B: No, I haven't finished it yet.
③ A: What do the Korean people call the moon?
   B: It is called Dal.
④ A: Who bought the vase?
   B: It was bought by Kevin.
⑤ A: Was this building built by Richard?
   B: Yes, it wasn't built by Richard.

13 다음 밑줄 친 ⓐ~ⓔ 중 어법상 어색한 것은?

> There was a car accident on the street last night. A woman ⓐwas hit by a car. The woman was crossing the road when the car crashed into her. She ⓑwas seen falling by me, so I called the police. An ambulance took her to the hospital and I ⓒwas worried about her. The woman ⓓwas heard get well this morning, so I ⓔam pleased with the news.

① ⓐ   ② ⓑ   ③ ⓒ
④ ⓓ   ⑤ ⓔ

14 다음 중 수동태로 바르게 바꾼 것은?

① My dad bought me some chocolate.
　→ Some chocolate was bought to me by my dad.

② You should cook the pasta well.
　→ The pasta should cooked well.

③ This shop does not allow dogs to enter.
　→ Dogs is not allowed to enter this shop.

④ My teacher taught me to be honest.
　→ I was taught to be honest by my teacher.

⑤ I saw her run away from her house.
　→ She was seen run away from her house by me.

15 다음 중 어법상 어색한 문장끼리 짝지어진 것은?

ⓐ He is known by his talent of drawing.
ⓑ The TV was produced by the workers.
ⓒ The book is read by many people.
ⓓ The car wasn't drove by its owner.
ⓔ This necklace is made of gold.

① ⓐ, ⓑ　　② ⓐ, ⓓ　　③ ⓑ, ⓓ
④ ⓑ, ⓔ　　⑤ ⓒ, ⓔ

16 우리말과 뜻이 같도록 괄호 안의 말을 이용하여 문장을 완성하시오.

어제 콘서트에서 그 음악은 밴드에 의해 연주되었다. (play)

The music _____ _____ by the band at the concert yesterday.

17 두 문장의 뜻이 같도록 각각 알맞은 전치사를 쓰시오.

The bottle is filled _____(A)_____ orange juice.
= The bottle is full _____(B)_____ orange juice.

(A) _____　(B) _____

18 다음 문장을 수동태 문장으로 바꿔 쓰시오.

The police stopped my motorcycle this morning.

→ _____

_____

[19~20] 우리말과 뜻이 같도록 괄호 안의 말을 바르게 배열하시오.

19
그 소녀는 내가 시켜서 설거지를 하게 되었다.
(made, the girl, wash, by, me, was, the dishes, to)

_____

_____

20
이 시계는 Tom에 의해 내게 주어졌다.
(watch, this, given, to, was, by, me, Tom)

21 다음 문장에서 어법상 어색한 부분을 고쳐 완전한 문장을 쓰시오.

Dinner will be able to prepare soon.

→ _____

[22~24] 다음 문장에서 어법상 어색한 부분을 찾아 바르게 고치시오.

22 I invited to Mirae's birthday party.

_____ → _____

23 Did your luggage delivered by him last night?

_____ → _____

24 English is speaking in many countries.

_____ → _____

[25~27] 다음 문장을 지시대로 바꿔 쓰시오.

25 This book is read by Jake. (능동태로)

→ Jake _____ this book.

26 The strawberries are grown in the field. (의문문으로)

→ _____ the strawberries _____ in the field?

27 She made me water the plants every morning. (수동태로)

→ I _____ the plants every morning.

28 다음 밑줄 친 ⓐ~ⓔ 중 어법상 어색한 것의 기호를 쓰고 바르게 고쳐 쓰시오. (답2개)

A: ⓐDid the flower ⓑbought by Julia?
B: No, it ⓒdidn't. It ⓓwas bought by Jeremy.
A: Oh, how romantic he is! I ⓔam touched by his kindness.

_____ → _____

_____ → _____

29 주어진 |조건|을 이용하여 아래 문장을 바꿔 쓰시오.

┤조건├
1. 수동태를 사용할 것
2. 주어를 the umbrella로 할 것
3. 12단어를 사용할 것

She brought me the umbrella because it was raining.

→ _____

_____

30 다음 밑줄 친 ⓐ~ⓔ 중 어법상 어색한 것의 기호를 쓰고 바르게 고쳐 쓰시오.

Do you know Walt Disney? He was an animator and film producer. The popular animations such as *Pinocchio*, *Cinderella* and *Bambi* ⓐwere produced by him. He ⓑwas born in 1901. He ⓒwas interested in drawing when he was a child. He ⓓwas presented with many awards including five Academy Awards. He also opened Disneyland in 1955. Every Disneyland around the world ⓔare visiting by many people every year now.

_____ → _____

to부정사

to부정사의 명사적 용법 1 – 주어, 보어

동사를 명사(~하기, ~하는 것)처럼 사용하려면 〈to＋동사원형〉의 형태로 만들어야 해요.

명사 역할 – 주어	명사 역할 – 보어
To become a scientist takes years.	My dream is to become a scientist.

우리말과 같은 뜻이 되도록 괄호 안의 말을 배열하여 문장을 완성하시오.

01 이 수학 문제를 푸는 것은 쉽지 않다. (problem, this, is, solve, to, math)

_____ not easy.

02 Jenny의 특기는 노래를 작곡하는 것이다. (is, songs, to, write)

Jenny's talent _____ .

03 그녀의 소망은 외국에서 공부하는 것이다. (abroad, study, to)

Her wish is _____ .

04 내 꿈은 수의사가 되는 것이다. (a, to, become, vet)

My dream is _____ .

05 우리 엄마의 직업은 학생들에게 영어를 가르치는 것이다. (English, to, teach, to students)

My mom's job is _____ .

06 다른 사람들을 도와주는 것이 오늘의 교훈이다. (is, others, help, to)

_____ today's lesson.

UNIT 02 **가주어 It**

to부정사 주어는 문장 뒤로 옮길 수 있는데, 이때 가(짜)주어 It을 주어 자리에 넣어야 해요.

to부정사를 주어 자리에 쓸 때	가주어 It을 쓸 때
To become a scientist takes years.	It takes years to become a scientist.

우리말과 같은 뜻이 되도록 괄호 안의 말과 가주어 It을 이용하여 문장을 완성하시오.

01 행복한 가정을 꾸리는 것이 Joy의 소망이다. (have)

_____ Joy's wish _____ a happy family.

02 초코 쿠키를 굽는 것은 쉽지 않다. (bake)

_____ easy _____ chocolate cookies.

03 너와 친구가 된 것은 축복이다. (be)

_____ a blessing _____ friends with you.

04 날씨를 예측하는 것은 어렵다. (predict)

_____ difficult _____ the weather.

05 그곳까지 버스를 타고 가는 것은 가능하지 않다. (go)

_____ possible _____ there by bus.

UNIT 03　to부정사의 명사적 용법 2 – 목적어

to부정사를 목적어(명사)로 쓸 수 있는 기본 동사들을 파악하세요.

want/would like 원하다	hope 바라다	plan 계획하다	refuse 거절하다
wish 소망하다	promise 약속하다	choose 선택하다	learn 배우다
expect 예상하다	agree 동의하다	decide 결정하다	need ~할 필요가 있다

참고 명사를 주어, 목적어, 보어 자리에 쓰듯이, 명사적 용법의 to부정사도 목적어 자리에 쓸 수 있어요.

우리말과 같은 뜻이 되도록 괄호 안의 말을 이용하여 문장을 완성하시오.

01 그는 제시간에 오겠다고 약속했다. (be, promise)　→ He _____ on time.

02 나는 그 파티에 가고 싶다. (like, go)　→ I would _____ to the party.

03 네게 부탁하고 싶은 게 하나 있다. (ask, wish)　→ I _____ you a favor.

04 그는 내게 비밀을 말해 주기를 거절했다. (tell, refuse) → He _____ me the secret.

05 나는 시험에 통과하기를 희망한다. (pass, hope)　→ I _____ the exam.

06 그녀는 버스를 잡기 원했다. (catch, want)　→ She _____ the bus.

UNIT 04　의문사+to부정사

의문사 뒤에 to부정사를 써서 하나의 명사처럼 쓸 때, 문맥에 맞게 알맞은 의문사를 써야 해요.

what+to부정사	무엇을 ~할지	when+to부정사	언제 ~할지
which+to부정사	어느 것을 ~할지	where+to부정사	어디에서 ~할지
who(m)+to부정사	누가[누구를] ~할지	how+to부정사	어떻게 ~할지, ~하는 법

우리말과 같은 뜻이 되도록 괄호 안의 말과 to부정사를 이용하여 문장을 완성하시오.

01 슈퍼마켓에서 무엇을 사야 할지 저에게 말씀해 주세요. (buy)

Please tell me _____ at the supermarket.

02 지금 누구를 도와야 할지 알려줄 수 있나요? (help)

Could you tell me _____ now?

03 오늘의 주제는 환경을 위해 무엇을 해야 하는가 입니다. (do)

Today's topic is _____ for the environment.

04 너는 언제 일을 시작할지 결정해야 한다. (start)

You need to decide _____ your work.

05 그녀는 내게 쿠키 굽는 방법을 보여 주었다. (bake)

She showed me _____ cookies.

06 선생님은 스페인어를 읽고 쓰는 방법을 설명해 주셨다. (read, write)

The teacher explained _____ Spanish.

UNIT 05 to부정사의 명사적 용법 3 – 목적격보어

목적격보어로 to부정사를 쓰는 동사들을 외워 두세요.

어순	주어	to부정사를 목적격보어로 쓰는 5형식 동사	목적어	목적격보어(to부정사)
예문	I	want, ask, tell, expect, allow, advise, order, get, help	him	to come

주의 help는 목적격보어로 to부정사와 원형부정사 둘 다 써요.

우리말과 같은 뜻이 되도록 괄호 안의 말을 이용하여 문장을 완성하시오.

01 그는 그 군인들에게 그 스파이를 쏘지 말라고 명령했다. (order. the soldiers. shoot)

He _____ the spy.

02 그 선생님이 Sera가 말하기 시합을 이기도록 도와주실 것이다. (win. help)

The teacher _____ the speech contest.

03 그들은 아들들에게 더 많은 우유를 마시도록 격려했다. (encourage. drink)

They _____ more milk.

04 그 남자는 방문객들에게 여기서 사진을 찍지 말라고 부탁한다. (ask. take pictures)

The man _____ here.

UNIT 06 to부정사의 형용사적 용법

to부정사는 형용사처럼 명사를 꾸밀 수 있는데, 이때 어순에 주의하세요.

어순	형용사	명사	형용사	형용사 역할 to부정사
일반적인 명사의 경우	many	books		to read
-thing/-one/-body의 경우		something	interesting	(~해야 할, ~할)

우리말과 같은 뜻이 되도록 괄호 안의 말을 배열하여 문장을 완성하시오.

01 Kelly에게는 가지고 놀 장난감이 충분히 없다. (play. toys. to. with)

Kelly doesn't have enough _____.

02 그 박물관에는 감상할 만한 훌륭한 그림들이 많이 있다. (appreciate. paintings. great. to)

The museum has a lot of _____.

03 그는 마실 당근 주스 한 컵을 주문했다. (juice. to. drink. carrot)

He ordered a cup of _____.

04 우리는 해야 할 숙제가 많이 있다. (homework. do. to)

We have a lot of _____.

05 이 문제를 해결할 만한 누군가가 없나? (anyone. to. problem. solve. this)

Is there _____?

UNIT 07   to부정사의 부사적 용법 1

 to부정사가 주어, 목적어, 보어가 아니라면, 부사의 역할을 하는 것으로 판단하세요.

~하기 위해서(목적)	I exercise to lose weight.	= in order to[so as to] lose weight
~하지 않기 위해서(목적)	I try hard not to fail.	= in order not to[so as not to] fail

우리말과 같은 뜻이 되도록 괄호 안의 말을 이용하여 to부정사가 포함된 문장으로 완성하시오.

01 나는 잼을 좀 사기 위해 빵집에 갔다. (some, buy, jam)

I went to a bakery _____ .

02 나는 엄마를 도와드리기 위해 일찍 왔다. (my, help)

I came early _____ .

03 감기에 안 걸리기 위해 이것을 입어라. (cold, a, catch)

Wear this _____ .

04 그는 배우가 되기 위해 여기 왔다. (an, be, actor)

He came here _____ .

05 지구를 구하기 위해 뭘 해야 할까? (the, earth, save)

What should we do _____ ?

06 Jane은 살을 빼기 위해 날마다 조깅을 한다. (weight, lose)

Jane jogs every morning _____ .

UNIT 08   to부정사의 부사적 용법 2

'~하기 위해서(목적)'라는 뜻 이외에도 다음과 같은 의미로 쓰이므로 문맥에 맞게 해석해야 해요.

~하게 되어 ···한	감정의 원인	I'm happy to see you again.
~하기에 ···한	형용사 수식	This sentence is hard to understand.
~하다니 ···한	판단의 근거	She must be clever to think of such an idea.
~해서 (결국) ···하다	결과	The poor girl grew up to be a famous star.

|A| |보기|와 같이 to부정사를 이용하여 두 문장을 한 문장으로 연결하시오.

> |보기|
>
> I hear the news. + I am sorry.   → I am sorry to hear the news.

01 Jimin went to a concert. + Jimin was happy. → _____

02 I call you so late. + I am sorry.   → _____

03 Emily saw a lizard. + Emily was surprised. → _____

04 Lucas got an A. + Lucas was pleased.   → _____

05 I say bye to you. + I am sad.   → _____

06 You have a new bike. + You must be happy. → _____

|B| 우리말과 같은 뜻이 되도록 괄호 안의 말을 배열하여 문장을 완성하시오.

01 우리가 백세가 넘을 때까지 살 수 있을까? (more than, live, to, be)

Can we _____ one hundred?

02 나는 집에 돌아와 내가 혼자라는 걸 발견했다. (to, myself, find, alone)

I came back home _____.

03 그렇게 좋은 차를 사다니 그는 틀림없이 부자이다. (car, buy, to, such a nice)

He must be rich _____.

04 나는 커서 유명한 영화배우가 되고 싶다. (movie star, to, be, a famous)

I want to grow up _____.

05 그 벌레는 도망치려 노력했지만, 매번 실패했다. (fail, each time, to)

The bug tried to get away, only _____.

06 하버드대에 들어가다니 지민이는 틀림없이 훌륭한 학생이다. (Harvard university, enter, to)

Jimin must be a good student _____.

UNIT 09 to부정사의 의미상 주어

to부정사의 행위를 하는 주체가 따로 있을 경우, 그 행위의 주체자를 표시하는 방법을 알아 두세요.

〈for+행위자〉	The book is hard for children to read. 그 책은 아이들이 읽기 어렵다.	to read의 행위자 → children
〈of+행위자〉	It was nice of her to take me home. 나를 집까지 데려다주다니 그녀는 멋지구나.	to take의 행위자 → her

참고 일반적으로 〈for+행위자〉를 사용하나, 사람의 성질, 태도를 나타내는 형용사(kind, wise, polite, honest, nice, clever 등)가 오는 경우 의미상의 주어로 〈of+행위자〉로 써야 해요.

우리말과 같은 뜻이 되도록 괄호 안의 말과 of 또는 for를 이용하여 문장을 완성하시오.

01 우리가 다른 사람을 배려하는 것이 필요하다. (be considerate, necessary)

It is _____ of others.

02 그런 소문을 퍼뜨리다니 그녀는 어리석었다. (foolish, spread)

It was _____ the rumors.

03 나에게 너의 우산을 빌려주다니 너는 친절하구나. (lend, nice)

It is _____ your umbrella.

04 우리들에게는 학교에 가는 것이 즐겁다. (school, fun, go)

It is _____.

05 이곳에서는 모두가 헬멧을 쓰는 것이 필수적이다. (everyone, wear, necessary)

It is _____ a helmet here.

06 내가 교실 청소하는 것을 도와주다니 너는 친절하다. (help, kind)

It is _____ clean the classroom.

UNIT 10 | too ~ to = so ~ that

 〈too ~ to부정사〉를 〈so ~ that〉 구문으로 바꿔 쓸 수 있어야 해요.

too ~ to ...	…하기에는 너무 ~하다	I was too <u>tired</u> to <u>study</u>.
so ~ that ...	매우 ~해서 …하다	= I was so <u>tired</u> that <u>I couldn't study</u>.

🗨️ 주의 〈so ~ that ...〉 구문에서 that 이하는 시제와 문맥에 맞게 쓰세요.

우리말과 같은 뜻이 되도록 괄호 안의 말과 to부정사를 이용하여 문장을 완성하시오.

01 그 작품은 그가 사기에는 너무 비쌌다. (expensive, buy, him)

The artwork was _____.

02 나는 지금 나가 놀기에는 너무 피곤하다. (tired, go)

I am _____ out to play.

03 Jenny는 너무 흥분돼서 잠이 들 수가 없었다. (excited, fall)

Jenny was _____ asleep.

04 이 책은 내가 이해하기에는 너무 어렵다. (difficult, me, understand)

This book is _____.

05 이 물은 우리가 수영하기에는 너무 얕다. (shallow, us, swim)

This water is _____ in.

UNIT 11 | ~ enough to = so ~ that

 〈~ enough+to부정사〉 역시 〈so ~ that〉 구문으로 바꿔 쓸 수 있어야 해요.

~ enough to ...	…하기에 충분히 ~하다	He is <u>smart</u> enough to <u>solve it</u>.
so ~ that ...	매우 ~해서 …하다	= He is so <u>smart</u> that <u>he can solve it</u>.

우리말과 같은 뜻이 되도록 괄호 안의 말과 enough to를 이용하여 문장을 완성하시오.

01 우리 학교는 내가 걸어서 갈 수 있을 만큼 충분히 가깝다. (walk, me, for, close)

My school is _____ there.

02 이 음식은 아기도 먹을 수 있을 만큼 충분히 부드럽다. (baby, a, eat, soft)

This food is _____.

03 이 컵은 우리가 주스를 다 담을 수 있을 만큼 충분히 크다. (big, us, pour)

This cup is _____ all the juice in.

04 나는 혼자 여행할 수 있을 만큼 충분히 용감하다. (travel, brave)

I am _____ alone.

05 이 책가방은 우리가 살 수 있을 만큼 충분히 저렴하다. (buy, us, cheap)

This backpack is _____.

[01~03] 다음 빈칸에 들어갈 말로 알맞은 것을 고르시오.

01
> My sister wanted _____ to K-pop music.

① listen   ② listened   ③ listening
④ to listen   ⑤ listens

02
> You have to study hard _____ the test.

① passing   ② pass
③ to pass   ④ so that to pass
⑤ in order to passing

03
> Mom told _____ home early today.

① I come   ② I coming
③ me to come   ④ me coming
⑤ me to coming

04 다음 중 빈칸에 들어갈 말이 나머지 넷과 <u>다른</u> 것은?

① It's difficult _____ me to understand math.
② It was brave _____ you to save that dog.
③ It's hard _____ me to believe it.
④ It may be easy _____ you to solve the problem.
⑤ It can be helpful _____ him to learn English.

[05~06] 다음 중 밑줄 친 부분의 용법이 나머지 넷과 <u>다른</u> 것을 고르시오.

05 ① I want to buy a new car <u>to drive</u>.
② Do you have anything <u>to drink</u>?
③ It's wonderful <u>to visit</u> Disneyland.
④ We need something <u>to eat</u>.
⑤ It's time <u>to get up</u> not to be late.

06 ① Mom went to the hospital <u>to see</u> a doctor.
② She has left for Mexico <u>to get</u> a job.
③ He saved money <u>to buy</u> a present for her.
④ John likes <u>to write</u> letters in English.
⑤ We went to the beach <u>to swim</u> in the sea.

07 다음 문장의 밑줄 친 부분과 용법이 같은 것은?

> He went to the restaurant <u>to have</u> dinner.

① <u>To climb</u> the mountain wasn't easy.
② She decided not <u>to go</u> for a walk.
③ His goal was <u>to become</u> a scientist.
④ <u>To be</u> a lawyer, he has studied very hard so far.
⑤ I expected Junho <u>to visit</u> my house tonight.

08 다음 문장의 밑줄 친 부분과 용법이 다른 것은?

> My father's hobby is to go fishing with his friends every Sunday.

① He couldn't decide where to go for his vacation.
② Sarah rode on the bus to leave for Sokcho.
③ Jinsu allowed his dog to enter his room.
④ To study history is always boring.
⑤ Danny agreed to go hiking this weekend.

09 두 문장의 뜻이 같도록 빈칸에 들어갈 알맞은 말은?

> Helen was brave enough to try bungee jumping.
> = Helen was _____ brave that she could try bungee jumping.

① too   ② to   ③ in order to
④ so as to   ⑤ so

10 다음 우리말을 영어로 바르게 옮긴 것은?

> 내가 겨울 바다에서 수영하기에는 너무 춥다.

① It is too cold to swim in the winter sea.
② It's too cold for me to swim in the winter sea.
③ To swim in the winter sea is enough cold to me.
④ It's too cold to me to swim in the winter sea.
⑤ To swim in the winter sea is too cold to me.

[11~12] 다음 중 어법상 올바른 문장을 고르시오.

11 ① The movie was so sad that I couldn't watch.
② There is a bench for my grandmother to sit.
③ He was too busy to come to the party.
④ I want cool something to drink.
⑤ I don't know what say to her.

12 ① How about going to skiing tomorrow?
② His dream is become a movie star.
③ Walk on the frozen lake is not safe.
④ Will you be able to going to my house?
⑤ They expect to see her next week.

13 다음 중 밑줄 친 부분의 용법이 같은 것끼리 바르게 짝지어진 것은?

> ⓐ It is difficult not to make an error in writing.
> ⓑ I know the best way to get to the river.
> ⓒ They built a gallery to collect many artworks.
> ⓓ I found the perfect place to live.
> ⓔ I love to eat pancakes for my breakfast.

① ⓐ, ⓑ   ② ⓐ, ⓒ   ③ ⓑ, ⓓ
④ ⓑ, ⓔ   ⑤ ⓓ, ⓔ

14 다음 대화의 빈칸에 들어갈 말이 바르게 짝지어진 것은?

> A: It's time for you ____(A)____ breakfast.
> B: I'm late for school! Can I skip breakfast, Mom? I'm too busy ____(B)____ anything.
> A: No, you can't. I told you ____(C)____ to bed late last night.

	(A)	(B)	(C)
①	to have	to eat	not to go
②	to have	not to eat	not going
③	to have	not to eat	not go
④	have	to eat	not to go
⑤	have	not to eat	to go

15 다음 중 어법상 어색한 문장의 개수는?

> ⓐ It costs a lot of money to raise a pet.
> ⓑ He let me know how I should to get to the post office.
> ⓒ I'm really excited to hear the news.
> ⓓ Mom made me to wash the dishes.

① 없음　② 1개　③ 2개　④ 3개　⑤ 4개

16 우리말과 뜻이 같도록 괄호 안의 말을 이용하여 문장을 완성하시오.

> 선생님은 우리에게 조용히 하라고 말씀하셨다.
> (tell, be)

The teacher _____ us _____
_____quiet.

17 우리말과 뜻이 같도록 괄호 안의 말을 바르게 배열하시오.

> 나는 이야기할 사람 한 명이 필요하다.
> (someone, I, with, to, talk, need)

_____

_____

[18~19] 다음 문장에서 <u>어색한</u> 부분을 고쳐 완전한 문장을 쓰시오.

18 Jane has a lot of apples to eat them.

→ _____

_____

19 Brian bought some pasta so to cook.

→ _____

_____

20 다음 문장을 지시대로 바꿔 쓰시오.

We chose to swim in the sea. (to부정사를 부정하는 부정문으로)

→ _____

_____

[21~24] 다음 밑줄 친 to부정사의 용법이 무엇인지 |보기|에서 골라 각각에 해당하는 기호를 쓰시오.

> ┤보기├
> ⓐ 명사적 용법　　ⓑ 형용사적 용법　　ⓒ 부사적 용법

21 I allowed him <u>to play</u> computer games.

→ _____

22 To work in Germany, I have studied German for a year.

→ _____

23 She wants a cup of tea to drink now.

→ _____

24 His grandfather lived to be eighty.

→ _____

[25~26] 두 문장의 뜻이 같도록 괄호 안의 말을 이용하여 문장을 완성하시오.

25 The water was so cold that I couldn't take a shower. (too ~ to)

= The water _____

_____.

26 Cleo searched how to play the guitar on the Internet. (how, should)

= Cleo _____

_____.

[27~28] 다음 문장에서 어법상 어색한 부분을 찾아 바르게 고치시오.

27 I'm planning taking a trip to Italy.

_____ → _____

28 It is fantastic of him to meet his favorite baseball player.

_____ → _____

29 주어진 |조건|을 이용하여 우리말을 영어로 바꾸시오.

┌─ 조건 ─────────────────────┐
1. to부정사를 사용할 것
2. 가주어 It을 사용할 것
3. 단어 dangerous, try, skydiving을 사용할 것
4. 6단어를 사용할 것
└───────────────────────────┘

스카이다이빙을 해 보는 것은 위험하다.

→ _____

_____

30 다음 대화의 (A)~(E) 중 빈칸에 들어갈 말이 나머지 넷과 다른 것을 골라 기호를 쓰고 바르게 고치시오.

┌───────────────────────────┐
A: I have a problem with my cell phone. It got locked and I don't know ____(A)____ unlock it.
B: Did you enter the password?
A: Yes. But it didn't work.
B: I don't know ____(B)____ solve this problem, either. We should know ____(C)____ ask help for this kind of problem. Oh, there's a service center over there. We can ask ____(D)____ fix it.
A: Great. I don't know ____(E)____ thank you.
└───────────────────────────┘

_____ → _____

“
내가 가장 취약한 부분에 대해
요점 정리를 해 보세요.
”

05

동명사와 분사

명사로 쓰이는 동명사 1 – 주어, 보어

동사를 명사처럼 쓸 때는 동사를 to부정사로 만들거나 동명사(V-ing)로 만드세요.

| 의미 | ~하는 것, ~하기 | 형태 | 동사원형+-ing |

두 문장이 같은 뜻이 되도록 동명사를 이용하여 빈칸에 알맞은 말을 쓰시오.

01 It can be interesting to live in a foreign country.

= _____ can be interesting.

02 It is a good habit to exercise regularly.

= _____ is a good habit.

03 Emily's hobby is to play musical instruments.

= Emily's hobby is _____ .

04 It was exciting to watch the soccer game.

= _____ was exciting.

05 My goal is to master three foreign languages.

= My goal is _____ .

06 It is important to brush your teeth after meals.

= _____ is important.

UNIT 02 **명사로 쓰이는 동명사 2 – 동사의 목적어**

to부정사만 목적어로 쓸 수 있는 동사들이 있듯이, 동명사만 목적어로 쓰는 동사들을 파악하세요.

enjoy 즐기다	keep 계속 ~하다	imagine 상상하다	practice 연습하다
avoid 피하다	quit 그만 두다	deny 부정하다	give up ~을 포기하다
finish 마치다	mind 신경 쓰다	suggest 제안하다	stop ~하기를 멈추다

우리말과 같은 뜻이 되도록 괄호 안의 말을 이용하여 문장을 완성하시오.

01 오늘 우리는 공 던지는 연습을 했다. (practice, throw)

Today, we _____ a ball.

02 너는 테니스 동아리에 가입할 것을 고려해 볼 수 있다. (join, consider)

You can _____ the tennis club.

03 그 소년은 아빠의 차를 세차하는 것을 끝마쳤다. (finish, wash)

The boy _____ his dad's car.

04 의사는 7시 이후에는 아무것도 먹지 않을 것을 제안했다. (suggest, not, eat)

The doctor _____ anything after seven o'clock.

05 그들은 함께 노래하고 춤추는 것을 좋아한다. (sing, dance, enjoy)

They _____ and _____ together.

동명사와 to부정사 목적어 – 의미가 같은 경우

동사에 따라 목적어를 to부정사를 쓸지, 동명사를 쓸지, 아니면 둘 다 쓸 수 있는지를 파악하세요.

to부정사만 목적어로 취하는 동사	want, wish, expect, hope, promise, need, plan, choose, decide, refuse, learn, agree
동명사만 목적어로 취하는 동사	enjoy, keep, imagine, practice, avoid, quit, deny, give up, finish, mind, suggest, stop
둘 다를 목적어로 취하는 동사	like, love, hate, prefer, begin, start, continue

우리말과 같은 뜻이 되도록 괄호 안의 말을 이용하여 문장을 완성하시오.

01 나는 그 어려운 소설을 읽는 것을 포기했다. (read, gave, up)

I _____ the difficult novel.

02 우리는 상을 받을 거라고 예상하지 못했다. (get, expect)

We _____ the award.

03 우리 할아버지가 담배를 끊으실 수 있을까? (quit, smoke)

Is my grandfather able to _____?

04 우리는 이번 겨울 방학에 유럽을 방문하기를 바라고 있다. (hope, visit)

We _____ Europe this summer vacation.

05 나는 식사를 끝마치고 나서 밖에 나가 놀 것이다. (finish, eat)

I will play outside after I _____.

06 나는 여자 의사 선생님을 (보는 것을) 더 선호한다. (prefer, see)

I _____ a female doctor.

동명사와 to부정사 목적어 – 의미가 다른 경우

목적어가 to부정사일 때와 동명사일 때 의미가 달라지는 동사에 주의하세요.

remember	+ to부정사	~할 것을 기억하다	try	+ to부정사	~하려고 노력하다
	+ 동명사	~한 것을 기억하다		+ 동명사	시험 삼아 ~해 보다
forget	+ to부정사	~할 것을 잊다	regret	+ to부정사	~하게 되어 유감이다
	+ 동명사	~한 것을 잊다		+ 동명사	~한 것을 후회하다

다음 밑줄 친 부분의 의미를 우리말로 쓰시오.

01 We should stop using plastic bags and bottles. _____

02 I forgot to tell her the news about the event. _____

03 You should try to go to bed early for your health. _____

04 Remember to turn off all the lights when you go out. _____

05 On my way home, I stopped to borrow books from the library. _____

06 I regret not attending the seminar. _____

to부정사 목적어와 동명사 목적어에 대해 종합적으로 학습하세요.

동사+to부정사	want, wish, expect, hope, promise, need, plan, choose, decide, refuse, learn, agree
동사+동명사	enjoy, keep, imagine, practice, avoid, quit, deny, give up, finish, mind, suggest, stop
동사+둘 다	like, love, hate, prefer, begin, start, continue *둘 다 취하고 의미가 같음.
동사+둘 다	remember, forget, try, regret *둘 다 취하지만 의미가 달라짐.

우리말과 같은 뜻이 되도록 괄호 안의 말을 이용하여 문장을 완성하시오.

01 우리들 중 누구도 이 경기에서 이길 것이라고 예상하지 않았다. (expect. win)

None of us _____ this game.

02 Emily는 영국에 있는 옥스퍼드 대학교에 입학하기를 희망한다. (enter. hope)

Emily _____ Oxford University in England.

03 잊지 말고 네 선생님께 이메일 보내. (forget. send)

Don't _____ an email to your teacher.

04 전화 좀 받아 주실래요? (mind. answer)

Do you _____ the phone?

05 어려움에 처하면 내게 전화할 것을 기억해. (remember. call)

_____ me if you have any trouble.

동명사와 자주 쓰이는 관용표현을 외워 두세요.

go -ing	~하러 가다	be worth -ing	~할 만한 가치가 있다
How[What] about -ing?	~하는 게 어때?	have trouble -ing	~하는 데 어려움을 겪다
be busy -ing	~하느라 바쁘다	feel like -ing	~하고 싶다
spend+시간/돈+-ing	~하는 데 시간/돈을 쓰다	It is no use -ing	~해 봐야 소용없다
look forward to -ing	~하기를 기대하다	on[upon] -ing	~하자마자(= as soon as)
be used to -ing	~하는 것에 익숙하다	cannot help -ing	~할 수밖에 없다
Thank you for -ing	~한 것에 대해 감사하다	by -ing	~함으로써

우리말과 같은 뜻이 되도록 괄호 안의 말과 동명사 관용표현을 이용하여 문장을 완성하시오.

01 그녀는 주차하는 데 어려움을 겪었다. (park) → She _____ her car.

02 스키 타러 가는 게 어때? (go) → _____ skiing?

03 그 장소는 방문할 가치가 있다. (visit) → The place is _____ .

04 그 소식을 듣자마자, 그녀는 떠났다. (hear) → _____ the news. she left.

05 그녀에게 부탁해봐야 소용없다. (ask) → It is _____ her.

06 나는 그들을 만나는 것을 고대한다. (meet) → I _____ them.

UNIT 07 현재분사 vs. 과거분사

동사를 형용사(명사 수식, 보어 역할)처럼 쓰기 위해서는 현재분사나 과거분사로 만들어야 해요.

	현재분사	과거분사
형태	동사+-ing	과거분사형(-ed 또는 불규칙 형태)
의미	~하는(능동)	~된, ~당한(수동)

우리말과 같은 뜻이 되도록 괄호 안의 말을 이용하여 문장을 완성하시오.

01 이 탑이 언제 지어졌니? (build) → When was this tower _____?

02 방은 분홍색과 회색으로 칠해졌다. (paint) → The room was _____ pink and gray.

03 나무 식탁 위에서 촛불이 타고 있다. (burn) → The candles are _____ on the table.

04 그 건물은 화재로 인해 파괴되었다. (destroy) → The building was _____ by the fire.

05 Dennis는 큰 목소리로 말하고 있었다. (speak) → Dennis was _____ in a loud voice.

UNIT 08 명사를 앞뒤에서 수식하는 분사

분사는 목적어나 부사(구)를 취할 수 있고, 이때 명사를 뒤에서 수식한다는 것을 알아 두세요.

현재분사	명사 앞	Do you know the running dog? 달리고 있는 개
	명사 뒤	Do you know the dog running in the park? 공원에서 달리고 있는 개
과거분사	명사 앞	My uncle will fix the broken window. 깨진 창
	명사 뒤	My uncle will fix the window broken by a boy. 소년에 의해 깨진 창

주어진 문장과 같은 뜻이 되도록 다음 문장을 완성하시오.

01 He is reading a book. It is written in English.

= He is reading a book _____.

02 My mom sent me some pictures. They were taken by my dad.

= My mom sent me _____.

03 A book is placed on the sofa. It is my favorite.

= _____ is my favorite.

04 Children are playing basketball. They are my brothers.

= _____ are my brothers.

05 I know the man. The man is cleaning the window.

= I know _____.

06 A list shows this year's best students. It was posted on the school website.

= _____ shows this year's best students.

보어로 쓰이는 분사

분사를 형용사처럼 보어로 쓸 때, 주어나 목적어와의 관계가 능동인지 수동인지 파악하세요.

주격	현재분사	The news is surprising. 놀라게 하는, 놀라운	news = surprising 관계
보어	과거분사	We are surprised by the news. 놀람을 당한, 놀란	We = surprised 관계
목적격	현재분사	I heard someone calling my name. 부르는	someone = calling 관계
보어	과거분사	I heard my name called. 불려지는	my name = called 관계

우리말과 같은 뜻이 되도록 괄호 안의 말을 이용하여 문장을 완성하시오.

01 우리는 선생님께서 우리가 안 보일 때까지 손을 흔들어 인사하고 계신 것을 보았다. (see, wave)

We _____ our teacher _____ goodbye until we were out of sight.

02 Mandy는 경기에서 졌을 때 우울함을 느꼈다. (feel, depress)

Mandy _____ when she lost the game.

03 Joy는 엄마가 그녀의 이름을 부르고 계신 것을 들었다. (hear, call)

Joy _____ her mom _____ her name.

04 나는 내일 치과에 가서 사랑니가 뽑히도록 할 것이다. (have, pull)

I will go to a dentist to _____ my wisdom tooth _____ out.

05 나는 Lucas가 버스 정류장에서 버스를 기다리고 있는 모습을 보았다. (see, wait)

I _____ Lucas _____ for a bus at the bus station.

06 우리 아빠는 자동차가 수리되도록 하셔서 우리는 지금 시내에 갈 수 있다. (have, repair)

My dad _____ our car _____, so we can go downtown now.

감정 분사 리스트: 현재분사, 과거분사

감정 동사를 분사로 만들 때, 감정을 유발하는지, 느끼는지를 판단하여 분사의 형태를 결정하세요.

감정을 표현하는 동사	감정을 유발 → 현재분사	감정을 느낌 → 과거분사
interest 흥미를 끌다	interesting 흥미를 갖게 하는	interested 흥미를 느끼는
excite 신나게 하다	exciting 신나게 하는	excited 신이 난

우리말과 같은 뜻이 되도록 괄호 안의 말을 이용하여 문장을 완성하시오.

01 그녀는 그 머리 모양이 지루하다. (bore) → She is _____ with her hairstyle.

02 그 공원에 가는 것은 신난다. (excite) → Going to the park is _____.

03 나는 그녀의 말에 실망했다. (disappoint) → I was _____ with her words.

04 나는 지구를 구하는 데 관심이 있다. (interest) → I am _____ in saving the earth.

05 나는 그의 설명에 혼란스럽다. (confuse) → I feel _____ by his explanation.

06 나는 할머니와 편안한 시간을 보냈다. (relax) → I had a _____ time with my grandma.

07 Ted는 June의 선물에 놀랐다. (surprise) → Ted was _____ at June's present.

현재분사와 동명사는 형태가 같아서, 문맥상 그 쓰임과 의미를 구분할 수 있어야 해요.

	현재분사	동명사
명사 앞	running man 뛰고 있는 남자	running shoes 달리기 신발 *뛰고 있는 신발(X)
	washing woman 세탁하고 있는 여자	washing machine 세탁기 *세탁하고 있는 기계(X)
be의 보어	The news is surprising. 소식은 놀랍다	My hobby is dancing. 취미는 춤추기이다
	The movie was boring. 영화는 지루했다	The plan is going to Jeju. 계획은 가는 것이다

|A| 밑줄 친 부분의 쓰임이 동명사인지 현재분사인지 고르시오.

01 Cooking for my parents is my hobby. (현재분사 / 동명사)

02 You should check the meeting place. (현재분사 / 동명사)

03 You need some running shirts. (현재분사 / 동명사)

04 Joy lost her dancing shoes on the way home. (현재분사 / 동명사)

05 Be careful of the boiling water! (현재분사 / 동명사)

06 Don't forget to bring your swimming wear. (현재분사 / 동명사)

|B| 다음 문장의 밑줄 친 부분이 형용사인지 동명사인지를 고르고, 문장을 우리말로 해석하시오.

01 The movie was so interesting.
(현재분사 / 동명사) → _____

02 Looking after children is not easy.
(현재분사 / 동명사) → _____

03 How about going to a movie tonight?
(현재분사 / 동명사) → _____

04 Look at that barking dog.
(현재분사 / 동명사) → _____

05 Going on a trip alone was a thrilling experience for me.
(현재분사 / 동명사) → _____

06 I heard my dad snoring.
(현재분사 / 동명사) → _____

[01~02] 다음 빈칸에 들어갈 말로 알맞은 것을 고르시오.

01

My job is _____ care of old people.

① take　　　② took　　　③ taking
④ takes　　　⑤ to taken

02

I thought her voice was very _____.

① to fascinate　　　② fascinate
③ fascinated　　　④ fascinating
⑤ to be fascinated

[03~04] 다음 중 빈칸에 들어갈 말이 바르게 짝지어진 것은?

03

· She looked very ____(A)____ by his return.
· I'm tired of ____(B)____ all day.

　　(A)　　　　　(B)
① surprising － not to study
② surprising － to study
③ surprising － studying
④ surprised － to study
⑤ surprised － studying

04

A: What time is the flight tomorrow? I'm really looking forward to ____(A)____ to Jeju.
B: It's 10:30 in the morning. You should remember ____(B)____ at the airport on time.

　　(A)　　　　　(B)
① go　　－　to arrive
② go　　－　arriving
③ going － to arrive
④ going － not arriving
⑤ going － not to arrive

[05~06] 다음 우리말을 영어로 바르게 옮긴 것을 고르시오.

05

나는 어제 놀이터에서 놀았던 것을 기억한다.

① I remember playing at the playground yesterday.
② I remember to play at the playground yesterday.
③ I remember play at the playground yesterday.
④ I remember to playing at the playground yesterday.
⑤ I remembered play at the playground yesterday

06

그녀는 자고 있는 고양이를 소파로 옮겼다.

① She moved the cat slept to the sofa.
② She moved the slept cat to the sofa.
③ She moved cat the sleeping to the sofa.
④ She moved the sleeping cat to the sofa.
⑤ She moved the sleeped cat to the sofa.

[07~08] 다음 중 밑줄 친 부분의 용법이 나머지 넷과 다른 것을 고르시오.

07 ① She was <u>singing</u> in the park.
② I heard him <u>singing</u> a pop song.
③ They were <u>singing</u> together.
④ My hobby is <u>singing</u> in my room.
⑤ Who is <u>singing</u> in the garden?

08 ① Jaemin enjoys <u>drawing</u> sketches of fruit.
② They suggested not <u>having</u> dinner outside.
③ He disliked <u>trying</u> new things such as durian.
④ She avoided <u>riding</u> a bike at night.
⑤ I saw her <u>walking</u> on the roof at night.

09 다음 대화의 빈칸에 들어갈 말로 알맞은 것은?

A: We must hurry for the dinner with Jack.
B: OK, I'll call the taxi.
_____
A: Don't worry. I won't forget.

① Forget to bring the present for him.
② Remember bringing the present for him.
③ Don't forget bringing the present for him.
④ Remember to bring the present for him.
⑤ Don't remember to bring the present for him.

10 다음 짝지어진 문장의 의미가 서로 <u>다른</u> 것은?

① My dream is to travel around the world.
→ My dream is traveling around the world.
② I can't but miss my dog in the hospital.
→ I can't help missing my dog in the hospital.
③ Amy stopped swimming in the pool.
→ Amy stopped to swim in the pool.
④ It is good to drink a cup of coffee a day.
→ Drinking a cup of coffee a day is good.
⑤ Jack started chasing the thief to catch him.
→ Jack started to chase the thief to catch him.

11 다음 중 밑줄 친 부분의 용법이 같은 것끼리 바르게 짝지어진 것은?

ⓐ Did you buy the <u>coloring</u> book yesterday?
ⓑ I was <u>enjoying</u> learning how to bake an apple pie.
ⓒ I was <u>disappointed</u> because I couldn't see the magic show.
ⓓ She touched the <u>burning</u> candle with her hands.
ⓔ <u>Reading</u> many books is a very good way to improve your knowledge.

① ⓐ, ⓑ   ② ⓐ, ⓒ   ③ ⓑ, ⓓ
④ ⓑ, ⓔ   ⑤ ⓓ, ⓔ

12 다음 중 어법상 올바른 것은?

① I picked up a broken box on the street.
② She made the freezing yogurt for me.
③ Sally saw the artist painted the bridge.
④ The river was shone with the moonlight.
⑤ The movie about Helen Keller was touched.

13 다음 중 어법상 <u>어색한</u> 것은?

① Playing the piano in a big concert hall have been my goal.
② Do you mind opening the window for me?
③ Kevin is not used to speaking with foreigners.
④ I couldn't help choosing the last bread.
⑤ Mary practiced not falling from the bike.

14 다음 대화의 빈칸에 들어갈 말이 바르게 짝지어진 것은?

> A: How about going hiking this weekend? I'm trying ___(A)___ if anyone can go with me.
> B: I'm sorry. I'm busy ___(B)___ to my new apartment this week. I'm sorry for making you ___(C)___ .
> A: It's okay. I can find someone else.

	(A)	(B)	(C)
①	finding	moving	disappointed
②	finding	moving	disappointing
③	to find	moving	disappointed
④	to find	to move	disappointing
⑤	to find	to move	disappointed

15 다음 중 어법상 <u>어색한</u> 문장의 개수는?

> ⓐ Don't be afraid of diving in the sea.
> ⓑ How about jogging tomorrow morning?
> ⓒ I wore shoes making of rubber.
> ⓓ He was confused by her mistake.

① 없음   ② 1개   ③ 2개   ④ 3개   ⑤ 4개

16 우리말과 뜻이 같도록 괄호 안의 말을 이용하여 문장을 완성하시오.

> Sally에 의해 만들어진 그 장갑은 아름답다. (make)

The gloves _____ by Sally were beautiful.

17 우리말과 뜻이 같도록 괄호 안의 말을 바르게 배열하시오.

> 그 외국인은 젓가락을 사용하는 데 어려움을 겪었다. (chopsticks, the, using, trouble, had, foreigner)

_____

_____

[18~20] 다음 밑줄 친 동명사의 용법이 무엇인지 |보기|에서 골라 각각에 해당하는 기호를 쓰시오.

> |보기|
> ⓐ 주어   ⓑ 보어
> ⓒ 동사의 목적어   ⓓ 전치사의 목적어

18 He is worried about <u>catching</u> a cold.

→ _____

19 He is enjoying <u>drinking</u> a glass of wine.

→ _____

20 <u>Drinking</u> warm water helps you get better.

→ _____

[21~23] 다음 문장에서 어법상 <u>어색한</u> 부분을 찾아 바르게 고치시오.

21 Don't forget finishing your homework by tomorrow.

_____ → _____

22 Building a hospital are one of his dreams.

_____ → _____

23 You can earn money by read books to old people.

_____ → _____

[24~25] 다음 문장에서 어법상 <u>어색한</u> 부분을 고쳐 완전한 문장을 쓰시오.

24 It is no use to talk about it.

→ _____

_____

25 I'm used to live in the rural area.

→ _____

_____

26 다음 문장을 지시대로 바꿔 쓰시오.

Susan's goal is holding her own exhibition. (동명사의 의문문으로)

→ _____

_____

[27~28] 다음 괄호 안의 말을 이용하여 문장을 완성하시오.

27 I look forward _____ her at school tomorrow. (see)

28 _____ me, my dog ran to me. (see)

[29~30] 주어진 |조건|을 이용하여 우리말을 영어로 바꾸시오.

29 ┤조건├
　1. 동사 regret의 목적어를 문장의 의미에 맞게 사용할 것
　2. 단어 regret, tell, this news를 사용할 것
　3. 7단어를 사용할 것

나는 너에게 이 뉴스를 말하게 되어 유감이다.

→ _____

_____

30 ┤조건├
　1. 현재분사(진행)와 과거분사(수동)의 형태를 사용할 것
　2. 단어 eat, the grapes, grow, the farmer를 활용하여 쓸 것
　3. 8단어를 사용할 것
　4. 필요시 축약형을 써도 됨

나는 그 농부가 키운 포도를 먹고 있다.

→ _____

_____

대명사, 형용사, 부사

부정대명사 1

부정대명사 one, all, both의 쓰임을 알아 두세요.

one / ones	정해지지 않은 대상을 가리킴	all	모든, 전부
it / they	정해진 대상을 가리킴	both	둘 다(의), 양쪽 모두

우리말과 같은 뜻이 되도록 |보기|에서 알맞은 말을 골라 빈칸에 쓰시오.

| 보기 |
| one   ones   it   all   both |

01 그들 모두 다 그 파티를 즐겼다. → _____ of them enjoyed the party.

02 그녀는 돈을 전부 다 도둑맞았다. → She had _____ of her money stolen.

03 그의 부모님은 두 분 다 일하신다. → _____ of his parents work.

04 빨간 점들이 있는 것들을 주세요. → Can I have the _____ with red dots?

05 그녀는 그 소파를 팔고, 새 것을 샀다. → She sold the sofa and got a new _____.

UNIT 02 **부정대명사 2**

정해진 범위(2개, 3개) 내에서 하나씩 가리킬 때 one, another, the other를 써요.

구분	부정대명사	의미	수	예문
둘 중에서	one	하나	단수	One is red.
	the other	나머지 하나		The other is blue.
셋 중에서	one	하나		One is red.
	another	또 다른 하나		Another is blue.
	the other	나머지 하나		The other is yellow.

참고 other(그 밖의 다른, 그 밖의 다른 것) 앞에 the가 붙으면 특정한 것이 되므로 '나머지 하나는'이라는 의미가 돼요.

우리말과 같은 뜻이 되도록 |보기|에서 알맞은 말을 골라 빈칸에 쓰시오.

| 보기 |
| one   ones   the other   another   others |

01 너는 휴대폰이 이미 있는데, 왜 또 하나가 더 필요하니?

You already have a mobile phone. so why do you need _____?

02 우리는 다른 사람들을 돕도록 늘 노력해야 한다.

We should always try to help _____.

03 그녀에게는 형제가 두 명 있다. 한 명은 오빠고, 나머지 한 명은 남동생이다.

She has two brothers. _____ is older than her. and _____ is younger than her.

04 나는 색연필 세 자루가 있다. 하나는 빨강, 또 다른 하나는 노랑, 나머지 하나는 초록이다.

I have three colored pencils. _____ is red. _____ is yellow. and _____ is green.

UNIT 03 부정대명사 3

대상이 여러 개의 경우, 쓸 수 있는 부정대명사의 표현을 알아 두세요.

some ~, others ...	(정해지지 않은 수에서) 어떤 사람들은 ~하고, 또 어떤 사람들은 ···하다
some ~, the others ...	(정해진 수에서) 어떤 사람들은 ~하고, 나머지 모두는 ···하다
each other	(둘 사이에서) 서로
one another	(셋 이상일 때) 서로서로

우리말과 같은 뜻이 되도록 괄호 안의 말과 부정대명사를 이용하여 문장을 완성하시오.

01 어떤 아이들은 용감하지만, 다른 아이들은 그렇지 않다.

_____ are brave. but _____ are not.

02 Emily와 그녀의 친구들은 서로를 껴안았다. (hug)

Emily and her friends _____.

03 엄마랑 나는 자주 서로 통화한다. (call)

My mom and I _____ frequently.

04 몇몇 학생들은 영어 공부를 즐겼지만, 다른 학생들은 그렇지 않았다. (enjoy)

_____ studying English. but _____ didn't.

05 세 자매는 서로 닮았다. (resemble)

The three sisters _____.

06 몇몇 사람들은 집에 머물렀지만, 나머지 모든 사람들은 밖에 나가 놀았다. (go out)

_____ people stayed at home. and _____ to play.

UNIT 04 부정대명사 4

다양한 부정대명사의 쓰임을 알아 두세요.

each	(하나하나) 각각(의)	some	몇몇(의), 약간(의) (긍정, 권유)
every	매, 다, 모든	any	어떤 ~도, 조금이라도 (부정, 의문)

우리말과 같은 뜻이 되도록 |보기|에서 알맞은 말을 골라 빈칸에 쓰시오.

| 보기 |

each	every	some	any

01 그는 아프리카의 일부 지역을 방문했다. → He visited _____ parts of Africa.

02 다른 질문이라도 있니? → Are there _____ other questions?

03 우리는 방학마다 할머니 댁을 방문한다. → We visit our grandma _____ vacation.

04 각각의 텐트는 모양이 다 다르다. → _____ tent is different in shape.

05 나는 책 몇 권을 반납해야 한다. → I must return _____ books.

06 각각의 학생은 재능을 가지고 있다. → _____ of the students has a talent.

UNIT 05 재귀대명사

재귀대명사를 어떤 경우에 사용하는지 파악하세요.

재귀	주어와 동일 목적어일 때	I love myself. (○) *I love ~~me~~. (×)	목적어이므로 생략 ×
강조	'직접'이라는 의미로 주어/목적어를 강조할 때	We (ourselves) made the cake (ourselves).	강조 역할로 생략 ○

😊 참고 단수일 때는 인칭대명사 뒤에 -self, 복수일 때는 -selves를 붙여서 써야 해요.

우리말과 같은 뜻이 되도록 괄호 안의 말과 재귀대명사를 이용하여 문장을 완성하시오.

01 그 꼬마 여자아이는 스스로가 제일 예쁘다고 생각한다. (think)

The little girl _____ the most beautiful.

02 내 여동생은 스스로 이 컴퓨터를 고칠 수 있다. (fix)

My sister can _____ this computer _____.

03 네가 직접 그녀에게 진실을 말하는 게 좋겠다. (tell)

You'd better _____ the truth to her _____.

04 그 아이들은 스스로를 달콤한 아이스크림으로 가득 채웠다. (fill)

The children _____ with sweet ice cream.

05 네가 직접 나를 위해 이 생일 케이크를 만들었니? (make)

Did you _____ this birthday cake for me _____?

UNIT 06 재귀대명사 관용표현

재귀대명사를 포함한 다음 관용표현을 알아 두세요.

for oneself	혼자 힘으로, 스스로	talk to oneself	혼잣말하다
by oneself	홀로, 혼자서(= alone)	enjoy oneself	즐거운 시간을 보내다
of itself	저절로	make oneself at home	편하게 지내다
in itself	본래, 그 자체가	help oneself to	~을 마음껏 먹다
beside oneself	제정신이 아닌	kill oneself	자살하다

우리말과 같은 뜻이 되도록 재귀대명사 관용표현을 이용하여 문장을 완성하시오.

01 원하는 것은 어느 것이든 마음껏 드세요. → _____ anything you want.

02 너희들은 파티에서 즐거운 시간을 보냈니? → Did you _____ at the party?

03 그의 삶은 그 자체로 예술이었다. → His life was an art _____.

04 그는 혼자 힘으로 그것을 끝마칠 수 없었다. → He couldn't finish it _____.

05 너는 혼자 영화 보러 가니? → Do you go to a movie _____?

06 여기 계시는 동안, 편하게 지내세요. → _____ while you are here.

UNIT 07   -thing + 형용사

명사를 수식하는 형용사의 위치를 잘 파악하세요.

형용사+명사	a useful book 유용한 책
명사+형용사구	a book useful for kids 아이들에게 유용한 책
-thing/-one/-body+형용사	nothing wrong 잘못된 것이 없음
-thing/-one/-body+형용사+to부정사(형용사적 용법)	something important to know 알아야 할 중요한 것

우리말과 같은 뜻이 되도록 괄호 안의 말과 -thing 또는 -one을 이용하여 문장을 완성하시오.

01 Tomas는 다른 사람들에게 나에 대해 뭔가 안 좋은 이야기를 했다. (bad)

Tomas told others _____ about me.

02 그에게는 특별한 뭔가가 있어 보이지 않는다. (special)

He doesn't seem to have _____.

03 나의 목표는 매일 무언가 새로운 것을 배우는 것이다. (new)

My goal is to learn _____ every day.

04 거짓말을 하는 것에는 좋은 게 하나도 없다. (good)

There is _____ about telling a lie.

05 내 여동생은 단 것을 아주 좋아한다. (sweet)

My younger sister is very fond of _____.

06 중요한 할 말 있으면 언제든지 내게 전화해. (to say, important)

If you have _____. call me anytime.

UNIT 08   수량형용사

명사의 수와 양을 나타내는 수량형용사를 기억해 두세요.

많은	+ 명사	조금/약간 있는	+ 명사	거의 없는	+ 명사
many	+ 복수명사	a few	+ 복수명사	few	+ 복수명사
much	+ 셀 수 없는 명사	a little	+ 셀 수 없는 명사	little	+ 셀 수 없는 명사

주의 '많은'은 명사에 상관없이 a lot of를 쓸 수 있고, '약간'은 명사에 상관없이 some(긍정, 권유)이나 any(부정, 의문)를 쓸 수 있어요.

우리말과 같은 뜻이 되도록 괄호 안의 말과 수량형용사를 이용하여 문장을 완성하시오.

01 그녀는 오늘 책을 몇 권 빌렸다. (book)   → She borrowed _____ today.

02 실수가 거의 없었다. (mistake)   → There were _____.

03 그는 가족과 지낼 시간이 거의 없다. (time)   → He has _____ to spend with his family.

04 어떤 문제가 있나요? (problem)   → Are there _____ ?

05 그녀는 많은 변화를 겪었다. (changes)   → She went through _____.

부사의 역할과 형태

부사가 수식하는 말들과 부사의 위치를 알아 두세요.

형용사 수식	형용사 바로 앞	He is my very good friend.
다른 부사 수식	수식하는 부사 바로 앞	He speaks too slowly.
동사 수식	문장 뒤	Snails move slowly.
문장 전체 수식	문장 앞	Fortunately, there is a solution.

우리말과 같은 뜻이 되도록 괄호 안의 말을 이용하여 문장을 완성하시오.

01 그는 매우 빠른 달리기 선수이다. (fast, very) → He is a _____ runner.

02 너는 너무 빨리 운전하고 있다. (fast, too) → You are driving _____.

03 다행히도, 아무도 다치지 않았다. (lucky) → _____, no one was injured.

04 그 가수는 부드럽게 노래했다. (soft) → The singer sang _____.

05 그녀는 쉽게 상처를 받는다. (easy) → Her feelings get hurt _____.

06 우리 아빠는 아침 일찍 일어난다. (early) → My dad gets up _____ in the morning.

UNIT 10 **빈도부사**

얼마나 자주(빈도)인지에 따라서 부사를 알맞게 선택해야 해요.

빈도	100%	80–90%	60%	30–40%	10%	0%
부사	always	usually	often	sometimes	hardly/seldom	never
	항상	보통, 대개	종종, 자주	가끔, 때때로	거의 ~않다	절대 ~않다

주의 빈도부사는 be동사 뒤, 일반동사 앞에 쓰고, 조동사가 있다면 조동사 뒤에 써요.

우리말과 같은 뜻이 되도록 괄호 안의 말을 배열하여 문장을 완성하시오.

01 Jessica는 제시간에 오는 경우가 거의 없다. (seldom, on, time, arrives)

Jessica _____.

02 그는 남동생의 숙제를 자주 도와줬다. (brother, often, helped, his)

He _____ with his homework.

03 그녀는 주로 긴 치마와 티셔츠를 입는다. (long, usually, wears, skirts)

She _____ and T-shirts.

04 우리 가족과 나는 매년 겨울 방학마다 늘 산에 간다. (mountains, to, go, always, the)

My family and I _____ every winter vacation.

05 우리 선생님은 좀처럼 우리에게 화를 내지 않으신다. (us, angry, with, hardly, gets)

My teacher _____.

[01~02] 다음 빈칸에 들어갈 말로 알맞은 것을 고르시오.

01

A: Do you have any red chillies?
B: No. We only have green _____.

① some   ② one   ③ it
④ them   ⑤ ones

02

There is _____ water in the pond.

① a few   ② few   ③ a little
④ one   ⑤ many

03 다음 밑줄 친 부분과 바꿔 쓸 수 있는 말은?

I could pick lots of strawberries in the countryside.

① much   ② many   ③ a few
④ some   ⑤ few

[04~05] 다음 빈칸에 들어갈 말이 바르게 짝지어진 것을 고르시오.

04

Sumi invited us to her party. _____ of us have come, but _____ haven't come.

① Some – ones   ② Ones – others
③ The ones – some ④ Some – others
⑤ Some – the others

05

• There are _____ places to ride a bike around our house.
• I _____ eat vanilla ice cream.

① a little – hardly   ② many – hard
③ little – hardly   ④ few – hardly
⑤ a few – hard

06 다음 문장의 밑줄 친 재귀대명사와 용법이 같은 것은?

I should finish my homework myself.

① She herself won the prize at the game.
② I said to myself, "I can do it!"
③ He stayed up all night by himself.
④ My sister wore the socks for herself.
⑤ Mary looked at herself in the mirror.

07 다음 우리말을 영어로 바르게 옮긴 것은?

Tom은 종종 자신의 방에서 혼잣말을 했다.

① Tom often talks to himself in his room.
② Tom often talked to himself in his room.
③ Tom often talks to him in his room.
④ Tom often talked to him in his room.
⑤ Tom often talked himself in his room.

08 다음 중 밑줄 친 long의 쓰임이 나머지 넷과 <u>다른</u> 것은?

① The king lived very <u>long</u>.
② He gave me a <u>long</u> dress.
③ I waited so <u>long</u> for the subway.
④ How <u>long</u> have you lived in Incheon?
⑤ The hot weather lasts <u>long</u> this summer.

[09~10] 다음 중 어법상 <u>어색한</u> 것을 고르시오.

09 ① She wrote the story herself.
② Help yourself to the pasta and salad.
③ He wrote a letter to hisself in the camp.
④ I enjoyed myself listening to the music.
⑤ She herself heard the strange voice yesterday.

10 ① There isn't any milk left in the cup.
② Any dogs were barking at the thief at night.
③ Do you have a lot of friends in your class?
④ I heard that some students went to the hospital.
⑤ Exercising for a few hours every day helps your health.

11 다음 중 어법상 올바른 것은?

① You have to be polite to others people.
② I ate this meatball spaghetti and I like one.
③ Each the cats in the room were sleeping.
④ Some people are happy, but anothers are sad.
⑤ I want one more apple. Can you pass me another?

12 다음 중 어법상 <u>어색한</u> 문장의 개수는?

ⓐ Let me introduce myself to you.
ⓑ Both of my parents like to travel a lot.
ⓒ I saw her in your room a little days ago.
ⓓ My friend and I go often to see a movie.

① 없음   ② 1개   ③ 2개   ④ 3개   ⑤ 4개

13 다음 중 수식하는 대상이 같은 것끼리 짝지어진 것은?

ⓐ I'm <u>truly</u> sorry for my mistake.
ⓑ He has <u>enough</u> time to travel.
ⓒ I studied <u>late</u> until the moon rose.
ⓓ She is a <u>lovely</u> girl in my class.
ⓔ I have to leave <u>early</u>.
ⓕ The table made by him is <u>hard</u>.

① ⓐ, ⓑ   ② ⓐ, ⓕ   ③ ⓑ, ⓓ
④ ⓑ, ⓔ   ⑤ ⓓ, ⓔ

14 다음 대화의 빈칸에 들어갈 말이 바르게 짝지어진 것은?

A: Please help ___(A)___ to sandwiches.
B: Thank you. I'll have ___(B)___.
A: Would you like ___(C)___ milk?
B: No, thanks.

	(A)		(B)		(C)
①	you	–	it	–	any
②	yourself	–	one	–	any
③	you	–	it	–	some
④	yourself	–	one	–	some
⑤	you	–	it	–	some

15 다음 밑줄 친 ⓐ~ⓔ 중 어법상 <u>어색한</u> 것은?

> It's the second year of middle school. I'm looking forward to having ⓐ<u>a lot of</u> friends. Luckily, I was able to join a dance club. ⓑ<u>All</u> the members are friendly. We ⓒ<u>always</u> practice K-pop dances ⓓ<u>hardly</u> every Friday evening. Now I can have ⓔ<u>both</u> good friends and good health!

① ⓐ   ② ⓑ   ③ ⓒ
④ ⓓ   ⑤ ⓔ

[16~17] 다음 괄호 안에 주어진 빈도부사를 문장 중간의 알맞은 위치에 넣어 문장을 다시 쓰시오.

16 He thinks of other people's feelings. (always)

→ _____

_____

17 Text messaging can be a convenient way of communication. (sometimes)

→ _____

_____

[18~20] 다음 |보기|에서 알맞은 말을 골라 빈칸에 각각 쓰시오.

> ┌ 보기 ┐
> one   ones   it   them

18 I made three wooden toys. Do you want me to show you _____?

19 I lost my pencil. Can I borrow _____ from you?

20 My old shoes are too small for me now. I need to buy new _____.

21 우리말과 뜻이 같도록 괄호 안의 말을 바르게 배열 하시오.

> 그들은 그 소식 때문에 제정신이 아니었다.
> (themselves, the, were, because, news, they, beside, of)

_____

_____

[22~25] 다음 |보기|에서 알맞은 말을 골라 빈칸에 각각 쓰시오.

┌─|보기|──────────────────────┐
│ many   much   a little   a few │
└──────────────────────────────┘

22 I saw so _____ birds in the sky.

23 How _____ money do you need to buy a wallet?

24 Only _____ students passed the test.

25 When you boil eggs, put _____ salt in the water.

[26~27] 다음 문장에서 어법상 어색한 부분을 찾아 바르게 고치시오.

26 Every guest need to arrive on time.

_____ → _____

27 You had better not eat too many sugar.

_____ → _____

[28~29] 다음 문장에서 어법상 어색한 부분을 고쳐 완전한 문장을 쓰시오.

28 It's very hot, and there's few water to drink.

→ _____

_____

29 There was expensive nothing to buy on the list.

→ _____

_____

30 주어진 |조건|을 이용하여 우리말을 영어로 바꾸시오.

┌─|조건|──────────────────────┐
│ 1. 빈도부사 seldom을 사용할 것 │
│ 2. 단어 watch, TV, nowadays, can을 사용 │
│   할 것 │
│ 3. 6단어를 사용할 것 │
└──────────────────────────────┘

그는 요즘 TV를 좀처럼 보지 못한다.

→ _____

_____

비교 표현

UNIT 01 원급 비교

'~만큼 …한[하게]'는 〈as+형용사/부사+as〉로 표현하세요.

형용사	She is	as	kind	as	him[he is].
부사	She can swim		well		him[he can].

주의 부정문(~만큼 …하지 않은[않게])은 〈not as[so]+형용사/부사+as〉로 쓸 수 있어요.

우리말과 같은 뜻이 되도록 괄호 안의 말을 이용하여 문장을 완성하시오.

01 이 상자는 커다란 돌만큼이나 무겁다. (be, heavy)

This box _____ a large rock.

02 오늘도 어제만큼 덥다. (be, hot)

Today _____ yesterday.

03 그들은 축구만큼 배구를 즐기지는 않는다. (enjoy, much)

They _____ volleyball _____ soccer.

04 나는 우리 엄마만큼 일찍 일어날 수는 없다. (get up, early)

I can't _____ my mom.

05 나는 우리 언니만큼 키가 크고 싶다. (be, tall)

I want to _____ my sister.

06 이곳의 음식은 우리 엄마의 음식만큼 맛있지 않다. (taste, good)

The food here does _____ my mom's.

UNIT 02 as+형용사/부사+as possible

〈as+형용사/부사+as〉를 이용한 다음 표현을 익혀 두세요.

as ~ as possible	가능한 한 ~하게	Please call me as quickly as possible.
as ~ as 주어+can[could]	주어가 할 수 있는 만큼 ~하게	Please call me as quickly as you can.

주의 〈as ~ as〉 뒤에 〈주어+can[could]〉를 쓸 때 알맞은 주어와 시제에 유의하세요.

두 문장의 뜻이 같도록 문장을 완성하시오.

01 Ants dig as deep as they can.　　　　= Ants dig _____.

02 You should talk as quietly as possible. = You should talk _____.

03 Send this message as fast as you can. = Send this message _____.

04 They took a walk as often as possible. = They took a walk _____.

05 Eat junk food as little as you can.　　 = Eat junk food _____.

06 Stay as close as possible.　　　　　　= Stay _____.

형용사나 부사의 비교급과 최상급을 만드는 방법을 알아 두세요.

원급	tall	nice	early	famous
비교급	taller	nicer	earlier	more famous
최상급	tallest	nicest	earliest	most famous

불규칙 변화하는 형용사/부사의 비교급과 최상급은 암기해야 해요.

good / well	better – best	many / much	more – most
bad / ill / badly	worse – worst	little	less – least

다음 단어들의 비교급과 최상급을 쓰면서 외우시오.

01	화난	angry	–	_____	–	_____
02	나쁜	bad	–		–	
03	아름다운	beautiful	–		–	
04	큰	big	–		–	
05	따분한	boring	–		–	
06	바쁜	busy	–		–	
07	조심하는	careful	–		–	
08	위험한	dangerous	–		–	
09	근면한, 성실한	diligent	–		–	
10	더러운	dirty	–		–	
11	쉬운	easy	–		–	
12	쉽게	easily	–		–	
13	뚱뚱한	fat	–		–	
14	상냥한	friendly	–		–	
15	좋은	good	–		–	
16	무거운	heavy	–		–	
17	뜨거운	hot	–		–	
18	아픈	ill	–		–	
19	게으른	lazy	–		–	
20	가벼운	light	–		–	
21	양이 적은	little	–		–	
22	사랑스러운	lovely	–		–	
23	많은	many/much	–		–	
24	예쁜	pretty	–		–	
25	빨리	quickly	–		–	
26	슬픈	sad	–		–	
27	화창한	sunny	–		–	
28	맛있는	tasty	–		–	
29	잘	well	–		–	

UNIT 04 | 비교급

비교 표현 '~보다 더 …한[하게]는 〈비교급+than ~〉으로 써야 해요.

비교급+than (~보다)	She is <u>taller than</u> her mom.	그녀는 그녀의 엄마보다 더 키가 크다.
비교급 강조(훨씬)	She is <u>much taller than</u> her mom.	그녀는 그녀의 엄마보다 훨씬 더 키가 크다.

🙁주의 비교급을 강조하여 '훨씬 더'라고 할 때, 비교급 앞에 much, even, far, still, a lot을 써요.
*very는 쓸 수 없음에 주의하세요.

우리말과 같은 뜻이 되도록 괄호 안의 말을 이용하여 문장을 완성하시오.

01 그는 전보다 더 건강해 보인다. (look, healthy) → He _____ before.

02 이것이 저것보다 훨씬 더 싸다. (cheap, far) → This is _____ that.

03 그녀는 나의 목숨보다 더 귀하다. (valuable) → She is _____ my life.

04 그는 나보다도 훨씬 더 무겁다. (heavy, a lot) → He is _____ me.

05 어제보다는 기분이 좀 나아졌니? (feel, good) → Do you _____ yesterday?

06 그녀는 보이는 것보다 더 강하다. (strong) → She is _____ she looks.

UNIT 05 | 배수사 비교

'~보다 …배 더 ~한[하게]'는 〈as+원급+as〉 또는 〈비교급+than〉 앞에 배수사를 붙이세요.

주어+동사	배수(사)	원급/비교급	비교 대상	의미
Regular pizza is	three times	as thick as	thin pizza.	얇은 피자보다 3배 더 두꺼운
		thicker than		

두 문장이 같은 뜻이 되도록 원급 또는 비교급을 이용하여 문장을 완성하시오.

01 Jane's hair was three times longer than mine.

= Jane's hair was _____ as mine.

02 These shoes are five times as light as yours.

= These shoes are _____ than yours.

03 My pet bird lived three times as long as my dog.

= My pet bird lived _____ than my dog.

04 That watch is nine times more expensive than this watch.

= That watch is _____ as this watch.

05 This lake is six times bigger than the one in my town.

= This lake is _____ as the one in my town.

06 Mr. Kim spends four times as much money as his friends.

= Mr. Kim spends _____ money than his friends.

UNIT 06 비교급 표현

다음 비교급을 이용한 유용한 표현을 알아 두세요.

표현	〈the+비교급 ~, the+비교급 ...〉	〈비교급+and+비교급〉
의미	~하면 할수록 더 …하다	점점 더 ~한[하게]

두 문장이 같은 뜻이 되도록 〈the+비교급, the+비교급〉을 이용하여 문장을 완성하시오.

01 If you exercise more often. you will become healthier.

= _____ you exercise, _____ you will become.

02 As I knew more about her. I liked her more.

= _____ I knew about her, _____ I liked her.

03 As they became busier. they felt less relaxed.

= _____ they became, _____ they felt.

04 When the bus was more crowded. the passengers' voices got louder.

= _____ the bus was, _____ the passengers' voices got.

05 As we loved each other more. we met more often.

= _____ we loved each other, _____ often we met.

UNIT 07 최상급

다음 최상급 표현을 알아 두세요.

표현	〈the+최상급〉	〈one of the+최상급+복수명사〉
의미	가장 ~한[하게]	가장 ~한 것들 중 하나

참고 최상급 뒤에는 〈in+단수명사(장소나 집단): ~에서〉 또는 〈of+복수명사(~들 중에서)〉가 올 수 있어요.

우리말과 같은 뜻이 되도록 괄호 안의 말을 이용해 문장을 완성하시오.

01 그녀는 가장 유명한 모델 중 한 명이다. (famous. model)

She is _____.

02 Joy는 학교에서 최고의 학생이다. (good, student)

Joy is _____ in her school.

03 가장 인기 있는 직업 중 하나는 수의사다. (popular. job)

_____ is a vet.

04 그는 회사에서 가장 열심히 일한다. (hard, work)

_____ in the company.

05 오늘은 올해 중에 가장 행복한 날이다. (happy. day. year)

Today is _____.

UNIT 08 최상급 표현

원급과 비교급을 이용하여 최상급의 의미를 표현하는 방법을 알아 두세요.

원급	No (other) ~ as[so]+원급+as	비교급	No (other) ~ 비교급+than 비교급+than any other+단수명사 비교급+than all the other+복수명사

두 문장이 같은 뜻이 되도록 문장을 완성하시오.

01 No other sports attracted her more than figure skating.

= _____ her the most.

02 Taemin can dance the best.

= No other _____ than Taemin.

03 No other musician is as great as Amadeus Mozart.

= Amadeus Mozart _____ other musician.

04 A dog is the most beloved pet.

= No other _____ as a dog.

05 My mom's chicken soup is the most delicious food.

= _____ as my mom's chicken soup.

06 Football is the most popular sport in Brazil.

= _____ as football.

UNIT 09 원급 vs. 비교급 vs. 최상급

형용사/부사의 원급, 비교급, 최상급에 관한 기본 사항을 표에서 확인한 후 종합적으로 연습하세요.

구분	형태	의미	참고
원급	as ~ as ...	…만큼 ~한[하게]	as ~ as 사이에는 원급을 써요.
비교급	-er[more ~] than ...	…보다 더 ~한[하게]	전치사 than과 함께 써요.
최상급	the -est[most ~] of/in ...	…에서/중에서 가장 ~한[하게]	최상급 앞에 the를 붙여요.

우리말과 같은 뜻이 되도록 괄호 안의 말을 이용하여 문장을 완성하시오.

01 그것은 내가 생각한 것만큼 뜨거웠다. (hot) → It was _____ I expected.

02 그의 목소리가 그녀의 것보다 부드럽다. (soft) → His voice is _____.

03 피카소는 가장 위대한 예술가였다. (great) → Picasso was _____.

04 그는 가능한 한 조심스럽게 걸었다. (carefully) → He walked _____.

05 이 시계가 이 가게에서 가장 비싸다. (expensive) → This watch is _____.

06 신용카드가 현금보다 편리하다. (convenient) → Credit cards _____ cash.

[01~02] 다음 빈칸에 들어갈 말로 알맞은 것을 고르시오.

01

> He can run as _____ as his coach.

① fastest　　② faster　　③ fast
④ most fast　　⑤ more fast

02

> My grandfather is the _____ in my family.

① old　　② older　　③ old enough
④ too old　　⑤ oldest

03 다음 중 원급 – 비교급 – 최상급 형태가 <u>잘못된</u> 것은?

① little – less – least
② lazy – lazier – laziest
③ ill – worse – worst
④ bright – more bright – most bright
⑤ busy – busier – busiest

04 다음 중 빈칸에 들어갈 말로 알맞지 <u>않은</u> 것은?

> Shawn sings _____ better than anyone else.

① still　　② far　　③ very
④ much　　⑤ a lot

05 다음 중 빈칸에 들어갈 말이 바르게 짝지어진 것은?

> _____ you save, _____ you will become.

① The most – the richest
② More – richer
③ The more – the richest
④ The more – the richer
⑤ More – the richest

06 다음 우리말을 영어로 바르게 옮긴 것은?

> 눈이 점점 더 심하게 내렸다.

① The snow fell hard and harder.
② The snow fell more hard and hard.
③ The snow fell harder and harder.
④ The snow fell harder and the harder.
⑤ The snow fell the harder and the harder.

07 다음 중 주어진 문장과 의미가 같은 것은?

> This watermelon is bigger than that melon.

① That melon is smaller than this watermelon.
② That melon isn't smaller than this watermelon.
③ This watermelon is as small as that melon.
④ That melon is bigger than this watermelon.
⑤ That melon is bigger than all the other fruits.

08 다음 중 문장의 의미가 나머지 넷과 <u>다른</u> 것은?

① Ivan is the smartest boy in my school.
② No other student is as smart as Ivan in my school.
③ No other student is smarter than Ivan in my school.
④ Ivan isn't smarter than any other student in my school.
⑤ Ivan is smarter than all the other students in my school.

09 다음 중 어법상 올바른 것은?

① This town is quiet than my hometown.
② She earned much more money as I did.
③ This chocolate is still more delicious than that candy.
④ She is the a lot best singer in Korea.
⑤ I'm smallest student in my classroom.

10 다음 중 어법상 <u>어색한</u> 것은?

① His strength is far stronger than mine.
② She is one of the prettiest girl in our town.
③ Mount Everest is higher than all the other mountains in the world.
④ The weather is getting hotter and hotter.
⑤ I ate more apples than Sarah did.

11 다음 중 어법상 올바른 문장의 개수는?

ⓐ My father's foot is bigger than my uncle.
ⓑ The many medals you get, the famous you become.
ⓒ Wonho is as not tall as Junho.
ⓓ This is one of the biggest balloons I've ever seen.

① 없음   ② 1개   ③ 2개   ④ 3개   ⑤ 4개

12 다음 중 어법상 <u>어색한</u> 문장의 개수는?

ⓐ Please call me back as soon as possible.
ⓑ Using that knife seems even dangerous.
ⓒ Your hair is three times longer than me.
ⓓ He is one of braver captains in our camp.

① 없음   ② 1개   ③ 2개   ④ 3개   ⑤ 4개

13 다음 중 빈칸에 들어갈 말이 바르게 짝지어진 것은?

A: I'd like to buy these shoes. Can I try them on?
B: Of course.
A: They are ____(A)____ for me. Do you have a ____(B)____ size?
B: I'm sorry, but it is the ____(C)____ in our store.

	(A)	(B)	(C)
①	large	– smaller	– largest
②	large	– smaller	– smallest
③	small	– smaller	– largest
④	larger	– small	– largest
⑤	small	– large	– smallest

14 다음 가격표를 보고 올바르게 설명한 것은?

pencil	color pen	notebook	eraser
$1.50	$2	$2.50	$1

① A pencil is cheaper than an eraser.
② A color pen is more expensive than a notebook.
③ A pencil is the cheapest one.
④ An eraser is cheaper than all the other things.
⑤ A notebook is the biggest one.

15 다음 문장들 중 무거운 순서대로 알맞게 나열한 것은?

• Tom is much heavier than Jina.
• Jina is the lightest one of the four.
• Sophie isn't as heavy as Tom.
• Sophie is less heavier than Sam.
• Sam is as heavy as Tom.

① Tom 〉 Sam 〉 Jina
② Sophie 〉 Tom 〉 Jina
③ Sam 〉 Sophie 〉 Jina
④ Sam 〉 Tom 〉 Sophie
⑤ Tom 〉 Sam 〉 Sophie

[16~17] 다음 괄호 안에 주어진 말을 알맞은 형태로 고쳐 쓰시오.

16 Today is the _____ day in my life. Everything went wrong. (bad)

17 The magic show was as _____ as the football game. (exciting)

[18~19] 우리말과 뜻이 같도록 괄호 안의 말을 이용하여 문장을 완성하시오.

18 나의 아빠는 점점 더 늙으신다. (old)

My father is getting _____ and _____.

19 샘이 춤을 오래 출수록, 그는 더 신나 보였다. (long, excited)

_____ Sam danced, _____ he looked.

20 다음 문장과 뜻이 같도록 possible을 이용하여 문장을 완성하시오.

I passed the ball to Linda as quickly as I could.

= I passed the ball to Linda _____ _____.

[21~23] 다음 |보기|에서 알맞은 말을 골라 빈칸에 각각 쓰시오.

|보기|
| very | far | as | more |

21 No bag is _____ expensive as this bag.

22 I think I love you much _____ than he does.

23 This movie is _____ more interesting than that movie.

24 우리말과 뜻이 같도록 괄호 안의 말을 바르게 배열하시오.

> 그는 나보다 메달을 세 배나 많이 받았다.
> (received, as, me, he, medals, three times, as, many)

_____

_____

[25~27] 다음 문장에서 어법상 <u>어색한</u> 부분을 찾아 바르게 고치시오.

25 I like sandwiches as more as hamburgers.

_____ → _____

26 Her lemon pie is the most tasty in this bakery.

_____ → _____

27 My textbook is cleaner than Mike.

_____ → _____

[28~29] 다음 문장에서 어법상 <u>어색한</u> 부분을 고쳐 완전한 문장을 쓰시오.

28 Jack is much famous than any other artist in Europe.

→ _____

_____

29 Mina and I are twins, but she is so healthy not as me.

→ _____

_____

30 주어진 |조건|을 이용하여 우리말을 영어로 바꾸시오.

> ┤조건├
> 1. 비교급을 강조하는 단어 even을 사용할 것
> 2. 단어 store, noisy, than, other를 활용하여 쓸 것
> 3. 8단어를 사용할 것

그의 가게는 다른 가게들보다 훨씬 시끄럽다.

→ _____

_____

의문사 의문문

UNIT 01   who/what 의문문

사람 또는 사물에 대한 구체적인 정보를 요구할 때 쓰는 의문사를 알아 두세요.

누구	보어	Who is she?	무엇	보어	What is this?
누가	주어	Who knows you?	무엇이	주어	What makes you mad?
누구를	목적어	Who(m) do you know?	무엇을	목적어	What do you like?

참고 어떤 것, 어느 쪽을 물을 때는 which를 사용하고 선택 가능한 것들을 or로 연결해요.

우리말과 같은 뜻이 되도록 괄호 안의 말을 배열하여 문장을 완성하시오.

01 너는 여름 방학 동안에 무엇을 했니? (do, did, what, you)

_____ during the summer vacation?

02 주스와 아이스크림 중에 어느 것이 더 좋니? (prefer, you, do, which)

_____, juice or ice cream?

03 그녀가 가장 좋아하는 노래는 뭐니? (like, she, song, what, does)

_____ the most?

04 네가 염두에 둔 게 뭐니? (have, do, what, you)

_____ in mind?

05 너는 파티에서 누구를 만났니? (meet, did, who, you)

_____ at the party?

06 네가 가장 좋아하는 작가는 누구니? (author, is, your, who, favorite)

_____?

UNIT 02   when/where/why/how 의문문

다양한 정보를 물을 수 있는 의문사들을 알아 두세요.

| when(언제) | When is the exam? | why(왜) | Why are you sad? |
| where(어디, 어디서) | Where is the bathroom? | how(어떻게) | How do you go there? |

우리말과 같은 뜻이 되도록 괄호 안의 말을 이용하여 문장을 완성하시오.

01 그녀는 어떻게 병원에 갈까? (get to) → _____ the hospital?

02 너는 언제 우리 집에 들를 거야? (stop by) → _____ my house?

03 오늘 도쿄의 날씨는 어떠니? (weather) → _____ today in Tokyo?

04 오늘 그 가게가 왜 문을 닫았니? (closed) → _____ the shop _____ today?

05 다음 버스는 언제 있니? (next, be) → _____ bus?

06 그들은 어떻게 수수께끼를 풀었니? (solve) → _____ the mystery?

UNIT 03 <how+형용사/부사> 의문문

'얼마나 ~한[하게]'라고 물을 때는 〈how+형용사/부사〉로 쓰세요.

얼마나 ~한[하게]	How+형용사/부사	How often do you see her?
(수) 얼마나 많이	How+many+셀 수 있는 명사	How many books do you read?
(가격/양이) 얼마(나 많이)	How+much+셀 수 없는 명사	How much water do you drink?

우리말과 같은 뜻이 되도록 괄호 안의 말을 이용하여 문장을 완성하시오.

01 너는 우유를 얼마나 많이 마시니? → _____ drink?

02 버스는 얼마나 자주 오지? → _____ the bus _____ ?

03 그는 얼마나 많은 언어를 아니? (language) → _____ does he know?

04 그녀는 이곳에 얼마나 오래 머무를까? (stay) → _____ here?

05 당신은 일이 얼마나 많나요? (have) → _____ you _____ ?

06 너의 학교는 얼마나 머니? → _____ ?

UNIT 04 how come 의문문

how come은 why와 비슷한 의미지만, 뒤에 나오는 어순이 다른 점에 주의하세요.

의미	How come	+ 평서문 어순	Why	+ 의문문 어순
도대체 왜,	How come	you are angry?	= Why	are you angry?
어째서, 어쩌다	How come	you called her?	= Why	did you call her?

우리말과 같은 뜻이 되도록 괄호 안의 말을 이용하여 문장을 완성하시오.

01 도대체 왜 Thomas는 전학을 간 거야? (how come, to, moved)

_____ another school?

02 어째서 그가 시험에 떨어졌을까? (failed, how come)

_____ the exam?

03 왜 항상 George가 1등을 하는 거야? (win, prize, first, how come)

_____ all the time?

04 오늘 너는 왜 이렇게 집에 일찍 돌아왔니? (home, why, come)

_____ so early today?

05 도대체 왜 문이 안 열리는 거야? (the, door, how come, does, not)

_____ open?

06 도대체 왜 그들은 서로에게 아무 말도 안 하는 거지? (do, not, how come, talk)

_____ to each other?

감탄문은 의문사 what 또는 how로 만들 수 있어요.

구분	감탄의 대상		어순	참고
What 감탄문	명사	셀 수 없을 때	What(+형용사)+명사(+주어+동사)!	〈주어+동사〉는 생략하는 경우가 많음
		셀 수 있는 단수	What+a/an(+형용사)+단수명사(+주어+동사)!	
		셀 수 있는 복수	What(+형용사)+복수명사(+주어+동사)!	
How 감탄문	형용사/부사		How+형용사/부사(+주어+동사)!	

우리말과 같은 뜻이 되도록 괄호 안의 말을 배열하여 문장을 완성하시오.

01 그녀는 정말 똑똑한 소녀구나! (smart, what, she, is, girl, a)

_____

02 그 남자는 정말 공손하구나! (polite, how, is, the man)

_____

03 이 꽃들은 정말 아름답구나! (how, these flowers, beautiful, are)

_____

04 그것은 정말 오래된 미술관이구나! (museum, it, an, what, is, old)

_____

05 그들은 정말 좋은 사람들이구나! (nice, are, people, they, what)

_____

06 그 소녀는 정말 아름답게 노래를 부르는구나! (the girl, beautifully, how, sings)

_____

07 정말 신선한 공기네! (what, is, fresh, it, air)

_____

08 그녀의 이야기는 정말 재미있군요! (interesting, is, how, her story)

_____

[01~02] 다음 빈칸에 들어갈 말로 알맞은 것을 고르시오.

01

_____ will you fly to Paris?

① Who　② Where　③ When
④ What　⑤ Which

02

_____ an exciting summer vacation these children had!

① How　② Why　③ Whom
④ Where　⑤ What

[03~04] 다음 중 빈칸에 들어갈 말이 바르게 짝지어진 것을 고르시오.

03

_____ class I should take if I want to learn _____ to play the guitar?

① What – what　② How – what
③ Where – how　④ Which – how
⑤ Where – what

04

· _____ did you do last Saturday?
· _____ often do you play tennis?

① What – What　② How – What
③ What – How　④ Where – How
⑤ What – How come

05 다음 중 빈칸에 공통으로 들어갈 말로 알맞은 것은?

· _____ made this cake?
· _____ is your girlfriend among them?

① How　② Who　③ When
④ Where　⑤ Which

[06~07] 다음 우리말을 영어로 바르게 옮긴 것을 고르시오.

06 너는 어떤 종류의 음식을 좋아하니?

① How kind of food do you like?
② Some kind of food do you like?
③ How come kind of food you like?
④ What kind of food do you like?
⑤ How come kind of food do you like?

07 수박과 멜론 중에 어떤 과일을 좋아하니?

① What fruit do you like, watermelon or melon?
② Which fruit do you like, watermelon or melon?
③ Which fruit you like, watermelon or melon?
④ What fruit you like, watermelon or melon?
⑤ Which fruit you like more, watermelon or melon?

08 다음 중 빈칸에 들어갈 말이 나머지 넷과 <u>다른</u> 것은?

① _____ beautiful earrings you wear!

② _____ nice he looks with a new jacket!

③ _____ lucky we could find the shelter!

④ _____ friendly he is to foreigners!

⑤ _____ fluently he can talk in English!

09 다음 중 어법상 올바른 것을 <u>모두</u> 고르면?

① Where were you when we called?

② What clever your dog is! He understands everything.

③ Which is bigger, a cherry or an avocado?

④ What are the smallest animal in the world?

⑤ When you were getting colder and colder?

10 다음 중 어법상 <u>어색한</u> 것은?

① How can I ride a bike on the sand?

② What is the first goal of your life?

③ Where was the last place you traveled?

④ When time do you open your shop?

⑤ When was the last time you visited Paris?

11 다음 중 질문에 대한 답으로 <u>어색한</u> 것은?

A: Which do you watch more often, action movies or horror movies?

B: _____

① I often go to the theater alone.

② I don't like watching movies.

③ I prefer horror movies.

④ I like both of them.

⑤ I watch action movies more often than horror movies.

12 다음 중 어법상 올바른 문장의 개수는?

ⓐ Where did you get that banana pudding?

ⓑ Why didn't you do your homework?

ⓒ What kind daughters you have!

ⓓ How long it takes to get to the shopping mall?

① 없음   ② 1개   ③ 2개   ④ 3개   ⑤ 4개

13 다음 중 어법상 <u>어색한</u> 문장의 개수는?

ⓐ Which clothes do you prefer, jeans and a dress?

ⓑ How old Brian is when he won first prize?

ⓒ How come do the sky and the sea look blue?

ⓓ How careful your sister carries the baby!

① 없음   ② 1개   ③ 2개   ④ 3개   ⑤ 4개

14 다음 중 빈칸에 들어갈 의문사가 나머지 넷과 <u>다른</u> 것은?

① A: _____ do you for a living?
B: I'm a fashion designer.
② A: _____ did do last night?
B: I went to see a movie.
③ A: _____ are you late for school?
B: I got up late.
④ A: _____ color is your favorite?
B: I like yellow the most.
⑤ A: _____ were you thinking?
B: I thought about my grandmother.

15 다음 중 빈칸에 들어갈 말이 바르게 짝지어진 것은?

A: Nice to meet you. _____(A)_____ do you do?
B: I'm a scientist.
A: Oh, _____(B)_____ an interesting job! _____(C)_____ did you decide to become a scientist?
B: It's because I wanted to explore space when I was young.

	(A)		(B)		(C)
①	What	–	how	–	How come
②	What	–	what	–	Why
③	How	–	how	–	When
④	How	–	what	–	Why
⑤	How	–	how	–	How come

[16~17] 우리말과 뜻이 같도록 괄호 안의 말을 이용하여 문장을 완성하시오.

16
> Sarah는 어제 왜 수업에 늦었니? (be)

Why _____ Sarah late for class yesterday?

17
> 너는 언제 여기에 방문할 예정이니? (visit)

When _____ you _____ here?

[18~21] 다음 |보기|에서 알맞은 단어를 골라 빈칸에 각각 쓰시오.

|보기|
Who   How   What   When   Where   Why

18 _____ long will the concert be?

19 _____ can I do for you, sir?

20 _____ are you crying all day?

21 _____ do you leave for Tokyo?

22 우리말과 뜻이 같도록 괄호 안의 말을 바르게 배열하시오.

> 어느 쪽이 그의 아내이죠, Mary인가요, Susan인가요?
> (is, Mary, one, or, his, which, Susan, wife)

_____

_____

[23~25] 다음 |보기|에서 알맞은 말을 골라 빈칸에 각각 쓰시오.

| 보기 |
| Why   How come   How   What |

23 _____ you can't eat raw fish? It really tastes good, so you should try it!

24 _____ important information it is!

25 _____ difficult this question is to solve!

[26~27] 다음 문장에서 어법상 어색한 부분을 찾아 바르게 고치시오.

26 When did you came home last night?

_____ → _____

27 How quiet she moves her body!

_____ → _____

28 다음 문장에서 어법상 어색한 부분을 고쳐 완전한 문장을 쓰시오.

How much tables did he make last Friday?

→ _____

_____

29 다음 문장을 지시대로 바꿔 쓰시오.

The police officer saved your life from the accident.
(의문사 who을 사용한 의문문으로)

→ _____

_____

30 주어진 |조건|을 이용하여 우리말을 영어로 바꾸시오.

| 조건 |
1. 의문사 How come을 사용할 것
2. 단어 like, the book, so, much를 사용할 것
3. 8단어를 사용할 것

너는 어째서 그 책을 그렇게 많이 좋아하니?

→ _____

_____

CHAPTER

09

문장의 형식

UNIT 01 문장의 요소

문장을 구성하는 5대 요소, 즉 주어, 동사(서술어), 목적어, 보어, 수식어를 외워 두세요.

주어	문장의 주체 (~은/는, ~이/가)	보어	주어나 목적어 보충 설명
동사(서술어)	주어의 상태, 동작 서술 (~이다, ~하다)	수식어	명사, 동사, 문장 수식
목적어	동작의 대상 (~을/를, ~에게)		

밑줄 친 부분이 문장의 어떤 요소인지 쓰시오.

01 I love <u>my school</u> a lot. → _____

02 She <u>waters</u> flowers every Saturday. → _____

03 Please give me <u>a chance</u>. → _____

04 Everyone calls her <u>Little Giant</u>. → _____

05 Did <u>Jessie</u> show some photos to you? → _____

06 My mom's pizza always tastes <u>good</u>. → _____

UNIT 02 1형식 & 2형식

〈주어+동사〉 뒤에 어떤 말이 오는가에 따라 1, 2, 3형식으로 구분하세요.

1형식	2형식	3형식
〈주어+동사〉	〈주어+동사〉+보어	〈주어+동사〉+목적어

우리말과 같은 뜻이 되도록 괄호 안의 말을 배열하여 문장을 완성하고, 몇 형식인지 쓰시오.

01 내가 가장 좋아하는 계절은 봄이다. (favorite, my, is, season, spring)

_____ [　　] 형식

02 이 상자는 너무 무겁다. (heavy, box, this, is, too)

_____ [　　] 형식

03 다음 주 월요일은 Sam의 생일이다. (birthday, Monday, next, is, Sam's)

_____ [　　] 형식

04 Tom과 그의 가족은 아프리카에서 산다. (live, Tom, and, his, family)

_____ in Africa. [　　] 형식

05 부산에는 아직도 눈이 내리고 있다. (snowing, still, is, it)

_____ in Busan. [　　] 형식

06 큰 비가 갑자기 그쳤다. (stopped, rain, the, heavy)

_____ suddenly. [　　] 형식

UNIT 03　감각동사+형용사

be동사와 감각동사가 취하는 보어의 종류와 그 의미를 파악하세요.

	보어를 취하는 동사	보어
be동사	be, am, are, is, was, were	명사, 형용사
감각동사	feel, look, sound, smell, taste	형용사
일반동사	keep, get, become, turn, remain, appear	

참고　감각동사 뒤에 명사를 쓰려면 〈감각동사+like+명사〉로 쓰면 돼요.

He looks smart. → He looks like a smart person.

우리말과 같은 뜻이 되도록 괄호 안의 말을 이용하여 문장을 완성하시오.

01　그들은 오늘 매우 행복해 보인다. (happy)　→ They ＿＿＿＿＿＿＿＿＿＿＿ today.

02　그 꽃들에서는 달콤한 향기가 났다. (sweet)　→ The flowers ＿＿＿＿＿＿＿＿＿＿＿.

03　그의 설명은 지루하게 들렸다. (boring)　→ His explanation ＿＿＿＿＿＿＿＿＿＿＿.

04　그녀는 그 결과에 화가 남을 느꼈다. (angry)　→ She ＿＿＿＿＿＿＿＿＿ about the result.

05　오늘 너는 네 아빠처럼 보여. (dad)　→ You ＿＿＿＿＿＿＿＿＿ today.

06　엄마의 파스타는 환상적인 맛이다. (fantastic) → Mom's pasta ＿＿＿＿＿＿＿＿＿.

UNIT 04　3형식 & 4형식

3형식과 4형식 문장의 차이를 알아 두세요.

문장 형식	동사	목적어
3형식	want, like, know, call 등	'~에게' 또는 '~을'(목적어 1개)
4형식	give, make, show, send, ask, tell, lend, get, bring, teach, buy, cook 등	'~에게', '~을'(목적어 2개)

우리말과 같은 뜻이 되도록 괄호 안의 말을 바르게 배열하여 문장을 완성하시오.

01　우리 가족은 다 함께 공포 영화를 보았다. (a horror movie, watched)

My family ＿＿＿＿＿＿＿＿＿＿＿ together.

02　아빠가 어제 우리에게 새 신발을 사 주셨다. (new shoes, bought, us)

My dad ＿＿＿＿＿＿＿＿＿＿＿ yesterday.

03　매주 토요일 엄마는 우리에게 치킨 수프를 요리해 주신다. (chicken soup, us, cook)

My mom ＿＿＿＿＿＿＿＿＿＿＿ every Saturday.

04　내게 책가방을 좀 찾아 줄 수 있니? (me, find, my backpack)

Can you ＿＿＿＿＿＿＿＿＿＿＿, please?

05　그녀는 나에게 스웨터와 장갑을 만들어 줬다. (me, a sweater and gloves, made)

She ＿＿＿＿＿＿＿＿＿＿＿.

3~4형식 전환

4형식 문장을 3형식 문장으로 바꿔 쓸 수 있는데, 이때 어순과 전치사에 주의하세요.

3형식 어순	일반 수여동사	직접목적어	to	간접목적어
	get, make, buy, cook, build, find	(~을)	for	
	ask, inquire	question, favor	of	

3형식 문장은 4형식으로, 4형식 문장은 3형식으로 바꿔 쓰시오.

01 I will get you a taxi. → _____

02 You can give carrots to the rabbits. → _____

03 She told us a funny fairy tale. → _____

04 Will you buy me a new bag? → _____

05 Emily sent a card to her parents. → _____

06 Could you find my book for me? → _____

5형식 1 – 명사, 형용사

목적격보어로 명사나 형용사를 쓰는 5형식 동사를 알아 두세요.

5형식 어순	명사/형용사를 목적격보어로 쓰는 5형식 동사	목적어	목적격보어
	make, call, name, find, keep, elect, think, believe, consider 등	~을, ~이/가	명사, 형용사

우리말과 같은 뜻이 되도록 괄호 안의 말을 바르게 배열하여 문장을 완성하시오.

01 Luna의 노력은 그녀를 최고의 발레리나로 만들었다. (the best ballerina, made, her)

Luna's effort _____.

02 문은 계속 열어 놔 주세요. (keep, open, the doors)

Please _____.

03 이 노래는 그녀를 세계적으로 유명한 가수로 만들었다. (her, made, a world-famous singer)

This song _____.

04 Leo는 스스로 매우 운이 좋다고 여긴다. (himself, considers, very lucky)

Leo _____.

05 Teddy는 테니스 수업이 너무 어렵다고 생각했다. (too hard, the tennis class, found)

Teddy _____.

06 어떻게 하면 우리가 이 방을 시원하게 유지할 수 있을까? (this room, keep, cool)

How can we _____?

UNIT 07 5형식 2 – to부정사

목적격보어로 to부정사를 쓰는 동사들을 알아 두세요.

	to부정사를 목적격보어로 쓰는 5형식 동사	목적어	목적격보어
5형식 어순	want, ask, tell, expect, enable, encourage, allow, advise, order, get, permit, force 등	~에게, ~이/가	to부정사 (~하기를/~하라고)

참고 to부정사의 부정은 to 앞에 not을 쓰면 돼요.

우리말과 같은 뜻이 되도록 괄호 안의 말을 이용하여 문장을 완성하시오.

01 그는 내가 그것을 끝내기를 기대한다. (expect, finish)

He _____ it.

02 그녀는 그들에게 운동하라고 조언했다. (advise, exercise)

She _____ .

03 그는 Emma한테 입을 벌리라고 요청했다. (ask, open)

He _____ her mouth.

04 나는 Noah에게 내 가방을 가져오라고 말했다. (tell, bring)

I _____ my bag.

UNIT 08 5형식 3 – 지각동사

지각동사가 취할 수 있는 목적격보어의 종류와 그 의미를 잘 파악하세요.

	지각동사	목적어	목적격보어	의미
5형식 어순	feel, see, watch, hear, listen to, smell, notice 등	~이/가	원형부정사	목적어가 ~하는 것을(능동)
			현재분사	목적어가 ~하고 있는 것을(진행 강조)

|보기|와 같이 두 문장을 한 문장으로 연결하시오.

|보기|
I saw a cat. It was climbing over the fence. → I saw a cat climbing over the fence.

01 Leo smelled some clothes. They were burning.

→ _____

02 They felt the ground. It was shaking and moving.

→ _____

03 I heard you and Tommy. You were talking about me.

→ _____

04 Julie watched her daughter. She was playing with dolls.

→ _____

UNIT 09 　5형식 4 – 사역동사

사역동사(~에게 …하도록 시키다)는 목적격보어로 원형부정사나 과거분사를 쓰세요.

5형식 어순	사역동사	목적어	목적격보어	의미
5형식 어순	make, have (~이 …하게 시키다)	~이/가	원형부정사	목적어가 ~하게 만들다/시키다
			과거분사	목적어가 ~되도록 만들다/시키다
	let (~이 …하게 두다)		원형부정사	목적어가 ~하게 두다
			to be 과거분사	목적어가 ~되도록 두다

우리말과 같은 뜻이 되도록 괄호 안의 말을 이용하여 문장을 완성하시오.

01 선생님은 우리가 일렬로 줄을 서게 하셨다. (make, stand)

The teacher _____ in a line.

02 엄마는 항상 내가 아침 7시에 일어나게 하신다. (get up, make)

My mom always _____ at seven in the morning.

03 Jessica는 왜 그녀의 강아지가 밤새 짖도록 두었지? (let, bark)

Why did Jessica _____ all through the night?

04 그 버스 기사는 승객들에게 창문을 닫아 달라고 요청했다. (ask, close)

The bus driver _____ the passengers _____ the windows.

05 그 슬픈 영화는 우리가 영화를 보는 내내 울게 만들었다. (make, cry)

The sad movie _____ through the whole movie.

06 나는 Lily가 그 문제에 대해 내게 조언하도록 했다. (let, give)

I _____ me advice about the problem.

UNIT 10 　5형식 5 – help/get

help와 get의 목적격보어에 주의하세요.

help의 목적격보어	get의 목적격보어
원형부정사, to부정사, (to) be 과거분사	to부정사, 과거분사

우리말과 같은 뜻이 되도록 괄호 안의 말과 help 또는 get을 이용하여 문장을 완성하시오.

01 그는 내가 일기를 쓰도록 도와줬다. (keep) → He _____ a diary.

02 그녀는 우리가 웃는 걸 멈추게 하셨다. (stop) → She _____ laughing.

03 내가 답을 찾는 걸 도와줘. (find) → _____ the answer.

04 그는 그 라디오가 고쳐지게 했다. (fix) → He _____ .

05 그녀는 모두가 떠나도록 했다. (leave) → She _____ .

06 그들은 그가 일어나도록 도왔다. (get up) → They _____ .

목적격보어의 다양한 형태 확인

대표적인 5형식 동사들의 주요 목적격보어의 형태를 전체적으로 확인하세요.

동사	목적격보어
make, call, name, find, keep, elect, think, believe, consider	명사, 형용사
want, ask, tell, expect, enable, encourage, allow, advise, order, get, permit, force	to부정사
지각동사 feel, see, watch, hear, listen to, smell, notice	원형부정사, 현재분사
사역동사 make, have, let	원형부정사, 과거분사
help	원형부정사, to부정사
get	to부정사, 과거분사

우리말과 같은 뜻이 되도록 괄호 안의 말을 이용하여 문장을 완성하시오.

01 내가 생일 파티 준비하는 것을 도와줄 수 있겠니? (prepare, help)

Can you _____ a birthday party?

02 의사 선생님은 Luke에게 따뜻한 물을 자주 마시라고 조언했다. (advise, drink)

The doctor _____ warm water often.

03 나는 어떤 할머니가 무거운 수레를 끌고 가시는 것을 도와드렸다. (pull, help)

I _____ an old lady _____ a heavy cart.

04 네 선생님이 네가 집으로 돌아올 수 있게 하셨니? (let, come back)

Did your teacher _____ home?

05 그의 정직함이 그를 훌륭한 지도자로 만들었다. (a, leader, good, make)

His honesty _____ .

06 우리 엄마는 내게 늘 예의 바르게 행동하라고 말씀하신다. (behave, tell)

My mom _____ politely all the time.

[01~02] 다음 빈칸에 들어갈 말로 알맞은 것을 고르시오.

01

> This fried chicken tastes too _____.

① spice　　② oil　　③ big
④ much　　⑤ oily

02

> She asked Jack _____ to a movie next weekend.

① went　　② to go　　③ go
④ gone　　⑤ going

[03~04] 다음 빈칸에 들어갈 말로 알맞지 <u>않은</u> 것을 고르시오.

03

> She _____ the girls laughing out loud at the comedy show.

① watched　　② heard　　③ saw
④ let　　⑤ listened to

04

> Mr. Park _____ the boy scouts to dig a hole.

① wanted　　② told　　③ asked
④ had　　⑤ helped

05 다음 중 빈칸에 들어갈 말이 바르게 짝지어진 것은?

> • The bad news _____ me sad.
> • He _____ us turn around the corner.

① made – told　　② made – made
③ told – made　　④ told – told
⑤ got – got

06 다음 중 빈칸에 공통으로 들어갈 말로 알맞은 것은?

> • Please keep this room _____.
> • The weather turned _____ in April.

① easy　　② warm　　③ lately
④ easily　　⑤ warmly

07 다음 중 우리말을 영어로 바르게 옮긴 것은?

> 하민이는 그 새로운 요리사가 잘생겼다고 생각했다.

① Hamin found the handsome chef new.
② Hamin founded the new chef handsome.
③ Hamin found the new chef handsome.
④ Hamin taught the new chef handsome.
⑤ Hamin thought the handsome chef new.

08 다음 중 문장의 형식이 나머지 넷과 <u>다른</u> 것은?

① A bomb explosion happened last night.
② Helen finally becomes a doctor.
③ The pizza and pasta really tasted good.
④ The girl looked very shy on the stage.
⑤ The table must always be clean.

09 다음 중 어법상 올바른 것은?

① This pumpkin soup tastes very cream.
② He asked me lend some money.
③ We felt boring during the math class.
④ Sarah gave a love letter for Michael at school.
⑤ The police officer made them tell the truth.

10 다음 중 어법상 <u>어색한</u> 것을 <u>모두</u> 고르면?

① This pecan pie smells like nutty.
② I watched a boy shouting at me over there.
③ The diamond ring will shine forever.
④ The farmer showed his onion farm us.
⑤ She finished her homework before midnight.

11 다음 중 어법상 올바른 문장의 개수는?

ⓐ The Mexican food tasted especially good.
ⓑ The scarf felt very softly.
ⓒ The news of his marriage sounds craziness.
ⓓ This town looks peacefully.

① 없음 ② 1개 ③ 2개 ④ 3개 ⑤ 4개

12 다음 중 어법상 <u>어색한</u> 문장의 개수는?

ⓐ David sent me a traditional Korean fan.
ⓑ I was very nervously when I took that exam.
ⓒ Can you read me the letter from my father?
ⓓ I found the book very interesting.

① 없음 ② 1개 ③ 2개 ④ 3개 ⑤ 4개

13 다음 중 빈칸에 들어갈 말이 바르게 짝지어진 것은?

A: Good evening. Welcome to my house.
B: Thank you for inviting me. Take this.
A: What is it?
B: I brought a cake ____(A)____ you.
A: Thanks. Please help yourself to the dishes.
B: Wow, it smells ____(B)____ !
A: Let's eat together. Could you pass your plate ____(C)____ me?

	(A)		(B)		(C)
①	for	–	tasty	–	of
②	to	–	nice	–	for
③	for	–	nicely	–	to
④	to	–	good	–	to
⑤	for	–	taste	–	of

14 다음 문장의 밑줄 친 get과 쓰임이 같은 것은?

> They always <u>get</u> me to come home early.

① The apples <u>get</u> bigger and bigger.
② I want to <u>get</u> his autography this time.
③ They'll never <u>get</u> her to understand it.
④ Could you <u>get</u> me a cup of water, please?
⑤ I really need to <u>get</u> this job to earn money.

15 다음 밑줄 친 ⓐ~ⓔ 중 어법상 어색한 것을 모두 고르면?

> When I was home alone last night, ⓐ <u>I heard someone walking</u> on the second floor. So ⓑ <u>I felt like scared</u> very much. ⓒ <u>I called Sujin and asked her to come over.</u> We checked my house together, but there was nobody. We ⓓ <u>found it a sound of breeze</u> and ⓔ <u>it made me feel safely.</u>

① ⓐ   ② ⓑ   ③ ⓒ   ④ ⓓ   ⑤ ⓔ

[16~17] 우리말과 뜻이 같도록 괄호 안의 말을 이용하여 문장을 완성하시오.

16
> 그녀는 나의 개가 그 상점에 들어가도록 허락해 주었다. (enter)

She allowed my dog _____ the shop.

17
> 그는 내가 약속을 지키도록 했다. (keep)

He had me _____ the promise.

[18~21] 다음 밑줄 친 말의 문장 성분을 |보기|에서 골라 각각 알맞은 기호를 쓰시오.

> |보기|
> ⓐ 주어   ⓑ 동사   ⓒ 목적어
> ⓓ 보어   ⓔ 수식어

18 My father is <u>an English teacher</u>.

→ _____

19 This store offers <u>its customers</u> a free gift.

→ _____

20 My aunt had her children <u>stop yelling at her</u>.

→ _____

21 She bought a new PC <u>to take online lessons</u>.

→ _____

[22~23] 우리말과 뜻이 같도록 괄호 안의 말을 바르게 배열하시오.

22
> 그 경호원은 대통령을 안전하게 지킨다.
> (safe, the, the, guard, keeps, president)

_____

_____

23

> 당신에게 반 고흐의 진품 명작을 보여 드리겠습니다.
> (real, Van Gogh, you, of, the, let, show, me, masterpiece)

_____

_____

[24~25] 다음 문장에서 어법상 <u>어색한</u> 부분을 찾아 바르게 고치시오.

24 He told me a shocked story today.

_____ → _____

25 Every dog makes its owner happiness.

_____ → _____

[26~27] 다음 |보기|와 같이 두 문장을 한 문장으로 만드시오.

> | 보기 |
> I saw Jane. She was dancing on the stage.
> → I saw Jane dancing on the stage.

26 I was standing in line. The flight attendant told me to do that.

→ The flight attendant _____

_____.

27 Tom moved the boxes. His boss made him do that.

→ Tom's boss _____

_____.

28 다음 문장에서 어법상 <u>어색한</u> 부분을 고쳐 완전한 문장을 쓰시오.

It tastes the strawberry cake made by my grandmother.

→ _____

_____

29 다음 문장을 지시대로 바꿔 쓰시오.

He lent me his special edition of Avatar.
(3형식 문장으로)

→ _____

_____

30 주어진 |조건|을 이용하여 우리말을 영어로 바꾸시오.

> | 조건 |
> 1. 사역동사 let을 사용할 것
> 2. 단어 the kids, stay up, late, night를 사용할 것
> 3. 10단어를 사용할 것
> 4. 축약형을 사용하지 말 것

그 아이들을 밤늦게까지 깨어 있게 하지 마라.

→ _____

_____

접속사

UNIT 01 등위접속사

앞뒤에 오는 말의 의미를 파악하여 접속사 and(그리고), but(그러나), or(또는)로 연결하세요.

and	~와, 그리고	but	~이지만, 그러나	or	~이거나, 또는

빈칸에 and, but, or 중 알맞은 접속사를 쓰시오.

01 Would you like some juice. _____ ice cream?

02 I wanted to go outside. _____ it was snowing heavily.

03 Which season do you like better. summer _____ winter?

04 We bought watermelons. apples. _____ peaches at the supermarket.

05 I usually have breakfast _____ I skipped it today.

06 Lily's cake looks beautiful _____ tastes good.

UNIT 02 상관접속사

서로 상관이 있는 것들을 묶어 주는 상관접속사의 종류와 의미를 알아 두세요.

상관접속사	의미	상관접속사	의미
both A and B	A와 B 둘 다	not A but B	A가 아니라 B
either A or B	A 또는 B	not only A but (also) B	A뿐만 아니라 B도
neither A nor B	A도 B도 아닌	= B as well as A	A와 마찬가지로 B도

우리말과 같은 뜻이 되도록 괄호 안의 말과 상관접속사를 이용하여 문장을 완성하시오.

01 Zoey는 예쁠 뿐만 아니라 친절하기까지 하다. (pretty. kind)

Zoey is _____.

02 나는 오늘 말고 내일 병원에 갈 것이다. (tomorrow. today)

I will go to see a doctor _____.

03 당신은 펜이나 연필로 편지를 쓸 수 있다. (a pencil. with. a pen)

You can write a letter _____.

04 남자아이들뿐만 아니라 여자아이들도 극한 운동을 즐길 수 있다. (boys. girls. well)

_____ can enjoy extreme sports.

05 John과 Stella 둘 다 오늘 우리 집에 올 것이다.

_____ will visit my house today.

06 운동하는 것뿐만 아니라 가볍게 먹는 것도 필요했다. (exercising. lightly. eating. only)

_____ was needed.

부사절 접속사 1 - 시간

시간을 나타내는 부사절 접속사를 익혀 두세요.

when	~할 때, ~하면	after	~한 후에	as	~할 때, ~하면서
before	~하기 전에	while	~하는 동안	until	~할 때까지

우리말과 같은 뜻이 되도록 괄호 안의 말과 접속사를 이용하여 문장을 완성하시오.

01 자전거를 타면서 우리는 대화를 나눴다. (bikes, rode, we)

We talked to each other _____.

02 야채와 과일을 먹기 전에 잘 씻어라. (them, eat, you)

Wash fruits and vegetables _____.

03 외롭고 슬프게 느껴질 때 너는 무엇을 하니? (feel, you, lonely, sad, and)

What do you do _____?

04 물이 끓을 때까지 기다려라. (boils, the water)

Wait _____.

05 방을 청소하는 동안, 그녀는 음악을 들었다. (was, the room, cleaning, she)

_____, she listened to music.

부사절 접속사 2 - 조건

앞뒤 문맥을 확인하여, if를 써야 하는지 반대의 의미인 unless를 써야 하는지를 판단하세요.

if	~한다면	unless	~하지 않는다면(= if ~ not)

우리말과 같은 뜻이 되도록 괄호 안의 말을 이용하여 문장을 완성하시오.

01 만약 더우시면, 편하게 에어컨을 켜세요. (if, feel)

Feel free to turn on the air conditioner _____.

02 열심히 노력하지 않는다면, 너는 꿈을 이룰 수 없다. (unless, hard, try)

You can't achieve your dream _____.

03 상태가 좋지 않다면, 너는 당장 병원에 가 보는 게 좋을 것이다. (unless, good, feel)

You'd better go see a doctor right now _____.

04 날마다 패스트푸드를 먹는다면, 너는 살이 찌게 될 것이다. (every day, eat, fast food)

You will gain weight _____.

05 옷이 비싸지 않다면, 나는 옷을 몇 벌 살 것이다. (unless, expensive, are)

I will buy some clothes _____.

06 지금 당장 그 일을 시작한다면 우리는 오늘 안에 끝마칠 수 있다. (right now, start, it)

We can finish the work within today _____.

명령문 + and/or

명령문 뒤에 and를 쓸 때와 or를 쓸 때 반대의 의미가 되는 것에 주의해야 해요.

명령문, and	~해라, 그러면 ~할 것이다	명령문, or	~해라, 그렇지 않으면 ~할 것이다

다음 두 문장이 같은 뜻이 되도록 문장을 완성하시오.

01 If you don't take the subway. you cannot get there on time.

= Take the subway. _____.

02 If you forgive others. you can have a lot of friends.

= Forgive others. _____.

03 Unless you go to bed right now. you will get up late tomorrow morning.

= Go to bed right now. _____.

04 If you come to my house today. we will have a good time together.

= Come to my house today. _____.

05 If you don't bring your umbrella. you will get wet.

= Bring your umbrella. _____.

UNIT 06 **부사절 접속사 3 - 원인과 결과**

앞뒤 문맥에 맞게 접속사 so(그래서 ~)를 쓸지, because(~ 때문에)를 쓸지 판단하세요.

so+결과	그래서 ~	because+원인	~ 때문에(= as[since])

우리말과 같은 뜻이 되도록 괄호 안의 말을 이용하여 문장을 완성하시오.

01 나는 그 자전거가 너무 비싸기 때문에 살 수 없었다. (expensive. it. too)

I couldn't buy that bicycle _____.

02 오늘은 밖이 너무 더워서 우리는 소풍을 가지 않았다. (a picnic. go. on)

It was too hot today. _____.

03 나는 옷이 더러워져서 옷을 갈아입어야 했다. (they. dirty. get. since)

I had to change my clothes _____.

04 Emily는 오늘 시험 때문에 무척 긴장하고 있다. (today's test)

Emily is so nervous _____.

05 우리 아빠는 너무 일이 바빠서 집에 늦게 오셨다. (because. so. busy. work. with)

My dad came back home late _____.

06 Ted는 오늘 아침에 늦게 일어나서 학교 버스를 놓쳤다. (the school bus. miss)

Ted got up late this morning. _____.

UNIT 07   so that ~ & so ~ that ...

〈so that ~〉과 〈so ~ that ...〉의 쓰임과 의미를 혼동하지 마세요.

so that ~	~하도록, ~하기 위해서	so 형용사/부사 that ...	너무[매우] ~해서 …하다

우리말과 같은 뜻이 되도록 괄호 안의 말을 이용하여 문장을 완성하시오.

01 나는 내 목표를 이루기 위해 최선을 다해 노력했다. (achieve, my goal)

I tried my best _____.

02 Chloe는 너무 바빠서 오늘 여기에 올 수 없었다. (busy, come here)

Chloe was _____.

03 우리 엄마는 우리에게 수프를 요리해 주시기 위해 채소를 좀 사셨다. (cook, for, us, soup)

My mom bought some vegetables _____.

04 Aiden은 조언을 좀 구하기 위해 선생님께 찾아갔다. (get, advice, some)

Aiden went to see the teacher _____.

05 콘서트 표가 너무 비싸서 나는 그것을 살 수 없었다. (expensive, buy)

The concert ticket was _____.

UNIT 08   부사절 접속사 4 - 양보

'비록 ~이지만, 비록 ~일지라도'라는 양보의 표현은 접속사 though를 쓰세요.

though (비록 ~이지만)	Though she failed several times, she never gave up. = Although[Even though] she failed several times, she never gave up.

우리말과 같은 뜻이 되도록 괄호 안의 말을 이용하여 문장을 완성하시오.

01 Jennie는 매우 수줍었음에도, 무대 위에서 춤을 아주 잘 추었다. (so, feel, shy)

_____, she danced so well on the stage.

02 그 자동차는 매우 비싼데도 불구하고, 인기가 많다. (car, expensive, so)

_____, it is popular.

03 우리 할머니는 연세가 많으시지만, 여전히 건강하시다. (grandma, old, very)

_____, she is still healthy.

04 그녀의 집은 학교에서 멀지만, 그녀는 학교까지 걸어간다. (house, school, far from)

_____, she walks to school.

05 밤늦은 시각이었지만, Joy는 전혀 졸리지 않았다. (late, night, at)

_____, Joy didn't feel sleepy at all.

06 Henry는 키가 작은데도 불구하고, 농구를 잘한다. (short)

_____, he is good at playing basketball.

접속사 that(~하다는 것) 뒤에 하나의 절(문장)을 써서 하나의 명사처럼 사용하세요.

that절	의미: 그가 늦게 일어난다는 것	주의
주어	That he gets up late is unbelievable.	that절은 단수 취급
목적어	No one knows (that) he gets up late.	목적어 that절의 that은 생략 가능
보어	The truth is that he gets up late.	

참고 주어 자리의 that절은 가주어 It을 그 자리에 쓰고, 진짜 주어는 문장 뒤로 옮길 수 있어요.

It is unbelievable that he gets up late.

|A| 다음 두 문장을 한 문장으로 연결하시오.

01 I don't remember her face. + That is the truth.

→ The truth is _____.

02 We should exercise regularly. + It is important.

→ _____ is important.

03 I should get up early tomorrow. + I know that.

→ I know _____.

04 Gianna couldn't speak any French. + That was the problem.

→ The problem was _____.

05 She is still alive somewhere. + It is certain.

→ _____ somewhere.

06 James could recover soon. + I hoped so.

→ I hoped _____.

07 They did their best. + That was the important thing.

→ The important thing was _____.

08 Jack and Jill will get married tomorrow. + It is true.

→ _____ Jack and Jill will get married tomorrow.

|B| 우리말과 같은 뜻이 되도록 괄호 안의 말을 이용하여 문장을 완성하시오.

01 당신이 아직도 내 이름을 기억한다는 것이 놀라워요. (still, remember)

_____ surprising.

02 Lucas가 그 경기에서 이겼다는 것은 좋은 뉴스이다. (the game, win)

The good news _____.

03 그녀가 유명한 가수가 되었다는 것을 믿을 수 없다. (have become, a famous singer)

We can't believe _____.

04 우리가 이번 주말에 놀이공원에 갈 것이라는 것이 흥미진진하다. (will, go, exciting)

_____ the amusement park this weekend.

접속사 각각의 의미를 다시 한번 확인하세요.

and	~와, 그리고	but	~이지만, 그러나	or	~이거나, 또는
not only A but (also) B (= B as well as A)	A뿐만 아니라 B도	both A and B	A와 B 둘 다	either A or B	A 또는 B
neither A nor B	A도 B도 아닌	not A but B	A가 아니라 B	when	~할 때, ~하면
before	~하기 전에	after	~한 후에	while	~하는 동안
as	~할 때, ~하면서	until	~할 때까지	if	~한다면
unless	~하지 않는다면	because/as/ since	~ 때문에	so	그래서 ~
so that ~	~하도록, ~하기 위해서	so ~ that	너무[매우] ~해서 …하다	(even) though	비록 ~일지라도 (= although)
명령문, and	~해라, 그러면	명령문, or	~해라, 안 그러면	명사절 that	~하다는 것

우리말과 같은 뜻이 되도록 괄호 안의 말을 이용하여 문장을 완성하시오.

01 Joy는 피곤했지만, 일찍 잠자리에 들지 않았다. (early. go to. bed)

Joy felt tired. _____.

02 그 아기는 엄마가 그녀에게 다시 돌아올 때까지 계속 울었다. (come back. her mom. to her)

The baby kept crying _____.

03 우리 할아버지는 젊은 시절에 정말 미남이셨다. (young)

My grandpa was very good-looking _____.

04 너는 오늘 밖에 나갈 거니, 아니면 집에 있을 거니? (stay. at home)

Will you go out _____?

05 소라는 영어와 독일어 모두 잘할 수 있다. (speak. German)

Sora can _____.

06 James는 숙제를 다 하고 나서 저녁을 먹을 것이다. (his homework. finish)

James will have dinner _____.

07 나는 점심으로 피자 또는 양송이 수프를 먹고 싶다. (mushroom soup. lunch)

I want to eat _____.

08 우리 할머니는 몸이 너무 약하셔서 자주 편찮으셨다. (weak. get ill)

My grandma was _____.

[01~02] 다음 빈칸에 들어갈 말로 알맞은 것을 고르시오.

01

Would you like some bread _____ cookies?

① nor   ② but   ③ so
④ both   ⑤ or

02

_____ you were sleeping, Santa Clause visited!

① Until   ② While   ③ If
④ Before   ⑤ Because

03 다음 빈칸에 들어갈 말로 알맞은 것을 모두 고르면?

_____ you failed the exam, it was worth trying your best.

① Though   ② As   ③ Although
④ If   ⑤ Because

04 다음 중 빈칸에 들어갈 말이 바르게 짝지어진 것은?

• You can go to the pool _____ it rains.
• Put this coat on, _____ you will get a cold.

① if – or   ② although – and
③ after – or   ④ unless – or
⑤ when – and

05 다음 중 빈칸에 공통으로 들어갈 말로 알맞은 것은?

• _____ you are rich, you can buy anything.
• Please come back _____ soon as possible.

① As[as]   ② If[if]
③ And[and]   ④ Because[because]
⑤ Since[since]

06 다음 중 우리말을 영어로 바르게 옮긴 것은?

나 혹은 Tom 중 하나가 저녁 식사 비용을 지불해야 한다.

① Either I or Tom have to pay for the dinner.
② Either I nor Tom have to pay for the dinner.
③ Neither I nor Tom has to pay for the dinner.
④ Either I or Tom has to pay for the dinner.
⑤ Both I and Tom have to pay for the dinner.

07 다음 문장의 밑줄 친 that과 쓰임이 같은 것은?

I understand that you can't join our club.

① What I know is that you broke the window.
② Can you believe that he ate ten pieces of chocolate cake?
③ It is amazing that we can meet again!
④ Can you see that meeting room next to the front door?
⑤ You can't enter that building because it's closed now.

08 다음 빈칸에 들어갈 말로 알맞은 것은?

> _____ cleans the classroom today.

① Either Carrie or I
② Both I and Sunny
③ Not only I but also Jerry
④ Neither I nor you
⑤ All the students, as well as Mr. Han,

09 다음 중 밑줄 친 부분의 의미가 나머지 넷과 <u>다른</u> 것은?

① Bobby has to find another job <u>as</u> he lost his.
② <u>As</u> Marilyn loves Jack, she can do anything for him.
③ He was able to go to the exhibition <u>as</u> he got a ticket.
④ You can use my pencil <u>as</u> I don't use it now.
⑤ <u>As</u> he entered the room, he said hi to everyone.

10 다음 중 어법상 올바른 것은?

① She changed her plans because the weather.
② Unless I have a passport, I can go abroad.
③ Don't forget to lock the door until you go out.
④ I felt worried so that I couldn't sleep last night.
⑤ Let's hurry to school before it starts raining.

11 다음 중 어법상 <u>어색한</u> 것은?

① This sofa is both comfortable and big.
② I can play neither the violin nor the piano.
③ Both you and John makes me happy.
④ Not you but Jake is going to Jeju with me.
⑤ They'll have either a sandwich or a hamburger.

12 다음 중 어법상 올바른 문장의 개수는?

> ⓐ I couldn't pass the exam as I studied hard.
> ⓑ I don't go to the beach if it will rain.
> ⓒ I went to the library so that I could borrow some books.
> ⓓ I visited Italy when I was seven.

① 없음　② 1개　③ 2개　④ 3개　⑤ 4개

13 다음 중 어법상 <u>어색한</u> 문장의 개수는?

> ⓐ We ate peaches as well as apples at the picnic.
> ⓑ I ordered not only pizza but fried chicken.
> ⓒ Please call me if you will have any problems.
> ⓓ I was taking a shower when you called me.

① 없음　② 1개　③ 2개　④ 3개　⑤ 4개

14 다음 짝지어진 문장의 의미가 서로 <u>다른</u> 것은?

① I woke up early so that I can take a walk.
  → I woke up early so as to take a walk.

② It is false that water boils under 0 ℃.
  → That water boils under 0 ℃ is false.

③ You have to tell the truth, or you will go to jail.
  → If you don't tell the truth, you will go to jail.

④ I couldn't see my dog since it was too dark.
  → I couldn't see my dog as it was too dark.

⑤ I'd like to see not only Jane but also Amy.
  → I'd like to see either Jane or Amy.

15 다음 중 같은 의미로 쓰인 접속사가 들어간 문장끼리 짝지어진 것은?

ⓐ We could read some Spanish words after we learned them.
ⓑ Do you know that we solved the hard math problem?
ⓒ She won an Academy Award as she acted so well.
ⓓ This ring is special to me because my grandmother gave it to me.
ⓔ I was called Bambi when I was young.
ⓕ I can introduce you to Sally since we are friends.

① ⓐ, ⓑ, ⓒ   ② ⓐ, ⓒ, ⓔ   ③ ⓑ, ⓓ, ⓕ
④ ⓒ, ⓓ, ⓕ   ⑤ ⓑ, ⓒ, ⓔ

16 우리말과 뜻이 같도록 괄호 안의 말을 이용하여 문장을 완성하시오.

나는 Jenny를 좋아하지만, 내 여동생은 그녀를 미워한다. (hate)

I like Jenny, _____ my sister _____ her.

[17~19] 다음 |보기|에서 알맞은 단어를 골라 빈칸에 각각 쓰시오.

| 보기 |
either   both   or   and   neither   nor

17 We have to do it. _____ Shawn _____ Smith has to do it.

18 _____ Mickey _____ Minnie are popular characters. Every child loves them.

19 Among the three, _____ popularity _____ money is more important than health. Health is the most important thing.

[20~22] 다음 밑줄 친 <u>that</u>의 문장 성분을 |보기|에서 골라 각각 알맞은 기호를 쓰시오.

| 보기 |
ⓐ 주어   ⓑ 보어   ⓒ 목적어

20 You should know <u>that</u> you hurt my feelings.
  → _____

21 It is exciting <u>that</u> we can go to the same high school.
  → _____

22 Your fault is <u>that</u> you ignored his advice.
  → _____

[23~25] 다음 |보기|에서 알맞은 접속사를 골라 빈칸에 각각 쓰시오.

| 보기 |

if   before   until   while   after

23 _____ I watched the movie yesterday, I became the main character's fan.

24 I want you to wait _____ I call you back.

25 Ben sent me a message _____ I was chatting online.

26 우리말과 뜻이 같도록 괄호 안의 말을 바르게 배열하시오.

그 그림은 비싸긴 했지만, 살 만한 가치가 있었다.
(buying, though, even, worth, it, the, was, was, painting, expensive)

_____

_____

[27~28] 다음 문장에서 어법상 어색한 부분을 찾아 바르게 고치시오.

27 I enjoy both listening to music and to go hiking on weekends.

_____ → _____

28 I can't hear you if you turn down the radio.

_____ → _____

29 다음 문장에서 어색한 부분을 고쳐 완전한 문장을 쓰시오.

She has known him as she was young.

→ _____

_____

30 주어진 |조건|을 이용하여 우리말을 영어로 바꾸시오.

| 조건 |
1. 접속사 not A but B를 사용할 것
2. 단어 want, go, to Japan, to Vietnam을 쓸 것
3. 10단어를 사용할 것

나는 일본이 아니라 베트남에 가고 싶다.

→ _____

분사구문

UNIT 01　현재분사

동사를 형용사(명사 수식, 보어 역할)처럼 쓰기 위해서는 동사에 -ing를 붙여 현재분사로 만드세요.

형태	V+-ing	의미	~하는(능동)

참고 분사란 동사에 -ing(현재분사)나 -ed(과거분사)를 붙여서, 형용사처럼 사용할 수 있는 말이에요.

우리말과 같은 뜻이 되도록 괄호 안의 말을 배열하여 문장을 완성하시오.

01 마당에서 꽃에 물을 주고 있는 저 소녀는 Lisa다. (flowers, watering, the girl)

_____ in the yard is Lisa.

02 그녀의 미소 짓는 얼굴은 많은 사람들을 행복하게 한다. (her, makes, face, smiling)

_____ a lot of people happy.

03 나를 향해 걸어오고 있는 사람은 우리 아빠다. (the man, toward, walking, me)

_____ is my dad.

04 스테이크를 요리하고 있는 저 여자는 유명한 요리사다. (the woman, steak, cooking)

_____ is a famous chef.

05 Ava가 호감을 주는 성격을 가지고 있다는 것은 사실이다. (pleasing, a, has, personality)

It is true that Ava _____.

UNIT 02　과거분사

동사를 수동의 의미를 나타내는 형용사로 쓸 때는 동사의 과거분사형을 활용하세요.

형태	과거분사형(-ed 또는 불규칙 형태)	의미	~된, ~당한(수동)

우리말과 같은 뜻이 되도록 괄호 안의 말을 배열하여 문장을 완성하시오. (단, 형태를 바꿀 것)

01 깨친 창문 조심하세요. (window, the, break)

Be careful of _____.

02 식탁 위에는 갓 구워진 쿠키와 케이크가 놓여 있었다. (bake, cookies, were, there, freshly)

_____ and cake on the table.

03 모든 사람들은 갑작스러운 큰 소음에 깜짝 놀랐다. (by, everyone, was, surprise)

_____ the sudden loud noise.

04 간호사들은 부상당한 군인들을 돌봤다. (care, took, of, wound, the, soldiers)

Nurses _____.

05 우리는 우리 차를 수리하고 있다. (repair, our car, having)

We are _____.

06 그의 장난감들이 한 줄로 정리돼 있었다. (toys, were, his, arrange)

_____ in a row.

분사구문 만드는 법

부사절 〈접속사+주어+동사〉를 분사를 이용하여 간결하게 줄여 쓰는 방법을 익히세요.

	분사구문 만드는 법	
1	부사절의 접속사 생략	~~As~~ Jane got off the bus, she said goodbye.
2	부사절과 주절의 주어가 같다면, 부사절 주어 생략	~~Jane~~ got off the bus, she said goodbye.
3	부사절의 동사를 현재분사(-ing)로 바꿈	Getting off the bus, Jane said goodbye.

주어진 부사절을 분사구문으로 바꿔 문장을 완성하시오.

01 When I opened the door → _____ . I found a little box.

02 As she was brushing her teeth → _____ . Gina answered my call.

03 After he finished the book → _____ . he fell asleep.

04 As he walked on the street → _____ . Ted ate a sandwich.

05 Because she was hungry → _____ . Ellie ate two plates.

06 Since we ran in the rain → _____ . we got all wet.

분사구문 1 - 때, 이유

접속사가 없는 분사구문은 주절과의 관계를 파악하여 문맥에 맞게 해석해야 해요.

분사구문	주절과의 관계	의미
Arriving there, she saw Tom.	때	= When she arrived there, 도착했을 때
Being tired, he went to bed.	이유	= Because[Since / As] he was tired, 피곤했기 때문에

참고 부사절이 부정문이면 분사 앞에 not이나 never를 써야 해요.

다음 문장의 분사구문을 부사절로 바꿔 쓰시오.   Tip: 접속사와 시제에 주의하세요.

01 Waking up in the morning. she stretches. → _____

02 Fighting hard. they didn't talk. → _____

03 Making a mistake. he always apologizes. → _____

04 Not knowing the answer. Mina felt upset. → _____

05 Entering the room. he found Jim. → _____

06 Being too busy. I often skip meals. → _____

분사구문 2 – 조건, 양보

분사구문이 의미상 '~하면'의 조건이나 '비록 ~일지라도'라는 양보를 나타낼 때를 주의하세요.

Turning right, you will see it.	조건	= If you turn right,
Though[Although] being young, she is thoughtful.	양보	= Though[Although] she is young,

참고 양보를 나타내는 분사구문은 의미를 명확히 하기 위해 접속사를 생략하지 않고 쓰는 경우가 많아요.

우리말과 같은 뜻이 되도록 괄호 안의 말과 분사구문을 이용하여 문장을 완성하시오.

01 나는 오늘 매우 바쁘지만, 너와 함께 놀고 싶다. (busy, very, be, today, though)

_____. I want to play with you.

02 모퉁이에서 오른쪽으로 돌면, 너는 화장실을 발견할 것이다. (turn, right, corner, the, at)

_____, you will find the restroom.

03 Annie를 매우 자주 봤지만, 나는 그녀의 전화번호는 모른다. (often, very, see, though)

_____, I don't know her phone number.

04 지금 밖에 나가면, 너는 비에 다 젖을 것이다. (go, now, right, out)

_____, you will get wet in the rain.

05 따뜻한 차를 좀 마시면, 너는 기분이 훨씬 더 좋아질 것이다. (hot, some, drink, tea)

_____, you will feel much better.

분사구문 3 – 동시동작, 연속상황

분사구문으로 '~하는 동안, ~하면서'의 동시동작이나 '~하고 나서'라는 연속상황을 나타낼 수 있어야 해요.

Driving a car, you shouldn't eat.	동시동작	= While[As] you drive a car, 운전하면서
He studied hard, passing the exam.	연속상황	= and passed the exam 그리고 합격했다

두 문장이 같은 뜻이 되도록 분사구문을 이용하여 문장을 완성하시오.

01 The man had a bite of the steak, and nodded his head.

= The man had a bite of the steak, _____.

02 While Lucas wrote a letter to Emily, he broke into tears.

= _____, Lucas broke into tears.

03 As my dad drives his car, he listened to the radio.

= _____, my dad listened to the radio.

04 As she had an interview, she shook with anxiety.

= _____, she shook with anxiety.

05 As the children played on the swings, they whistled.

= _____, the children whistled.

[01~02] 다음 빈칸에 들어갈 말로 알맞은 것을 고르시오.

01

> The movie we saw yesterday was really _____.

① excite
② exciting
③ excited
④ excitement
⑤ excitedly

02

> _____ nothing about the place, I got nervous.

① Know
② Knew
③ To know
④ Knowing
⑤ Be knowing

03 다음 빈칸에 공통으로 들어갈 말로 알맞은 것은?

> • I watched Tommy _____ away from the police.
> • He started _____ when I called him.

① ran
② run
③ running
④ to run
⑤ has run

[04~05] 다음 중 빈칸에 들어갈 말이 바르게 짝지어진 것을 고르시오.

04

> • I heard your name _____ just before.
> • The soldier was _____ by the enemy.

① called – attacked
② call – attack
③ called – attacking
④ to call – to attack
⑤ calling – attacking

05

> • _____ German, I can't read this book.
> • I have _____ Brian for ten years.

① Known – known
② To know – known
③ Knowing – knowing
④ Not knowing – knowing
⑤ Not knowing – known

[06~07] 다음 우리말을 영어로 바르게 옮긴 것을 고르시오.

06

> 샤워를 하면서 나는 음악을 들었다.

① Taking a shower, I listened to music.
② Being a shower, I listened to music.
③ Take a shower, I listened to music.
④ Being taken a shower, I listened to music.
⑤ While being a shower, I listened to music.

07

> 몸이 아플지라도 그녀는 운동하는 것을 그만두지 않았다.

① Been sick, she didn't stop exercising.
② Though be sick, she didn't stop exercising.
③ Though having sick, she didn't stop exercising.
④ Being though sick, she didn't stop exercising.
⑤ Though being sick, she didn't stop exercising.

08 다음 중 밑줄 친 부분의 쓰임이 나머지 넷과 <u>다른</u> 것은?

① It is no use <u>crying</u> over spilt milk.
② The news was <u>surprising</u> to me.
③ It is <u>interesting</u> that the Earth is round.
④ She was <u>holding</u> my hands when I cried.
⑤ The man <u>wearing</u> sunglasses is my uncle.

09 다음 중 어법상 올바른 것은?

① That sounds a plan.
② I'm worrying about my grandfather's health.
③ Born in Spain, she is fluent in Spanish.
④ Not tiring, I went to bed early last night.
⑤ The event will be holding in Myeongdong.

10 다음 중 어법상 어색한 것은?

① I'm honored to receive this award.
② You must be tired as you worked hard.
③ I can see the bear licking honey.
④ Felt like listening to music, he turned on the radio.
⑤ Using good ingredients, the chef made a wonderful dish.

11 다음 중 밑줄 친 부분의 의미가 <u>어색한</u> 것은?

① <u>Stealing the ring</u>, he ran away.
   (= After he stole the ring)
② <u>Although being old</u>, she is childish.
   (= Although she is old)
③ <u>Listening to music</u>, I cooked pasta.
   (= While I listened to music)
④ <u>Cleaning the room</u>, she sang a song.
   (= As she cleaned the room)
⑤ <u>Being sick</u>, she couldn't come to my party.
   (= So she was sick)

12 다음 중 어법상 올바른 문장의 개수는?

ⓐ Though not been pretty, Sarah is very charming.
ⓑ Being friendly, Jake is loved by everyone.
ⓒ Not known her well, I couldn't ask for a favor.
ⓓ I heard someone to knock on the door.

① 없음　② 1개　③ 2개　④ 3개　⑤ 4개

13 다음 중 밑줄 친 부분을 바르게 고친 것은?

① Sera is in the living room <u>watched</u> TV.
   (→ watch)
② <u>Took</u> a shower, she cleaned the bathroom.
   (→ Taken)
③ <u>Knowing not</u> the result, we were very nervous. (→ Not knowing)
④ <u>Exercised</u> hard, I drank cold water.
   (→ As exercising)
⑤ <u>Rode</u> on my bike, I felt the breeze.
   (→ Ridden)

14 다음 중 어법상 <u>어색한</u> 문장의 개수는?

ⓐ This bag is making in a factory.
ⓑ Are you satisfied with our service?
ⓒ I'm sorry to make you disappointment.
ⓓ He is surprising at the big news.

① 없음　② 1개　③ 2개　④ 3개　⑤ 4개

15 다음 빈칸에 들어갈 말이 바르게 짝지어진 것은?

> A: What is this?
> B: It is a present ____(A)____ from Minsu.
> A: Oh, is it a sculpture?
> B: Yes, he gave me this sculpture ____(B)____ by him.
> A: It ____(C)____ you. I think that he is a great artist.

	(A)	(B)	(C)
①	send	– carve	– is resembled
②	sending	– carved	– resembles
③	sent	– carving	– resemble
④	sending	– carving	– is resembled
⑤	sent	– carved	– resembles

[16~18] 우리말과 뜻이 같도록 괄호 안의 말을 분사의 형태로 바꿔 문장을 완성하시오.

16
> Mary는 그가 사준 책을 받았다. (buy)

Mary got a book _____ by him.

17
> 영화 '반지의 제왕'은 많은 사람들에게 사랑 받는다. (love)

The movie *The Lord of the Rings* is _____ by many people.

18
> 숲으로 가면 너는 토끼를 볼 수 있을 것이다. (go)

_____ to the forest, you will be able to see a rabbit.

[19~20] 우리말과 뜻이 같도록 괄호 안의 말을 바르게 배열하시오.

19
> 엄마를 보자마자, 아기는 울기 시작했다.
> (mother, baby, seeing, crying, his, the, started)

_____

_____

20
> 달걀이 하나도 없어서, 나는 식료품점에 갔다.
> (any, I, the, grocery, having, eggs, went, store, not, to)

_____

_____

[21~22] 우리말과 뜻이 같도록 밑줄 친 분사구문을 부사절로 바꿔 쓰시오.

21
> 그의 주소를 몰랐기 때문에 나는 그의 집에 방문하지 못했다.
> <u>Not knowing his address</u>, I couldn't visit his place.

→ _____

_____, I couldn't visit his place.

22
> 공원에서 조깅을 한 후에 우리는 아침을 먹었다.
> <u>Jogging in the park</u>, we had breakfast.

→ _____

_____, we had breakfast.

[23~25] 다음 문장에서 어법상 <u>어색한</u> 부분을 찾아 바르게 고치시오.

23 I was confusing because of the difficult problem.

_____ → _____

24 To become dark, the moon shone very brightly.

_____ → _____

25 Took Mr. Kim's class, I asked many questions.

_____ → _____

26 다음 문장을 올바른 분사구문으로 고쳐 다시 쓰시오.

Although be old, my grandfather is very healthy.

→ _____

_____

[27~28] 다음 문장에서 <u>어색한</u> 부분을 고쳐 완전한 문장을 쓰시오.

27 Closed her eyes, Lucy remembered visiting Disneyland.

→ _____

_____

28 To exercise regularly, you will become healthier.

→ _____

_____

[29~30] 주어진 |조건|을 이용하여 우리말을 영어로 바꾸시오.

29 ┤조건├
1. 분사를 사용할 것
2. 단어 find, the oranges, pick, mom을 활용하여 쓸 것
3. 8단어를 사용할 것

나는 우리 엄마가 딴 오렌지들을 발견했다.

→ _____

_____

30 ┤조건├
1. 분사구문을 사용할 것
2. 단어 hungry, eat, the leftover pizza, make를 활용하여 쓸 것
3. 10단어를 사용할 것
4. 분사를 생략하지 말 것

그는 배가 고파서 내가 만든 남은 피자를 먹었다.

→ _____

_____

CHAPTER

12

관계사

UNIT 01　주격 관계대명사 1 - 사람

두 개의 문장에 같은 사람이 있을 때, 관계대명사 who[that]를 써서 두 문장을 연결하세요.

I met the boy. 나는 그 소년을 만났다.	관계대명사로	I met the boy who[that] knows you.
He knows you. 그는 너를 안다.	연결	나는 너를 아는 그 소년을 만났다.

우리말과 같은 뜻이 되도록 괄호 안의 말과 관계대명사를 이용하여 문장을 완성하시오.

01 저기서 잠을 자는 저 소년은 귀엽다. (there, sleep)

The boy _____ is cute.

02 캐나다에서 사는 Mary가 전화했다. (live)

Mary _____ called.

03 그 경기에서 우승한 사람은 나였다. (win, the game)

The man _____ was me.

04 여기서 일하는 사람들은 바빠 보인다. (here, work)

The people _____ look busy.

05 나는 춤에 능숙한 한 소녀를 안다. (be good at)

I know a girl _____.

UNIT 02　주격 관계대명사 2 - 사물

두 개의 문장에 같은 사물이 있을 때, 관계대명사 which[that]를 써서 두 문장을 연결하세요.

I like the shirt. 나는 그 셔츠를 좋아한다.	관계대명사로	I like the shirt which[that] has no buttons.
It has no buttons. 그것은 단추가 없다.	연결	나는 단추가 없는 그 셔츠를 좋아한다.

우리말과 같은 뜻이 되도록 괄호 안의 말과 관계대명사 which나 that을 이용하여 문장을 완성하시오.

01 주방에서 요리하고 있는 사람은 우리 삼촌이다. (cook, in the kitchen)

The man _____ is my uncle.

02 우리는 싸고 맛있는 음식을 원한다. (delicious, cheap)

We want _____.

03 이것이 이 호텔에서 가장 큰 방이다. (the biggest, hotel)

This is the room _____.

04 가장 돈을 많이 버는 직업은 무엇인가? (make, the most money)

What is _____?

05 치킨 수프는 내게 에너지를 주는 음식이다. (energy, give)

Chicken soup is _____.

06 식탁 위에 있는 생일 케이크는 특별해 보인다.

The birthday cake _____ looks special.

UNIT 03 　목적격 관계대명사

관계대명사가 목적격 대명사의 역할을 할 때는 목적격 관계대명사를 쓰세요.

The boy knows you. 그 소년은 너를 안다. I met him. 나는 그를 만났다.	관계대명사로 연결	The boy who(m)[that] I met knows you. 내가 만난 그 소년은 너를 안다.

우리말과 같은 뜻이 되도록 괄호 안의 말과 관계대명사를 이용하여 문장을 완성하시오.

01 그들은 그들이 직접 나무에서 딴 사과를 먹고 있다. (from the tree, pick)

They are eating the apples _____ for themselves.

02 Joy는 내가 6년 동안 알고 지낸 나의 가장 친한 친구다. (have known)

Joy is my best friend _____ for six years.

03 Katie는 Jessica가 던진 작은 공을 받았다. (throw)

Katie catched the little ball _____.

04 우리는 엄마가 만든 커다란 크리스마스트리 앞에서 사진을 찍었다.

We took a picture in front of the tall Christmas tree _____.

05 함께 모인 그 아이들은 모두 미국인이었다. (together, gather)

All the children _____ were Americans.

UNIT 04 　소유격 관계대명사

두 문장의 공통된 부분이 소유의 관계일 때, 소유격 관계대명사 whose를 쓰세요.

The boy knows you. 그 소년은 너를 안다. His eyes are big. 그의 눈은 크다.	관계대명사로 연결	The boy whose eyes are big knows you. 눈이 큰 그 소년이 너를 안다.

다음 두 문장을 관계대명사 whose를 이용하여 한 문장으로 만드시오.

01 Emily is a girl. + Her dream has come true.

→ Emily is a girl _____.

02 She is a designer. + Her clothes are special.

→ She is a designer _____.

03 I found an animal. + Its house was burnt.

→ I found an animal _____.

04 I know a girl. + Her voice is beautiful.

→ I know a girl _____.

05 The man is rich. + His house is on a hill.

→ The man _____ is rich.

06 The tourist looks sad. + Her bag is missing.

→ The tourist _____ looks sad.

주격, 목적격, 소유격 관계대명사 종합

선행사의 종류에 따른 주격, 목적격, 소유격 관계대명사를 종합적으로 연습하세요.

	사람 선행사	사물 선행사	사물 또는 사람
주격 관계대명사	who	which	that
목적격 관계대명사	who(m)	which	
소유격 관계대명사	whose		

다음 두 문장을 관계대명사를 이용하여 한 문장으로 만드시오.

01 This is the song. + My favorite singer wrote and sang the song.

→ This is the song _____ .

02 I know the girl. + You are going to meet her.

→ I know the girl _____ .

03 There is a box. + It has a lot of presents in it.

→ There is a box _____ in it.

04 The person is my grandma. + Her food always makes me happy.

→ The person _____ is my grandma.

05 I like the worker. + He always works very hard.

→ I like the worker _____ .

06 We are watching a movie. + Our teacher recommended it to us.

→ We are watching a movie _____ to us.

UNIT 06 관계대명사 that을 주로 쓰는 경우

관계대명사 who(m)나 which가 아닌, that을 주로 쓰는 다음의 선행사들에 유의하세요.

사람+사물	최상급이나 서수	-thing인 대명사
the only, the very, the same 등		all, much, little, any, no 등

우리말과 같은 뜻이 되도록 괄호 안의 말과 관계대명사를 이용하여 문장을 완성하시오.

01 그것은 내가 시도해 본 첫 태국 음식이다. (Thai, try) → It is _____ .

02 나는 네가 좋아하는 모든 색깔을 좋아한다. (like) → I like _____ .

03 너는 나를 도와준 첫 친구다. (help) → You are _____ .

04 나는 뭔가 말하고 싶은 것이 있다. (say) → There is _____ .

05 네가 원하는 어느 것이든 골라. (pick, anything) → Pick _____ .

06 그것은 내가 봤던 가장 높은 탑이다. (tower) → It's _____ .

관계대명사 that vs. 접속사 that

that의 역할이 관계대명사인지 명사절을 이끄는 접속사인지를 구분하세요.

관계대명사 that	형용사적 역할 – 선행사 수식	접속사 that	명사적 역할 – 주어, 목적어, 보어

우리말과 같은 뜻이 되도록 괄호 안의 말과 that을 이용하여 문장을 완성하시오.

01 나는 도서관에서 빌려온 그 책을 재미있게 읽었다. (borrow)

I enjoyed reading the book _____ from the library.

02 Natalie는 그녀가 제시간에 파티에 올 수 없다고 말했다. (come)

Natalie said _____ on time.

03 이것은 예전에 우리 할머니 댁에 있던 의자다. (used to)

This is the chair _____ in my grandma's house.

04 나는 내가 병원에 가야 한다고 생각하지 않는다. (have to, go to see)

I don't think _____ a doctor.

05 그의 의견은 우리가 오늘은 실내에 머물러야 한다는 것이다. (inside, stay, should)

His opinion is _____ today.

UNIT 08 관계대명사의 생략

관계대명사를 생략할 수 있는 경우들을 알아 두세요.

목적격 관계대명사 생략 가능		The boy who(m) I met knows you.	
관계대명사의 동사가 진행형일 때	〈관계대명사+be동사〉 생략 가능	The boy who is singing is Ben.	분사가 명사를 뒤에서 수식하는 문장이 됨
관계대명사의 동사가 수동태일 때		The boy who is invited is Ben.	

우리말과 같은 뜻이 되도록 괄호 안의 말을 배열하여 관계대명사를 생략한 문장을 완성하시오.

01 네가 수업 시간에 그린 그림 좀 내게 보여 줘. (the picture, painted, you, during class)

Please show me _____.

02 나는 운동장에서 야구를 하고 있는 저 아이들을 안다. (playing, children, baseball, those)

I know _____ in the playground.

03 일본어로 쓴 이 표지판 읽을 수 있니? (this sign, in Japanese, written)

Can you read _____?

04 이것은 네가 다섯 살 때 내게 써 준 편지다. (wrote, you, the letter, to me)

This is _____ when you were five.

05 밀크쉐이크를 마시고 있는 그 소년이 우리 반 반장이다. (drinking, the boy, a milkshake)

_____ is our class president.

06 내가 가장 존경하는 사람은 우리 영어 선생님이시다. (I, respect, the most, the person)

_____ is my English teacher.

UNIT 09 관계대명사 what

선행사가 없을 때는 관계대명사 what을 쓰세요.

관계대명사 that	관계대명사 what
The movie (that) I saw was fun.	What I saw was fun.
내가 본 그 영화는 재미있었다.	내가 본 것은 재미있었다.

참고 관계대명사 what은 '~한 것'의 의미로, the one[thing] that[which]로 바꿔 쓸 수 있어요.

우리말과 같은 뜻이 되도록 괄호 안의 말과 that 또는 what을 이용하여 문장을 완성하시오.

01 Sophia가 되고 싶은 것은 모델이다. (be) → _____ is a model.

02 그것이 Mike가 사고 싶은 자전거다. → It is the bike _____.

03 이것이 우리가 TV에서 들은 것이다. → This is _____ on TV.

04 이것이 그가 말하고 싶었던 것이다. (say) → This is _____.

05 내가 해야 하는 숙제는 어렵다. (must) → The homework _____ is hard.

06 너는 오늘 배운 것을 이해했구나. (learn) → You understood _____.

UNIT 10 관계부사 1 – when, where

선행사가 시간, 장소인 경우에는 〈접속사+부사(구)〉의 역할을 하는 관계부사를 쓰세요.

when	The 25th is the day.	The 25th is the day when we first met.
	We first met on that day.	
where	This is the park.	This is the park where we had fun.
	We had fun in the park.	

다음 두 문장을 관계부사를 이용하여 한 문장으로 연결하시오.

01 May 8 is the day. We give some presents to our parents on that day.

→ May 8 is the day _____ to our parents.

02 It was the only room. She could stay for one day in that room.

→ It was the only room _____.

03 This is the place. The car accident happened at this place.

→ This is _____.

04 Today is the day. We are going on a picnic on this day.

→ Today is _____.

05 Busan is the city. You can enjoy a lot of water activities in this city.

→ Busan is the city _____.

06 Tomorrow is the day. My family and I are planning to go to the amusement park on that day.

→ Tomorrow is the day _____.

관계부사 2 – why, how

선행사가 이유나 방법인 경우에도 〈접속사+부사(구)〉의 역할을 하는 관계부사를 쓰세요.

관계부사	두 문장	관계부사가 있는 한 문장	주의
why	That is the reason. He is mad for that reason.	That is the reason why he is mad.	〈접속사+부사구(for that reason)〉 역할
how	I found the way. He solved it in that way.	I found the way ~~how~~ he solved it. I found ~~the way~~ how he solved it.	the way, how 둘 중 하나만 써요.

😊참고 the reason과 같이 일반적인 선행사는 선행사나 관계부사 둘 중 하나만 써도 돼요.

This is the reason why [the reason / why] he is mad.

우리말과 같은 뜻이 되도록 괄호 안의 말과 관계부사를 이용하여 문장을 완성하시오.

01 네가 왜 Tim이랑 싸웠는지 이유를 내게 얘기해 줘. (have a fight)

Please tell me the reason _____ .

02 모든 사람들이 그 요리사가 국수를 요리하는 방법을 알고 싶어 한다. (the chef. the noodles)

Everyone wants to know _____ .

03 우리가 제주도에 가기로 한 날을 잊지 마. (are going to)

Don't forget _____ Jeju Island.

04 이 TV를 고치는 방법을 우리에게 보여 줘. (fix)

Show us _____ .

05 네가 왜 수업에 지각했는지 이유를 내게 알려 줘. (late for class)

Give me the reason _____ .

06 그것이 바로 그녀가 수의사가 되기로 결심한 이유다. (a vet. decide to)

That's the reason _____ .

the way와 관계부사 how는 함께 쓸 수 없음을 기억해야 해요. 또한, 구어체에서는 관계부사 why의 선행사 the reason을 생략하기도 한답니다.

[01~02] 다음 빈칸에 들어갈 말로 알맞은 것을 고르시오.

01

> I like the flowers _____ Tom gave.

① whom   ② thing   ③ what
④ which   ⑤ whose

02

> This is my classroom _____ I study.

① the place   ② which   ③ when
④ which   ⑤ where

03 다음 빈칸에 들어갈 말로 알맞은 것을 모두 고르면?

> I know the boy _____ Sarah likes.

① that   ② whose   ③ whom
④ which   ⑤ who

[04~05] 다음 빈칸에 공통으로 들어갈 말을 고르시오.

04

> • _____ do you do for a living?
> • This cell phone is _____ I bought at the store yesterday.

① What[what]   ② When[when]
③ How[how]   ④ That[that]
⑤ Where[where]

05

> • I remember the day _____ I first met him.
> • I learned the way _____ my mom bakes lemon pies.

① which – how   ② that – in which
③ when – in which   ④ when – which
⑤ what – how

06 다음 우리말을 영어로 바르게 옮긴 것은?

> 나는 그가 보낸 문자 메시지를 받았다.

① I got the text message what he sent.
② I got the text message he sent.
③ I got the text message in which he sent.
④ I got the text message of which he sent.
⑤ I got the text message in that he sent.

07 다음 두 문장을 한 문장으로 바르게 연결한 것은?

> • I have a dog.
> • It is very lovely and lively.

① I have a dog and is very lovely and lively.
② I have a dog what is very lovely and lively.
③ I have a dog that is very lovely and lively.
④ I have a dog how is very lovely and lively.
⑤ I have a dog whom is very lovely and lively.

08 다음 중 밑줄 친 that의 쓰임이 나머지 넷과 다른 것은?

① Do you see the bird that is sitting on the branch?
② It is exciting that we can go to the beach.
③ I like the posture that you did on the stage.
④ It is the novel that he wrote two years ago.
⑤ The students that study math are serious.

09 다음 밑줄 친 단어 중 생략이 가능하지 않은 것은?

① You saw that I got ten points at the game.
② I know the man who Minho is working with.
③ He is the boy whom I met right before.
④ The book that I borrowed is interesting.
⑤ I saw a dancer who is performing in the show.

10 다음 문장의 밑줄 친 what과 쓰임이 같은 것은?

> You can't always get what you want.

① What do you want for dinner?
② I don't know what to say.
③ He asked me what kind of juice I wanted.
④ I asked him what to eat for dinner.
⑤ What I heard is that Tom loves Jane.

11 다음 중 어법상 올바른 것은?

① We saw a goat that eating a lot of grass.
② This is that I told you yesterday.
③ Where is the worst city what you have visited?
④ He'll come back to the place where he was born.
⑤ She is a teacher who teach us English.

12 다음 중 어법상 어색한 것은?

① I heard the music that the artist played.
② You don't know anything that he wants.
③ I missed my friend used to play with me.
④ Do you remember the woman he met?
⑤ I know what you ate for dinner.

13 다음 중 어법상 바르게 고치지 않은 것은?

① I was the last one which arrived here.
    (→ that)
② She is satisfied with for that she looks.
    (→ how)
③ How I need is a piece of thick paper.
  (→ What)
④ I met the guy whom wearing a red hat.
    (→ who)
⑤ He is the one who height is 160 cm.
    (→ whose)

14 다음 중 어법상 어색한 문장의 개수는?

> ⓐ This year is the year she reaches adulthood.
> ⓑ I recognize your sister whose hat is red.
> ⓒ What is the last trip whom you had?
> ⓓ The kids who sings a song are cute.

① 없음 ② 1개 ③ 2개 ④ 3개 ⑤ 4개

15 다음 밑줄 친 관계대명사의 쓰임이 같은 것끼리 짝지어진 것은?

> ⓐ I visited her house that is near my house.
> ⓑ I know a man whose painting is famous.
> ⓒ You can tell me anything that you need.
> ⓓ I'll get the book that you asked for.
> ⓔ Give me the book which is on the desk.
> ⓕ He made a desk that I can use.

① ⓐ, ⓑ, ⓔ ② ⓐ, ⓓ, ⓕ ③ ⓑ, ⓒ, ⓓ
④ ⓐ, ⓔ, ⓕ ⑤ ⓒ, ⓓ, ⓕ

[16~17] 다음 괄호 안의 말과 관계대명사를 이용하여 문장을 완성하시오.

16 There are five boys _____ _____ the baseball game. (watch)

17 Can you show me _____ you and Henry _____ yesterday? (make)

[18~20] 다음 밑줄 친 관계대명사의 역할을 |보기|에서 골라 각각에 해당하는 기호를 쓰시오.

> |보기|
> ⓐ 주격   ⓑ 소유격   ⓒ 목적격

18 I love my dog that always comes when I need him.

→ _____

19 She published the book which she had written two years ago.

→ _____

20 I met a friend whose name is the same as mine.

→ _____

[21~23] 다음 |보기|에서 알맞은 관계부사를 골라 빈칸에 각각 쓰시오.

> |보기|
> how   when   where   why

21 I'll tell you the place _____ we'll meet tomorrow.

22 Can you guess _____ he is angry?

23 Let me know _____ you solved this problem. Did you use a calculator?

24 우리말과 뜻이 같도록 괄호 안의 말을 바르게 배열하시오.

> 나는 Brown 선생님께서 가르친 것을 이해할 수 있다.
> (understand, taught, Mr. Brown, what, can, I)

_____

_____

25 |보기|와 같이 다음 두 문장을 관계대명사를 이용하여 한 문장으로 만드시오.

> ┤보기├
> • This is the fable.
> • I liked it very much when I was young.
> → This is the fable that I liked very much when I was young.

• I'm satisfied with my room.
• I painted it yesterday.

→ _____

_____

[26~27] 다음 문장에서 어법상 **어색한** 부분을 찾아 바르게 고치시오.

26 That is the reason for why she loves him very much.

_____ → _____

27 He is the youngest son what is very smart and wise.

_____ → _____

28 다음 문장에서 어법상 **어색한** 부분을 고쳐 완전한 문장을 쓰시오.

They work in the building which have a cafeteria on the first floor.

→ _____

_____

[29~30] 주어진 |조건|을 이용하여 우리말을 영어로 바꾸시오.

29
> ┤조건├
> 1. 관계대명사를 사용할 것
> 2. 단어 like, the boy, meet, the summer camp를 활용하여 쓸 것
> 3. 11단어를 사용할 것

그녀는 여름 캠프에서 만났던 그 소년을 좋아한다.

→ _____

30
> ┤조건├
> 1. 관계부사를 사용할 것
> 2. 단어 grandmother's home, feel, the most relaxed를 사용할 것
> 3. 10단어를 사용할 것
> 4. 선행사를 생략할 것

나의 할머니의 집은 내가 가장 편안함을 느끼는 장소이다.

→ _____

_____

> 내가 가장 취약한 부분에 대해
> 요점 정리를 해 보세요.

가정법

현재 사실의 반대를 가정할 때는 가정법 동사(일반동사 과거형, be동사 were)를 쓰세요.

현재 사실	I don't have time, so I can't go.	시간이 없어서 갈 수 없다.
반대 가정	┌ don't have의 반대/과거 If I had time, I could go. └ can't go의 반대/과거	내가 시간이 있다면, 갈 수 있을 텐데. (현재 사실과 반대되는 가정)

다음 문장을 가정법 문장으로 바꿔 쓰시오.

01 As she is not a baby, she may not like it.

→ _____, she might like it.

02 Since I don't have time, I can't watch TV.

→ _____, I could watch TV.

03 As I don't live close, I can't walk to school.

→ _____, I could walk to school.

04 As he isn't old enough, he can't ride it.

→ _____, he could ride it.

05 Since he isn't here, he can't tell us.

→ _____, he could tell us.

'만약 ~이라면 좋을 텐데'라고 할 때는 〈I wish＋가정법 동사〉로 표현하세요.

현재 사실	I don't have a brother.	형제가 없다.
유감/아쉬움	I wish I had a brother. └ 가정법 과거(현재 사실의 반대)	형제가 있다면 좋을 텐데. (현재 사실과 반대되는 일을 소망)

다음 두 문장이 같은 뜻이 되도록 문장을 완성하시오.

01 I'm sorry (that) I don't have sunglasses and a hat.

= I wish _____.

02 I'm sorry (that) I can't play the violin well.

= I wish _____.

03 I wish my art teacher liked my painting.

= I'm sorry (that) _____.

04 I'm sorry (that) you don't want to be a doctor.

= I wish _____.

05 I wish she wouldn't move to another school.

= I'm sorry (that) _____.

UNIT 03 as if+가정법 과거

'마치 ~인 것처럼'이라고 쓸 때는 〈as if+가정법 동사〉로 표현하세요.

현재 사실	He can't do it now.	지금 할 수 없다.
마치 ~처럼	He acts as if he ~~did~~ could do it now. ↳ 조동사를 과거로 써요.	지금 할 수 있는 것처럼 행동한다. (실제로는 아님)

다음 두 문장이 같은 뜻이 되도록 문장을 완성하시오.

01 In fact, today is not Christmas. = It seems _____ .

02 In fact, she can't run fast. = She talks _____ .

03 In fact, Sara is not good at math. = Sara acts _____ .

04 In fact, he is not a doctor. = He behaves _____ .

05 In fact, Amy is not a soccer fan. = Amy talks _____ .

06 In fact, she doesn't like English. = She speaks _____ .

UNIT 04 if+가정법 과거완료

과거 사실의 반대를 가정할 때는 가정법 동사를 과거완료형으로 쓰세요.

과거 사실	I didn't have time, so I couldn't go.	시간이 없어서 갈 수 없었다.
반대 가정	┌ didn't have의 반대 had+have의 완료형 had If I had had time, I could have gone. 　　　　　　 ↳ couldn't go의 반대/완료형	시간이 있었다면, 갈 수 있었을 텐데. (과거 사실과 반대되는 가정)

우리말과 같은 뜻이 되도록 |보기|에서 알맞은 말을 골라 빈칸에 알맞은 형태로 쓰시오.

|보기|

answer	tell	be	win	watch	take

01 그가 내게 더 천천히 얘기해 줬더라면, 나는 그의 말을 이해할 수 있었을 텐데.

_____ me more slowly. I could have understood his words.

02 내가 나이가 더 많았더라면, 강아지를 돌볼 수 있었을 텐데.

If I had been older, _____ care of a dog.

03 그가 우승을 했더라면, 그는 많은 상금을 받을 수 있었을 텐데.

_____ , he could have had a lot of prize money.

04 그녀가 일찍 자지 않았더라면, 내 전화를 받았을 텐데.

If she had not gone to sleep early, _____ my call.

05 내가 아프지 않았더라면, 너와 함께 놀이공원에 갈 수 있었을 텐데.

_____ sick. I could have gone to the amusement park with you.

06 내가 숙제를 다 끝마쳤더라면, 내가 제일 좋아하는 TV 프로그램을 볼 수 있었을 텐데.

If I had finished my homework, _____ my favorite TV program.

UNIT 05 　I wish+가정법 과거완료

'만약 ~였다면 좋았을 텐데'라고 할 때는 〈I wish+가정법 과거완료〉로 표현하세요.

과거 사실	I didn't see him.	그를 못 봤다.
유감/아쉬움	I wish I had seen him. └ 가정법 과거완료(과거 사실의 반대)	그를 봤다면 좋았을 텐데. (과거 사실과 반대되는 일을 소망)

다음 두 문장이 같은 뜻이 되도록 문장을 완성하시오.

01 I wish I had learned Spanish. 　　= I'm sorry that ＿＿＿＿＿＿＿＿＿＿＿＿.

02 I'm sorry that I didn't remember the song. = I wish ＿＿＿＿＿＿＿＿＿＿＿＿.

03 I wish we had had lunch. 　　　　= I'm sorry that ＿＿＿＿＿＿＿＿＿＿＿＿.

04 I'm sorry that you didn't have enough time. = I wish ＿＿＿＿＿＿＿＿＿＿＿＿.

05 I wish we had watched the game. 　= I'm sorry that ＿＿＿＿＿＿＿＿＿＿＿＿.

06 I'm sorry that we didn't play together. = I wish ＿＿＿＿＿＿＿＿＿＿＿＿.

UNIT 06 　as if+가정법 과거완료

'마치 ~이었던 것처럼'이라고 쓸 때는 〈as if+가정법 과거완료〉로 표현하세요.

과거 사실	He didn't see me.	나를 못 봤다.
마치 ~처럼	He talks as if he had seen me. └ 과거 사실의 반대 가정	마치 나를 봤던 것처럼 말한다. (실제로는 아니었음)

우리말과 같은 뜻이 되도록 괄호 안의 말을 이용하여 문장을 완성하시오.

01 우리 할아버지는 마치 Harvard 대학교를 졸업했던 것처럼 말씀하신다. (talk, graduate from)

My grandpa ＿＿＿＿＿＿＿＿＿＿＿＿＿＿＿＿＿＿.

02 너는 마치 네가 내게 거짓말을 하지 않았던 것처럼 행동한다. (tell me a lie, act)

You ＿＿＿＿＿＿＿＿＿＿＿＿＿＿＿＿＿＿.

03 Teddy는 마치 자신이 방 청소를 했던 것처럼 이야기한다. (talk, clean his room)

Teddy ＿＿＿＿＿＿＿＿＿＿＿＿＿＿＿＿＿＿.

04 그 가수는 마치 그것이 자기의 마지막 콘서트였던 것처럼 말한다. (his last concert, talk)

The singer ＿＿＿＿＿＿＿＿＿＿＿＿＿＿＿＿＿＿.

05 Helena는 마치 자기가 롤러코스터를 탔던 것처럼 이야기한다. (talk, ride the roller coaster)

Helena ＿＿＿＿＿＿＿＿＿＿＿＿＿＿＿＿＿＿.

06 학생들은 마치 오전에 쉬는 시간을 보내지 않은 것처럼 행동한다. (behave, have a morning break)

The students ＿＿＿＿＿＿＿＿＿＿＿＿＿＿＿＿＿＿.

[01~02] 다음 빈칸에 들어갈 말로 알맞은 것을 고르시오.

01
> If it _____ tomorrow, we will cancel our plans.

① rained ② will rain ③ rains
④ rain ⑤ would rain

02
> I wish I _____ a whale in the ocean.

① were ② would be ③ am
④ was ⑤ have been

03 다음 빈칸에 공통으로 들어갈 말로 알맞은 것은?

> A: What _____ you do if you met the little match girl in this story?
> B: I _____ hug her.

① do ② will ③ can
④ would ⑤ could

[04~05] 다음 중 빈칸에 들어갈 말이 바르게 짝지어진 것을 고르시오.

04
> • I would take a taxi if it _____ .
> • I wish you _____ to my party yesterday.

① rains – had come
② rains – came
③ rained – have come
④ rained – had come
⑤ will rain – come

05
> • If you _____ hard, you could pass the test.
> • You look as if you _____ a good time last weekend.

① study – had ② study – had had
③ studied – had ④ studied – had had
⑤ will study – have had

[06~07] 다음 우리말을 영어로 바르게 옮긴 것을 고르시오.

06
> 내가 나의 지갑을 잃어버리지 않았었더라면 좋았을 텐데.

① I wish I lost my wallet.
② I wish I have lost my wallet.
③ I wish I didn't lost my wallet.
④ I wish I haven't lost my wallet.
⑤ I wish I hadn't lost my wallet.

07
> 내가 Tom보다 키가 더 크다면, 농구선수가 될 수 있을 텐데.

① If I were taller than Tom, I can become a basketball player.
② If I was taller than Tom, I could become a basketball player.
③ If I were taller than Tom, I could become a basketball player.
④ If I was taller than Tom, I can become a basketball player.
⑤ If I am taller than Tom, I could become a basketball player.

08 다음 주어진 문장을 가정법으로 바르게 옮긴 것은?

> I had no money, so I couldn't buy it.

① If I had money, I could buy it.
② If I had had money, I could buy it.
③ If I had money, I could have bought it.
④ If I had had money, I could have bought it.
⑤ If I have had money, I could have bought it.

09 다음 중 빈칸에 들어갈 말이 나머지 넷과 다른 것은?

① I would run _____ I saw a bear in the forest.
② _____ you go to Paris, try this restaurant.
③ I'll fail the test _____ I study hard.
④ _____ you trust her, you can tell her.
⑤ I could have lunch _____ he let me go.

10 다음 중 어법상 올바른 것을 모두 고르면?

① I wish I was the captain of our team.
② She wishes she had earned a lot of money.
③ If he had known it, he would tell us.
④ I could see stars if the weather was great.
⑤ If I were a pilot, I could travel anywhere.

11 다음 중 어법상 어색한 것은?

① If we saved more money, we could buy it.
② I wish I could fly in the sky like a bird.
③ If he were kind, I would have liked him.
④ Phillip acts as if he had seen my boss.
⑤ If my sister had arrived early, she could have met my friend.

12 다음 중 어법상 바르게 고치지 않은 것은?

① If you get up late, you had been on time.
   (→ won't be)
② If she wasn't ill, she would go there.
   (→ weren't)
③ As you knew him well, you would like him.
   (→ If)
④ If I exercise more, I could become slim.
   (→ had exercised)
⑤ He looks as if he sees a ghost.
   (→ had seen)

13 다음 중 올바른 문장의 개수는?

> ⓐ I wish he replied to my text message.
> ⓑ He looks as if he hasn't eaten for a week.
> ⓒ I would be glad if you come to my home.
> ⓓ If I hadn't lost the key, I could have entered my house.

① 없음　② 1개　③ 2개　④ 3개　⑤ 4개

14 다음 중 어법상 어색한 문장의 개수는?

> ⓐ If I had slept early, I could have got up early.
> ⓑ She acts as if she had been sick now.
> ⓒ If I had a pet, I'll take care of it very well.
> ⓓ If it rains, I'll drive you to school.

① 없음　② 1개　③ 2개　④ 3개　⑤ 4개

15 다음 중 빈칸에 들어갈 말이 바르게 짝지어진 것은?

> A: What would have happened if we
> _____(A)_____ ?
> B: I can't imagine that we don't know
> each other.
> A: I would be unhappy if I ____(B)____
> you.
> B: Me too. I wish we ____(C)____
> together forever.

	(A)		(B)		(C)

① haven't met – can't see – will be
② hadn't met – couldn't see – could be
③ haven't met – could see – are
④ had met – couldn't see – had been
⑤ hadn't met – could see – can be

[16~18] 우리말과 뜻이 같도록 괄호 안의 말을 이용하여 문장을 완성하시오.

16

> 그 건물은 마치 그 산보다 더 커 보인다. (be)

The building looks as if it _____
taller than the mountain.

17

> 만약 내가 너라면, 나는 그에게 그것에 대해서 이야기할 텐데. (talk)

If I _____ you, I _____
_____ to him about it.

18

> 네가 지금 올 수 있다면 좋을 텐데. (come)

I wish you _____ _____
now.

[19~20] 우리말과 뜻이 같도록 괄호 안의 말을 바르게 배열하시오.

19

> 그녀가 지난주보다 더 건강하다면 좋을 텐데.
> (wish, last, healthier, she, were, I, than week)

_____

_____

20

> 그녀는 자신이 스타인 것처럼 행동한다.
> (acts, were, star, if, she, a, as, she)

_____

_____

[21~22] 다음 주어진 문장과 뜻이 같도록 문장을 완성하시오.

21

> I regret that I didn't go there.

= I wish I _____.

22

> Sunny is too busy to go hiking.

= If Sunny _____,
she _____.

[23~24] 다음 |보기|와 같이 가정법 문장으로 바꿔 쓰시오.

|보기|

He gained weight, so he decided to go on a diet.
→ If he hadn't gained weight, he wouldn't have decided to go on a diet.

23 As I don't know how to play Baduk, I can't play with you.

→ If _____

_____ .

24 She was very sick, so she couldn't attend the meeting.

→ If _____

_____ .

[25~26] 다음 문장에서 어법상 <u>어색한</u> 부분을 찾아 바르게 고치시오.

25 I would buy this skirt right now if it had been cheaper.

_____ → _____

26 I wish I could have joined you tomorrow.

_____ → _____

27 다음 문장을 as if 가정법을 이용하여 바꿔 쓰시오.

He is not handsome, but he acts like he is.

→ _____

_____

28 다음 문장에서 어법상 <u>어색한</u> 부분을 고쳐 가정법 문장으로 쓰시오.

I donated to the poor if I had money.

→ _____

_____

[29~30] 주어진 |조건|을 이용하여 우리말을 영어로 바꾸시오.

29 **|조건|**
1. wish를 사용할 것
2. 단어 be good at, math, like, Tom을 활용하여 쓸 것
3. 9단어를 사용할 것

내가 Tom처럼 수학을 잘하면 좋을 텐데.

→ _____

_____

30 **|조건|**
1. if를 사용할 것
2. 단어 more careful, get hurt를 활용하여 쓸 것
3. 12단어를 사용할 것

만약 내가 좀 더 조심했다면, 나는 다치지 않았을 것이다.

→ _____

_____

일치와 화법

UNIT 01 시제 일치

 주절의 시제와 종속절의 시제의 기본적인 관계를 알아 두세요.

주절 시제	종속절의 시제	예문
현재	모든 시제 가능	He knows that you are honest.
과거	과거나 과거완료 가능	He thought that she was in London.

우리말과 같은 뜻이 되도록 괄호 안의 말을 이용하여 문장을 완성하시오.

01 나는 그 의사 선생님이 모두에게 매우 친절하다는 것을 알게 됐다. (find, kind)

I _____ that the doctor _____ to everyone.

02 Emily는 자기가 파티에 올 수 없다고 말하고 있다. (say, come to)

Emily _____ that she _____ the party.

03 나는 Tom이 왜 그런 말을 했는지 궁금하다. (say, wonder, such a thing)

I _____ why Tom _____.

04 그 가수는 자기가 직접 그 노래를 작곡했다고 우리에게 말했다. (write, tell, the song)

The singer _____ us that he _____ himself.

05 간호사 선생님은 내게 휴식을 취해야 한다고 말씀하셨다. (tell, take a rest)

The nurse _____ me that I _____.

06 Jennie는 그녀의 엄마가 어떻게 수프를 요리하실지 알고 싶었다. (want to, make soup)

Jennie _____ know how her mom _____.

UNIT 02 시제 일치의 예외

 항상 현재시제를 쓰는 경우와 항상 과거시제를 쓰는 경우에 유의하세요.

항상 현재	진리, 사실, 속담, 현재의 습관 등	항상 과거	역사적 사실

다음 문장의 주절의 시제를 과거로 바꿔 문장을 완성하시오.

01 Even my youngest sister knows that the sun rises in the morning.

→ Even my youngest sister _____ in the morning.

02 The book says that the first Olympic Games took place in Greece.

→ The book _____ in Greece.

03 I hear that my grandma always gets up at six o'clock.

→ I _____ at six o'clock.

04 The staff tells us that the shuttle bus goes every ten minutes.

→ The staff _____.

05 He tells us that about 64 million people died in World War II.

→ He _____ in World War II.

UNIT 03 조동사 do의 쓰임

do는 조동사로도 쓰일 수 있다는 것을 알아 두세요.

본동사 do의 쓰임	조동사 do의 쓰임		
～하다	강조 용법 '정말'	부정문	의문문

참고 조동사가 있는 문장에는 항상 동사원형을 써요.

우리말과 같은 뜻이 되도록 괄호 안의 말과 조동사 do를 이용하여 문장을 완성하시오.

01 그는 정말 수업에 왔다. (come)　　→ He _____ to the class.

02 나는 네가 정말 보고 싶었다. (miss)　→ I _____ you.

03 나의 강아지의 털은 정말로 부드럽다. (feel) → My puppy's hair _____ soft.

04 그녀는 정말로 열심히 공부했다. (study) → She _____ hard

05 그는 나에게 전화하지 않는다. (call)　→ He _____ me.

06 그녀는 너를 아니? (know)　　　　→ _____ you?

UNIT 04 도치

부사(구)나 전치사구를 강조하기 위해 문장 앞에 쓸 때, 그 뒤는 〈동사+주어〉의 어순으로 도치시키세요.

〈Here/There+동사+주어〉	〈전치사구+동사+주어〉
Here comes the bus.	Across the street is the shop.
There goes the last bus.	Down the hill ran the boy.

주의 Here나 There의 경우 주어가 대명사일 때는 그대로 〈주어+동사〉가 돼요.

Here it comes. / There it goes.

괄호 안의 말을 바르게 배열하여 부사구를 강조하는 도치 문장으로 쓰시오.

01 많은 나무와 꽃들이 정원에서 자란다. (trees and flowers, a lot of, the garden, grows, in)

_____

02 그들이 여기에서 자고 있다. (they, are, here, sleeping)

_____

03 아름다운 꽃병이 식탁 위에 놓여 있었다. (a beautiful vase, the table, on, lay)

_____

04 밤새 비가 내렸다. (came, the rain, all night, down)

_____

05 당신이 주문한 오렌지 주스 여기 있습니다. (the orange juice, you, here, is, ordered)

_____

06 아이들이 수영장 안으로 뛰어들었다. (the children, the pool, into, jumped)

_____

UNIT 05 직접화법과 간접화법 1

 직접화법의 문장을 간접화법으로 바꿔 쓸 때 주의해야 할 시제 및 부사(구)를 알아 두세요.

전달 동사의 시제	현재(say)	따옴표 안의 동사 = 간접화법 that절의 동사
	과거(said)	현재 → 과거 / 과거 → 과거완료 / 현재완료 → 과거완료

now → then	today → that day	tonight → that night
this[these] → that[those]	here → there	ago → before
yesterday → the previous day	tomorrow → the next day	last night → the previous night

다음 문장을 간접화법으로 바꿔 쓰시오.

01 Ava said, "I will exercise hard from today."

→ Ava _____ that _____ .

02 Tom said, "I woke up late this morning."

→ Tom _____ that _____ .

03 James said, "I will go to the park today."

→ James _____ that _____ .

04 Lucas said to his mom, "I got a perfect score."

→ Lucas _____ that _____ .

UNIT 06 직접화법과 간접화법 2

의문사가 있을 때는 의문사를 그대로 쓰지만, 의문사가 없다면 접속사 if나 whether를 쓰세요.

의문사 있음	직접화법	She said to him, "Where do you live now?"
	간접화법	She asked him where he lived then.
의문사 없음	직접화법	He said to me, "Have you been to Busan?"
	간접화법	He asked me if[whether] I had been to Busan.

다음 문장을 간접화법으로 바꿔 쓰시오.

01 He said to her, "When will you come?"

→ He _____ her _____ .

02 I said to him, "Can you open it?"

→ I _____ him _____ .

03 He said, "How do you feel today?"

→ He _____ me _____ .

04 She said to me, "Do you understand me?"

→ She _____ me _____ .

UNIT 07 간접의문문

의문사가 있는 의문문을 평서문 어순으로 써서 '~인지 말해 줘', '~인지 궁금해'와 같이 쓰세요.

의문사 여부	직접의문문	간접의문문	
의문사 있음	Where did you stay?	Tell me where you stayed.	어디 묵었는지 말해 줘.
		I wonder where you stayed.	어디 묵었는지 궁금해.
의문사 없음	Did you stay here?	Tell me if you stayed here.	여기 묵었는지 아닌지 말해 줘.
		I wonder whether you stayed here.	여기 묵었는지 아닌지 궁금해.

🗨️주의 의문사가 없는 의문문은 if/whether를 써서 간접의문문을 만들어요.

의문사가 주어인 경우에는 어순이 바뀌지 않아요. She wanted to know who wrote the essay.

생각이나 추측을 나타내는 동사(think, believe, imagine, guess, suppose)의 간접의문문에 주의하세요.

직접 의문문	think, believe 등의 동사가 있는 간접의문문	
Where did you stay?	Do you think where he stayed? (X)	
	Where do you think he stayed. (O)	그가 어디에 묵었다고 생각해?
Who is she?	Do you suppose who she is? (X)	
	Who do you suppose she is? (O)	그녀가 누구라고 추측해?

|A| 다음 두 문장을 간접의문문으로 만들 때, 빈칸에 알맞은 말을 쓰시오.

01 Can you tell me? + Why are you angry?

→ Can you tell me _____ ?

02 I am not sure. + Did I pass the test?

→ I am not sure _____ .

03 I don't know. + Does Kevin like Susie?

→ I don't know _____ .

04 I wonder. + When is Jessie's birthday?

→ I wonder _____ .

05 I want to know. + Where are we now?

→ I want to know _____ .

06 We want to know. + Who won the contest?

→ We want to know _____ .

|B| 다음 두 문장을 한 문장으로 연결하시오.

01 Do you think? + What is his name?　　→ _____

02 Do you believe? + When will she come?　→ _____

03 Do you think? + Who will get the prize?　→ _____

04 Do you guess? + Why is he late?　　→ _____

평서문 뒤에 '그렇지?' 또는 '그렇지 않니?'라고 확인을 구하는 부가의문문의 사용법을 알아 두세요.

	평서문	+ 부가의문문		평서문	+ 부가의문문
be동사	긍정	+ 부정 의문 be동사	일반동사	긍정	+ 부정 의문 do동사
	부정	+ 긍정 의문 be동사		부정	+ 긍정 의문 do동사

주의 대답은 긍정이면 무조건 Yes, 부정이면 무조건 No로 해야 해요.

A: She is wise, isn't she? **B:** Yes, she is. (현명함) / No, she isn't. (현명하지 않음)

부가의문문과 그에 맞는 대답으로 대화를 완성하시오.

01 A: You studied hard. _____? **B:** _____. So I am tired today.

02 A: He doesn't live in Seoul. _____? **B:** _____. He lives in Busan.

03 A: You don't want to buy it. _____? **B:** _____. I don't have money.

04 A: This is your favorite song. _____? **B:** _____. I like its melody.

05 A: You know this story. _____? **B:** _____. I don't know about it.

06 A: Sam isn't good at tennis. _____? **B:** _____. He is a great player.

조동사가 있는 문장이나, 명령문, 청유문의 부가의문문을 만드는 방법에 유의하세요.

	평서문	+ 부가의문문		평서문	+ 부가의문문
조동사	긍정	+ 부정 의문 조동사	명령문	긍정/부정	will you?
	부정	+ 긍정 의문 조동사	청유문		shall we?

주의 부가의문문에서 am의 부정은 aren't로 한다는 것에 주의하세요. I <u>am</u> too late, aren't I?

우리말과 같은 뜻이 되도록 괄호 안의 말과 부가의문문을 이용하여 문장을 완성하시오.

01 너는 영어로 쓸 수 있어, 그렇지 않니? (write)

_____ in English. _____?

02 그들은 10분 내에 도착할 거야, 안 그래? (arrive)

_____ in 10 minutes. _____?

03 내가 카트 미는 걸 도와줘, 그래 줄래? (help, push)

_____ the cart. _____?

04 이 신발 멋져 보인다, 안 그래? (look)

_____ good. _____?

05 그의 음악을 들어보자, 어때? (listen to)

_____ his music. _____?

[01~02] 다음 빈칸에 들어갈 말로 알맞은 것을 고르시오.

01

They are good students, _____ they?

① are   ② do   ③ aren't
④ will   ⑤ were

02

I don't know _____ Tom is here.

① whether   ② who   ③ when
④ what   ⑤ where

03 다음 빈칸에 공통으로 들어갈 말로 알맞은 것은?

• Open the window, _____ you?
• I promise that I _____ study hard.

① and   ② will   ③ may
④ or   ⑤ should

[04~05] 다음 중 빈칸에 들어갈 말이 바르게 짝지어진 것을 고르시오.

04

• She told me that she _____ it for me.
• What do you _____ it is?

① keep – guess   ② kept – know
③ keep – believe   ④ kept – think
⑤ to keep – imagine

05

A: Sarah said that she _____ go to school early this morning.
B: I guess she _____ study for the exam.

① would – has to   ② will – would
③ has to – would   ④ would – have to
⑤ has to – have to

06 다음 질문에 대한 답으로 알맞은 것은?

A: We can't make dinner on time, can we?
B: _____

① Yes, we can't.   ② No, we can.
③ Yes, we can.   ④ Yes, we will.
⑤ No, we won't

07 다음 우리말을 영어로 바르게 옮긴 것은?

나는 Jim에게 국수가 먹고 싶은지 물었다.

① I asked Jim whether he wanted to eat noodles.
② I asked Jim which he wants to eat noodles.
③ I asked Jim where he wanted to eat noodles.
④ I asked Jim how he wanted to eat noodles.
⑤ I asked Jim if he wants to eat noodles.

08 다음 주어진 문장을 간접화법으로 바르게 바꾼 것은?

> He said to us, "Bring your plates and have dinner."

① He told us to bring your plates and have dinner.
② He told to us to bring my plates and have dinner.
③ He told us to bring our plates and had dinner.
④ He told us to bring your plates and had dinner.
⑤ He told us to bring our plates and have dinner.

09 다음 주어진 문장을 직접화법으로 바르게 바꾼 것은?

> I asked her when she was going to arrive there.

① I asked her, "When you are going to arrive here?"
② I said to her, "When are you going to arrive here?"
③ I said to her, "When is she going to arrive here?"
④ I said her, "When am I going to arrive here?"
⑤ I asked to her, "When are you going to arrive here?"

10 다음 중 어법상 올바른 것은?

① He asked me if I have a bike.
② There goes she up the hill.
③ Can you tell me what is this?
④ On the table was an apple.
⑤ I did told you not to be late.

11 다음 중 어법상 어색한 것은?

① I realized that he had stolen my wallet.
② Did she do her best in the race?
③ In front of the mirror smiled the girl.
④ I learned that the moon reflects the sun.
⑤ He said he wants to stay there longer.

12 다음 중 주어진 문장의 밑줄 친 단어와 쓰임이 같은 것은?

> She did look wonderful today.

① You should do your best in the race.
② She does not like swimming in the pool.
③ I do like the apple pie made by my mom.
④ Did you do the dishes after dinner?
⑤ What would you do for love?

13 다음 중 어법상 바르게 고치지 않은 것은?

① Do you know what I have for dinner yesterday?　(→ had)
② Christine can play the guitar, does she?　(→ can't)
③ He asked me what time was it.　(→ it was)
④ Across the street a dog is running.　(→ is a dog running)
⑤ You will take a taxi, will you?　(→ won't)

14 다음 중 올바른 문장의 개수는?

> ⓐ Up in the air fly the eagles.
> ⓑ I wondered how she had entered the room.
> ⓒ I do love my boyfriend because he is kind.
> ⓓ Can you tell me what your favorite color?

① 없음 ② 1개 ③ 2개 ④ 3개 ⑤ 4개

15 다음 중 빈칸에 들어갈 말이 바르게 짝지어진 것은?

> A: We're not late, are we?
> B: Yes, we ___(A)___ . Hurry up! We must arrive at the classroom by 9:00 a.m. What time is it?
> A: It's 8:30. Joe told me that the bus ___(B)___ at 8:30.
> B: Here ___(C)___ the bus! We can make it!

	(A)	(B)	(C)
①	are	leaves	comes
②	aren't	leave	goes
③	are	left	comes
④	aren't	leaves	goes
⑤	are	left	comes

[16~17] 다음 빈칸에 들어갈 알맞은 부가의문문을 쓰시오.

16 We had a great time at the party last night, _____ _____ ?

17 He won't come to see us, _____ _____ ?

[18~19] 우리말과 뜻이 같도록 괄호 안의 말을 이용하여 문장을 완성하시오.

18
> 그는 그 소파가 너무 더러워서 누울 수 없다고 말했다. (be)

He said that the sofa _____ too dirty to lie down on.

19
> 우리는 우리가 1등을 할 수 있다고 믿었다. (win)

We believed we _____ _____ first prize.

20 우리말과 뜻이 같도록 괄호 안의 말을 바르게 배열하시오.

> Mia는 바다에서 수영하는 것을 매우 좋아한다.
> (like, sea, Mia, in, does, the, swimming)

_____

_____

21 다음 두 문장의 의미가 같도록 빈칸에 알맞은 말을 쓰시오.

> James walked down the street
> = Down the street _____ .

[22~23] 다음 |보기|와 같이 간접화법을 이용하여 문장을 바꿔 쓰시오.

> |보기|
> He said, "We have to fix the machine."
> → He said that we had to fix the machine.

22 He said to me, "Don't push me hard!"

→ _____

_____

23 She said to me, "Did you enjoy the concert?"

→ _____

_____

[24~25] 다음 문장에서 어법상 <u>어색한</u> 부분을 찾아 바르게 고치시오.

24 I wondered why he won't tell me the truth.

_____ → _____

25 I learned that water boiled at 100℃.

_____ → _____

26 다음 두 문장을 한 문장으로 바꿔 쓸 때, <u>어색한</u> 부분을 고쳐 완전한 문장을 쓰시오.

Do you guess? + Who is the winner?
→ Do you guess who is the winner?

→ _____

_____

27 다음 문장에서 어법상 <u>어색한</u> 부분을 고쳐 완전한 문장을 쓰시오.

On the top of the mountain a big rock was.

→ _____

_____

[28~29] 주어진 |조건|을 이용하여 우리말을 영어로 바꾸시오.

28 |조건|
1. 간접화법을 사용할 것
2. 단어 clean, the house를 활용하여 쓸 것
3. 10단어를 사용할 것

그는 내게 그때 집을 청소하는 중이라고 말했다.

→ _____

_____

29 |조건|
1. there를 문두에 쓰고 주어 동사를 도치시킬 것
2. 단어 there, live, a beautiful girl, in our town을 활용하여 쓸 것
3. 8단어를 사용할 것

한 아름다운 소녀가 우리 동네에 살았다.

→ _____

_____

30 다음 밑줄 친 ⓐ~ⓔ 중 어법상 <u>어색한</u> 것의 기호를 쓰고 바르게 고쳐 쓰시오.

My family was on the beach in my dream. My father ⓐasked me if I wanted to swim in the sea. I said I ⓑwanted to catch fish instead. My brother told me that he could see a whale ⓒthen. I was very excited and told my family that I ⓓwill catch that whale. We ⓔspent a great time trying to catch it in the water. It was a wonderful dream.

_____ → _____

EBS

MY GRAMMAR COACH

내신기출 N제 중2

수학 **꽉** 잡아

중학 수학 완성

EBS 선생님 **무료강의 제공**

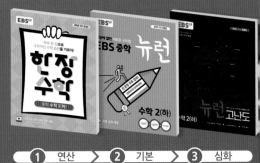

사뿐

중학 사회
중학 역사

사회를 한 권으로
가뿐하게!

중학 사회

① - 1   ② - 1   ① - 2   ② - 2

중학 역사

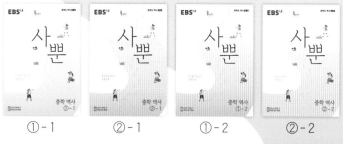

① - 1   ② - 1   ① - 2   ② - 2

인류사에서 뒷이야기만큼 흥미로운 것은 없다!

EBS 오디오 콘텐츠팀 지음 | EBS BOOKS | 값 각 15,000원

꽁꽁 숨겨져 있던 비하인드 스토리로 배우는 흥미진진 역사와 과학

한 권의 추리소설을 읽듯 스릴 넘치는 반전의 역사와 과학 수업

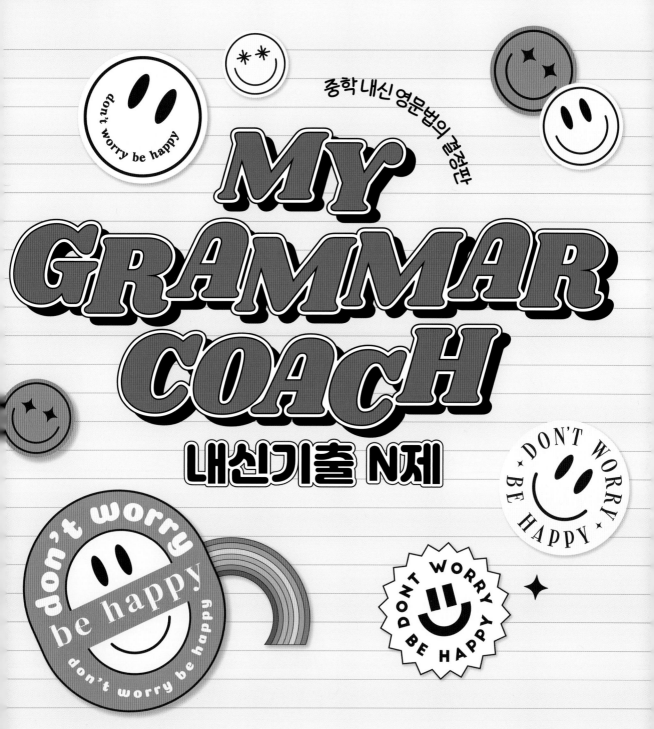

중·학·도·역·시 **EBS**

중학 내신 영문법의 끝장판

MY GRAMMAR COACH

내신기출 N제

정답과 해설

MY GRAMMAR COACH

내신기출 N제 중 **2**

정답과 해설

CHAPTER
[01 시제]

Unit 01 .... p. 15

A

01 accepted – accepted
02 accomplished – accomplished
03 agreed – agreed
04 allowed – allowed
05 believed – believed
06 borrowed – borrowed
07 carried – carried
08 closed – closed
09 collected – collected
10 copied – copied
11 covered – covered
12 cried – cried
13 decided – decided
14 depended – depended
15 delayed – delayed
16 disagreed – disagreed
17 dropped – dropped
18 enjoyed – enjoyed
19 entered – entered
20 failed – failed
21 finished – finished
22 founded – founded
23 happened – happened
24 hoped – hoped
25 hurried – hurried
26 joined – joined
27 laughed – laughed
28 learned – learned
29 lied – lied
30 looked – looked
31 married – married
32 moved – moved
33 needed – needed
34 passed – passed
35 planned – planned

36 played – played
37 preferred – preferred
38 pulled – pulled
39 pushed – pushed
40 raised – raised
41 remembered – remembered
42 saved – saved
43 showed – showed
44 smelled – smelled
45 smiled – smiled
46 sounded – sounded
47 started – started
48 stayed – stayed
49 stopped – stopped
50 studied – studied
51 thanked – thanked
52 touched – touched
53 tried – tried
54 used – used
55 visited – visited
56 waited – waited
57 walked – walked
58 wanted – wanted
59 washed – washed
60 watched – watched
61 worked – worked
62 worried – worried

B

01 was – been	13 bought – bought
02 were – been	14 caught – caught
03 became – become	15 chose – chosen
04 began – begun	16 came – come
05 bet – bet	17 cost – cost
06 bound – bound	18 cut – cut
07 bit – bitten	19 did – done
08 bled – bled	20 drew – drawn
09 blew – blown	21 drank – drunk
10 broke – broken	22 drove – driven
11 brought – brought	23 ate – eaten
12 built – built	24 fell – fallen

25 fed – fed
26 felt – felt
27 fought – fought
28 found – found
29 flew – flown
30 forgot – forgotten
31 forgave – forgiven
32 got – got[gotten]
33 gave – given
34 went – gone
35 grew – grown
36 had – had
37 heard – heard
38 hit – hit
39 held – held
40 hurt – hurt
41 kept – kept
42 knew – known
43 laid – laid
44 led – led
45 left – left
46 lent – lent
47 let – let
48 lay – lain
49 lost – lost
50 made – made
51 meant – meant
52 met – met
53 paid – paid
54 put – put
55 read – read

56 rode – ridden
57 rang – rung
58 rose – risen
59 ran – run
60 said – said
61 saw – seen
62 sold – sold
63 sent – sent
64 shot – shot
65 shut – shut
66 sang – sung
67 sat – sat
68 slept – slept
69 spoke – spoken
70 spent – spent
71 spread – spread
72 stood – stood
73 stole – stolen
74 swam – swum
75 took – taken
76 taught – taught
77 told – told
78 thought – thought
79 threw – thrown
80 understood – understood
81 woke – waken
82 wore – worn
83 won – won
84 wrote – written

내신 기출 ①

Unit 02   p. 19

A

01 is – was
02 finds – found
03 keeps – kept
04 reads – read
05 watches – watched

06 forgives – forgave
07 believes – believed
08 flies – flew
09 hits – hit
10 leaves – left

11 does – did
12 lets – let
13 hides – hid
14 feeds – fed
15 goes – went

16 has – had
17 stops – stopped
18 knows – knew
19 studies – studied
20 makes – made

B

01 wake
02 play
03 sent
04 goes
05 arrive
06 has

07 started
08 does
09 didn't
10 is
11 finishes

C

01 Are
02 am
03 did not[didn't] have
04 bought
05 love

06 will give
07 Do / want
08 Are / going to have
09 ate
10 was

내신 기출 ③

Unit 03   p. 21

A

01 arriving
02 baking
03 beginning
04 believing
05 bringing
06 calling
07 camping
08 climbing
09 closing
10 coming
11 controlling
12 dancing
13 dying
14 driving
15 flying
16 getting
17 giving
18 having

19 lying
20 listening
21 loving
22 making
23 playing
24 putting
25 reading
26 riding
27 running
28 saving
29 saying
30 shopping
31 singing
32 sitting
33 smiling
34 stopping
35 studying
36 swimming

37 taking

38 teaching

39 winning

40 writing

Unit 04   p. 22

A

01 is raining

02 are going

03 is opening

04 was snowing

05 are running

06 were swimming

07 was buying

08 are singing

09 am taking

10 was drinking

11 were playing

12 are laughing

13 is eating

14 were standing

15 was closing

16 were listening

B

01 am sweeping

02 was watering

03 were introducing

04 Are / having

05 Is / waiting

06 was / baking

07 am not talking

08 Was / cooking

09 were not[weren't]
     cleaning

Unit 05   p. 23

A

01 read

02 written

03 heard

04 come

05 seen

06 bought

07 have been

08 been

B

01 have raised

02 have / visited

03 has / decided

04 has gone

05 have / learned

06 had

07 has been

08 moved

내신기출 ①

Unit 06   p. 24

A

01 for

02 since

03 since

04 for

05 since

06 for

07 for

08 since

09 for

10 since

11 since

12 for

13 since

14 since

B

01 has liked animals

02 since last year

03 have played baseball

04 has worked

05 for ten years

06 since we were children[since childhood]

07 has driven this car

08 has known

09 has been four months

Unit 07   p. 25

A

01 has already left

02 has just bought

03 Have you finished

04 have not[haven't] received / yet

05 has just got[gotten]

06 Has she already washed

07 have not[haven't] arrived yet

08 has already come

B

01 has already begun

02 have not[haven't] decided yet

03 have just read

04 just come back

05 Have / just finished

06 has just started

07 has already told

08 has just become

09 has not[hasn't] opened yet

Unit 08   p. 26

A

01 before

02 once

03 never

04 ever

05 never

06 before

07 never

08 ever

B

01 has never lost

02 have visited / once

03 has raised / before

04 Have / ever been

05 has never ridden

06 Have / ever tried

07 you ever met

08 has tried / once

09 have never been

Unit 09   p. 27

A

01 have gone   04 Has / gone

02 have been   05 has gone

03 Have / been

B

01 have lost   06 has gone

02 has gone   07 has taken

03 has stolen   08 have been

04 has left   09 has forgotten

05 has lost

Unit 10   p. 28

A

01 not finished / yet [완료]

02 How long / studied [계속]

03 have lost [결과]

04 have been to / times [경험]

B

01 Have you ever visited

02 has not opened yet

03 We have already finished

04 has never lost a game

05 have studied / since

06 has already sent us

내신 기출   ③ → was

객관식 정답 [01~25]

01 ③	02 ③	03 ④	04 ②, ③	05 ②, ④
06 ④	07 ①	08 ①	09 ③	10 ⑤
11 ①	12 ③	13 ③	14 ②	15 ④
16 ②	17 ④	18 ⑤	19 ③	20 ④
21 ③	22 ②	23 ④	24 ③	25 ①

주관식 정답 [26~50]

26 traveled

27 bought

28 haven't played → didn't play

29 since → for 또는 his entire life → he was born

30 am → was

31 Have you ever played this game

32 It has snowed a lot since last month.

33 hasn't / finished

34 were / dancing

35 has / already / closed

36 have / had / for

37 has / gone

38 Thomas Edison invented the phonograph in 1877.

39 We will be late if we are stuck in a traffic jam!

40 (1) ○ (2) has written → wrote (3) for → since

41 (1) has lost → lost (2) ○ (3) ○

42 The train has already left the station.

43 He has known her for ten years.

44 My father has gone to Russia for his work.

45 Cathy has loved to sing since she was young.

46 I have never heard such a funny story.

47 (1) She has not[hasn't] worked as a pilot.
   (2) Has she worked as a pilot?

48 (1) They have not[haven't] arrived home (yet).
   (2) Have they already arrived home?

49 ⓔ → visit

50 has grown flowers / have eaten a waffle / has not[hasn't, has never] seen a dolphin

01 wait의 동사변화형은 wait-waited-waited이다.

02 will과 같은 미래시제 표현은 〈be going to+동사원형〉이다.

03 현재완료의 경험적 용법 〈have/has been to: ~에 가 본 적이 있다〉

04 have, smell, taste, think와 같은 상태동사, 감각동사는 진행형으로 쓰지 못한다. ① 과거진행형이다. ④ think가 행위로 쓰일 때는 진행형이 가능하다. ⑤ 과거진행형이다.

05 ①, ③, ⑤ this morning, last night, this morning이라는 특정 시점에 맞춰 과거형 took, read, woke를 썼다. ② '눕다'라는 의미의 lie의 과거형 lay를 써야 한다. lie-lay-lain으로 변화한다. *lie-lied-lied: 거짓말하다 ④ last week라는 과거 시점에 맞춰 win의 과거형 won을 써야 한다.

06 ④는 현재완료의 계속적 용법이고 나머지는 완료적 용법이다.

07 ①은 현재완료의 결과적 용법이고 나머지는 경험적 용법이다.

08 now에 맞게 현재진행형 am listening을 써야 한다.

09 현재완료의 계속적 용법(어제부터 계속 말을 하지 않고 있다)이므로 hasn't talked를 써야 한다.

10 '이 케이크를 언제 만들었니?'라는 뜻의 의문문은 과거시제를 써서 When did you bake this cake?라고 해야 한다.

11 특정 과거 시점 yesterday에 맞게 break의 과거형 broke를 써야 한다.

12 swim의 과거분사형 swum을 써야 한다.

13 문장1은 현재(now) 상태이므로 is, 문장2는 in 1989이라는 과거 시점을 나타내는 시간 부사(구)가 있으므로 과거시제 was, 문장3은 현재완료 계속적 용법이므로 has written을 써야 한다.

14 현재완료의 계속적 용법 〈have/has+과거분사+for+기간〉. ① 현재완료의 완료적 용법. 미완료 시에는 부사 yet을 쓴다. ③ 기간에는 for를 쓴다. ④ 특정 과거 시점에는 since를 쓴다. ⑤ ago는 주로 과거시제와 함께 쓰이므로 see의 과거형 saw를 써야 한다.

15 현재완료의 경험적 용법 〈have/has never been to: ~에 가 본 적이 없다〉 ① begin의 과거분사형은 begun, ② '그를 언제 만났니?'라는 뜻의 의문문은 과거시제를 써서 When did you meet him?, ③ How long은 주로 완료시제와 함께 사용하므로 현재완료의 계속적 용법의 의문문 어순 〈How long+have+주어+과거분사 ~?〉에 따라 How long have you played, ⑤ Chris는 3인칭 단수이므로 has를 써야 한다.

16 현재 시점을 나타내는 now와 어울리는 현재진행형. ① next week에 맞게 미래시제인 will leave를 써야 한다. ③ 현재진행형이 가까운 미래에 예정된 일을 표현하기도 하므로 tomorrow에 맞게 are you coming을 써야 한다. ④ 〈be going to+동사원형〉은 미래시제인데, last weekend가 나왔으므로 I went shopping을 써야 한다. 또는 last weekend를 next weekend로 바꿀 수도 있다. *go shopping: 쇼핑하러 가다 ⑤ ago는 주로 과거시제와 함께하므로 arrive의 과거형 arrived를 써야 한다.

17 〈for+기간〉으로 표현한 현재완료 계속적 용법. ① 〈have/has+과거분사+for+기간〉이기 때문에 has worked를 써야 한다. ② 〈have+과거분사+since+특정 시점〉이기 때문에 have saved를 써야 한다. ③ last year는 과거시제와 주로 쓰는 시간의 부사(구)로서 travel의 과거형 traveled를 써야 한다. ⑤ in 2001처럼 구체적 시간을 나타내는 부사(구)는 과거시제와 주로 쓰이므로 invent의 과거형 invented를 쓴다.

18 특정 과거 시점인 last year에 맞게 since를 써야 한다.

19 문장2의 현재완료의 부정문은 〈have/has+not+과거분사〉이므로 has not eaten, 문장3의 현재완료 계속적 용법의 의문문은 〈How long+have/has+주어+과거분사 ~?〉이므로 How long has it rained?로 써야 한다.

20 문장4는 시간의 부사(구) last night에 맞게 study의 과거형 studied를 써야 한다.

21 문장2의 ago는 주로 특정 과거 시점을 나타내므로 send의 과거형 sent, 문장4의 특정 시점 yesterday에는 buy의 과거형 bought를 써야 한다.

22 ⓑ 특정 과거 시점 last week에 맞게 visit의 과거형 visited, ⓒ 특정 과거 시점 in 2019에 맞게 win의 과거형 won을 써야 한다.

23 in 2018이라는 구체적 과거 시점은 과거시제와 주로 쓰므로 give의 과거형 gave를 쓴다.

24 '여행의 마지막 날'이라는 특정 과거 시점이므로 과거시제 의문문 What did you do ~?로 써야 한다.

25 (A) 과거 시점 When I saw와 어울리는 과거진행형 was walking, (B) 현재완료의 계속적 용법으로서 for days(며칠 동안) 찾고 있으므로 have looked, (C) 현재완료의 완료적 용법의 미완료로 haven't found를 써야 한다. *look for: ~을 찾다

26 현재완료의 경험적 용법으로 travel의 과거분사형인 traveled를 써야 한다.

27 현재완료시제 의문문이므로 buy의 과거분사형 bought를 써야 한다.

28 when 부사절이 과거를 의미하므로 과거시제로 쓴다.

29 his entire life(그의 평생)이라는 의미이므로 〈have/has+과거분사+for+기간〉의 형태로 for를 써야 한다. since를 쓰려면 since he was born이 되어야 한다.

30 when 부사절이 과거를 의미하므로 과거진행형을 써야 한다.

31 현재완료 경험적 용법의 의문문은 〈Have+you+ever+과거분사 ~?〉로 쓴다.

32 현재완료의 계속적 용법이다.

33 현재완료의 완료적 용법에서 미완료 어순 〈have/has not+과거분사+yet〉으로 쓴다.

34 과거진행시제로 과거 특정 시점의 일을 물었으므로 과거진행형을 써야 한다.

35 현재완료의 완료적 용법은 〈have/has+already+과거분사〉로 쓴다.

36 현재완료의 계속적 용법은 〈have+과거분사+for+기간〉으로 쓴다.

37 현재완료의 결과적 용법으로, '~에 가 버려서 없다'는 have/has gone to로 쓴다.

38 in 1877이라는 구체적 과거 시점은 과거시제와 함께 쓰므로 invent의 과거형 invented를 쓴다.

39 조건의 if절에서는 현재시제로 미래를 나타내므로 will be가 아니라 are로 쓴다.

40 (2) in 1813이라는 구체적 과거 시점은 주로 과거시제와 함께 쓴다. 따라서 write의 과거형 wrote로 쓴다. (3) 특정 과거 시점에는 for가 아니라 since를 쓴다.

41 (1) last month(특정 과거 시점)는 주로 과거시제와 쓰이므로 lose의 과거형 lost를 쓴다.

42 현재완료의 완료적 용법의 어순 〈have/has+already+과거분사〉로 쓴다.

43 현재완료의 계속적 용법의 어순 〈have/has+과거분사+for+기간〉으로 쓴다.

44 현재완료의 결과적 용법으로 '~에 가 버려서 없다'는 have/has gone to를 쓴다.

45 현재완료의 계속적 용법이다.

46 현재완료의 경험적 용법의 부정문은 〈have/has+not+과거분사〉 또는 〈have/has+never+과거분사〉로 쓸 수 있는데, 조건에서 never를 쓰라고 했으므로 have never heard로 쓴다.

47 현재완료의 부정문 어순 〈have/has+not+과거분사〉, 의문문 어순 〈have/has+주어+과거분사 ~?〉

48 현재완료의 완료적 용법의 부정문 〈have+not+과거분사+(yet)〉, 의문문 〈have+주어+과거분사 ~?〉

49 조건의 if절에서는 현재시제로 미래를 나타내므로 visit을 쓴다.

50 현재완료의 경험적 용법이다.

05 should ask

06 should not[shouldn't] eat

Unit 06 p. 41

A

01 wouldn't like to

02 had better

03 would like to

04 would / like to

05 would like to

06 had better not

07 would like to

08 had better not

B

01 had better listen

02 would you like to travel

03 had better not make

04 had better go

05 would like to have

06 Would you like to sit

Unit 07 p. 42

A

01 used to

02 used to

03 used to / would

04 used to

05 used to

06 used to

07 used to

08 used to / would

B

01 used to

02 would[used to]

03 used to

04 used to

05 would[used to]

06 used to

중간고사 · 기말고사 실전문제 pp. 43~48

객관식 정답 [01~25]

01 ③	**02** ②	**03** ②	**04** ①	**05** ④
06 ③	**07** ①	**08** ④	**09** ③	**10** ③
11 ⑤	**12** ③	**13** ③	**14** ⑤	**15** ②
16 ⑤	**17** ④	**18** ③	**19** ④	**20** ④
21 ③	**22** ①	**23** ③	**24** ②	**25** ④

주관식 정답 [26~50]

26 could

27 had / better / take

28 doesn't / have / to

29 Could you pass me the salt, please? 또는 Could you please pass me the salt?

30 How much do I have to pay?

31 ⓑ

32 ⓐ

33 ⓒ

34 Would you like some more water?

35 I would like to order a cheeseburger.

36 mays went → may go

37 would → used to

38 will can → will be able to

39 being → be

40 (1) ○ (2) using → use (3) ○

41 (1) musts → must (2) being → be (3) have to → has to

42 He could watch the movie yesterday.

43 I will have to move to another place next year.

44 Must Eric fill in the form for immigration?

45 He had better not bring an umbrella.

46 Are you going to visit Vietnam this summer?

47 I would like to travel all around the world.

48 Should we call an ambulance?

49 couldn't / could / couldn't

50 ⓒ → cannot[can't]

해설

01 '~하는 게 낫다'는 의미의 〈had better+동사원형〉을 써야 한다.

02 '~할 수 있다(능력)'는 의미의 can의 과거부정형 couldn't를 써야 한다.

03 문장1은 '~하면 안 된다'는 금지의 must not, 문장2는 '~임에 틀림없다'는 강한 추측의 must를 써야 한다.

04 문장1에서 Can은 허가의 의미, 문장2에서 can은 부정의 강한 추측의 의미, 문장3에서 can은 요청의 의미이다.

05 want to와 바꿔 쓸 수 있는 말은 〈would like to+동사원형〉이다.

06 '~하면 안 된다'는 금지의 may not은 can't와 의미가 같다.

07 '~할 필요가 없다'는 의미의 don't have to를 써야 한다.

08 '~일지도 모른다'는 의미의 약한 추측인 may를 써야 한다. must는 강한 추측을 나타낸다.

09 'Can I ~?(해도 되나요?)'로 물으면 답은 'Yes, you can ~' 혹은 'No, you can't ~'로 한다.

10 '~하지 않는 것이 더 낫다'는 〈had better not+동사원형〉을 쓴다.

11 used to는 과거에 반복하던 행동을 지금은 더 이상 하지 않을 때 쓰므로 I don't play it any longer.로 쓴다.

12 ③은 '~임이 틀림없다'는 강한 추측을 나타낸다. 나머지는 '~해야 한다'는 의무를 나타낸다.

13 '~하는 게 낫다'의 had better 뒤에는 동사원형을 써야 한다. ① yesterday라는 과거시점에 맞게 can의 과거부정형 couldn't, ② 조동사 must 뒤에는 동사원형 leave, ④ 과거를 나타내는 부사절에 맞게 can의 과거형 could, ⑤ 3인칭 단수주어와 현재시제를 나타내는 now에 맞게 has to로 써야 한다.

14 '~해야 한다'는 의미의 조동사 should 뒤에는 동사원형을 쓴다. ① 조동사 must 뒤에는 동사원형 take, ② 조동사 can뒤에는 동사원형 fly, ③ 조동사 can의 과거형 could 뒤에는 동사원형 run, ④ 조동사끼리는 연달아 나올 수 없으므로 will be able to로 써야 한다.

15 ②에서 would는 문맥상 '피자를 먹곤 했다'는 의미이므로 would eat으로 써야 하는데 〈would like to+동사원형〉은 '~하기를 원하다'의 의미이므로 like to를 삭제해야 한다.

16 '시험에 통과하고 싶으면 열심히 공부해야 한다'는 문장이므로 의무나 조언을 나타내는 had better, should, must, have to를 써야 한다.

17 과거의 습관적인 행위를 나타낼 때는 would와 used to를 모두 쓸 수 있지만, 상태(be)를 나타낼 때는 used to만 쓸 수 있다.

18 (A)는 요청하는 의미의 can, (B)는 '~하기를 원하다'는

의미의 would like to, (C)는 '~해야 한다'는 의미의 have to이다.

19 '~해야 한다'는 의무의 have to를 3인칭 단수주어에 맞춰 has to로 썼다. ⓐ '~해야 한다'는 의무의 must, ⓑ '~할 필요 없다'의 don't have to, ⓒ '~임에 틀림없다'는 강한 확신의 must, ⓔ yesterday에 맞춰 '~해야 한다'는 의무의 have to를 과거형 had to로 써야 한다.

20 문장1에서 과거의 상태를 나타낼 때는 used to를 쓴다.

21 문장3은 〈had better+동사원형〉이므로 arrive를 써야 한다. 문장4는 can만 쓰거나 〈be able to+동사원형〉이므로 can을 빼고 is able to를 써야 한다.

22 어법상 어색한 문장이 없다.

23 문장1은 〈used to+동사원형〉이므로 live로 써야 한다. 문장4는 〈had better+동사원형〉이므로 형용사 careful 앞에 be를 써야 한다.

24 Sarah는 과거에도 현재에도 매일 목욕을 하므로 현재시제(습관)로 쓸 수 있다. ① 과거에만 탔으므로 would[used to] ride, ③ 과거에도 현재에도 하지 않는다. ④ 현재만 하는 행위이므로 feeds her dog, ⑤ 과거에는 하지 않았으므로 didn't feed her dog로 써야 한다.

25 '~하지 말아야 한다'의 should not을 바르게 쓴 문장이다. ① Jake가 해야 할 일이다. ② Hannah가 해야 할 일이다. ③ Jake가 하지 말아야 할 일은 play computer games too much이다. ⑤ play computer games는 하지 말아야 할 일이다.

26 can의 과거형을 써야 한다.

27 〈had better+동사원형〉으로 써야 하므로 동사원형 take를 써야 한다.

28 '~할 필요가 없다'이므로 don't have to를 3인칭 단수주어에 맞게 써야 한다.

29 정중한 요구에는 Could를 사용한다.

30 have to 의문문은 〈(의문사+)Do+주어+have to+동사원형 ~?〉으로 만든다.

31 '~하면 안 된다'는 금지를 나타내는 can't이다.

32 '~할 수 있다'는 can의 능력·가능의 의미이다.

33 '~해 줄 수 있니?'는 can의 요청의 의미이다.

34 want와 바꿔 쓸 수 있는 〈would like+명사〉로 써야 한다.

35 want to와 바꿔 쓸 수 있는 〈would like to+동사원형〉으로 써야 한다.

36 조동사는 주어의 인칭에 상관없이 원형으로 쓴다. 조동사 may 뒤에는 동사원형 go를 쓴다.

37 과거의 상태를 나타낼 때는 would를 쓰지 못하고 used to만 쓸 수 있다.

38 조동사를 연달아 쓸 수 없으므로 can과 바꿔 쓸 수 있는 be able to를 써야 한다.

39 조동사 should 뒤에는 동사원형을 써야 한다.

40 (2) 〈had better not+동사원형〉으로 원형 use를 쓴다.

41 (1) 조동사는 주어의 인칭과 상관없이 항상 원형으로 쓰기 때문에 must로 쓴다.

　(2) '~하곤 했다'는 의미의 used to는 〈used to+동사원형〉으로 쓰므로 be동사의 원형 be를 쓴다.

　(3) 3인칭 단수주어에 맞게 have to를 has to로 쓴다.

42 조동사 뒤에는 동사원형을 쓰므로 watched를 watch로 써야 한다.

43 조동사를 연달아 쓸 수 없으므로 must와 같은 뜻인 have to를 써야 한다.

44 조동사 의문문은 〈(의문사+)조동사+주어+동사원형 ~?〉으로 쓴다.

45 〈had better+동사원형〉의 부정문은 〈had better not+동사원형〉이다.

46 be going to 의문문은 〈(의문사+)be동사+주어+going to+동사원형 ~?〉으로 쓴다.

47 want to는 〈would like to+동사원형〉으로 바꿔 쓸 수 있다.

48 조동사 의문문은 〈(의문사)+조동사+주어+동사원형 ~?〉의 어순으로 쓴다.

49 '~할 수 없다'의 과거형은 couldn't로, '~할 수 있다'의 과거형은 could로 써야 한다.

50 '~할 수 없다'는 불가능을 나타내는 cannot[can't]으로 쓴다.

CHAPTER 03 수동태

Unit 01 p. 50

A

01 invited
02 typed
03 performed
04 spoken
05 delivered
06 recycled
07 cleaned
08 sung
09 protected
10 grown / eaten

B

01 are delivered
02 are baked by
03 are screened
04 are trained / by
05 are invented and used
06 are left

C

01 is cleaned by Ted
02 is messed up by my little brother
03 is respected (by people)
04 are copied by many women
05 is led by Dr. White
06 is done by robots
07 is made by
08 are supported by

내신기출 ④, ⑤

Unit 02 p. 52

A

01 was invented
02 wrote
03 was built
04 planted
05 was baked
06 was stolen
07 was cooked
08 designed
09 invented
10 was written
11 built
12 were planted
13 baked
14 stole
15 cooked
16 was designed

B

01 Over 500 works were composed by Mozart
02 The Eiffel Tower was built by
03 The opera was performed (by them)

04 Our trip was canceled (by us)

05 *The Mona Lisa* was painted

06 His speech was broadcasted (by them)

Unit 03 p. 53

A

01 will be repaired

02 will be served

03 will be built

04 will be finished

05 will be sold

06 will be introduced

07 will be planted

B

01 will be awarded

02 will be delivered

03 will be moved

04 will be solved by

05 will be dried

06 will be sent

내신기출 ④

Unit 04 p. 54

A

01 will be saved (by us)

02 was raised by

03 The elevator will be repaired by

04 This artwork was painted by

05 is spoken (by people)

06 will be provided (by them)

07 was installed by him

08 will be kept (by me)

B

01 was made by

02 are saved

03 was established

04 will not[won't] be collected

05 was written by

06 will be announced

Unit 05 p. 55

A

01 with

02 of

03 to

04 at

05 with

06 from

07 in

08 of

09 with

10 with

B

01 am interested in

02 is made from

03 will be excited about

04 is made of

05 were pleased with

06 will be surprised at

내신기출 ③

Unit 06 p. 56

A

01 should be protected

02 must be kept

03 could be delayed

04 may be finished

05 can be solved

06 must be returned

07 can be prepared

08 should be carried

B

01 Right decisions should be made (by us)

02 This fish can be eaten (by us)

03 Wild animals might be found (by us)

04 The speed limit must be observed by drivers

05 This mirror should be wiped softly (by you)

06 The island can be seen from far away (by us)

Unit 07 p. 57

A

01 The train was not[wasn't] delayed.

02 Will the book be printed in Korea?

03 Rooms are not[aren't] cleaned every day.

04 Is it delivered in the morning?

05 The letter was not[wasn't] written by me.

06 Was the ring found on the bed?

07 You will not[won't] be surprised at the news.

08 Are they invited to the party?

B

01 cannot be moved

02 was not[wasn't] painted by

03 will / be served

04 cannot be done

05 was not[wasn't] satisfied with

06 Is / spoken

Unit 08 p. 58

A

01 to

02 of

03 to

04 to

05 for

06 for

07 to

08 to

09 to

10 of

11 to

B

01 was shown to me (by her)

02 was sent to me (by someone)

03 were bought for Rosy by Mr. Jeon

04 was cooked for us by the chef

05 was made for him by his girlfriend

06 was given flowers (by them)

07 was asked my name by a stranger

C

01 was given a lot of opportunities

02 was told a warm story by

03 were written to you by

04 was bought for her by

05 were shown Picasso's great paintings

06 were asked of the singer

내신기출 was told the news / was told to me

Unit 09 · p. 60

A

01 is called Little Bunny (by people)

02 is kept clean by

03 were made happy by

04 was elected the president by

05 was taught to be kind by

06 was found alive (by them)

07 were told to exercise by

08 was asked not to run by

B

01 are asked to fasten

02 was made angry by

03 were warned not to touch

04 was told not to leave

05 were warned to stay away

06 are advised not to travel

Unit 10 · p. 61

A

01 to enter

02 to stay

03 shopping

04 to feel

05 breaking

B

01 I am made to sing along by her song

02 The thief was seen stealing the shoes (by us)

03 Some dogs were heard barking outside (by us)

04 The workers were made to move the stone (by them)

05 A man was seen driving too fast by the police

06 I was made to wear a life jacket by the instructor

내신기출 to

Unit 11 · p. 62

A

01 for

02 off

03 over

04 down

05 out

B

01 were looked down on by

02 was laughed at by

03 are taken care of by

04 were brought up

05 was put off

06 was paid for by

중간고사 · 기말고사 실전문제 · pp. 63~68

객관식 정답 [01~25]

01 ②	**02** ③	**03** ④	**04** ⑤	**05** ②
06 ①	**07** ⑤	**08** ①	**09** ④	**10** ③
11 ③	**12** ④	**13** ⑤	**14** ①	**15** ②
16 ④	**17** ①	**18** ④	**19** ⑤	**20** ②
21 ③	**22** ①	**23** ⑤	**24** ③	**25** ②

주관식 정답 [26~50]

26 was / turned / on

27 was / put / off

28 (A) done (B) collected

29 with

30 of

31 about

32 from

33 of

34 Many fish are caught by the fisherman.

35 My father was taken care of by the nurse for one week.

36 I was taken to the library by my aunt.

37 The enemy was attacked by the soldiers.

38 built → was built

39 are → were

40 Was → Did

41 By who(m) was this song written? 또는 Who wrote this song?

42 Junho had the blue bird.

43 (1) wear (2) for (3) ○

44 (1) was found (2) be saved (3) in

45 (1) made this cupcake
(2) was made by Jina

46 (1) read this newspaper
(2) was read by my brother

47 must not be

48 was given to me

49 The pizza was cooked for me by the chef.

50 ⓒ → asked

해설

01 3인칭 단수주어에 맞는 올바른 수동태는 〈is/was+과거분사〉이므로 was moved로 써야 한다.

02 3인칭 단수주어에 맞는 올바른 수동태는 〈is/was+과거분사〉이므로 was made로 써야 한다.

03 (A)는 능동태이므로 steal의 과거형 stole을. (B)는 주어가 It(my wallet)이므로 수동태 〈be+과거분사〉에 따라 was stolen으로 쓴다.

04 be surprised at '~에 놀라다', be interested in '~에 흥미가 있다'

05 be known as '~으로서 알려져 있다', be known for '~으로[때문에] 알려져 있다', be known to '~에게 알려져 있다'

06 drown은 '익사하다'라는 뜻의 동사원형으로 과거분사형이 아니고 의미도 맞지 않다.

07 be worried about '~에 대해 걱정하다', be excited about '~에 흥분해 있다'

08 ①은 be covered with '~으로 덮여 있다'이고 나머지는 모두 by를 써야 한다.

09 ③은 be satisfied with '~에 만족하다'이고 나머지는 모두 of를 써야 한다.

10 능동태 과거시제이기 때문에 wear의 과거형 wore를 써야 한다.

11 수동태 과거시제 〈was/were+과거분사〉에 따라 was kept clean으로 써야 한다. ④는 '청소되었다'는 뜻이므로, '깨끗이 유지되었다'와는 의미가 다르다.

12 주어가 this roof로서 3인칭 단수이므로 수동태 의문문 어순인 〈의문사+be동사+주어+과거분사 ~?〉로 쓴다.

13 ①~④는 수동태로 쓸 수 없는 동사들이다.

14 수동태 의문문의 어순 〈(의문사)+be동사+주어+과거분사 ~?〉에 맞는 문장이다. ② 수동태 부정문은 be동사 뒤에 not을 붙이므로 was not built가 되어야 한다. ③ find의 과거분사형 found로 써야 한다. ④ 〈will+be able to+동사원형〉의 수동태 의문문이므로 be able to be given으로 써야 한다. ⑤ 수동태 부정문에서 조동사가 있는 경우. 조동사 뒤에 not을 붙이므로 could not be로 쓴다.

15 bring은 목적어가 2개인 4형식 동사로서 직접목적어가 주어인 수동태로 바꿀 경우, 간접목적어 앞에는 전치사 to가 필요하다.

16 주어가 She이고 능동태이므로 could not ride로 써야 한다.

17 사역동사 make를 수동태로 바꿀 때는 목적어를 주어로 보내고 목적격보어를 to부정사로 만들어야 하므로 to borrow로 써야 한다.

18 동사구 hand in은 '~을 제출하다'는 의미로 한 단어처럼 사용되기 때문에 수동태는 be handed in by가 되어야 한다.

19 3인칭 단수주어인데 동사가 cut인 것으로 보아 과거시제이므로 수동태에서 was cut으로 써야 한다.

20 문장1에서 make는 목적어가 2개인 4형식 동사로서 직

접목적어가 주어인 수동태로 바꿀 경우, 간접목적어 앞에는 전치사 for가 온다. 문장3에서 be동사가 빠졌으므로 is/was sent로 써야 한다. 문장4에서도 be동사가 빠졌으므로 was discovered로 써야 한다.

21 문장3은 'be covered with(~으로 덮여 있다)'이므로 by를 쓰면 안 된다. 문장4의 fit은 수동태로 쓸 수 없기 때문에 is fit이 아니라 fits로 써야 한다.

22 ⓐ send는 목적어가 2개인 4형식 동사로서 직접목적어가 주어인 수동태로 바꿀 경우, 간접목적어 앞에는 전치사 to가 필요하다. ⓑ 3인칭 단수주어에 맞게 was, 수동태이므로 was done으로 써야 한다.

23 문장1은 주어가 The tall tree이고 수동태 〈be+과거분사〉가 필요하므로 was cut으로 써야 한다. 문장2는 주어가 소설(Gulliver's Travels)이므로 3인칭 단수로 취급하여 was로 써야 한다. 문장3은 People이 주어일 경우 능동태이므로 speak로, Chinese가 주어일 경우 수동태이므로 is spoken을 써야 한다. 문장4는 break의 과거분사형 broken으로 써야 한다.

24 문장1은 paint의 과거분사형 painted로 써야 한다. 문장3은 5형식 문장을 수동태로 바꿀 때는 목적어를 주어로 보내고 명사, 형용사, to부정사 같은 목적격보어는 수동태 동사 뒤에 그대로 오므로 be를 삭제하고 happy만 써야 한다.

25 '~에 흥미가 있다'는 의미의 be interested in으로 써야 한다.

26 동사구 turn on은 한 단어처럼 사용되기 때문에 모두 써야 한다.

27 동사구 put off는 한 단어처럼 사용되기 때문에 모두 써야 한다.

28 do의 과거분사형, collect의 과거분사형을 써야 한다.

29 be pleased with '~에 기뻐하다'

30 재료의 성질이 변하지 않는 물리적 변화에는 be made of를 쓴다.

31 be worried about '~에 대해 걱정하다'

32 재료의 성질이 변하는 화학적 변화에는 be made from을 쓴다.

33 be tired of '~에 싫증이 나다'

34 fish는 단수, 복수형이 같은 단어로 Many fish에 맞춰 복수동사 are caught로 써야 한다.

35 동사구 take care of는 한 단어처럼 사용되기 때문에 함

께 쓰고 by를 생략하면 안 된다.

36 3형식 문장의 수동태 어순은 목적어를 주어로 두고 〈주어+be+과거분사+by+행위자〉로 쓴다. *take A to B: A를 B로 데려가다

37 3형식 문장의 수동태 어순은 목적어를 주어로 두고 〈주어+be+과거분사+by+행위자〉로 쓴다.

38 가게가 지어진 것이므로 수동태 〈be+과거분사〉로 쓴다.

39 태어난 것은 과거의 일이므로 are의 과거형 were로 써야 한다.

40 appear는 수동태로 쓸 수 없는 동사로 조동사 Do/Does/Did를 사용해서 의문문을 만든다.

41 Who(m)는 수동태에서 노래를 작사한 행위자를 말하므로 by를 생략하면 안 된다. 또는 능동태 Who wrote this song?으로도 쓸 수 있다.

42 have는 수동태로 쓸 수 없다.

43 (1) 주어가 안경을 쓰는 주체인 '나'이므로 능동태이고, 조동사 의문문 〈조동사+주어+동사원형 ~?〉으로 쓴다.
(2) '~으로[때문에] 알려져 있다'는 의미는 be known for를 써야 한다.

44 (1) 금은 셀 수 없는 명사이므로 단수동사 was, 발견된 것이므로 수동태 was found로 써야 한다.
(2) 조동사가 있는 수동태의 어순은 〈조동사+be+과거분사〉이다. 조동사 should 뒤에는 동사원형이 오므로 be동사의 원형 be와 save의 과거분사형 saved를 쓴다.
(3) 만들어진 장소를 표현할 때는 made in을 쓴다.

45 (1)은 행위의 주체가 주어이므로 능동태, (2)는 사물이 주어이므로 수동태로 써야 한다.

46 (1)은 행위의 주체가 주어이므로 능동태, (2)는 사물이 주어이므로 수동태로 써야 한다.

47 〈조동사+not+be+과거분사〉로 써야 한다.

48 give는 목적어가 2개인 4형식 동사로서 직접목적어가 주어인 수동태로 바꿀 경우, 간접목적어 앞에 전치사 to를 쓴다.

49 cook은 목적어가 2개인 4형식 동사로서 직접목적어가 주어인 수동태로 바꿀 경우, 간접목적어 앞에는 전치사 for가 온다. 또한 cook은 간접목적어가 주어인 수동태로 쓸 수 없다.

50 요청한 주체는 화자인 나(I)이므로 수동태가 아닌 능동태로 써야 한다.

CHAPTER 04 to부정사

Unit 06

p. 75

A

01 to waste
02 to do
03 understand me
04 to talk
05 to stop
06 to use
07 to think

B

01 something important to tell you
02 pretty dress to wear
03 season to enjoy skiing
04 something cold to drink
05 bad habit to get rid of
06 someone nice to talk with

Unit 07

p. 76

A

01 to pass
02 to buy
03 to send
04 to learn
05 to stay
06 to arrive
07 to win
08 to ask

B

01 to see the sunrise
02 so as not to fall
03 to get back home
04 in order not to be late
05 to buy the ticket
06 in order to take a walk

Unit 08

p. 77

A

01 b. 배우기에
02 c. 그런 말을 하다니
03 d. (결국) 어머니처럼 되다
04 b. 혼자 여행하기에
05 d. (결국) 실패했다
06 b. 읽기에
07 a. 이렇게 말하게 되어
08 d. (결국) 소방관이 되었다
09 b. 파티에서 입기에
10 a. 너와 친구가 되어
11 b. 아침에 먹기에
12 a. 선물을 받게 되어
13 b. 만족시키기에
14 b. 돌보기에
15 b. 마시기에

B

01 We were happy to win the contest

02 He was glad to meet his teacher again
03 I am disappointed not to have the opportunity
04 I was pleased to be invited to the party
05 They were really excited to go to the amusement park
06 Everyone was surprised to hear the sudden noise

C

01 to become a great scientist
02 woke up to hear
03 to catch such a large fish
04 to be late for school
05 to fail the exam
06 to travel by herself

내신 기출 ②

Unit 09

p. 79

A

01 of
02 for
03 of
04 for
05 of
06 of
07 of
08 for

B

01 kind of you to explain
02 easy for Koreans to study
03 honest of you to tell
04 dangerous for children to swim
05 generous of him to forgive
06 wise of you to seek advice

Unit 10

p. 80

A

01 too late / to call
02 too young to watch
03 so dark that I could not[couldn't] read
04 too hot for her to eat
05 too short to be
06 so big that you cannot[can't] wear
07 so cold that we cannot[can't] swim

B

01 too far for me to walk

02 so sad that I could not[couldn't] stop

03 too spicy for little children to eat

04 too slow to win

05 so long that we cannot[can't] memorize

06 too sleepy to concentrate

Unit 11 .... p. 81

A

01 so strong that I can lift

02 is brave enough to fight back

03 so rich that he can buy

04 healthy enough to go out

05 fast enough to catch

06 so hard that they could pass

B

01 early enough to catch

02 honest enough for everyone to believe

03 ripe enough for us to eat

04 old enough to take

05 warm enough for us to go

06 well enough to be

내신기출 to

중간고사 · 기말고사 실전문제   pp. 82~88

객관식 정답 [01~25]

01 ④	02 ③	03 ②	04 ③	05 ⑤
06 ③	07 ⑤	08 ①	09 ②	10 ①
11 ⑤	12 ③	13 ④	14 ③	15 ①
16 ②	17 ⑤	18 ⑤	19 ②	20 ④
21 ③	22 ③	23 ①	24 ②	25 ④

주관식 정답 [26~50]

26 learning / to / cook

27 Let's plan when to meet at the park.

28 She decided not to go to the mountain this summer.

29 ⓑ

30 ⓓ

31 ⓐ

32 I told my sister to pass me the ball.

33 I ask him to lend me a pen to write with.

34 He goes on a diet in order to lose weight.

35 for

36 to

37 too

38 of

39 to

40 strong enough to lift heavy stones.

41 It costs a lot of money to study psychology.

42 where

43 when

44 how

45 what

46 (1) so as to not → so as not to
    (2) enough → too (3) what → how

47 (1) ○ (2) ○ (3) of → for

48 The house was too big to clean by myself.

49 I don't know what to say to him.

50 ⓓ → (to) exercise

해설

01 '어떻게 ~하는지, ~하는 법'은 〈how+to부정사〉로 써야 한다.

02 to부정사의 부정은 to 앞에 not을 쓴다.

03 〈형용사/부사+enough+to부정사〉는 '~하기에 충분히 …한'이라는 의미이다.

04 가주어 It이다. ① 날씨에 쓰이는 비인칭주어 It, ② 시간에 쓰이는 비인칭주어 It, ④, ⑤는 지시대명사이다.

05 to부정사의 행위의 주체를 밝히고자 할 때는 to부정사 앞에 〈for+인칭대명사의 목적격〉을 쓰는데, ①~④는 사람의 성격이나 성품을 나타내므로 〈of+인칭대명사의 목적격〉으로 의미상 주어를 나타낸다.

06 ③은 목적을 나타내는 부사적 용법이다. 나머지는 형용사적 용법이다.

07 ⑤는 목적을 나타내는 부사적 용법이다. 나머지는 명사적

용법이다.

08 주어진 문장과 ①은 감정의 원인을 나타내는 to부정사의 부사적 용법이다. ②는 결과를 나타내는 부사적 용법, ③은 형용사를 수식하는 부사적 용법, ④는 목적을 나타내는 부사적 용법, ⑤는 형용사를 수식하는 부사적 용법이다.

09 주어진 문장은 부사적 용법이다. ② 가주어 It을 사용한 명사적 용법이다. 나머지는 부사적 용법이다.

10 주어진 문장은 ask의 목적격보어로 명사적 용법이다. ① 부사적 용법이다.

11 〈의문사+주어+should+동사원형〉은 〈의문사+to부정사〉로 바꿔 쓸 수 있다.

12 space를 꾸미는 to부정사의 형용사적 용법이다. space가 to부정사의 전치사의 목적어이므로 전치사 on을 생략하지 않고 반드시 써야 한다. enough는 명사 앞, 형용사나 부사 뒤에 온다.

13 '너무 ∼해서 …하지 못하다'의 의미로 〈too+형용사/부사+to부정사〉의 어순으로 쓴다. 부정의 의미이지만 not을 쓰지 않도록 주의한다.

14 전체 문장은 It is not good for you not to get up early.이고, ©자리에는 to부정사를 부정하는 not이 to앞에 와야 하므로 not을 써야 한다.

15 decide의 목적어는 to부정사로 쓰며, to부정사의 부정은 to 앞에 not을 쓴다. ② refuse의 목적어는 to부정사를 쓴다. ③ 조동사의 부정은 조동사 뒤에 not을 쓴다. ④ so as to의 부정은 to 앞에 not을 쓴다. ⑤ fat은 형용사로 to 뒤에 be동사의 원형인 be를 쓴다.

16 want의 목적어는 to부정사로 쓴다. ① and로 이어진 동사 play는 hope의 목적어로 to부정사로 써야 한다. ③ to부정사의 명사적 용법(주어)이므로 To watch나 Watching으로 쓴다. ④ tell은 to부정사를 목적격보어로 쓰므로 to clean으로 쓴다. ⑤ refuse의 목적어는 to부정사이므로 to go로 쓴다.

17 places를 꾸며줄 형용사적 용법의 to부정사가 필요하므로 to play로 써야 한다.

18 -thing/-one으로 끝나는 대명사가 형용사와 to부정사의 수식을 동시에 받을 때는 〈-thing/-one+형용사+to부정사〉로 쓰므로 something warm to wear로 쓴다.

19 '불가능한'이라는 의미의 형용사 impossible은 사람의

성격이나 성품이 아니므로 의미상 주어에 for를 쓴다.

20 ⓐ want의 목적격보어는 to부정사이므로 to talk를 써야 한다. ⓑ be known to는 '∼에게 알려져 있다'는 뜻인데 여기서 to는 부정사와 상관없는 전치사로서 뒤에 알려진 대상이 바로 나와야 하므로 be는 삭제해야 한다. ⓒ promise의 목적어는 to부정사이므로 to get up으로 써야 한다.

21 ⓑ order는 to부정사를 목적격보어로 쓰므로 to go가 필요하다. ⓒ ready를 꾸미는 to부정사 to eat이 필요하다.

22 ⓐ, ⓓ 부사적 용법(목적), ⓑ, ⓒ 명사적 용법, ⓔ 형용사적 용법

23 '그가 너무 피곤해서 밤을 새지 못했다'는 의미이므로 〈too+형용사/부사+to부정사〉를 써야 한다. be tired of ∼ing는 '∼에 싫증이 나다'는 뜻이다.

24 (A)는 '∼하는 법, 어떻게 ∼하는지'의 how to, (B)는 ask의 목적격보어 to부정사. (C)는 '무엇을 ∼할지'의 what to를 써야 한다.

25 ⓐ 명사적 용법(목적어), ⓑ 형용사적 용법(앞의 명사 many opportunities 수식), ⓒ 부사적 용법(목적), ⓓ 형용사적 용법(앞의 명사 some documents 수식), ⓔ 명사적 용법(목적어)

26 '∼하는 중이다'의 의미를 담은 현재진행형이 필요하므로 learning을 쓰고, learn은 to부정사를 목적어로 취하므로 to cook을 쓴다.

27 plan은 to부정사를 목적어로 취하는 동사이고, '언제 ∼할지'는 when to로 쓴다.

28 decide는 to부정사를 목적어로 취하는 동사이고 to부정사의 부정은 to 앞에 not을 붙인다.

29 to부정사의 부사적 용법 중 결과(∼해서 결국 …하다)이다.

30 to부정사의 부사적 용법 중 판단(∼하다니 …한)이다.

31 to부정사의 부사적 용법 중 감정의 원인(∼하게 되어 …한)이다.

32 to부정사는 주어에 상관없이 〈to+동사원형〉으로 써야 한다.

33 to부정사가 수식하는 명사가 to부정사구의 전치사의 목적어일 때는 전치사를 반드시 같이 써야 하므로 write 다음에 with를 생략하면 안 된다.

34 '∼하기 위해서'는 〈in order to+동사원형〉으로 쓴다.

35 가주어 It의 진주어 to부정사(to check ~)의 의미상의 주어는 〈for+목적격〉으로 쓴다.

36 '~하기 위해서'라는 to부정사의 부사적 용법 중 목적의 의미이다.

37 '너무 꽉 닫혀 있어서 열 수 없다'라는 의미이므로 tightly 앞에 too를 쓴다.

38 형용사가 사람의 성격이나 성품을 나타낼 때는 의미상의 주어를 〈of+목적격〉의 형태로 써야 한다. 여기서 mean 은 '비열한'이라는 형용사이다.

39 명사 one of the easiest ways를 수식하는 to부정사의 형용사적 용법이다. for teenagers는 to부정사의 의미상 주어이다.

40 〈so+형용사+that+주어+can[could]〉는 〈형용사/부사+enough+to부정사〉로 바꾸어 쓸 수 있다.

41 주어가 길어지면 가주어 It을 주어 자리에 두고 진짜 주어는 뒤로 보낸다.

42 어디로 가야 할지를 물으므로 where to(어디에서 ~할지)를 쓴다.

43 시간으로 답하므로 when to(언제 ~할지)를 쓴다.

44 '어떻게 ~할지, ~하는 법'을 물을 때는 how to를 쓴다.

45 '무엇을 ~할지'는 what to를 쓴다.

46 (1) so as to의 부정은 to 앞에 not을 붙여야 한다.
(2) '너무 ~해서 …하지 못하다'의 의미이므로 too를 써야 한다.
(3) '어떻게 ~할지, ~하는 법'을 물을 때는 〈how+to부정사〉를 써야 한다.

47 (3) to부정사의 의미상 주어를 밝힐 때는 to부정사 앞에 〈for+인칭대명사의 목적격〉을 쓰는데, 사람의 성격이나 성품을 나타낼 때는 〈of+목적격〉으로 쓴다. 여기서 meaningful은 성격이나 성품이 아니므로 for를 쓴다.

48 〈so+형용사+that+주어+can't[couldn't]〉는 〈too+형용사/부사+to부정사〉로 바꿔 쓸 수 있다.

49 '무엇을 ~할지'의 의미로 what to를 써야 한다.

50 exercise는 tell의 목적격보어 to부정사 to study와 and로 연결되므로 to exercise로 써야 한다. 또는 앞에 나온 to study의 to에 이어진다고 보고 exercise만 쓸 수도 있다.

CHAPTER

[05] 동명사와 분사

Unit 01   p. 90

A

01 going
02 Listening
03 becoming
04 Taking
05 teaching
06 Drinking
07 Eating

B

01 Learning foreign languages
02 going to a movie
03 drawing pictures of her dog
04 Keeping a friendship
05 designing cars and motorbikes
06 Winning first place

Unit 02   p. 91

A

01 ⓒ
02 ⓐ
03 ⓒ
04 ⓐ
05 ⓑ

B

01 mind eating
02 enjoy doing
03 cannot[can't] imagine working
04 can finish writing
05 will not[won't] give up doing
06 should avoid wearing

내신 기출 ②

Unit 03   p. 92

A

01 playing
02 to leave
03 to come
04 going
05 saying
06 to go / going
07 seeing
08 to rain / raining
09 to meet
10 eating

B

01 chose to stay

02 started to get[getting] dark

03 kept taking a walk

04 agreed to delay

05 mind turning off

06 enjoys watching

내신기출 ①

Unit 04　　　　　　　　　　　p. 93

A

01 먹기 위해 멈췄다

02 사야 한다는 것을 기억하다

03 알리게 되어 유감이다

04 먹어야 한다는 것을 잊지 않다

05 듣지 않았던 것을 후회하다

06 방문했던 것을 기억하다

B

01 going
02 having
03 making
04 to bring
05 behaving
06 to call
07 to take
08 using

Unit 05　　　　　　　　　　　p. 94

A

01 O
02 promise to do
03 enjoy traveling
04 O
05 imagine having

B

01 started crying[to cry]
02 stop to think
03 want to study hard
04 remember learning
05 need to help
06 avoid becoming

내신기출 ③

Unit 06　　　　　　　　　　　p. 95

A

01 could not[couldn't] help falling

02 went camping

03 What about searching

04 is worth being praised

05 is no use crying

06 On arriving at

B

01 is used to getting up

02 is / busy doing

03 spend much time playing

04 has trouble making

05 look forward to meeting

06 feels like staying

C

01 are responsible for taking care of

02 Thank you for giving

03 is good at composing

04 prevented us from arriving

05 dream of traveling

06 are interested in doing

07 were excited about going

내신기출 ② She apologized for not keeping her promise.

Unit 07　　　　　　　　　　　p. 97

A

01 sitting
02 standing
03 made
04 used
05 locked
06 broken
07 named
08 leaving

B

01 running
02 left
03 repaired
04 written
05 invited
06 shaking

Unit 08　　　　　　　　　　　p. 98

A

01 walking dictionary
02 crying baby
03 songs made
04 book written
05 fallen tree
06 girl singing
07 rotten egg
08 trembling voice

B

01 the boy leaning against a tree

02 toys displayed on the shelf

03 apples picked this morning

04 The president elected yesterday

05 A woman introducing him

06 A woman waiting at the gate

Unit 09
p. 99

A

01 cut

02 exhausted

03 broken

04 boring

05 broken

06 called

07 interesting

08 dancing

B

01 became shocked

02 saw / swimming[swim]

03 found / opened

04 had / washed

05 got / painted

06 found / left

Unit 10
p. 100

A

01 boring

02 disappointed

03 embarrassing

04 satisfied

05 confusing

06 moving

07 fascinating

08 tired

09 interesting

10 embarrassing [puzzling]

11 satisfying

12 amazed

13 disappointing

14 excited

15 amazing[surprising]

16 exciting

17 depressed

18 surprising

19 puzzled

20 relaxed

B

01 surprising

02 satisfying

03 moved

04 shocked

05 embarrassing

06 depressed

C

01 fascinating / were fascinated by

02 were satisfied with / satisfying

03 was pleased with / pleasing

04 were frightened by / frightening

내신기출 ③

Unit 11
p. 102

A

01 동명사

02 동명사

03 동명사

04 현재분사

05 현재분사

06 동명사

07 동명사

08 현재분사

B

01 동명사 / 내 취미는 줄넘기다.

02 동명사 / 아프리카의 많은 사람에게 깨끗한 식수가 필요하다.

03 동명사 / 나는 드레스를 디자인하는 일에 관심이 있다.

04 현재분사 / 그 작은 소녀는 짖는 개 때문에 겁을 먹었다.

05 동명사 / 그녀의 목표는 올림픽에서 금메달을 따는 것이다.

06 동명사 / 너는 대기실에서 네 차례를 기다려야 한다.

▌중간고사 · 기말고사 실전문제
pp. 103~108

객관식 정답 [01~25]

01 ②	**02** ④	**03** ③	**04** ⑤	**05** ①
06 ③	**07** ⑤	**08** ③	**09** ⑤	**10** ②
11 ④	**12** ②	**13** ④	**14** ④	**15** ⑤
16 ③	**17** ②	**18** ①	**19** ③	**20** ②
21 ⑤	**22** ③	**23** ②	**24** ③	**25** ④

주관식 정답 [26~50]

26 written

27 couldn't / help

28 I will have my hair cut this weekend.

29 My grandmother liked growing flowers in the garden.

30 It is no use apologizing for your mistake.

31 interested → interesting

32 to turn → turning

33 turning → to turn

34 do → doing

35 give → giving

36 painting

37 baked

38 built

39 made

40 I'm not used to using a knife and fork together.

41 It is a sword used in the battle with France.

42 The horror movie made me frightened.

43 (1) ○ (2) to skip → skipping (3) ○

44 (1) ○ (2) doing → to do (3) help → helps

45 ⓑ

46 ⓒ

47 ⓐ

48 I saw her dancing the Tango yesterday.

49 They gave up climbing the mountain because of the weather.

50 ⓐ → buying

해설

01 '~할 것을 기억하다'는 〈remember+to부정사〉로 쓴다.

02 수식하는 대상인 his bicycle이 도난당한 것이므로 수동의 의미인 stolen을 쓴다.

03 수식하는 대상(experience)이 감정을 유발하거나 감정을 느끼게 만드는 주체이므로 현재분사 exciting(신나게 하는)으로 쓴다.

04 plan은 to부정사만 목적어로 취한다.

05 keep은 동명사만을 목적어로 취하는 동사이므로 shopping, 전치사 without의 목적어로는 (동)명사가 필요하므로 knocking으로 써야 한다.

06 '~하려고 노력하다'는 〈try+to부정사〉로 써야 한다.

07 '~하는 데 어려움이 있다'는 동명사 관용표현 〈have trouble -ing〉와 '~없이'라는 의미의 전치사 without이 필요하다.

08 '~할 수밖에 없다'는 의미의 동명사 관용표현 〈cannot help -ing〉는 〈cannot help but+동사원형〉으로 바꿔 쓸 수 있다.

09 〈forget+동명사〉는 '(과거에) ~했던 것을 잊다'는 의미이다. '(앞으로) ~할 것을 잊다'는 〈forget+to부정사〉이다.

10 주어진 문장과 ②는 진행의 의미를 나타내는 현재분사이다. ① 동명사 관용표현 〈go -ing(~하러 가다)〉, ③ 동명사 관용표현 〈spend+시간/돈+-ing(시간/돈을 ~하는 데 쓰다)〉, ④ 동명사 관용표현 〈on[upon] -ing(~하자마자)〉, ⑤ 주어로 쓰인 동명사이다.

11 ④는 sister를 뒤에서 수식하는 현재분사이다. 나머지는 용도의 의미로 쓰인 동명사이다.

12 ②는 진행의 의미로 쓰인 현재분사이다. 나머지는 동명사이다.

13 〈stop+to부정사〉는 '~하기 위해 멈추다'이고, 〈stop+동명사〉는 '~하던 것을 멈추다'는 의미이다. 나머지는 부정사와 동명사 모두 목적어로 취하는 동사이다.

14 '~하기를 기대하다'는 의미의 look forward to에서 to는 전치사이므로 동명사를 목적어로 취한다.

15 ⓐ 명사를 뒤에서 수식하는 현재분사, ⓑ 전치사 without의 목적어인 동명사, ⓒ 수식하는 news가 감정을 유발하는 주체이므로 현재분사, ⓓ 동사 hate의 목적어로 쓰인 동명사, ⓔ 동명사 관용표현 〈How[What] about -ing ~?(~하는 게 어때?)〉이다.

16 동명사가 주어일 때는 3인칭 단수로 취급한다. ① 동명사의 부정은 동명사 앞에 not을 붙이므로 Not being, ② 동명사가 주어일 때는 3인칭 단수로 취급해야 하므로 is, ④ 동명사의 부정은 동명사 앞에 not을 붙이므로 not eating, ⑤ 현재분사가 보어로 쓰인 의문문이므로 be동사의 3인칭 단수형인 Is로 시작해야 한다.

17 '시험 삼아 ~해 보다'는 〈try+동명사〉이다. ① '~한 것을 기억하다'는 〈remember+동명사〉, ③ '~할 것을 잊다'는 〈forget+to부정사〉, ④ '~한 것을 후회하다'는 〈regret+동명사〉, ⑤ '~하기 위해 멈추다'는 〈stop+to부정사〉로 쓴다.

18 수식을 받는 chicken이 튀겨지는 수동의 의미이므로 과거분사 fried로 써야 한다.

19 '~하고 싶다'는 의미의 〈would like to+동사원형〉이므로 to drink로 써야 한다.

20 avoid는 동명사를 목적어로 취하는 동사이므로 sleeping을 써야 한다.

21 수식하는 대상인 festival이 감정을 유발하거나 감정을 느끼게 만드는 주체이므로 현재분사 amazing(놀라운)을 써야 한다.

22 ⓑ keep은 동명사를 목적어로 취하는 동사이며, ⓓ 분사가 서술하는 대상이 감정을 느끼는 객체인 I이므로 과거분사 satisfied(만족한)가 되어야 한다.

23 ⓓ mind는 동명사를 목적어로 취하는 동사이다.

24 (A) 수식하는 대상인 music이 감정을 유발하거나 감정을 느끼게 만드는 주체이므로 touch의 현재분사 touching(감동적인)을 써야 한다. (B) 수식하는 대상인 playing(연주)이 감정을 유발하거나 감정을 느끼게 만드는 주체이므로 fascinate의 현재분사 fascinating(매력적인)으로 써야 한다. (C) 수식하는 대상인 woman을 뒤에서 형용사처럼 수식하는 현재분사로서 standing을 써야 한다.

25 ⓐ 동사 want의 목적어로 쓰인 to부정사로서 명사. ⓑ 동명사 관용표현 〈feel like -ing(~하고 싶다)〉로서 전치사 like의 목적어인 명사. ⓒ 동사 need의 목적어로 쓰인 to부정사로서 명사. ⓓ 진행의 의미를 갖는 현재분사로서 형용사. ⓔ 동사 forget의 목적어로 쓰인 to부정사로서 명사이다.

26 수식하는 대상이 novel이므로 수동의 의미인 과거분사를 써야 한다.

27 동명사 관용표현 〈cannot help -ing(~할 수밖에 없다)〉의 과거형이므로 couldn't help를 써야 한다.

28 명사 hair를 뒤에서 수식하는 분사로 수동의 의미인 과거분사 cut을 써야 한다.

29 like는 동명사와 to부정사를 모두 목적어로 취한다.

30 '~해 봐야 소용없다'는 의미의 동명사 관용표현은 〈It is no use -ing〉이다.

31 수식하는 대상이 감정을 유발하거나 감정을 느끼게 만드는 일이므로 현재분사 interesting(흥미를 갖게 하는)으로 써야 한다.

32 mind는 동명사를 목적어로 취하는 동사이다.

33 〈forget+to부정사〉는 '~할 것을 잊다'는 의미이다. 여기서는 '집을 나갈 때 불을 끌 것을 잊었다'는 의미이므로 to turn을 써야 한다.

34 동사 finish는 동명사를 목적어로 취하는 동사로서 washing과 and로 이어진 동사 do도 동명사 doing으로 써야 한다.

35 전치사 for의 목적어로 쓰인 동명사이므로 giving으로 써야 한다.

36 The man을 뒤에서 수식하는 형용사 역할의 분사 중 그림을 그리는 주체이므로 능동을 의미하는 현재분사를 써

37 This cake를 뒤에서 수식하는 형용사 역할의 분사 중 구워진 객체이므로 수동을 의미하는 과거분사를 써야 한다.

38 this store를 뒤에서 수식하는 형용사 역할의 분사 중 지어진 객체이므로 수동을 의미하는 과거분사를 써야 한다.

39 The chair를 뒤에서 수식하는 형용사 역할의 분사 중 만들어진 객체이므로 수동을 의미하는 과거분사를 써야 한다.

40 〈be used to -ing(~에 익숙하다)〉의 부정문은 be동사 뒤에 not을 쓴다.

41 수식하는 대상이 a sword로서 사용된 객체이므로 수동의 의미인 과거분사 used로 써야 한다.

42 분사가 수식하는 대상이 감정을 느끼는 객체인 me이므로 과거분사 frightened(겁먹은)로 써야 한다.

43 (2) mind는 동명사를 목적어로 취한다.

44 (2) '~하려고 노력하다'는 의미의 〈try+to부정사〉를 써야 한다.
(3) 동명사가 주어일 때는 3인칭 단수로 취급하므로 helps로 써야 한다.

45 보어 역할을 하는 동명사이다. ⓑ 보어 역할을 하는 현재분사이다.

46 동사의 목적어 역할을 하는 동명사이다. ⓒ 동사의 목적어 역할을 하는 to부정사이다.

47 주어 역할을 하는 동명사이다. ⓐ 주어 역할을 하는 to부정사이다.

48 분사 dancing이 지각동사 see의 목적격보어로 쓰인 것으로, 목적어인 그녀가 춤을 추는 능동이므로 현재분사로 쓴다.

49 give up은 동명사를 목적어로 취하는 동사이다.

50 consider는 동명사를 목적어로 취하는 동사이다.

CHAPTER 06 대명사, 형용사, 부사

Unit 01
p. 110

A

01 it

02 ones

03 It

04 one / one

05 ones

06 it

B

01 Both

02 one

03 Both

04 All

05 it

06 ones

Unit 02
p. 111

A

01 one / another

02 the other

03 it

04 One / another / the other

B

01 one

02 it

03 ones

04 another

05 One / the other

06 One / another / the other

Unit 03
p. 112

A

01 another → the other

02 the others is → are

03 the other → the others[others]

04 is → are

B

01 hardly / know / each / other

02 another / cup / of / tea

03 Some / laptop / computers / others

04 One / the / other

05 help / one / another

내신 기출 ③

Unit 04
p. 113

A

01 some → any

02 teams → team

03 Any → Some

04 were → was

05 is → are

06 some → any

B

01 some

02 every

03 some

04 any

05 Each

내신 기출 ① → child   ② → is able to

Unit 05
p. 114

A

01 yourself [X]

02 yourself [O]

03 themselves [O]

04 myself [X]

05 herself [O]

06 yourself [X]

B

01 love yourselves

02 angry at himself

03 myself / take care of

04 likes summer itself

05 make it ourselves

Unit 06
p. 115

A

01 herself

02 Help

03 in

04 myself

05 yourself

06 themselves

B

01 beside himself

02 of itself

03 by herself

04 help yourself to

05 for himself

06 make herself at home

내신 기출 yourself

Unit 07
p. 116

A

01 something good

02 nothing worse

03 anything cold

04 main thing

05 someone special

06 something funny

07 heavy things

08 anything interesting

B

01 someone famous

02 anything serious

03 nothing important

04 easy thing

05 something interesting

06 someone beautiful

07 anyone reliable to look after

Unit 08 .... p. 117

A

01 friend → friends

02 any → some

03 were → was

04 little → few

05 much → many

06 times → time

07 question → questions

08 few → little

B

01 little water

02 many students

03 some time

04 a little[some] milk

05 a few minutes

06 any information

Unit 09 .... p. 118

A

01 beautiful

02 simple

03 strange

04 quick

05 happily

06 Fortunately

07 carefully

08 peacefully

B

01 lately (부사)

02 high (부사)

03 late (형용사)

04 highly (부사)

05 late (부사)

06 high (형용사)

C

01 Suddenly

02 Nearly

03 hard

04 hardly

05 long

06 long

[내신기출] ④

Unit 10 .... p. 120

A

01 ②

02 ②

03 ①

04 ①

05 ①

06 ①

B

01 can be usually seen

02 am always ready to run

03 often goes fishing

04 will never give up

05 hardly snowed last winter

06 sometimes does something strange

▌중간고사 · 기말고사 실전문제   pp. 121~126

객관식 정답 [01~25]

01 ②	**02** ④	**03** ①	**04** ①	**05** ⑤
06 ②	**07** ③	**08** ③	**09** ⑤	**10** ②, ④
11 ①	**12** ③	**13** ④	**14** ④	**15** ③
16 ②	**17** ①	**18** ③	**19** ②	**20** ③
21 ③	**22** ①	**23** ④	**24** ④	**25** ③

주관식 정답 [26~50]

26 She couldn't find anything special in his art.

27 There are many exciting things to experience in Korea.

28 I will never forget this moment in my life.

29 She often loses confidence when she is criticized.

30 I told him to make himself at home.

31 We should not spend too much time playing computer games.

32 Did you often watch cartoons on TV when you were young?

33 any

34 a few[some]

35 little

36 few / some

37 one

38 the others

39 Some

40 One / The other

41 another

42 myself → me[herself]

43 the others → others

44 We don't have much light to find the gold earrings.

45 Those cats are very cute! I like the white cat and the two orange ones.

46 (1) some → any　(2) ○　3) ○

47 (1) ○　(2) one → ones　(3) one → it

48 I have lots of things to do now.

49 A few years later, he came back from the journey. 또는 He came back from the journey a few years later.

50 ⓔ → herself

해설

01 복수명사와 셀 수 없는 명사를 수식하는 수량형용사 any는 부정문에 쓴다.

02 '또다른'의 의미를 가지는 another를 써야 한다.

03 '많은'이라는 뜻의 a lot of, lots of는 셀 수 없는 명사 information을 꾸미는 수량형용사 much로 바꿔 쓸 수 있다.

04 lovely는 '사랑스러운'이라는 의미의 형용사로 동사 is smiling을 수식하면서 부사 very의 수식을 받을 수 없다. 나머지는 부사이다.

05 (A) 정해지지 않은 불특정한 사람이나 물건은 부정대명사 one으로, (B) '나머지 하나'는 the other로 쓴다.

06 '약간의'라는 뜻의 부정형용사 중 (A) 부정문에는 any를 쓴다. (B) 긍정의 평서문에는 some을 쓴다.

07 pretty는 '예쁜'을 뜻하는 형용사로 명사를 수식한다. 나머지는 동사를 수식하는 부사이다.

08 '가끔'을 의미하는 빈도부사는 sometimes이다.

09 '거의 없는'을 의미하는 수량형용사 중 셀 수 없는 명사

money를 수식할 때는 little을 쓴다.

10 ②, ④ 재귀대명사의 재귀적 용법으로 문장에서 목적어 역할을 하므로 생략할 수 없다. 나머지는 강조적 용법이다.

11 seldom은 '거의 ~않다'는 의미이므로 문맥상 every day와 어울리지 않는다.

12 빈도부사 often은 be동사나 조동사 뒤에, 일반동사 앞에 써야 한다. ① 주어가 3인칭 단수이므로 eats, ② 빈도부사 never(절대 ~않다)에 이미 부정의 의미가 있으므로 can't가 아닌 can, ④ 빈도부사는 be동사나 조동사 뒤에, 일반동사 앞에 쓰므로 sometimes meet, ⑤ 빈도부사 hardly(거의 ~않다)에는 이미 부정의 의미가 있으므로 couldn't가 아닌 could로 쓴다.

13 권유할 때는 수량형용사 some을 쓴다. ① 부정문에는 any, ② 평서문(긍정)에는 some, ③ 의문문에는 any와 셀 수 있는 명사의 경우 복수형(questions)으로, ⑤ 평서문(긍정)에는 some을 쓴다.

14 every는 '모든'을 의미하는 부정형용사로 뒤에는 셀 수 있는 명사의 단수형이 온다.

15 빈도부사는 be동사나 조동사 뒤에, 일반동사 앞에 쓰므로 is always로 써야 한다.

16 things는 형용사가 앞에서 수식하므로 many interesting things가 되어야 한다.

17 양발(2개)이므로 '둘 다 모두'를 나타내는 both와 복수동사를 써야 하므로 were를 써야 한다.

18 권유를 나타낼 때는 some을 쓴다.

19 ⓑ 의문문에는 any를 쓴다.

20 ⓒ 빈도부사 hardly(거의 ~않다)에는 이미 부정의 의미가 있으므로 not 없이 could로 써야 한다. ⓓ each는 '각각(의)'을 의미하며 단수 취급하므로 was로 쓴다.

21 ⓐ 형용사 '늦은', ⓑ 부사 '빠르게', ⓒ 부사 '충분히', ⓓ 형용사 '긴'으로 부사는 형용사, 다른 부사, 문장 전체, 동사를 수식할 수 있지만, 형용사처럼 주어를 보충 설명할 수는 없다. ⓐ, ⓓ는 주어를 보충 설명하는 주격보어이다.

22 (A) 정해지지 않은 불특정한 사람이나 물건을 가리킬 때는 부정대명사 one, (B) 셀 수 없는 명사를 수식하는 수량형용사 much, (C) 셀 수 있는 명사를 수식하는 수량형용사 many를 써야 한다.

23 (A) each other는 '둘이 서로', (B) 앞에 언급한 ball을 가리키는 대명사이므로 it, (C) one another는 '셋 이상일 때 서로'를 나타낸다.

24 Jack은 봄에만 공원에 가므로 '거의 ~않다'의 의미인 seldom이 맞다. ①, ⑤ Sarah는 모든 계절에 가므로 always를 써야 한다. ② Tom은 공원에 전혀 가지 않으므로 never를 써야 한다. ③ Amy는 봄, 가을에 공원에 가므로 never는 맞지 않는다.

25 의문문에는 any를 쓴다. ⓐ 부정문이므로 any, ⓑ 앞의 to wash the dishes를 언급한 것이므로 대명사 it, ⓓ 앞의 my jeans를 가리키는 대명사이므로 ones가 아니라 them이 와야 한다. ⓔ '어딘가'의 의미로 평서문(긍정)에는 somewhere를 써야 한다.

26 anything처럼 -thing으로 끝나는 대명사를 수식할 때는 형용사가 뒤에 온다.

27 things는 형용사가 앞에서 수식해야 한다.

28 빈도부사는 be동사나 조동사 뒤에, 일반동사 앞에 쓴다.

29 빈도부사는 be동사나 조동사 뒤에, 일반동사 앞에 쓴다.

30 '편하게 지내다'는 재귀대명사 관용표현 make oneself at home으로 쓴다.

31 '~하는 데 시간/돈을 쓰다'는 의미의 〈spend+시간/돈/+-ing〉를 쓰면서 셀 수 없는 명사인 time에는 much를 써야 한다.

32 빈도부사 often은 과거시제 의문문에서 〈(의문사+)Did+주어+often+동사원형 ~?〉으로 쓴다.

33 의문문에는 any를 쓴다.

34 긍정문으로 부사 only(겨우)가 앞에 있고 뒤에 셀 수 있는 명사 people이 있으므로 '약간의, 조금의'를 뜻하는 a few나 some을 써야 한다.

35 목이 마른 상태인데 but으로 이어지므로 부정의 의미가 이어져야 한다. '거의 없는'을 뜻하는 형용사 중 셀 수 없는 명사 water를 수식하는 little을 써야 한다.

36 새로 사야 한다고 하므로 '거의 없는'을 뜻하는 형용사 중 셀 수 있는 명사 onion을 수식하는 few를 쓰고, 불특정한 다수로서 '몇몇, 약간'을 의미하는 some을 써야 한다.

37 쌍둥이 두 명 중 하나이므로 one을 쓴다.

38 '나머지 다른 것들'의 의미이므로 the others를 쓴다.

39 불특정 다수(몇몇, 일부)의 의미는 부정대명사 some을 써야 한다.

40 두 명(개) 중 하나를 칭할 때는 one, 나머지 하나를 칭할 때는 the other를 써야 한다.

41 단수의 '또 다른 하나'를 뜻하는 another를 써야 한다.

42 주어가 She여서 목적어인 myself와 재귀의 관계가 아니므로 재귀대명사가 아닌 I의 목적격인 me를 쓰거나, 재귀용법으로 주어(She) 자신을 나타내는 재귀대명사 herself를 써야 한다.

43 the others는 '나머지 사람들 (전부)'을 뜻하므로 불특정인 '다른 사람들'은 others로 써야 한다.

44 셀 수 없는 명사 light에는 much를 써야 한다.

45 불특정 다수에는 ones를 쓴다.

46 (1) 의문문에는 any를 쓴다.

47 (2) sunglasses가 복수이므로 ones를 쓴다.

(3) 앞에 언급한 a message를 특정해서 가리키는 것이기 때문에 it을 써야 한다.

48 수량형용사 lots of(=a lot of)는 '많은'을 의미한다.

49 셀 수 있는 시간의 단위인 year에는 a few를 쓴다.

50 주어인 She(Ms. Franklin)가 자기 자신을 자랑스러워하는 것이므로 재귀대명사 herself를 써야 한다.

CHAPTER 07 비교 표현

Unit 01   p. 128

A

01 as[so] well as
02 as[so] diligently as
03 is as deep as
04 as fast as
05 is not[isn't] as[so] important as

B

01 your → yours
02 highly → high
03 is → does
04 me → mine
05 없음
06 are → do
07 well → as[so] well
08 was → did

Unit 02   p. 129

A

01 as often as possible
02 as hard as we can
03 as much as possible
04 as loud as possible
05 as fast as you can
06 as young as possible

B

01 as slowly as she could
02 as quickly as possible
03 as soon as you can
04 as cool as possible
05 as early as possible
06 as politely as we could

내신기출 ⑤ → could

Unit 03   p. 130

A

01 abler – ablest
02 angrier – angriest
03 worse – worst
04 worse – worst
05 more beautiful – most beautiful

06 bigger – biggest
07 more boring – most boring
08 braver – bravest
09 brighter – brightest
10 busier – busiest
11 more careful – most careful
12 more carefully – most carefully
13 cheaper – cheapest
14 cleaner – cleanest
15 colder – coldest
16 more comfortable – most comfortable
17 more dangerous – most dangerous
18 more delicious – most delicious
19 more difficult – most difficult
20 more diligent – most diligent
21 dirtier – dirtiest
22 easier – easiest
23 more easily – most easily
24 more exciting – most exciting
25 more expensive – most expensive
26 more famous – most famous
27 fatter – fattest
28 more foolish – most foolish
29 fresher – freshest
30 friendlier – friendliest
31 better – best
32 more handsome – most handsome
33 happier – happiest
34 harder – hardest
35 healthier – healthiest
36 heavier – heaviest
37 more helpful – most helpful
38 hotter – hottest
39 worse – worst
40 more important – most important
41 more interesting – most interesting
42 lazier – laziest
43 lighter – lightest
44 less – least
45 longer – longest

46 lovelier — loveliest

47 lower — lowest

48 luckier — luckiest

49 more — most

50 more — most

51 nicer — nicest

52 noisier — noisiest

53 older — oldest

54 politer — politest

55 poorer — poorest

56 more popular — most popular

57 prettier — prettiest

58 quieter — quietest

59 richer — richest

60 ruder — rudest

61 sadder — saddest

62 safer — safest

63 more serious — most serious

64 shallower — shallowest

65 skinnier — skinniest

66 slower — slowest

67 more slowly — most slowly

68 sunnier — sunniest

69 tastier — tastiest

70 more terrible — most terrible

71 thicker — thickest

72 thinner — thinnest

73 uglier — ugliest

74 more useful — most useful

75 more valuable — most valuable

76 weaker — weakest

77 better — best

78 wider — widest

79 wiser — wisest

80 younger — youngest

Unit 04
p. 133

A

01 smart

02 shorter

03 cleaner

04 much

05 did

07 Jack can

06 expensive

B

01 even more important than

02 smell better than

03 more popular than

04 is easier than

05 sings better than

내신기출 ②

Unit 05
p. 134

A

01 twice as long

02 six times as large

03 five times more expensive

04 three times older

05 seven times better

06 twice as bright

B

01 three times as fast

02 eight times more books

03 a hundred times prettier

04 ten times as easy

05 four times as big

06 twelve times heavier

Unit 06
p. 135

A

01 hotter and hotter

02 faster and faster

03 stronger and stronger

04 More and more

05 more and more expensive

06 more and more excited

B

01 The more / the more

02 The more / the happier

03 The more / the more relaxed

04 The more / the cleaner

05 The darker / the colder

06 The later / the more difficult

Unit 07   p. 136

A

01 the best moment

02 the youngest of three sisters

03 one of the most beloved partners

04 one of the best inventions

05 the most diligent student

06 one of the busiest cities in the world

B

01 best → better

02 high → highest

03 beautiful island → most beautiful islands

04 singer → singers

05 of → in

06 man → men

07 in → of

08 song → songs

Unit 08   p. 137

A

01 understand me the best[understand me better than any other friend, understand me better than all the other friends]

02 way is shorter and easier

03 more important than any

04 thing is as difficult

05 season is more beautiful

06 than any other invention[than all the other inventions]

B

01 dress is as beautiful

02 more than all the other subjects

03 No other student swims as fast

04 more than any other dessert

05 No other song is more popular

06 more attractive than any other

07 person feels happier than I do

08 No other planet is larger than

Unit 09   p. 138

A

01 very → much[even, far, still, a lot]

02 city → cities

03 fastest → fast

04 more → so[as] 또는 as → than

05 harder → the harder

06 bright → as bright 또는 bright as → brighter than

07 teachers → teacher

B

01 as delicious as

02 much better than

03 twice as big as[twice bigger than]

04 one of the most popular movies

05 the more confident

06 No (other) country is as large

내신 기출 ①

중간고사 · 기말고사 실전문제   pp. 139~144

객관식 정답 [01~25]

01 ③	**02** ②	**03** ④	**04** ②	**05** ④
06 ①	**07** ④	**08** ⑤	**09** ④	**10** ⑤
11 ②	**12** ①	**13** ④	**14** ②	**15** ③
16 ②	**17** ④	**18** ③	**19** ④	**20** ④
21 ②	**22** ④	**23** ④	**24** ⑤	**25** ②

주관식 정답 [26~50]

26 She earns ten times more money than he does.

27 Science is one of the most difficult subjects.

28 the fastest

29 happier

30 better

31 more important

32 No / busier

33 The more / the smarter

34 even

35 less

36 than

37 very

38 as

39 (1) the most comfortable

(2) more comfortable

(3) comfortable

40 Sarah cannot[can't] ride a bike as[so] well as I can.

41 possibly → possible

42 high → higher

43 kindest → kind 또는 a very → the

44 The computer was much[even, a lot, still, far] more expensive than I expected.

45 He hopes to become more handsome than before.

46 (1) 문장 끝의 question → questions 또는 all the → any

(2) players → player 또는 the → one of the

(3) ○

47 (1) ○ (2) city → cities

(3) as → than 또는 fresher as → as fresh as

48 The bag slowly got heavier and heavier.

49 She is the best person for the job.

50 ⓓ → the smartest dogs

【해설】

01 '가벼운'을 뜻하는 light의 비교급 변화는 light-lighter-lightest이다.

02 뒤에 than이 나왔으므로 boring의 비교급 more boring으로 써야 한다.

03 뒤에 than이 나왔으므로 big의 비교급 bigger로 써야 한다.

04 문장1은 뒤에 than이 나왔으므로 비교급인 faster, 문장 2는 원급 비교 표현인 〈as+형용사/부사의 원급+as〉이므로 원급 sharp를 써야 한다.

05 문장1은 비교급 bigger가 나왔으므로 than, 문장2는 '~ 만큼 …하지 못하는'이라는 원급 비교 표현의 부정형인 〈not as[so] ~ as〉이므로 so 또는 as로 써야 한다.

06 handsome의 최상급은 the most handsome이다.

07 배수사 비교 중 〈배수사+as+원급+as〉 형태이다.

08 양을 표현하는 much의 비교급이면서 비교급을 만들 때 쓰는 more가 필요하다.

09 보기의 문장과 ④는 '훨씬 더'라는 의미로 비교급을 강조할 때 쓰는 much이다. ①, ②, ③은 수량형용사, ⑤는 '많이'라는 뜻의 부사이다.

10 보기의 문장은 '이 게임은 저 책보다 덜 지루하다'는 의미이므로 ⑤의 '저 책이 이 게임보다 더 지루하다'와 같다.

11 ②는 '망고는 다른 과일들만큼 달다'라는 의미이며, 나머지 문장은 '망고가 가장 단 과일이다'라는 최상급의 의미이다.

12 ② 〈as+형용사/부사+as possible〉 표현으로 possibly 가 아닌 possible, ③ 소유격으로 쓴 앞의 비교 대상에 호응하여 소유대명사인 hers, ④ '~만큼 …하지 못하는' 이라는 원급 비교 표현의 부정문은 〈not as[so] ~ as〉이 므로 is not as, ⑤ 형용사 slow가 아닌 동사 speak를 수식하는 부사 slowly를 써야 한다.

13 ① convenient의 비교급은 more convenient, ② 〈as+형용사/부사의 원급+as possible〉 표현이므로 than이 아닌 as, ③ '훨씬 더'라는 의미로 비교급을 강조할 때 very는 쓸 수 없다. ⑤ '점점 더 ~한[하게]'는 〈비교급+and+비교급〉으로 쓴다.

14 '~하면 할수록 더 …하다'는 〈the+비교급 ~. the+비교급 …〉으로 The more ~, the poorer …로 써야 한다. ③ '우리 팀에서'는 on our team으로 쓴다.

15 a lot은 비교급을 강조하므로 very를 써야 한다.

16 bad의 최상급은 worst이다.

17 ⓓ '가장 ~한 것[사람]들 중 하나'라는 표현은 〈one of the+최상급+복수명사〉이므로 the most ~로 써야 한다.

18 ⓐ 뒤에 than이 있으므로 well의 비교급 better를 써야 한다. ⓓ '어떤 ~도 …보다 더 ~하지 않은[않게]'이란 뜻의 비교급을 이용한 최상급 표현으로 〈No (other)+비교급+than〉을 쓰므로 as가 아니라 than을 쓰거나 〈No (other)+as+원급+as〉로 as funny as를 써야 한다.

19 ⓐ, ⓑ '가장 ~한 것들 중 하나'라는 표현은 〈one of the+최상급+복수명사〉로 쓴다. ⓒ 비교 대상 중 앞의 동사가 과거형이므로 뒤의 동사도 과거형 did로 써야 한다.

20 (A)는 비교급을 강조하는 a lot, (B)는 부사 beautifully를 수식하는 부사 very, (C)는 원급 비교 표현인 〈as+형용사/부사의 원급+as〉이므로 as를 써야 한다.

21 (A)는 B가 지난주에 교통사고를 당했다고 했으므로 '아픈'의 의미인 ill, (B)는 '지금은 상태가 나아졌니?'라는 의미이므로 well의 비교급인 better, (C)는 '매우'를 뜻하는 very를 쓰거나 '더 조심해야 한다'는 의미로 more를 써야 한다.

22 첫 번째 문장은 그녀의 딸이 아들보다 키가 크다는 것이고, 두 번째 문장은 그녀의 아들이 딸만큼 키가 작다는 것이므로 의미가 다르다.

23 Steve의 키가 Jimmy보다 크다.

24 Sheryl은 Judy보다 더 무겁다.

25 ⓐ '지호의 점수가 소라의 점수보다 높았다.'와 ⓓ '소라의 점수는 지호의 점수만큼 높지 않았다.'가 같은 뜻이다.

26 '~보다 …배 더 ~한[하게]'라는 비교를 하고 싶을 때는 〈배수사+비교급+than〉으로 쓸 수 있다.

27 〈one of the+최상급+복수명사〉를 쓴다.

28 fast의 최상급을 써야 한다.

29 happy의 비교급을 써야 한다.

30 뒤에 than이 나왔으므로 비교급 better를 써야 한다.

31 뒤에 than이 나왔으므로 비교급을 써야 한다.

32 '어떤 ~도 …보다 더 ~하지 않은[않게]'이란 뜻의 비교급을 이용한 최상급 표현으로 〈No (other)+비교급+than〉을 쓴다.

33 비교급을 이용한 〈the+비교급 ~, the+비교급 …〉 표현이다.

34 비교급을 강조할 때 even을 쓸 수 있다.

35 '~보다 덜'이라는 열등 비교는 〈less+형용사/부사의 원급+than〉으로 쓴다.

36 비교급을 썼으므로 비교 대상 앞에 than이 와야 한다.

37 부사의 원급 much를 꾸미는 부사 very가 와야 한다.

38 '~만큼 …하지 못하는'이라는 원급 비교 표현의 부정문은 〈not as[so] ~ as〉이다.

39 (1) '그의 방에서 가장 편안한'의 의미이므로 최상급, (2) than이 나왔으므로 비교급, (3) 부사 very가 꾸며 주는 형용사 원급을 써야 한다.

40 비교 표현의 부정문은 동사에 not을 붙인다. '~만큼 …하지 않다[못하다]'는 〈not as[so] ~ as〉로 쓴다.

41 〈as+형용사/부사 원급+as+possible〉 표현으로 possibly가 아닌 possible을 써야 한다.

42 뒤에 than이 나왔으므로 high의 비교급 higher로 써야 한다.

43 very는 형용사 kind를 수식하는 부사이며, 최상급과 함께 쓰지 않는다. 또는 최상급을 써서 She is the kindest person.으로도 쓸 수 있다.

44 비교급을 강조할 때 very는 쓸 수 없다.

45 뒤에 than이 나왔으므로 비교급으로 써야 한다.

46 (1) 비교급을 이용한 최상급 표현은 〈비교급+than all the other+복수명사〉 또는 〈비교급+than any other+단수명사〉로 쓴다.

(2) He를 지칭하는 주격보어이므로 단수명사 형태로 써야 한다. 혹은 one of the greatest football players로 써도 된다.

47 (2) '가장 ~한 것들 중 하나'라는 표현은 〈one of the+최상급+복수명사〉이므로 cities로 쓴다.

(3) fresh의 비교급인 fresher를 썼으므로 than을 써야 한다. 또는 as fresh as로 써도 된다.

48 '점점 더 ~한[하게]'는 〈비교급+and+비교급〉이므로 heavier and heavier로 쓴다.

49 good의 최상급은 best이다.

50 '가장 ~한 것들 중 하나'라는 표현은 〈one of the+최상급+복수명사〉이므로 dogs로 쓴다.

CHAPTER

[08] 의문사 의문문

객관식 정답 [01~25]

01 ⑤	**02** ②	**03** ⑤	**04** ③	**05** ③
06 ②	**07** ②	**08** ④	**09** ③	**10** ⑤
11 ③	**12** ④	**13** ⑤	**14** ④	**15** ②
16 ②	**17** ①	**18** ③	**19** ②	**20** ②
21 ③	**22** ④	**23** ①	**24** ⑤	**25** ③

주관식 정답 [26~50]

26 happened

27 Does / like

28 How

29 What

30 Where

31 When

32 Who

33 Who will be able to be the next winner?

34 How come you stayed up late last night?

35 What

36 Which

37 How

38 What

39 What is[What's] her dog's name?

40 When did they visit Disneyland?

41 How long has Heejin lived in Italy?

42 Why → How come 또는 you didn't → didn't you

43 do → are

44 Whom → Who

45 What did you see when you were out?

46 Which do you want to eat, pizza or fried chicken?

47 (1) ○
(2) How → How come 또는 How you don't → Why don't you
(3) What → When

48 How tall is the new building in Hanoi?

49 Which direction do you mean, North or South?

50 ⓓ → How

해설

01 '누가'라는 의미가 나와야 하므로 Who를 써야 한다.

02 '왜'라는 의미가 나와야 하는데 〈조동사(didn't)+주어〉의 어순이므로 Why를 써야 한다.

03 문장1은 시간 정보, 만나는 주체, 만나는 대상이 이미 나왔으므로 Where, 문장2는 '왜'라는 의미가 어울리므로 Why를 써야 한다.

04 문장1은 time을 수식하는 What, 문장2는 '어떻게'라는 방법을 물으므로 How를 쓴다.

05 문장1은 문맥상 '어떻게/왜/언제 제주도에 갔니?'가 가능하다. 문장2에서 날짜(시간) 정보를 물으므로 '언제'의 의미인 When을 써야 한다.

06 ②는 be동사 Were을 써야 한다. 나머지는 Did를 쓴다.

07 ②는 감탄사 What이다. 나머지는 의문사 What이다.

08 '얼마나 ~한[하게]'라고 물을 때는 〈how+형용사/부사+조동사+주어+동사원형 ~?〉의 어순으로 쓴다.

09 '도대체 왜, 어째서 ~?'라고 물을 때는 How come을 쓸 수 있으며, 〈How come+주어+동사 ~?〉의 어순으로 쓴다.

10 〈How often+조동사+주어+동사원형 ~?〉은 빈도를 묻는 질문이고, 체육관에서 운동하는 빈도를 물었으므로 ⑤가 가장 적절하다. 빈도를 물었는데 Yes 또는 No로 답할 수는 없기 때문에 ①, ④는 오답이다.

11 What do/does/did+주어+do for a living?은 '직업이 무엇입니까?'라는 의미로 ③은 어울리지 않는다.

12 방법, 수단으로 답하므로 '어떻게'를 묻는 how를 쓴다.

13 ① 선택지를 주는 질문이 아니므로 what, ② '무슨 일이 일어났던 거지?'는 What happened?, ③ 선택지를 주는 질문은 which, ④ '이 집에 있는 방들'이라는 제한된 선택 범위가 있는 질문은 which를 쓴다.

14 ① 〈How+형용사+주어+동사!〉의 어순으로 써야 한다. ② 〈Why+조동사(didn't)+주어+동사원형 ~?〉으로 써야 한다. ③ 명사가 단수일 때는 〈What+a+형용사+명사+주어+동사!〉이기 때문에 a를 붙여야 한다. ⑤ Which로 물을 때 뒤의 선택지는 or로 연결한다.

15 왜 좋아하냐고 묻는 말에 많이 좋아한다는 대답은 어색하다.

16 의문사는 3인칭 단수 취급하므로 동사도 brings로 쓴다.

17 복수형 interesting movies이므로 it is가 아니라 they

are가 되어야 한다.

18 ⓐ 둘 중 하나를 묻는 경우에는 which를 쓴다. ⓑ 명사가 단수일 때는 〈What+a+형용사+명사+주어+동사!〉로 쓰기 때문에 a huge waterfall로 쓴다.

19 What do you do?는 '직업이 무엇입니까?'라는 뜻이고 What are you doing?은 '뭐 하니?'라는 뜻이다.

20 ⓐ 킬로그램과 그램은 무게의 단위이므로 heavy의 비교급 heavier로 써야 한다.

21 ⓐ London에 비가 매일 온다는 빈도를 표현했으므로 How often으로 물어야 한다. ⓒ 사람의 키는 tall로 쓴다. long은 주로 시간, 사물의 길이 등을 표현할 때 쓴다.

22 Mr. Choi가 가르치는 과목은 영어이다.

23 (A) 뒷부분의 어순이 〈did+주어+동사원형 ~?〉이므로 Why를 써야 한다. (B) 이어지는 A의 대답이 사람이므로 '누구'를 뜻하는 Who이다. (C) 〈형용사+주어+동사!〉의 어순이 뒤따를 때는 앞에 How를 써야 한다.

24 (A) time을 수식하는 What, (B), (C) '얼마나 ~한[하게]'라고 물을 때는 〈How+형용사/부사+동사+주어?〉로 쓴다.

25 be동사가 있는 의문사 의문문은 〈의문사+be동사+주어 ~?〉의 어순으로 써야 한다.

26 last night에 맞춰 과거형으로 써야 한다.

27 일반동사 의문문은 〈Do/Does/Did+주어+동사원형 ~?〉의 어순으로 써야 한다.

28 '얼마나 ~한[하게]'라고 물을 때는 〈How+형용사/부사〉를 쓴다.

29 size를 수식하는 What을 써야 한다.

30 뒷부분에 '정문 옆'이라는 장소를 언급했으므로 '어디서'를 의미하는 Where를 써야 한다.

31 '언제'를 의미하는 When을 써야 한다.

32 '누구'를 의미하는 Who를 써야 한다.

33 '누구'를 뜻하는 의문사 Who가 주어인 의문문을 써야 한다.

34 '도대체 왜?'라고 물을 때 〈How come+주어+동사〉을 쓴다.

35 '무엇'을 의미하는 What을 써야 한다.

36 '책장의 책들'이라는 한정된 선택지를 주고 물으므로 Which를 써야 한다.

37 '얼마나 ~한[하게]'라고 물을 때는 〈How+형용사/부사+동사+주어 ~?〉이다.

38 '날씨가 어때?'는 What is the weather like?로 쓸 수 있다. like가 없을 때는 How is the weather?로 쓴다.

39 '무엇'을 의미하는 〈의문사 what+be동사+주어 ~?〉의 어순으로 써야 한다.

40 '언제'를 의미하는 〈의문사 when+조동사+주어+동사원형 ~?〉의 어순으로 써야 한다.

41 시간의 길이(for 10 years)가 있으므로 How long을 쓴다.

42 '왜'를 묻는 의문문이면서 뒤의 어순이 〈주어+동사〉이므로 How come을 쓰거나, 주어와 동사의 순서를 바꿔서 Why didn't you ~?를 쓴다.

43 출신지를 물을 때는 Where are you from?을 쓴다.

44 Whom은 목적격으로 쓰는 의문사인데, 여기서는 주어 역할이므로 Who로 써야 한다.

45 일반동사가 있는 의문사 의문문은 〈의문사+do/does/did+주어+동사원형 ~?〉의 어순으로 쓴다.

46 선택지를 주는 의문문에서는 의문사 Which를 써야 하고, or로 선택지를 연결해야 한다.

47 (2) '도대체 왜'라고 물을 때는 〈How come+주어+동사 ~?〉 또는 〈Why+조동사+주어+동사원형 ~?〉을 쓴다.
(3) '언제'를 의미하는 의문사 When을 써야 한다.

48 '얼마나 ~한[하게]'라고 물을 때는 〈How+형용사/부사+동사+주어 ~?〉로 쓴다.

49 선택지를 주는 의문문에서는 의문사 Which를 써야 하고, or로 선택지를 연결한다.

50 '학교는 어땠니?'라는 질문이므로 How를 쓴다.

CHAPTER
09 문장의 형식

Unit 01
p. 158

A

01 [O] **09** [V]
02 [V] **10** [O]
03 [S] **11** [V]
04 [C] **12** [C]
05 [V] **13** [S]
06 [C] **14** [C]
07 [O] **15** [S]
08 [S] **16** [O]

B

01 The class starts in five minutes
02 Both my parents are teachers
03 This food doesn't smell good
04 Birds are singing on a branch
05 He bought her one hundred roses

Unit 02
p. 159

A

01 He/became/a great scientist. 주어+동사+보어
02 The show/ends/in one hour. 주어+동사+수식어구
03 Water/freezes/at 0 ℃. 주어+동사+수식어구
04 Her face/turned/red. 주어+동사+보어
05 Joy/looks/happy/today. 주어+동사+보어+수식어구

B

01 The full moon rose [1]
02 They are the most famous singers [2]
03 Teddy woke up late [1]
04 The horror movie was very scary [2]
05 My older sister is a high school student [2]
06 Her little baby was crying [1]

Unit 03
p. 160

A

01 sadly → sad
02 sourly → sour

03 comfortably → comfortable
04 salt → salty
05 sound like → sound
06 looks → looks like

B

01 looked like a real
02 feel good
03 smells awesome
04 look like a princess
05 sound strange
06 tastes like milk

내신기출 ④ → nervous

Unit 04
p. 161

A

01 me mail [4]
02 her friend money [4]
03 Tony the way [4]
04 going there [3]
05 the shop [3]
06 my math homework [3]
07 the dishes [3]
08 him a present [4]

B

01 made the same mistake
02 made me a carrot cake
03 give us some water
04 told me her secret
05 asks me a lot of questions
06 bring me another drink

Unit 05
p. 162

A

01 for **05** for
02 to **06** to
03 of **07** for
04 to **08** to

B

01 Lucas, pass another player the ball right now
02 Did you make this birthday card for me

03 He taught me how to play the violin

04 The driver showed his driver's license to the police

05 Tom asked me a lot of questions

06 She reads bedtime stories to her baby

Unit 06   p. 163

A

01 her alone

02 the cat Mia

03 interesting

04 me a genius

05 happy

06 him a hero

07 clean

08 him a leader

B

01 made me confident

02 will keep you healthy

03 call James Mr. Know-It-All

04 found the game really difficult

05 call America a melting pot

06 kept me warm

Unit 07   p. 164

A

01 use → to use

02 taking → to take

03 secret it → it secret

04 being → be

05 happily → happy

06 win → to win

07 becoming → to become

08 stayed → to stay

B

01 want you to join

02 asked me to open

03 ordered the robbers to put

04 do not[don't] allow me to play

05 keep ourselves clean

06 advised me to get

Unit 08   p. 165

A

01 sad

02 scratch

03 sing

04 burn / burning

05 knock / knocking

06 to buy

07 cry / crying

08 touch

B

01 I smelled the food burning in the kitchen

02 Aiden felt someone looking at him

03 Emma heard her dog barking in a loud voice

04 We listened to a parrot speaking some words

05 Bella watched several elephants crossing the road

06 I saw Charles running at the park

Unit 09   p. 166

A

01 to talk

02 play[playing]

03 plant

04 clean

05 have

06 come

B

01 made us stay

02 had / serve

03 not let me travel

04 made Joy look

05 Let me think

내신기출 ③, ⑤

Unit 10   p. 167

A

01 to arrive

02 move / to move

03 to make

04 clean

05 feel

06 to wash

07 to take

B

01 help us (to) relax and sleep

02 let strangers come

03 got / to wear

04 helps / (to) keep

05 made me feel

06 got me to say hello

Unit 11

p. 168

A

01 to pick
02 give
03 shake[shaking]
04 (to) take
05 to win
06 to clean

B

01 had me walk
02 tells us to practice
03 call / Marine Boy
04 asked / to give
05 made his friends wait
06 helps you (to) keep / cool

C

01 saw a lot of dolphins swimming[swim]
02 helped Susie (to) finish
03 watched Levi win[winning] first place
04 helped my mom (to) arrange books
05 made Jack order
06 heard Ava[her] play[playing] the violin
07 helped a blind man (to) cross the street

D

01 call Mila Little Snow White
02 got me to call him
03 expect her to keep her promise
04 found / so interesting
05 felt someone pull[pulling]

내신 기출 ②

중간고사 · 기말고사 실전문제
pp. 170~176

객관식 정답 [01~25]

01 ②	**02** ④	**03** ③	**04** ②	**05** ⑤
06 ③	**07** ①	**08** ②	**09** ③	**10** ②
11 ①	**12** ④	**13** ①	**14** ②	**15** ③
16 ④	**17** ②	**18** ①	**19** ③	**20** ④
21 ⑤	**22** ②	**23** ④	**24** ①	**25** ⑤

주관식 정답 [26~50]

26 sing(ing)
27 cry
28 ⓔ
29 ⓔ
30 ⓓ
31 ⓒ
32 ⓔ
33 Please keep your kids quiet. 또는 Keep your kids quiet, please.
34 My grandfather always called me a hero.
35 of
36 to
37 for
38 to
39 heard Mary singing the song.
40 told me not to allow dogs to come in.
41 Did he show you his photo album?
42 Have you bought a present for your parents before?
43 me → to me 또는 that white towel me → me that white towel
44 looked → looked like
45 to arrive → arrive
46 We sang cheerfully at the concert altogether last weekend.
47 The new president made people live better than before.
48 (1) being → to be 또는 myself being → to be (2) sounds → sounds like (3) ○
49 Only you can make me happy when I am sad. 또는 When I am sad, only you can make me happy.
50 ⓒ, ⓓ

해설

01 think는 형용사나 명사를 목적격보어로 취한다.

02 ask는 to부정사가 목적격보어로 오는 5형식 동사이다.

03 감각동사의 보어로 부사 calmly는 쓸 수 없다.

04 get은 to부정사나 과거분사를 목적격보어로 쓸 수 있다. 나머지는 목적격보어로 원형부정사를 쓴다.

05 문장1은 4형식으로 〈get+간접목적어+직접목적어(간접목적어에게 직접목적어를 얻어 주다)〉, 문장2는 5형식으로 〈get+목적어+to부정사(목적어가 ~하도록 하다)〉이다.

06 문장1에서 ask는 to부정사가 목적격보어로 온다. 문장2의 사역동사 let은 목적격보어로 원형부정사가 온다.

07 문장1의 사역동사 let은 원형부정사가 목적격보어로 온다. 문장2의 지각동사 see는 원형부정사 혹은 현재분사가 목적격보어로 온다.

08 want는 to부정사를 목적격보어로 쓰는 5형식 동사로 〈주어+동사+목적어+목적격보어(to부정사)〉로 쓴다.

09 5형식 동사 make로 〈주어+make+목적어+목적격보어(명사, 형용사)〉를 쓴다. ①번은 '그 히트곡은 그녀를 유명하게 만들었다'는 의미로 문제와 조금 다르다.

10 ②는 1형식이고 나머지는 2형식이다.

11 ①은 4형식이고 나머지는 〈직접목적어+전치사+간접목적어〉인 3형식이다.

12 주어진 문장과 ④는 1형식이다. ①, ③ 3형식, ②, ⑤ 2형식이다.

13 주어진 문장과 ①은 3형식이다. ② 1형식, ③ 4형식, ④, ⑤ 5형식이다.

14 ②는 for을 써야 하고 나머지는 to를 쓴다.

15 call은 5형식 동사로 〈주어+call+목적어+목적격보어(명사, 형용사)〉로 쓴다. ① 2형식 감각동사 뒤에는 like 없이 바로 형용사가 온다. ② 4형식 수여동사 buy는 3형식으로 바꿀 때 간접목적어 앞에 for를 쓴다. ④ 지각동사 listen to의 목적격보어는 원형부정사나 현재분사를 쓴다. ⑤ 감각동사 뒤에는 형용사가 오므로 friendly로 쓴다.

16 3형식 문장이다. ① 5형식으로 〈get+목적어+to부정사(목적어가 ~하도록 하다)〉로 쓴다. ② 1형식 동사 smile을 수식하는 부사 brightly로 쓴다. ③ 주어가 The potato chips이므로 taste로 쓴다. ⑤ 5형식 make의 목적격보어는 명사 혹은 형용사(attractive)로 쓴다.

17 ①, ②, ④ 4형식 수여동사 give, write, lend를 3형식으로 바꿀 때는 간접목적어 앞에 to를 쓴다. ③ make를 3형식으로 바꿀 때는 간접목적어 앞에 for를 쓴다. ⑤ 4형식일 때는 목적어에 전치사를 쓰지 않으므로 to를 삭제해야 한다.

18 4형식 수여동사 build를 3형식으로 바꿀 때는 간접목적어 앞에 for를 쓴다.

19 5형식 사역동사 make의 목적격보어는 원형부정사이므로 find 앞의 to를 삭제해야 한다.

20 ⓓ 5형식 사역동사 make는 목적격보어로 원형부정사 smile을 쓴다.

21 ⓐ 사역동사 have는 목적격보어로 원형부정사를 쓰므로 listen으로 쓴다. ⓑ order는 목적격보어로 to부정사 즉, to finish를 쓴다. ⓒ 동사 help는 목적격보어로 to부정사나 원형부정사를 쓰고 현재분사는 쓰지 않는다. ⓓ 5형식으로 쓰인 make로서 목적격보어는 원형부정사 feel로 쓴다.

22 ⓐ, ⓒ는 1형식, ⓑ는 5형식, ⓓ, ⓔ는 3형식이다.

23 보기의 문장은 4형식으로 〈make+간접목적어+직접목적어(간접목적어에게 직접목적어를 만들어 주다)〉이다. ①, ②는 5형식 〈make+목적어+목적격보어(목적어가 ~하게 만들다)〉이며, ③, ⑤는 3형식으로 〈make+목적어(~을 만들다)〉이다.

24 (A) 2형식 감각동사의 보어는 형용사를 쓰고 문맥상 '날씬한'인 slim을 써야 한다. (B) advise는 to부정사를 목적격보어로 쓰는 5형식 동사이다. (C) 2형식 감각동사의 보어는 형용사를 쓴다.

25 ⓔ 2형식 감각동사의 보어는 형용사 free로 써야 한다.

26 5형식 지각동사의 목적격보어는 동사원형이나 현재분사로 쓴다.

27 5형식 사역동사의 목적격보어는 원형부정사로 쓴다.

28 '아침에'라는 수식어이다.

29 '배에서'라는 수식어이다.

30 5형식 사역동사 make의 목적격보어이다.

31 4형식 tell의 직접목적어이다.

32 '사실은, 솔직히 말해서'라는 뜻으로 문장을 수식하는 수식어이다.

33 keep은 형용사나 명사를 목적격보어로 가지는 5형식 동사로 〈keep+목적어+목적격보어〉로 쓴다.

34 call은 형용사나 명사를 목적격보어로 가지는 5형식 동사로 〈주어+call+목적어+목적격보어〉로 쓴다.

35 4형식 수여동사 ask는 3형식으로 바꿀 때 간접목적어 앞에 of를 쓴다.

36 4형식 수여동사 send은 3형식으로 바꿀 때 간접목적어 앞에 to를 쓴다.

37 4형식 수여동사 buy는 3형식으로 바꿀 때 간접목적어 앞에 for를 쓴다.

38 4형식 수여동사 pass는 3형식으로 바꿀 때 간접목적어 앞에 to를 쓴다.

39 지각동사 hear은 〈hear+목적어+목적격보어(원형부정사 혹은 현재분사)〉로 쓴다.

40 〈tell+목적어+목적격보어〉에서 목적격보어는 to부정사로 쓰며, to부정사의 부정은 to 앞에 not을 쓴다.

41 4형식 수여동사 show는 〈주어+동사+간접목적어+직접목적어〉의 어순으로 쓴다.

42 4형식 수여동사 buy를 3형식으로 바꿀 때는 간접목적어 앞에 for를 쓴다.

43 bring을 3형식으로 쓸 때는 간접목적어 앞에 to를 쓴다. 4형식으로 쓸 때는 간접목적어가 직접목적어 앞에 온다.

44 감각동사의 보어로 명사를 쓸 때는 명사 앞에 like를 쓴다.

45 사역동사 have는 원형부정사가 목적격보어로 온다.

46 sang을 수식하는 부사 cheerfully를 써야 한다.

47 5형식 make는 목적격보어로 원형부정사가 온다.

48 (1) 5형식 동사 want는 목적격보어로 to부정사를 쓴다. 또는 3형식 〈want+to부정사〉로도 쓸 수 있다.
　　(2) 감각동사의 보어로 명사가 올 때는 〈감각동사+like+명사〉로 쓴다.

49 5형식 동사 make를 쓴 문장으로 이때 목적격보어는 명사나 형용사를 쓴다.

50 ⓐ 2형식, ⓑ 3형식, ⓒ, ⓓ 5형식, ⓔ 4형식이다.

Unit 01　　　　　　　p. 178

A

01 and
02 or
03 and
04 or
05 but
06 but
07 and
08 but

B

01 a winner and a loser
02 Busan, Jeju, or Gangwon
03 or (you can) come with me
04 but (he) didn't cry
05 practiced hard and became
06 but I love you

Unit 02　　　　　　　p. 179

A

01 or
02 but
03 and
04 not
05 or
06 nor
07 either
08 neither

B

01 neither meet nor call
02 not only Spanish but (also) German[German as well as Spanish]
03 either a mobile phone or a camera
04 not only delicious but (also) cheap[cheap as well as delicious]
05 by both kids and adults
06 not a doctor but a vet

C

01 are → is
02 is → are
03 in → for
04 are → is
05 also → but (also)
06 watching → watch
07 or → nor
08 were → was

D

01 Neither / nor

02 either / or

03 Both[Not only] / and[but (also)]

04 not / but

05 not only / but (also)

06 both[not only] / and[but (also)]

내신기출 ②

Unit 03

p. 181

A

01 after   **05** after

02 before   **06** as

03 while   **07** until

04 when   **08** When

B

01 before you dive into the pool

02 after she finished eating

03 When I was little

04 As[When/While] I walked to school

05 while[when/as] you are driving

06 until he feels sleepy

Unit 04

p. 182

A

01 if / unless   **05** unless / if

02 if / unless   **06** unless / if

03 unless / if   **07** if / unless

04 if / unless

B

01 unless we hurry

02 if you have free time

03 if you want to go there

04 if it is too cold outside

05 if you do not[don't] arrive on time

Unit 05

p. 183

A

01 and   **02** or

03 and   **05** and

04 or

B

01 and you will be safe

02 or you may fall on the street

03 and you will feel better

04 or she will get angry at you

05 or you will catch a cold

06 and you will be the champion someday

내신기출 ②

Unit 06

p. 184

A

01 so I go to the library

02 because of air pollution

03 As Lucas is kind to everyone

04 so his face turned red

05 Since Linda is my best friend

B

01 because of the huge fire

02 because I love animals

03 because of the noise

04 because she loves skiing

05 because he was sick

내신기출 ③

Unit 07

p. 185

A

01 so that I could arrive early

02 so tired that I could not[couldn't] get up early

03 so spicy that I cannot[can't] eat it

04 so that she could get a good mark

B

01 so loud that I could not[couldn't] hear your voice

02 so that she could enter the house

03 so bitter that children cannot[can't] drink it

04 so that they can see better

05 so deep that we cannot[can't] swim in it

06 so that we could watch the sunrise

내신 기출 so

Unit 08
p. 186

A

01 Though
02 Though
03 Because
04 Though
05 Because
06 Though
07 Because
08 Though

B

01 Though[Although, Even though] it will snow a lot
02 Though[Although, Even though] Ella is beautiful
03 Though[Although, Even though] the song is very old
04 Though[Although, Even though] he is a world-famous star
05 Though[Although, Even though] Minsu is (a) Korean
06 Though[Although, Even though] we are sisters

Unit 09
p. 187

A

01 (that) no one is perfect
02 that our team won the gold medal
03 disappointing that he didn't join us
04 that you should not break the rules
05 That he won an Oscar
06 (that) you need some time to take a rest
07 That kimchi is good for your health
08 (that) he made a mistake
09 that we don't have enough time
10 unexpected that Ted gave me a present

B

01 that meat is not good for your health
02 That dolphins help the sick members
03 that we have no leader
04 that there are many homeless people
05 that he broke his promise
06 that our country will hold
07 that the Internet is one

C

01 Do you think (that) this is
02 That I have a good friend like you is
03 was sad that a lot of children lost
04 is that I should be a doctor
05 is interesting that some cats have

내신 기출 ③

Unit 10
p. 189

A

01 this → that
02 like → likes
03 after → before
04 Unless → If 또는 don't 삭제
05 or → and 또는 can → can't
06 can → could
07 because → because of

B

01 neither too hot nor too cold
02 unless you have a ticket
03 or you may catch a cold
04 It hurt so much that
05 I think (that) we need to do
06 Though[Although, Even though] the work is not[isn't] easy

중간고사 · 기말고사 실전문제
pp. 190~196

객관식 정답 [01~25]

01 ③	**02** ①	**03** ③, ④	**04** ②	**05** ④
06 ②	**07** ①	**08** ④	**09** ③	**10** ④
11 ⑤	**12** ③	**13** ⑤	**14** ②	**15** ⑤
16 ①	**17** ③	**18** ②	**19** ②	**20** ②
21 ④	**22** ③	**23** ①, ⑤	**24** ④	**25** ①, ②

주관식 정답 [26~50]

26 (Al)Though / I'm / busy
27 Neither / nor / passed
28 Unless
29 When

30 Since

31 if

32 I danced not with Jim but with Jack at the party.

33 I was so thrilled with the music that I couldn't say anything.

34 ⓑ

35 ⓒ

36 ⓐ

37 If you try to help others, you can make the world better.

38 We have to save water so that we can protect the planet.

39 because

40 because[when]

41 friend → friendly

42 goes → go

43 it → that

44 You should knock on the door before you enter.

45 She[Eunhee] took an online class after she fed her dog.

46 She[Eunhee] took a rest before she had lunch.

47 (1) ○

   (2) Though → Because[Since, As] 또는 can't → can

   (3) ○

48 This rope is thick as well as long.

49 Unless you are sick, you can go to the concert.

50 ⓐ, ⓓ

[해설]

01 두 문장이 상반되는 의미이므로 '~이지만, 하지만'을 뜻하는 but을 써야 한다.

02 '비록 ~이지만, 비록 ~일지라도'라는 양보의 표현은 접속사 though, although, even though를 써야 한다.

03 '~때문에'는 since/as/because로 쓸 수 있다.

04 and는 '그리고'라는 뜻이며 〈명령문+and〉는 '~해라, 그러면 …할 것이다'라는 의미이다.

05 문장1은 '그래서'의 의미인 so, 문장2는 '너무[매우] ~해서 …하다'를 뜻하는 〈so+형용사/부사+that ...〉이다.

06 문장1은 both A and B(A와 B 둘 다), 문장2는 either A or B(A, B 둘 중 하나)를 써야 한다.

07 문장1은 '~때문에'의 의미인 since, 문장2는 '그래서'의 의미인 so를 써야 한다.

08 'A뿐만 아니라 B도'는 not only A but (also) B 또는 B as well as A로 쓸 수 있다.

09 '~할 때'는 as/when을 써야 한다. excite는 '흥분하게 하다'라는 동사이므로, '흥분하게 된'은 excited로 쓴다.

10 ① 보어로 쓰이는 명사절 접속사 that, ②, ⑤ '저, 그'의 의미인 지시형용사 that, ③ 가주어 It의 진주어 that절, ④ 목적어로 쓰이는 명사절 접속사 that이다.

11 '~하지 않으면'은 if ~ not, 또는 unless로 쓴다.

12 ③은 '~이래로'의 의미, 나머지는 '~때문에'라는 뜻이다.

13 주어진 문장과 ⑤의 as는 절을 이끄는 접속사이다. ① 전치사 as로 뒤에 명사가 온다. as a child는 '어린 시절에, 어렸을 때'의 의미이다. ②, ③ 원급 비교에 쓰는 as이다. ④ 전치사 as로 '~으로서'의 뜻이며 뒤에 명사가 온다.

14 주어진 문장은 '~해라, 그렇지 않으면 …할 것이다'의 의미인 〈명령문+or〉이다. ① '~때문에'의 의미인 because/since/as이다. ② either A or B(A, B 둘 중 하나)를 써야 한다. ③ 목적어로 쓰이는 명사절 접속사 that이다. ④ 〈명령문+and〉는 '~해라, 그러면 …할 것이다'이다. ⑤ both A and B(A와 B 둘 다)를 써야 한다.

15 '~하기 전에'의 의미인 before를 썼다. ① 'A뿐만 아니라 B도'는 not only A but (also) B이다. ②, ③ '비록 ~이지만, 비록 ~일지라도'라는 양보의 표현은 though, although, even though를 쓴다. ④ neither A nor B(A, B 둘 다 아닌)는 동사를 B에 맞추므로 doesn't로 써야 한다.

16 '숙제를 마쳐라, 그러면 너는 유튜브를 볼 수 있다'는 의미이므로 or가 아닌 and를 써야 한다. 〈명령문+and〉는 '~해라, 그러면 …할 것이다'라는 뜻이다. or로 연결하려면 you can't ~가 되어야 한다.

17 시간을 나타내는 after절은 현재시제가 미래시제를 대신하므로 will be가 아니라 is로 써야 한다.

18 '불을 끄고 나서 나갔다'는 의미이므로 '~한 후에'를 의미하는 시간의 부사절 접속사 after를 써야 한다.

19 ⓒ both A and B(A, B 둘 다)와 while(~하는 동안)을 쓴 올바른 문장이다. ⓐ '너무[매우] ~해서 …하다'의 의미는 〈so+형용사/부사+that …〉이다. ⓑ neither A nor B(A, B 둘 다 아닌)는 동사를 B에 맞추므로 was, ⓓ '밥을 먹지 않았으면'은 어색하므로 Unless가 아니라 After나 Before 등을 써야 한다.

20 ⓑ 명사 앞에는 because of를 쓴다.

21 ⓑ 목적어로 쓰이는 명사절 접속사는 that이다. ⓒ 시간을 나타내는 after절은 현재시제가 미래시제를 대신하므로 after I finish가 되어야 한다. ⓓ '너무[매우] ~해서 …할 수 없다'는 〈too~to부정사〉 혹은 〈so+형용사/부사+that+주어+can't+동사〉로 쓸 수 있다.

22 ⓐ not only A but (also) B(A뿐만 아니라 B도), ⓑ neither A nor B(A, B 둘 다 아닌), ⓒ B as well as A(A뿐만 아니라 B도). ⓓ either A or B(A, B 둘 중 하나)이므로 호랑이와 곰을 둘 다 볼 수 있다는 ⓐ와 ⓒ가 같다.

23 ① '~때문에'는 because/as/since를 쓴다. ② 〈too~to부정사〉는 '너무~해서 …할 수 없다'이고, 〈so that ~〉은 '~하도록'이다. ③ not A but B는 'A가 아니라 B'라는 뜻이고, B as well as A는 'A뿐만 아니라 B도'라는 뜻이다. ④ '서둘러라. 그러면 너는 기차를 탈 수 있을 것이다'의 의미가 되려면 if를 써야 한다. ⑤ '~할 때'는 when/as를 쓴다.

24 (A) '또는, ~이거나'의 의미인 or, (B) '~이지만, 하지만'의 의미인 but, (C) Why로 질문했으므로 이유를 답하는 because/since/as를 써야 한다.

25 ⓐ 문맥상 '그리고'를 의미하는 and를 써야 한다. ⓑ either A or B(A, B 둘 중 하나) 또는 both A and B(A, B 둘 다)가 되어야 한다.

26 '비록 ~이지만, 비록 ~일지라도'라는 양보 표현은 접속사 though, although, even though를 쓴다.

27 neither A nor B(A, B 둘 다 아닌)를 써야 한다.

28 '~하지 않으면'의 의미인 Unless를 쓴다.

29 '~할 때'의 의미인 When을 쓴다.

30 '~때문에'의 의미인 Since를 쓴다.

31 '~하면'의 의미인 if를 쓴다.

32 'A가 아니라 B'의 의미인 not A but B를 쓴다.

33 '너무[매우] ~해서 …하지 못하다'는 〈so+형용사/부사+that+주어+can't/couldn't+동사〉로 써야 한다.

34 주어로 쓰인 명사절 접속사 that이다.

35 보어로 쓰인 명사절 접속사 that이다.

36 목적어로 쓰인 명사절 접속사 that이다.

37 〈명령문+and〉는 '~해라, 그러면 …할 것이다'의 의미이므로 '~한다면'을 뜻하는 〈If+주어+동사, 주어+동사 ~〉로 쓸 수 있다.

38 to부정사의 부사적 용법 중 '~하기 위해서'라는 목적의 의미로 〈주어+동사+so that+주어+can+동사〉와 같다.

39 '~때문에'라는 뜻의 as이므로 because와 바꿔 쓸 수 있다.

40 '~때문에' 또는 '~할 때'를 뜻하는 as이므로 because/when과 바꿔 쓸 수 있다.

41 상관접속사 not only A but (also) B(A뿐만 아니라 B도)로 연결된 A와 B는 형태가 같아야 하므로 앞의 kind처럼 성격을 나타내는 형용사 friendly로 써야 한다.

42 B as well as A(A뿐만 아니라 B도)가 주어일 때는 동사를 B에 맞춘다.

43 목적어로 쓰인 명사절 접속사는 that을 써야 한다.

44 들어오기 전에 노크를 해야 하므로, '~하기 전에'라는 의미의 before를 쓴다.

45 개에게 먹이를 준 후 온라인 수업을 들었으므로, after를 사용하여 문장을 완성한다.

46 점심을 먹기 전에 휴식을 취했으므로, before를 이용하여 문장을 완성한다.

47 (2) '내가 시간이 없기 때문에 너를 데리러 갈 수 없다'라는 뜻이 되려면 Though 대신 Because/Since/As를 쓰고, '내가 시간이 없지만 너를 데리러 갈 수 있다'라는 뜻이 되려면 can't를 can으로 바꾼다.

48 'A뿐만 아니라 B도'의 의미는 B as well as A이다.

49 '~하지 않는다면'을 뜻하는 unless를 쓸 때는 not을 쓰지 않는다.

50 '~때문에'의 의미로 쓰인 접속사들(as, since)이다. ⓑ '~할 때'를 의미하는 시간의 접속사 when, ⓒ '~한다면'의 의미인 조건의 접속사 if, ⓔ '비록 ~이지만, 비록 ~일지라도'의 의미인 양보의 접속사 although이다.

[11] 분사구문

Unit 01 p. 198

A

01 dancing
02 standing
03 surprising
04 interesting
05 writing
06 talking

B

01 disappointing performance
02 Who is this girl sitting next to
03 sounds too boring
04 take care of that crying baby
05 knocking on the door

Unit 02 p. 199

A

01 puzzled
02 raised
03 tiring
04 worried
05 thrilling
06 shocked

B

01 has become interested in
02 was folded in half
03 The present sent to me
04 was deeply moved by the movie
05 I heard someone crying
06 the roof covered with snow

내신기출 disappointed / embarrassing

Unit 03 p. 200

A

01 Looking at me
02 Having a lot to do
03 Meeting you again
04 (Being) surprised
05 Reaching the top
06 Saying hello to me
07 Relaxing
08 (Being) short

B

01 Leaving the house
02 Singing a song
03 Hoping to get a ticket
04 Arriving at the airport
05 Going straight one block
06 Having enough time

Unit 04 p. 201

A

01 Missing the train
02 Finding me
03 Taking a bath
04 Taking a walk

B

01 Spilling the hot water
02 Not keeping my promise
03 Sitting in our car
04 Playing basketball outside
05 Sitting on the bench

내신기출 ③

Unit 05 p. 202

A

01 Though I live near the sea
02 If you exercise regularly
03 If you listen to this music
04 Although she felt hungry

B

01 Though feeling so cold
02 Reading this book
03 Practicing hard every day
04 Though smiling brightly
05 Turning off all the lights

내신기출 ③

Unit 06 p. 203

A

01 Looking at the sky
02 going out
03 Calling my name
04 boarding the plane
05 Saying "cheese,"
06 cleaning the house

B

01 looking at himself in the mirror
02 Having lunch

03 jumping into the sea

04 giving a big smile

05 Surfing the Internet

06 arriving in Seoul at four

객관식 정답 [01~25]

01 ③	**02** ⑤	**03** ③	**04** ③	**05** ④
06 ①	**07** ②	**08** ④	**09** ①	**10** ②
11 ④	**12** ⑤	**13** ①	**14** ②	**15** ④
16 ④	**17** ①	**18** ②	**19** ②	**20** ②
21 ①	**22** ④	**23** ⑤	**24** ⑤	**25** ①, ⑤

주관식 정답 [26~50]

26 drawn

27 Walking

28 Touched

29 ⓐ

30 ⓓ

31 ⓑ

32 The flowers growing in the garden are blooming.

33 Not having any snacks, she became thin.

34 If you are not busy now

35 While[As, When] my father watches[is watching] the news program

36 After it was built in 1925

37 Crossed → Crossing

38 Got → Getting

39 annoying → annoyed

40 Turned → Turning

41 Walking to her office, she was talking on the phone.

42 Finding an old coin in his pocket, he was curious.

43 Decorated with flowers, the shop looked fascinating.

44 (1) painting → painted (2) ○
(3) Don't → Not

45 (1) smiles → smiling (2) sat → sitting (3) ○

46 We made some products by using recycled plastic.

47 Injured in the war, the soldier had scars.

48 (Al)though hungry, I did not eat anything.

49 While[As, When] lying on her lap, her dog felt safe and loved.

50 ⓐ Before ⓑ Before ⓒ Because ⓓ When ⓔ Because

해설

01 the woman과 꾸며 주는 분사의 관계가 능동이므로 현재분사 sitting을 써야 한다.

02 목적어와 목적격보어의 관계가 수동이므로 과거분사 written을 써야 한다.

03 '그는 부자이지만, 매우 외롭다'는 분사구문으로 '~에도 불구하고'라는 양보의 접속사 though/although/even though를 써야 한다.

04 분사구문은 〈접속사+주어+동사〉를 분사 형태로 바꾼 것으로, 능동의 의미인 현재분사 Putting on을 써야 한다.

05 '~하는 동안'을 의미하는 시간의 접속사 While을 쓴다.

06 문장1은 주어 She가 감정을 느끼는 객체이므로 과거분사 depressed, 문장2는 be filled with(~으로 가득 차 있다)를 사용한 수동태 구문이므로 과거분사 filled를 쓴다.

07 첫 번째 빈칸은 '~하는 것을 멈추다'의 의미로 〈stop+동명사〉, 두 번째 빈칸은 감정을 느끼게 하는 주체에는 현재분사를 쓰므로 '지루한'을 뜻하는 boring을 써야 한다.

08 현재시제이므로 is, 수동의 의미이므로 과거분사 called를 써야 한다.

09 '~하고 나서'의 의미인 연속상황의 분사구문이다.

10 ②는 동명사이고 나머지는 현재분사이다.

11 조건을 나타내는 분사구문으로 〈if+주어+동사〉로 쓰고, 조건의 if절에서는 현재시제가 미래시제를 대신한다.

12 분사구문은 〈접속사+주어+동사〉를 분사 형태로 바꾼 것으로, 능동의 의미인 현재분사 Falling을 써야 한다.

13 파이는 만들어진 것이므로 수동의 의미인 과거분사

made를 써야 한다. ② 진행의 의미인 현재분사 going, ③ 현재완료는 〈have+과거분사〉이므로 과거분사 shown, ④ '받았다'는 의미이므로 수동의 의미인 과거분사 given, ⑤ to 이하가 진주어로서 감정을 느끼게 하는 주체이므로 현재분사 exciting을 쓴다.

14 분사구문은 분사로 바꿔야 하며 to부정사로 바꿀 수 없다. Not studying hard가 되어야 한다.

15 분사구문에서 능동의 의미인 현재분사 Spending을 써야 한다.

16 조건을 나타내는 분사구문이므로 '좌회전한다면, ~'으로 해석한다.

17 help는 목적격보어로 원형부정사 또는 to부정사를 쓰고 현재분사는 쓸 수 없다.

18 Though가 아니라 이유의 접속사 Because가 와야 한다.

19 감정을 느끼는 객체일 때는 과거분사 Interested를 써야 한다. ① 능동의 의미인 현재분사 Entering, ③ raise는 '키우다'는 의미이므로, 수동의 의미인 Raised, ④ 감정을 느끼는 객체일 때는 과거분사 Shocked, ⑤ 능동의 의미인 현재분사 Walking을 써야 한다.

20 ⓐ having이 아니라 being이어야 하며, 문맥상 Not을 삭제해야 한다. ⓑ 진행의 현재분사 Chewing, ⓒ Not having이나 Having no로 바꿔야 한다.

21 어법상 어색한 문장이 없다.

22 ⓑ 주어가 The chocolate cookies이므로 3인칭 단수에 상응하는 taste로 써야 한다.

23 문장1은 '~한 후에'를 의미하는 접속사 After, 문장2는 분사구문의 분사 자리로서 능동의 의미인 현재분사 Meeting, 문장3은 분사구문으로 바꿀 때 be동사는 Being으로 쓴다.

24 (A) '매력적인'이라는 뜻의 분사는 fascinating, (B) tickets와 분사는 수동의 관계이므로 given, (C) consider는 동명사를 목적어로 갖는다.

25 ⓐ 우리가 집을 떠날 때, 비가 내리고 있다는 것을 알게 되었으므로 Leaving the house가 되어야 한다. ⓔ 우리가 산에 올라서 산장에 머물렀다는 연속상황이므로 stayed가 아니라 staying으로 분사구문을 만든다.

26 목적어와 목적격보어의 관계가 수동이므로 과거분사를 써야 한다.

27 분사구문은 〈접속사+주어+동사〉를 분사 형태로 바꾼 것으로, 주어인 I가 걸어가는 것이므로 능동의 의미인 현재분사를 써야 한다.

28 주어가 감정을 느끼는 객체이므로 '감동 받은'이라는 의미의 과거분사 Touched를 쓴다.

29 '~ 때문에'의 의미인 이유의 분사구문이다.

30 '~한다면'의 의미인 조건의 분사구문이다.

31 '~에도 불구하고'의 의미인 양보의 분사구문이다.

32 '자라다'는 의미의 동사 grow의 현재분사 growing이 뒤에서 수식하는 형태를 써야 한다.

33 분사구문의 부정문은 분사 앞에 not을 쓴다.

34 분사구문은 〈접속사+주어+동사〉의 부사절로 바꿀 수 있으며, 여기서는 조건의 접속사 if를 써야 한다.

35 분사구문은 〈접속사+주어+동사〉의 부사절로 바꿀 수 있으며, 여기서는 동시동작을 의미하므로 while이나 as, 또는 '~할 때'라는 의미의 when을 쓸 수 있다.

36 분사구문은 〈접속사+주어+동사〉의 부사절로 바꿀 수 있으며, 여기서는 '~한 후에'의 의미인 접속사 after를 쓴다.

37 Cindy가 팔짱을 낀 것이므로 능동의 의미인 현재분사를 써야 한다.

38 I가 지겨워하는 주체이므로 능동의 의미인 현재분사를 써야 한다.

39 me는 감정을 느끼는 객체이므로 수동의 의미를 나타내는 과거분사 annoyed를 쓴다.

40 she가 라디오를 켰으므로 능동의 의미인 현재분사 Turning을 써야 한다.

41 동시동작을 나타내는 분사구문으로 능동의 의미인 현재분사 Walking을 써야 한다.

42 이유를 나타내는 분사구문으로 능동의 의미인 현재분사 Finding을 써야 한다.

43 이유를 나타내는 분사구문으로 수동의 의미인 과거분사 Decorated를 써야 한다.

44 (1) 수동의 의미이므로 과거분사 painted를 쓴다.
(3) 분사구문의 부정문은 분사 앞에 Not을 쓴다.

45 (1) 동시동작의 분사구문으로 능동의 의미인 현재분사를 쓴다.

(2) 주어 The man을 뒤에서 수식하는 분사가 능동의 의미이므로 현재분사 sitting이 되어야 한다.

46 분사와 plastic과의 관계는 수동이므로 과거분사 recycled를 쓴다.

47 the soldier는 전쟁에서 부상을 당한 것이므로 수동의 의미인 과거분사 Injured를 쓴다.

48 분사구문은 〈접속사+주어+동사〉를 분사 형태로 바꾼 것으로 양보의 접속사 Al(though)를 쓴다. 분사구문에서 hungry 앞의 being은 생략 가능하다.

49 '~하는 동안'을 의미하는 시간의 접속사 While을 넣는다. 접속사 As나 When도 가능하다.

50 ⓐ, ⓑ '~하기 전에'를 의미하는 시간의 접속사 Before, ⓒ, ⓔ '~때문에'를 의미하는 이유의 접속사 Because, ⓓ '~할 때'를 의미하는 시간의 접속사 When이 생략되었다.

CHAPTER
[12] 관계사

Unit 01 p. 212

A
01 who[that] is kind to me
02 who[that] sings well
03 who[that] is 2 years older
04 who[that] was wearing a hat

B
01 who[that] used to be my English teacher
02 who[that] attend this university are
03 who[that] is standing next to the tree
04 the man who[that] is wearing glasses
05 who[that] writes mystery novels

내신 기출 ③

Unit 02 p. 213

A
01 has　　　　　　**04** wants
02 which　　　　　**05** that
03 raises　　　　　**06** who

B
01 which[that] was made by herself
02 something that[which] makes him special
03 someone that[who] resembles you
04 which[that] is about the importance
05 a fashion designer who[that] loves clothes
06 one problem which[that] must be solved

내신 기출 who / which

Unit 03 p. 214

A
01 who(m)[that] I saw yesterday
02 which[that] we climb often
03 which[that] many tourists visit
04 who(m)[that] I like
05 which[that] he bought for me
06 which[that] we used to sing together

B

01 who(m)[that] I like

02 which[that] I take for a cold

03 who(m)[that] I respect the most

04 who[that] wrote many best-selling books

05 which[that] Annie sent to me

Unit 04   p. 215

A

01 whom → who[that]

02 who → which[that]

03 whom → whose

04 which → that

05 who → which[that]

06 who → whose

B

01 whose eyes are blue

02 whose roof is painted red

03 whose name is Ken

04 whose hair is white and long

05 whose cover is green

06 whose advice is always helpful

Unit 05   p. 216

A

01 which[that]

02 who(m)[that]

03 whose

04 who[that]

05 whose

B

01 who[that] was selected as the MVP

02 which[that] my dad wants to buy

03 whose heart is full of thanks

04 who(m)[that] I can always trust

05 which[that] Emily used to wear

06 which[that] wags its tail

내신기출 it 삭제 / it 삭제

Unit 06   p. 217

A

01 that   **05** that

02 that   **06** who

03 which   **07** that

04 that   **08** that

B

01 everything that they need

02 the only word that she knew

03 the first love letter that I received

04 the second point that we need to discuss

05 the woman and her dog that were crossing

06 everything that makes her baby happy

Unit 07   p. 218

A

01 ⓑ   **03** ⓑ

02 ⓐ   **04** ⓐ

B

01 the money that I lent her

02 that you are too young to do it

03 everything that I have

04 that we should follow the rules

내신기출 ③

Unit 08   p. 219

A

01 who is   **05** that are

02 who   **06** which

03 who is   **07** which was

04 that   **08** that

B

01 the girl cleaning the classroom

02 all the songs composed by her

03 soup made of chicken

04 the cute dog wearing a green sweater

05 a tower built one hundred years ago

06 the necklace her parents had bought for her

Unit 09
p. 220

A

01 The one[thing] that[which] I want

02 What I ordered

03 the one[thing] that[which] we can do

04 What she wanted

05 What made me mad

06 what I need

B

01 what I am[I'm] saying

02 What makes him special

03 my dog which I have raised

04 what she did yesterday

05 what I usually do in my free time

내신 기출 ①

Unit 10
p. 221

A

01 where   **04** when

02 when   **05** where

03 where   **06** when

B

01 when the Korean War broke out

02 where a lot of rich people live

03 (the day) when we moved to a new house

04 where you can buy the ticket

05 when you should give your opinion

Unit 11
p. 222

A

01 why   **04** why

02 how   **05** how

03 how   **06** why

B

01 the way[how] you get back home

02 the way[how] she takes good pictures

03 (why) leaves turn red in fall

04 the way[how] you became good at math

05 the reason why[the reason, why] you failed the test

중간고사 · 기말고사 실전문제
pp. 223~228

객관식 정답 [01~25]

01 ⑤	**02** ④	**03** ⑤	**04** ②	**05** ③
06 ④	**07** ①	**08** ④	**09** ③	**10** ①
11 ②	**12** ⑤	**13** ②	**14** ②	**15** ⑤
16 ②	**17** ③	**18** ①	**19** ③	**20** ⑤
21 ⑤	**22** ①	**23** ②	**24** ②	**25** ④

주관식 정답 [26~50]

26 which[that] / stands

27 which[that] / is

28 ⓑ

29 ⓒ

30 ⓐ

31 ⓐ

32 What is the best thing that you bought?

33 A panda is an animal which enjoys eating bamboo.

34 My mom didn't tell me (the reason) why my sister was angry.

35 He taught his kids how his grandfather sailed the boat.

36 It is Kate who[that] is singing in the yard.

37 She is the only one that Matt has been waiting for.

38 He misses his hometown where he was born.

39 I don't remember the day when we first met.

40 who → whose

41 who → which[that]

42 for → in 또는 for which → where 또는 for which 삭제

43 ⓒ

44 ⓑ

45 ⓑ

46 A library is the place in which people read books. 또는 A library is the place where people read books.(the place나 where 중 하

나만 써도 됨)

47 Can you tell me the reason for which you lied? 또는 Can you tell me the reason why you lied?(the reason이나 why 중 하나만 써도 됨)

48 (1) which → what (2) O

49 A lot of people love how he plays the guitar.

50 ⓐ, ⓒ, ⓔ

해설

01 관계대명사절에서 주어 역할을 하므로 사람 선행사(Sam) 뒤에 주격 관계대명사 that이나 who가 온다.

02 관계대명사절에서 주어 역할을 하므로 사물 선행사(a book) 뒤에 주격 관계대명사 that이나 which가 온다.

03 관계부사 how의 선행사는 the way인데, the way와 how는 같이 쓰지 않고 둘 중 하나만 써야 한다. how는 in which로 바꿔 쓸 수 있다.

04 관계대명사 which는 선행사가 사물일 때 쓴다.

05 문장1은 접속사 that으로 시작하는 부사절이 목적어로 쓰였으며, 문장2에는 주격 관계대명사 that이 필요하다.

06 선행사(The elderly lady)는 관계대명사절에서 목적어 역할을 하므로 사람이 선행사인 목적격 관계대명사 who(m)이나 that을 쓸 수 있고, 대화한 시점이 before이므로 동사는 과거형으로 써야 한다.

07 문장1은 선행사를 포함하는 관계대명사 what(=the one[thing] that[which])이고, 문장2는 관계대명사가 관계대명사절에서 the girl's name을 의미하므로 소유격 관계대명사 whose를 써야 한다.

08 선행사(That girl)가 3인칭 단수로서 관계대명사절에서 주어여서 〈주격 관계대명사+3인칭 단수동사〉가 필요하므로 who[that] is eating으로 쓴다.

09 목적격 관계대명사는 생략할 수 있지만 선행사는 생략할 수 없다. 선행사를 포함하는 관계대명사는 what으로 쓴다.

10 ① 부사절이 목적어로 쓰인 접속사 that, ② 지시형용사 that, ③ 진주어 that, ④, ⑤ 주격 관계대명사 that이다.

11 선행사(grapes)가 사물이고 관계대명사절에서 목적어 역할이므로 that이나 which를 쓴다.

12 선행사(an umbrella)가 사물이고 관계대명사절에서 주어 역할이므로 that이나 which를 사용하고 3인칭 단수 주어에 맞춰 동사는 helps로 써야 한다.

13 ②는 the bus를 수식하는 관계부사로 쓰인 where이고, 나머지는 의문사 where이다.

14 ②는 의문사로 쓰인 who이고, 나머지는 관계대명사 who이다.

15 보기의 문장과 ⑤는 주격 관계대명사, 나머지는 목적격 관계대명사이다.

16 보기의 문장과 ②는 목적격 관계대명사 that, ① 진주어 that, ③, ④ 목적어로 쓰이는 접속사 that, ⑤ 지시형용사 that이다.

17 선행사에 서수가 있다면 관계대명사 that을 쓴다. ① the day와 같은 시간을 선행사로 갖는 관계부사 when은 〈in[at/on]+which〉로 바꿔 쓸 수 있으나 〈전치사+that〉은 쓸 수 없다. ② 관계대명사가 관계대명사절에서 friend's name을 의미하므로 소유격 관계대명사 whose를 쓴다. ④ 관계대명사절에서 주어 역할을 하므로 사람 선행사(The girl) 뒤에 주격 관계대명사 that이나 who를 쓴다. ⑤ 관계부사 how의 선행사는 the way인데, the way와 how는 둘 중 하나만 쓴다.

18 관계대명사절에서 주어 역할을 하는 사물 선행사(the story)에는 주격 관계대명사 which 혹은 that을 쓴다.

19 선행사가 장소(the city)이므로 관계부사 where이고, where은 〈in[at/on]+which〉로 바꿔 쓸 수 있으나 〈전치사+that〉은 쓸 수 없다.

20 이유를 선행사로 갖는 관계부사 why는 〈for+which〉로 바꿔 쓸 수 있으나 〈전치사+that〉은 쓸 수 없다.

21 ① 선행사가 장소(the third floor)인 경우에는 관계부사 where, ② 관계대명사절에서 주어 역할을 하는 사람 선행사(Tom)에는 주격 관계대명사 who 혹은 that, ③ 관계대명사절에서 주어 역할을 하는 사람 선행사(role model)에는 주격 관계대명사 who 혹은 that, ④ 관계대명사절에서 주어 역할을 하는 사물 선행사(his, 그의 것)에는 주격 관계대명사 which 혹은 that을 쓴다.

22 ⓐ 선행사(The only thing)가 3인칭 단수이므로 동사는 changes, ⓑ 선행사에 서수가 있으면 관계대명사 that, ⓒ 선행사(Joe)가 관계대명사절에서 주어이므로 3인칭

단수주어에 맞도록 동사는 exercises, ⓓ 선행사가 everything이므로 관계대명사 that을 쓴다.

23 ⓑ what이 아니라 the dress가 선행사인 목적격 관계대명사 that이나 which를 써야 한다.

24 (A) 선행사(the film)가 사물이고 관계대명사절에서 목적어이므로 that이나 which, (B) 선행사(dog)가 사물이고 관계대명사절에서 주어이므로 that이나 which, (C) 선행사가 시간(next Thursday)이므로 관계부사 when이나 〈in[at/on]+which〉로 써야 한다.

25 ⓓ 선행사가 The inventions로 복수이므로 which 다음에 are를 쓴다.

26 선행사가 사물(the snowman)이고 주어이므로 주격 관계대명사를 써야 한다.

27 선행사가 사물(the road)이고 관계대명사절에서 주어이므로 주격 관계대명사를 써야 한다.

28 선행사를 포함하는 관계대명사이다.

29 선행사가 시간(the month)인 관계부사 when이다.

30 '어떻게'의 의미인 의문사 how이다.

31 '어디서'의 의미인 의문사 where이다.

32 선행사가 사물(the best thing)이고 관계대명사절에서 목적어 역할을 하는 주격 관계대명사 that을 쓴 문장이다.

33 선행사가 사물(an animal)이고 관계대명사절에서 주어 역할을 하는 주격 관계대명사 which를 쓴 문장이다.

34 이유(the reason)를 선행사로 갖는 관계부사는 why이다. the reason이나 why 둘 중 하나는 생략 가능한데, 문제에서 관계부사를 사용하라고 했으므로 the reason이 생략 가능하다.

35 방법(the way)을 선행사로 갖는 관계부사는 how이며, the way와 how는 둘 중 하나만 써야 하는데 문제에서 관계부사를 사용하라고 했으므로 the way를 생략한다.

36 생략된 부분은 〈주격 관계대명사+be동사〉이므로 be동사를 꼭 같이 써야 한다.

37 목적격 관계대명사는 자주 생략되는데, 선행사에 only가 있으므로 관계대명사 that을 쓴다.

38 선행사가 장소(his hometown)이므로 관계부사 where를 쓴다.

39 선행사가 시간(the day)이므로 관계부사 when을 쓴다.

40 관계대명사가 관계대명사절에서 my brother's friend's name을 의미하므로 소유격 관계대명사를 써야 한다.

41 소설 제목이므로 선행사는 사물(novel)에 맞도록 which 혹은 that을 써야 한다.

42 장소(the place)를 선행사로 갖는 관계부사 where은 〈in[at/on]+which〉로 바꿔 쓸 수 있다. 그러므로 This city is the place where she was ~로도 쓸 수 있고 선행사 the place만 써도 된다.

43 목적어로 쓰이는 명사절 that이다.

44 목적격 관계대명사 that이다.

45 목적격 관계대명사 that이다.

46 관계부사 where은 〈in[at/on]+which〉로 바꿔 쓸 수 있는데, 문제에서처럼 〈전치사+관계부사〉로는 쓸 수 없다.

47 관계부사 why는 〈for+which〉로 바꿔 쓸 수 있다.

48 (1) 선행사가 없으므로 관계대명사 what을 쓴다.

49 방법은 관계부사 how로 표현한다.

50 ⓐ 관계대명사절에서 목적격 관계대명사는 생략 가능하다. ⓒ, ⓔ 관계부사와 선행사 둘 중 하나는 생략 가능하다. ⓑ, ⓓ 관계대명사절에서 주격 관계대명사는 be동사와 함께 생략 가능하며, 주격 관계대명사만 생략할 수는 없다.

[13 가정법]

Unit **01** .... p. 230

A

01 were / would go **04** were / would help
02 knew / would talk **05** were not / could spend
03 went / would play **06** learned / could talk

B

01 If you wanted juice
02 If I knew the way to the station
03 If I were an eagle
04 If there were not[weren't, were no] air
05 If we were not[weren't] healthy
06 If he were not[weren't] kind to everyone

C

01 If I were in America
02 we could swim
03 we will play catch
04 If you had good eyesight
05 I would not[wouldn't] regret
06 If I did not[didn't] have a good friend
07 If my parents are free

D

01 were **04** won
02 had **05** were
03 would **06** would

내신 기출 ②

Unit **02** .... p. 232

A

01 were **05** snowed
02 had **06** were
03 could travel **07** could spend
04 bought

B

01 I could speak a lot of foreign languages
02 there are not[aren't] many students in this class
03 I were good at eating spicy food

04 I cannot[can't] go skiing with you
05 I could enter Harvard University
06 I cannot[can't] help you clean the classroom

Unit **03** .... p. 233

A

01 as if I were a baby
02 as if I were flying in the sky
03 as if he were a chef
04 as if she were an American
05 as if he knew everything
06 as if we were in heaven

B

01 as if he understood me well
02 as if they did not[didn't] enjoy playing computer games
03 as if I were younger than you
04 as if there were not[weren't] a serious problem
05 as if you knew everything about life
06 as if he were a famous movie star

Unit **04** .... p. 234

A

01 had had / would have called
02 had practiced / could have won
03 had been / could have used
04 had walked / might not have fallen
05 had woken up / could have caught
06 had snowed / would have enjoyed

B

01 If we had lived
02 my mom would have baked
03 If I had spoken
04 we could have played
05 If I had been
06 we would not[wouldn't] have fallen

C

01 If I had lived / I could have seen
02 Because[As/Since] you did not[didn't] tell / I did not[didn't] congratulate

03 If the weather had been / we would have gone

04 Because[As/Since] he did not[didn't] run / he could not[couldn't] win

05 If the math exam had not[hadn't] been / I could have got[gotten]

D

01 have felt

02 had had

03 been able

04 would

05 could

내신 기출 ③

Unit 05

p. 236

A

01 had been

02 had behaved

03 had exercised

04 had read

05 had joined

06 had not[hadn't] forgotten

07 had attended

08 had opened

B

01 I did not[didn't] wake up early

02 I had not[hadn't] spilled the water

03 I did not[didn't] listen to my parents

04 you had been satisfied with our food

05 there was not[wasn't] enough time

06 I had brought my umbrella

Unit 06

p. 237

A

01 you did not[didn't] live in

02 as if you had helped me

03 he did not[didn't] become a president

04 as if she had done her best

05 Michael did not[didn't] arrive on time

06 as if she had seen a UFO

07 you had lunch

08 as if he had participated in

B

01 speaks as if he had won the game

02 talks as if he had solved all the problems

03 talks as if she had finished reading the book

04 acts as if she had cooked the food herself

05 talk as if they had not[hadn't] broken the window

06 talk as if you had taken the art class

중간고사 · 기말고사 실전문제
pp. 238~244

객관식 정답 [01~25]

01 ①	**02** ④	**03** ⑤	**04** ④	**05** ②
06 ③	**07** ①	**08** ⑤	**09** ④	**10** ③
11 ④	**12** ⑤	**13** ③	**14** ③	**15** ⑤
16 ③	**17** ⑤	**18** ③	**19** ②, ③	**20** ③
21 ①	**22** ④	**23** ③	**24** ①	**25** ④

주관식 정답 [26~50]

26 were

27 knew / would be

28 could

29 If

30 As

31 would

32 I wish I had been healthier.

33 If I knew where his house is, I would go there now.

34 If my house had been bigger, I could have raised a big dog.

35 he had not[hadn't] spent too much money, he would not[wouldn't] have become poor.

36 today[it] were Friday.

37 it had not[hadn't] rained a lot, we would not[wouldn't] have canceled the game.

38 were older, he could play with his sisters.

39 had saved enough money to buy the pants.

40 had had → had

41 tell → will tell 또는 I → I'll

42 met → had met

43 is → were

44 had → had not[hadn't] 또는 would → would not[wouldn't]

45 He talks as if he had not[hadn't] done anything wrong before.

46 If I had not left early yesterday, I could have met you.

47 (1) wasn't → were not[weren't]
(2) can → could (3) ○

48 If the weather were good, I could go fishing.

49 He acts as if he had been a detective.

50 ⓑ → I would become a writer

해설

01 현재 사실의 반대를 가정하는 If 가정법 과거로 〈If+주어+동사의 과거형, 주어+would/could/might+동사원형〉이므로 win의 과거형 won을 써야 한다.

02 '마치 ~인 것처럼'이라는 의미로 지금 실제가 아닌 일을 표현하는 as if 가정법 과거 〈주어+동사의 현재형+as if+주어+동사의 과거형〉에 따라 were을 쓴다.

03 '~한다면'의 의미인 조건의 접속사 if이므로 현재시제를 써야 한다.

04 문장1은 '~때문에'의 의미인 as, 문장2는 as if 가정법이므로 as를 써야 한다.

05 문장1은 If 가정법 과거완료, 문장2는 I wish 가정법 과거완료형으로 〈had+과거분사〉 형태로 써야 하므로 문맥상 가장 맞는 had had를 써야 한다.

06 문장1은 If 가정법 과거로, if절의 동사는 과거형 found, 문장2는 I wish 가정법 과거로 〈I wish+주어+동사의 과거형〉이므로 had를 써야 한다.

07 두 문장 모두 가정법 과거로 문장1은 과거형 knew, 문장2는 if절의 동사가 be동사이므로 were로 써야 한다.

08 If 가정법 과거완료 〈If+주어+had+과거분사, 주어+would/could/might+have+과거분사〉이므로 If절은 had seen, 주절은 would have called를 쓴다.

09 I wish 가정법 과거는 〈I wish+주어+동사의 과거형〉으로 쓰므로 문맥상 could help로 써야 한다.

10 현재 실제가 아닌 일을 표현하는 as if 가정법 과거 〈주어+동사의 현재형+as if+주어+동사의 과거형〉으로 쓴다.

11 현재 사실의 반대를 가정하는 If 가정법 과거 〈If+주어+동사

12 직설법 평서문에서 3인칭 복수주어의 be동사 과거형으로 쓰였고, 나머지는 가정법에 쓴 were이다.

13 I wish 가정법 과거로 현재 이룰 수 없거나 현재 사실과 반대되는 일에 대한 소망을 나타내며 〈I wish+주어+동사의 과거형〉의 어순으로 쓴다.

14 현재 사실의 반대를 가정하는 If 가정법 과거 〈If+주어+동사의 과거형, 주어+would/could/might+동사원형〉이다.

15 '(지금) 바쁘지 않으면 좋겠다'라는 의미로 were not so busy로 써야 한다.

16 ① If 가정법 과거로 if절의 be동사는 were로 써야 한다. ② doesn't know를 didn't know 혹은 hadn't known으로 써야 한다. ④ now라고 했으므로 현재의 상황과 반대되는 I wish 가정법 과거를 써서 were로 써야 한다. ⑤ '거기 있는 것처럼'의 의미로서 현재 사실의 반대를 가정하므로 as if절의 be동사를 were로 써야 한다.

17 현재 사실의 반대를 가정하므로 as if절의 be동사를 were로 써야 한다.

18 가정법 과거완료가 되려면 looked를 had looked로, 가정법 과거가 되려면 would have found를 would find로 써야 한다.

19 ② If 가정법 과거완료 〈If+주어+had+과거분사, 주어+would/could/might+have+과거분사〉에 따라 wouldn't have let, ③ 사역동사 let의 목적격보어는 시제에 관계없이 동사원형이므로 do the job으로 쓴다.

20 사실의 반대를 가정한 것이 아니라 단순 조건문이다. 따라서 if절로 바꿀 때 If you don't study hard, you can't get good scores.가 되어야 한다.

21 now가 있으므로 현재 사실과 반대되는 소망을 나타내는 I wish 가정법 과거에 따라 〈I wish+주어+동사의 과거형(could watch)〉을 쓴다.

22 ⓒ If 가정법 과거라면 would give로, if 가정법 과거완료라면 if I had had it으로 써야 한다.

23 ⓐ '높게, 높이'라는 뜻의 부사는 high이고 highly는 '매우'라는 의미의 부사이다. ⓓ 현재 사실의 반대를 가정하는 If 가정법 과거 〈If+주어+동사의 과거형, 주어+would/could/might+동사원형〉에 따라 could travel로 써야 한다.

24 (A) 현재 이루어질 가능성이 적은 일을 표현하는 I wish

가정법 과거 〈I wish+주어+동사의 과거형〉인데 be동사이므로 were, (B) 주절에 〈would+동사원형〉이 있는 If 가정법 과거인데 〈If+주어+동사의 과거형, 주어+would/could/might+동사원형〉의 어순으로 쓰므로 과거형 went, (C) 가정법 과거를 쓴 의문문에 대한 답이므로 would를 쓴다.

25 ⓓ 현재 사실의 반대를 나타내므로 as if 절에 가정법 과거 didn't miss를 써야 한다.

26 '마치 ~인 것처럼'이라는 의미로 현재 실제가 아닌 일을 표현하는 as if 가정법 과거 〈주어+동사의 현재형+as if+주어+동사의 과거형〉인데 be동사이므로 were를 쓴다.

27 현재 사실의 반대를 가정하는 If 가정법 과거이므로 〈If+주어+동사의 과거형, 주어+would/could/might+동사원형〉으로 써야 한다.

28 현재 사실과 반대되는 소망을 나타내는 I wish 가정법 과거이므로 could를 쓴다.

29 현재 사실의 반대를 가정하는 If 가정법 과거 〈If+주어+동사의 과거형, 주어+would/could/might+동사원형〉이다.

30 '나는 돈이 없었기 때문에 재킷을 살 수 없었다'는 직설법 문장이므로 '~때문에'라는 의미의 접속사 as를 쓴다.

31 가정법 과거로 would visit으로 써야 한다.

32 과거에 이룰 수 없었거나 과거 사실과는 반대되는 일에 대한 소망을 나타내는 I wish 가정법 과거완료 〈I wish+주어+had+과거분사〉를 쓴다.

33 현재 사실의 반대를 가정하는 If 가정법 과거 〈If+주어+동사의 과거형, 주어+would/could/might+동사원형〉이다.

34 If 가정법 과거완료로서 〈If+주어+had+과거분사, 주어+would/could/might+have+과거분사〉의 어순으로 쓴다.

35 과거 사실의 반대를 가정하는 If 가정법 과거완료로 〈If+주어+had+과거분사, 주어+would/could/might+have+과거분사〉의 어순으로 쓴다.

36 현재 이룰 수 없거나 사실과 반대되는 일에 대한 소망을 나타내는 I wish 가정법 과거 〈I wish+주어+동사의 과거형 (be동사의 경우 were)〉이다.

37 과거 사실의 반대를 가정하는 If 가정법 과거완료 〈If+주어+had+과거분사, 주어+would/could/might+have+과거분사〉의 어순으로 쓴다.

38 현재 사실에 반대되는 일을 가정하는 If 가정법 과거 〈If+

주어+동사의 과거형, 주어+would/could/might+동사원형〉으로 be동사는 were를 쓴다.

39 과거에 이루지 못했거나 사실과는 반대되는 일에 대한 소망을 나타내는 I wish 가정법 과거완료 〈I wish+주어+had+과거분사〉의 어순으로 쓴다.

40 부사 now에 맞춰 현재 사실에 반대되는 일을 가정하는 If 가정법 과거 〈If+주어+동사의 과거형, 주어+would/could/might+동사원형〉이므로 had로 써야 한다.

41 '~한다면'의 의미인 조건절 If이므로 주절은 will tell을 써야 한다.

42 과거에 이룰 수 없었거나 과거 사실과는 반대되는 일에 대한 소망을 나타내는 I wish 가정법 과거완료 〈I wish+주어+had+과거분사〉이므로 had met을 쓴다.

43 as if 가정법 과거에는 be동사 자리에 were를 쓴다.

44 '우리가 버스를 잡지 못했다면, 지각했을 것이다'나 '우리가 버스를 잡았다면 지각하지 않았을 것이다'라는 의미의 if 가정법 과거완료 〈If+주어+had+과거분사, 주어+would/could/might+have+과거분사〉가 되어야 한다.

45 as if절에 before가 있으므로 주절보다 과거의 일을 나타내는 가정법 과거완료를 쓴다.

46 과거 사실에 반대되는 일을 가정하는 If 가정법 과거완료 〈If+주어+had+과거분사, 주어+would/could/might+have+과거분사〉이다.

47 (1) 현재 사실에 반대되는 일을 가정하는 If 가정법 과거 〈If+주어+동사의 과거형, 주어+would/could/might+동사원형〉에서 if절의 be동사는 were로 쓴다.
(2) 현재 사실에 반대되는 일을 가정하는 If 가정법 과거 〈If+주어+동사의 과거형, 주어+would/could/might+동사원형〉이므로 could have를 쓴다.

48 현재 사실의 반대를 가정하는 If 가정법 과거는 〈If+주어+동사의 과거형, 주어+would/could/might+동사원형〉이다.

49 '마치 ~이었던 것처럼'이라는 의미로, 실제가 아닌 과거의 일을 표현하는 as if 가정법 과거완료이므로 〈주어+동사의 현재형+as if+주어+had+과거분사〉로 써야 한다.

50 ⓑ 현재 사실에 반대되는 일을 가정하는 If 가정법 과거는 〈If+주어+동사의 과거형, 주어+would/could/might+동사원형〉이므로 would become으로 써야 한다.

CHAPTER

[14 일치와 화법]

Unit 01

p. 246

A

01 knew / felt
02 said / had heard
03 told / were
04 found out / was
05 believed / would win
06 hoped / were
07 thought / had left
08 was / might be

B

01 thought / was interesting
02 knew / had left for
03 believe / did their best
04 are / will succeed
05 realized / had made a mistake
06 know / is held yearly

Unit 02

p. 247

A

01 turned → turn
02 is → was[had been]
03 had broken → broke
04 froze → freezes
05 was → is
06 did → do
07 gathered → gathers

B

01 knew that Shakespeare wrote about 37 plays
02 learned that the biggest planet is Jupiter
03 learned that Mount Everest is the tallest mountain
04 found out that a spider has eight legs
05 said that Dokdo is a Korean island
06 said that Queen Victoria became queen at the age of 18

내신기출 had discovered → discovered

Unit 03

p. 248

A

01 ⓐ
02 ⓐ
03 ⓑ
04 ⓑ
05 ⓐ
06 ⓑ
07 ⓑ

B

01 did try not to
02 did smell
03 do always trust
04 do like
05 do believe in
06 did taste

Unit 04

p. 249

A

01 Under a tree played the baby
02 Behind the tower is the bank
03 On my shoulder is the bird
04 Under the bed hid the dog
05 Up the hill walked the children
06 There went our school bus
07 There she comes

B

01 Into the crowd ran a monkey
02 In the sky is a rainbow
03 Behind the clouds disappeared the moon
04 There goes the last bus for Incheon
05 At the top of the mountain was our tent
06 Under the bridge flows the Han River

Unit 05

p. 250

A

01 the next[following] day
02 that
03 there
04 then

B

01 told me / she wanted me to join her
02 told us / she was happy with our present
03 said / she had to change her clothes
04 said / he had got[gotten] up at seven that morning
05 said / they had enjoyed the party
06 told me / she liked my painting

C

01 said to me / I had a heavy lunch
02 said / I can pass the test today
03 said / We don't like this food
04 said to us / I will go to France next week

05 said to me / I am sorry for being rude

06 said to me / I saw you on TV last night

D

01 had been → was **03** said → told

02 can → could **04** has → had

내신기출 ③

Unit 06

p. 252

A

01 have → had **05** told → asked (me)

02 will → would **06** helped → had helped

03 can → could **07** that → if[whether]

04 was I → I was **08** was it → it was

B

01 asked / why I had chosen that school

02 asked who was making a noise then

03 asked / if[whether] he might sit next to her

04 asked / what I was interested in

05 asked / if[whether] I had got[gotten] my hair cut

06 asked / how long we were staying there

C

01 What are you doing now

02 Do you like your school

03 Is your family doing well

04 Where are you planning to visit

05 Who makes you feel angry

06 How can I get to the bank

07 Did you finish your homework

D

01 if[whether] I had learned Chinese

02 what I had for lunch

03 if[whether] I had enjoyed the Mexican food

04 when I could get the next bus

05 if[whether] the cake tasted good

06 if[whether] she had taken the medicine

Unit 07

p. 254

A

01 if[whether] you are ready

02 how old you are

03 what this book is about

04 how you will fix this problem

B

01 What do you think it is

02 Who do you believe can help you

03 How do you think I can keep warm

04 What time do you suppose she will arrive

05 Where do you think you lost the bag

06 Why do you guess this is not[isn't] working

C

01 Do you know what happened

02 Please tell me where I should get

03 The doctor knew why I had

04 I'm not sure whether Sam will like

05 Can you tell me where you saw

06 I wonder how much you love

07 It is doubtful if he will keep

08 No one knows if the weather will be

D

01 did you tell → you told

02 How do you think old → How old do you think

03 When do you know → Do you know when

04 told → asked

05 Do you believe who → Who do you believe

내신기출 ③

Unit 08

p. 256

A

01 isn't she **05** doesn't he

02 didn't you **06** doesn't it

03 do they **07** wasn't it

04 are you **08** aren't they

B

01 doesn't she / No, she doesn't

02 were you / Yes, I was

03 are they / No, they aren't

04 weren't you / Yes, I was

05 did she / No, she didn't

06 aren't they / No, they aren't

Unit 09   p. 257

A

01 won't you   **05** can you

02 should she   **06** shall we

03 can't he   **07** shouldn't we

04 will you   **08** will you

B

01 We can catch / can't we

02 so smart / aren't I

03 You should not[shouldn't] play soccer / should you

04 Let's not talk about / shall we

05 Be more patient / will you

내신 기출 ②

중간고사 · 기말고사 실전문제   pp. 258~264

객관식 정답 [01~25]

01 ②	**02** ④	**03** ③	**04** ③	**05** ⑤
06 ①	**07** ③	**08** ⑤	**09** ①	**10** ④
11 ②	**12** ④	**13** ⑤	**14** ④	**15** ③
16 ③	**17** ①	**18** ⑤	**19** ④	**20** ④
21 ①, ③	**22** ②	**23** ②	**24** ⑤	**25** ②

주관식 정답 [26~50]

26 shall we

27 couldn't he

28 will / go 또는 am / going

29 had / seen

30 Jimmy asked me if I had slept enough.

31 How long do you guess he can run?

32 Can you tell me why you cried last night?

33 How do you suppose he became a super star?

34 I did remember what my teacher had told me.

35 We do see the thousands of stars in the sky.

36 is coming the bus now

37 the stage she was singing

38 I said to her, "Have you read this novel?"

39 He said, "I can join you today."

40 won't → wouldn't 또는 wondered → wonder

41 will Matt → Matt will

42 called → call

43 comes it → it comes

44 Paul said to me, "Please call me now."

45 Can you tell me when the show ends?

46 (1) will → would 또는 hoped → hope
     (2) ○ (3) could → can

47 what your hobbies are

48 how long you have taught at a school of music

49 Max does trust Tom among his friends.

50 ⓐ, ⓔ, ①

해설

01 긍정문에 대한 부가의문문은 부정으로 써야 한다.

02 주절의 시제가 과거이므로 종속절은 과거 혹은 과거완료로 써야 한다. would를 쓰려면 동사원형 be를 함께 써서 would be가 되어야 한다.

03 강조의 조동사 do가 가장 어울린다.

04 문장1과 같은 역사적 사실은 과거 시제로 쓴다. 문장2는 주절의 시제가 과거이므로 종속절은 과거 혹은 과거완료로 써야 한다.

05 ①, ④, ⑤ 주절에 과거나 현재완료시제를 쓰면 종속절에는 과거 또는 과거완료시제를 써야 한다. ② 주절에 미래시제가 오려면 종속절도 미래시제로 쓴다. ③ 주절에 현재시제를 쓰려면 3인칭 단수주어 She에 따라 tells를 쓴다.

06 문장1은 주절의 시제(과거)에 맞춰 was going to로 써야 한다. 문장2는 주어로 쓰인 의문사로 '누구'의 의미인 who를 써야 한다.

07 문장1은 as if 가정법이고, 문장2는 '~인지 아닌지'라는

의미의 간접의문문의 접속사 if이다.

08 첫 번째 문장에서 긍정 I'm ~에 대한 부가의문문은 aren't I?로 쓴다. 두 번째 문장에서 부가의문문에 대한 대답으로 부정이면 무조건 No를 쓴다. No가 나왔으므로 부정의 의미인 aren't를 써야 한다.

09 의문사가 있는 간접의문문은 〈의문사+주어+동사〉의 어순으로 쓴다.

10 주어진 우리말을 직접화법으로 쓰면 화자의 입장으로 써야 하므로 He said to me, "Return my chair today."로 쓴다. 간접화법으로 쓰면 said to me는 told me로, my chair는 his chair로, today는 that day로 바꾼다. 따라서 He told me to return his chair that day.로 쓴다.

11 답변이 '그녀의 공책에 써 있었다'이므로 그녀의 이름이 '무엇'인지 아느냐는 질문이 나와야 하고, 간접의문문에서 종속절은 〈의문사+주어+동사〉의 어순으로 쓴다.

12 ④는 조건(~하면)의 뜻인 접속사 if이고, 나머지는 '~인지 아닌지'의 뜻인 의문사가 없는 간접의문문의 접속사 if이다.

13 전달동사 said to는 told로, that절의 인칭대명사는 전달자의 입장으로, now는 then으로 바꿔야 한다.

14 전달동사 said는 said로, that절의 인칭대명사와 동사는 전달자의 입장으로, tomorrow는 the next day로 바꿔야 한다.

15 생각이나 추측을 나타내는 동사 think, believe, imagine, guess, suppose 등이 쓰인 문장에서 간접의문문이 목적어로 쓰일 때, 간접의문문의 의문사는 문장 맨 앞으로 가야 한다.

16 ① 강조의 조동사 do를 과거형 did로 쓰면 뒤에는 동사원형 practice가 와야 한다. ② 부가의문문의 동사는 문장의 시제와 일치해야 하므로 wasn't, ④ 역사적 사실은 항상 과거시제로 써야 하므로 started, ⑤ How come(어째서)으로 시작하는 의문문은 〈How come+주어+동사 ~?〉의 어순이므로 you broke로 써야 한다.

17 3인칭 단수주어에 맞게 동사는 enjoys로 써야 한다.

18 부가의문문은 앞 문장과 시제와 형태가 일치해야 하므로 does she?로 써야 한다.

19 부가의문문의 대답은 긍정(훔쳤다)이면 무조건 Yes, 부정(훔치지 않았다)이면 무조건 No로 쓴다.

20 ⑤ think, believe, imagine, guess, suppose 등이 쓰인 문장에서 간접의문문이 목적어로 쓰일 때, 간접의문문의 의문사는 문장 맨 앞으로 가야 하며, 어순은 〈주어+동사〉이므로 that girl is로 쓴다.

21 ① 의문사가 없는 간접의문문은 〈if[whether](~인지 아닌지)+주어+동사〉의 어순으로 쓰므로 if he ate, ③ 강조의 조동사 did이므로 did appear로 쓴다.

22 ④ Here가 문장 앞에 오면서 주어가 대명사일 때는 〈Here+대명사 주어+동사〉로 쓴다.

23 ⑤ 강조의 조동사 do/does/did는 동사원형이 뒤에 와야 하므로 did enjoy로 써야 한다.

24 (A) 주절의 시제가 과거일 때 종속절은 과거나 과거완료가 되어야 하므로 had 혹은 had had, (B) '어떻게' 화해할지 묻는 문장이므로 How, (C) say 뒤에 청자가 나올 때는 to를 써야 하고 say to는 tell로 쓸 수 있다.

25 ⑤ 주절의 시제가 과거일 때 종속절은 과거나 과거완료가 되어야 하므로 was 또는 had been이 된다.

26 제안문의 부가의문문은 항상 shall we?로 쓴다.

27 긍정문에 대한 부가의문문은 부정으로 써야 한다.

28 시간의 부사가 next month(다음 달)이므로 미래시제로 쓴다. 진행시제로도 미래를 나타낼 수 있다.

29 말하는 시점보다 낯선 사람을 본 것이 이전이므로 과거완료시제로 쓴다.

30 의문사가 없는 간접의문문은 〈if[whether]+주어+동사〉로 쓰며, 주절이 과거이므로 종속절도 과거 혹은 과거완료로 쓴다.

31 추측을 나타내는 동사 guess가 쓰인 문장에서 간접의문문이 목적어로 쓰일 때, 간접의문문의 의문사는 문장 맨 앞으로 가야 하며, 어순은 〈주어+동사〉로 써야 한다.

32 의문사가 있는 간접의문문은 〈의문사+주어+동사〉의 어순으로 써야 한다.

33 추측을 나타내는 동사 suppose가 쓰인 문장에서 간접의문문이 목적어로 쓰일 때 간접의문문의 의문사는 문장 맨 앞으로 가야 하며, 어순은 〈주어+동사〉로 써야 한다.

34 강조의 조동사 do/does/did 뒤에는 동사원형을 써야 하므로 did remember가 된다.

35 강조의 조동사 do 뒤에는 동사원형을 써야 하므로 do

see로 써야 한다.

36 Here이 문장 앞에 오면 〈동사+주어〉가 온다.

37 장소 전치사구가 문두에 오면 주어와 동사를 도치시키지만. 주어가 대명사(She)일 때는 〈주어+동사〉로 쓴다.

38 직접화법에서 청자가 있으면 〈say to+청자〉로 쓰며, 주절에 콤마와 인용부호(" ")를 넣고 화자의 입장에서 인칭대명사(she)를 you로 바꾸고 시제도 발화 시점인 현재완료로 써야 한다.

39 직접화법에서 청자가 없는 경우는 say를 쓰고, 주절에 콤마와 인용부호(" ")를 넣고 화자의 입장에서 인칭대명사(he, us)를 I, you로 바꾸고, that day는 today로 바꿔야 한다.

40 주절의 시제가 과거라면 종속절에는 won't의 과거형 wouldn't를 쓴다. 주절의 시제가 현재라면 종속절에는 모든 시제가 가능하다.

41 간접의문문은 평서문처럼 〈주어+조동사+동사원형〉의 어순으로 쓴다.

42 강조의 조동사 do/does/did 뒤에는 동사원형을 쓴다.

43 Here이 문장 앞에 오더라도 주어가 대명사라면 도치하지 않고 〈Here+대명사 주어+동사〉로 쓴다.

44 say 뒤에 청자가 나올 때는 to를 쓴다.

45 의문사가 있는 간접의문문은 〈의문사+주어+동사〉로 쓴다.

46 (1) 주절이 과거시제이므로 종속절도 will의 과거형 would를 써야 한다. 또는 주절을 현재시제로 바꿀 수도 있다.

(3) 사실. 진리. 현재의 습관은 언제나 현재시제로 써야 하므로 주절이 과거시제여도 종속절에는 현재시제를 쓴다.

47 의문사가 있는 간접의문문은 〈의문사+주어+동사〉의 순으로 쓰며, 답변이 취미에 대한 것이므로 '취미가 무엇입니까?'인 what are your hobbies?의 간접의문문 형태 what your hobbies are로 써야 한다.

48 의문사가 있는 간접의문문은 〈의문사+주어+동사〉의 순으로 쓰며, 답변이 경력에 대한 것이므로 '음악 학교에서 얼마나 오래 가르쳤습니까?'인 How long have you taught at a school of music?의 간접의문문 형태 how long you have taught at a school of music

으로 써야 한다.

49 주어가 3인칭 단수(Max)이므로 강조의 조동사 do를 does로 쓰고 조동사 다음에는 동사원형 trust를 쓴다.

50 ⓐ 의문사가 있는 간접의문문은 〈의문사+주어+동사〉로 쓰므로 whom he invited, ⓔ 강조의 조동사 do 뒤에는 동사원형을 쓰고, do는 3인칭 단수주어에 맞춰야 하므로 does like로 쓴다. ⓕ 장소 전치사구가 문두에 오면 주어와 동사를 도치하는데, 주어가 대명사라면 도치하지 않고 〈장소 전치사구+대명사 주어+동사〉의 어순으로 쓴다.

MY GRAMMAR COACH

내신기출 N제 중 2

Workbook

정답과 해설

CHAPTER [01] 시제

Unit 01   p. 4

A

01 accepted – accepted
02 accomplished – accomplished
03 agreed – agreed
04 allowed – allowed
05 believed – believed
06 borrowed – borrowed
07 carried – carried
08 closed – closed
09 collected – collected
10 copied – copied
11 covered – covered
12 cried – cried
13 decided – decided
14 depended – depended
15 delayed – delayed
16 disagreed – disagreed
17 dropped – dropped
18 enjoyed – enjoyed
19 failed – failed
20 finished – finished
21 founded – founded
22 happened – happened
23 hoped – hoped
24 hurried – hurried
25 joined – joined
26 laughed – laughed
27 learned – learned
28 lied – lied
29 looked – looked
30 married – married
31 planned – planned
32 played – played
33 preferred – preferred
34 raised – raised
35 remembered – remembered

36 saved – saved
37 smiled – smiled
38 stayed – stayed
39 stopped – stopped
40 studied – studied
41 thanked – thanked
42 touched – touched
43 tried – tried
44 used – used
45 visited – visited
46 waited – waited
47 walked – walked
48 wanted – wanted
49 washed – washed
50 watched – watched
51 worked – worked
52 worried – worried

B

01 was – been
02 were – been
03 became – become
04 began – begun
05 broke – broken
06 brought – brought
07 built – built
08 bought – bought
09 caught – caught
10 chose – chosen
11 came – come
12 cost – cost
13 cut – cut
14 did – done
15 drew – drawn
16 drank – drunk
17 drove – driven
18 ate – eaten
19 fell – fallen
20 felt – felt
21 fought – fought

22 found – found
23 flew – flown
24 forgot – forgotten
25 forgave – forgiven
26 got – got[gotten]
27 gave – given
28 went – gone
29 grew – grown
30 had – had
31 heard – heard
32 hit – hit
33 hurt – hurt
34 kept – kept
35 knew – known
36 laid – laid
37 led – led
38 left – left
39 lent – lent
40 let – let
41 lay – lain
42 lost – lost

43 made – made
44 meant – meant
45 met – met
46 paid – paid
47 put – put
48 read – read
49 rode – ridden
50 rang – rung
51 rose – risen
52 ran – run
53 paid – paid
54 said – said
55 saw – seen
56 sold – sold
57 sent – sent
58 sang – sung
59 sat – sat
60 slept – slept

61 spoke – spoken
62 spent – spent
63 spread – spread
64 stood – stood
65 stole – stolen
66 swam – swum
67 took – taken
68 taught – taught
69 told – told
70 thought – thought
71 threw – thrown
72 understood
   – understood
73 woke – waken
74 wore – worn
75 won – won
76 wrote – written

Unit 02 p. 6

01 found
02 rain
03 freezes
04 eat
05 visited
06 said
07 was
08 am
09 rode
10 comes

Unit 03 p. 6

01 arriving
02 beginning
03 believing
04 bringing
05 climbing
06 closing
07 coming
08 controlling
09 dying
10 driving
11 flying
12 getting
13 giving
14 lying
15 playing
16 putting
17 riding
18 running
19 saying
20 shopping
21 sitting
22 stopping
23 studying
24 swimming

Unit 04 p. 7

01 was reading
02 are playing
03 were taking
04 What are / doing
05 was not[wasn't] watching
06 are not[aren't] exercising
07 Were / looking
08 was not[wasn't] driving
09 was not[wasn't] stretching

Unit 05 p. 7

01 did not[didn't] wash
02 got
03 have / finished
04 wrote
05 have not[haven't] eaten
06 had
07 Have / been
08 watched
09 has worked

Unit 06 p. 8

01 have not[haven't] seen
02 have had this bag
03 since I was
04 have known
05 has been here
06 since last week
07 has worked
08 since last year
09 have they stayed

Unit 07 p. 8

01 has already become
02 have just bought
03 has already left
04 has just started
05 have just finished
06 has just broken down

07 has already bought

08 Have you already got

09 Haven't you finished

Unit 08 p. 9

01 has never made / before

02 have watched / twice

03 ever bought

04 has been / three times

05 has ridden / before

06 you ever seen

07 have gone / several times

08 have never played

09 ever spoken

Unit 09 p. 9

01 has gone

02 has moved

03 has lost

04 has left

05 have left

Unit 10 p. 10

A

01 경험

02 계속

03 완료

04 계속

05 결과

B

01 have raised / before

02 have gone to

03 How long has it rained

04 has gone out

05 I have lost

06 has taught science / for

■ 중간고사 · 기말고사 실전문제 pp. 11~14

객관식 정답 [01~15]

01 ④	**02** ③	**03** ③	**04** ④	**05** ②
06 ③	**07** ⑤	**08** ③	**09** ⑤	**10** ⑤
11 ④	**12** ①	**13** ④	**14** ⑤	**15** ②

주관식 정답 [16~30]

16 fallen

17 finished

18 left

19 knew → have known

20 already → yet

21 spended → spent

22 is / to

23 When my father was on his way home, a bell was ringing on the hill.

24 hasn't been to

25 How long have you studied math?

26 has gone to

27 have lived in

28 has worked

29 Tom is going to close his bakery.

30 They have not met their relatives since last year.

해설

01 make의 동사변화형은 make-made-made이다.

02 현재완료의 계속적 용법이므로 have played를 써야 한다.

03 현재완료시제인 〈have+과거분사〉로 질문했고, No라고 답했으므로 현재완료의 부정문으로 대답해야 한다.

04 ④는 '가지다'라는 의미의 일반동사 have이며, 나머지는 현재완료시제의 have이다.

05 ②는 미래시제인 〈be going to+동사원형〉이 아니라 go to church의 현재진행형이다.

06 last evening(어제 저녁)이라는 부사(구)는 주로 과거시제와 함께 쓰므로 help의 과거형 helped를 써야 한다.

07 ⑤는 현재완료의 결과적 용법이고, 나머지는 경험적 용법이다.

08 ③은 현재완료의 결과적 용법이고, 나머지는 계속적 용법이다.

09 in the 17th century(17세기에)라는 구체적인 시간을 나타내는 부사(구)는 주로 과거시제와 함께 쓰므로 write의 과거형 wrote를 써야 한다.

10 조건의 if절에서는 현재시제가 미래시제를 대신하므로 will snow를 snows로 써야 한다.

11 yesterday는 주로 과거시제와 함께 쓰이는 시간의 부사 (구)이다. ① When절이 과거시제이므로 is를 was로 고

쳐야 한다. ② ago는 주로 과거시제와 함께 쓰이는 시간의 부사(구)이다. ③ 현재완료의 계속적 용법으로 last month라는 기간의 시작점이 쓰였으므로 since를 써야 한다. ⑤ 현재완료의 계속적 용법으로 two years라는 기간이 쓰였으므로 for를 써야 한다.

12 현재 시점을 나타내는 these days(최근)에 맞게 현재진행형으로 써야 한다. ② in 2009처럼 구체적 시간을 나타내는 부사(구)는 과거시제와 주로 쓰이므로 die의 과거형 died를 쓴다. ③ 현재(now)를 나타내므로 teaches를 쓴다. ④ ago는 주로 과거시제와 함께 쓰이는 시간의 부사(구)이므로 read의 과거형 read를 써야 한다. ⑤ 불변의 진리, 과학적 사실 등은 현재시제를 써야 하므로 rises를 쓴다.

13 ⓐ 특정 과거 시점 yesterday에 맞게 went로 써야 한다. ⓒ 현재완료의 부정문은 〈have/has +not+과거분사〉이므로 don't를 haven't로 써야 한다. ⓓ 현재완료의 의문문은 〈Have/Has+주어+과거분사 ~?〉이므로 hear의 과거분사형 heard를 써야 한다.

14 조건의 if절에서는 현재시제가 미래시제를 대신하므로 is를 쓴다.

15 ⓐ last night은 주로 과거시제에 쓰이는 부사(구)로 과거형 came. ⓒ 기간 앞에는 since가 아니라 for. ⓔ 특정 과거 시점 yesterday에 맞게 leave의 과거형 left로 써야 한다.

16 fall의 과거분사형 fallen을 써야 한다.

17 finish의 과거분사형 finished를 써야 한다.

18 '떠나다'라는 의미의 leave의 과거형 left를 써야 한다.

19 현재완료의 계속적 용법으로 knew의 과거분사형 have known을 써야 한다.

20 현재완료의 완료적 용법으로 아직 돌아오지 않았다는 의미로 yet을 써야 한다.

21 spend의 과거분사형 spent를 써야 한다.

22 will과 같은 의미의 〈be going to+동사원형〉 형태로 바꾸어 쓸 수 있으며, 주어가 3인칭 단수이므로 be동사를 is로 써야 한다.

23 when 부사절이 과거를 의미하므로 과거진행형을 써야 한다.

24 현재완료의 부정문 〈haven't/hasn't+과거분사〉의 형태로 써야 한다.

25 현재완료의 계속적 용법의 의문문은 〈How long+have +주어+과거분사 ~?〉의 형태로 써야 한다.

26 현재완료의 결과적 용법이다.

27 현재완료의 계속적 용법이다. *live in: ~에 살다

28 현재완료의 계속적 용법이다.

29 미래의 일은 〈be going to+동사원형〉의 형태로 나타낼 수 있다.

30 현재완료의 계속적 용법으로 meet의 과거분사형 met을 써야 한다.

Unit 04

01 had to
02 Do / have to
03 had to
04 did / have to
05 do not[don't] have to

Unit 05

01 should see
02 should hurry up
03 should not[shouldn't] make fun of
04 What should / buy
05 should go back

Unit 06

01 had better give
02 would not like to return
03 had better take a rest
04 would like to hear
05 had better not go
06 would like to move

Unit 07

01 would[used to] go to the beach
02 used to be
03 would[used to] read
04 used to understand
05 used to have
06 used to hate

중간고사 · 기말고사 실전문제

객관식 정답 [01~15]

01 ④	**02** ③	**03** ④	**04** ①	**05** ②
06 ④	**07** ⑤	**08** ②	**09** ①	**10** ③
11 ⑤	**12** ②	**13** ①	**14** ④	**15** ②

주관식 정답 [16~30]

16 had better
17 would like
18 Do / have to
19 couldn't
20 You should exercise every day if you want to be healthy. 또는 If you want to be healthy, you should exercise every day.

21 I wasn't able to find any food in the kitchen.
22 Was he able to get to the top of the mountain?
23 don't have to → must not
24 has better → had better
25 must be
26 don't have to read
27 may not be
28 had to go
29 I'm able to go to Jongro by myself.
30 There used to be a post office here.

해설

01 조동사는 주어의 인칭과 수에 상관없이 같은 형태로 쓰므로 would like to와 바꿔 쓸 수 있다.

02 be able to는 '~할 수 있다'라는 뜻이며 be는 주어와 시제에 따라 형태를 바꾼다. 주어가 3인칭 단수이므로 과거의 부정형 wasn't able to로 써야 한다.

03 첫 번째 문장의 Would you ~?는 '~해 주시겠어요?'라는 요청, 두 번째 문장은 '~하곤 했다'라는 의미로 과거의 반복적인 행동을 나타내는 would이다.

04 주어진 문장과 ①의 may는 허가의 의미이며, ②, ③, ④, ⑤는 추측의 의미이다.

05 허가의 의미의 Can은 May와 바꿔 쓸 수 있다.

06 '~해서는 안 된다'라는 의미로 must not, can't, should not이 있다. ① must는 '~해야 한다'라는 의미이므로 must not을 써야 한다. ② don't have to는 '~할 필요가 없다'라는 의미이다. ③ can의 부정형 can't에 not을 또 쓰면 안 된다. ⑤ must의 부정형은 must not이다.

07 must는 '~임에 틀림없다'라는 의미로 강한 추측을 나타낸다. ①, ④의 used to와 would는 '~하곤 했다'라는 의미로 과거의 상태나 반복적인 동작을 나타낸다. ②의 can't는 '~하면 안 된다'라는 의미이다. ③ may는 '~일지도 모른다'라는 의미이다.

08 ②는 허가의 의미이며, 나머지는 능력의 의미이다.

09 have/has to의 부정형은 don't/doesn't have to이며, 주어가 3인칭 단수이므로 doesn't have to로 써야 한다.

10 '~하고 싶다'라는 의미의 would like to는 〈would like+명사〉 또는 〈would like to+동사원형〉 어순이므로 Would you like to go ~?로 고쳐야 한다.

11 조동사 will 뒤에 동사원형 stay를 바르게 썼다. ① 조동사 can 뒤에는 동사원형 swim, ② 조동사 will 뒤에는 동사원형 come, ③ 조동사 may 뒤에는 동사원형 use, ④ 조동사는 주어의 인칭과 수에 상관없이 원형으로만 쓰므로 may를 써야 한다.

12 must의 부정형은 must not이다. ① can의 부정형 can't 뒤에 not을 중복하여 쓸 수 없다. ③ doesn't만 쓰거나 may not을 써야 한다. ④ have to의 부정형은 don't have to로 써야 한다. ⑤ had better의 부정형은 had better not으로 써야 한다.

13 don't have to는 '~할 필요가 없다', must not은 '~하면 안 된다'라는 의미이다.

14 '다행히도, 제시간에 도착할 수 있었다'라는 의미가 되어야 하므로, should가 아니라 could가 되어야 한다.

15 현재에 run fast가 O이므로 맞는 말이다. ① 과거에 O이므로, could sing well. ④ 과거에 X이므로 couldn't. ③, ⑤ 과거에도 현재에도 X이므로 couldn't play/can't play이다.

16 '~하는 게 낫다'라는 의미의 〈had better+동사원형〉을 써야 한다.

17 '~하고 싶다'라는 의미의 〈would like to+동사원형〉을 써야 한다.

18 '~해야 한다'라는 의미인 have to의 의문문 어순은 〈Do/Does+주어+have to ~?〉로 써야 한다.

19 '볼 수 없었다'는 과거 부정형이므로 can의 과거 부정형인 couldn't로 써야 한다.

20 '~해야 한다'라는 뜻으로 충고나 제안을 할 때 조동사 should를 사용한다.

21 can의 과거 부정형인 couldn't는 wasn't able to와 바꿔 쓸 수 있다.

22 〈be able to+동사원형〉의 의문형은 〈be+주어+able to+동사원형 ~?〉이다.

23 '~하면 안 된다'라는 의미의 강한 금지를 나타내는 must not을 써야 한다.

24 had better는 주어의 인칭과 수에 상관없이 항상 같은 형태로 쓴다.

25 '~임에 틀림없다'라는 의미의 must를 써야 한다.

26 '~할 필요가 없다'라는 의미의 don't have to를 써야 한다.

27 '~일지도 모른다'라는 의미의 약한 추측인 may를 사용한다.

28 '~해야 한다'라는 의미의 have to로 나타낼 수 있으며, 과거시제이므로 had to로 써야 한다.

29 can이 능력을 의미할 때 be able to와 바꾸어 쓸 수 있다.

30 〈used to+동사원형〉은 과거에는 사실이었지만 현재는 사실이 아닌 일에 대해 말할 때도 사용한다.

CHAPTER
[03 수동태]

Unit 01
p. 26

01 are written by
02 are caught
03 are provided
04 was scolded / by
05 is consumed
06 are loved by

Unit 02
p. 26

01 were found
02 was loved by a lot of girls
03 were planned by Joy's friends
04 was signed by him
05 was spread by people
06 was posted by the school

Unit 03
p. 27

01 will be performed
02 will be baked by my mom
03 will be played
04 will be selected by
05 will be printed
06 will be watched by

Unit 04
p. 27

01 will be served
02 was delivered by
03 are displayed
04 was discovered by
05 will be planted
06 will be sent

Unit 05
p. 28

01 was known to
02 was surprised at
03 were filled with
04 is covered with
05 am tired of
06 will be satisfied with

Unit 06
p. 28

01 My homework can be finished (by me).
02 It can be done by Teresa.
03 The computer should be fixed (by them).
04 The plans might be changed (by them).
05 His new song might be released (by him).
06 This should be kept in a refrigerator (by you).

Unit 07
p. 29

01 When was / invented
02 Are / pleased with
03 Is / interested in
04 is not[isn't] finished
05 will not[won't] be erased
06 Can / be baked

Unit 08
p. 29

01 was bought for my dad by
02 was given lots of medicine by
03 was sent to me by
04 will be given to you
05 are taught math by

Unit 09
p. 30

01 should be kept clean
02 was called an angel by
03 was advised to eat
04 is expected to arrive
05 was named / by
06 was told to sit down

Unit 10
p. 30

01 The students are made to practice jumping rope by their teacher.
02 The phone was heard ringing in her pocket (by her).
03 I am made to wipe the floor by Mom every Saturday.
04 You were seen to arrive at the airport (by me).
05 The building was seen shaking heavily (by people).

Unit 11
p. 31

01 was turned down
02 were taken care of by
03 were put off by
04 were always turned down by
05 was looked down on by
06 was run over by
07 must be handed in

■ 중간고사 · 기말고사 실전문제
pp. 32~35

객관식 정답 [01~15]

01 ④	**02** ②	**03** ②	**04** ③	**05** ③
06 ①	**07** ③	**08** ⑤	**09** ①	**10** ④
11 ③	**12** ⑤	**13** ④	**14** ④	**15** ②

주관식 정답 [16~30]

16 was played
17 (A) with (B) of
18 My motorcycle was stopped by the police this morning.
19 The girl was made to wash the dishes by me.
20 This watch was given to me by Tom.
21 Dinner will be able to be prepared soon.
22 invited → was invited
23 Did → Was
24 speaking → spoken
25 reads
26 Are / grown
27 was made to water
28 ⓐ → was / ⓒ → wasn't
29 The umbrella was brought to me by her because it was raining.
30 ⓔ → is visited

해설

01 be satisfied with는 '~에 만족한다', be covered with는 '~로 덮여 있다'라는 의미이다.

02 '가르치다'라는 의미인 teach의 과거형과 과거분사형인 taught를 써야 한다.

03 수동태 과거시제 〈was/were＋과거분사〉에 따라 was taken으로 써야 한다.

04 수동태를 능동태로 바꾸는 방법은 수동태 문장 〈주어＋be＋과거분사＋by＋행위자〉에서 수동태의 주어를 능동의 목적어로, 행위자를 능동태의 주어로 바꾼다. 즉 〈행위자＋(be생략) 동사＋주어(목적격)〉로 써야 한다.

05 소유나 상태를 나타내는 타동사 have는 수동태로 쓸 수 없다.

06 행위자가 일반인이거나 중요하지 않을 경우 〈by＋행위자(목적격)〉를 생략할 수 있다.

07 첫 번째 문장은 '잡다' catch의 수동 표현 was caught, 두 번째 문장은 '닫다' close의 수동 표현의 미래 시제 will be closed, 세 번째 문장은 wear의 주어가 사람이므로 능동 의미의 과거형 wore를 써야 한다.
*wear a necklace: 목걸이를 하다

08 수동태를 올바르게 썼다. ① news는 단수형이므로 was를, ② pay의 과거분사형인 paid를, ③ take의 과거분사형인 taken을, ④ The CD가 주어이므로 '발매되었다'라는 의미의 was released를 써야 한다.

09 동사구 look after는 한 단어처럼 취급하므로 함께 쓰고, by를 생략하면 안 된다. ② 수동태의 미래시제의 어순은 〈will＋be＋과거분사〉이므로 will be released로 써야 한다. ③ 의문사가 있는 수동태의 의문문은 〈의문사＋be＋주어＋과거분사 ~?〉이므로 did를 was로 바꿔야 한다. ④ 수동태의 과거시제 〈was/were＋과거분사〉에 따라 was eaten으로 써야 한다. ⑤ 수동태의 미래시제이므로 will be sung으로 써야 한다.

10 조동사가 있는 수동태의 어순은 〈조동사＋be＋과거분사〉이므로 must be followed로 써야 한다.

11 4형식 동사 make는 직접목적어만을 수동태의 주어로 취하므로, 수동태는 다음과 같이 the wine만 주어로 쓸 수 있다. The wine with grapes was made for Jina by Tom.

12 Yes로 대답했으므로 it was로 써야 한다.

13 지각동사 hear의 목적격보어로 쓰인 원형부정사는 수동태의 문장에서 〈to＋동사원형〉 형태가 되어야 하므로 was heard to get well로 써야 한다.

14 5형식 문장을 수동태로 만들려면, 목적어를 주어로 보내고, 명사, 형용사, to부정사 같은 목적격보어는 수동태 동사 뒤에 그대로 온다. ① buy는 목적어가 2개인 4형식 동사로서 직접목적어가 주어인 수동태로 바꿀 경우, 간접목적어 앞에 전치사 for를 쓴다. ② 조동사의 수동태형은 〈조동사＋be＋과거분사〉이므로 should be cooked로 써야 한다. ③ Dogs가 복수이므로 are로 써야 한다. ⑤ 지각동사 see의 목적격보어로 쓰인 원형부정사는 수동태의 문장에서 〈to＋동사형〉 형태가 되어야 하므로 to run으로 써야 한다.

15 ⓐ 유명해진 이유가 나와야 하므로 '~로[때문에] 알려져 있다'라는 의미의 be known for를 써야 한다. ⓓ drive의 과거분사형은 driven으로 써야 한다.

16 yesterday에 맞춰 수동태의 과거시제의 어순 〈was/were＋과거분사〉로 써야 한다.

17 '~으로 가득 차 있다'는 be filled with = be full of이다.

18 〈주어＋be＋과거분사＋by＋행위자〉의 어순으로 써 준다.

19 사역동사 make를 수동태로 만들려면 목적어를 주어로, 목적격보어를 to부정사로 만들어야 한다.

20 give는 목적어가 2개인 4형식 동사로서 직접목적어가 주어인 수동태로 바꿀 경우, 간접목적어 앞에 전치사 to를 쓴다.

21 〈will＋be able to＋동사원형〉의 수동태형이므로 to be prepared로 써야 한다.

22 수동태의 과거시제 〈was/were＋과거분사〉에 따라 invite의 과거분사형 was invited를 써야 한다.

23 수동태의 의문문은 〈(의문사＋)be동사＋주어＋과거분사 ~?〉 형태이므로 Did를 Was로 써야 한다.

24 speak의 과거분사형 spoken을 써야 한다.

25 read의 3인칭 단수 주어에 맞도록 reads로 써야 한다.

26 수동태의 의문문은 〈(의문사＋)be동사＋주어＋과거분사 ~?〉의 어순으로 써야 한다.

27 사역동사 make를 수동태로 만들려면 목적어를 주어로, 목적격보어를 to부정사로 만들어야 한다.

28 ⓐ 수동태의 의문문은 〈(의문사＋)be동사＋주어＋과거분사 ~?〉 형태이므로 Did를 Was로 써야 한다. ⓒ 주어가 it(= the flower)이므로 수동인 wasn't로 써야 한다.

29 bring은 목적어가 2개인 4형식 동사로서 직접목적어가 주어인 수동태로 바꿀 경우, 간접목적어 앞에 전치사 to를 쓴다.

30 Every Disneyland는 단수 취급하기 때문에 is, 방문되는 것이므로 수동태 형태의 is visited로 고쳐야 한다.

03 big enough for us to pour

04 brave enough to travel

05 cheap enough for us to buy

객관식 정답 [01~15]

01 ④	**02** ③	**03** ③	**04** ②	**05** ③
06 ④	**07** ④	**08** ②	**09** ⑤	**10** ②
11 ③	**12** ⑤	**13** ③	**14** ①	**15** ③

주관식 정답 [16~30]

16 told / to be

17 I need someone to talk with.

18 Jane has a lot of apples to eat.

19 Brian bought some pasta so as to cook.

20 We chose not to swim in the sea.

21 ⓐ

22 ⓒ

23 ⓑ

24 ⓒ

25 was too cold to take a shower

26 searched how she should play the guitar on the Internet

27 taking → to take

28 of → for

29 It is dangerous to try skydiving.

30 (C) → where to

해설

01 want는 to부정사를 목적어로 취하는 동사이다.

02 '~하기 위해서'라는 목적의 의미를 가지는 to부정사의 부사적 용법이다.

03 tell은 to부정사를 목적격보어로 취하는 동사이다.

04 문장에서 사람의 성격이나 성품을 나타내는 형용사가 오는 경우 의미상의 주어를 〈of+인칭대명사의 목적격〉 형태로 써야 한다.

05 ③은 가주어 it을 사용한 명사적 용법이며, 나머지는 형용사적 용법이다.

06 ④는 동사 like의 목적어로 명사적 용법이며, 나머지는 부사적 용법이다.

07 주어진 문장과 ④는 목적을 나타내는 부사적 용법이며, 나머지는 명사적 용법이다.

08 주어진 문장은 명사적 용법이다. ②는 형용사적 용법이며, 나머지는 명사적 용법이다.

09 〈형용사/부사+enough+to부정사〉는 '~할 만큼 충분히 …한'이라는 의미로 〈so+형용사/부사+that+주어+can[could]〉로 바꾸어 쓸 수 있다.

10 〈too+형용사/부사+to부정사〉 형태로 배열하며, 가주어 It과 to부정사의 의미상의 주어 〈for+목적격〉을 모두 써야 한다.

11 '그가 너무 바빠서 파티에 오지 못했다'라는 의미이므로 〈too+형용사/부사+to부정사〉를 써야 한다. ① watch 뒤에 목적어 it(the movie)을 써야 한다. ② to부정사가 수식하는 명사가 to부정사구의 전치사의 목적어일 경우 to부정사 뒤에 전치사를 반드시 같이 써야 하므로 sit on을 써야 한다. ④ -thing/-one으로 끝나는 대명사가 형용사와 to부정사의 수식을 동시에 받을 경우 〈-thing/-one+형용사+to부정사〉로 쓰므로 something cool to drink로 쓴다. ⑤ 〈의문사+to부정사〉의 어순이므로 what to say를 써야 한다.

12 expect의 목적어는 to부정사로 쓴다. ① go skiing은 '스키를 타러 가다'라는 의미이므로 to를 삭제해야 한다. ② 주격보어 역할을 하는 to부정사이므로 to become으로 써야 한다. ③ 주어 역할을 하는 to부정사이므로 To walk로 써야 하며, 주어 역할을 하는 동명사 Walking 또한 올 수 있다. ④ 〈be able to+동사원형〉 형태이므로 to go를 써야 한다.

13 ⓐ 명사적 용법, ⓑ 형용사적 용법, ⓒ 부사적 용법, ⓓ 형용사적 용법, ⓔ 명사적 용법

14 (A)는 to have, (B)는 〈too+형용사/부사+to부정사〉 구문으로 to eat, (C)는 tell의 목적어로 not to go를 써야 한다.

15 ⓑ 조동사 should 뒤에는 동사원형이 와야 하므로 to를 삭제해야 한다. ⓓ 사역동사 make는 동사원형을 목적격보어로 취하므로 wash로 써야 한다.

16 tell은 to부정사를 목적격보어로 취한다.

17 to부정사가 수식하는 명사가 to부정사구의 전치사의 목적어일 경우 to부정사 뒤에 반드시 전치사를 함께 써야 한다.

18 명사 apples를 수식하는 to부정사의 형용사적 용법으로 eat의 목적어 apples가 앞에 나왔으므로 them을 삭제해야 한다.

19 '~하기 위해서'라는 목적을 나타내는 to부정사는 목적을 더 강조하기 위해 〈so as to+동사원형〉으로 쓸 수 있다.

20 to부정사의 부정은 to 앞에 not을 써야 한다.

21 allow의 목적격보어로 명사적 용법이다.

22 목적을 나타내는 부사적 용법이다.

23 a cup of tea를 수식하는 형용사적 용법이다.

24 결과를 나타내는 부사적 용법이다.

25 〈so+형용사/부사+that+주어+can't[couldn't]〉는 〈too+형용사/부사+to부정사〉로 바꿔 쓸 수 있다.

26 〈의문사+to부정사〉는 〈의문사+주어+should[can]+동사원형〉으로 바꿔 쓸 수 있다.

27 plan은 to부정사를 목적어로 취하는 동사이다.

28 to부정사 행위의 주체를 밝히고자 할 때 to부정사 앞에 〈for+인칭대명사의 목적격〉을 쓰며, 사람의 성격이나 성품을 나타내는 형용사가 오는 경우 〈of+목적격〉으로 쓴다. 여기서 fantastic은 성격이나 성품이 아니므로 of를 for로 고쳐야 한다.

29 주어가 길어지면, 가주어 It을 주어 자리에 두고 진짜 주어는 뒤로 보낸다.

30 (C)는 where to이고, 나머지는 how to이다.

[CHAPTER 05 동명사와 분사]

02 some pictures taken by my dad

03 The book placed on the sofa

04 The children playing basketball

05 the man cleaning the window

06 The list posted on the school website

Unit 09 p. 54

01 saw / waving[wave]   **04** have / pulled

02 felt depressed   **05** saw / waiting[wait]

03 heard / calling[call]   **06** had / repaired

Unit 10 p. 54

01 bored   **05** confused

02 exciting   **06** relaxing

03 disappointed   **07** surprised

04 interested

Unit 11 p. 55

A

01 동명사   **04** 동명사

02 동명사   **05** 현재분사

03 동명사   **06** 동명사

B

01 현재분사 / 그 영화는 매우 흥미로웠다.

02 동명사 / 아이들을 돌보는 것은 쉽지 않다.

03 동명사 / 오늘 밤 영화 보러 가는 거 어때요?

04 현재분사 / 저 짖고 있는 강아지를 봐.

05 현재분사 / 혼자서 여행을 갔던 것은 나에게 떨리는 경험이었다.

06 현재분사 / 나는 우리 아빠가 코고는 소리를 들었다.

중간고사 · 기말고사 실전문제
pp. 56~59

객관식 정답 [01~15]

01 ③	**02** ④	**03** ⑤	**04** ③	**05** ①
06 ④	**07** ④	**08** ⑤	**09** ④	**10** ③
11 ③	**12** ①	**13** ①	**14** ③	**15** ②

주관식 정답 [16~30]

16 made

17 The foreigner had trouble using chopsticks.

18 ⓓ

19 ⓒ

20 ⓐ

21 finishing → to finish

22 are → is

23 read → reading

24 It is no use talking about it.

25 I'm used to living in the rural area.

26 Is Susan's goal holding her own exhibition?

27 to seeing

28 On[Upon] seeing

29 I regret to tell you this news.

30 I'm eating the grapes grown by the farmer.

해설

01 보어 역할을 하는 동명사이다.

02 수식하는 대상이 감정을 유발하거나 감정을 느끼게 만드는 주체이므로 fascinate의 현재분사 fascinating(매력적인)을 써야 한다.

03 첫 번째 문장은 분사가 서술하는 대상이 감정을 느끼는 객체인 She이므로 과거분사 surprised(놀란)를 써야 하며, 두 번째 문장은 전치사 of의 목적어인 동명사 studying을 써야 한다.

04 빈칸 (A)에는 '~하기를 기대하다'라는 의미의 〈look forward to+동명사〉, 빈칸 (B)에는 '~할 것을 기억하다'라는 의미의 〈remember+to부정사〉로 나타낸다.

05 '~한 것을 기억하다'라는 의미의 〈remember+동명사〉로 나타낸다.

06 분사는 형용사처럼 명사를 앞뒤에서 수식할 수 있으며, '자고 있는'이라는 능동의 의미이므로 현재분사 sleeping이 와야 한다.

07 ④는 보어 역할을 하는 동명사이며, 나머지는 현재분사이다.

08 ⑤는 현재분사, 나머지는 동사의 목적어 역할을 하는 동명사이다.

09 '선물을 가져가는 것을 기억해라(= 잊지 말아라)'라는 의미의 문장이 들어가야 하므로, 〈Remember+to부정사〉이거나 〈Don't forget+to부정사〉로 써야 한다.

10 〈stop+to부정사〉는 '~하기 위해 멈추다'라는 의미이고, 〈stop+동명사〉는 '~하는 것을 멈추다'라는 의미이다.

11 ⓐ coloring book(색칠하기 위한 책)은 용도의 의미로 쓰인 동명사, ⓑ 진행의 의미로 쓰인 현재분사, ⓒ 감정을 나타내는 과거분사, ⓓ 명사를 수식하는 현재분사, ⓔ 주어 역할을 하는 동명사이다.

12 '부서진'이라는 수동의 의미로 box를 수식하므로 과거분사 broken을 써야 한다. ② '얼린'이라는 수동의 의미로 yogurt를 수식하므로 과거분사 frozen을 써야 한다. ③ '~하고 있는' 의미로 the artist를 수식하므로 현재분사 painting을 써야 한다. ④ shine이 '빛나다'라는 의미로 쓰일 때는 수동태를 쓸 수 없는 자동사이므로 현재분사 shining을 써야 한다. ⑤ 수식하는 대상인 movie가 감정을 유발하는 주체이므로 현재분사 touching(감동적인)을 써야 한다.

13 동명사가 주어일 때는 3인칭 단수로 취급하므로 have를 has로 써야 한다.

14 (A) '~하려고 노력하다'는 〈try+to부정사〉이다. (B) 〈be busy -ing〉는 '~하느라 바쁘다'라는 동명사 관용표현으로 moving을 써야 한다. (C) 수식하는 대상인 you가 감정을 느끼는 객체이므로 과거분사 disappointed(실망한)를 써야 한다.

15 ⓒ shoes를 뒤에서 수식하는 형용사 역할의 분사 중 '만들어진' 객체이므로 수동을 의미하는 과거분사 made를 써야 한다.

16 the gloves를 뒤에서 수식하는 분사로서, 수동의 의미인 과거분사 made를 써야 한다.

17 동명사의 관용표현 〈have trouble -ing(~하는 데 어려움을 겪다)〉이다.

18 전치사 about의 목적어로 쓰인 동명사이다.

19 enjoy는 동명사를 목적어로 취하는 동사이다.

20 주어 역할을 하는 동명사이다.

21 〈forget+to부정사〉는 '~할 것을 잊다'라는 의미이다. 여기서는 Don't가 붙어 '숙제 끝내는 것을 잊지 말아라'라는 의미이므로 to finish를 써야 한다.

22 동명사가 주어일 때는 3인칭 단수로 취급하므로 are를 is로 써야 한다.

23 전치사 by의 목적어이므로 동명사를 써야 한다. 〈by -ing〉는 '~함으로써'의 의미이다.

24 '~해 봐야 소용없다'라는 의미는 〈It is no use+동명사〉로 나타낸다.

25 동명사의 관용표현 〈be used to -ing(~에 익숙하다)〉이다.

26 주격보어로 쓰인 동명사의 의문문이므로 〈Is+주어+동명사 ~?〉의 어순으로 써야 한다.

27 '~하기를 기대하다'라는 의미는 〈look forward to+동명사〉로 나타낸다.

28 '~하자마자'라는 의미는 on[upon] -ing로 나타낸다.

29 〈regret+to부정사〉는 '~하게 되어 유감이다'라는 의미이다.

30 '~하는 중이다'라는 의미로 현재진행형 am eating으로 써야 하며, 수식의 대상인 the grapes가 키워진 것이므로 수동의 의미인 과거분사 grown과 〈by+행위자〉로 by the farmer로 써야 한다.

CHAPTER
[06] 대명사, 형용사, 부사

Unit 05
p. 64

01 thinks herself   **04** filled themselves
02 fix / herself   **05** make / yourself
03 tell / yourself

Unit 06
p. 64

01 Help yourself to   **04** for himself
02 enjoy yourselves   **05** by yourself
03 in itself   **06** Make yourself at home

Unit 07
p. 65

01 something bad   **05** sweet things
02 anything special   **06** something important to say
03 something new
04 nothing good

Unit 08
p. 65

01 some[a few] books   **04** any problems
02 few mistakes   **05** many[a lot of] changes
03 little time

Unit 09
p. 66

01 very fast   **04** softly
02 too fast   **05** easily
03 Luckily   **06** early

Unit 10
p. 66

01 seldom arrives on time
02 often helped his brother
03 usually wears long skirts
04 always go to the mountains
05 hardly gets angry with us

중간고사 · 기말고사 실전문제
pp. 67~70

객관식 정답 [01~15]

01 ⑤	02 ③	03 ②	04 ⑤	05 ④
06 ①	07 ②	08 ②	09 ③	10 ②
11 ⑤	12 ③	13 ③	14 ④	15 ④

주관식 정답 [16~30]

16 He always thinks of other people's feelings.
17 Text messaging can sometimes be a convenient way of communication.
18 them
19 one
20 ones
21 They were beside themselves because of the news.
22 many
23 much
24 a few
25 a little
26 need → needs
27 many → much
28 It's very hot, and there's little water to drink.
29 There was nothing expensive to buy on the list.
30 He can seldom watch TV nowadays.

해설

01 부정대명사 one은 정해지지 않은 불특정한 사람이나 물건을 가리킨다. chillies가 복수이므로 ones로 써야 한다.

02 water는 셀 수 없는 명사이므로 '약간 있는'을 뜻하는 수량형용사 a little을 써야 한다.

03 '많은'이란 뜻의 lots of는 셀 수 있는 명사 strawberries를 꾸미는 수량형용사 many로 바꿔 쓸 수 있다.

04 첫 번째 빈칸은 불특정한 '몇몇'을 나타내므로 부정대명사 Some으로, 두 번째 빈칸은 나머지 사람들을 나타내므로 the others를 써야 한다.

05 첫 번째 빈칸은 셀 수 있는 명사인 places에 맞는 수량형용사를 써야 하므로 many, few, a few가 올 수 있다. 두 번째 빈칸은 '거의 ~않다'라는 뜻의 hardly를 써야 한다.

06 주어진 문장과 ①은 재귀대명사의 강조적 용법이며, ②, ③, ④, ⑤는 재귀적 용법이다.

07 재귀대명사의 관용표현 중 '혼잣말하다'라는 뜻의 talk to oneself이다.

08 ②는 명사를 수식하는 형용사이며, 나머지는 부사이다.

09 he의 재귀대명사는 himself이다.

10 '약간(의), 몇몇(의)'를 의미하는 단어 중 긍정문에 쓰이는 some을 써야 한다.

11 '다른 하나, 하나 더'라는 의미의 another를 써야 한다. ① '다른'의 의미로 people을 꾸미는 형용사인 other를 써야 한다. others는 '다른 사람들'이다. ② 앞에서 언급한 동일한 명사를 가리킬 때 '(동일한 바로) 그것'의 의미의 대명사 it을 써야 한다. ③ 부정대명사 each는 항상 단수로 취급하므로 '모든'을 나타내는 all을 써야 한다. ④ '다른 사람들'을 뜻하는 others를 써야 한다.

12 ⓒ 셀 수 있는 명사 day에는 a few를 써야 한다. ⓓ 빈도부사(often)는 조동사나 be동사 뒤, 일반동사 앞에 써야 한다.

13 ⓐ 부사 '진심으로', ⓑ 형용사 '충분한', ⓒ 부사 '늦게', ⓓ 형용사 '사랑스러운', ⓔ 부사 '일찍', ⓕ 형용사 '열심히'의 의미로, 부사는 형용사, 다른 부사, 문장 전체, 동사를 수식할 수 있지만, 형용사처럼 명사는 수식할 수 없다.

14 (A)는 '~을 마음껏 먹다'라는 의미의 재귀대명사 관용표현 help oneself to, (B)는 여러 개의 sandwiches 중 정해지지 않은 불특정 한 개의 sandwich이므로 one, (C)는 권유나 요청의 의문문에 사용할 수 있는 some을 써야 한다.

15 '열심히'라는 의미의 부사는 hard이고, hardly는 '거의 ~ 않다'를 뜻한다.

16 빈도부사(always)는 be동사나 조동사 뒤에, 일반동사 앞에 써야 한다.

17 빈도부사(sometimes)는 be동사나 조동사 뒤에, 일반동사 앞에 써야 한다.

18 앞에 언급한 wooden toys를 가리키는 대명사 them을 써야 한다.

19 불특정한 물건을 가리키므로 one을 써야 한다.

20 shoes는 복수명사이고, 불특정한 물건을 나타내므로 ones를 써야 한다.

21 '제정신이 아닌'이라는 뜻의 재귀대명사 관용표현은 beside oneself이다.

22 부사 so(너무)가 앞에 있으므로 '많은'이라는 의미를 써야 하고, 셀 수 있는 명사 bird가 있으므로 수량형용사 many가 알맞다.

23 셀 수 없는 명사 money에는 의문문에 자주 쓰이는 수량형용사 much를 써야 한다.

24 부사 only(겨우)가 앞에 있으므로 '약간의, 조금의'라는

의미를 써야 하고, 셀 수 있는 명사 student가 있으므로 수량형용사 a few가 알맞다.

25 셀 수 없는 명사 salt에는 '조금의, 약간의' 의미인 수량형용사 a little을 써야 한다.

26 every는 '모든'이라는 의미의 형용사로 뒤에는 셀 수 있는 명사의 단수형과 단수동사가 온다.

27 셀 수 없는 명사 sugar에는 수량형용사 much를 써야 한다.

28 '거의 없는'이라는 의미의 셀 수 없는 명사 water를 꾸미는 수량형용사로 little이 알맞다.

29 nothing처럼 -thing으로 끝나는 대명사를 수식할 때는 형용사가 뒤에 온다.

30 빈도부사(seldom)는 be동사나 조동사 뒤에, 일반동사 앞에 써야 한다.

CHAPTER 07 비교 표현

Unit 01 p. 72

01 is as heavy as
02 is as hot as
03 do not[don't] enjoy / as[so] much as
04 get up as[so] early as
05 be as tall as
06 not taste as[so] good as

Unit 02 p. 72

01 as deep as possible
02 as quietly as you can
03 as fast as possible
04 as often as they could
05 as little as possible
06 as close as you can

Unit 03 p. 73

01 angrier – angriest
02 worse – worst
03 more beautiful – most beautiful
04 bigger – biggest
05 more boring – most boring
06 busier – busiest

07 more careful – most careful

08 more dangerous – most dangerous

09 more diligent – most diligent

10 dirtier – dirtiest

11 easier – easiest

12 more easily – most easily

13 fatter – fattest

14 friendlier – friendliest

15 better – best

16 heavier – heaviest

17 hotter – hottest

18 worse – worst

19 lazier – laziest

20 lighter – lightest

21 less – least

22 lovelier – loveliest

23 more – most

24 prettier – prettiest

25 more quickly – most quickly

26 sadder – saddest

27 sunnier – sunniest

28 tastier – tastiest

29 better – best

Unit 04   p. 74

01 looks healthier than   **04** a lot heavier than

02 far cheaper than   **05** feel better than

03 more valuable than   **06** stronger than

Unit 05   p. 74

01 three times as long   **04** nine times as expensive

02 five times lighter   **05** six times as big

03 three times longer   **06** four times more

Unit 06   p. 75

01 The more often / the healthier

02 The more / the more

03 The busier / the less relaxed

04 The more crowded / the louder

05 The more / the more

Unit 07   p. 75

01 one of the most famous models

02 the best student

03 One of the most popular jobs

04 He works the hardest

05 the happiest day of the year

Unit 08   p. 76

01 Figure skating attracted

02 person can dance better

03 is greater than any

04 pet is beloved as much

05 No other food is as delicious

06 No other sport in Brazil is as popular

Unit 09   p. 76

01 as hot as

02 softer than hers

03 the greatest artist

04 as carefully as possible

05 the most expensive in this store

06 are more convenient than

중간고사 • 기말고사 실전문제   pp. 77~80

객관식 정답 [01~15]

01 ③	**02** ⑤	**03** ④	**04** ③	**05** ④
06 ③	**07** ①	**08** ④	**09** ③	**10** ②
11 ②	**12** ④	**13** ②	**14** ④	**15** ③

주관식 정답 [16~30]

16 worst

17 exciting

18 older / older

19 The longer / the more excited

20 as quickly as possible

21 as

22 more

23 far

24 He received three times as many medals as me.

25 more → much

26 most tasty → tastiest

27 Mike → Mike's

28 Jack is much more famous than any other artist in Europe.

29 Mina and I are twins, but she is not as[so] healthy as me.

30 His store is even nosier than other stores.

해설

01 〈as+형용사/부사의 원급+as〉 형태이므로 원급인 fast를 써야 한다.

02 the 뒤에는 최상급 표현이 와야 하므로 oldest로 써야 한다.

03 '밝은'을 뜻하는 bright의 비교급 변화표는 bright - brighter - brightest이다.

04 '훨씬 더'라는 의미로 비교급을 강조할 때 very는 쓸 수 없다.

05 〈the+비교급+주어+동사 ~, the+비교급+주어+동사 …〉 형태이므로 The more ~, the richer …가 와야 한다.

06 '점점 더 ~핸[하게]'는 〈비교급+and+비교급〉으로 표현한다.

07 주어진 문장은 'this watermelon이 that melon보다 크다'이므로 ①의 'that melon이 this watermelon보다 작다'가 같은 의미이다.

08 ①, ②, ③, ⑤는 Ivan이 가장 똑똑하다는 의미의 문장이며, ④가 같은 의미가 되려면 isn't를 is로 바꿔야 한다.

09 '훨씬 더'라는 의미로 비교급을 강조할 때 still을 쓸 수 있다. ① 원급이 아닌 비교급 quieter를 써야 하고, ② as 대신 than을 써야 하며, ④ a lot은 비교급을 강조할 때 사용하므로 삭제, ⑤ 최상급 표현 앞에 the를 붙여야 한다.

10 '가장 ~한 것들 중 하나'라는 표현은 〈one of the+최상급+복수명사〉이므로 girls로 써야 한다.

11 ⓐ 소유격으로 쓴 앞의 비교 대상에 호응하여 소유격인 uncle's를 써야 하며, ⓑ 〈the+비교급+주어+동사 ~, the+비교급+주어+동사 …〉 어순이 되어야 하므로 the more medals ~, the more famous …로 써야 한다. ⓒ '~만큼 …하지 못하는'이라는 원급 비교 표현의 부정문은 〈not as[so] ~ as〉이므로 is not as로 써야 한다.

12 ⓑ even은 비교급을 강조할 때 사용하므로 very를 쓰거나 삭제해야 하며, ⓒ 소유격으로 쓴 앞의 비교 대상 your hair에 호응하여 소유대명사 mine으로, ⓓ 〈one of the+최상급+복수명사〉이므로 the bravest로 써야 한다.

13 빈칸 (A)와 (B)는 반대 내용(크면 더 작은 사이즈를, 작으면 더 큰 사이즈를 찾음)이 나와야 하고, 빈칸 (C)는 (B)와 상통하는 내용이 나와야 하므로 large - smaller - smallest가 정답이다.

14 ① pencil은 eraser보다 비싸므로 more expensive, ② color pen은 notebook보다 저렴하므로 cheaper로 써야 한다. ③ 가장 싼 것은 pencil이 아닌 eraser이며, ⑤ 사이즈는 내용과 무관하다.

15 문장들을 종합해 무게 순으로 나열하면 Tom = Sam 〉 Sophie 〉 Jina와 같다.

16 the 뒤에는 bad의 최상급 worst가 와야 한다.

17 〈as+형용사/부사의 원급+as〉이므로 원급을 써야 한다.

18 '점점 더 ~핸[하게]'는 〈비교급+and+비교급〉으로 표현한다.

19 '~하면 할수록 더 …하다'는 〈the+비교급+주어+동사 ~, the+비교급+주어+동사 …〉로 표현한다.

20 〈as+형용사/부사+as+주어+can[could]〉는 〈as+형용사/부사+as+possible〉로 바꾸어 쓸 수 있다.

21 〈as+형용사/부사의 원급+as〉이므로 as를 써야 한다.

22 뒤에 than이 나왔으므로 much의 비교급 more을 써야 한다.

23 '훨씬 더'라는 의미로 비교급을 강조하는 far를 써야 한다.

24 배수사 비교 중 〈배수사+as+원급+as〉 형태이다.

25 〈as+형용사/부사의 원급+as〉이므로 원급인 much를 써야 한다.

26 tasty의 최상급은 tastiest이다.

27 소유격으로 쓴 앞의 비교 대상 My textbook에 호응하여 소유격인 Mike's를 써야 한다.

28 famous의 비교급은 more famous이다.

29 '~만큼 …하지 못하는'이라는 원급 비교 표현의 부정형인 〈not as[so] ~ as〉로 써야 한다.

30 noisy의 비교급은 noisier이고, '훨씬 더'라는 의미로 비교급을 강조할 때 even을 쓸 수 있다.

CHAPTER 08 의문사 의문문

07 What fresh air it is!
08 How interesting her story is!

중간고사 • 기말고사 실전문제   pp. 85~88

객관식 정답 [01~15]

01 ③	**02** ⑤	**03** ④	**04** ③	**05** ②
06 ④	**07** ②	**08** ①	**09** ①, ③	**10** ④
11 ①	**12** ④	**13** ⑤	**14** ③	**15** ②

주관식 정답 [16~30]

16 was
17 will / visit
18 How
19 What
20 Why
21 When
22 Which one is his wife, Mary or Susan?
23 How come
24 What
25 How
26 came → come
27 quiet → quietly
28 How many tables did he make last Friday?
29 Who saved your life from the accident?
30 How come you like the book so much?

해설

01 목적지가 Paris로 언급되었으므로 Where는 오답이며, 언제 갈 것이냐는 When이 알맞다.

02 an exciting summer vacation을 강조하는 감탄문이므로 What이 들어가야 한다.

03 질문의 답이 될 만한 대상 가운데 한 가지를 선택하여 '어떤 것, 어느 쪽'을 물을 때는 Which를 사용한다. '어떻게 ~하는지, ~하는 법'은 〈how+to부정사〉로 써야 한다.

04 첫 번째 문장에는 '무엇'을 묻는 의문사 What, 두 번째 문장에는 '얼마나 ~한[하게]'이라고 묻는 〈how+형용사/부사〉를 쓰므로 How가 알맞다.

05 첫 번째 문장과 두 번째 문장 모두 '누가'라는 의미가 나와야 하므로 Who를 써야 한다.

06 '어떤 종류의 ~을 …하니?'는 〈What kind of+명사+do+주어+동사원형 ~?〉으로 표현한다.

07 질문의 답이 될 만한 대상 가운데 한 가지를 선택하여 '어떤 것, 어느 쪽'을 물을 때는 Which를 사용한다.

08 감탄문에서 〈형용사+명사+주어+동사〉의 어순일 때는 What을 쓰며, 나머지는 How를 써야 한다.

09 ② What이 아닌 How를 써야 한다. ④ 주어가 the smallest animal이므로 is를 써야 한다. ⑤ be동사가 들어간 의문사 의문문은 〈의문사+be동사+주어 ~?〉로 써야 한다.

10 When이나 What time이 되어야 한다.

11 선택에 관한 질문에 대해 '나는 종종 극장에 혼자 간다.'라고 응답하는 것은 어색하다.

12 ⓓ '~ 가는 데 얼마나 걸리니?'라는 의미의 How long does it take to ~?로 써야 한다.

13 ⓐ Which로 물을 때 뒤의 선택지는 or로 연결해야 한다. ⓑ '얼마나 ~한[하게]'이라고 물을 경우 〈How+형용사/부사+동사+주어 ~?〉 형태이므로 won과 시제를 일치시켜 How old was Brian으로 써야 한다. ⓒ do를 삭제해야 한다. ⓓ 동사 carry를 수식하는 부사 형태인 carefully로 써야 한다.

14 '왜'라는 의미의 의문사 Why를 써야 하며, 나머지는 '무엇'을 의미하는 What을 써야 한다.

15 (A) '무슨 일을 하십니까?. 직업이 무엇입니까?'를 물을 때는 What do you do?로 쓴다. (B) 〈What+a/an+형용사+명사(+주어+동사)!〉의 감탄문 어순이다. (C) 뒤에 나오는 대답이 이유를 설명하므로 '왜'를 의미하는 Why를 써야 한다.

16 yesterday와 3인칭 단수 주어에 맞춰 was를 써야 한다.

17 조동사가 있는 의문문의 경우 〈의문사+조동사+주어+동사원형 ~?〉으로 써야 한다.

18 '얼마나 ~한[하게]'이라고 물을 때는 〈How+형용사/부사+동사+주어 ~?〉이다.

19 '무엇을 도와드릴까요?'는 What can I do for you?라고 표현한다.

20 '왜'라는 의미의 의문사 Why를 써야 한다.

21 '언제'를 의미하는 의문사 When을 써야 한다.

22 질문의 답이 될 만한 대상 가운데 한 가지를 선택하여 '어떤 것, 어느 쪽'을 물을 때는 Which를 사용한다.

23 '도대체 왜 ~?. 어째서 ~?'라고 물을 때는 How come을 사용할 수 있으며, 〈How come+주어+동사 ~?〉의 어순으로 써야 한다.

24 감탄문 중 〈형용사+명사+주어+동사!〉의 어순일 때는 What을 써야 한다.

25 감탄문 중 〈형용사+주어+동사!〉의 어순일 때는 How를 써야 한다.

26 일반동사의 의문사 의문문은 〈의문사+do/does/did+주어+동사원형 ~?〉의 어순으로 써야 한다.

27 동사 move를 수식하는 부사 quietly로 써야 한다.

28 tables는 셀 수 있는 명사이므로 many를 써야 한다.

29 누구인지를 묻는 의문문이 되어야 하므로 who를 써서 〈의문사(Who)+동사+주어 ~?〉의 어순으로 써야 한다.

30 〈How come+주어+동사 ~?〉의 어순으로 써야 한다.

Unit 04
p. 91

01 watched a horror movie

02 bought us new shoes

03 cooks us chicken soup

04 find me my backpack

05 made me a sweater and gloves

Unit 05
p. 92

01 I will get a taxi for you.

02 You can give the rabbits carrots.

03 She told a funny fairy tale to us.

04 Will you buy a new bag for me?

05 Emily sent her parents a card.

06 Could you find me my book?

Unit 06
p. 92

01 made her the best ballerina

02 keep the doors open

03 made her a world-famous singer

04 considers himself very lucky

05 found the tennis class too hard

06 keep this room cool

Unit 07
p. 93

01 expects me to finish

02 advised them to exercise

03 asked Emma to open

04 told Noah to bring

Unit 08
p. 93

01 Leo smelled some clothes burning.

02 They felt the ground shaking and moving.

03 I heard you and Tommy talking about me.

04 Julie watched her daughter playing with dolls.

Unit 09
p. 94

01 made us stand

02 makes me get up

03 let her dog bark

04 asked / to close

05 made us cry

06 let Lily give

Unit 10
p. 94

01 helped me (to) keep

02 got us to stop

03 Help me (to) find

04 got the radio fixed

05 got everyone to leave

06 helped him (to) get up

Unit 11
p. 95

01 help me (to) prepare

02 advised Luke to drink

03 helped / (to) pull

04 let you come back

05 made him a good leader

06 tells me to behave

중간고사 • 기말고사 실전문제
pp. 96~99

객관식 정답 [01~15]

01 ⑤	02 ②	03 ④	04 ④	05 ②
06 ②	07 ③	08 ①	09 ⑤	10 ①, ④
11 ②	12 ②	13 ④	14 ③	15 ②, ⑤

주관식 정답 [16~30]

16 to enter

17 keep

18 ⓓ

19 ⓒ

20 ⓓ

21 ⓔ

22 The guard keeps the president safe.

23 Let me show you the real masterpiece of Van Gogh.

24 shocked → shocking

25 happiness → happy

26 told me to stand in line

27 made Tom move the boxes

28 It tastes like the strawberry cake made by my grandmother.

29 He lent his special edition of Avatar to me.

30 Do not let the kids stay up late at night.

해설

01 맛을 나타내는 형용사를 써야 한다. ①, ②는 명사, ③은 크기를 나타내는 형용사, ④는 부사이다.

02 ask는 to부정사가 목적적보어로 오는 5형식 동사이다.

03 사역동사 let은 원형부정사가 목적격보어로 와야 한다.

04 사역동사 have는 원형부정사가 목적격보어로 와야 한다.

05 첫 번째 문장에는 형용사 sad를 목적격보어로 가지는 5형식 동사 make. 두 번째 문장에는 원형부정사 turn을 목적격보어로 가지는 사역동사 make를 써야 한다.

06 첫 번째 문장의 keep은 형용사나 명사를 목적격보어로 가지는 5형식 동사이기 때문에, 빈칸에 형용사가 와야 한다. 두 번째 문장의 turn은 2형식 동사이고 주격보어로 형용사나 명사를 써야 하므로 두 문장의 문맥상 공통의 의미인 warm을 써야 한다.

07 find는 think와 같은 뜻으로 형용사나 명사를 목적격보어(여기서는 handsome)로 가지는 5형식 동사이다.

08 ①은 1형식이고, 나머지는 2형식이다.

09 사역동사 make는 원형부정사가 목적격보어로 와야 한다. ① 2형식 감각동사의 보어는 형용사만 쓸 수 있으므로 creamy로 쓴다. ② ask는 to부정사가 목적적보어로 오는 5형식 동사이다. ③ 감정을 느끼는 객체이므로 과거분사 bored로 쓴다. ④ 4형식 수여동사 give는 3형식으로 바꿀 때 간접목적어 앞에 전치사 to를 쓴다.

10 ① like 뒤에는 명사가 와야 하는데 nutty는 형용사이므로 like를 삭제하고, ④ 4형식 수여동사 show는 3형식으로 바꿀 때 간접목적어 앞에 전치사 to를 쓴다.

11 2형식 감각동사의 보어는 형용사만 쓸 수 있으므로 ⓑ는 soft, ⓒ는 crazy, ⓓ는 peaceful로 써야 한다.

12 ⓑ 2형식 문장의 주격보어는 형용사나 명사만 쓸 수 있으므로 nervous로 써야 한다.

13 (A) 4형식 수여동사 bring은 3형식으로 바꿀 때 간접목적어 앞에 전치사 to를 쓴다. (B) 2형식 감각동사의 보어는 형용사만 쓸 수 있다. (C) 4형식 수여동사 pass는 3형식으로 바꿀 때 간접목적어 앞에 전치사 to를 쓴다.

14 주어진 문장은 5형식으로 to부정사가 목적격보어로 오는 경우이다. ①은 2형식으로 〈get+보어(~해지다, ~하다)〉, ②, ⑤는 3형식으로 〈get+목적어(~을 얻다)〉, ③은 5형식으로 〈get+목적어+목적격보어(to부정사)(목적어가 ~하게 하다)〉, ④는 4형식으로 〈get+간접목적어+직접목적어(간접목적어에게 직접목적어를 얻어주다)〉이다.

15 ⓑ, ⓔ 2형식 감각동사 feel의 보어로 형용사가 와야 한다.

16 allow는 to부정사가 목적격보어로 오는 5형식 동사이다.

17 사역동사 have는 원형부정사가 목적격보어로 온다.

18 2형식 문장의 주어를 설명하는 보어이다.

19 4형식 수여동사 offer의 간접목적어이다.

20 5형식 사역동사 have의 목적격보어이다.

21 '~ 하기 위해서'를 의미하는 to부정사의 부사적 용법이며, 부사는 수식어이다.

22 keep은 형용사나 명사를 목적격보어로 가지는 5형식 동사이다.

23 show는 4형식 수여동사로 〈주어+동사+간접목적어+직접목적어〉의 어순으로 쓴다.

24 감정을 느끼게 하는 주체인 경우 수식하는 형용사는 현재분사로 써야 한다.

25 5형식 동사 make의 목적격보어로 명사 happiness(행복)는 사람이 될 수 없는 것이므로 형용사 happy(행복한)로 써야 한다.

26 〈tell+목적어+목적격보어〉로 이때 목적격보어는 to부정사를 써야 한다.

27 사역동사 make는 목적격보어로 원형부정사를 쓴다.

28 2형식 감각동사 뒤에 명사를 써서 '~처럼'의 뜻으로 쓸 경우 〈감각동사+like+명사〉로 써야 한다.

29 4형식 수여동사 lend를 3형식으로 바꿀 때는 〈주어+lend+직접목적어+to+간접목적어〉로 써야 한다.

30 사역동사 let은 원형부정사가 목적격보어로 와야 한다.

CHAPTER 10 접속사

Unit 01   p. 102

01 or   **04** and
02 but   **05** but
03 or   **06** and

Unit 02
p. 102

01 kind as well as pretty[not only pretty but (also) kind]

02 not today but tomorrow

03 either with a pen or with a pencil

04 Girls as well as boys

05 Both John and Stella

06 Not only exercising but (also) eating lightly

Unit 03
p. 103

01 as we rode bikes

02 before you eat them

03 when you feel lonely and sad

04 until the water boils

05 While she was cleaning the room

Unit 04
p. 103

01 if you feel hot

02 unless you try hard

03 unless you feel good

04 if you eat fast food every day

05 unless they are expensive

06 if we start it right now

Unit 05
p. 104

01 or you cannot get there on time

02 and you can have a lot of friends

03 or you will get up late tomorrow morning

04 and we will have a good time together

05 or you will get wet

Unit 06
p. 104

01 because[as/since] it was too expensive

02 so we did not[didn't] go on a picnic

03 since they got dirty

04 because of today's test

05 because he was so busy with work

06 so he missed the school bus

Unit 07
p. 105

01 so that I could achieve my goal

02 so busy that she could not[couldn't] come here

03 so that she could cook soup for us

04 so that he could get some advice

05 so expensive that I could not[couldn't] buy it

Unit 08
p. 105

01 Though[Although/Even though] Jennie felt so shy

02 Though[Although/Even though] the car is so expensive

03 Though[Although/Even though] my grandma is very old

04 Though[Although/Even though] her house is far from the school

05 Though[Although/Even though] it was late at night

06 Though[Although/Even though] Henry is short

Unit 09
p. 106

A

01 that I don't remember her face

02 That we should exercise regularly

03 (that) I should get up early tomorrow

04 that Gianna couldn't speak any French

05 It is certain that she is still alive

06 (that) James could recover soon

07 that they did their best

08 It is true that

B

01 That you still remember my name is

02 is that Lucas won the game

03 (that) she has become a famous singer

04 It is exciting that we will go to

Unit 10
p. 107

01 but he did not[didn't] go to bed early

02 until her mom came back to her

03 when he was young

04 or stay at home today

05 speak both English and German

06 after he finishes his homework

07 either pizza or mushroom soup for lunch

08 so weak that she often got ill

객관식 정답 [01~15]

01 ⑤	**02** ②	**03** ①, ③	**04** ④	**05** ①
06 ④	**07** ②	**08** ③	**09** ⑤	**10** ⑤
11 ③	**12** ③	**13** ②	**14** ⑤	**15** ④

주관식 정답 [16~30]

16 but / hates

17 Either / or

18 Both / and

19 neither / nor

20 ⓒ

21 ⓐ

22 ⓑ

23 After

24 until

25 while

26 Even though the painting was expensive, it was worth buying. 또는 The painting was worth buying even though it was expensive.

27 to go → going

28 if → unless

29 She has known him since she was young.

30 I want to go not to Japan but to Vietnam.

해설

01 '또는, ~이거나'라는 의미의 or가 알맞다.

02 '~하는 동안'이라는 의미의 While이 알맞다.

03 '비록 ~이지만, 비록 ~일지라도'라는 양보의 표현으로 접속사 though, although, even though를 쓴다.

04 첫 번째 문장은 '~하지 않는다면'이라는 의미의 unless, 두 번째 문장은 '~해라, 그렇지 않으면 …할 것이다'라는 의미의 〈명령문, or ~〉이다.

05 첫 번째 문장은 '~ 때문에'라는 의미의 As, 두 번째 문장은 '가능한 한 빠르게'라는 의미의 as soon as possible이다.

06 'A, B 둘 중 하나'라는 의미의 〈either A or B〉로 나타내며, 주어로 쓰일 때 동사는 B에 일치시킨다.

07 주어진 문장과 ②의 that은 목적어로 쓰인 that절이다. ①은 보어로 쓰인 that절, ③은 진주어 that절, ④, ⑤는 '저, 그'라는 의미인 지시형용사이다.

08 주어진 문장의 동사가 cleans이므로 3인칭 단수 주어가 나와야 하는데, 상관접속사로 연결된 말이 주어로 오면, 〈either A or B〉, 〈neither A nor B〉, 〈not A but B〉, 〈not only A but (also) B〉, 〈B as well as A〉는 동사를 모두 B에 일치시키지만, 〈both A and B〉는 복수 취급한다.

09 ⑤는 '~할 때'라는 의미의 as이고, 나머지는 '~ 때문에'라는 의미의 as이다.

10 '~하기 전에'라는 의미의 before를 알맞게 사용했다. ① (동)명사 앞에는 because가 아닌 because of를 써야 한다. ② '~하지 않는다면'의 unless가 아닌 '~한다면'의 if를 쓰거나 unless를 쓴다면 주절에 can't를 써야 한다. ③ until이 아닌 when이나 before를 써야 한다. ④ '너무[매우] ~해서 …하다'는 〈so+형용사/부사+that ~〉이고, 〈so that ~〉은 '~하도록, ~하기 위해서'이다.

11 〈both A and B〉가 주어로 오면 '둘 다 모두'라는 의미로 복수 취급하므로 동사는 make로 써야 한다.

12 ⓐ as 대신 although, though, even though를 써야 한다. ⓑ 조건을 나타내는 if절은 현재시제가 미래시제를 대신하므로 will rain이 아닌 rains가 알맞다.

13 ⓒ 조건을 나타내는 if절은 현재시제가 미래시제를 대신하므로 will을 쓰면 안 된다.

14 ⑤ 〈not only A but (also) B〉는 〈B as well as A〉로 바꿔 쓸 수 있으므로 Amy as well as Jane으로 써야 한다.

15 ⓐ '~한 후에'를 의미하는 시간의 부사절 접속사 after, ⓑ 목적어로 쓰이는 명사절 접속사 that, ⓒ, ⓓ, ① '~ 때문에'를 의미하는 원인의 부사절 접속사 as/because/since, ⓔ '~할 때'를 의미하는 시간의 부사절 접속사 when이다.

16 '~이지만'을 의미하는 접속사 but을 써야 한다.

17 동사가 3인칭 단수의 형태이므로 〈either A or B(A, B 둘 중 하나)〉를 써야 한다.

18 동사가 1, 2인칭 혹은 3인칭 복수의 형태이므로 복수를 의미하는 〈both A and B(A와 B 둘 다)〉를 써야 한다.

19 '인기, 돈, 건강 3가지 중 건강이 가장 중요하고, 나머지는 건강보다 더 중요하지 않다'는 의미이므로 〈neither A nor B(A, B 둘 다 아닌)〉를 써야 한다.

20 동사 know의 목적어로 쓰인 명사절 접속사 that이다.

21 가주어 it의 진주어 that절이다.

22 보어로 쓰인 명사절 접속사 that이다.

23 '~한 후에'라는 의미의 After를 써야 한다.

24 '~할 때까지'라는 의미의 until을 써야 한다.

25 '~하는 동안'이라는 의미의 while을 써야 한다.

26 '비록 ~이지만, 비록 ~일지라도'라는 양보의 표현으로 접속사 though, although, even though를 쓴다.

27 〈both A and B〉에서 A와 B의 형태는 같아야 하며 enjoy의 목적어로는 동명사가 와야 하므로 going을 써야 한다.

28 '~하지 않는다면'을 뜻하는 unless를 써야 한다.

29 '~부터'라는 의미일 때는 since와 as를 바꿔 쓸 수 없으므로 since로 써야 한다.

30 'A가 아니라 B'라는 의미의 〈not A but B〉로 나타낸다.

CHAPTER

11 분사구문

■ 중간고사 • 기말고사 실전문제   pp. 117~120

객관식 정답 [01~15]

01 ②	**02** ④	**03** ③	**04** ①	**05** ⑤
06 ①	**07** ⑤	**08** ①	**09** ③	**10** ④
11 ⑤	**12** ②	**13** ③	**14** ④	**15** ⑤

주관식 정답 [16~30]

16 bought   **17** loved   **18** Going

19 Seeing his mother, the baby started crying.

20 Not having any eggs, I went to the grocery store.

21 Because[As/Since] I did not[didn't] know his address

22 After we jogged in the park

23 confusing → confused

24 To become → Becoming

25 Took → Taking

26 Although (being) old, my grandfather is very healthy.

27 Closing her eyes, Lucy remembered visiting Disneyland.

28 Exercising regularly, you will become healthier.

29 I found the oranges picked by my mom.

30 Being hungry, he ate the leftover pizza made by me.

해설

01 감정을 유발하는 주체가 주어인 경우, 현재분사를 쓴다.

02 분사구문은 〈접속사+주어+동사〉를 분사 형태로 바꾼 것으로, 능동의 의미인 현재분사 Knowing을 써야 한다.

03 첫 번째 문장은 지각동사 watch의 목적격보어인 현재분사 running, 두 번째 문장은 start의 목적어로 쓰인 동명사 running을 써야 한다.

04 첫 번째 문장은 '네 이름이 불린 것'이므로 수동의 의미를 갖는 과거분사 called, 두 번째 문장은 '적에게 공격을 당한'이라는 수동의 의미이므로 과거분사 attacked가 알맞다.

05 첫 번째 문장은 분사구문 문장으로 부정문의 경우, 분사 앞에 not을 붙여야 한다. 두 번째 문장은 현재완료형으로 〈have+과거분사〉의 형태로 써야 한다.

06 부사절 While I was taking a shower를 분사구문으로 바꾼 것이다.

07 분사구문은 〈접속사+주어+동사〉를 분사 형태로 바꾼 것으로, 의미를 분명히 하기 위해 접속사를 생략하지 않고 쓰기도 한다.

08 ①은 동명사이고, 나머지는 분사이다.

09 Being이 생략된 분사구문으로, 태어난 것은 과거분사 born을 쓴다. ① 2형식 감각동사 뒤에 명사가 오면 〈감각동사+like+명사(~처럼)〉 형태로 써야 한다. ② 〈be

worried about ~(~에 대해 걱정하다)〉은 수동태 문장이므로 worried로 쓴다. ④ 부사절 Because I was tired를 분사구문으로 바꾸면 (Being) tired가 되어야 한다. ⑤ '이벤트가 열리는'의 수동의 의미이므로 과거분사 held를 써야 한다.

10 〈feel like+동명사(~하고 싶다)〉 구문으로 주어인 he가 느낀 것이므로 Feeling으로 써야 한다.

11 '~ 때문에'라는 의미의 because/since/as를 써야 한다.

12 ⓐ Though not being pretty가 되어야 한다. ⓒ 주어인 I가 아는 것이므로 능동의 의미인 현재분사 knowing, ⓓ 지각동사 hear의 목적격보어는 현재분사 혹은 원형부정사를 써야 한다.

13 부사절이 부정문인 경우, 분사구문의 분사 앞에 not이나 never를 써야 한다. ① 동시동작의 분사구문이고, 능동이므로 watching, ② 동시동작의 분사구문이고, 능동이므로 현재분사 Taking, ④ 의미상 접속사는 After나 While이 들어가야 한다. ⑤ 동시동작의 분사구문이고, 능동이므로 현재분사 Riding을 써야 한다.

14 ⓐ 수동의 의미인 made, ⓒ you가 감정을 느끼는 주체이므로 과거분사 disappointed, ⓓ 주어 He가 감정을 느끼는 주체이므로 과거분사 surprised를 써야 한다.

15 (A) 선물과 분사의 관계가 수동이므로 과거분사 sent, (B) 목적어인 조각과 목적격보어의 관계가 수동이므로 과거분사 carved, (C) resemble은 수동태로 쓰지 않는 동사로 주어가 it이므로 resembles를 써야 한다.

16 a book을 꾸미는 분사와의 관계가 수동이므로 과거분사 bought를 써야 한다.

17 주어와 보어의 관계가 수동이므로 과거분사 loved를 써야 한다.

18 분사구문은 〈접속사+주어+동사〉를 분사 형태로 바꾼 것으로, 능동의 의미인 현재분사 Going을 써야 한다.

19 분사구문은 〈접속사+주어+동사〉를 분사 형태로 바꾼 것으로, 능동의 의미인 현재분사 Seeing을 써야 한다.

20 분사구문은 〈접속사+주어+동사〉를 분사 형태로 바꾼 것으로, 부사절이 부정문인 경우, 분사구문의 분사 앞에 Not이나 Never를 써야 한다.

21 분사구문은 〈접속사+주어+동사〉로 쓸 수 있으며 이유를 나타내므로 Because/As/Since를 써 준다.

22 분사구문은 〈접속사+주어+동사〉로 쓸 수 있으며 '~한 후에'를 뜻하는 접속사 After를 써 준다.

23 주어가 감정을 느끼는 주체이므로 과거분사 confused로 써야 한다.

24 분사구문은 〈접속사+주어+동사〉를 분사 형태로 바꾼 것으로, 능동의 의미인 현재분사 Becoming을 써야 한다.

25 분사구문은 〈접속사+주어+동사〉를 분사 형태로 바꾼 것으로, 능동의 의미인 현재분사 Taking을 써야 한다.

26 분사구문으로 바꿀 때 be동사는 being으로 써 주되, 양보를 나타내는 분사구문은 의미를 명확히 하기 위해 접속사를 생략하지 않고 쓰는 경우가 많다.

27 주어인 Lucy가 눈을 감는 것이므로 능동의 의미인 현재분사 Closing을 써야 한다.

28 조건을 나타내는 분사구문으로 능동의 의미인 현재분사 Exercising을 써야 한다.

29 목적어와 목적격보어의 관계가 수동이므로 과거분사 picked를 써야 한다.

30 분사구문은 〈접속사+주어+동사〉를 분사 형태로 바꾼 것으로, be동사는 Being으로 써 주되, 생략이 가능하지만, 조건에 따라 Being을 써야 한다.

[CHAPTER 12 관계사]

Unit 08 p. 125

01 the picture you painted during class

02 those children playing baseball

03 this sign written in Japanese

04 the letter you wrote to me

05 The boy drinking a milkshake

06 The person I respect the most

Unit 09 p. 126

01 What Sophia wants to be

02 that Mike wants to buy

03 what we heard

04 what he wanted to say

05 that I must do

06 what you learned today

Unit 10 p. 126

01 when we give some presents

02 where she could stay for one day

03 (the place) where the car accident happened

04 (the day) when we are going on a picnic

05 where you can enjoy a lot of water activities

06 when my family and I are planning to go to the amusement park

Unit 11 p. 127

01 why you had a fight with Tim

02 the way[how] the chef cooks the noodles

03 (the day) when we are going to

04 the way[how] you fix this TV

05 why you were late for class

06 why she decided to become a vet

중간고사 · 기말고사 실전문제 pp. 128~131

객관식 정답 [01~15]

01 ④	**02** ⑤	**03** ①, ③, ⑤	**04** ①
05 ③	**06** ②	**07** ③	**08** ②	**09** ⑤
10 ⑤	**11** ④	**12** ③	**13** ④	**14** ③
15 ⑤			

주관식 정답 [16~30]

16 who[that] watch

17 what / made

18 ⓐ

19 ⓒ

20 ⓑ

21 where

22 why

23 how

24 I can understand what Mr. Brown taught.

25 I'm satisfied with my room which[that] I painted yesterday.

26 why → which 또는 for 삭제

27 what → that

28 They work in the building which has a cafeteria on the first floor.

29 She likes the boy who(m)[that] she met at the summer camp.

30 My grandmother's home is where I feel the most relaxed.

해설

01 선행사가 사물(the flowers)인 목적격 관계대명사는 which나 that을 써야 한다.

02 선행사가 장소(my classroom)일 경우에는 관계부사 where를 써야 한다.

03 선행사가 사람(the boy)인 목적격 관계대명사는 who(m)이나 that을 써야 한다.

04 첫 번째 문장의 빈칸에는 의문사 What, 두 번째 문장의 빈칸에는 관계대명사 what을 쓴다.

05 첫 번째 문장에서는 선행사가 시간(the day)이므로 관계부사 when을 써야 한다. 두 번째 문장에서는 선행사가 방법(the way)이므로 how를 쓰는데, the way how라고 쓰지 않고 the way와 how 중 하나만 써야 한다. 이때, how를 〈in+which〉로 바꾸어 쓸 수 있다.

06 선행사가 사물(the text message)인 목적격 관계대명사는 which나 that을 쓰는데, 이는 생략이 가능하다.

07 동물(a dog) 선행사는 주격 관계대명사로 which나 that을 쓴다.

08 ②는 진주어를 이끄는 접속사 that이고, 나머지는 관계대 명사이다.

09 주격 관계대명사는 생략할 수 없고, 〈주격 관계대명사 +be동사〉의 경우에만 생략이 가능하다. ①은 목적어로 쓰인 접속사 that, ②, ③, ④는 목적격 관계대명사로 생략 이 가능하다.

10 주어진 문장과 ⑤는 선행사를 포함하는 관계대명사 what(= the thing which[that])이고, 나머지는 의문사 what이다.

11 ① 관계대명사의 동사가 없으므로 that을 삭제하거나 eating을 was eating, ② 문장에 선행사가 없으므로 선 행사를 포함하는 관계대명사 what, ③ 선행사 the worst city가 있으므로 관계대명사는 that, ⑤ 선행사가 a teacher이므로 teaches로 써야 한다.

12 관계대명사절에서 주어 역할을 하므로 선행사(my friend) 뒤에 주격 관계대명사 that이나 who를 써 줘야 한다.

13 관계대명사절의 동사 부분에 현재분사가 쓰였으므로 whom을 삭제하거나, 생략이 가능한 〈주격 관계대명사 +be동사〉의 형태인 who is로 써야 한다.

14 ⓒ the last가 선행사에 쓰인 경우는 관계대명사 that, ⓓ 선행 사가 kids이므로 복수형 동사 sing을 써야 한다.

15 ⓐ, ⓔ는 주격 관계대명사, ⓑ는 소유격 관계대명사, ⓒ, ⓓ, ⓕ는 목적격 관계대명사이다.

16 선행사가 사람(five boys)이고 주어 역할을 하므로 주격 관계대명사 who 또는 that을 써야 한다.

17 빈칸 앞에 선행사가 없으므로 선행사를 포함하는 관계대 명사 what을 써야 하고, yesterday에 맞춰 과거시제 made를 써야 한다.

18 관계대명사가 관계대명사절에서 주어 역할을 하므로 주격이다.

19 관계대명사가 관계대명사절에서 목적어 역할을 하므로 목 적격이다.

20 밑줄 친 whose가 a friend's를 의미하므로 소유격이다.

21 선행사가 장소(the place)이므로 관계부사 where를 써 야 한다.

22 선행사가 이유(the reason)이므로 관계부사 why를 써야 한다.

23 선행사가 방법(the way)이므로 관계부사 how를 써야

한다.

24 선행사를 포함하는 관계대명사 what(= the thing[one] which[that])을 써야 한다.

25 관계대명사가 관계대명사절에서 목적어 역할을 하므로 사 물(my room)을 선행사로 하는 목적격 관계대명사 which나 that을 써야 한다.

26 관계부사 why는 〈for+which〉로 바꿔 쓸 수 있는데, 여 기서처럼 〈전치사+관계부사〉로는 쓸 수 없다.

27 관계대명사가 관계대명사절에서 주어 역할을 하므로 사람 (the youngest son)을 선행사로 하는 주격 관계대명사 that 을 써야 한다. 최상급이 선행사일 때는 주로 that을 쓴다.

28 선행사(the building)가 단수이므로 동사의 3인칭 단수 형태 has를 써야 한다.

29 관계대명사가 관계대명사절에서 목적어 역할을 하므로 사 람(the boy)을 선행사로 하는 목적격 관계대명사 who(m) 나 that을 써야 한다.

30 장소가 선행사인 문장으로 선행사(the place)나 관계부 사 where 중 하나를 생략할 수 있는데, 조건 4)에 따라 선행사를 생략해야 한다.

CHAPTER
[13 가정법]

Unit 01 .... p. 134

01 If she were a baby
02 If I had time
03 If I lived close
04 If he were old enough
05 If he were here

Unit 02 .... p. 134

01 I had sunglasses and a hat
02 I could play the violin well
03 my art teacher does not[doesn't] like my painting
04 you wanted to be a doctor
05 she will move to another school

Unit 03

p. 135

01 as if today were Christmas
02 as if she could run fast
03 as if she were good at math
04 as if he were a doctor
05 as if she were a soccer fan
06 as if she liked English

Unit 04

p. 135

01 If he had told
02 I could have taken
03 If he had won
04 she would have answered
05 If I had not[hadn't] been
06 I could have watched

Unit 05

p. 136

01 I did not[didn't] learn Spanish
02 I had remembered the song
03 we did not[didn't] have lunch
04 you had had enough time
05 we did not[didn't] watch the game
06 we had played together

Unit 06

p. 136

01 talks as if he had graduated from Harvard University
02 act as if you had not[hadn't] told me a lie
03 talks as if he had cleaned his room
04 talks as if it had been his last concert
05 talks as if she had ridden the roller coaster
06 behave as if they had not[hadn't] had a morning break

중간고사 · 기말고사 실전문제

pp. 137~140

객관식 정답 [01~15]

01 ③	02 ①	03 ④	04 ④	05 ④
06 ⑤	07 ③	08 ④	09 ③	10 ②, ⑤
11 ③	12 ④	13 ③	14 ④	15 ②

주관식 정답 [16~30]

16 were
17 were / would talk
18 could come
19 I wish she were healthier than last week.
20 She acts as if she were a star.
21 had gone there
22 were not[weren't] busy / could go hiking
23 I knew how to play Baduk, I could play with you
24 she had not[hadn't] been sick, she could have attended the meeting
25 had been → were
26 could have joined → could join
27 He acts as if he were handsome.
28 I would donate to the poor if I had money.
29 I wish I were good at math like Tom.
30 If I had been more careful, I would not have got hurt.

해설

01 조건의 접속사 if절의 동사는 미래 대신 현재시제로 써야 한다.

02 〈I wish+주어+동사의 과거형(be동사의 경우 were)〉은 '만약 ~이라면 좋을 텐데'의 의미로 현재 이룰 수 없거나 실현 가능성이 높지 않은 일에 대한 소망을 나타낸다.

03 〈If+주어+동사의 과거형 ~, 주어+would/could/might+동사원형 …〉은 '만약 ~이라면, …할 텐데'라는 의미로, 현재의 사실에 반대되는 일을 가정한다. 여기서는 이 이야기의 성냥팔이 소녀를 만나면 무엇을 하겠냐는 질문에, 안아 주겠다고 대답하고 있으므로, 빈칸에는 would가 알맞다.

04 첫 번째 문장은 '만약 ~이라면, …할 텐데'라는 의미로, 현재의 사실에 반대되는 일을 가정하는 가정법 과거로 동사는 과거형 rained로 써야 한다. 두 번째 문장은 I wish 가정법 과거완료형으로 〈had+과거분사〉 형태로 써야 하므로 had come이 알맞다.

05 첫 번째 문장은 주절이 〈could+동사원형〉 형태이므로, if 가정법 과거이다. 이때 if절은 동사의 과거형을 써야 하므로 studied. 두 번째 문장은 '마치 ~였던 것처럼'이라는 의미로, 실제로는 아닌 과거의 일을 표현하는 as if 가정법

과거완료이므로 had had로 써야 한다.

06 '만약 ~였다면 좋았을 텐데'라는 의미로, 과거에 이룰 수 없거나 과거 사실과 반대되는 일에 대한 소망을 나타내는 I wish 가정법 과거완료형으로 hadn't lost를 써야 한다.

07 '만약 ~이라면, …할 텐데'라는 의미로, 현재의 사실에 반대되는 일을 가정하는 if 가정법 과거로 〈If+주어+동사의 과거형(were) ~, 주어+would/could/might+동사원형 …〉의 형태를 갖는다. 여기서는 '~할 수 있을 것이다'의 가능의 의미를 나타내므로 could를 써야 한다.

08 if 가정법 과거완료 〈If+주어+had+과거분사 ~, 주어+would/could/might+have+과거분사 …〉('만약 ~였다면, …했었을 텐데')의 어순으로 쓴다.

09 ③은 '~하지 않는다면'의 의미인 unless(= if not)가 알맞고, 나머지는 if가 알맞다.

10 ① be동사는 were로 써야 한다. ③ 주절에 would have told로 써야 한다. ④ if절의 was를 were로 써야 한다.

11 현재의 사실에 반대되는 일을 가정하므로 주절의 동사는 would like로 써야 한다.

12 주절이 〈could+동사원형〉이므로, if절은 과거형인 exercised로 써야 한다. ⑤에는 가정법 과거 동사 saw를 써도 좋다.

13 ⓑ '(실제로는 아니었지만) 마치 ~였던 것처럼'의 as if 가정법 과거완료로 hadn't eaten으로 써야 한다. ⓒ 〈If+주어+동사의 과거형 ~, 주어+would/could/might+동사원형 …〉이므로 if절의 동사는 과거형 came으로 써야 한다.

14 ⓑ now라는 부사가 현재의 사실이 아님을 표현하므로 were를 써야 한다. ⓒ if 가정법 과거이므로 주절에 would를 써야 한다.

15 (A) 주절에 〈would+have+과거분사〉를 썼으므로 if 가정법 과거완료인 〈If+주어+had+과거분사 ~, 주어+would/could/might+have+과거분사〉('만약 ~였다면, …했었을 텐데')의 어순에 따라 hadn't met. (B) 주절에 〈would+동사원형〉을 썼으므로 if 가정법 과거인 〈If+주어+동사의 과거형 ~, 주어+would/could/might+동사원형 …〉의 어순에 따라 couldn't see. (C) 영원히(forever) 함께 하는 것은 불가능하므로 현재 이루어

질 가능성이 적은 I wish 가정법 과거인 〈I wish+주어+동사의 과거형〉의 어순에 따라 could be를 써야 한다.

16 '마치 ~인 것처럼'이라는 의미로 실제가 아닌 현재의 일을 표현하는 〈주어+동사의 현재형+as if+주어+동사의 과거형(were)〉의 어순으로 써야 한다.

17 if 가정법 과거 〈If+주어+동사의 과거형(were) ~, 주어+would/could/might+동사원형 …〉('만약 ~이라면, …할 텐데')의 어순으로 쓴다.

18 '만약 ~이라면 좋을 텐데'라는 의미로 현재에 이룰 수 없거나 현재 사실과 반대되는 일에 대한 소망을 나타내는 I wish 가정법 과거로 〈I wish+주어+동사의 과거형〉의 어순이므로 could come으로 써야 한다.

19 '만약 ~이라면 좋을 텐데'라는 의미로 현재에 이룰 수 없거나 현재 사실과 반대되는 일에 대한 소망을 나타내는 I wish 가정법 과거로 〈I wish+주어+동사의 과거형(were)〉의 어순으로 쓴다.

20 as if 가정법 과거로 〈주어+동사의 현재형+as if+주어+동사의 과거형(were)〉의 어순으로 쓴다.

21 '만약 ~였다면 좋았을 텐데'라는 의미로 과거에 이룰 수 없거나 과거 사실과 반대되는 일에 대한 소망을 나타내는 I wish 가정법 과거완료 〈I wish+주어+had+과거분사〉의 어순으로 써야 한다.

22 현재의 사실에 반대되는 일을 가정하는 if 가정법 과거 〈If+주어+동사의 과거형(were) ~, 주어+would/could/might+동사원형 …〉의 어순으로 쓴다. 여기서는 '~할 수 있을 것이다'의 가능을 나타내므로 조동사 could를 써야 한다.

23 현재 사실에 반대되는 일을 가정하는 if 가정법 과거 〈If+주어+동사의 과거형 ~, 주어+would/could/might+동사원형 …〉의 어순으로 쓴다.

24 과거 사실에 반대되는 일을 가정하는 if 가정법 과거완료 〈If+주어+had+과거분사 ~, 주어+would/could/might+have+과거분사 …〉의 어순으로 쓴다.

25 주절에 now가 있으므로 현재 사실에 반대되는 일을 가정하는 if 가정법 과거 〈If+주어+동사의 과거형(were) ~, 주어+would/could/might+동사원형 …〉의 어순으로 표현한다.

26 '내일 합류할 수 있기를 바란다'는 의미로 현재 사실의 반

대를 소망하는 I wish 가정법 과거이므로 could join이 되어야 한다.

27 '마치 ~였던 것처럼'이라는 의미로 실제로는 아닌 현재의 일을 표현하는 as if 가정법 과거 〈주어+동사의 현재형+as if+주어+동사의 과거형(were)〉의 어순으로 쓴다.

28 '만약 ~이라면, …할 텐데'라는 의미로 현재 사실과 반대되는 일을 가정하는 if 가정법 과거 〈If+주어+동사의 과거형 ~, 주어+would/could/might+동사원형 …〉의 어순으로 쓴다.

29 I wish 가정법 과거로 〈I wish+주어+동사의 과거형(were)〉의 어순으로 써야 한다.

30 if 가정법 과거완료 〈If+주어+had+과거분사 ~, 주어+would/could/might+have+과거분사 …〉의 어순으로 쓴다.

[
CHAPTER
14 일치와 화법
]

Unit 01 p. 142

01 found / was very kind
02 is saying / cannot[can't] come to
03 wonder / said such a thing
04 told / had written the song
05 told / should take a rest
06 wanted to / would make soup

Unit 02 p. 142

01 knew that the sun rises
02 said that the first Olympic Games took place
03 heard that my grandma always gets up
04 told us that the shuttle bus goes every ten minutes
05 told us that about 64 million people died

Unit 03 p. 143

01 did come
02 did miss
03 does feel
04 did study
05 does not[doesn't] call
06 Does she know

Unit 04 p. 143

01 In the garden grows a lot of trees and flowers.
02 Here they are sleeping.
03 On the table lay a beautiful vase.
04 Down came the rain all night.
05 Here is the orange juice you ordered.
06 Into the pool jumped the children.

Unit 05 p. 144

01 said / she would exercise hard from that day
02 said / he had woken late that morning
03 said / he would go to the park that day
04 told his mom / he had got[gotten] a perfect score

Unit 06 p. 144

01 asked / when she would come
02 asked / if[whether] he could open it
03 asked / how I felt that day
04 asked / if[whether] I understood her

Unit 07 p. 145

A

01 why you are angry
02 if[whether] I passed the test
03 if[whether] Kevin likes Susie
04 when Jessie's birthday is
05 where we are now
06 who won the contest

B

01 What do you think his name is?
02 When do you believe she will come?
03 Who do you think will get the prize?
04 Why do you guess he is late?

01 didn't you / Yes, I did

02 does he / No, he doesn't

03 do you / No, I don't

04 isn't it / Yes, it is

05 don't you / No, I don't

06 is he / Yes, he is

01 You can write / can't you

02 They will arrive / won't they

03 Help me (to) push / will you

04 These shoes look / don't they

05 Let's listen to / shall we

중간고사 · 기말고사 실전문제   pp. 147~150

객관식 정답 [01~15]

01 ③	**02** ①	**03** ②	**04** ④	**05** ①
06 ③	**07** ①	**08** ⑤	**09** ②	**10** ④
11 ⑤	**12** ③	**13** ④	**14** ④	**15** ①

주관식 정답 [16~30]

16 didn't we

17 will he

18 was

19 could win

20 Mia does like swimming in the sea.

21 walked James

22 He told me not to push him hard.

23 She asked me if[whether] I had enjoyed the concert.

24 won't → wouldn't

25 boiled → boils

26 Who do you guess the winner is?

27 On the top of the mountain was a big rock.

28 He told me that he was cleaning the house then.

29 There lived a beautiful girl in our town.

30 ⓓ → would

해설

01 긍정문에 대한 부가의문문은 부정으로 써야 한다.

02 의문사가 없는 간접의문문은 〈if[whether](~인지 아닌지)+주어+동사〉로 써야 한다.

03 첫 번째 문장에서 명령문의 부가의문문은 will you로 써야 한다. 두 번째 문장에서는 주절의 시제가 현재이므로 종속절은 어떤 시제이든지 나올 수 있으므로 '~할 것이다'라는 의지의 표현인 will이 알맞다.

04 첫 번째 문장에서는 주절의 시제가 과거이고 종속절에는 과거 혹은 과거완료를 써야 하므로 kept, 두 번째 문장에서는 생각이나 추측을 나타내는 동사 think, believe, imagine, guess, suppose 등이 쓰인 문장 안에서 간접의문문이 목적어로 쓰일 때, 간접의문문의 의문사가 문장의 맨 앞에 위치하게 된다.

05 첫 번째 문장에서는 주절의 시제가 과거이므로 종속절에는 과거 혹은 과거완료를 써야 하고, 두 번째 문장에서는 주절의 시제가 현재이므로 종속절에는 모든 시제를 쓸 수 있다.

06 부가의문문의 대답이 긍정(제 시간에 준비할 수 있다)이면 Yes, 부정(제 시간에 준비할 수 없다)이면 No로 써야 한다.

07 의문사가 없는 간접의문문은 〈if[whether](~인지 아닌지)+주어+동사〉로 써야 하며, 주절이 과거이므로 종속절도 과거로 써야 한다.

08 명령문의 간접화법 전환 방법은 said to는 전달동사 told로 바꾸고, 명령문의 동사원형을 to부정사로 바꾼다. 인칭대명사는 전달자(us)의 입장으로 바꾸어 your를 our로 바꿔야 한다.

09 say 뒤에 말을 하는 대상이 나오면 to를 써 줘야 하며, 직접화법 문장의 주어는 듣는 사람 입장으로 바꿔야 하므로 you를 쓰고, there은 here로, 시제는 현재로 바꿔야 한다.

10 장소 또는 방향을 나타내는 부사(구)가 강조를 위해 문두에 올 경우, 〈부사(구)+동사+주어〉의 어순으로 도치된다. ① 과거시제로 had를 써야 한다. ② There 뒤에 주어가 대명사일 경우, 도치가 아닌 〈There+대명사 주어+동사〉 형태로 써야 한다. ③ 의문사가 있는 간접의문문의 경우, 〈의문사+주어+동사〉의 어순이 되어야 하므로 what this is로 써야 한다. ⑤ 강조의 조동사 do/does/did 뒤에는 동사원형을 써야 하므로 did tell이 되어야 한다.

11 주절의 동사가 과거시제이므로 종속절도 과거 혹은 과거 완료를 써야 한다.

12 주어진 문장과 ③은 강조의 의미를 갖는 조동사 do로 쓰였고, 나머지는 본동사 do로 썼다.

13 장소 또는 방향을 나타내는 부사(구)가 강조를 위해 문두에 올 경우 〈부사(구)+동사+주어〉의 어순으로 도치하므로 is running 전체를 도치하여 is running a dog으로 써야 한다.

14 ⓓ 의문사가 있는 간접의문문의 경우, 〈의문사+주어+동사〉의 어순이 되어야 하므로 what your favorite color is로 써야 한다.

15 (A) 부가의문문의 답으로 Yes라고 대답할 경우 긍정이므로 are. (B) 종속절이 현재의 습관, 일반적인 사실, 반복적으로 일어나는 일인 경우는 주절이 과거이더라도 종속절은 항상 현재시제로 나타내므로 leaves를 써야 한다. (C) Here이 문장 앞에 오면 〈동사+주어〉의 어순으로 도치되며 버스가 온다는 의미이므로 comes를 써야 한다.

16 긍정문에 대한 부가의문문은 부정으로 쓰며, 동사가 과거형이므로 didn't we를 써야 한다.

17 부정문에 대한 부가의문문은 긍정으로 써야 한다.

18 주절의 시제가 과거이므로 종속절의 동사인 be동사도 3인칭 단수 주어에 맞는 과거 was로 써야 한다.

19 주절의 시제가 과거이므로 종속절도 과거인 could win으로 써야 한다.

20 강조의 의미를 갖는 조동사 do를 3인칭 단수 주어에 일치시켜 〈does+동사원형〉으로 써야 한다.

21 장소 또는 방향을 나타내는 부사(구)가 강조를 위해 문두에 올 경우, 〈부사(구)+동사+주어〉의 어순으로 도치된다.

22 명령문의 간접화법 전환 방법은 said to를 told로 바꾸고, 명령문의 동사원형을 to부정사로 바꾼다. 부정문의 경우 to 앞에 not을 붙인다.

23 의문사가 없는 간접의문문은 〈if[whether](~인지 아닌지)+주어+동사〉로 써야 하며, 과거에 질문하는 시점보다 질문의 내용이 더 과거(콘서트를 즐긴 것은 질문 받는 시점보다 과거)이므로 과거완료로 써야 한다.

24 주절의 시제가 과거이므로 종속절도 과거시제로 써야 한다.

25 일반적인 사실이나 불변의 진리는 항상 현재시제로 써야

한다.

26 생각이나 추측을 나타내는 동사 think, believe, imagine, guess, suppose 등이 쓰인 문장에서 간접의문문이 목적어로 쓰일 때, 간접의문문의 의문사는 문장의 맨 앞에 위치하며, 〈의문사+do you+생각, 추측 동사+주어+동사〉 형태로 써야 한다.

27 장소 또는 방향을 나타내는 부사(구)가 강조를 위해 문두에 올 경우 〈부사(구)+동사+주어〉의 어순으로 도치된다.

28 평서문의 간접화법으로 전환 방법은 said to를 told로 전달 동사를 바꾸고, 시제는 여는 중이라고 했으므로 과거진행형. '지금'을 의미하는 now는 then으로 바꿔야 한다.

29 There가 강조를 위해 문장의 맨 앞에 올 경우, 주어 앞에 동사가 먼저 나와야 한다.

30 주절의 시제가 과거이므로 종속절도 과거인 would로 써야 한다.

MY GRAMMAR COACH

내신기출 N제 중2